DEMOCRACY IN
LATIN AMERICA
1760–1900

Morality and Society Series
Edited by Alan Wolfe

DEMOCRACY IN LATIN AMERICA
1760–1900

*Volume 1, Civic Selfhood and
Public Life in Mexico and Peru*

CARLOS A. FORMENT

The University of Chicago Press   Chicago and London

The University of Chicago Press, Chicago 60637
The University of Chicago Press, Ltd., London
© 2003 by The University of Chicago
All rights reserved. Published 2003.
Paperback edition 2013
Printed in the United States of America

22 21 20 19 18 17 16 15 14 13   2 3 4 5 6

ISBN-13: 978-0-226-25715-0 (cloth)
ISBN-13: 978-0-226-10141-5 (paperback)
ISBN-13: 978-0-226-11290-9 (e-book)
DOI: 10.7208/chicago/9780226112909.001.0001

Library of Congress Cataloging-in-Publication Data

Forment, Carlos A.
    Democracy in Latin America, 1760–1900 / Carlos A. Forment.
    v. cm.—(Morality and society series)
    Includes bibliographical references and index.
    Contents: v. 1. Civic selfhood and public life in Mexico and Peru
    ISBN: 0-226-25715-0 (v. 1 : cloth : alk. paper)
    1. Mexico—History—19th century. 2. Peru—History—19th century.
    3. Democracy—Mexico—History. 4. Democracy—Peru—History. I. Title.
    II. Morality and society.

    F1232.F683 2003
    320.98′09′034—dc21

                                          2002152501

Let us not turn to America in order slavishly to copy the institutions she has fashioned for herself, but in order that we may better understand what suits us; let us look there for instruction rather than models; let us adopt the principle rather than the details of her laws.
  —*Alexis de Tocqueville*

Spanish Americans have, through study and inclination, assimilated the aspirations and ideas that form part of universal culture, but the world that moves beneath their feet is different from the one they now carry in their heads. This is the reason why they consider it improper to discuss the great issues confronting humanity in light of their own experiences. . . . Flashes of lightning emanate from our heads, but our feet remain covered in hobnailed boots. . . . This is the source of our infinite sadness.
  —*José Martí*

Without a Tradition—which selects and names, which hands down and preserves, which indicates where the treasures are and what their worth is— there seems to be no willed continuity in time and, hence, humanly speaking, neither past nor future. . . . In this gap between the past and future, we find our place in time when we think, that is, when we are sufficiently removed from the past and future. . . .
  —*Hannah Arendt*

Contents

Illustrations

TABLES

MAPS

Preface

Surveying the public landscape of Latin America from the mid-eighteenth to the late nineteenth century has persuaded me, contrary to other interpretations, that civic democracy, understood in Tocquevillian terms as a daily practice and form of life rooted in social equality, mutual recognition, and political liberty, was by the mid-nineteenth century rooted in the region. Citizens across the continent organized thousands of civic, political, and economic associations, providing themselves a place in which to give textured form and contoured shape to their yearnings at a time when the vast majority of state and church officials remained hostile or indifferent to them. Men and women, elite and commoner, from rural and urban areas and from different socio-ethnic backgrounds, transformed these voluntary groups into "models of" and "models for" democratic life, to borrow from Clifford Geertz. These enclaves of democracy surfaced alongside bastions of authoritarianism, the two sometimes coexisting and sometimes clashing. The thick residues of these encounters shaped the alternative pathways taken by Mexicans, Peruvians, Argentines, and Cubans in their century-long effort to establish democratic life.

The democratic tradition in Latin America is far more robust than most scholars have claimed. It has also been imperfect. Civic Republicanism in this part of the world never experienced the Golden Age it seems to have enjoyed for brief moments in various small areas of western Europe and North America. In Latin America, really-existing democracy was distinctive in several ways. First, it was radically disjointed. Citizens invested their sense of sovereignty horizontally in each other rather than vertically in government institutions, thereby provoking a disjuncture between daily practices and institutional structures. Second, it was radically asymmetrical. Citizens practiced democracy more readily and intensely in civil society than in any of the other public terrains (economic society, political society, and the public sphere), thereby making democratic life in the region lopsided. Third, it was radically fragmented. Latin Americans were the first group of citizens in the modern West to have failed in their attempt to reconcile social equality with cultural differences, thereby causing public life in the continent to become socio-ethnically fissured. Fourth, democratic life in Latin America was culturally hybrid. Catholicism was the language of public life in the region. Citizens used its narrative resources to create new democratic meanings from old religious terms, thereby fusing the two to create an alternative vocabulary—call it Civic Catholicism. Some of these traits are also discernible in other democracies in the modern West, but only in Latin America did the four of them appear together and in such a pronounced manner as to create a unique form of life, one that remains palpable in the region to this day.

My study takes readers on the southern route, on the road not taken by Tocqueville, and explores how daily practices shaped and were shaped in their turn by institutional structures across civil society, economic society, political society, and the public sphere in nineteenth-century Mexico, Peru, Argentina, and Cuba. The democratic tradition I have unearthed has provided generations of citizens in the region with an alternative to state- and market-centered forms of life that surfaced alongside it and continue to claim our loyalties today, in addition to national populism, a twentieth-century creation. Studying the shifting fortunes of these four traditions would be tantamount to writing a "total history" of the region —a daunting task which only a French scholar with a well-stocked wine cellar would dare to undertake and one which, in any case, is beyond my reach.

I have tried to reconstruct Latin America's democratic tradition without relying on the self-images of the age. A large portion of the scholarly and popular works on the subject of "democratization" published in the last two decades are themselves an expression of the moral and socio-political crisis that afflicts the region rather than a critical reflection on it. The arguments and counterarguments we write and rewrite, read and reread, and then repeat to each other again and again in countless conference papers, newspaper articles, books, and hastily edited volumes are as much an expression of the crisis as are the terrifying reports of human rights abuses published in the last two decades by the various Truth Commissions that have appeared throughout the continent. The democratic tradition in Latin America is in greater disarray than ever before. Skeptics are invited to compare our own "thin" conception of democratic life with the "thick" conception that prevailed among nineteenth-century Mexicans, Peruvians, Argentines, and Cubans. Skeptics are also invited to compare recent works on "transitions" and "consolidation" with those that appeared in the postwar period following the de-Nazification and Stalin-ization of western and eastern Europe.

My aim in proposing a Tocquevillian account of Latin America's "first" democratic wave is to encourage scholars working on the "third" wave to rethink their own understanding of it, based as it is on Schumpeterian notions of state governance, elite pacts, and low-intensity elections. But in studying the history of democratic life in nineteenth-century Latin America, I have resisted the temptation to turn the past into an appendage of the present and to explain the relationship between the two by invoking one or another "scientific law," as is customarily done among scholars in the fields of comparative politics and sociology. Sociopolitical situations change, and because citizens develop new ways of acting and thinking, it is foolhardy to use the past as a "laboratory" in which to test our "hypotheses." Studying the past has no "exchange value." Its only "use" value is in its capacity to enlarge and enrich our political imagination beyond the here and now.

For more than a century now, scholars and public intellectuals have attributed Latin America's recurrent bouts with authoritarianism in the nineteenth and twentieth century to the "colonial legacy." Admittedly, the majority of Latin Americans who appear in this study were born and raised in antidemocratic milieux at home, in their schools, in their church parishes and workplaces. But by century's end, if not before, many of them were already acting and speaking like democratic citizens of a sovereign republic. For example, in the 1840s, Mexicans in mutual-aid associations practiced self-rule (democracy) for the first time in their lives by participating in meetings, voting for officials, making those officials accountable to the other members of the group, deliberating about common concerns, paying their dues in a timely manner, and serving on juries that were responsible for enforcing the norms and statutes of the group. Mexicans in community development groups, to take a second example, practiced collective sovereignty (nationalism) by wearing domestic-made trousers, shoes, and petticoats and by encouraging local notables to boycott foreign-made carriages, furniture, and liquor. Throughout Mexico, commoner and elite imagined and practiced democracy and nationalism in strikingly similar ways, indicating that they had become embedded in daily life.

Among contemporary thinkers, John Dewey and Nelson Goodman (like Tocqueville in the nineteenth century) have done much to redirect the study of public life from issues of "choice and information" to matters of "habit and inculcation." Although the first approach remains dominant in the fields of comparative politics and sociology, a growing group of scholars have been trying since the 1980s to correct this imbalance. Pierre Bourdieu has been at the forefront of this effort. His trailblazing work on "habitus" has been an inspiration to many of us; however, there is no denying that it remains rooted in precisely the type of "theoretical knowledge" he is seeking to challenge. Hubert Dreyfus and Paul Rabinow's broad-minded criticism of Bourdieu's work is instructive in more than one way:

> We call metaphysical any . . . account that claims to know . . . what it is to be a human being. For example, the meaning of human being might be that man is created by God to serve . . . him, or that man is the highest manifestation of the will to power. . . . Bourdieu . . . denies . . . the manifold significance [that] practices have to the practitioners [themselves]. . . . Behind them he [always] finds the [same] explanatory reality . . . [namely,] the struggle for [power]. . . . In order to preserve . . . Bourdieu's insight . . . one must abandon the claim to [be] . . . doing . . . science and . . . the symbolic capital that accompanies this privileged position. . . . There is no position from which to do an objective, detached study of one's sense of reality.[1]

Scholars committed to "practical knowledge" are going back to the work of Goodman, Dewey, and other pragmatists. But in returning to them, all of us have also tried to push their arguments in a different direction by raising a host of new questions, such as: How do habits emerge and change over time? What makes some habits more durable than others? How do people break with old habits and acquire new dispositions? How do they circulate and spread among large groups of people? What stories do people use in daily life to describe their own habits? What are some of the social, moral, cultural, institutional, political, and economic resources citizens use to give materiality to their habits and embed them in "reality?" And so on. My study takes up some of these questions, and even tries to answer a few of them.

Socio-moral practices played a key role in the emergence of civic democracy in nineteenth-century Latin America. As Charles Taylor argues so convincingly, moral frameworks enable us to make sense of our shared differences in public life: "To know who you are is to be oriented in moral space. . . . To think, feel, and judge within such a framework is to function with the sense that some action, mode of life or mode of feeling is incomparably higher than the others which are more readily available to

1. Hubert Dreyfus and Paul Rabinow, "Can There Be a Science of Existential Structure and Social Meaning," in *Bourdieu: Critical Perspectives*, ed. Craig Calhoun, Edward LiPuma, and Moishe Postone (Chicago: University of Chicago Press, 1993), 35–44.

us." [2] In borrowing from Taylor, my aim is to extend his argument beyond the confines of western Europe and a handful of distinguished philosophers in order to show how everyday forms of moral judgments enabled elite and non-elite groups throughout Latin America to restructure their habits. Citizens in this part of the world who practiced democracy skillfully in public life received special recognition from their compatriots. Senior democrats (elite and commoner) distinguished themselves by their uncanny capacity to make "substantive claims and qualitative distinctions [about] what is good and bad . . . what is worth doing and what is not, what has meaning . . . and what is trivial." [3] As stewards of the public good, senior democrats were responsible for initiating novices into the democratic "paradigm" and providing them with the "tacit knowledge" and "practical skills" they would need to become part of this community. In other words, emulation was far more important than imitation (mimicry) in enabling Latin Americans to break with authoritarian habits and acquire democratic inclinations.

However, as in any interpretive community, the meaning of democracy in Latin America was fluid and subject to contestation by those who had been deemed competent to do so. In challenging each other's conceptions, senior democrats were at the same time challenging each other's claim to authority and in doing so conveying to the rest of the citizenry who among them deserved special recognition in public life. Moral authority in public life in nineteenth-century Latin America, I submit, is best understood as an example of practical judgment, as a "conflict of interpretation" in Paul Ricoeur's sense, rather than as an example of "self-evident truth," as Hannah Arendt would have us believe. Despite her fierce hostility toward all forms of determinism, Arendt remained trapped within her own self-made "iron cage," as evidenced by her tendency to dichotomize moral practices into "traditional" (objective truth) and "modern" (subjective interpretation) and to depict public life as a stage for the performance of great deeds by the virtuous few rather than a form of life constituted by the many in the course of practicing "everyday heroism."

In Latin America, democratic selfhood emerged in civic, economic, and political associations and developed out of the interpersonal dynamics among members. Associations provided Latin Americans with a vehicle for shuttling back and forth between public and private life. But these groups and the formal and informal networks that grew out of them were more than organizational facts; they were the concrete materialization of

2. Charles Taylor, *Sources of the Self* (Cambridge: Harvard University Press, 1989), 19, 30.
3. Taylor, *Sources of the Self*, 4, 28.

democratic forms of life. In these temples, members took turns "representing" democracy, thereby compelling each other to find novel ways of
communicating their own particular understanding of self-rule (and collective sovereignty) intersubjectively. The routinization of these practices
eventually provided Mexicans, Peruvians, Cubans, and Argentines with
shared standards by which to evaluate each other's actions in public life.
In the course of practicing democracy in daily life, Latin Americans were
in fact constituting it.

In her seminal essay on the "crisis of authority," Arendt also argued
that associative life was the most effective safeguard available to modern
democracy against the threat of totalitarianism. I concur with her on this
second point. While her argument was embraced by Tocquevillians who
studied western Europe and North America, those who studied Third
World countries found it unpersuasive. In reaction to the spread of nationalism and populism across Africa, Asia, India, and Latin America, an
entire generation of scholars, led by Samuel P. Huntington, appropriated
bits and pieces of Arendt's argument but did so in order to develop an
alternative state-centered interpretation of postcolonial life. According
to them, the process of economic modernization throughout the Third
World had already weakened or destroyed associative life based on racial,
ethnic, religious, and communal and other traditional ties, leaving citizens
of these countries isolated, disconnected, and inclined to act in predatory
ways. In order to repair the socio-moral fabric of these countries, political leaders across the Third World, with support from leaders in the First
World, would need to create highly centralized and autonomous states beyond the control of their citizenry, enabling the government officials that
staffed them to resist the vicious forms of life that flourished all around
them and to implement policies aimed at propagating "virtue" among the
citizenry. What began in the postwar period as a discussion of associative
life and its role in strengthening democracy was turned during the decol-
onization period into a Liberal-Leninist argument in support of "enlightened despotism." With the collapse of the Soviet Union and the demise of
state socialism across the world, we now have an opportunity to shift the
discussion on postcolonial life from Hobbes and Huntington to Tocqueville and Arendt.

The practice-centered (performative) perspective I have outlined here
might provide Tocquevillian scholars an alternative to the existing approaches based on "socio-psychological orientation" (David Riesman);
"compulsive habits" (Edward Banfield); "deep norms" (Gabriel Almond
and Sidney Verba); "institutional domination" (Samuel Huntington);
"simple speech" (Robert Bellah); "social trust" (Francis Fukuyama); and,
most recently, "strategic rationality" (Robert Putnam).

Initially, I had planned to use only secondary sources in this study, but after reading countless monographs I realized that the type of evidence I needed had not yet been collected. I spent a year or so doing primary research in each country. I began my research in Mexico City, at the National Archives, where I was shocked and dismayed to discover that government officials in the nineteenth century, in contrast to their European and North American counterparts, had never compiled a national directory nor even a simple list of voluntary groups for any one region in the country. Neither had government officials in Peru, Argentina, and Cuba. This made my work doubly difficult.[4] In order to correct their oversight, I pored over numerous newspapers, reading them day by day, week by week, month by month, and year by year. I kept a detailed record on each association, the way a birdwatcher keeps a log of all his sightings. My databank, the first of its kind, contains records on 7,056 voluntary groups (Argentina: N = 1,567; Cuba: N = 2,186; Mexico: N = 2,291; Peru: N = 912). I collected additional information on associative life and one or another group from the hundreds of partisan pamphlets, tabloids, journals, private letters, and travelogues published during the nineteenth century to create my own "archive" on democratic life.

Because the bulk of my data came from newspapers, readers might find it useful to know more about them. Most voluntary groups were too poor to publish their own tabloid. Instead, they paid local newspapers to have their documents featured in the advertisement section on the back or inside back page, alongside other announcements for hair tonics, farm tools, stagecoach schedules, regional fairs, and the like. These notices appeared intermittently and accounted for roughly 2 percent of the column space, based on a random sample (N = 100) I did of *Siglo XIX*, Mexico's leading daily, for the years 1842 and 1882. The information published on each association was written in a telegraphic style (to save money) and the prose was hermetic, suggesting that it was read primarily by other members rather than aimed at the public at large. This might also have served to protect the group from state officials; however, as I noted above, the capacity of such officials to monitor public life (Foucault's governmentality) remained quite limited throughout most of the period under study.

Newspapers, I discovered gradually, were more than just a source of primary information; they were embedded in and constitutive of demo-

---

4. The *Censo General de Población, Edificación, Comercio e Industria de la Ciudad de Buenos Aires* (Buenos Aires, 1887) gives the total number of associations in the province of Buenos Aires but does not have any information on them, not even their names. The "Registro de Asociaciones" in Havana's National Archive has documents on associations that were licensed by the government between 1880 and 1890. The *Censo* and "Registro" remain woefully incomplete even within their own declared parameters.

cratic life. Associative practices in Latin America surfaced somewhere between the world of the "hidden" and the "official" transcript and formed
part of what James Scott calls the "intermediate domain," the domain
where citizens use semipublic and peaceful methods to subvert the dominant moral and sociopolitical order. Associative life in Latin America, I
am convinced, occupied a place in the public landscape different from the
one it came to occupy in postcolonial India and Africa as demonstrated
by Partha Chatterjee and Mahmood Mamdani in their recent, ground-
breaking work.

My reliance on newspapers worked reasonably well except during periods of prolonged censorship (i.e., Juan M. Rosas's dictatorship in Argentina from 1831 to 1852) and foreign rule (i.e., French occupation of
Mexico, 1861–1867), when the number of dailies in the affected country
dropped and their coverage of associative life declined. For such periods,
I relied mainly on semiclandestine tabloids, handbills, and pamphlets.
Comparing the number of groups organized during the crisis with the
number that appeared before and after it convinced me that the decline in
associative life was real and not just an indication of reduced availability
of media during these moments of duress.

I encountered a second problem. In assembling my databank, I relied
heavily on newspapers published in the national capitals. Mexico City
and Havana dailies provided extensive coverage of associative life in the
provinces (itself an indication of nationhood); those published in Lima
and Buenos Aires, in contrast, did not. In order to correct for this bias,
I reviewed half a dozen newspapers from Arequipa, Cuzco, and Piura in
Peru, and a similar number from Santa Fe and Cordoba in Argentina.
Roughly 70 percent of the associations that now appear in my databank
were organized by local residents from across the provinces. Nevertheless, my coverage of associative life in small towns and hamlets across the
provinces remains spotty. Anyone seeking to remedy this problem should
plan on spending no less than five years in each country visiting local
archives and rummaging through the catalogued—and piles of uncata-
logued—manuscripts and documents in their collections.

My study is limited in several ways. Despite my best efforts, for most
associations I did not find reliable demographic information on the class
and ethnicity of members. Postcolonial governments banned the use of
ethnic and racial categories in public life, even purging such references
from their own documents (population censuses, voting lists, tax rolls). In
some cases, the institutional context itself provided me with the indirect
evidence I needed to establish the socio-ethnic composition of an association; for example, an artisan in a mutual-aid society in the provinces was
almost certain to be a dark-skinned mixed blood. At other times this type

of information could be deduced from the sources themselves, by examining the forms of address (citizen, don, doña, excelencia) used by members; the descriptions of clothing (ragged or elegant, coarse cotton or fine linens, and so on); and the presence or absence of a surname (indigenous peoples rarely used them). The only way of knowing whether an association was civic or not is by studying its practices. This led me to exclude from my list any group that did not fit my criteria, although I decided to include all those associations whose practices were an amalgam of democratic and authoritarian elements. I also had difficulty gathering data on kinship, residential patterns, and workplace relations, and how these shaped social networks and associative life. Once again, the sources themselves provided the information I needed to make reasonable inferences. I have not presented data on the ratio of citizens who were active in associative life in selected cities and towns across the continent.[5] It will take me another year to verify these estimates, and I could no longer afford to delay publication of this volume. In any case, because I am primarily interested in studying the emergence of democratic life ("natality" in Arendtian terms) rather than its full flowering, this information is not crucial to my argument.

In order to make the book readable and of interest to a general audience, I have taken several small liberties. In translating Spanish quotes into English, I found it necessary sometimes to simplify the wording, syntax, and grammatical structure of the passage while remaining faithful to the meaning of the text. Purists who take special delight in reading baroque and romantic prose can consult the original passage. The country maps that appear in the historical chapters were drawn according to the administrative divisions and geopolitical boundaries that were in place in 1880 after they had become stable. For the sake of consistency, I used the term "state," which was used only in Mexico, to discuss administrative life in Peru, Argentina, and Cuba, even though in these countries the appropriate term would have been "department" or "province." I used the term "province" when discussing public life outside the nation's capital. My specific usage of these and other technical terms will become apparent in the empirical chapters.

The book is divided into four parts. The first consists of an introductory and a theoretical chapter that are based on a revised and edited version of the field-notes I kept while working on this project. I relied on those notes

5. "Asociaciones Mutualistas," *El Socialista* (26 September 1882), 1–2. Roughly 20 percent of residents in Mexico City were dues-paying members in a mutual-aid group; another 15 percent were active in other types of voluntary associations—cultural, religious, patriotic, and so on.

to keep track of my inchoate thinking (autobiography is not my métier). Without these notes, it would have been impossible for me to retrace my steps and find my way back to familiar territory. In chapter 1, I situate the recent debate on Latin American "transitions" within the broader democratic tradition in the region in order to challenge our understanding of them. In chapter 2, I locate my study of Latin American public life in relation to recent Tocquevillian debates on the relationship between civil society, economic society, political society, and the public sphere and democratic life; in relation to comparativists who study the social origins of dictatorship and democracy in the region; in relation to postcolonialists who account for the frail and fragile nature of democracy in Third World countries in terms of the colonial legacy; and in relation to democratic theorists who have proposed guidelines for evaluating "polyarchical" regimes. My work stands at the juncture of these four discussions and seeks to make a contribution to each.

Part 2 offers an overview of the Latin American public landscape during the late colonial period (1750s to 1820s). Chapter 3 gives a brief outline of institutional practices across civil, economic, and political society and in the public sphere. This will enable readers to acquire a working knowledge of Latin American public life and to evaluate the extent and depth of authoritarianism in the region. Chapter 4 examines the various anticolonial movements that broke out in different parts of Mexico and Peru. Although these movements have been the subject of numerous studies, I am interested in understanding the cultural and social practices they generated. Mexican and Peruvian rebels, and the colonial rulers they challenged, employed the same Catholic terminology and tropes rooted in traditional notions of "passion," "reason," and "judgment" to develop alternative conceptions of selfhood and nationhood. The anticolonial movements that swept Mexico and Peru need to be interpreted, first and foremost, as a cultural revolution rather than as a political upheaval. Popular movements continued to appear periodically throughout the remainder of the nineteenth century in both countries; however, after gaining independence in the 1820s the majority of citizens of the two countries began to organize all types of voluntary associations and to use them as the main vehicle for democratizing everyday life.

Parts 3 (chapters 5–10) and 4 (chapters 11–16) form the empirical core of my study. In these sections, I provide a "semi-thick" description of associative life in postcolonial Peru and Mexico. I have emphasized the links between the implicit practices and the explicit self-understandings that Latin Americans had of associative life and how these shaped their conception of modern democracy. The discussion in parts 3 and 4 move back and forth between countries (Peru and Mexico) and contrapuntally among the various public terrains (civil society, economic society, political society, and the public sphere). Chapters 5 to 10 examine public practices during the first half of the nineteenth century. Latin Americans relied on these civic, economic, and political associations to give materiality to their newly acquired civic habits. In providing a numerical estimate and description of daily life in these groups, my aim has been to show the extent and depth to which democratic practices had become rooted in each country. For the sake of simplicity I have discussed institutional structures and sociocultural practices separately, but in real life they were one and the same. In general terms, Mexicans were far more successful than Peruvians in practicing democracy in daily life.

Part 4 is organized very much like part 3, but the chapters focus on the second half of the century, when associative life had become institutionalized alongside the newly centralized state and national markets. Although Mexicans and Peruvians now used the resources of all three to improve their life chances, my discussion remains focused on the first. In order to evaluate the type of democracy that became rooted in Mexico and Peru, I examine the capacity of citizens in each country to: (a) create new and different types of associations in all four public terrains; (b) develop increasingly complex, extensive, and durable social networks based on a variety of ties (strong/weak; direct/indirect; local/regional/national); (c) protect the institutional autonomy of public life from external threats posed by the central state, the Catholic Church, national markets and family clans; and (d) use civic terminology in everyday life to make sense of each other. Once again, Mexicans proved far more successful than Peruvians in democratizing public life, although the latter were able to break with many of their authoritarian habits and to develop civic ones.

I have divided my empirical discussion of democratic life in Mexico and Peru into three different moments, but in reality the forms of life that crystallized during each extended well into the next. The practices that emerged at each moment resemble the superimposed layers of rock that form part of a single geological formation. Instead of tracing each set of practices all the way back to their original source (according to some scholars, the origins of democratic life in Latin America are rooted in sixteenth-century Castile), I am mainly interested in exploring how they emerged, how they sprang forth and succeeded in moving beyond their points of origin.

In the "Concluding Remarks," I put forward a Tocquevillian account of Latin American democracy and a Latin American account of Tocqueville. This is my version of what might have taken place if Tocqueville and a group of public intellectuals from across Latin America had gathered on the banks of the Rio Grande to discuss the differences and similarities in the type of democratic life that had become rooted in the northern and southern halves of the continent. Tocqueville and his followers, including Huntington, Bellah, and Putnam, have, in my judgment, misunderstood these differences and in doing so misconstrued the nature of postcolonial life. I hasten to add that their shortcomings cannot be attributed solely to "ideology"; recall that the founders of liberal utilitarianism, James Mill and his son, John Stuart, and the founders of radical socialism, Karl Marx and Vladimir Lenin, were even more shortsighted (and brutal) in their assessments.

Our inability to understand postcolonial life is related, I think, to what scholars now call, somewhat inaccurately, the "Enlightenment problem" —that is, the habit of using abstract models to make sense of particular forms of life. Tocqueville was one of the first to draw our attention to this problem when he suggested that the Jacobin Terror in France had been inspired by the type of theoretical rationalism that had become dominant among public intellectuals in the pre-revolutionary period. Following the Holocaust, thinkers as dissimilar as Hannah Arendt, François Furet, Theodor Adorno, and Jean Starobinski, to list just a few, have tried to make explicit the subterranean links between technocratic rationalism and human barbarism. While I do not subscribe to all their arguments, I am convinced that, like the guillotine blade and the gas chamber in Europe, the "disappearances" that took place under the recent dictatorships in Latin America are closely related to the triumph of "civilization" in the region, to reverse the terms of discussion that have been dominant since the nineteenth century, when Domingo F. Sarmiento, Argentina's most influential thinker, argued in favor of exterminating indigenous peoples in order to prepare the way for the "new man." Although I do not delve into any of these complex and polemical issues, I wrote this book in the darkness of their shadows.

In studying the Latin American case, I join a small but growing group of scholars who are committed to decolonizing area studies and deprovincializing modern theory. I continue to find it odd, despite the endless talk about globalism and multiculturalism, that colleagues who study, say, England, France, Germany, or the United States are automatically considered bona fide, card-carrying "comparativists," while those of us who study peripheral countries are classified as mere "area specialists" regardless of the intellectual ambitions of each. I also find it puzzling that my colleagues who work on North America and Europe ignore even the best works on peripheral societies, while those of us who study the Third World are expected, and often required, to be familiar with even their most unambitious work. I also find it perplexing that "theory" in the academy today has become simply a byword for technical discussions on relatively minor (sometimes trivial) issues related to, say, rational choice and state theory, postmodernism and queer theory, or whatever else is in fashion, rather than a broad-minded and critical assessment of the intellectual traditions that have defined the West, the non-West, and the relationship between the two over the ages. I am especially disturbed that many scholars who work on Third World countries have, in reaction against the type of symbolic violence leveled against them by these so-called theorists, saturated their texts with brute facts or, even worse, identified with their aggressors and embraced their scientistic models. I could go on (and on, and on) with this list of observations, but I will not. I have written this study in the hope that it might contribute to developing a "new science of politics."

I am currently preparing the second volume, a comparison of daily practices and public life in nineteenth-century Cuba and Argentina. In contrast to Peru and Mexico, which were "old nations" in the process of becoming modern democracies, Cuba and Argentina were "new nations" in the process of becoming sovereign republics. Colonial habits in the first two countries were far more entrenched than in the second two. Comparing all four will give us a greater appreciation for the variable relationship that exists between the colonial legacy and the development of democratic selfhood in Latin America. In the concluding chapter of this second volume, I analyze Tocqueville's writings on Latin America, North Africa, the U.S. South, Ireland, the French-speaking West Indies, and India. His study of these areas, I maintain, inspired Tocqueville to explore the relationship between modern democracy and colonial rule. A close and internal reading of his writings on peripheral peoples has led me to believe that he was in the process of identifying a third type of regime: postcolonial. Although it bears a family resemblance to the aristocratic and democratic types he had already discussed in his published books, the postcolonial regime he was grappling with differed from them and would come to occupy an increasingly prominent place in the modern world. During the July monarchy of Louis Bonaparte, Tocqueville abandoned his study of postcolonial life to become artificer of French colonial policy in Algeria. That most scholars continue to ignore or downplay the significance of these writings might itself be another expression of the colonial legacy.

Acknowledgments

I begin "in medias res," with the three persons who influenced me the most and caused me the greatest unease. Daniel Bell enabled me to understand the differences between a "causal explanation" and one that is "adequate at the level of meaning." He also steered me away from those self-described students of cultural life who have abandoned the study of meaning for the study of strategic power, abstract norms, self-interest, institutional structures, or whatever else they deem important. All of these factors are, of course, relevant, but they do not determine cultural practices in the first or last instance. Dan also launched an enfilade against some of my most cherished sociopolitical beliefs. After completing his search-and-destroy mission, he introduced me to the work of Alexis de Tocqueville and left me alone in the privacy of my study to ponder his argument.

I am also indebted to William J. Richardson for providing me a haven in which to explore the relationship between language and selfhood, and to Gerald E. Weinstein for encouraging me to explore how practical judgment shapes daily practices.

Other colleagues accompanied me on the first stretch of this long and solitary journey. Seyla Benhabib reanimated my long-term concern with the study of moral life and led me to alter my understanding of the human sciences. Alessandro Pizzorno shared with me his ideas about collective identity during our vigorous walks along the back roads of Trespiano (Florence), side streets of Cambridge (Massachusetts), and pavements of New York City. Harrison C. White undermined my longtime commitment to Levi-Straussian structuralism and trained me to see the hurly-burly of life beneath even the most seemingly stable structures.

Clifford Geertz, Albert Hirschman, Joan Scott, and Michael Walzer invited me to spend a year with them at the School for Social Science at the

Institute for Advanced Study. My time at the School was magical and be-
witching. My conversations with the permanent and visiting faculty led
me to overcome the worst intellectual habits I had acquired from years
in the academy and led me to overhaul my entire argument. I had fewer
pages of my book written at the end of my term at the Institute than when
I arrived! My debt to the School's permanent faculty is documented in the
footnotes, but it goes well beyond them. The second volume of my book
is dedicated to them. I spent my year at the Institute with a remarkable
group of scholars, including Ji Wei Ci, Martina Kessler, and Mohammed
Naciri.

James Scott and William Sewell Jr. gave me the benefit of the doubt
when I most needed it. Their scholarship and, even more importantly,
their expansive humanity has inspired me. Jorge I. Domínguez, Mark Granovetter, and Charles Tilly commented on key chapters, and persuaded
me to trim three hundred pages of text from the original manuscript even
at the risk of depriving skeptical readers of additional evidence. Partha
Chatterjee, Mahmood Mamdani, and the other members of our "Postcolonial Democracy" study group criticized my argument with the same
fierce intelligence and generosity of spirit that characterizes all their work.
David Swartz set me right on Pierre Bourdieu; Robert Westbrook reviewed
my remarks on John Dewey. My friends Samer Shehata and Shamil Jep-
pie gave me detailed comments on the entire manuscript. Dilip Gaonkar,
co-director of the Center for Transcultural Studies; Beth Povinelli, co-
editor of *Public Culture;* and all the colleagues they have brought together
into an international network provided me with the type of intellectual
stimulation and encouragement I needed to continue with my work. It was
through the Center that I was able to discuss my work with Charles Taylor. His writings played a central role in the development of my project.

Douglas Mitchell, Robert Devens, Leslie Keros, and Mark Heineke, all
at the University of Chicago Press, were the finest midwives any pregnant
author would want. They delivered my book with care and competence.
Evan P. Young copyedited my manuscript with skill and care. I am indebted to Claudio Lomnitz, Frank Safford, and a third, anonymous reviewer for their thoughtful comments on the manuscript and for saving
me from making some very foolish mistakes. If ever there were an award
for best reviewer, they would surely deserve it. Alan Wolfe, editor of the
Morality and Society Series at the University of Chicago Press, was
unswerving in his support of my project from start to finish. Alan is also
one of the most independent-minded scholars that I know, and he proved
it to me when he stood up for my manuscript at the Press and persuaded
the editors to get it reviewed again after an early reviewer judged it unworthy of publication. So it goes.

The following scholars taught me all I know about nineteenth-century Latin American history; some of them also criticized the chapters dealing with the country they know best. Nils Jacobsen, Carmen McEvoy, Ulrich Muecke, and Victor Peralta Ruiz tutored me in Peruvian history; Fernando Escalante Gonzalbo, Peter Guardino, Alan Knight, and Eric Van Young tutored me in Mexican history; Carmen Barcia, Jorge Ibarra, Manuel Barcia, and Pablo Riaño tutored me in Cuban history; and Pilar González Bernaldó, Hilda Sábato, Ricardo Salvatore, and Oscar Chamosa tutored me in Argentine history. None of them bears any responsibility for whatever errors of fact or judgment may remain in my work.

Peter Johnson, the Latin American bibliographer at Firestone Library in Princeton University, guided me through the subterranean world of special collections in the United States and Latin America, and more. Francisco Fonseca, also of Firestone, helped in important ways, as did the entire staff of the interlibrary office and photocopying services. I am also indebted to the staff at the Bancroft Library at the University of California at Berkeley; the Beinecke Library at Yale University; Widener Library at Harvard University; the Sutro Collection of the California State Library; the Biblioteca Nacional and the Archivo General de la Nación in Mexico City; the Instituto Riva-Aguero, the Archivo Histórico Municipal, and the Biblioteca Nacional in Lima; the Biblioteca Nacional José Martí and the Archivo Nacional in Havana; and the Archivo Nacional, the Biblioteca Nacional, and the Museo Mitre in Buenos Aires, to list only those institutions where I did the bulk of my primary research.

Numerous colleagues provided me with a public forum in which to present portions of my work. The criticisms and comments I received from them and from other members of the audience were especially helpful. In recognition of this, I list the institutions that made this possible: the Program in Agrarian Studies at Yale University; the Center for the Study of Social Change at the New School for Social Research; the Divinity School at the University of Chicago; the Latin American Studies Program at the University of Chicago; the Center for Mexican Studies at the University of California-San Diego; the Program in Latin American Culture at the University of Pennsylvania; the Instituto de Estudios Peruanos, Universidad de San Marcos, and Universidad Católica del Perú; the Universidad Torcuato di Tella, Universidad de Buenos Aires, and Facultad Latinoamericana de Ciencias Sociales (Buenos Aires); the Colegio de México and Universidad Nacional Autónoma de México; and the Instituto de Historia and Universidad de la Habana.

During the last phase of this study, I had the privilege of working in each country alongside a group of talented junior scholars. Without their assistance, I would not have been able to complete my databank on associative life in nineteenth-century Latin America in a timely manner. In Mexico, I worked with the incomparable Cecilia Riquelme; in Peru, with the ever resourceful Eduardo Quintana Sánchez; in Argentina, with Sonia Tedeschi and Pablo Vagliente; and in Cuba, with Adrián López-Denis. In addition to designing my databanks and providing me with technical support, Francisco Hirsch, María Marta Sobico, and Lucas Cadena taught me what little I know about computer software. Lunia Vera assisted me in revising and checking all my footnotes.

Over the years, I received financial support for my project from the following: the Social Science Research Council; the National Endowment for the Humanities; the American Philosophical Society; the American Sociological Association; the American Political Science Association; the Fulbright Commission; Princeton University's Committee on Faculty Research and the Lewis Fund, which is administered by the Center of International Affairs; and the Center for Caribbean Studies of the John Hopkins University.

I lived for nearly two years in Ayahualulco (Veracruz, Mexico), a village community perched high up in the Sierra Madre Oriental near the "Pico de Orizaba," in a Christian Base Community, alongside a group of public intellectuals active in the Catholic Church and various radical groups. After the Tlatelolco massacre in 1968, they, like so many others of their generation, abandoned Mexico City for the countryside and went "directly to the people," reminiscent of the nineteenth-century Russian Narodniks studied by Franco Venturi. By the time I joined them in early fall 1976, they had established several other base communities, including in San Miguel Zinacapan in Cuetzalan, Puebla, the heartland of indigenous life. During the two years that I worked and lived in the highlands of Ayahualulco, the entire region was teeming with Mexican narodniks, especially along the border between the states of Veracruz and Puebla, and between Morelos and Guerrero. Our work consisted in providing local residents with primary and adult education programs, cooperatives, credit unions, and political organization, and, in some places, leading land takeovers. Some of those I met in the region eventually became disenchanted with this type of work; the majority of them returned to the city, and the remaining few joined one or another of the short-lived guerrilla groups that had been active in the area.

This generated enormous concern among municipal, state, and federal officials loyal to the Institutionalized Revolutionary Party (PRI). After President José López Portillo took office in January 1977, the PRI launched a "low-intensity" campaign aimed at pacifying the countryside. Fortunately, Ayahualulco was not a hot spot, so it was not targeted. However, fallout from the campaign reached us as well, and made daily life extremely difficult. PRI bosses led witch hunts against anyone in the region they considered disloyal to them. Friends and neighbors accused each other of "subversion," using this as an opportunity to settle age-old feuds. After the crisis had passed, I returned to Mexico City and took courses at the Museum of History and Anthropology in order to make sense of what I had lived through. The other members of the community remained in Ayahualulco for another decade; some of them continue to work in the countryside. A study evaluating key aspects of our sociopolitical work in Ayahualulco can be found in an article that appeared in *Relaciones,* a leading social science journal in Mexico.[6] The lessons I learned in democratic living from Enrique, Gabriel, Valerio, Artemio, and Guillebaldo remain with me to this day.

In 1990 I spent four months in Hungary and Poland, where I had the opportunity to have numerous conversations with Miklos Sukosd and other ex-members of the Free Democrats in Budapest, and members of the East-Central European Study Group in Cracow, Warsaw, and Poltusk. Their insights on the nature of civil society, democratic life, and authoritatianism is discernible in my work.

My salute to all these people, and to my two oldest friends, César V. Cauce and Juan de Armendi, who are forever present in their absence. My ex-neighbors in Lake Lane, Hume Feldman, the great cosmologist and sailor from Haifa, and the Mediterranean humanist extraordinaire Stathis Gourgourian, have now become new friends.

I dedicate the first volume of this study to my wife, Silvia María, an anthropologist by profession, and to my daughters, Amanda Raquel and Cecilia Antonia. Silvia's affection for daily life and sense of reciprocity taught me the meaning of both. She also provided me with "a room with a view" in which to pursue my work. The door to this room, however, was always open and Amanda and Cecilia visited me all too often. Their lives have kept me rooted in the present and have renewed my faith in the future.

My gratitude to one and all.

. . . Caminante no hay camino, se hace camino al andar. . . .

6. Miguel J. Hernández Madrid, "Conflicto social y movilización campesina en un Municipio del estado de Veracruz: El caso de Ayahualulco (1973–1983)," *Relaciones* 6, no. 24 (autumn 1985): 111–33.

PART ONE

INTRODUCTION

CHAPTER 1

Common Sense and Democracy
in Latin America Today

Working on this study has been extremely difficult. Some of the reasons for this are all too familiar: a lack of clarity about my own argument; the breadth of the project itself; the constant search for the proper phrase to convey an elusive idea; and a lack of financial support for libraries and archives in Latin America that makes research on the nineteenth century an exercise in fortitude. But the single greatest challenge I faced, the one that confused me the most and took me the longest to recognize, is what I now call, not without affection, the problem of "common sense." Common sense is another way of saying: "this is the way we do things here." Common sense is what remains untouched after we have submerged all our other ideas and beliefs in an acid bath of criticism and purified them of any personal prejudices. Common sense is rarely remarked upon because it is constitutive of who we are.[1]

Common Sense: Popular and Academic

While doing research in each country, I spent a large part of my time in conversation with cabbies, bus drivers, schoolteachers, skilled workers, shopkeepers, policemen, professionals, housewives, journalists, and semi-employed squatters.[2] In the course of these conversations, I came to realize that the most recent "return to democracy" in Latin America was radically different from all previous such movements in one fundamental respect: it has not been accompanied by a renascence in democratic prac-

1. Clifford Geertz, "Common Sense as a Cultural System," in *Local Knowledge: Further Essays in Interpretive Anthropology* (New York: Basic Books, 1983), 73–93.
2. Pierre Bourdieu, *Leçon sur la leçon* (Paris: Editions de Minuit, 1982), 10: "the sociology of . . . intellectual life . . . takes the analytical categories that define and limit the subject of study and makes them as much a part of the investigation as the object of analysis itself."

tice or thought. The democratic tradition in Latin America is in a more advanced state of disrepair than ever before.[3]

Prior to now, the tradition had suffered both momentary setbacks and long-lasting reversals, especially in the 1930s and 1940s during the era of "national populism." But from the late 1960s onward, the democratic tradition began unraveling under the pressures exerted by those of us who were directly engaged in, or were indirect supporters of, guerrilla socialism and military authoritarianism. I am speaking, of course, about the majority of us. Recall that in the early 1970s, more than half of all residents of Cordoba, Argentina—one of Latin America's most "modern" cities, with a highly skilled labor force and a stable middle class—supported guerrilla warfare.[4] Also recall than in May 1995, voters in Tucuman, Argentina, the province most brutalized during the early years of the dictatorship, elected as state governor the same General "Mad Dog" Bussi who had been responsible for implementing the "dirty war" in the region.[5] The strange mixture of dread, courage, helplessness, and self-importance that afflicted all of us who lived through this period seems to have diminished our capacity to imagine and practice democracy.

After clarifying my views about the demise of democracy in Latin America, I began to discuss them with friends, strangers, colleagues, and acquaintances in corner cafes, in public parks, at scholarly conferences and private gatherings. All of them claimed that my assessment of democratic life in their country was off target, and by a wide margin. In Argentina, for example, I recall an especially spirited discussion with long-time Peronist militants, mainly shopkeepers, construction workers, and bus drivers. Although opposed to the government of President Carlos Menem for having privatized and denationalized the economy, they continued to be loyal to the Justicialista Party. The wave of public demonstrations, "supermarket" riots, highway blockades, and popular rebellions that swept the country in the early 1990s was, they claimed, proof that democracy had finally returned to this troubled country.

3. Alasdair MacIntyre, *After Virtue: A Study in Moral Theory* (Notre Dame, Ind.: University of Notre Dame Press, 1981), 222: "A living tradition . . . is a historically extended, socially embodied argument, and an argument precisely in part about the goods which constitute the tradition. . . . Traditions, when vital, embody continuities in conflict. . . ." My understanding of tradition derives from the work of Hans Georg Gadamer and Alasdair McIntyre rather than from the work of Richard Morse or Howard Wiarda on the "Iberian-Corporate" tradition that is dominant among Latin Americanists.

4. "Opinionmetro-Medición sistemática de tendencias de la opinión pública (Ola I, Ola II)," in Guillermo O'Donnell, *Bureaucratic Authoritarianism: Argentina, 1966–1973 in Comparative Perspective*, trans. James McGuire with Rae Flory (Berkeley: University of California Press, 1988), 308–10.

5. Alejandro Isla, "Terror, Memory and Responsibility in Argentina," *Critique of Anthropology* 18, no. 2 (1998): 134–56.

I heard similar accounts during my stay in Lima in the early 1990s, soon after President Alberto Fujimori had begun dismantling Peru's bloated state and slashing social spending. The "Fuji-shocks," as his program came to be called, wreaked havoc among the poorest of the poor living in Lima's shantytowns, many of whom were indigenous peoples who had been forced to abandon their rural communities to escape the crossfire between "Shining Path" guerrillas and the army's counterinsurgent forces. Immigrants led the way in organizing soup kitchens in Lima's shantytowns, providing daily sustenance to more than 2 million residents. The local organizers and journalists with whom I spoke were convinced that these self-help groups were proof that the country's poor were now capable of practicing self-rule. Democracy, according to them, had finally found a place in Latin America's most oligarchic city.

During my visits to Cuba in the mid-1990s, it was apparent that the Communist Party had "liberalized" public life but by adopting a different strategy. The Party decriminalized ownership of U.S. dollars and granted business licenses, thereby legalizing the island's underground economy. The Party also encouraged foreign investors, mainly Canadian, Western European, and Mexican, to establish joint ventures with state firms (roughly 350 of them) and cleared the way for emigres to send remittances ($500 million per year) to their relatives on the island. Many of them used these monies as start-up capital, establishing small businesses of all types. When I was there, *paladares*—mom-and-pop diners that operated in the living rooms of private homes—had sprouted all over Havana; by 1998, there were roughly 800 of them. These diners had a large and loyal clientele that paid for their food in dollars, enabling owners to hire a small army of farmers, fishermen, plumbers, and electricians to keep them going, inducing many others to abandon the public for the private sector. The Cubans I spoke with, including several mid- and lower-level members of the Party, were convinced that economic globalization was unstoppable and would soon compel the Party to recognize property rights and reinstate the rule of law on the island.

The Mexican and Argentine voters I spoke with described elections as the jewel in the crown of post-authoritarian democracy. Although all of them acknowledged that political parties in their country continued to be "oligarchic" and that the majority of officials in all three branches of government continued to be corrupt and unresponsive to their needs, these voters remained unswerving in their commitment to the electoral process. In my conversations with members of the "Alianza Civica," a civic group in Mexico whose 40,000 members were responsible in 1994 for monitoring voting practices in more than 10,000 polling stations across the country, it became evident to me that they were now investing elections with a symbolic importance that went far beyond their actual significance. In the late summer of that year, I was in Buenos Aires on election day and had the opportunity to accompany my wife to the voting station in our neighborhood (Moldes). After she had voted, we stayed and mingled with other residents, and in our conversations we were struck by their sense of loyalty to the electoral process. My wife and I spent the remainder of the day at a private gathering at the home of a friend. Predictably enough, much of the discussion that afternoon focused on the elections and, more broadly, the issue of constitutional rule in Argentina. The staunchest defender of both turned out to be, I found out later on, an ex-Montonero who had recently returned from exile. Every six years or so, Mexicans and Argentines enter the voting booth and once inside transform themselves, if only for a few minutes, into citizens. Those who partake in this ritual do so for different reasons. For some, it is an opportunity to reaffirm their commitment to democracy; for others, it enables them to express their sense of shame and remorse at having been disloyal to democracy.

But from my Tocquevillian perch, these examples seemed to me a confirmation rather than a refutation of my interpretation of the crisis of democracy in the region. Contrary to what post-marxists now claim, democracy cannot be reduced to the brief moments of hyperactivism that characterize most "new" social movements in the region; nor can it be sustained over the long run by the type of low-intensity elections endorsed by political reformers; nor can the rule of law ensure democracy's survival. The mass movements, self-help groups, presidential elections, and economic-legal reforms struck me as the shattered fragments and incoherent remains of what once had been a vital (albeit flawed) democratic tradition. They reminded me of the rubbled walls, truncated pyramids, and weed-covered paths that mark the places where the great Mayan and Incan civilizations once flourished but today are nothing more than archaeological sites. Although we continue to admire these ancient ruins, few of us can even conjure, much less understand, the forms of life they once sustained.

Sociologists and political scientists have produced their own brand of common sense. For the past decade or so, they have been scrambling across the continent chasing after late-breaking events in order to develop a "theory" of democratization.[6] The number of monographs that have appeared on the subject is simply staggering and cannot be reviewed here. Three views predominate. "Rationalists" focus on the way military and civilian groups created elite pacts and negotiated the transfer of power

6. Albert O. Hirschman, "The Search for Paradigms as a Hindrance to Understanding," *World Politics* 22 (April 1970): 329–43.

during and after the transition, and on how this has shaped the new civilian government.[7] "Parliamentarians" focus on the ways government reformers have tried to create strong and autonomous legislatures capable of curbing the executive and preventing it from centralizing power.[8] Finally, "party-centered" scholars focus on the demise of the party system. The demise of mass parties has, on the one hand, undermined the socioelectoral foundations of single-party states and, on the other hand, made it impossible for voters to make politicians responsive and to hold them accountable.[9]

These scholars have trained our attention on key aspect of public life, but they have done so by subordinating the issue of democracy itself, what Tocqueville called "sovereignty of the people," to matters of state governance. Although all of them claim to be borrowing from Robert Dahl's classic studies on "polyarchy," they have done so in an exceedingly biased and selective manner, either ignoring or downplaying his concern for associative life, public deliberation, civic selfhood, socioeconomic equality, and accountability in the workplace, school, and other arenas of public life.[10] On closer inspection it becomes clear that their main debt is to Joseph Schumpeter.[11] That most of these scholars are unable to distinguish civic from market models of democracy is itself indicative of the crisis of democracy in the region.

Even Guillermo O'Donnell, by far the most insightful scholar in this group, too often expresses his criticism in overly narrow terms.[12] Although he shares many of Dahl's concerns, including a normative commitment to

7. Guillermo O'Donnell, Philippe Schmitter, and Laurence Whitehead, *Transitions from Authoritarian Rule* (Baltimore, Md.: Johns Hopkins University Press, 1986).

8. Juan J. Linz and Arturo Valenzuela, *The Failure of Presidential Democracy* (Baltimore, Md.: Johns Hopkins University Press, 1994).

9. Scott Mainwaring and Timothy Scully, *Building Democratic Institutions: Party Systems in Latin America* (Stanford, Calif.: Stanford University Press, 1995).

10. See the following works by Robert Dahl: *Democracy and Its Critics* (New Haven, Conn.: Yale University Press, 1989), 91, 221–22; *Polyarchy: Participation and Opposition* (New Haven, Conn.: Yale University Press, 1971), 10–11, 84, 227–40; *A Preface to Economic Democracy* (Chicago: University of Chicago Press, 1956), 13; *Dilemmas of Pluralist Democracy: Autonomy versus Control* (New Haven: Yale University Press, 1982), 32. For an assessment of Dahl's works: Ian Shapiro and Grant Reher, *Power and Inequality: Essays in Honor of Robert Dahl and Democratic Politics* (Boulder, Colo.: Westview Press, 1988).

11. David Held, *Models of Democracy* (Cambridge: Polity Press, 1987) for a comparison of Dahl's and Schumpeter's analyses of democracy.

12. It is impossible to analyze the development of Latin American Studies since the 1970s without considering Guillermo O'Donnell's influence. In his early work, O'Donnell adopted a "structuralist determinist" approach to explain the emergence of bureaucratic authoritarian regimes in the Southern Cone; in his later work, he adopted a "microrationalist" perspective to explain democratic transitions in the region. Each time he shifted his intellectual orientation, a great many Latin Americanists followed suit. Whether this reflected a fundamental change in the nature of public life in the region or was mainly the result of professional dynamics in the field is a question that requires further study.

democracy, the bulk of his work focuses on the incapacity or unwilling-
ness of government officials to rationalize the state and to use its legal-
administrative resources to implant democracy on what he deems to be
an otherwise populist society composed of unruly citizens.[13] Instead of
exploring how they actually practice democracy in daily life and how this
practice shapes and is in turn shaped by institutions, O'Donnell, after
countless twists and turns in his argument, almost always ends up granting primacy to state officials, until his next essay, when he then accuses
them of acting even more irrationally than the citizenry itself. It usually
takes O'Donnell several years (or articles) to complete an entire cycle.
His shift from a statist to an antistatist conception of democracy and
back again is reminiscent of Weber's description of modern politics, with
periods of "bureaucratic rationality" interrupted by brief moments of
"charismatic meaning." O'Donnell's vacillations are also reminiscent of
the intellectual and political swings one finds in the writings of nineteenth-
century Latin American intellectuals. Their unswerving belief in the power
of laws and institutions to usher in democracy was shattered time and
again by the seemingly irrational practices of the citizenry itself.[14] This was
also, of course, the main issue underlying all of Tocqueville's work and the
issue I have tried to explore in this book.

   This is not the time to attempt a comprehensive evaluation of the democratic tradition in Latin America; that task belongs to the next generation
of scholars and thinkers. But in the meantime, we can clear the ground
by challenging old and new "certainties" and providing them with what
Albert Hirschman calls "possibilistic" accounts of democratic life in the
region.[15]

Tocquevillians and Sovereignty of the People

The recent worldwide resurgence in Tocquevillianism is now poised to
fill the intellectual and sociopolitical vacuum left by the demise of marxism. The Tocquevillian revival began in Central Europe and was initiated
by Bronislaw Geremek, Václav Havel, George Konrad, and other public
intellectuals in Poland, Czechoslovakia, and Hungary during the last years
of the old regime. The discussion became especially animated after the

---

   13. Guillermo O'Donnell, *Counterpoints: Selected Essays on Authoritarianism and Democratization* (Notre Dame, Ind.: University of Notre Dame Press, 1999), focuses on democracy. Most of his other works focus on the emergence and demise of authoritarian
regimes.
   14. See Brian Loveman, *The Constitution of Tyranny: Regimes of Exception in Spanish America* (Pittsburgh, Pa.: University of Pittsburgh Press, 1993) for an overview.
   15. Albert O. Hirschman, *Rival Views of Market Society and Other Recent Essays* (Cambridge: Harvard University Press, 1992), 171–75.

demise of state socialism and after the opposition gained power and was faced with the daunting task of creating democratic life from the rubble of totalitarian rule.[16] The "civil society" argument, as it came to be called, was put forward by Central Europeans who, in living with their "backs toward the state," were seeking to undermine peacefully and from within the most autocratic and stable regime to have appeared in the modern period.

By the mid-1990s the center of Tocquevillianism had migrated from central Europe to North America and western Europe, and from public intellectuals to professional scholars in major research universities and private foundations. In addition to shifting the discussion from issues related to the emergence of democracy in post-totalitarian settings to those pertaining to the problems confronting mature democracies, these scholars and policy makers altered the grammar and syntax of the debate, for better and for worse. They improved on it by challenging Havel's antipolitical model of public life, made famous by his phrase, "civil society against the state." All of us now know that participation in political society is as important to the development of democratic life as is participation in civil society, economic society, and the public sphere. But the second generation also impoverished the discussion by using liberalism to domesticate democracy.[17] In the United States, for example, scholars, policy makers, and think-tank analysts steered the discussion on civic democracy away from the issue of "sovereignty of the people," which had been at the center of the debate in central Europe and at the heart of Tocqueville's work, to issues related to "communal cohesion," "individual rights," "big government," and "welfare relief."[18]

But modern democracy has no foundations, liberal or otherwise, nor should we be trying to provide it with any. As Claude Lefort argues, what makes democratic regimes so radically new and distinct from all other

16. See Jeffrey C. Goldfarb, *Civility and Subversion: The Intellectual in Democratic Society* (Cambridge: Harvard University Press, 1998), and his *After the Fall: The Pursuit of Democracy in Central Europe* (New York: Basic Books, 1992) for a broad-minded account.

17. Christopher Beem, *The Necessity of Politics: Reclaiming American Public Life*, with a foreword by Jean Bethke Elshtain (Chicago: University of Chicago Press, 1999), surveys the debate in the United States. For a perceptive account of how the collapse of state socialism represented a major challenge to the liberal imagination, see Peter Sherwood, "The Errata of History," *Times Literary Supplement*, 20 March 1992, 10. For a remarkably obtuse and intolerant discussion of the same, see Paul Starr, "Liberalism after Socialism," *The American Prospect* 7 (fall 1991): 13.

18. Alexis de Tocqueville, *Democracy in America*, trans. George Lawrence, ed. J. P. Mayer (Garden City, N.Y.: Doubleday, 1969), 397: "sovereignty of the people is not an isolated doctrine. . . . [T]his is the great maxim on which rests political and civil society. . . . Thus . . . the generative principle of the republic is the same which directs the majority of human action."

regimes is their capacity to "institutionalize uncertainty."[19] In the course of practicing democracy, citizens give sociopolitical form and cultural meaning to the otherwise hollow phrase "sovereignty of the people." Popular sovereignty in democratic regimes is never the exclusive patrimony of any one group (business elite, industrial workers, middle class, peasants); nor is sovereignty always produced in the same way or from the exact same places (social movements in civil society); nor is sovereignty always transferred from the ruled to the rulers in the same manner (political parties and elections); nor is sovereignty deposited each and every time in the same institution (legislature, judiciary, executive).

The way sovereignty is lived in democratic regimes contrasts starkly with how it is experienced in aristocratic and Leninist regimes, which have been, historically and politically, its principal rivals. In aristocratic regimes, the monarch, by virtue of his direct link to God, is made the embodiment of sovereignty, therefore making it unnecessary for him and for members of his court to deliberate publicly and to justify their policies to their subjects. According to the doctrine of divine will, monarchs are the only ones who know where sovereignty resides (in the throne) and what it means (rule by the few). In Leninist regimes, the vanguard plays an analogous role. The party, by virtue of its scientific knowledge of the "laws and motion" of history (dialectical materialism), is the final arbiter in all matters related to sovereignty. The cadre in regimes of this type is responsible for establishing what is "true" and "false" consciousness at any time and for implementing whatever policies are needed to advance the general and universal interests of humanity (read: proletariat). Despite their obvious differences, monarchists and Leninists assume that they, and only they, occupy a place outside history and beyond the ebb and flow of sociopolitical life.

Tradition against Common Sense

My effort to break with common sense eventually took its toll on me. Each time I returned from doing fieldwork, I would spend several months in my office sifting through mountains of photocopied documents and the reams of notes I had transcribed, but unable to make any sense of them in light of the recent debates on democratization in the field of Latin American Studies. David Lehman's description of them is worth quoting here:

19. Claude Lefort, "The Question of Democracy," in *Democracy and Political Theory* (Minneapolis: University of Minnesota Press, 1989), 9–20: "democracy institutionalizes and maintains itself through the dissolution of certainty. It inaugurates a history in which men are subjected to a final indetermination as to the foundation of power, law and knowledge, and the basis of the relationship between them in every aspect of social life."

the (discussion) has been hijacked by the highly professionalized and self-consciously model-based discipline of comparative politics, which has thrived in recent years. . . . The "comparative" element consists in drawing material in an a-historical way from variegated experiences distributed often indiscriminately across time and space, resulting in the replacement of a multi-faceted . . . account . . . with rational choice models constructed around tightly drawn conceptual questions about institutions. . . .[20]

In contrast to the postwar generation, who took their intellectual cues from public life, contemporary scholars working on Latin America take theirs from professional debates rooted in the academy. The abstracted empiricism, hyperpresentism, jargonistic cant, and scientism that passes for common sense in Latin American Studies, I now recognize, prevented me from making sense of democratic life in the region.

The confusion I experienced reminded me of a passage from E. M. Forster's *Two Cheers for Democracy,* in which the author describes the sense of disorientation he and members of his generation felt on the eve of the Second World War:

> 1941 is not a good year in which to sum up anything. Our judgements, to put it mildly are not at their prime. We are all of us upon the Leaning Tower. . . . We cannot judge the landscape properly . . . for everything is tilted. Isolated objects are not so puzzling; a tree, a wave, a hat, a jewel, an old gentlemen's bald head look as they always did. But the relation between objects—that we cannot estimate, and that is why the verdict must be left to another generation.[21]

I lost my intellectual and moral moorings midway into my project, and I did not become re-anchored until I had the opportunity to reread Michael Walzer's little book on social criticism. According to him,

> Social criticism is less the practical offspring of scientific knowledge than the educated cousin of common complaint. We become critics naturally . . . by elaborating on existing moralities and telling stories about a society more just than, though never entirely different from, our own.[22]

This time my connection to Walzer's book was immediate and strong. After reading it, I became convinced of the need to use the narrative resources already contained in the democratic tradition of Latin America

20. David Lehman, "Mr. Bountiful Takes Charge," *Times Literary Supplement,* 28 April 2000, 30.

21. E. M. Forster, *Two Cheers for Democracy* (New York: Harcourt, Brace and World, 1951), 251.

22. Michael Walzer, *Interpretation and Social Criticism* (Cambridge: Harvard University Press, 1987), 65.

to expose and criticize its shortcomings from within. I continued doing archival research, gathering new evidence and poring over my old notes, but this time around I found myself pausing and listening carefully to the concerns expressed by nineteenth-century Latin Americans in the documents they had left behind. I now accorded these citizens the very same authority that I had previously been willing to grant only to contemporary scholars in the field of Latin American Studies.

This "conversational" approach led me to revise my interpretation many times over, with each new "fact" altering my understanding of all the rest. Rebuilding my framework was even more bewildering.[23] This two-way dialogue is now reflected in the structure of the book. My conversation with fellow scholars appears mainly in chapter 1, chapter 2, and the "Concluding Remarks"; my conversation with nineteenth-century citizens of the region appears in chapters 3 to 15. In other words, this book resembles the same type of animated discussion we often have with each other about the issues we care most about, discussions that nourish and sustain public life. Whether I have also succeeded in reviving the democratic tradition in Latin America is for readers to judge.

While working on this project, I was struck by the subterranean connections between the forms of life I saw all around me and the descriptions of public life contained in the nineteenth-century documents housed in the libraries and archives I visited. This connection, it is safe to say, will prove no less elusive and complex to the next generation of scholars as they attempt to study the spread of authoritarianism and the demise of democracy in late-twentieth-century Latin America. In the transition from living memory to archival documents, neither they nor we can overlook the moral meaning and sociopolitical choices that confronted those citizens who lived through both periods. As Arendt noted, it is impossible to understand democratic life by relying on the type of scientistic methods commonly used by political scientists and sociologists, since these are themselves based on authoritarian premises.[24] The struggle for democratic life is as much a struggle over "research methodology" as over the right to participate in public affairs. Only after I had become aware of the

23. See Hans Georg Gadamer, *Truth and Method,* trans. Garrett Barden and John Cummings (New York: Seabury Press, 1975), 5–6, 87–89, 236–37, 240–53, 311–12, 332–36, 407–12 for a discussion of "fusion of horizons."

24. Hannah Arendt, *Between Past and Future: Eight Exercises in Political Thought* (New York: Penguin Books, 1977), 239, 241: "Seen from the viewpoint of politics, truth has a despotic character. . . . The mode of thought and communication that deal with truth, if seen from the political perspective, are necessarily domineering; they don't take into account other people's opinions, and taking these into account is the hallmark of all strictly political thinking."

connection between democracy and methodology was I able to regain my own sense of "author-ity."

Contemporary theorists have already leveled telling criticisms against scientism; I need not review them here.[25] Anyone who insists on evaluating my work in these terms will be disappointed. I have collected a significant body of evidence in order to challenge our own belief in the irrelevance of history, the existence of invariant laws, and the need for social engineering.[26] In the 1970s, these three "myths," in Walter Benjamin's sense, inspired a generation of socialists to embrace guerrilla warfare and in doing so to sacrifice the imperfect present for an idyllic future, in the same way that today neoliberals are destroying the future and past in order to prepare the way for that new time zone pundits call the "end of history," where rational truth is supposed to have triumphed over subjective delusion.[27] In order to emancipate us from the burdens of time and tradition, guerrilla socialists and neoliberals have relied on the "will to power" and "self-interest." The "new man" that inspired the former and the "greedy consumer" so dear to the latter are in reality nothing more than latter-day incarnations of the "egoist," as originally described by Tocqueville. Throughout Latin America, egoists now populate the public landscape and occupy major positions in all the key institutions of the region, including the national congress and central bank, labor unions and the national university, the Catholic Church and the Communist Party, and even nongovernmental organizations.

I have written this study from inside the breach that now exists in the democratic tradition with the goal of salvaging whatever treasures remain scattered in the wreckage that is Latin American public life. "History is mere history," said the Argentine poet Jorge Luis Borges. "Myths are what matter: They determine the type of history a country is bound to create and repeat." I have assembled a significant body of "empirical evidence" in order, paradoxically, to enable us to look beyond the facts themselves. Only by reconfiguring our myths will we be able to reckon with the reality of democratic life in Latin America. In surveying the nineteenth cen-

---

25. Richard Bernstein, *The Restructuring of Social and Political Theory* (Philadelphia: University of Pennsylvania Press, 1976), and his *Praxis and Action* (Philadelphia: University of Pennsylvania Press, 1971).

26. See Irving Wohlfarth, "Re-fusing Theology," *New German Critique* 39 (fall 1986): 17 for a critical rereading of Benjamin.

27. On guerrilla socialism, see Jorge Castañeda, *Utopia Unarmed: The Latin American Left after the Cold War* (New York: Alfred A. Knopf, 1993). On neoliberalism, see Javier Santiso, "Political Sluggishness and Economic Speed: A Latin American Perspective," *Social Science Information* 39, no. 2 (2000): 233–53.

tury, I have followed Hannah Arendt's advice and like a pearl diver have descended to the ocean floor,

> not to excavate the bottom and bring it to light but to pry loose from the rich and strange, the pearls and the corals . . . and carry them to the surface. . . . [This type] of thinking delves into depths of the past—but not in order to resuscitate it the way it was and to contribute to the renewal of extinct ages. What guides this thinking is the conviction that although the living is subject to the ruin of time, the process of decay is at the same time a process of crystallization. . . .[28]

The strengths and shortcomings of my study are to be found in the way I have woven together the interpretive and historical strands that now constitute this seamless work.[29] This is where I take my stand, and this is where my argument will persuade readers or not.

Only toward the end of my study did I find the words I needed to describe the common sense that from the start had been in front of my eyes but outside my field of vision. Common sense got between me and my work, and I have written this introduction in the hope that it will not prevent you, the reader, from appreciating the "counterfactual" argument of this book.

28. Hannah Arendt, *Men in Dark Times* (New York: Harcourt, Brace and World, 1968), 205–6.

29. Rogers M. Smith, "Science, Non-Science and Politics," and Craig Calhoun, "The Rise and Domestication of Historical Sociology," in *The Historic Turn in the Human Sciences*, ed. Terence J. McDonald (Ann Arbor: University of Michigan Press, 1996), 119–60 and 305–37, criticize the way political scientists and sociologist such as Theda Skocpol and Charles Tilly use the historical record as a "laboratory" for testing "scientific theories," thereby draining both of their critical and emancipatory potential.

CHAPTER 2

Social Equality and Political Liberty as Forms of Life

My work on Latin American democracy is in dialogue with the following four groups of scholars: Tocquevillians who study the changing character of public life; Latin Americanists who study the origins of authoritarianism in the area; postcolonialists who study the negative effects the colonial legacy had on democracy in Third World countries; and political theorists who study polyarchical regimes in the modern world. Scholars in any one of these groups rarely engage those in the others, although I found the work of all four to be directly relevant to my own. The ideas outlined in this chapter are nothing more than landmarks. Their purpose is to provide readers with a road map of the historical thicket that lies ahead. Adventurous readers who enjoy trekking through the wilderness without a guide can skip this chapter and return to it whenever they feel the need (or not at all).

Tocquevillians and Public Life

Tocquevillians are currently debating the relative importance of each of the four public terrains—civil society, political society, economic society, and the public sphere—in the development of democratic life.[1] Four views predominate. Scholars in the first group grant primacy to civil society.[2]

1. My interpretation owes much to Michael Walzer, "The Concept of Civil Society," in his *Toward a Global Civil Society* (Providence, R.I.: Berghahn Books, 1995), 7–28.
2. David Riesman, with Nathan Glazer and Reuel Denney, *The Lonely Crowd: A Study of the Changing American Character* (New Haven, Conn.: Yale University Press, 1950); Edward C. Banfield, *The Moral Basis of a Backward Society* (Glencoe, Ill.: The Free Press, 1958); Richard Sennett, *The Fall of Public Man: On the Social Psychology of Capitalism* (New York: Vintage Books, 1978); Michèle Odeye-Finzi, *Les associations en villes africaines* (Paris: L'Harmâttan, 1985); Robert Bellah, Richard Madsen, William M. Sullivan, Ann Swidler, and Steve Tipton, *Habits of the Heart: Individualism and Commitment in*

According to them, membership in religious, work-based, neighborhood, educational, ethnic-racial, recreational, and other types of associations provides citizens a stable place in which to forge ties of solidarity and to recognize each other as members of the same community. In these groups, citizens also acquire the practical and deliberative skills they need to become competent citizens. These authors claim that despite its importance, civil society is fast unraveling as a result of efforts by state officials and economic managers to "colonize" it. Civil society's demise has undermined the moral and social foundations of democratic life.

Scholars in the second group ascribe similar importance to political society.[3] According to them, participating in elections, political parties, interest groups, and mass movements provides citizens an opportunity to influence government officials and to use the institutional resources they have to improve their life chances, enabling them to redistribute socioeconomic and cultural power from the privileged "few" to the "many." Acting collectively enables even the poor and marginalized citizens to use political power to democratize public life. However, according to scholars in this group, the wealthy and powerful have been far more successful in gaining control of the political arena. They have accomplished this by organizing themselves into lobby groups and by using their economic

---

American Life (Berkeley: University of California Press, 1985); Renato Boschi, *A Arte de Associação* (Rio de Janeiro: IUPERJ, 1987); Alan Wolfe, *Whose Keeper: Social Science and Moral Obligation* (Berkeley: University of California Press, 1989); Fernando Escalante Gonzalbo, *Ciudadanos Imaginarios* (Mexico City: El Colegio de México, 1993); Robert Putnam, *Making Democracy Work: Civic Traditions in Modern Italy* (Princeton, N.J.: Princeton University Press, 1993); Adolf Bibic and Gigi Graziano, *Civil Society, Political Society and Democracy* (Ljubljana: Slovenina Political Science Association, 1994); and Robert Wuthnow, *Loose Connections: Joining Together in America's Fragmented Communities* (Cambridge: Harvard University Press, 1998).

3. Hannah Arendt, *On Revolution* (New York: Viking Press, 1963); Seymour M. Lipset, *The First New Nation: The United States in Historical and Comparative Perspective* (New York: Basic Books, 1963); Samuel P. Huntington, *Political Order in Changing Societies* (New Haven, Conn.: Yale University Press, 1968); Morris Janowitz, *The Reconstruction of Patriotism: Education for Civic Consciousness* (Chicago: University of Chicago Press, 1983); Natalio R. Botana, *La tradición republicana: Alberdi, Sarmiento y las ideas políticas de su tiempo* (Buenos Aires: Editorial Sudamericana, 1984); Alfred Stepan, *Rethinking Military Politics: Brazil and the Southern Cone* (Princeton, N.J.: Princeton University Press, 1988); Pierre Rosanvallon, *Le sacre du citoyen: Histoire du suffrage universel en France* (Paris: Gallimard, 1992); Víctor Pérez Díaz, *The Return of Civil Society: The Emergence of Democratic Spain* (Cambridge: Harvard University Press, 1993); J. W. Harbeson, D. Rothchild, and N. Chazan, *Civil Society and the State in Africa* (Boulder, Colo.: L. Rienner Publishers, 1994); Augustus R. Norton, *Civil Society in the Middle East*, 2 vols. (Leiden: Brill, 1996); Michael Sandel, *Democracy's Discontent: America in Search of a Public Philosophy* (Cambridge: Harvard University Press, 1996); Hilda Sábato, *La política en las calles: Entre el voto y la movilización* (Buenos Aires: Editorial Sudamericana, 1998); Michael Schudson, *The Good Citizen: A History of American Civic Life* (New York: Martin Kessler Books, 1998); and Larry Diamond, *Developing Democracy: Toward Consolidation* (Baltimore, Md.: Johns Hopkins University Press, 1999).

resources to support one or another congressional or presidential candidate, undermining the capacity of all other citizens to do the same, making the electorate at large increasingly apathetic and leading many citizens to abandon political society.

A third group of neo-Tocquevillians claim that economic society is the foundation of democracy.[4] Market capitalism, they argue, contributes to decentralizing wealth, thereby providing citizens the power they need to defend themselves against state officials and to preserve liberty in the modern world. Market-driven societies are also unique in their unmatched capacity to soften racial, ethnic, and religious differences by compelling citizens to respect the laws of "supply and demand." Even when the market fails to accomplish all of this, it has its own built-in mechanisms that lead it to correct its own imperfections automatically. But according to critics, the proliferation of large corporations and multinational firms throughout economic society has led to a centralization and monopolization of wealth and other types of material and symbolic resources, making it impossible for citizens to practice democracy in economic society or any other public terrain.

A fourth group of scholars argue that the public sphere is the central axis of public life.[5] Deliberating in public according to "universal rules" exposes citizens to competing viewpoints and in doing so teaches them to become critical and tolerant. Public debates enable citizens to transform

4. Michael Novak, *The Spirit of Democratic Capitalism* (New York: Simon and Schuster, 1982); Peter L. Berger, *The Capitalist Revolution: Fifty Propositions About Prosperity, Equality and Liberty* (New York: Basic Books, 1986); C. M. Hann, *Market Economy and Civil Society in Hungary* (London: F. Cass, 1990); Paul Hirst, *Associative Democracy: New Forms of Economic and Social Governance* (Amherst: University of Massachusetts Press, 1994); Ernest Gellner, *Conditions of Liberty: Civil Society and Its Rivals* (London: Hamish Hamilton, 1994); Frances Fukuyama, *Trust: The Social Virtues and the Creation of Prosperity* (New York: Free Press, 1996); Robert Kuttner, *Everything for Sale: The Virtues and Limits of Market* (New York: Alfred A. Knopf, 1997); and Neil J. Mitchell, *The Conspicuous Corporation: Business, Public Policy and Representative Democracy* (Ann Arbor: University of Michigan Press, 1997).

5. Gabriel Almond and Sidney Verba, *The Civic Culture* (Boston: Little, Brown, 1965); Jane Mansbridge, *Beyond Adversary Democracy* (Chicago: University of Chicago Press, 1983); Angel Rama, *La ciudad letrada* (Montevideo: Arca, 1984, 1995); Jurgen Habermas, *The Structural Transformation of the Public Sphere* (Cambridge, Mass.: MIT Press, 1989); Michael Warner, *The Letters of the Republic* (Cambridge: Harvard University Press, 1990); Vladimir Tismaneanu, *Political Culture and Civil Society in the Soviet Successor States* (Armonk, N.Y.: M. E. Sharpe, 1995); Dominique Colas, *Civil Society and Fanaticism: Conjoined Histories* (Stanford, Calif.: Stanford University Press, 1997); Alicia del Aguila Peralta, *Callejones y mansiones: espacios de opinión pública y redes sociales y políticas en Lima del 900* (Lima: Pontífica Universidad Católica del Perú, 1997); Dean Alger, *Megamedia: How Giant Corporations Dominate Mass Media, Distort Competition and Endanger Democracy* (Lanham, Md.: University Press of America, 1998); and Claudio Lomnitz, *Deep Mexico, Silent Mexico: An Anthropology of Nationalism* (Minneapolis: University of Minnesota Press, 2001).

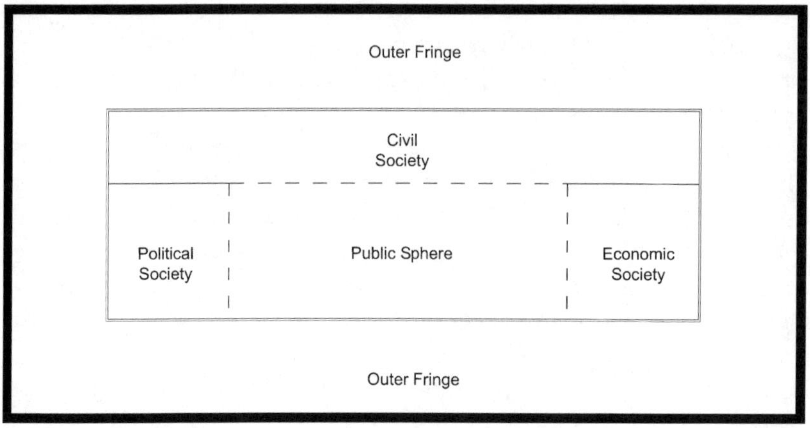

Figure 2.1   Public Life in Latin America: A Tocquevillian Perspective

their "particularistic" concerns into "universal" ones. In addition, the public sphere, more than any of the other domains, provides women, as well as racial, ethnic, and other marginalized groups, a way of broadening the public agenda and therefore a way of gaining access and entry into public life. These changes have democratized the public sphere, but they have also contributed to the decline of critical deliberation and to the spread of "mass entertainment." On their account, democracy has been turned into a "spectator sport" to be viewed in the privacy of one's home.

My conception of public life in Latin America is influenced by the work of these Tocquevillians.[6] I have divided the public landscape into four terrains: Civil Society; Economic Society; Political Society; Public Sphere (fig. 2.1).[7]

My study of Latin American public life focuses on democratic practices across the core and ignores the fringe where authoritarianism continued to be dominant and widespread. This might seem odd. After all, in the nineteenth century the majority of Mexicans and Peruvians continued

6. I have bracketed the issue of liberalism and its relationship to democracy in Latin America for the same reasons given by Robert Dahl, *Dilemmas of Pluralist Democracy: Autonomy vs. Control* (New Haven, Conn.: Yale University Press, 1982), 4–13.

7. My Tocquevillian model differs from the Habermasian one developed by Jean Cohen and Andrew Arato, *Civil Society and Political Theory* (Cambridge, Mass.: MIT Press, 1992). Whereas they focus on the public sphere and its capacity to influence policy makers, I grant coeval importance to all four terrains. Whereas they are concerned with "rational deliberation," I am mainly interested in how narrative practices shape selfhood. Whereas they grant primacy to new social movements during "moments of crisis," I focus on daily practices in voluntary associations during "ordinary periods." Finally, whereas they are mainly interested in how these movements contribute to integrating the "life-world" with "systemic structures," I am concerned with the disjuncture between daily habits and institutional structures.

to live and work on private estates and in indigenous communities as salaried peons, tenant farmers, and villagers.[8] I have focused on the core rather than the fringe because I am interested in studying the emergence of democratic habits, not the reproduction of authoritarian forms of life. In any case, scholars have already published countless monographs on daily life across the latter, but they have not yet given us an overview of everyday practices in the former. The double line separating the core from the fringe serves as a reminder to readers that my study is meant to be a partial rather than an exhaustive account of public life in nineteenth-century Latin America.

Tocqueville's description of everyday life in the core and fringe areas of the United States is pertinent to our discussion of Latin America. Here is Tocqueville's description of how New Englanders behaved in everyday life across the democratic core:

> [Because the] code [of conduct] is uncertain, to contravene it is no longer a crime. . . . So the substance of behavior comes to count for more than the form. . . . [New Englanders] have a habit of considering the feelings and opinions of those whom they meet more than their [formal] manners.[9]

Tocqueville's description of daily life across the authoritarian fringe is also relevant. They live as if they are complete

> strangers to each other. . . . [For these citizens, their] children and . . . private friends constitute . . . the whole of mankind; as for the rest of his fellow citizens, he is close to them, but he sees them not, he touches them, but he feels them not; he exists but in himself and for himself alone; and if his kindred still remain to him, he may be said to have lost his country.[10]

Although they lived in a democratic republic, these citizens were not a part of it.[11]

---

8. Arnold J. Bauer, "Rural Workers in Spanish America: Problems of Peonage and Oppression," *Hispanic American Historical Review* 59 (1979): 34–63; and Alan Knight, "Mexican Peonage: What Was It and Why Was It?" *Journal of Latin American Studies* 18 (1995): 41–74.

9. Alexis de Tocqueville, *Democracy in America*, trans. George Lawrence, ed. J. P. Mayer (Garden City, N.Y.: Doubleday, 1969), 568. Hereafter abbreviated as *DA* followed by page number.

10. Tocqueville, *DA*, 692.

11. Tocqueville, *DA*, 556–57. In New England, daily life along the economic fringe remained authoritarian: "while the mass of the nation is turning toward democracy, that particular class which is engaged in industry becomes more aristocratic. . . . [Having been] chased out of political society, they have taken refuge in some parts of the world of industry and established its sway there in another shape." For antidemocratic practices along the political and social areas of the fringe, see *DA*, 692 and 343.

Studying Public Life

Tocquevillian scholars, as I noted above, disagree on the relative importance of each public terrain for democratic life, but they do so by relying
on similar assumptions—assumptions that in my judgment are not altogether useful. In my discussion of them, I have deliberately blurred (as
in a Monet painting) the work of individual authors in order to clarify the
main ideas that serve to frame the general discussion.

First: Tocquevillians portray democratic regimes as institutionally
monocentric, leading them to establish a hierarchical chain of command
among the various public terrains with the one on top responsible for
all the rest.[12] But as I suggested above, modern democratic life is by definition structured vertically and pluralistically, with each terrain semi-
independent from the others and daily life in each organized according
to a different standard—mutual recognition, in the case of civil society;
collective participation, in the case of political society; socioeconomic decentralization, in the case of economic society; and deliberation, in the
case of the public sphere.[13] Instead of attributing a priori significance to
one or another terrain at the expense of the others, I have tried to understand why Latin Americans were inclined to practice democracy more
readily and intensely in some terrains than in others, and how this inclination varied over time and differed among Mexicans and Peruvians. As
with states and markets, democratic life in Latin America expanded and
contracted, and took on an astonishing variety of shapes and sizes, and
these have to be examined sociohistorically and comparatively rather than
deduced from abstract and a priori claims.

Second: Tocquevillians depict the relationship between associative life
and the central state in zero-sum terms—the more of one, the less of the
other. For "localists," the most effective way for citizens to safeguard democracy is by organizing local associations and using them to prevent the
state from intruding in their community. "Collectivists" disagree, arguing
that democracy is best served when citizens organize nationwide associations and use them to control government officials.[14] But from a Tocque-

12. For examples of this problem, see: Gellner, *Conditions of Liberty;* Boschi, *Arte de
associação;* and Rosanvallon, *Sacre du citoyen.*
13. My understanding of democratic life is indebted to the work of Michael Walzer,
Spheres of Justice: A Defense of Pluralism and Equality (New York: Basic Books, 1983) and
of Luc Boltanski and Laurent Thévenot, *De la justification: les economies de la grandeur*
(Paris: Gallimard, 1991).
14. For the localist approach, see Sandel, *Democracy's Discontent.* Schudson's *Good
Citizen* and Wolfe's *Whose Keeper* focus on nationwide associations but disagree on whether
establishing ties with the state benefits or undermines modern democracy. Schudson gives a
positive assessment, Wolfe a negative assessment. For a summary of this debate as it applies
to the United States: Theda Skocpol, Marshall Ganz, and Ziad Munson, "A Nation of Or-

villian perspective, whether an association has local or national constituents, and whether it actively pursues or avoids forming any ties with state officials is secondary to whether these and other practices contribute to the development of "sovereignty of the people."[15] Sovereignty of the people—social power for short—is the type of power citizens generate whenever they organize themselves into stable and cohesive groups and find ways of resolving their differences among themselves in a civic manner.[16] For Tocquevillians, social power is the most reliable and potent type of power available to citizens in a modern democracy, more so than any other type, including those based on institutional domination, military violence, and economic exploitation. In the words of Hannah Arendt,

> Power is never the property of an individual; it belongs to a group and remains in existence only so long as the group keeps together. . . . All political institutions are manifestations and materializations of power; they petrify and decay as soon as the living power of the people ceases to uphold them.[17]

In my study, I examine the daily practices and collective strategies that surfaced within a large number of voluntary groups in each of the countries I consider in order to gauge the citizenry's capacity to generate social power in civil society, economic society, political society, and the public sphere.

Third: Tocquevillians describe macro-institutional structures as inert fixtures on the horizon, rarely studying how daily practices shaped and were in turn shaped by them.[18] My study examines these practices as they were in motion and unfolding, before they congealed into stable structures. Drawing on Bourdieu's work on "fields and habitus," I have divided each Public Terrain (Civil Society, Economic Society, Political Society, Public Sphere) into several discrete Fields, each of which is subdivided into even smaller, compact Subfields.[19] Table 2.1 below lists the various Ter-

---

ganizers: The Institutional Origins of Civic Voluntarism in the United States," *American Political Science Review* 94, no. 3 (September 2000): 527–46.

15. Tocqueville, *DA,* 397 and 669.

16. Albert O. Hirschman, "Social Conflicts as Pillars of Democratic Market Society," *Political Theory* 22 (1994): 206: "social ties [are what] . . . hold democratic societies together and provide them with the strength and cohesion they need."

17. Hannah Arendt, *On Violence* (New York: Harcourt, Brace and World, 1970), 44. In developing Tocqueville's argument on social power, Arendt also distorts it by focusing on "heroic" deeds rather than everyday life and by ignoring the importance of economic power. For a review of her work, see Hannah Fenichel Pitkin, *The Attack on the Blob: Hannah Arendt's Concept of the Social* (Chicago: University of Chicago Press, 1998).

18. The following are illustrative of this problem: Stepan, *Rethinking Military Politics;* Wuthnow, *Loose Connections;* and Diamond, *Developing Democracy.*

19. Pierre Bourdieu, "The Genesis of the Concepts of 'Habitus' and 'Fields,'" *Socio-Criticism* 2, no. 2 (1985): 11–24. For a critical assessment, see David Swartz, *Culture and Power: The Sociology of Pierre Bourdieu* (Chicago: University of Chicago Press, 1997), 117–42 and 290–93.

Table 2.1   Latin American Public Life: Terrains, Fields, and Subfields

Public Terrains	Fields	Subfields
Civil society	Cultural	Literary-scientific
		Educational
		Professional
	Societal	Mutual-aid
		Artisan
		Racial-ethnic
		Patriotic
		Masonic
		Community-development
	Public service	Charity-welfare
		Fire brigade
	Religious	Moral improvement
		Church
	Recreational	Hobby-leisure
		Social
Economic society	Financial organizations	Bank and insurance companies
		Savings and loans
	Credit networks	Cooperatives
	Business	Family firms
		Joint stock companies
Political society	Electoral clubs	
	Municipal townships	
	Mass movements	
Public sphere	Literate	Reading and writing practices
		Newspapers
	Oral	Rumor and gossip networks
	Visual	Theater
		Clothing

rains, Fields, and Subfields; the historical chapters of my study are organized accordingly.

Consider the terrain of Civil Society and three of its Fields—Social, Cultural, and Religious. In the social Field, citizens organized mutual-aid societies and practiced solidarity by attending meetings, electing officers, and providing each other with unemployment and medical relief. In the cultural Field, citizens organized literary and scientific associations to provide public intellectuals the moral and artistic support they needed to break with "European aesthetics" and develop a "creole" style of their own. In the religious Field, citizens organized moral improvement groups in order to challenge corrupt parish priests. The players, practices, and resources in each Subfield were just as varied as those that appeared in each field. The boundaries between the various domains were, admittedly, porous, but even when external influences filtered through, they were transformed by local practices; the absence of such transformation is itself an indicator that the domain was in crisis and in the process of unraveling. The Terrains, Fields, and Subfields in Mexico and Peru (and Argentina and Cuba) appeared and disappeared and expanded and contracted over time. Tracking these changes enables us to compare and evaluate the development of democratic life among the various countries of the region.

Fourth: Tocquevillians depict everyday practices (habits) as static and compulsive.[20] In my study, I have portrayed them, following the work of John Dewey, as Janus-faced, with one side anchored in our memory of the past and the other in our vision of the future.[21] Like cables on a suspension bridge, the past and future sustain us in the present, and they do so by connecting us to the "not-here." Our actions in everyday life are influenced by prior experience and by our changing expectations about the future. In the course of "in-habiting" the present, we also alter our relation to the past and the future, leading us to select only those experiences that help us on the one hand to make sense of the present, and on the other to modify our future goals in light of our present situation. The attempt to reconcile our memory of the past with our vision of the future in light of the opportunities and constraints we face in the present is what Charles Taylor and other neo-Aristotelians call "practical judgment."[22] Mexicans and Peruvians who had been in the same authoritarian networks sometimes broke away and went on to become active in democratic ones; likewise, citizens who were active in dissimilar networks (authoritarian or democratic) sometimes converged and became active in similar networks. Practical judgments—not just rational choice or network ties—enabled Latin Americans to maneuver across public life in new and creative ways.

20. Despite their differences, Banfield, *Moral Basis of a Backward Society,* Huntington, *Political Order in Changing Societies,* Putnam, *Making Democracy Work* share a static conception of habits. They disagree, though, on how they can be changed. Banfield claims they are resistant to change. Huntington and Putnam claim that they can be altered, with the first emphasizing the role of institutional domination and the second the role of self-interest.

21. John Dewey, *Human Nature and Conduct* (New York: Henry Holt, 1922), 31–34, 40–46, 61–69, 73–89, 194–95; his "The Need for a Recovery of Philosophy," in *The Philosophy of John Dewey,* ed. John J. McDermott (Chicago: University of Chicago Press, 1981), 61–69; and his *Art as Experience* (New York: Minton, Balch and Co., 1958), 104. On the influence that "forward" and "backward" effect have on decision making, see Jon Elster and George Loewenstein, "Utility from Memory and Anticipation," in *Choice over Time,* ed. J. Elster and G. Lowenstein (New York: Russell Sage Foundation, 1992), 213–34.

22. Charles Taylor, *Sources of the Self* (Cambridge: Harvard University Press, 1989); and Ronald Beiner, *Political Judgement* (Chicago: University of Chicago Press, 1983). Practical judgment and theoretical knowledge differ in several ways. Scholars drawn to the first approach emphasize the role of local and informal practices in shaping public life (stochastic models). According to them, immersion in a given way of life is our only means of gaining an understanding of it. Scholars drawn to the second approach emphasize the role of codified rules and abstract principles in enabling us to make sense of public life. According to them, the only way to gain objective knowledge of these principles and to suppress one's personal biases is by using the scientific method.

Practical judgment is what enabled Latin Americans to disassociate their imagined selves from their past selves.[23] And in exercising their judgment and transforming themselves, they also contributed to restructuring the public landscape.

Fifth: Tocquevillians often depict the public sphere as a unitary place, and public opinion as a rational discussion among a select number of elites about the "general will."[24] But in Latin America, there were as many deliberative sites as there were social groups, and the communicative practices that flourished in each one were shaped by local practices. In the words of Peter Stallybrass and Allan White,

> [Deliberative practices] are regulated through the forms of corporate assembly in which they are produced . . . each place of assembly is a different site of intercourse requiring different manners and morals. . . . [The] formation of new [meanings] . . . can be traced through the emergence of new public sites . . . and the transformation of old ones.[25]

In my study, I have tried to show how the "little stories" citizens told each other in daily life in civil, economic, and political society were related to the "grand narratives" produced by public intellectuals in the public sphere.[26] Citizens who were active in associative life used colloquial terms to discuss, for example, monthly dues, the moral qualifications of applicants, and whether or not the group should become active in regional politics, but without ever pausing to ponder the deeper or broader significance of these terms. Citizens in associative life simply talked, expressing themselves in a somewhat staccato and telegraphic style because they were already familiar with each other's "assumptions" and "expectations," to recall Basil Bernstein's argument.[27] Communicative practices in the pub-

23. Jerold D. Siegel, "Problematizing the Self," in *Beyond the Cultural Turn*, ed. Victoria E. Bonnell and Lynn Hunt (Berkeley: University of California Press, 1999), 281–314 for an intelligent and lucid discussion of the debate.

24. Habermas, *Transformation of the Public Sphere;* Rama, *Ciudad letrada;* and Mansbridge, *Beyond Adversary Democracy* exemplify this shortcoming.

25. Peter Stallybrass and Allan White, *The Politics and Poetics of Transgression* (Ithaca, N.Y.: Cornell University Press, 1986), 80. Also see John Dewey, *The Public and Its Problems* (New York: Henry Holt and Co., 1954), 38–39, 62–72, 75–84, 110–42, 206–17.

26. Paul Ricoeur, "The Narrative Function," in *Hermeneutics and the Human Sciences* (Cambridge: Cambridge University Press, 1981), 278. Ricoeur does not deny the importance of "power" (Foucault), nor does he deny the role of "validity claims" (Habermas) in public debates. But Ricoeur does not take sides in this debate since he is interested in studying the relationship between stories and narrative, or "emplotment"—that is, the way various groups "represented" power and truth in public life.

27. Basil Bernstein, "Elaborated and Restricted Codes: Their Social Origins and Some Consequences," *American Anthropologist* 66 (1964): 55–69.

lic sphere were slightly different. Parish priests, schoolteachers, country lawyers, scribblers, newspapers writers, and other intellectuals used terms and phrases similar to those employed by citizens in daily life. But because they were trying to reach a broader audience about whom they knew very little, these public intellectuals had to discuss public affairs in a relatively explicit and coherent manner. In the historical chapters, I focus on the interplay between the little stories that circulated in daily life among citizens in associations and the grand narratives that were produced by intellectuals in the public sphere in order to understand the development of public opinion in postcolonial Mexico and Peru.

Sixth and last: Tocquevillians assume that democracy is based on a set of abstract and universal norms derived from either the Anglo-Puritan or the French Republican tradition.[28] But when Latin Americans practiced democracy in daily life, they did so by relying on their own narrative resources rooted in Civic Catholicism. Citizens used the same religious terms—reason, passion, free will, and so on—but pronounced them slightly differently. Whether these terms acquired democratic or authoritarian connotations in everyday life was the result of "pragmatic usage" rather than "semantic meaning."[29] In the words of Marshall Sahlins,

> history is culturally ordered, differently so in different societies, according to meaningful schemes. . . . The converse is also true: cultural schemes are historically ordered since to a greater or lesser extent the meanings are revalued as they are practically enacted. . . . And to that extent, the culture is historically altered in action. . . . [The] larger idea . . . may be summed up in the assertion that what anthropologist call "structure"—the symbolic relations of cultural order—is an historical object.[30]

What Samuel Huntington describes as a "clash of civilizations" is best understood, following Paul Ricoeur, as a "conflict of interpretations" within the same narrative tradition.[31]

---

28. For examples of this limitation, see Almond and Verba, *Civic Culture;* Pérez Díaz, *Return of Civil Society;* and Fukuyama, *Trust.*

29. Paul Ricoeur, "Structure, Word, Event," in *The Conflict of Interpretation* (Evanston, Ill.: Northwestern University Press, 1974), 84–93 on the relationship between "pragmatic usage" and "semantic meaning."

30. Marshall Sahlins, *Islands of History* (Chicago: University of Chicago Press, 1985), 86. Also see his *Historical Metaphors and Mythical Realities* (Ann Arbor: University of Michigan Press, 1981), 35.

31. Samuel P. Huntington, *The Clash of Civilizations and the Remaking of World Order* (New York: Simon and Schuster, 1996). Compare his Parsonian account of cultural traditions with the hermeneutical account developed by Hans Georg Gadamer, *Truth and Method,* trans. Garrett Barden and John Cummings (New York: Seabury Press, 1975).

Democratic life in Latin America, as I have portrayed it in this section, was polycentric, particularistic, and processual, strikingly similar to John Dewey's conception of it.[32] His conception of democratic life is doubly relevant for scholars working on Third World countries where public life is radically asymmetrical, disjointed, and fissured. In the case of Latin America, democratic life bears a family resemblance to the millennium-old Chinese game of Go. The goal of the game is for each player—democrats and authoritarians in our case—to encircle the other and prevent them from gaining control of any part of the board. In this game, moves along the edges of the board are as important as those near the center. In moving from one quadrant to another, players also generate new sources of power, providing each with an opportunity to subvert the "balance of power" and causing the "center" of the game to become displaced from one place to another. Prior moves influence but do not necessarily determine future ones. In contrast to chess, Go players do not direct their moves against a single, semistationary target (king), nor do they rely on a simple "zero sum strategy" to plan them.

Origins of Authoritarianism in Latin America

Scholars have explained the origins of dictatorship (and lack of democracy) in Latin America in different ways.[33] In summarizing their interpretations, my aim is to introduce the nonspecialist to the debate.[34]

Claudio Véliz's *The Centralist Tradition* was the most influential Weberian account.[35] Véliz and like-minded scholars account for the lack of democratic life in the region in terms of three mutually reinforcing processes related to: (a) state-building, (b) urbanization, and (c) religion.[36]

32. John Dewey, "Creative Democracy: The Task Before Us," in *The Philosopher of the Common Man: Essays in Honor of John Dewey to Celebrate His Eightieth Birthday,* ed. Sidney Ratner (New York: G. P. Putnam's Sons, 1940), 220–28.

33. I do not discuss works published prior to the Cuban Revolution of 1959, including those by Daniel Cosío Villegas, *La constitución de 1857 y sus críticos* (Mexico City: Editorial Hermes, 1957); Ricardo Donoso, *Las idéas políticas en Chile* (Mexico City: Fondo de Cultura Económica, 1946); and José Luis Romero, *Las idéas políticas en Argentina* (Mexico City: Fondo de Cultura Económica, 1946). They were among the first to argue in favor of the existence of a distinctive democratic tradition in nineteenth-century Latin America, but in describing it they focused only on constitutional matters rather than on everyday practices as I do in my work.

34. See Carlos A. Forment, "Socio-Historical Models of Latin American Democratization: A Review and Reformulation," *Estudios Latinoamericanos* 14, no. 1 (1992): 213–39 for a detailed assessment.

35. Claudio Véliz, *The Centralist Tradition in Latin America* (Princeton, N.J.: Princeton University Press, 1980).

36. Richard Morse, *New World Soundings: Culture and Ideology in the Americas* (Baltimore, Md.: Johns Hopkins University Press, 1989); Howard Wiarda, *Political and Social Change in Latin America: The Distinct Tradition* (Amherst: University of Massachusetts

Castilian Spain, the first modern state to emerge in all of Europe, claimed the New World for itself and implanted a portion of its organizational apparatus on a colonial society that was relatively weak and disorganized. Backed by this mighty behemoth, colonial officials proceeded to gain direct control and exercise a virtual monopoly over land, labor, credit, and other sources of power, including mineral wealth (silver and gold), depriving the urban and rural elite of the opportunity to challenge them, as their counterparts had done in western Europe and North America. Urbanization reinforced the spread of authoritarian centralism throughout the region. In contrast to the case of western Europe, the colonial state established its main headquarters in urban centers and used its organizational resources to dominate the merchants, artisans, and other social groups that had played such a key role in ushering in democracy in the Old World, before moving out into the hinterlands and doing the same among the landed elite and indigenous villagers. State officials created a vast network of patrons and clients throughout the region, transforming Latin Americans into passive retainers of the state.[37] Catholic doctrine, with its organic, hierarchical, and corporatist notions of public life, served to legitimize absolutist rule in the region.[38] Churchmen instilled Latin Americans with fanatical and authoritarian notions, making them hostile to liberalism and democracy.[39] The "Hispanic legacy" is responsible for Latin America's "authoritarian" tradition and for turning the entire continent into an "iron cage."

Fernando H. Cardoso and Enzo Faletto provide the most compelling Marxian account of public life in the region.[40] Scholars in this school agreed on several basic points.[41] Late entry into the world market placed

Press, 1974), and his *The Continuing Struggle for Democracy in Latin America* (Boulder, Colo.: Westview Press, 1980); Glen Dealy, *The Public Man: An Interpretation of Latin America and Other Catholic Countries* (Amherst: University of Massachusetts Press, 1977); Alfred Stepan, *The State and Society: Peru in Comparative Perspective* (Princeton, N.J.: Princeton University Press, 1978); James Malloy, *Authoritarianism and Corporatism in Latin America* (Pittsburgh: University of Pittsburgh Press, 1977).

37. Véliz, *Centralist Tradition*, 4–11, 47–52, 62–81, 218–36.

38. Véliz, *Centralist Tradition*, 24, 189–216.

39. Véliz, *Centralist Tradition*, 11, 148, 163, 168, 179–82, 295.

40. Fernando H. Cardoso and Enzo Faletto, *Dependency and Development in Latin America* (Berkeley: University of California Press, 1979).

41. Marcelo Cavarozzi, "El desarollismo y las relaciones entre democracia y capitalismo dependiente," *Latin American Research Review* 17, no. 1 (1982): 152–71; Stanley and Barbara Stein, *The Colonial Heritage of Latin America* (Oxford: Oxford University Press, 1970); Peter Evans, *Dependent Development: The Alliance of Multinational, State and Local Capital* (Princeton, N.J.: Princeton University Press, 1979); Maurice Zeitlin, *The Civil Wars in Chile* (Princeton, N.J.: Princeton University Press, 1984); Charles W. Bergquist, *Coffee and Conflict in Colombia* (Durham, N.C.: Duke University Press, 1976); and Jeffrey Paige, *Coffee and Power: Revolution and the Rise of Democracy in Central America* (Cambridge: Harvard University Press, 1997).

Latin American entrepreneurs at a distinct disadvantage in relation to their western European and North American counterparts.[42] By the time the former had entered the market, the international division of labor had already developed a structure best suited to meet the socioeconomic needs of developed countries, undermining the ability of Latin American entrepreneurs to pull their countries out of economic backwardness. Incorporation into the world economy gave rise to export enclaves in Latin America that were used by foreign firms to siphon off wealth and control and "denationalize" the local economy.[43] All the countries of the region became poor and backward, although internal factors determined the extent of the decline. Chile and Argentina, for example, fared best due to their relative abundance of cheap labor, mineral resources, investment capital, and easy access to markets for their goods.[44] International and domestic factors "denationalized" the urban bourgeoisie, disorganized the working class, and undermined the state, making it difficult for any Latin American country to usher in democratic rule as had the nations in North America and western Europe.

Jorge I. Domínguez's *Insurrection and Loyalty* provides a Parsonian account of Latin American authoritarianism. For modernization theorists, the failure of Latin Americans to break with "traditional" norms and to acquire "modern" ones was due to two factors: personal frustration and institutional instability.[45] According to Domínguez, economic uncertainty in the export sector generated extreme frustration among the country's most powerful elite.[46] Instead of venturing forth into the market and taking calculated risks, the elite in Latin America retreated and turned for protection to the state, bringing the business and government elite into conflict with the "modern" elite who favored liberalization.[47] The country's traditional and modern elites struggled to control the state, and this struggle is responsible for the recurrent and bitter bouts of civil warfare

42. Cardoso and Faletto, *Dependency and Development,* 29–73.

43. Cardoso and Faletto, *Dependency and Development,* 69–76, 101–28, 173–74.

44. Cardoso and Faletto, *Dependency and Development,* 66–73.

45. Jorge I. Domínguez, *Insurrection or Loyalty* (Cambridge: Harvard University Press, 1980).

46. Also see: John J. Johnson, *Continuity and Change in Latin America* (Stanford, Calif.: Stanford University Press, 1964); Charles W. Anderson, *Politics and Economic Changes in Latin America* (Princeton, N.J.: Princeton University Press, 1967); Kalman H. Silvert, *The Conflict Society: Reaction and Revolution in Latin America* (New York: American Universities Field Staff, 1966); Martin C. Needler, *Latin American Politics in Perspective* (Princeton, N.J.: Princeton University Press, 1967); Gino Germani, *Política y sociedad en una época de transición* (Buenos Aires: Paidós, 1971); and the magisterial work of François-Xavier Guerra, *México: Del antiguo regimen a la revolución,* 2 vols. (Mexico City: Fondo de Cultura Económica, 1988).

47. Domínguez, *Insurrection or Loyalty,* 44–45, 111–21, 140–42, 242–47.

that plagued the region throughout the nineteenth century. Increased instability led the traditional elite to become even more entrenched in their antimodern views and even more dependent on the state, contributing to "institutional overload" and to erosion of the government's capacity to restore "law and order."[48] According to Domínguez, the Chilean and Cuban elite were the only ones to succeed in breaking out of this cycle. They accomplished this, however, not through their own effort but because their countries were invaded by foreign troops and the national elite were, during the occupation, deprived of access to the state and forced to enter the market and become forward-looking.[49] On Domínguez's account, foreign troops are responsible for introducing modern democracy into the region.

My study accounts for the emergence and development of democratic life in Latin America in terms of "sovereignty of the people" rather than as a structural byproduct of "state-building," "economic development," and "modernization." Associative life in the region was not, as I argue below, "causally related" to any of them. To begin with, associative life in Mexico and elsewhere surfaced several decades before the postcolonial state had granted juridical status to voluntary groups. Admittedly, the number of associations rose markedly after the state had granted them legal recognition, but the former did not "cause" the latter: recall that colonial law continued to be practiced until late in the century.[50] The relationship between economic markets and associative life is just as tenuous. Recall that associative life surfaced in the region about forty years prior to the turn-of-the-century formation of national markets. Moreover, associative life remained least developed in the export sector where commercialization was most advanced and flourished in parts of the country where economic life remained relatively underdeveloped. Furthermore, the correlation between income from the export sector, such as guano

48. Domínguez, *Insurrection or Loyalty,* 25, 84–105, 117–30, 189–95.
49. Domínguez, *Insurrection or Loyalty,* 140, 235.
50. On legal-juridical aspects see: Jorge Barrera Graf, "Historia del derecho de sociedades en México," in *Memoria del III Congreso de Historia del Derecho Mexicano,* ed. José Luis Soberanes Fernandes (Mexico City: Universidad Nacional Autónoma de México, Instituto de Investigaciones Jurídicas, 1984), 129–54; Benito Díaz, *Juzgados de paz de campaña de la provincia de Buenos Aires* (La Plata: Universidad Nacional de la Plata, 1959); Fernando de Trazegnies, *La idéa del derecho en el Perú republicano del siglo XIX* (Lima: Pontifica Universidad Católica del Perú, Fondo Editorial, 1992). On fiscal-administrative aspects, see: Oscar Oszlak, *La formación del estado argentino* (Buenos Aires: Editorial de Belgrano, 1982); Marcello Carmagnani, *Estado y mercado: La economía pública del liberalismo mexicano: 1850–1911* (Mexico City: El Colegio de México and Fondo de Cultura Económica, 1994); and Javier Tantaleán Arbulú, *Política económica y financiera y la formación del estado* (Lima: Centro de estudios para el desarollo y la participación, 1983).

(Peru), sugar (Cuba), wheat and beef (Argentina), and silver (Mexico), and associative life is not all that strong.[51] The relationship between modernization (migration, urbanization, literacy, and so on) and associative life is also weak, based on the very limited evidence I was able to gather.[52] As for the links between military occupation and associative life: the number of voluntary groups declined dramatically during the Chilean army's takeover of Peru (1879–1881) and the U.S. (1842–1845) and French (1862–1867) takeover of Mexico, as my historical chapters show.

Such leading scholars as Charles Tilly have argued forcefully and repeatedly that the modern West was shaped by the interplay of "states" and "markets."[53] While I do not deny their relevance, my study of public life across Latin America suggests that they are not the only influences that deserve our attention.

Comparing Public Life in Postcolonial Countries

By the early 1980s, the dependency paradigm had become influential in all the major universities of the First and Third Worlds. This marked the first time "local knowledge" from the periphery was recognized as "abstract theory" by the academic community from outside the area. But the "consumption" of dependency theory, argued Cardoso, also drained it of its critical edge, turning it into an example of "vulgar materialism," to use Marx's stinging phrase.[54] The critical-historical approach that had been central to the dependency perspective was replaced by formal arguments and abstract models, then repackaged and re-exported to Latin America and the rest of the Third World as so-called "political economy" and its

---

51. On national markets, see: John Coatsworth, *Los orígenes del atraso: Ensayos de historia económica de México en los siglos XVIII y XIX* (Mexico City: Alianza Editorial Mexicana 1990); Miron Burgin, *Economic Aspects of Argentine Federalism* (Cambridge: Harvard University Press, 1946); Nelson Manrique, *Mercado interno y región: La Sierra central, 1820–1930* (Lima: Centro de Estudios y Promoción del Desarollo, 1987); Stephen Haber, *How Latin America Fell Behind: Essay in the Economic Histories of Brazil and Mexico* (Stanford, Calif.: Stanford University Press, 1997).

52. On empirical indicators of modernization, see Clifford T. Smith, "Patterns of Urban and Regional Development in Peru on the Eve of the Pacific War," in *Region and Class in Modern Peruvian History,* ed. Rory Miller (Liverpool: Institute for Latin American Studies, 1987), 77–102; Mary Kay Vaughan "Economic Growth and Literacy n Late Nineteenth Century Mexico," in *Education and Economic Development since the Industrial Revolution,* ed. Gabriel Tortella (Valencia: Generalitat Valenciana, 1990), 89–111; and Antonio García Cubas, *Cuadro geográfico, estadístico, descriptivo e histórico de los Estados Unidos Mexicanos* (Mexico City: Oficina Tipográfica de la Secretariá de Fomento, 1884).

53. Charles Tilly, *Coercion, Capital and European States* (Cambridge: Basil Blackwell, 1990).

54. Fernando H. Cardoso, "The Consumption of Dependency Theory in the United States," *Latin American Research Review* 12, no. 3 (1977): 7–25.

poor cousin, "rational choice."[55] These economistic approaches, as exemplified in the work of neoliberals and neo-Marxists like Robert Bates and Adam Przeworski, signaled the resurgence of modernization theory in the field of comparative politics and sociology.[56] But their attempt to regain control of the field did not go unchallenged.

By the mid-1980s, the intellectual debate on postcolonial countries had migrated from Latin America to India, and its focus of attention had shifted from issues related to economic dependency to those related to sociocultural and political life.[57] Although the postcolonial perspective has already made deep inroads in North American and western European universities, it remains to be seen whether it will become as influential as the dependency approach came to be during its heyday.[58]

My study of Latin American public life is in conversation with the work of Partha Chatterjee on India and Mahmood Mamdani on Africa, who account for the stunted nature of postcolonial democracy in terms of the "colonial legacy."[59] According to Chatterjee, the British in India used racial categories to create a two-tiered system of public life, one for fair-skinned citizens and the other for dark-skinned colonials. Liberal rights were granted to those in the first tier but denied to those in the second. Indians resisted this type of caste democracy by withdrawing from public life and retreating to their villages, religious temples, family clans, and other arenas within the communal domain:

> the crucial break in the history of anti-colonial nationalism comes when the colonized refuse to accept membership in this civil society of subjects . . . and construct . . . a very different domain—a cultural domain. . . .[60]

The communal domain provided anticolonial Indians a place to cultivate and "reinvent" their own traditions and to use them to challenge British

55. Immanuel Wallerstein, "The Unintended Consequences of Cold War Area Studies," in *The Cold War and the University: Toward an Intellectual History of the Postwar Years,* ed. Noam Chomsky et al. (New York: W. W. Norton and Co., 1997), 195–231.

56. Robert Bates, "Areas Studies and the Disciplines," *PS: Political Science and Politics* 30, no. 2 (June 1997): 166–69 for a particularly strident example.

57. K. Sivaramakrishnan, "Situating the Subaltern: History and Anthropology in the Subaltern Studies," *The Journal of Historical Sociology* 8, no. 4 (December 1995): 395–429.

58. In their penchant for turgid language, political naiveté, and personal histrionics, some scholars in the field of postcolonial studies have failed to convey what is most insightful and enduring about this approach.

59. Partha Chatterjee, *The Nation and Its Fragments: Colonial and Postcolonial Histories* (Princeton, N.J.: Princeton University Press, 1993); Mahmood Mamdani, *Citizen and Subject: Contemporary Africa and the Legacy of Late Colonialism* (Princeton, N.J.: Princeton University Press, 1996).

60. Chatterjee, *Nation and Its Fragments,* 237–38.

liberalism, which they considered, by virtue of its racist, elitist, and evolutionary assumptions, to be no less "particularistic" than their own.

The anticolonial groups in India became divided in the 1890s, with a large number of them in favor of remaining in the communal domain and practicing cultural resistance against the British, and the rest in favor of entering political society and gaining control of its main institutions— judiciary, army, bureaucracy, and so on. This second group organized the Indian National Congress and used the same liberal notions (equality, fairness, liberty, rationality, sovereignty) they had learned from the British to secure their independence in 1945. Following independence, the Congress Party transformed itself from a mass movement into a "party-state" and for the next forty years ruled India, legitimizing itself by using many of the same racial arguments the British had used. Congress politicians and officials described themselves as "modern," "nationalist," and "rational," while depicting the citizenry in opposite terms—"superstitious," "communal," and "irrational."[61] In Chatterjee's judgment, colonial and postcolonial officials have always used the state to prevent civil society from becoming autonomous, thereby making it difficult for Indians to play a major role in public life.

The African experience with civil society, according to Mamdani, was quite different. In this part of the world, colonial officials were able to penetrate and gain control of the communal domain in a way that the British had never been able to do in India. Colonial rulers across Africa accomplished this by allying themselves with tribal chiefs. In exchange for preserving "law and order," these chiefs were granted absolute power in their own villages, which were thus transformed into personal fiefdoms. Colonial officials were now free to focus their attention on maintaining control in urban areas. Beginning in the 1920s, rural people had been migrating in large numbers to these areas in search of jobs and new opportunities. In order to retain control of these cities, colonial officials in South Africa and elsewhere herded black migrants into townships (apartheid) and segregated them by tribal and ethnic identity, making it difficult for them to have contact with each other. The countless burial societies, credit associations, sports clubs, and music groups that surfaced in each township strengthened the tribal and ethnic identities of migrants and discour-

---

61. Chatterjee, *Nation and Its Fragments,* 45: "[racial-ethnic-religious] solidarities and forms of authority deriving from pre-capitalist community inserted themselves into the representational process of [India's new] liberal, electoral democracy.... On the other hand, the state itself manipulated these 'pre-modern' forms of relations . . . to secure legitimacy for its developmental role.... The paradox in fact is that the very irrationality of the political process . . . continually works to produce legitimacy for the rational exercise of the planners."

aged them from developing a sense of nationhood or citizenship. Never-theless, migrants who returned to their villages carried with them the civic and organizational skills they had acquired in these urban-based associa-tions and used them to challenge tribal chiefs in their community. The spread of agricultural cooperatives, "popular" militias, and courts in these villages helped to democratize them and, just as importantly, made residents aware that the divisions between them were political and not just tribal.

The "detribalization" of village life was accompanied by the "deracial-ization" of urban life across the continent from Cape Town to Kampala. From the 1960s onward, the African National Congress (ANC) and other liberation movements sent organizers into townships to recruit members from local associations. By the time the ANC was "unbanned," it had a strong base among urban blacks, most of whom now identified them-selves in nationalist rather than ethnic or racial terms. Following inde-pendence, the ANC, like its counterpart in India, turned itself into a single party-state and used whatever legal and administrative power it had to dismantle the system of racial apartheid. The policy of "Africanization" they implemented was resisted by white supremacists and blacks who still identified themselves in tribal terms, which only strengthened government officials' determination to implement their policy. In order to do away with the legacy of apartheid, ANC officials were forced to take control over the same civic associations that had to that point remained autonomous:

> the collapse of an embryonic civil society of trade unions and autono-mous civic organizations [was brought about by] its absorption into po-litical society, [which was a consequence of] . . . state nationalism. . . .[62]

In Africa, as in India, civil society has never been anything more than a "marginal construct."

My work is in dialogue with the work of Chatterjee and Mamdani and seeks to determine the extent to which the colonial legacy in Latin Amer-ica shaped public life during the postcolonial period. Imperial Spain ruled over the New World for almost four hundred years, far longer than the British in India or any European power in Africa. This makes Latin Amer-ica an ideal place to assess the impact of colonial rule on public life. As in the Indian and African cases, Spanish rule in Latin America was based on racial and ethnic segregation and a combination of "direct" and "indi-rect" rule. Colonial officials and churchmen in Latin America had direct control of daily life in urban centers and exercised indirect control over the countryside, relying on village chiefs and estate owners to maintain

62. Mamdani, *Citizen and Subject*, 88.

control of rural peoples. As in Africa (but not India), Spanish colonialism also made deep inroads into the private-communal domain, relying on churchmen to exert moral influence on family life and even on the conscience of each individual via the confessional box.

This first volume of my work compares public life in Mexico and Peru, the core regions of Imperial Spain's empire in the New World.[63] These regions had, not coincidentally, the world's richest silver deposits and the largest concentration of indigenous peoples in the region; the indigenes were put to work in the mines nearby. Imperial Spain established its most important institutions (viceroy, supreme court, bishopric) in Mexico and Peru and from here ruled the entire continent. (Both appear shaded in map 2.1.) The legacy of colonialism was relatively strong in Mexico and Peru, but as my historical chapters show, citizens in the former were far more successful in institutionalizing democratic life than those in the latter.

The second volume compares public life in Cuba and Argentina. Located on the fringe, these areas lacked mineral wealth and manpower, which is why Imperial Spain never established its most important colonial institutions there. The colonial legacy was relatively weak in both. Despite these commonalities, Cubans and Argentines followed divergent paths in the way they democratized and institutionalized public life.

In contrast to Chatterjee and Mamdani, I have emphasized the discontinuities between colonial and postcolonial life by underscoring the way Latin Americans broke with their authoritarian habits and acquired democratic ones.

Evaluating Democratic Life in Latin America

Democratic life in Latin America was imperfect and incomplete in countless ways, and it falls far short of Robert Dahl's stringent standards for evaluating polyarchies. In this respect, the Latin American case is not all that different from democratic life in nineteenth-century North America and western Europe. Recall that even in New England, epicenter of democratic life, residents achieved only the most limited and restricted forms of: (a) socioeconomic and legal equality; (b) political contesta-

---

63. David Scott Palmer, *Peru: The Authoritarian Tradition* (New York: Praeger Publishers, 1980), uses twelve different indicators to evaluate the scope and degree of colonial penetration in Spanish America and then ranks all eighteen colonies accordingly. Mexico and Peru were the most colonized, followed by Argentina and Cuba, among others, with most Central American countries trailing far behind (and irrelevant to my work).

Map 2.1 Nineteenth-Century Latin America: Mexico, Peru, Argentina, and Cuba

tion and electoral participation; (c) critical deliberation; (d) associative forms of life; and (e) civic selfhood.[64] Although the United States, France,

64. On public life in the United States, see: Rogers M. Smith, *Civic Ideals: Conflicting Visions of Citizenship in U.S. History* (New Haven, Conn.: Yale University Press, 1997); Leon F. Litwack, *North of Slavery: The Negro in the Free States, 1790–1860* (Chicago: University of Chicago Press, 1961); Matthew Frye Jacobs, *Whiteness of a Different Color: European Immigrants and the Alchemy of Race* (Cambridge: Harvard University Press, 1998); Ed-

and England were not yet democratic, Dahl considers them to be "near polyarchies." [65]

Democratic life in Latin America was, admittedly, even more flawed, but its shortcomings bear a family resemblance to the imperfections that existed in all these countries. In other words, the differences between all these countries are of degree rather than kind, and this is why they are comparable. On a continuum from least to most democratic, I would rank the United States in the upper quartile, with England somewhere in the middle and France far below it and constantly oscillating from one extreme to the other; these would be followed by Mexico, Peru, Argentina, Cuba, and Spain.[66] All of these countries were proto-democracies in the nineteenth century; however, by the late twentieth century England, the United States, France, and Spain had democratized and moved closer to Dahl's standards, while the countries of Latin America had become fully authoritarian and moved farther away from them. In other words, it was in the twentieth century, not the nineteenth, that authoritarianism became rooted in the region. But this is a very different story from the one presented in the chapters ahead.

Studying the Latin American case might assist Tocquevillians in redirecting our attention from pure and pristine types of polyarchical regimes, the type found only in textbooks, to studies of deformed and polluted cases that are the norm in Third World countries and, I suspect, in other places as well. The remaining chapters explore the development of real-world democracy in late colonial and postcolonial Mexico and Peru.

---

ward Pessen, *Riches, Class and Power before the Civil War* (Lexington, Mass.: D.C. Heath, 1973); Robert H. Wiebe, *The Search for Order, 1877–1920* (New York: Hll and Wang, 1967); Culver H. Smith, *The Press, Politics and Patronage: The American Government's Use of Newspapers, 1789–1876* (Athens: University of Georgia Press, 1977); Joel H. Silbey, *The American Political Nation, 1838–1893* (Stanford, Calif.: Stanford University Press, 1991); and Martin Shefter, *Political Parties and the State: The American Historical Experience* (Princeton, N.J.: Princeton University Press, 1994).

65. Robert Dahl, *Polyarchy: Participation and Opposition* (New Haven, Conn.: Yale University Press, 1971), 10–11, and his *Democracy and Its Critics* (New Haven, Conn.: Yale University Press, 1989), 221–22 and 232–43.

66. For England, see: J. H. Plumb, *The Growth of Political Stability in England* (London: Macmillan, 1967); and David C. Moore, *The Politics of Deference: A Study of the Mid-Nineteenth Century English Political System* (Hassocks: Harvester Press, 1976). For France: Maurice Agulhon, *The Republican Experiment: 1848–1852,* trans. Janet Lloyd (Cambridge: Cambridge University Press, 1982), and Edward Berenson, *Populist Religion and Left-Wing Politics in France, 1832 to 1852* (Princeton, N.J.: Princeton University Press, 1984). For Spain: C.A.M. Hennessy, *The Federal Republic in Spain: Pí y Margall and the Federal Republic Movement, 1868–1874* (Oxford: Oxford University Press, 1962), and Juan Díaz del Moral, *Historia de las agitaciones Andaluzas* (Madrid: Alianza Editorial, 1969).

PART TWO

THE PUBLIC LANDSCAPE
OF LATE COLONIAL
LATIN AMERICA

CHAPTER 3

Alone in Public: Institutional Practices and Colonial Life

State officials, churchmen, settlers, foreign merchants, natural scientists, and travelers from the Old World to Latin America were struck by the peculiarities of colonial life. In the late 1760s, during his stay in Mexico City, Francisco Ajofrín, a Capuchin friar, described them with a certain sense of wonderment:

> This is indeed a New World, or at least the reverse of the Old World. A local wit has noted that everything here is the reverse of what we had in Europe: petticoats are worn on the outside; children are carried from behind; shoeless people hawk shoes; naked people peddle dresses; lakes give more meat than fish; and . . . volcanos are covered with snow instead of fire. . . . It is all very strange.[1]

Ajofrín is describing the loose-fitting cotton slip worn by indigenous women; shawl-wrapped babies carried by mothers on their backs; dirt-poor plebeians selling shoes and dresses to pedestrians; the meaty huachinango fish of Lake Texcoco; and the great Popocatepetl volcano.

The New World was peculiar in other ways as well. In contrast to the old regime in western Europe, public life in colonial Latin America was stunted from the outset and would remain so until after independence. The reasons for this are related to the particular type of absolutist state, aristocratic nobility, ethnic-racial relations, associative life, and colonial Catholic vocabulary that flourished in the region.

1. Francisco de Ajofrín, *Diario del viaje que por orden de la Sagrada Congregación de Propaganda Fide hizo a la América Septentrional en el Siglo XVIII*, vol. 1, ed. Vicente Castañeda y Alcover (Madrid: Real Academia de Historia, 1958–1959), 84.

Colonial-Absolutist State

By the end of the sixteenth century, long before the French Bourbons had centralized and rationalized power, Spain's Kingdom of Castile had already organized a modern state, western Europe's first, and implanted it in Latin America on a colonial society that was relatively weak and disorganized. State officials in the New World had little difficulty maintaining control over elite and non-elite groups in both urban and rural areas. The colonial state in Latin America expanded its bureaucratic capacity by subordinating and turning the Catholic Church into a government agency like any other. In exchange for assisting priests in converting indigenous peoples to Catholicism, state officials were granted the right to appoint the church's personnel, control its finances, advise on doctrinal and liturgical matters, adjudicate disputes among bishops and other members of the hierarchy, and negotiate directly with the pope over a broad range of policy-related matters.[2] By incorporating the Church, the colonial state doubled its administrative capacity, thereby enabling it to maintain tight control over public life.

The colonial-absolutist state was a mighty behemoth. The viceroy, supreme court, royal treasury, captain generals, intendants, and their administrative staff established headquarters in urban centers. In contrast to the free city-states of Europe, Latin American cities were controlled by state officials. Intendants controlled municipal townships across the region, including the most important ones in Mexico and Peru.[3]

State officials maintained "direct rule" in cities, but they relied on local officials and parish priests to maintain "indirect rule" in the countryside.

2. Mario Góngora, *El estado en le derecho indiano* (Santiago: Instituto de Investigaciones Histórico-culturales, Universidad de Chile, 1951); C. H. Haring, *The Spanish Empire in America* (New York: Harcourt, Brace and World, 1963); Magali Sarfatti Larson, *Spanish Bureaucratic Patrimonialism in America* (Berkeley: University of California Press, 1966); John Lynch, "The Institutional Framework of Colonial Spanish America," *Journal of Latin American Studies* 24 (1992): 69–81; David A. Brading, "Bourbon Spain and Its American Empire," in *Cambridge History of Colonial Spanish America,* vol. 1, ed. Leslie Bethell (Cambridge: Cambridge University Press, 1984), 112–62; Mark Burkholder and D. S. Chandler, *From Impotence to Authority: The Spanish Crown and the American Audiencias* (Columbia: University of Missouri Press, 1977).

3. John Lynch, *Spanish Colonial Administration, 1720–1810: The Intendant System in the Viceroyalty of the Rio de la Plata* (London: University of London, Athlone Press, 1958); David Brading, *Miners and Merchants in Bourbon Mexico: 1763–1810* (Cambridge: Cambridge University Press, 1971); John Preston Moore, *The Cabildo in Peru under the Bourbons: 1700–1824* (Durham, N.C.: Duke University Press, 1966); Reinhard Liehr, *Ayuntamiento y oligarquía en Puebla: 1780–1810* (Mexico City: Secretaría de Educación Pública, 1976); Peter Marzahl, *Town in the Empire: Government, Politics and Society in Popayan* (Austin: University of Texas Press, 1978); Hermes Tovar Pinzón, "El estado colonial frente al poder local y regional," *Nova Americana* 5 (1982): 39–77.

Although they were few in number and spread thinly across the hinterlands, officials and priests were unusually effective in collecting taxes and tithes, providing justice, maintaining social peace, and propagating Catholicism. Their success was in large part determined by their ability to forge alliances with village chiefs. Officials, priests, and chiefs were always developing and breaking ties amongst themselves and it was the intense factionalism they generated that, paradoxically, made administrative life across the hinterlands so stable.[4] The system of checks and balances they created greatly benefited rural peoples. In the words of the great Mexican Viceroy Carlos de Croix:

> Indians are customarily oppressed by priests and local officials with demands for services and taxes. When the two representatives in a district are united is when they most afflict the Indians. If they fall out, there is a stinking gush of complaints from the parish priest who vents his anger against the official by getting his Indian parishioners to initiate complaints against the latter.[5]

Petty factionalism in rural areas served to curb the power of local officials and priests and to improve the quality of indigenous people's lives.

Indigenous peoples also had access to local courts and frequently used them in order to protect their communal lands and customary rights from the threat of greedy landowners, zealous state officials, and corrupt priests.[6] Although litigation was a costly and time-consuming affair, and although state officials and parish priests often succeeded in preventing claimants from reaching the court, there is no denying that rural peoples were well served by the judiciary system:

4. William B. Taylor, *Landlord and Peasant in Colonial Oaxaca* (Stanford, Calif.: Stanford University Press, 1972); María Cecilia Cangiaño, *Curas, caciques y comunidades en el Alto Perú* (Tilcara: Proyecto ECIRA, Facultad de Filosofía y Letras, UBA-MLAL, 1987); Brooke Larson, "Caciques, Class Structure and the Colonial State in Bolivia," *Nova Americana* 2 (1979): 197–235; Nancy M. Farriss, *Maya Society under Colonial Rule: The Collective Enterprise of Survival* (Princeton, N.J.: Princeton University Press, 1984); Karen Spalding, "The Colonial Indian: Past and Future Research Perspective," *Latin American Research Review* 7 (1972): 47–76.

5. Carlos Francisco de Croix, *Instrucción del virrey . . . que deja a su succesor Antonio María Bucareli,* ed. Norman F. Martin (Mexico City: Editorial Jus, 1960), 56–57.

6. Steve Stern, *Peru's Indian Peoples and the Challenge of Spanish Conquest* (Madison: University of Wisconsin Press, 1982), 114–37; Karen Spalding, *Huarochiri: An Andean Society under Inca and Spanish Rule* (Stanford, Calif.: Stanford University Press, 1984), 204–9; Charles Gibson, *The Aztecs under Spanish Rule: 1519–1810* (Stanford, Calif.: Stanford University Press, 1964); Woodrow Borah, *Justice by Insurance* (Berkeley: University of California Press, 1983), 128–32; Diana Bonnett, *Los protectores de naturales en la audiencia de Quito: siglos XVII–XVIII* (Quito: Facultad Latinoamericano de Ciencias Sociales, 1992). See all the essays in Arij Ouwenweel and Simon Miller, eds., *The Indian Community of Colonial Mexico* (Amsterdam: CEDLA, 1990), and Bernard Lavalle, "Presión Colonial y Reivindicación indígena en Cajamarca, 1785–1820," *Allpanchis* [Lima] 35 (1990): 32–45.

the striking thing about the performance of late colonial judges is not how much land they despoiled from Indians and other peasants, but how often they confirmed the rights of the powerless, and particularly of communal landholding villages.[7]

The judicial system in Latin America was highly developed and would have surprised any Anglo-American jurist of the period. Colonial peoples were aware of their property rights and corporate privileges, and they were skilled in using the legal system to preserve them. The supreme tribunal (*audiencia*) and district courts occupied a key place in colonial society, making Latin Americans as litigious as the English. The judiciary in Latin America, as in Great Britain, contributed to sociopolitical stability by encouraging colonial peoples to individualize their struggles rather than to express them collectively outside the legal channels provided by the state.

Administrative rivalries and juridical struggles among and between state officials and colonial groups seem to have contributed to decentralizing power. But on closer inspection, the most significant shifts in power always took place within the institutional framework of the colonial absolutist state. The system of checks and balances that developed in Latin America served primarily to transfer power either horizontally, from, say, the judiciary to the church, or vertically, from the Viceroy and his staff stationed in urban areas to district officials in the countryside. But this system rarely enabled colonial groups to become autonomous by acquiring power or by developing new sources and using them to challenge state and church officials and their control of public life. In fact, state and church officials relied on colonial groups to strengthen their position within the government.

Landed Aristocracy

Under the old regime, the aristocracy in Europe had played a pivotal role in propagating civic practices across public life. In addition to "civilizing" the peasantry and instilling in them a sense of mutual reciprocity and duty, the aristocracy was responsible for preventing the king from centralizing power and for preserving communal autonomy. But Latin America never had a proper aristocracy. The nobility in this part of the world never had any of the feudal rights, corporate privileges, and legal immunities (Ban) that their counterparts had enjoyed in the Old World.[8] Furthermore,

7. Eric Van Young, "Conflict and Solidarity in Indian Villages: The Guadalajara Region in the Late Colonial Period," *Hispanic American Historical Review* 64 (February 1984): 55–79.
8. Mario Góngora, *Encomenderos y estancieros: 1580–1660* (Santiago: Universidad de Chile, Departamento de Historia, 1970), 118–27. Also see Doris M. Ladd, *The Mexican Nobility at Independence: 1780–1826* (Austin: University of Texas Press, 1976), 4–7, 17–18,

Latin America's gentry never had anything resembling an English Parliament, a French General Estate, nor even a Spanish Cortes in which to congregate, negotiate, and, if necessary, challenge the monarch.[9] Latin America's nobility was in reality nothing more than upwardly mobile merchants and miners who had purchased honorific titles relatively recently in an attempt to acquire prestige in colonial society. Few of them, however, actually acquired such prestige. They were ridiculed by their own peers and by commoners who worked for them, making the gentry all the more pretentious and anxious about their status. In any case, the majority of aristocratic families, even in Mexico and Peru where the wealthiest ones lived, were perpetually on the verge of bankruptcy. Their estates were heavily entailed to the Church, providing it enormous sums of money each year, which it used to finance religious and charitable work.[10] Bankruptcy rates among aristocratic families were so high that few of them lasted more than a couple of generations.

What little social cohesion Latin America's aristocracy was able to achieve derived from kinship ties rather than from public life.[11] Vicente Cañete, a civil servant with a long and distinguished career in the colonial bureaucracy and in the home office in Madrid, remarked:

56–62; and Guillermo Lohman Villeña, *Los Americanos en las órdenes nobilarias*, vol. 1 (Madrid: Consejo Superior de Investigaciones Científicas, 1947), xv–xxxi, lxxix–lxxix and his "Las Cortes en Indias," *Anuario de historia del Derecho Español* 18 (1947): 655–62.

9. Alexis de Tocqueville, *The Old Regime and the French Revolution*, trans. Stuart Gilbert (Gloucester, Mass.: Peter Smith, 1978). Also see Barrington Moore Jr., *Social Origins of Dictatorship and Democracy: Lord and Peasant in the Making of the Modern World* (Boston: Beacon Press, 1966), 415–20. For a restatement and further development of this argument see Brian Downing, *The Military Revolution and Political Change: Origins of Democracy and Autocracy in Early Modern Europe* (Princeton, N.J.: Princeton University Press, 1991), 11–13: "Across Medieval Western Europe, from England to the Scandinavian countries in the north, to the Spanish marshlands (excluding Castile) and Italian city-states in the south, across to Burgundy, the Swiss Confederation, and the Holy Roman Empire (excluding Muscovite Russia), you get parliaments responsible for controlling taxation and matters of war and peace. These local centers of power limited the strength of the crowd; contributed to independent judiciaries and the rule of law; guaranteed certain basic freedoms and rights for the entire population. Medieval constitutionalism, where it survived, laid the foundation for liberal democracy in the eighteenth and nineteenth century."

10. Arnold J. Bauer, "The Church and Spanish American Agrarian Structure: 1765– 1865," *The Americas* 28, no. 1 (1971): 78–98, and his "The Church in the Economy of Spanish America," *Hispanic American Historical Review* 63, no. 4 (1983): 707–29. Also see: Gisela von Wobser, *El crédito eclesiástico en la Nueva España, siglo XVIII* (Mexico City: Universidad Nacional Autónoma de México, 1994); Germán Colmenares, "Censos y capellanías: Formas de crédito en una economía agrícola," *Cuadernos americanos colombianos* [Bogotá] 2 (1974): 34–67; Alfonso Quiroz, "Reassessing the Role of Credit in Late Colonial Peru," *Hispanic American Historical Review* 74, no. 2 (May 1994): 193–230.

11. John Kicza, *Colonial Entrepreneurs: Family and Business in Bourbon Mexico City* (Albuquerque: University of New Mexico Press, 1984); Frederique Langue, "El círculo de las alianzas; estructuras familiares y estrategias económicas de la élite mantuana (siglo XVIII)," *Boletín de al Academia Nacional de la Historia* (January–March 1995): 97–121.

In Spain, there had been fraternity among [noble] families, and they had public and private ties to commoners, which had enabled them to advance their interests, attend to their needs and those of society. They were connected to each other and to the monarch. An electrical current traveled through the entire chain that linked them together, instilling in each person a sense of mutual dependency and reciprocity which served to unify and maintain a political balance and which led them to look after each other's civil interests. . . . The opposite of this has occurred in America. Each family considers itself an isolated island in the middle of the sea; each is concerned only with its own affairs. Citizens do not collaborate, and whatever ties they have developed are to [colonial] officials and magistrates. . . . This has made the latter arrogant and ambitious, and the former weak and sycophantic.[12]

The nobility in Latin America was weak, disorganized, and subservient to state and church officials.

Racial and Ethnic Fragmentation

Mixed bloods, fair-skinned creoles, indigenous peoples, and blacks mingled in public life but rarely forged stable ties with each other.[13] The system of ethnic-racial divisions and estates in Latin America was doubly divisive and far more rigid and complex than the system of corporate stratification in the Old World.[14]

Racial-ethnic distinctions permeated colonial society and were most pronounced at the bottom of the social ladder among mixed bloods, where they had become blurred and unstable due to miscegenation. Mixed bloods camouflaged their racial-ethnic identity in a variety of ways: bribing parish priests to falsify their birth certificate and baptismal document;

12. Vicente Cañete y Domínguez, *Clamor de la lealtad americana* (Lima, 1810), 2–3, 8–9.
13. See the following works by Magnus Morner: *Race Mixture in the History of Latin America* (Boston: Little, Brown, 1967); *Estado, razas y cambio social en la Hispanoamérica Colonial* (Mexico City: Secretaría de Educación Pública, 1974); and *Estratificación social Hispanoamericana durante el período colonial* (Stockholm: Institute of Latin American Studies, 1980). According to Claudio Fabregat, *El mestizaje en Iberoamérica* (Madrid: Alhambra, 1988), fair-skinned creoles represented 5 percent of the total population and lived mainly in urban areas across modern-day Mexico and Peru. Indigenous peoples accounted for 60 percent; the majority of them lived in rural areas across central and southern Mexico, Central America, and the Andean highlands. Mixed bloods accounted for another 30 percent; they were more or less evenly distributed throughout the region. Blacks (free and slave) accounted for the remaining 5 percent and lived mainly in the Caribbean islands and on the northern coast of Venezuela.
14. Cissie Fairchilds, *Domestic Enemies: Servants and Their Masters in Old Regime France* (Baltimore, Md.: Johns Hopkins University Press, 1986); and James R. Lehning, *Peasant and French: Cultural Contact in Rural France during the Nineteenth Century* (Cambridge: Cambridge University Press, 1995).

reporting a different identity to census-takers and local authorities each time they moved to a new neighborhood; wearing cotton trousers, shoes, and hats; learning to read and write, speak and behave like fair-skinned creoles; avoiding contact with darker-skinned persons; and so on.[15] Mixed bloods were living proof that racial-ethnic differences were a fiction, but it would be a mistake to consider them "multiculturalists" *avant la lettre*. In "whitening" themselves, mixed bloods were in fact contributing to this system of racial-ethnic stratification.

Racial-ethnic distinctions were also important among fair-skinned creoles at the top of the social ladder. But in contrast to the situation with mixed bloods, skin color undermined the internal cohesion of the elite. Alexander von Humboldt, the great Prussian naturalist, and his French companion, Aime Bonpland, after three years collecting flora and fauna throughout the region, noted:

> A sentiment of equality among the Whites has penetrated every bosom. . . . In the colonies, the color of the skin is the real badge of nobility. In Mexico as well as in Peru, in Caracas as in the island of Cuba, a barefooted fellow is often heard exclaiming: "Does that rich white man think himself whiter than me?" . . . The axiom, every "White man is noble" . . . must singularly wound the pretensions of a great number of ancient and illustrious European families.[16]

In colonial Latin America, skin color was as important as financial wealth in determining a person's social rank, making it difficult for the elite to distinguish themselves from fair-skinned commoners and to develop a sense of corporate identity.

The system of corporate estates in Latin America differed from that in the Old World.[17] Each group in colonial society—fair-skinned creoles,

15. Robert McCaa, Stuart B. Schwartz, and Arturo Grubesich, "Race and Class in Colonial Latin America: A Critique," and John K. Chance and William B. Taylor, "Estate and Class: A Reply," *Comparative Studies in Society and History* 21 (1979): 421–33 and 434–42, survey the discussion. Also see: Alberto Flores Galindo, "Los rostros de la plebe," *Revista Andina* 2 (December 1983): 315–52; David J. Robinson, *Migration in Colonial Spanish America* (Cambridge: ?????, 1990); Dennis Valdes, "The Decline of the Sociedad de Castas in Mexico City" (Ph.D. dissertation, University of Michigan, 1978); David Cahill, "Color by Numbers: Racial and Ethnic Categories in the Viceroyalty of Peru, 1532–1824," *Journal of Latin American Studies* 26 (1994): 325–46. Mario Góngora, "Urban Stratification in Urban Chile," *Hispanic American Historical Review* 55, no. 3 (August 1975): 421–46, shows that in the town of Valparaiso, 49 percent of all families in 1777 and 1778 altered their ethnic identity one or more times.
16. Alexander von Humboldt and Aime Bonpland, *Personal Narrative of Travels to the Equinoctial Regions of the New Continent during the Years 1799–1801*, vol. 3 (London, 1818), 476.
17. Marc Bloch, *Feudal Society*, trans. L. A. Manyon (Chicago: University of Chicago Press, 1961), 186–88; and Mario Góngora, *Studies in the Colonial History of Spanish America*, trans. Richard Southern (Cambridge: Cambridge University Press, 1975), 35–42.

churchmen, indigenous peoples, and blacks—had its own set of legal
rights and corporate privileges. But in contrast to the estate system in the
Old World, corporate groups in Latin America were not, strictly speaking, "constituted bodies" in Robert Palmer's sense, bodies that had the
right to represent themselves in front of the king. In Latin America, as I
noted above, municipal life was moribund and there was no nationwide
body such as a Parliament, General Estate, or Cortes that could be used
by colonial peoples to challenge the monarch.

> The state had a corporate character. Within it there were independently
> defined privileges and jurisdictions for general groups (Indians, Blacks,
> Europeans, Ecclesiastics) and for each subgroup, such as Indians in mis-
> sions, *pueblos de indios,* Indians on *encomiendas;* African slaves, col-
> ored freedmen; merchants, university students, artisans; regular clergy,
> inquisitorial officials, and so forth. [However], the medieval imprint that
> the system as a whole bore was not parliamentary representation, but
> that of pluralistic, compartmentalized privileges and of administrative
> paternalism.[18]

Colonial groups were kept divided, making it relatively easy for state officials to attack one or another group without having to worry that others
would come to its aid.

The system of racial-ethnic segregation and corporate estates I have
outlined here was, according to Alexander von Humboldt, a sociopolitical strategy used by the colonial-absolutist state to maintain law and order in Latin America:

> The want of sociability is universal in the Spanish colonies, and the ha-
> tred which divides the various castes of greatest affinity sheds much bit-
> terness over the life of the colonists; all this is due solely to the political
> principle by which these regions have been governed since the sixteenth
> century. [If ever an enlightened government were to gain power in the
> area, it] will have to overcome immense difficulties before it can render
> the inhabitants sociable and teach them to consider themselves mutually
> in the light of fellow citizens. . . . Until now, the mother country [Spain]
> has sought security in civil dissensions . . . and has fomented incessantly
> the spirit of party and hatred among the castes. . . . From this state of
> things, arises a rancor which disturbs the enjoyment of social life.[19]

The racial-ethnic divisions that kept groups internally divided were as
great as the corporate divisions that kept them separated from each

18. Richard Morse, *New World Soundings: Culture and Ideology in the Americas* (Baltimore, Md.: Johns Hopkins University Press, 1989), 98.

19. Alexander von Humboldt, *Political Essays on the Kingdom of New Spain,* vol. 1
(London, 1811), 258–62.

other.[20] Colonial life in the region resembled a shattered mosaic rather than a stained-glass window.

Associative Life

Religious confraternities were the single most important type of association in the region, and also the most common, providing elite and non-elite groups across the region a place to socialize outside the home and workplace.[21] Organized by parishioners devoted to the same saint, confraternities had close ties to the Church.

Membership in these groups was restricted to persons of the same racial-ethnic background and usually made up of individuals who were in the same trade or profession and lived in the same parish (silversmiths, carpenters, merchants, lawyers, doctors, and so on).[22] Confraternities charged members a small matriculation and monthly fee and in return provided them with credit and loans, welfare relief, and a modest stipend to cover burial costs and a monthly allowance for the widows and orphans of deceased members.[23] The wealthiest confraternities also owned and rented out their farms, cattle herds, textile mills, and landed estates, and drew a sizeable income from them.

Churchmen maintained a tight grip over urban-based confraternities, although they were not as successful in maintaining control of rural-based groups made up of indigenous peoples. They maintained their control of the urban groups in several ways. In order to be recognized as a confraternity, members had to apply to the Church for a "license" (*patente*), and these were rarely given unless the parish priest intervened on their behalf, which he did only if the members had already expressed loyalty and

20. Mary Douglas, *Natural Symbols* (New York: Vintage Books, 1973), 72–92 on institutional boundaries between (group) and within (grid) groups.

21. Asunción Lavrín, "La congregación de San Pedro: Una cofradía urbana del México colonial: 1604–1730," *Historia Mexicana* 116 (1980): 568.

22. Alicia Bazarte Martínez, *Las cofradías de españoles en la ciudad de México* (Mexico City: Universidad Autónoma Metropolitana, 1989); Susan Socolow, "Religious Participation of the Porteño Merchants: 1788–1810," *The Americas* 32 (1976): 373–401; A. Miguel de la Cruz, "Las cofradías de los negros en Lima" (Ph.D. dissertation, Pontífica Universidad Católica, 1985); George Reid Andrews, *The Afro-Argentines of Buenos Aires: 1800–1900* (Madison: University of Wisconsin Press, 1980), 139–55.

23. Asuncion Lavrin, "Rural Confraternities in the Local Economies of New Spain," in *The Indian Community of Colonial Mexico*, ed. Arij Ouweneel and Simon Miller (Amsterdam: CEDLA, 1990), 224–46; Albert Meyers and Diane E. Hopkins, *Manipulating the Saints: Religious Brotherhoods and Social Integration in Post-Conquest Latin America* (Hamburg: Wayasbah, 1989); Brian Belinger, "Secularization and the Laity in Colonial Mexico: 1598–1821," (Ph.D. dissertation, Tulane University, 1990), 5–14; María del Carmen Pareja Ortíz, "Religiosidad popular y caridad asistencial en las cofradías de Nueva España en el siglo XIX," *Hispania Sacra* 43 (July–December 1991), 625–46.

agreed to provide him with an income. Each confraternity had its own priests, who were responsible for attending to the religious and spiritual affairs of the members. Priests also attended monthly meetings, participated in discussions, intervened in annual elections for officers, and were always trying to get their hands on the ledger book in order to know how much money members could afford to pay them for their services. In the Old World, priests derived most of their income from tithes, but in Latin America they relied on confraternities—another indication of the close relationship between these groups and the Church.[24]

But even the most zealous priest had to exercise restraint. If they failed to do so, confraternity members could elect a new spiritual advisor, transfer the group to a different parish, or decide to boycott religious services and deprive the priest of an additional fee. In rural areas, members sometimes dissolved their confraternities and reorganized themselves into a "brotherhood."[25] Although the Church never gave them a license and refused to recognize their devotion to one or another saint, members flocked to these brotherhoods nonetheless, turning them into major centers of popular forms of religiosity. In the course of competing amongst themselves for financial and institutional control of these groups, priests were driven to grant them some independence. But the fact remains that state and church officials could, if they had to, abolish confraternities altogether. Recall that in 1791, the viceroy of Mexico banned roughly 430 of the 950 religious groups from public life, and that between 1805 and 1809, the state confiscated almost all the money from the remaining confraternities.[26] Despite the many examples of institutional autonomy that have been reported by scholars, on balance religious confraternities never

24. Adrian van Oss, *Catholic Colonialism: A Parish History of Guatemala* (Cambridge: Cambridge University Press, 1986), 89-1-9; Marcello Carmagnani, *El regreso de los dioses: El proceso de reconstitución de la identidad etníca en Oaxaca, siglos xvii–xviii* (Mexico City: Fondo de Cultura Económica, 1988); David Brading, *Church and State in Bourbon Mexico: 1749–1810* (Cambridge: Cambridge University Press, 1989), 131–49; Gary W. Graff, "Cofradias in the New Kingdom of Granada" (Ph.D. dissertation, University of Wisconsin, 1973), 40–94.

25. Serge Gruzinski, "Indian Confraternities, Brotherhoods and Mayordomias in Central New Spain," in *The Indian Community of Colonial Mexico*, ed. Arij Ouweneel and Simon Miller (Amsterdam: CEDLA, 1990), 207–11; Paul Charney, "A Sense of Belonging: Colonial Indian Cofradias and Ethnicity in the Valley of Lima, Peru," *The Americas* 54, no. 3 (January 1998), 379–408.

26. Serge Gruzinski, *La colonización del imaginario: Sociedades indígenas y occidentalización en el México español* (Mexico City: Fondo de Cultura Económica, 1991), 267–73; Brian R. Hamnett, "The Appropriation of Mexican Church Wealth by the Spanish Bourbon Government," *Journal of Latin American Studies* 1, no. 2 (1988): 85–113. Alejandro Díez Hurtado, *Fiestas y cofradías: Asociaciones religiosas e integración en la historia de la comunidad de Sechura; siglos XVII–XX* (Piura: Centro de Investigaciones y Promoción del Campesinado, 1993), 21–68.

succeeded in becoming independent from the Catholic Church and the colonial-absolutist state.

Catholicism, Selfhood, and Public Life

In the eighteenth century, Latin Americans used Catholic terminology to make sense of their differences in public life, in the same way that today most scholars and citizens resort to economic terminology to make sense of theirs.

Being in a Catholic World

Catholic doctrine sought to reconcile "divine determinism" and "human agency." In the Aristotelian terminology of the time, although God was both the "original source" and the "final outcome" of human history, each person was directly responsible for linking the two. Without human agency, God's influence on worldly affairs would remain unrealized, making it impossible for believers to attain eternal salvation.[27] But without divine guidance, human action would flounder and lose direction. God accompanied his people during their pilgrimage on earth, but human intervention shaped the actual course of the journey.

God had created human beings in his own image and likeness, imbuing them with a capacity for "rational faith." Catholics were encouraged to study natural science, mathematics, and philosophy in order to analyze the world around them, as it was said to contain hidden traces of God's divine intention (natural law). But because human beings were mortals and, therefore, flawed even at birth, having been tainted with "original sin," they could not be expected to behave like angels. Catholics accepted the fact that they would sometimes be tempted by Satan and his band of fallen angels.[28] In order to overcome their "irrational passions" and regain their capacity for free will, Catholics were expected to remain faithful to the Church and to obey all its teachings. The Church was there to enable even the most weak-willed of sinners to attain salvation.

One of the most stirring and memorable expressions of this struggle between the forces of rational faith and irrational passion is found in a poem

27. Etienne Gilson, *The Spirit of Mediaeval Philosophy*, trans. A.H.C. Downes (New York: Charles Scribner's Sons, 1940); and David Knowles, *The Evolution of Medieval Thought* (Baltimore, Md.: Helicon Press, 1962). Also see Otto Gierke, *Political Theories of the Middle Age*, trans. and intro. F. W. Maitland (Cambridge: Cambridge University Press, 1987), and John Finnis, *Natural Law and Natural Rights* (Oxford: Oxford University Press, 1980).

28. Fernando Cervantes, *The Devil in the New World: The Impact of Diabolism in New Spain* (New Haven, Conn.: Yale University Press, 1994).

written by the Jeronymite nun, Juana Inés (1651–1695), one of Mexico's greatest female writers:

> My soul is confusedly divided into two parts,
> One, a slave of passion, the other,
> measured by reason. Inflamed civil war importunately
> afflicts my bosom.[29]

To a late modern reader, the poem is about the author's unresolved tension between erotic pleasure and the life of the mind. Emancipated females of this period, especially cloistered nuns, felt this dilemma as intensely as did Max Weber and other late modern writers; however, in contrast to us, Sor Juana and her contemporaries made sense of it in Catholic rather than in Cartesian terms. For us, the poem is about the "mind-body" split; for her, it is about the contradictory pull she felt from her commitment to rational faith and her irrational passions, understood in Augustinian terms as the "libido dominandi," as the desire for power, glory, and fame that, according to Catholics, is a perfectly "natural" and therefore human tendency.[30] That Sor Juana did not include the adjectives "rational" and "irrational" in front of the terms "faith" and "passion," respectively, is another indication that she and we live in different worlds and speak different languages.

This tension between rational faith and unruly passions was not only an individual dilemma; it was also constitutive of the Catholic world system, as depicted in figure 3.1. From a Catholic perspective, the world was divided into three regions—core, semi-periphery, and periphery—with a country's place in the system determined by the capacity of its people and government to balance rational faith with human agency. Imperial Spain and Portugal were the only countries that had succeeded in balancing the two, which earned them a place in the system's core, where Grace, Prudence, and Moderation prevailed.[31]

---

29. Sor Juana Inés de la Cruz, "De amor y discreción," in *Obras Completas,* intro. and prologue by Francisco Monterde (Mexico City: Editorial Porrua, 1999), 112. See Octavio Paz, *Sor Juana; or, The Traps of Faith,* trans. Margaret Sayers Peden (Cambridge, Mass.: Belknap Press, 1988) for a broad-minded study of the author and her world.

30. Herbert A. Deane, *The Political and Social Ideas of St. Augustine* (New York: Columbia University Press, 1963), 44–56; and Etienne Gilson, *The Philosophy of St. Thomas Aquinas,* trans. Edward Bullough, ed. G. A. Elrington (Cambridge: W. Heffer, 1948), 284–303. Also see Sabine McCormick, *Religion in the Andes: Vision and Imagination in Early Colonial Peru* (Princeton, N.J.: Princeton University Press, 1991), 7–45.

31. Immanuel Wallerstein, *Unthinking Social Science: The Limits of Nineteenth Century Paradigms* (Cambridge: Polity Press, 1991), criticizes sociological theory for its inability to "historicize" itself, but then he fails to do the same in his own work on the capitalist world system by portraying market-centered forms of life as an almost natural and timeless phenomenon.

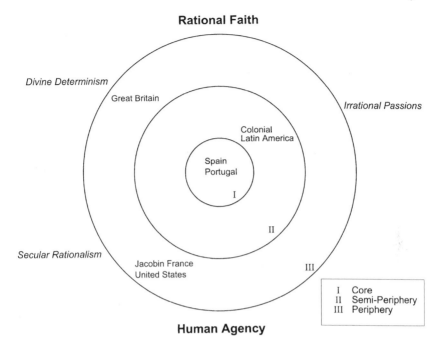

Figure 3.1 The Catholic World System

As one moved out from the core to the semi-periphery and periphery, the relationship between rational faith and human agency became progressively less balanced. Although Latin Americans were devout Catholics, they occupied the semi-periphery. Colonial peoples were considered too passionate to be able to exercise their rational faculties. Once they had learned to discipline themselves, Latin Americans would be able to move into the core and occupy a place alongside their Spanish and Portuguese brethren.

France, the United States, and Great Britain were on the periphery of the system. Prior to the revolution of 1789, France had been near the core, but after the Jacobins seized power and used it to attack the Catholic Church and to propagate rationalist and materialist doctrines, they were expelled from their previously central place and assigned to the periphery. Unlike the Ottoman "infidels," who had never known the one, true Catholic faith, French Jacobins had knowingly and deliberately turned away from the Church and transformed themselves into Godless "heretics." Across Latin America, parish priests mounted their pulpits on Sunday and sermonized against the French, describing them as "frenetic," "disorderly," and "confused," and accusing them of "establishing a reign of passion" in the modern West.[32] The people and government of the United States were relegated to the periphery for similar reasons.[33] Although Great Britain remained faithful to Puritanism, it also occupied the periphery. The Church of England, the official church, embraced the doctrine of predestination, which, from a Catholic perspective, was antihumanist insofar as it stripped people of any agency and assigned God a deterministic role in human affairs.[34] English Puritans would never be able to achieve salvation.

By the late eighteenth century, if not earlier, the Catholic world system was unraveling due to the moral, economic, and political pressures exerted on it by Jacobin France, the United States, and England. Catholicism was in decline across the Old World, but it remained dominant in Latin America.[35] Colonial peoples were destined to play a key role in the resurgence of Catholicism in the modern West:

> During certain epochs, passion . . . and virtue have coexisted in the world. . . . War, heresy, schisms, and sedition have never remained in their country of origin. In spreading to other places, they have also generated a counter-tendency and contributed to a resurgence in religiosity, enlightenment, and patriotism.[36]

But in seeking to reinvigorate the Catholic world system, Latin Americans contributed to its final demise—in the early nineteenth century, when they declared themselves independent from Spain—and to the consolidation of the capitalist world system.[37]

Latin Americans and Colonial Catholicism

In Latin America, colonial peoples continued to use Catholicism in public life at a time when it was no longer dominant in the rest of the Atlantic world. In Latin America, Catholicism and colonialism had been fused from the start and would remain indissoluble until independence:

32. "Carta pastoral," *Mercurio Peruano,* 26 January 1794, 59–66.
33. Samuel H. Beer, "The Rule of the Wise and the Holy: Hierarchy in the Thomistic System," *Political Theory* 14, no. 3 (August 1986): 391–422, discusses the main differences between Catholicism and U.S.-style republicanism.
34. Max Weber, *The Protestant Ethic and the Spirit of Capitalism,* trans. Talcott Parsons, with a foreword by R. H. Tawney (New York: Scribner's, 1958).
35. Anthony Pagden, *Spanish Imperialism and the Political Imagination* (New Haven, Conn.: Yale University Press, 1990), 5, claims that Catholicism was a spent force in international affairs by the sixteenth century. This might be true in economic and political terms, but not so in cultural terms, which is, after all, the subject of Pagden's book.
36. "Noticias de un nuevo periódico de Santa Fe de Bogotá," *Mercurio Peruano,* 28 April 1791, 306–8.
37. Immanuel Wallerstein, *The Modern World-System,* 3 vols. (New York: Academic Press, 1974–1988).

If we had to choose a single, irreducible idea underlying Spanish colonialism in the New World, it would undoubtedly be the propagation of the Catholic faith. Unlike such other European colonizing powers as England or the Netherlands, Spain insisted on converting the natives of the lands it conquered to its state religion.[38]

Colonial Catholicism in this part of the world was more than just a state religion; it was also the language of daily life. Elite and non-elite used its narrative resources to discuss public and private affairs. This does not mean that colonial peoples were any less venal, violent, or corrupt than any other group of people—only that they used colonial Catholic terminology to make sense of all their vices.

Selfhood in Colonial Latin America

Colonial Catholicism as imagined and practiced in Latin America was slightly different from Imperial Catholicism in Spain. Latin Americans were described as unruly children who were not yet capable of thinking and acting in a moderate and methodical manner.[39] They remained irrational because colonial life itself continued to be chaotic and uncivilized. The elite and non-elite acquired the same disorderly habits, which formed part of everyday life, and it was the task of state and church officials to assist them in overcoming them. The problem, they claimed, was endemic to the culture and to its social institutions, rather than a result of any biological or natural factors, as George Buffon, William Robertson, Cornelius de Pauw, G. F. Hegel, and other French, English, and German Enlightenment thinkers had proclaimed.[40] Small wonder that the majority of public intellectuals in Latin America from the late eighteenth to the early nineteenth century continued to use Catholic notions rooted in particularism rather than Enlightenment ideas based on rational universalism to discuss their own shortcomings.[41]

The detrimental influence of colonial habits and life manifested itself differently on each group. In the case of fair-skinned elites, faulty socialization at home and the ban that prohibited them from serving in the

38. Adrian van Oss, *Catholic Colonialism: A Parish History of Guatemala: 1524–1821* (Cambridge: Cambridge University Press, 1986), xi.

39. Lewis Hanke, *The Spanish Struggle for Justice in the Conquest of America* (Philadelphia: University of Pennsylvania Press, 1949); Anthony Pagden, *The Fall of Natural Man: The American Indian and the Origins of Comparative Ethnology* (Cambridge: Cambridge University Press, 1986).

40. Antonello Gerbi, *The Dispute of the New World: History of a Polemic, 1750–1900,* trans. Jeremy Moyle (Pittsburgh: University of Pittsburgh Press, 1973), remains the best study of its kind.

41. David A. Brading, *The First America: The Spanish Monarchy, Creole Patriots and the Liberal State: 1492–1867* (Cambridge: Cambridge University Press, 1991), 5, 293–502.

colonial bureaucracy had made them morally and cognitively backward. Elite children were customarily nursed, weaned, and raised by indigenous and black women, who instilled their own irrational impulses on the new generation of fair-skinned creole boys and girls. The consequences of this improper socialization were nowhere more evident than in the city of Cuzco in the Andean highlands. Although at this time Spanish was considered the language of reason and Quechua the language of passion, the city's elite were predisposed to use the latter:

> In the city of Cuzco, everyone speaks Quechua. . . . The most distinguished ladies also speak Spanish, but are more likely to speak [Quechua], which they consider to be their first tongue, even amongst themselves in family salons, having learned it from their own mothers, wet-nurses and maids. . . .[42]

Latin Americans were prohibited by law from serving in the colonial bureaucracy. Even Spanish officials recognized that this ban retarded the cognitive and moral development of their colonial subjects. In a report commissioned by the Spanish monarch, Antonio de Ullóa and Jorge Juan de Ullóa, both of whom had served for many years in Latin America, devoted many pages to a critique of the policy of banning any fair-skinned elite from pursuing professional careers in the colonial bureaucracy. Creoles are, they wrote,

> naturally endowed . . . however, between the ages of 25 and 30, they begin losing their rational faculties because they lack the incentive, honor and stimulation [they would have if they were allowed to work] in our administration.[43]

Family and public life discouraged the elite from becoming civilized and self-disciplined.

Among mixed bloods, miscegenation between individuals of different racial and ethnic backgrounds and rational capacities was responsible for making them impulsive and irrational. The children of mixed bloods inherited these same traits from their parents, and passed them on to their offspring. State and church officials considered miscegenation proof that

42. Concolorcorvo (Carlos Calixto), *El lazarillo de ciegos caminantes desde Buenos Aires hasta Lima* (1776; Buenos Aires, 1942), 96. Also see: Bernard Lavalle, "Del indio al criollo: Evolución y transformación de un imagen colonial," in *La imagen del indio en la europa moderna,* ed. Escuelas de estudios hispanoamericanos (Seville: Consejo Superior de Investigaciones Científicas, 1990), 319–42.

43. Jorge Juan and Antonio de Ullóa, *Relación histórica del viaje a la América Meridional,* vol. 1 (1748; Madrid: Fundación Universitaria Española, 1978), 46–47, and their *Noticias secretas de América* (1862; Madrid: Historia 16, 1991), 521–23. Also see: Juan José de Eguiara y Eguren, *Prólogo a la biblioteca mexicana,* ed. Ernesto de la Torre Villar (Mexico City: Universidad Nacional Autónoma de México, 1989), 142–43.

mixed bloods were not yet self-disciplined adults and felt compelled to put an end to it. In the late 1770s, state officials across Latin America approved and implemented the Royal Pragmatic Code, aimed at curbing interracial and interethnic breeding. From that point on, children would have to present evidence documenting their racial-ethnic stock and secure authorization from their parents and parish priests. Between 1785 and 1810, local magistrates in the province of Buenos Aires were presented with more than two hundred cases of suspected miscegenation. The judges approved 45 percent of the matches, declaring them "rational," and rejected the remaining 55 percent, declaring them "irrational."[44]

Indigenous peoples, or the "natural ones" as they were called in official documents in order to distinguish them from the "people of reason," were considered underage minors. Their moral and cognitive development was estimated to be that of a child of between seven and fifteen years of age. Colonial law prohibited them from entering into any contractual relationship; if they did, the agreement was considered invalid. Because the overwhelming majority of indigenous peoples could neither read nor write, church and state officials had to rely primarily on verbal, visual, and corporal methods to instill them with rational habits and inclinations.[45] In the confessional box, priests encouraged indigenous peoples to break with communal notions of action and selfhood by training them to speak in the active rather than in the passive voice, and by demanding that they individualize their actions. The most widely used confessional manual was written by Alonso de Molina and Juan de la Anunciación; it was translated into Nahuatl and various other indigenous languages and reissued many times. The manual instructed penitents to "never say that the devil

44. Susana Martínez López, Beatriz Rodríguez, and Dora Rodríguez, "Aplicación de la legislación sobre matrimonios de hijos de familia en Río de la Plata," in *III Congreso del Instituto Internacional de Historia del Derecho Indiano*, ed. Instituto Nacional de Estudios Jurídico (Madrid: Instituto Nacional de Estudios Jurídicos, 1973), 779–99. Daisy Rípodas Ardanaz, *El matrimonio en Indias: Realidad social y regulación jurídica* (Buenos Aires: Fundación para la Educación, la Ciencia y la Cultura, 1977), 307–14. Also see Verena Martínez-Alier, *Marriage, Class and Colour in Nineteenth Century Cuba* (Cambridge: Cambridge University Press, 1974), and Patricia Seed, *To Love, Honor and Obey in Colonial Mexico: Conflicts over Marriage Choice* (Stanford, Calif.: Stanford University Press, 1988), for studies of how the Pragmatic Code was implemented in societies with large numbers of indigenous peoples and blacks.

45. Vicente Cañete y Domínguez, *Guía histórica, geográfica, física, política, civil y legal del gobierno e intendencia de la provincia de Potosí* (Potosí: Editorial Potosí, 1952), 515–21; Josefina Cintrón Tiryakian, "La imagen económica del indio," in *Actas del XLI Congreso Internacional de Americanistas*, vol. 2 (Mexico City: Comisión de Publicación de las Actas y Memorias, 1976), 429–39; Ignacio González Casanovas, "La problemática social y económica de Charcas a fines del siglo XVIII," in *Ciencia, vida y espacio en Iberoamérica*, vol. 2, ed. José Luis Peset (Madrid: Consejo Superior de Investigaciones Científicas, 1989), 207–28.

had led me to do this, or that my friends and relatives have forced me to commit a sin. . . . [Instead], you must assume responsibility for your actions."[46]

Visual techniques were also used as pedagogical tools to propagate rational practices and forms of life among indigenous peoples and other nonliterate individuals. Religious and civic celebrations took up no less than 25 percent of the calendar year (not including Sundays).[47] In the late 1790s, after Bishop Antonio San Miguel banned religious celebrations in the small town of Silao in Mexico's Bajio region because they had degenerated into drunken revelry, the leaders of several indigenous confraternities met with the Bishop and requested that he lift the ban. The representatives were fluent in Nahuatl and Spanish, and they explained the importance of these celebrations to their confrères: "since the doors of their intellect are sealed against any discourse, entrance has to come through the senses if they are to perceive anything or form an idea of the mysteries of religion."[48] Civic and religious festivities were often accompanied by violent brawls, hard drinking, lewd dancing, and bawdy singing, activities that raised doubts as to the efficacy of the festival as a pedagogical tool for training nonliterate peoples to tame their passions.[49]

The Bishop of Cuzco, Juan A. Areche, also expressed concern regarding the way visual techniques were contributing to the spread of irrationality. The public display of Incan symbols and iconography rekindled their memory of conquest and served to stir their passions:

> We know that the Indian is a type of rational being who is impressed more by what he sees than by what he is told. [In Cuzco,] they have in front of their eyes images of their descendants, as well as the shields of their Kings and grandfathers, and their own noble titles to remind them of their past. . . . Is it any wonder that they continue to pay tribute and homage to their ancestors? They have succeeded in keeping their memory alive. . . .[50]

46. Serge Gruzinski, "Aculturación e individualización: Modalidades e impacto de la confesión entre los indios nahues de México, siglo XVI–XVIII," *Cuadernos para la historia de la Evangelización en América Latina* 1 (1986): 12–13.

47. Linda Curcio, "Saints, Sovereignty and Spectacle in Colonial Mexico" (Ph.D. dissertation, Tulane University, 1993); Rosa María Acosta Vargas, "Una aproximación al estudio de la fiesta colonial en le Perú" (Ph.D. dissertation, Universidad Católica, Lima, 1979), 23–40, 54–82; José Pedro Barrán, *Historia de la sensibilidad en el Uruguay*, vol. 1 (Montevideo: Ediciones de la Banda Oriental, 1989), 54–57.

48. Quoted in David Brading, "Tridentine Catholicism and Enlightened Despotism in Bourbon Mexico," *Journal of Latin American Studies* 15, no. 1 (1983): 19.

49. Hipólito Villareal, *Enfermedades políticas que padecen la capital de esta Nueva España* (Mexico City, 1785), 505–6.

50. Quoted in Jorge Hidalgo, "Amarus and Cataris: Aspectos mesiánicos de la rebelión de 1781 en Cuzco, Chayanta, La Paz y Arica," *Revista Chungara* (March 1983): 129. Also

During the late eighteenth century, Mexican viceroys prohibited parish priests from staging in the atrium of the church "The Conquest of Mexico" and other works for fear that this would "remind indigenous peoples and revive their memory of what had happened to their ancestors."[51]

State officials devised a socioeconomic method called "forced consumtion" (*repartimientos*) to "civilize" indigenous peoples living deep in the hinterlands. Local officials visited their villages at least once a year in order to update the census. Depending on the number of residents in each village, the community was forced to purchase a certain amount of clothes, tools, and liquor and to pay for them in cash, in this way forcing villagers to spend an ever greater number of days each year working for a salary in nearby estates. In compelling them to abandon their "uncivilized" way of life based on subsistence agriculture and barter exchange and to enter the "market," state officials were seeking to enable indigenous groups to overcome their own irrational habits and acquire self-discipline.[52]

Colonial Life and the Sociopolitical Pact

According to Catholic doctrine, God invested divine power (*potestas*) in the community and in the sovereign, and forbade each to wrest power from the other. But since ruler and ruled could not exercise their power simultaneously, they had to agree on how much they would transfer to the

see David Cahill, "Etnología e historia: Los danzantes rituales del Cuzco a finales de la Colonia" (Unpublished typescript, University of Liverpool, undated).

51. Villareal, *Enfermedades políticas*, 95; Germán Viveros, "El teatro como instrumento educativo en el México del siglo XVIII," *Estudios de Historia Novohispana* 12 (1999): 171–80; David Cahill, "Popular Religion and Appropriation: The Example of Corpus Christi in Eighteenth Century Cuzco," *Latin American Research Review* 31 (1996): 67–110; Sergio Rivera Ayala, "Lewd Songs and Dances from the Streets of Eighteenth Century New Spain," in *Rituals of Rule, Rituals of Resistance: Public Celebrations and Popular Culture in Mexico*, ed. William H. Beezley, Cheryl Martin, and William French (Wilmington, Del.: Scholarly Resources Books, 1994), 27–46. See also the suggestive work of Juan P. Viqueira Alban, *Relajados o reprimidos? Diversiones públicas y vida social en la ciudad de México durante el siglo de Las laces* (Mexico City: Fondo de Cultura Económica, 1987).

52. Brian Hamnett, *Politics and Trade in Southern Mexico* (Cambridge: Cambridge University Press, 1981); Alfredo Cebrian Moreno, *El corregidor de indios y la economía del siglo XVIII; los repartos forzosos de mercancía* (Madrid: Consejo Superior de Investigaciones Científicas, 1977); Javier Tord Nicolini, "El corregidor de indios del Perú: Comercio y tributos," *Historia y Cultura* 8 (1974): 173–214; Brooke Larson and Robert Wasserstrom, "Consumo forzoso en Cochabamba y Chiapas durante la época colonial," *Historia Mexicana* 31 (January–March 1982): 361–408. Also see: Juan Pérez de Tudela, "El problema moral en el trabajo minero del indio," and Paulino Castañeda Delgado, "El tema de las minas en la ética colonial española," in *La minería hispana e iberoamericana*, vol. 1 (León: Cátedra de San Isidoro, 1970), 355–71 and 333–54; Ignacio González Casanovas, "La problemática social y económica de Charcas a fines del siglo XVIII y el pensamiento liberal de la ilustración española," in *Ciencia, vida y espacio en Iberoamérica*, ed. José Luis Peset (Madrid: Consejo Superior de Investigaciones Científicas, 1989), 208–28.

other and how much they would retain. According to "regalists," the community transferred all its power to the monarch, and once they had agreed to do so the people could never reclaim it or divest the sovereign of it. "Communitarians" disagreed. They claimed that the community never surrendered all their power to the king, that instead the people transferred only a portion of it. Moreover, if the king violated the "natural rights" of the community, then its members were entitled to reclaim all their power and use it to overthrow the monarch (tyrant). On this account, God had imbued the community with natural rights, and these were "prepolitical" and not subject to any pact.[53]

But because in Latin America colonial peoples remained beholden to their irrational passions, as I explained earlier, they were disqualified from serving as a repository of divine power. The peculiarities of colonial life radically altered the Catholic interpretation of sociopolitical pacts. Latin Americans could neither transfer, nor invest the Spanish monarch with, any power because they had none. In figure 3.2 I outline the colonial Catholic conception of the pact between God, the Spanish king, and Latin Americans. Colonial peoples had natural rights like any other Catholic believer, but they were not yet eligible to enter into this pact because they remained unable to subdue their passions.

Colonial peoples had not yet constituted themselves into a "society," defined by Spain's Royal Academy as a "gathering of rational persons." [54] In fact, Latin Americans did not even begin to use the adjective "social" nor the term "society" until late in the eighteenth century.[55] And when they did, the terms had negative connotations because colonial peoples and the life they led continued to be portrayed as irrational. In 1813 Jose Fernández de Lizardi, Latin America's first novelist, published a newspaper article in Mexico City in which he discusses the vernacular meaning of the terms "society" and "sociable":

> we barely know the meaning of the word society except by name, which is why we associate this word with anything having to do with vain, deceitful and coarse behavior. Among commoners, the only persons who are described as sociable are those who are meddlesome, sycophantic,

53. Roger Labrousse, *La doble herencia politica de España* (Barcelona: Bosch, 1942); Bernice Hamilton, *Political Thought in Sixteenth Century Spain* (Oxford: Clarendon Press, 1963); O. Carlos Stoetzer, *The Scholastic Roots of the Spanish American Revolution* (New York: Fordham University Press, 1979); and Tulio Halperín Donghi, *Tradición política española e ideología revolucionaria de mayo* (Buenos Aires: Centro Editor de América Latina, 1985).

54. Real Academia Española, *Diccionario de la Lengua Castellana en que se explica el verdadero sentido de las voces, su naturaleza y calidad,* vol. 3 (1737; Madrid: Editorial Gredos, 1963), 133.

55. Gregorio Salvado, *Incorporaciones léxicas en el Español del siglo XVIII* (Oviedo: Facultad de Filosofía y Letras, 1973), 10.

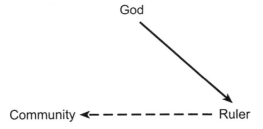

Figure 3.2 Colonial Catholicism and the Sociopolitical Pact

lewd, affected, brash, vicious, immoral and irreligious. But this is not the true meaning of the term. Society means nothing more than the intimate and fraternal ties among the inhabitants of a kingdom, a city or home. An example of what I mean by the word society is similar to the ties between husband and wife in a good marriage.[56]

The erroneous conception of society that predominated among the nonelite was rooted in irrational passions; the correct conception was based on intense affection such as the type of relations among family members and in other semiprivate domains. Neither conception had anything to do with either the Scottish Enlightenment notion based on "mutual sympathy" or the Rousseauist notion based on the "voluntary association."

Each kingdom in Latin America had the same juridical and political status as any other kingdom (Aragon, Navarre, Naples, Milan, Flanders, and so on) that was part of the Spanish empire. Although Latin America was an integral part of the Spanish empire, the king considered them to be a part of his own personal fiefdom. They were his vassals because they were still considered to be irrational children instead of a fully mature and constituted society like any other under the old regime. As I argued earlier, colonial peoples remained incapable of serving as a repository of divine power, nor could they be expected to partake in any sociopolitical pact with their monarch. Since they could not generate any social power, they were not entitled to have their own parliament nor to partake in any public affairs in Latin America. If the Spanish monarch had granted colonial peoples a parliament and a degree of self-rule, it would, ironically, have enabled the king to extract from them even more wealth without having to risk very much. But this alternative was never discussed because in the colonial Catholic framework colonial peoples continued to be construed as irrational children and, therefore, as unfit to practice self-rule.

56. José Joaquín Fernández de Lizardi, "Sociedad y Policía," in *Obras de José Joaquín Fernández de Lizardi,* ed. Jacobo Chencinsky and Luis M. Schneider (Mexico City: Universidad Nacional Autónoma de México, 1968), 216. Also see: Dieter Janik, "La noción de sociedad en el pensamiento de Lizardi y de sus contemporaneos," *Cahiers des Ameriques Latines* 10 (1990): 39–48.

However, after Napoleon invaded Spain and captured King Ferdinand VII, Latin Americans were invited to participate in the Cortes in Cadiz in recognition that a small portion of colonial peoples in the New World had reached adulthood. But because the majority of them remained beholden to their passions, Latin Americans were entitled to send only 1 delegate per 100,000 persons, while in Spain the ratio was 1 per 50,000.[57] The method of selecting delegates was also different. In Spain, the elections were direct and popular; even plebeians voted. In Latin America, only a tiny number of fair-skinned elites already active in municipal townships were permitted to participate in the elections. Latin Americans continued to be construed as children at a time when even the "lower orders" in Spain were already considered adults by the Liberal monarchists of the Cortes.[58] Commoners and plebeians in Spain were deemed higher up on the "Great Chain of Being" than any colonial person.[59]

Practical Judgment, Rationality, and Passion

Colonial peoples, state officials, and churchmen examined each other's behavior in public life in order to determine whether they were acting rationally or not. In the 1790s, members of "Concordia," Quito's leading salon, spent several sessions discussing the best way to study passions, and concluded:

> If you wish to know which passion is driving an individual . . . do the following: place whichever passions are relevant next to each other, and observe which of them is guiding the person's action. In revealing their preference, you will be able to understand their inclination. . . .[60]

The colonial elite and non-elite very rarely engaged in such explicit and systematic discussions of methodology, although as the examples below

---

57. Alvaro Flórez Estrada, *Examen imparcial de las disensiones de la América con la España* (Cádiz, 1812), 66–75, 145–48, 185; and María Teresa Berruezo, *La participación americana en las Cortes de Cádiz: 1810–1814* (Madrid: Centro de Estudios Constitucionales, 1986), esp. 28–29.

58. Teresa Servando de Mier, "Idea de la Constitución dada a las Américas, por los Reyes de España antes de la Invasión del antiguo despotismo," in *Obras completas,* intro. Edmundo O'Gorman and Jaime Rodriguez (Mexico City: Universidad Nacional Autónoma de México, 1981), 33–80; and Francisco Castillo Meléndez, Luisa J. Figallo Pérez, and Ramon Serrera Contreras, *Las cortes de Cádiz y la imagen de América: La visión etnográfica y geográfica del Nuevo Mundo* (Cádiz: Universidad de Cádiz, 1994). Also see María Cruz Seoane, *El primer lenguaje constitucional español en las cortes de Cádiz* (Madrid: Editorial Moneda y Crédito, 1968).

59. Arthur O. Lovejoy, *The Great Chain of Being: A Study of the History of an Idea* (Cambridge: Harvard University Press, 1936), 58–59.

60. "Historia literaria y económica," *Primicias de la Cultura,* 16 February 1792, reprinted in Francisco J. Eugenio de Santa Cruz y Espejo, *Escritos del Doctor . . . ,* vol. 2 (1792; Quito: Imprenta Municipal, 1912–1923), 57–63.

suggest, state officials, churchmen, fair-skinned creoles, and indigenous peoples used methods similar to this to evaluate each other's actions and motivations, and they expressed them publicly in the idiom of passion and reason.

The principal duty of state and church officials in Latin America was to rationalize colonial life and instill colonial peoples with habits of order and discipline. But like any mortal, state officials were the first to recognize, in proper Catholic fashion, that they were sinners like anyone else. In the 1780s, a state official stationed in Piura (in northern Peru) denounced his colleagues in the region:

> The passion of [local officials] . . . along with their own willfulness and stubbornness, has blinded and prevented them from recognizing how their own . . . appetites have dissolved all legal restraints. . . . Instead of acting benevolently as is expected of them, they have transformed themselves into beasts. . . .[61]

Church officials, too, were sinful mortals. Even Archbishop Jose Antonio de San Alberto, of La Plata, Argentina, one of the staunchest defenders of religious orthodoxy in Latin America, admitted to the Chiriguano Indians that the Carmelite friars they had kidnapped had behaved passionately:

> Don't think that our religion is any less saintly just because amongst its practitioners there are some who are sinful; this is not the fault of religion itself, which abhors and punishes all evil deeds, but the responsibility of those who behaved like children. You already know and have seen with your own eyes that good fathers are sometimes plagued by bad children. . . . The same is the case with our Catholic religion. It does not cease being holy simply because a few of its children have acted wrongly.[62]

San Alberto was able to persuade the Chiriguanos to release their captives. Church officials and priests stationed in rural parishes concurred that they sometimes acted like irrational children.[63]

State officials and creole elite also used the idiom of passion and rea-

---

61. Quoted in Anne Marie Brento, "Imaginaire politique et imaginaire economique chez un arbitriste peruvien," *Cahiers de Amérique Latine* 9 (1990): 38. Also see Francisco de Serra y Canals, *El Celo del Español y el Indiano Ilustrado* (1800; Buenos Aires: Facultad de Filosofía y Letras de la Universidad de Buenos Aires, 1979), 100, 191.

62. Josep Antonio de San Alberto, *Carta a los indios infieles Chiriguanos* (Madrid, 1788), 31–33.

63. Juan de Palafox y Mendoza, *Tratados Mejicanos*, vol. 1, ed. Francisco Sánchez Castañer (Madrid: Ediciones Atlas, 1968), 72–77; Pedro Borges Morán, *Misión y Civilización en América* (Madrid: Alhambra, 1987), 1–10, 39–40, 199–200; Manuel Marzal, *La transformación religiosa peruana* (Lima: Pontifica Universidad Católica del Perú, 1983), 343–78.

son to evaluate issues related to self-rule and imperial governance. At the end of his seven-year term as intendant of Venezuela, Jose de Abalos sent the king of Spain a report summarizing his years of service:

> Until now, my dear sirs, the Americas can be said to have been in their infancy . . . but now with the passage of time they have matured and grown and the previous impression which they [themselves] had inherited from their grandparents has [now] vanished. Their imagination is less encumbered than before and more capable . . . of reasoning freely without any fetters.[64]

Abalos was one of the few officials who was convinced that fair-skinned creoles had achieved adulthood and should be allowed to serve in the government bureaucracy. Juan Pablo Vizcardo y Guzman, a Jesuit who served in Peru until he was expelled in the late 1780s, was not the only one to describe Spain's relationship to Latin America in negative terms:

> Spain has been a malevolent tutor, and has grown accustomed to living . . . at the expense of its pupils. She is terrified that the time will soon come when nature, reason, and justice require that we put an end to this tyranny and demand emancipation. . . . Nature has placed a vast ocean between us to separate Peru from Spain. A child who lives far away from its parents would be a dolt if it always waited to hear from them before deciding anything.[65]

It is important to note that Vizcardo y Guzmán was arguing in favor of home rule but had never even considered the possibility of independence from Spain. Municipal officials in Mexico City and other townships across the region were in favor of local autonomy for similar reasons.[66]

The overwhelming majority of indigenous-led riots and rebellions in the countryside, including the largest of all, Tupac Amaru (1770), were organized in protest against zealous officials and the excessive demands of forced consumption.[67] Local officials and village chiefs were sometimes

---

64. Quoted in Maria T. Zubirí, "El cabildo de Caracas y la intendencia," in *Actas: Coloquio Internacional de Carlos III*, vol. 3 (Madrid: Universidad Complutense, 1990), 467–77.

65. Juan Pablo Vizcardo y Guzmán, *Carta Dirigida a los Españoles Americanos*, ed. Rubén Vargas Ugarte (Lima: Editorial del CIMP, 1954), 109, 118–19.

66. "Representación que hizo la ciudad de Mexico al Rey D. Carlos III en 1771," in *Colección de documentos para la historia de la guerra de independencia de México de 1808 a 1821*, vol. 1, ed. Juan E. Hernández y Dávalos (Mexico City: J. M. Sandoval, 1877–1882), 427–55.

67. John Coastworth, "Patterns of Rural Rebellion in Latin America," in *Riot, Rebellion and Revolution*, ed. Friedrich Katz (Princeton, N.J.: Princeton University Press, 1988),

accused of giving free rein to their own passions rather than contributing to the spread of civilization. In Chayanta, Bolivia, Aymara villagers organized a regional rebellion against local officials in the 1770s, and after their leader, Tomas Catari, was arrested and jailed, he was asked why they had taken up arms. He replied: "I am in jail simply because of the whim, the cruelty and passion with which Chayanta's local official (*corregidor*) administers our affairs."[68] Villagers rioted because they were convinced that officials were acting in an irrational manner. Parish priests in Cochabamba, Bolivia, and in other remote areas often accused landlords of acting irrationally and in their sermons persuaded indigenous peoples that it was rational to steal from them.[69]

In colonial Latin America, the elite and non-elite used similar methods to determine whether a person was acting rationally, but they evaluated their findings in light of the specific context and particular conditions in which they occurred. Even stealing, as I noted above, could be considered rational under certain circumstances. In other words, there was always a "phronetic gap," to borrow Charles Taylor's phrase, between the abstract definition of rationality and the "local knowledge" required to understand its particular meaning.[70]

In the same way that Immanuel Kant defined the "Enlightenment" as the "free use" of "theoretical reason," colonial peoples in Latin America relied on practical judgment to evaluate whether an action or utterance in public life was reasonable or not. According to Catholic doctrine, God's divine law was universally valid; however, because the human world was always in flux, this meant that people had to exercise their judgment in light of the particular situation and conditions facing them. The "discovery" of Latin America and the encounter with divergent cultures and peoples across the globe led members of the Jesuit order to come up with the doctrine of "probabilism" in the sixteenth century in order to make

21–62. Also see the monographic studies by Jurgen Golte, *Repartos y Rebeliones: Tupac Amaru y las contradicciones de la economía colonial* (Lima: Instituto de Estudios Peruanos, 1980); and Scarlett O'Phelan de Godoy, *Un siglo de rebeliones anticoloniales: Perú y Bolivia, 1700–1780* (Cuzco: Centro de Estudios Regionales Andinos "Bartolomé de las Casas," 1988).

68. Quoted in Sergio Serulnikov, *Reivindicaciones indígenas y legalidad colonial: La rebelión de Chayanta: 1777–1781* (Buenos Aires: IDES, 1989), 45.

69. In Juan Lope del Rodó, *Idea sucinta del probabilismo* (Lima, 1772), see the following unpaginated sections: "Prefacio," "Carta al Licenciado D. Francisco Álvarez," "Aprobación del P. Joseph Miguel Durán." Luis E. Bacigalupo, "El concepto moderno de la libertad y la tradición Católica" (Unpublished typescript, Instituto Riva-Agüero, 1993), discusses probabilism from the perspective of modern European philosophy.

70. Charles Taylor, "To Follow a Rule," in his *Philosophical Arguments* (Cambridge: Harvard University Press, 1995), 165–80.

sense of the new and modern world that had appeared on the horizon.[71] The Catholic Church accepted the doctrine and even encouraged believers who had a clean and clear conscience to exercise their judgment and follow the most "probable" path toward the good when dealing with situations that were not adequately accounted for by any existing doctrine.[72] When dealing with novelty, practical judgment was a better guide to human affairs than religious dogma.

In Latin America, the Jesuits introduced and were mainly responsible for propagating probabilism across the region, although other religious orders, including the Franciscans and the secular clerics in their parishes deep in the hinterlands, also contributed to disseminating it. From the 1780s onward, orthodox theologians (Jansenist) and state officials across the continent mounted a campaign against probabilism, claiming it promoted "laxity" and sinfulness among the faithful. Its moral precepts were now described as: "sacrilegious," because they assigned primacy to individual judgment and downplayed divine will; "seductive," because they contributed to the spread of social and moral ambiguity and disorder in public life; and "subversive," because they emphasized the right of individuals to challenge state and church officials.[73] By the turn of the century, colonial officials had expelled the Jesuit order from the region, banned the teaching of probabilism from every school and college, and prohibited parish priests from speaking out and sermonizing in favor of it. But it was too late. Probabilism was by now embedded in public life and was a social and moral habit among the elite and non-elite of the region. As I argue in the next chapter, probabilism provided Mexicans and Peruvians the narrative resources they needed to proclaim themselves rational adults.

I agree with those scholars who argue that Latin Americans achieved independence from Spain by working within their own Catholic tradition. But instead of focusing, as they do, on the ideological debate that broke out between "regalists" and "communitarians" across the region after the French army invaded the Iberian peninsula and captured King Ferdi-

---

71. Charles Taylor, *Sources of the Self: The Making of the Modern Identity* (Cambridge: Harvard University Press, 1989), does not discuss probabilism, although it was, arguably, the single most important doctrine produced by and for Catholics and also the most influential and widespread moral narrative in Latin America in the early modern and modern period.

72. Albert Jonsen and Stephen Toulmin, *The Abuse of Casuistry: A History of Moral Reasoning* (Berkeley: University of California Press, 1988), 137–227. John Mahoney, *The Making of Moral Theology* (Oxford: Oxford University Press, 1989), 180–84, 225–26, 240. Also see James F. Keenan, S.J., "Can a Wrong Action Be Good? The Development of Theological Opinion on Erroneous Conscience," *Eglise et Theologies* 24 (1993): 205–19. I am indebted to Keenan for clarifying the many questions I had regarding probabilism.

73. Lope del Rodó, *Idea Sucinta*, 2–3, 42–45, 61–75.

nand VII, my main concern in this chapter and the next is to understand how probabilism altered selfhood among colonial peoples in Mexico and Peru and how this, in turn, influenced the way they maneuvered through public life.[74] This story has not yet been told, and in my judgment it is just as significant as the other.

74. Stoetzer, *Scholastic Roots;* Morse, *New World Soundings;* Sergio Villalobos, "El bajo pueblo en el pensamiento de los precursores del 1810," *Anales de la Universidad de Chile* 68 (1960): 36–49; Ricardo Levene, *El mundo de las ideas y la revolución hispano-americana de 1810* (Santiago: Editorial Jurídica de Chile, 1956); Manuel Giménez Fernández, "Las ideas populistas en la independencia de hispanoamerica," *Anuario de estudios americanos* 3 (1947): 150–210; and Halperín Donghi, *Tradición política.*

CHAPTER 4

Becoming a Rational Person: Anticolonial Movements and the Emergence of a Public

The various anticolonial movements that broke out in Mexico and Peru in the 1810s and 1820s were the first in the modern West that sought to reconcile sociopolitical democracy with racial-ethnic differences. These movements formed part of what scholars now call the "age of democratic revolutions," which began in the United States in 1776 and soon spread through most of the countries on both sides of the Atlantic.[1] On Benedict Anderson's account, these movements were also responsible for giving birth to modern nationalism, foreshadowing by a century the different racial and ethnic movements that eventually swept throughout India, Asia, Africa, and the Middle East.[2]

True enough. But before Mexicans and Peruvians could even imagine themselves as citizens of a sovereign nation, they first had to construe themselves as rational adults. The anticolonial movements that erupted in Mexico and Peru were not, in my interpretation, merely efforts to gain independence from Spain. Rather, colonial peoples were through these movements asserting their adulthood and proclaiming to the world that they now deserved a place in the "family of nations." By channeling their most violent passions toward a single goal, self-rule, Mexicans and Peruvians were proving that they had acquired self-discipline. And by organizing a congress, they were proving themselves capable of resolving their differences by deliberation rather than brute force. The battle cry of New Englanders, French Jacobins, and Chartists in England against the Old Regime had been "no taxation without representation," "liberty, equality,

1. Victor Uribe, *State and Society in Spanish America during the "Age of Revolution": New Research on Historical Continuities and Changes, ca. 1750–1850s* (Durham, N.C.: Duke University Press, 2001).
2. Benedict Anderson, *Imagined Communities: Reflections on the Origin and Spread of Nationalism* (London: Verso, 1983).

and fraternity," and "in defense of the rights of free-born Englishmen."[3] When Mexicans and Peruvians rebelled against the Spanish King their slogan would be "we are rational adults."

In 1808, the French army invaded Spain and captured the king, thereby provoking a crisis for the monarchy. Commoners across Spain took to the barricades in defense of their nation and rallied around the rebel Parliament in Cadiz and the Liberal Constitution, the country's first. The anticolonial movements that erupted in Mexico and Peru in the 1810s and 1820s were, contrary to what some scholars claim, shaped by local dynamics in each colony rather than by recent events in Spain.[4] Mexicans responded to the demise of the Catholic world system by proclaiming their independence and declaring themselves rational adults. Peruvians, in contrast, responded by proclaiming their loyalty to the Spanish monarch but this time as adults. The rebel movements that broke out in both Mexico and Peru arose from interpersonal networks rather than from municipal townships (as in New England), political clubs (as in revolutionary France), or corresponding societies (as in Great Britain).[5] Associative life in Latin America had been too weak to provide rebels with a staging area for their movements. The rebel movements discussed below differed from the countless riots and rebellions that had occurred in the colonial period in several ways: they were multi-ethnic, multiclass, and multiregional in their social composition, relatively long-lasting and structured, made up of a civil and military wing.[6]

Mexican Popular Movements

My discussion is in two parts. The first examines the failed movements that surfaced in the Bajio Basin and Pacific Hotland region (see map 4.1); in the second I focus on the negotiations between insurgent and royalist

3. Pauline Maier, *From Resistance to Revolution: Colonial Radicals and the Development of American Opposition to Britain: 1765–1776* (New York: Vintage Books, 1961); E. P. Thompson, *The Making of the English Working Class* (New York: Pantheon Books, 1963); Emmett Kennedy, *A Cultural History of the French Revolution* (New Haven, Conn.: Yale University Press, 1989).

4. For works that emphasize sociopolitical dynamics within Spain rather than in Latin America, see: Timothy Anna, *Spain and the Loss of America* (Lincoln: University of Nebraska Press, 1983); Marie Laure Rieu-Millan, *Los diputados americanos en las Cortes de Cádiz: Igualdad o independencia* (Madrid: Consejo Superior de Investigaciones Científicas, 1990); and François-Xavier Guerra, *Modernidad e independencia: Ensayos sobre las revoluciones hispánicas* (Madrid: Editorial Mapfre, 1992).

5. Maier, *From Resistance to Revolution;* Thompson, *Making of the English Working Class;* Kennedy, *Cultural History of the French Revolution.*

6. Friedrich Katz, *Riot, Rebellion and Revolution* (Princeton, N.J.: Princeton University Press, 1988).

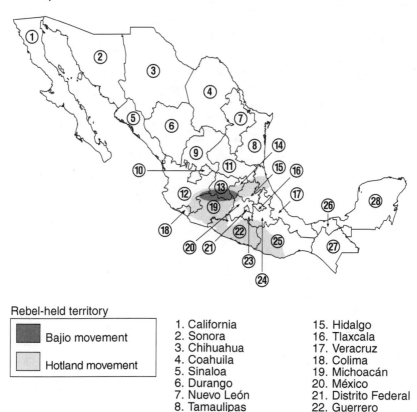

Rebel-held territory

▨ Bajio movement

▢ Hotland movement

1. California
2. Sonora
3. Chihuahua
4. Coahuila
5. Sinaloa
6. Durango
7. Nuevo León
8. Tamaulipas
9. Zacatecas
10. Aguascalientes
11. San Luis Potosí
12. Jalisco
13. Guanajuato
14. Querétaro

15. Hidalgo
16. Tlaxcala
17. Veracruz
18. Colima
19. Michoacán
20. México
21. Distrito Federal
22. Guerrero
23. Morelos
24. Puebla
25. Oaxaca
26. Tabasco
27. Chiapas
28. Yucatán

Map 4.1   Popular Movements, 1810–1821

troops in the battlefield, which culminated in Mexico's independence in 1821.

The rebel movement in the Bajio (September 1810 to January 1813) and Hotland (November 1812 to November 1815) differed in their political goals: the first sought home rule, the second demanded independence. Despite these differences, the two movements overlapped and were in fact different wings of the same movement. I focus on the social networks and political practices that shaped each of these movements and on Mexicans' understanding of them.[7]

7. Mexicanists have interpreted the war of independence from three perspectives: nationalist, radical, and antimodern. For nationalists such as Luis Villoro, *El proceso ideoló-*

Bajio and Hotland Movements

The Bajio and Hotland movement grew out of elite and non-elite networks. Merchants, landlords, textile mill owners, silver miners, country
lawyers, parish priests, militiamen, and local government officials and
their families gathered frequently in family salons to dance, sing, play card
games, and debate the burning issues of the day. Salon life in the towns of
Querétaro, Guanajuato, San Miguel, San Luis, and Valladolid had become
especially animated after the French captured Spain's monarch.[8] Members
visited and participated in each other's salons and organized a private
courier system in order to exchange documents and keep abreast of each
other's discussions. By 1810, there were roughly four hundred men active
in this network of salons.[9] The majority of them went on to participate in
the Bajio and Hotland movement. In addition to recruiting friends and
their employees, these men also donated large amounts of money to the
rebel cause.

Parish priests also played a key role in both movements. Nearly all the
priests who served in parishes across the Bajio and Hotland had studied
theology in one of three schools in Valladolid: San Nicolás, San Pedro,
and Tridentine.[10] Many of them had spent their formative years studying
together in the same school; those who had not were educated in natural
law, rationalism, and the doctrine of probabilism. A graduate of San Nico-

gico de independencia de la revolución (Mexico City: Universidad Nacional Autónoma de
México, 1967) and Ernesto Lemoine, Morelos y la revolución de 1810 (Morelia: Gobierno
del Estrado de Michoacán, 1979), the war was a nationalist revolution like the one in the
United States. For radicals such as M. S. Alperovich, Historia de la independencia de Méx-
ico 1810–1824, trans. Adolfo Sánchez Vázquez (Mexico City: Editorial Grijalbo 1967) and
John Tuttino, From Insurrection to Revolution in Mexico: Social Bases of Agrarian Violence
(Princeton, N.J.: Princeton University Press, 1986), it was a social revolution like the one that
broke out in France and led to the commercialization of land, labor, and capital. Guerra,
Modernidad e independencia, and Eric Van Young, The Other Rebellion (Stanford, Calif.:
Stanford University Press, 2001), claim that the war was the first reactionary and antimodern revolution to have taken place in the West where an entire nation (not just a few villages
as in the case of the Vendee) rebelled in defense of Catholicism, colonialism, and monarchical rule.
    8. Most of the primary sources I used in my work are published in the Colección de doc-
umentos para la historia de la guerra de independencia de México de 1808 a 1821, 6 vols.,
ed. Juan E. Hernández y Dávalos (Mexico City: J. M. Sandoval, 1877–1882), hereafter cited
as Colección followed by volume number and page numbers. On salons, see: "Declaración
de D. Juan Aldama," Colección 1.64–66; "Cuaderno Tercero de la causa instruída de Valladolid," Colección 1.253–407; and "Relación formada por el Sr. Michelena," Colección
2.5–7.
    9. "Extracto de los avisos dados desde la ciudad de Querétaro, sobre un proyecto de
sublevación en Dolores," in Colección 2.68–70.
    10. Agustín García Alcaraz, La cuna ideológica de la independencia (Morelia: Fimax
Publicistas, 1971), 87–92; and Germán Cardozo Galué, Michoacán en el siglo de las luces
(Mexico City: El Colegio de México, 1973), 12–66.

lás, Father Muñiz of Xocotitlán, recalled that his classmates had given their teacher, Pedro Flores, who was now a parish priest in Sultepec, the nickname "Fox," for his "dexterous use of Probabilism in arguments with them."[11] Roughly one-third of all priests in Mexico sided with the rebels. The majority of them served in the Bajio and Hotland region in poor parishes where they were in close contact with their congregations, which were composed mainly of tenant farmers, salaried peons, and indigenous villagers.[12] Rebel priests assisted the rebel cause in a variety of ways: preaching on their behalf; recruiting parishioners and leading them into battle; and collecting taxes and serving as local administrators in rebel-held areas.

Small farmers, salaried peons, and sharecroppers in the Bajio and Hotland region accounted for 40 percent of the rebel force.[13] Both areas had a large number of farmers. In the years prior to the rebellion, they had been successful in preventing large estate owners from encroaching on their land and competing against them by selling their crop in local markets.[14] The vast majority of rural peoples were salaried peons or tenant farmers in corn, wheat, and pulque estates in the Bajio, and in cotton and sugar plantations in the Hotland. The majority of estate owners lived in Mexico City, and a large number of the administrators who ran them joined the movement and led their peons and farmers into battle.[15]

Indigenous peoples also played a central role in the rebellion and accounted for almost 25 percent of the rebel force.[16] While it is true that by the turn of the century the majority of indigenous villages in the Bajio area had lost their communal lands, they remained relatively strong across other regions where the rebellion flourished, such as southern Michoacán (Patzcuaro, Zacapu, Yurira, Acambaro); in the area of Río Verde between San Luis Potosí and Guanajuato; in northern Veracruz around Papantla; and, of course, across the states of Oaxaca and Puebla, where village life was strong and accounted for 70 to 80 percent of the population. Whether a village joined the rebellion or not depended mainly on the social and moral relationship between the chief and members of the community over taxes, communal labor, distribution of land, and so on, rather than on

11. "Relación de la causa contra d. Miguel Hidalgo y Costilla," in *Colección* 2.78–92.
12. Van Young, *The Other Rebellion,* 204–12; Hugh Hamill, *The Hidalgo Revolt* (Gainesville: University of Florida Press, 1966), 170.
13. Van Young, *The Other Rebellion,* 63–64.
14. David Brading, *Haciendas and Ranchos in the Mexican Bajio: 1700–1860* (Cambridge: Cambridge University Press, 1978); and Claude Morín, *Michoacán en la Nueva España del siglo XVIII,* trans. Roberto Gómez (Mexico City: Fondo de Cultura Económica, 1979).
15. Brian R. Hamnett, *Roots of Insurgency: Mexican Regions, 1750–1824* (Cambridge: Cambridge University Press, 1986), 125–201.
16. Van Young, *The Other Rebellion,* 63–64.

status struggles between chiefs of noble lineage and commoners, which in so many places had already served to undermine village life from within. In southern Michoacán, most of the villages were led by commoners and joined in the rebellion; in contrast, the majority of villages in eastern Oaxaca, which also rebelled, were led by noblemen.[17] In San Luis Potosí, a dozen or so village chiefs joined ranks and organized a regional rebellion, whereas in northern Veracruz the villages became internally divided, with those who lived in the outlying hamlets (barrios) taking up arms against the head town (cabeceras), which remained loyal to the colonial regime.[18] No single factor can explain how all the villages responded; nevertheless, in most cases the relationship between chief and resident seems to have played a pivotal role.

Miners living in and around the city of Guanajuato and textile workers from San Miguel Allende, Celaya, and Querétaro accounted for roughly 30 percent of the rebel force in the region.[19] The largest mining camps (Valenciana, Catorce, Sirena, and Mellado) in Guanajuato employed 3,000 men. They were located close to each other and to smaller camps.[20] When the rebels marched through the area, Casimiro Chovello, Valenciana's much respected manager, joined them and brought along 3,000 miners. Textile workers from large factories and small workshops around San Miguel and other towns across the state of Querétaro also participated in large numbers. Roughly a fourth of all the men (40,000 or so) who worked in nearby factories and workshops joined the cause.[21]

The Bajio and Hotland movement was composed of a military and a civilian wing. The number of rebel insurgents grew from 40,000 in late 1810 to 80,000 in mid-1811, then dropped to 20,000 in mid-1812 and remained more or less at that level until mid-1815, when the movement unraveled. Although the size of the rebel force declined over time, its political and administrative influence spread from the Bajio and Hotland region to Oaxaca, Puebla, Morelos, Veracruz, and other areas indicated

17. François Chevalier, *Land and Society in Colonial Mexico; The Great Hacienda* (Berkeley: University of California Press, 1966), 17–19 and 164–65; William B. Taylor, *Landlord and Peasant in Colonial Mexico* (Stanford, Calif.: Stanford University Press, 1972), 20, 26–27, 89–97.

18. Van Young, *The Other Rebellion*, 111–25; and Michael Ducey, "Insurgent Politics in Papantla, Veracruz," *Hispanic American Historical Review* 79 (August 1999): 463–94.

19. Van Young, *The Other Rebellion*, 64–65.

20. David Brading, *Miners and Merchants in Bourbon Mexico: 1763–1810* (Cambridge: Cambridge University Press, 1971), 110–11, 147, 261–91; and Torcuato di Tella, "The Dangerous Classes in Early Nineteenth Century Mexico," *Journal of Latin American Studies* 5 (1973): 79–105.

21. H. G. Ward, *Mexico in 1827*, vol. 1 (London, 1828), 128. Also see Brading, *Miners and Merchants*, 232–35; and John C. Super, *La vida en Querétaro durante la colonia: 1521–1810* (Mexico City: Fondo de Cultura Económica, 1983), 79–140.

in map 4.1 above. The organizational shape of the movement also changed over time. At first, the movement did not have an organizational structure; residents from Dolores, Celaya, Silao, Leon, and other towns across the Bajio would join and quit the rebel force at will. But in response to the counterinsurgency strategy the Spanish army employed against them in 1812, insurgents fragmented into scores of guerrilla units. Most units were led by and composed of local residents. Each was autonomous from the rest and stayed within a thirty-mile radius of its own community.[22] Some of the most important units that emerged during this period, such as the one led by the members of the Villagrán clan from Querétaro, the Albino García group from Penjamo and Piedragorda (Guanajuato), and the Osorno clan in Apam (Puebla), were bandit groups like those studied by Anton Blok and Eric Hobsbawm.[23] These groups took advantage of the disorder in the region to loot estates, ransack farms, and settle old personal feuds against one or another resident. Bandit groups refused to subordinate themselves to the civil wing of the movement, which sought to give the rebellion political direction and instill military discipline.

The Bajio and Hotland movements organized a civil government to attend to administrative matters in rebel-held areas. They named each after the town in which it was established: Zitacuaro (1811–1813) and Chilpancingo (1813–1816). In a private letter to a parish priest who was sympathetic to the rebels, José Verduzco, a founding member of Zitacuaro, explained why they had organized a government:

> It is impossible, although I have tried incessantly, to change in a single blow the conduct of so many libertine men. . . . Even if the enemy is defeated, we will not succeed in controlling the unruly behavior of all those [who are on our side] and [who have] taken advantage of the revolution to impose their arbitrary will.[24]

Zitacuaro tried to establish political order by sending delegates to each guerrilla group. They were made responsible for appointing and promoting officials, disciplining and preventing them from looting and sacking

22. Lucas Alamán, *Historia de México desde los primeros movimiento que prepararon su independencia en el año 1808 hasta la época presente* (1849–1852; Mexico City: Editorial Jus, 1968–1969), 2.184, 190–91 and 4.255, lists the following guerrilla bands: Bernardo Huacal in Matehuala with 1,000 men; Muñiz in Patzcuaro with 5,000 men; Casimiro Gómez with 1,000 men; Guadalupe Victoria with 2,000 men; Hermenegildo Galeano with 1,000 men; Vicente Guerrero in Chilapa and Tixtla with 500 men; Nicolás Bravo in Oaxaca with 500 men; Rosains with 500 men; Vargas in Michoacán with 500 men; Carbajal in Valladolid with 500 men. See Van Young, *The Other Rebellion*, 60–61 for a discussion of the sociospatial relationship between rebels and their homes.
23. Hamnett, *Roots of Insurgency*, 125–201. Also see Anton Blok, *The Mafia of a Sicilian Village* (Oxford: Oxford University Press, 1964); and E. J. Hobsbawm, *Bandits* (London: Weidenfeld and Nicholson, 1969).
24. Quoted in Van Young, *The Other Rebellion*, 284–85.

private homes and estates, and pressuring commanders to turn over a portion of the funds in their treasuries to Zitacuaro.[25]

Zitacuaro also established a civil administration in rebel-held areas. The majority of administrators—including Luciano Navarrete, who served in Tuzantla, José Flores in Purungueo, and José Agrandar in Silao—had acquired their bureaucratic skills before the war in their capacity as parish priests, estate managers, and country lawyers.[26] Rebel administrators were responsible for collecting taxes from local residents, issuing passports, minting coins, organizing regional fairs and markets, confiscating and organizing production in agricultural estates owned by disloyal landlords, replacing royalist priests with rebel ones, and so on. Zitacuaro's administrative power in rebel-held areas was considerable: its tax collectors controlled 37 of 50 districts in the state of Michoacán.[27] Even more significant were the symbolic aspects of Zitacuaro's taxation policy. The rebels abolished the head tax, which to that point had been paid only by indigenous peoples, and replaced it with a flat 4 percent sales tax that everyone had to pay.[28] Taxation was perhaps the most important way for Zitacuaro to express its commitment to social equality. Through their actions, the rebels were affirming that all Mexicans were now rational adults. Zitacuaro dissolved in 1813 after the Spanish Army razed the town in which it had been established, forcing the rebel leaders to flee to different parts of the country.

The Chilpancingo government also tried to discipline the scores of guerrilla groups that remained scattered across the country. Like the previous government, Chilpancingo monitored each guerrilla unit, collected taxes, minted coins, regulated public markets, and organized production in private estates and mining camps. This government also tried to instill Mexicans with a different conception of themselves. The government sent the following proclamation to all its guerrilla commanders in the field and instructed them to read and discuss it with their men:

> We consider enemies of the nation . . . the wealthy, the nobility, high-ranking officials, creoles and Spaniards who have used the legal system to defend their own vices and passions. . . .[29]

25. Moisés Guzmán Pérez, *La Junta de Zitacuaro: 1811–1813* (Morelia: Universidad Michoacana de San Nicolás, 1994), 64–67, 70–73, 105–18.

26. Guzmán Pérez, *Junta de Zitacuaro*, 70–75, 126–29.

27. Alamán, *Historia de México*, 2.62, 151 and 4.197 estimated that the movement was spending 30,000 pesos daily in food, horses, weapons, salary, medical supplies, and clothing for rebel insurgents.

28. Alamán, *Historia de México*, 3.360; and Guzmán Pérez, *Junta de Zitacuaro*, 137–48.

29. "Medidas políticas que debe tomar los jefes de los ejércitos americanos," in *Colección* 5.271–72.

A person was considered rational to the extent that they supported nation-hood. In the Pacific Hotland, the insurgent government arrested and shot several guerrilla commanders for leading a "race war" against fair-skinned creoles in the movement. The insurgent government explained to their followers the harshness of their reaction:

> All of us are Americans; there are [no racial] distinctions amongst us. There is no reason for the so-called Castes to attack each other, nor for Whites to fight Blacks, nor Blacks to attack Natives. . . . Whites, recall, were . . . among the first to take up arms in defense of indigenous villages and other castes. . . . In the eyes of the Church and state, character and virtue are the only distinctions that exist among men.[30]

The Chilpancingo government deepened and broadened many of the policies begun by its predecessors while implementing new ones.

Chilpancingo introduced three major innovations in public life: popular elections, constitutional government, and public deliberation. By 1813, the rebels had their own state, Tecpan (modern-day Guerrero) and held congressional elections in all rebel-held areas, including Oaxaca, Mexico, Veracruz, Michoacán, and Puebla. In Tecpan, local officials refused to grant suffrage rights to indigenous peoples, but they were overruled by José María Morelos and other rebel leaders.[31] Composed of twenty delegates from rebel-held areas, the Congress of Chilpancingo was responsible for representing the "nation." It drafted a constitution and created legislative, judiciary, and executive wings. In her study of the Congress, Ana Macías concluded that for the rebels, "the creation of a legislature became as important as independence."[32] The Congress approved countless laws, which were sometimes challenged by residents in rebel courts, which were also extremely busy issuing rulings and decrees of their own.[33] The members of Congress elected Morelos as the country's first president. Each branch of the government served to check and balance the others, providing Mexicans their first taste of constitutional rule.

Chilpancingo also succeeded in recruiting the most influential public writers in the country. The rebels provided them with several printing presses, which they used to publish several tabloids aimed at convincing among its followers:

---

30. Ernesto Lemoine, *Morelos: Su vida revolucionaria a través de sus escritos y de otros testimonios de la época* (Mexico City: Universidad Nacional Autónoma de México, 1965), 13–31.

31. "Decreto del Sr. Morelos (5 October 1813)," in *Colección* 5.198: "they have the right to vote and run for office, even though they might not seem competent."

32. Ana Macías, *Génesis del gobierno constitucional de México: 1808–1820* (Mexico City: Secretaria de Educación Pública, 1973), 97.

33. Lemoine, *Morelos,* 258–90; and Anna Macías, *Génesis del gobierno,* 70–114.

The cruel and barbarous voices which you heard recently from our own enraged nation which at the beginning of the rebellion cried "death to the gachupín [Spaniard]," caused many of you to abandon us. . . . But today the nation has a government that is committed to urbanity and to respecting the rights of the public.[34]

But by late 1815, the executive and legislative branch were clashing constantly, causing the government to unravel from within. Soon after, several guerrilla groups from the state of Veracruz withdrew support, signaling the end of Chilpancingo. Juan Nepomuceno Rosains, an ardent supporter of the insurgent government, described the situation thus:

> our power has disappeared, public opinion has vanished and the legislative and executive branch are in conflict. Regional chieftains without any knowledge of the movement are now in control [of each guerrilla group]. . . . Each one has marked off and declared himself sovereign in his own area; they collect taxes, provide employment, expropriate property, and take lives arbitrarily. Our passions are boiling. Liberty has degenerated and become indistinguishable from libertinage. Our country is enveloped in chaos and confusion.[35]

After five years of civil war and enormous human and material losses, Mexico was still a colony. One out of every ten Mexicans (600,000) had perished as a result of the war, leaving behind countless widows, orphans, and aged parents without any means to provide for themselves. The war had also proven costly in economic terms, with damage and destruction to agricultural, textile, and mining production estimated at 887 million pesos. The thousands of rebels who had been granted amnesty returned home but found themselves without any work. The debacle was so great that many Mexicans began to wonder whether they were the rational adults they had thought themselves to be or still the unruly children Spanish officials considered them.

This public discussion attracted elite and non-elite groups and began soon after the rebellion had started. In 1810, nineteen indigenous chiefs from the state of Tlaxcala assembled all the residents in the main plazas of their respective villages and read to them a handbill the chiefs had drafted. It described the rebels as "motivated by the most vile passions."[36] In San Juan, the largest indigenous neighborhood in Mexico City (with some 20,000 residents), the chiefs described the rebels as suffering from "hallucinations" and read a similar proclamation:

34. José Mari Cos, "Proclama a los Españoles habitantes (21 October 1814)," in *Colección* 5.228.
35. Quoted in Alamán, *Historia de México*, 4.35–36.
36. "Proclama de los caciques y ayuntamiento de Tlaxcala contra la insurreción promovida por el Sr. Hidalgo (20 October 1810)," in *Colección* 2.172–73.

[We recognize] that due to his capture, [our king] deposited his sovereignty in us and that it is legitimately installed in us and that we recognize and swear loyalty to it, and that our Holy Religion does not allow
us to breach this oath, and summons us to honor this social pact . . .
[by] which we are governed in the name of our Holy mother the Virgin
of Guadalupe and Don Fernando VII.[37]

These chiefs seemed to be suggesting that indigenous peoples had become
rational adults and were eligible to enter into a "social pact" with the
monarch. Perhaps the loyalty oaths that they had taken in public may
have persuaded them that they were now capable of self-rule.[38]

In October 1810, government officials arrested Albino Vicente, the Indian governor of San Marco in the district of Tula, Mexico. A local resident reported that while the two traveled together along a country road
at night, Vicente had told him that

he did not owe any obedience to the magistrate or tax collector . . . that
only he ruled [the area], and that the [rebels] would make him governor
of all the Indians once they had eliminated all the shit-thieving, Spanish
pricks from the region.[39]

Indigenous peoples in the countryside were convinced that they were now
rational adults capable of self-rule, as this indigenous governor suggests.
The colonial state had protected village autonomy, but the villagers felt
that from now they would assume responsibility for it themselves by ensuring that residents practiced self-rule. Autonomy would now come from
the bottom rather than from the top.

Regalists who were against the uprising also used Catholic terms and
phrases, but they did so to claim that the uprisings were motivated by irrational passions. In the countryside, priests were ordered to read Agustín
Pomposo Fernández's *Memoria Cristiana Político* during Sunday sermon
to their faithful, many of whom were themselves insurgents or rebel sympathizers. The *Memoria* stated:

All who claim to be preserving our religion and protecting Ferdinand
VII [from the godless Jacobins] . . . have in fact given free rein to their
own passions. They have unleashed their furies [on society] and broken
whatever ties of reciprocal obligations had existed amongst us and between us and God.[40]

37. "Exposición de la parcialidad de San Juan (27 September 1810)," in *Colección*
2.115.
38. For a partial list of where these public ceremonies were held, see *Diario de México*,
11 August 1808, 1, and 6 October 1808, 1.
39. Quoted in Van Young, *The Other Rebellion*, 438.
40. Agustín Pomposo Fernández, "Memoria Cristiana Político," in *Colección* 3.749–51.

In January 1811, the regional office of the Inquisition interrogated Manuel Marcelino, Domingo de Berrio, Marco Antonio, and other residents of Querétaro to find out who among them had sympathized with the rebellion. All three were asked "whether [Hidalgo and his supporters] were insane, sick or suffering from inflamed passions, and which had prevented them from knowing what they were actually saying and doing."[41] The faculty at the University of Mexico commissioned one of their own, Luis Montana, to write a pamphlet expressing their views on the rebellion. It began like this:

> let us not deceive ourselves; passions more than calculation have guided our actions. In the last analysis, this is the true source of the revolution. . . . In convulsions of this type, there are basically two types of persons: those with vile passions [a reference to Hidalgo and all the other leaders] and the ignorant ones. The first type uses conversation and sophistry to attract each other; they use money and the promise of liberty to lure the second type. . . .[42]

In this account, rebel leaders were driven by a calculus of passion and reason, in contrast to their followers, who were impelled only by passion. The author went on to recognize that in Mexico there were a great many

> bad Spaniards who were devoid of reason and had mistreated the creoles. . . . [However,] because many of them were rational, they must not be allowed to become confused by the four crazies [leading the rebellion].[43]

Regalists used Catholic terminology to discredit the rebellion, whereas the insurgents used it to defend their cause.

Pedro Celestino, a royalist commander, was in charge of granting amnesty and interrogating rebel insurgents. A student of human nature, Celestino was famous for his capacity to uncover hidden motives and half-truths among those seeking pardon. One of them, José Salgado, a plebeian, explained why he had joined the rebellion:

> Because I am rational, I can be convinced by reason. . . . I now look forward to the future and regret the ills that have led me to follow the general will [instead of my own]. . . . A legitimate monarch is now back in his throne, but before that his absence and painful captivity gave rise to a situation in which each of us was free to obey the Viceroy

41. "Orden de los Inquisidores al comisario de Querétaro para que examine varios testigos," in *Colección* 1.151–63.
42. Luis Montana, *Reflexiones sobre los alborotos acaecidos en algunos pueblos de Tierradentro* (Mexico City, 1810), 5.
43. Montana, *Reflexiones,* 14–15.

or not, as his Majesty himself had declared . . . upon his departure from
France.[44]

Salgado's statement combines terminology from colonial Catholicism ("I
am rational") and French Republicanism ("general will") to explain the
rationality of his reasons for rebelling. The monarch's capture, judging
from Salgado's statement, generated considerable confusion among the
non-elite who now fancied themselves as rational adults.

In December 1816, José Álvarez de Toledo, who had fought in the Hotland movement, was granted amnesty. The royalists commissioned him to
write a pamphlet explaining his actions. It read, in part:

> Five years have gone by, and during this time I have discovered that the
> [rebels] were motivated only by inflamed passions and egoism. . . . You
> have transformed what was a war of liberty into a battle for self-gain;
> your chieftains are oppressive and are only interested in gold. They are
> motivated by ambition, greed, vengeance, and false pride rather than pa-
> triotism, religion, public morality, and respect for . . . human life.[45]

The colonial government suppressed this pamphlet because it was extremely critical of Spanish officials.

Rebel leaders were also convinced that their followers had lost the capacity to tame their passions. Morelos, the commander of the movement,
was invited by the members of the Chilpancingo Congress to address the
assembly. These are his words:

> Our worst enemy is the one that is in our midst. . . . The passions that
> have devoured our entrails and are killing us from within are fast lead-
> ing us to perdition. . . . Entire communities have succumbed to them. . . .
> I fear and tremble each time I confront the horror of war, but I am even
> more frightened by the anarchy that now surrounds us. . . .[46]

The bishop of Puebla, who had sympathized with the movement, explained in a letter to Morelos why he had abandoned the rebel cause:

> while it is easy to give movement to the machine of revolution, once it is
> in motion it will rapidly intensify and release passions which it can no
> longer control. In these cases, the wheels of the revolution will end up
> crushing the motor which is supposed to be driving it.[47]

44. Quoted in Van Young, *The Other Rebellion,* 176.
45. José Álvarez de Toledo, *Manifiesto o justificación dirigida a los mexicanos sobre las razones que lo impulsaron a abandonar la causa revolucionaria* (Philadelphia, 1816); see Lemoine, *Morelos,* 406–14 for a copy of this text.
46. "Razonamiento del Sr. Morelos en la apertura del congreso (18 September 1813)," in *Colección* 5.343.
47. "M. I. Campillo to Rayon and Morelos (15 September 1811)," in *Colección* 3.344.

Morelos and other rebel leaders had acted, following the doctrine of probabilism, with clear conscience and good intentions; many of the rebels, however, felt their leaders had taken them down the path of passion and irrationality.

From Rebellion to Resistance

Between 1816 and 1821, the vast majority of Mexicans practiced what James Scott calls "everyday forms of resistance."[48] Resistance against colonial rule became widespread in the countryside, urban areas, and battlefields, among estate workers and tenants, small farmers and indigenous villagers, white-collar professionals and low-level government officials. This resistance paved the way for the pact that was negotiated between Vicente Guerrero's rebel insurgents and Agustín Iturbide's royalist army in a remote area in the Hotland proclaiming Mexico to be a sovereign, independent nation. In practicing resistance, the elite and non-elite were expressing their belief that they were now rational adults capable of practicing self-rule, exercising sovereignty, and being a part of the great "family of nations."

From his large estate in San Luis Potosí, Antonio Pérez de Gálvez, one of the country's wealthiest landowners, complained to the intendant about the decline in social discipline among his peons:

> among employees and tenants, there is now a certain tone—call it insubordination—that had been unknown previously. This may be the result of poverty, hunger and deprivation . . . or it [may be due to the influence of] corruptors [in this area]; one often hears about them when they are denounced by good men. . . . If all the estate owners . . . would return to their own properties to encourage the employees, and remind [them of the virtues and benefits of loyalty] and the wickedness of the insurrection . . . there is no doubt that, given the affectionate respect that [tenants and laborers] have for their masters . . . there would be much progress in . . . attracting them back to the path of reason.[49]

According to Pérez Gálvez, other estate owners in San Luis Potosí and Durango were complaining of the same problem. Landowners in Oaxaca, Michoacán, Morelos, and Puebla also became troubled by the decline in social discipline among indigenous peoples and mixed bloods in the area.[50]

A large percentage of the 50,000 rebels pardoned by the government between 1816 and 1819 became bandits. They robbed silver convoys on

---

48. James C. Scott, *Domination and the Art of Resistance: Hidden Transcripts* (New Haven, Conn.: Yale University Press, 1990).
49. Quoted in Van Young, *The Other Rebellion*, 80.
50. Quoted in Van Young, *The Other Rebellion*, 98–105.

their way from the mines to the mint and passengers traveling by stage-coach, although they made most of their money from "protecting" estates and from a "toll tax" they collected on livestock, grain, and imported goods in transit from one part of the country to another.

> There is not a single man, who, fearing to see his fortune unravel, does not seek a link with the Insurgents and who does not aid the other side by giving them money, for without them no one can ship even a bag of flour or a barrel of wine.[51]

The Mexican elite became accustomed to transacting business with the rebels and bandits, who were (as I noted above) one and the same. The money the bandits made deprived the colonial state of revenue and contributed to the development of an underground economy. Even regional commanders, including Colonel Antonio de Linares, who was in charge of restoring law and order in Guanajuato, ended up transacting business with bandits in order to feed and clothe his troops.[52] Other regional commanders were forced to do likewise.

Everyday forms of resistance in Mexico and other cities were also widespread, and in each place resistance took on its own unique form. Viceroy Calleja, the most celebrated royalist commander, had defeated Hidalgo's force at Aculco, Allende's troops at Guanajuato, and their combined armies at Calderón; he had also burned to the ground the rebel-controlled town of Zitacuaro, for which he earned the nickname "butcher of Zitacuaro." He now realized that courage and ruthlessness were not enough to combat everyday forms of resistance among the urban elite and non-elite:

> Six millions, once decided for independence, do not need to convene or to agree; each one singly works for the universal project according to his own abilities and opportunities; the judge and his subalterns, covering up and dissimulating offenses; the priest persuading the justice of independence in the confessional, and often even in the pulpit; writers corrupting opinion; women seducing by their charms, even by prostituting themselves, to get government troops to join the rebels; the bureaucrat paralyzing and revising superior orders; the young man taking arms; the old man giving information and passing mails; the rich man

---

51. Quoted in Doris M. Ladd, *The Mexican Nobility* (Austin: University of Texas Press, 1976), 115.

52. Christon Archer, "Banditry and Revolution in New Spain: 1790–1821," *Biblioteca Americana* (November 1982): 59–89; Brian Hamnett, "Royalist Counter-insurgency and the Continuity of Rebellion: Guanajuato and Michoacan, 1813–1821," *Hispanic American Historical Review* 62, no. 1 (February 1982): 19–48; William Taylor, "Banditry and Insurrection: Rural Unrest in Central Jalisco: 1790–1816," in *Riot, Rebellion and Revolution: Rural Social Conflict in Mexico*, ed. Friedrich Katz (Princeton, N.J.: Princeton University Press, 1988), 521–60.

giving money; the literate giving advice and direction; corporations exacerbating the eternal divisions with the Europeans by never admitting one and by working against their popular election; making all aid to the government difficult; making it odious, under specious pretexts taking sides against it and its faithful agents . . . all, in short, toppling the edifice of the state.[53]

Resistance in daily life in rural and urban areas prepared the way for the rebel insurgents and royalist army to negotiate a pact in a remote and isolated area of the Hotland where they had been encamped for four years engaging each other in minor skirmishes but without scoring any decisive victories. The war was at a standstill.

Rebel insurgents and royalist soldiers traded, bartered, and exchanged all sorts of goods on the battlefield, and their commanders, including Guerrero and Iturbide, exchanged letters through their couriers. The distinguished historian Ernesto Lemoine described the situation:

> By 1819, once the battle line was drawn (with rebels camped on this side of Jaliaca and royalist on the far side of Teloloapan), the war became . . . routine and monotonous for those on either side. A curious situation developed between them . . . based on the personal ties they had established on the battlefield. At first, it was limited to soldiers stationed on the front, then to camp commanders on opposite sides. . . . Every so often, they would float a trial balloon to test each other's willingness to negotiate a pact . . . until they finally did.[54]

Iturbide, commander of the Regalist army, and Guerrero, chief of the insurgents, signed in March 1821 the "Plan of Iguala." It stated:

> The Mexican nation, which for three hundred years has had neither its own will nor free use of its voice, today leaves behind the oppression under which it had lived. . . . The nations which are now called great were at one time dominated by other ones until they were able to become emancipated themselves. The Europeans, who in our day have achieved the greatest civil development [*policia*], were once slaves of the Romans . . . until they matured, established their own families and became their head. . . . Our population has grown, our enlightenment has increased, our natural wealth has augmented . . . and all of these have taken place despite the harm that the crown has caused us due to its distance from our country.[55]

53. "Calleja to Minister of Grace and Justice (18 August 1814)," quoted in Alamán, *Historia de México,* 4.475.

54. Lemoine, *Morelos,* 360.

55. "Plan de Iguala," in *Agustín de Iturbide,* ed. Carlos Navarro y Rodrigo (Madrid: Editorial América, 1919), 58–64.

The army's long march from the Hotland to Mexico City was peaceful and orderly, as was the transition to sovereign nation in September 1821.

In disciplining their passions, Mexicans had proven that they were rational and had earned for themselves a place alongside the other adult nations of the modern West. But by July 1822, Iturbide proclaimed himself emperor, dissolved the Constitutional Congress, and staffed the central and state governments with soldiers loyal to him. This raised doubts in the minds of many as to whether the nation was indeed rational.[56] Prior to Iturbide's attack on Congress, Servando T. de Mier, representative from the state of Monterrey, said in a speech from the floor of the assembly:

> Turkey is independent and so are the Barbary states, but their people remain slaves. We desire independence not merely for its own sake, but for the sake of liberty. . . . We have not been staining the fields of Anahuac [Mexico] with our blood for the past ten years in order to secure an independence that is of no use to us. What we want is liberty, and if this is not attained, the war of independence has not yet ended.[57]

Sovereignty was not enough. The nation, which was now rational, was a republic and had entrusted its sovereign will to congress, not the executive or the military wing of the state. Guerrero and his insurgents concurred with this assessment.

> It is necessary, beloved compatriots, that the Congress should be protected, sustained, and aided by the entire heroic nation it represents. This is the one and only purpose for which I and my companions have once again lifted the sword.[58]

Constitutional rule was reestablished by March 1823.[59] For Mexicans, collective sovereignty (nationalism) by itself was not sufficient proof of rationality; they also required a nationwide congress as evidence that they were capable of self-rule (democracy).

During Iturbide's brief reign, public intellectuals continued to use colonial Catholic phrases. In honor of the Plan de Iguala, José Fernandez de Lizardi, the great satirist and Latin America's first novelist, wrote a series

---

56. See Timothy E. Anna, *The Mexican Empire of Iturbide* (Lincoln: University of Nebraska Press, 1999), for a detailed account of the year and a half of Iturbide's reign.

57. "Discurso de Fray Servando Teresa de Mier (15 July 1822)," in *La independencia de México: Textos de su historia,* ed. Miguel Gonzalez Avelar, vol. 3 (Mexico City: Secretaría de Educacion Pública, 1985), 35–37.

58. "El Ciudadano Guerrero a la Nación Mexicana (18 February 1828)," in *La Independencia de México,* 3.11–114.

59. Carlos M. de Bustamante, *Continuación del cuadro histórico: Historia del emperador Agustín de Iturbide y el establecimiento de la república popular federal* (Mexico City, 1846).

of pamphlets in the form of dialogues that circulated widely among plebeian readers. In one he wrote:

> Man has three ages: childhood, adulthood, and old age. As a child, he has to be cared for and educated; as an adult he has to take care of himself; and in old age he is once again like a child and must be cared for. . . . This is the natural order of things for persons; it is also the way political life unfolds. . . . After the conquest, Spain nourished us with her milk for 300 years. . . . Now we are adults and blessed with virility. This is an irrefutable fact. Spain, however, has become decrepit; now don't tell me that the old ought to subject the young to their needs.[60]

Lizardi was also in favor of congress and against Iturbide. He published several anonymous pamphlets urging Mexico City plebeians, the majority of whom were in favor of Iturbide, to support constitutional rule. Lizardi denounced Iturbide for having surrendered to his

> most degrading and vile passions and letting them undermine the foundations of our government and to push the nation into an abyss of horror. . . .[61]

Mexicans were now convinced that they were rational adults and that the nation was capable of governing itself.[62]

Peruvian Movements

In contrast to Mexicans, Peruvians wanted to remain a colonial kingdom of Spain. However, Generals Simón Bolívar and José de San Martín invaded their country and in 1824 compelled them to declare their independence. Prior to marching his troops into Lima, the capital of Peru, General San Martín published a proclamation in the city's leading daily explaining to the local elite his reasons for doing so:

> in order to preserve justice and security, I have employed the last resource that is available to reason, force. . . . Our victory will enable the people of this capital to come together and vote freely for their own rep-

60. José Fernández de Lizardi, *Chamorro y Dominguín: Dialogo joco-serio sobre la Independencia de América* (Mexico City, 1821), 3.

61. José Fernández de Lizardi, *Vivan las Cortes y Muera el Despotismo* (Mexico City, 1822), 1.

62. Guadalupe Jiménez Codinach, *México en 1821: Dominque de Pradt y el Plan de Iguala* (Mexico City: Ediciones El Cabellito, 1982), 131–43, is correct in noting de Pradt's influence on public intellectuals, but she overlooks the fact that de Pradt himself used colonial Catholicism to make sense of the independence movements across Latin America. Although he was French, de Pradt was also a Catholic priest and as such spoke the language of passion-reason.

resentatives, thereby signaling to the rest of the world that Peru is now a sovereign nation.[63]

The popular movement that broke out in Cuzco (August 1814 to April 1816) in support of home rule and the movement that took place in Huanta (December 1825 to June 1828) in favor of restoring colonial ties with Spain, I endeavor to show, were part of an ongoing discussion in Peru between those who claimed that they had become rational adults and those who denied this.[64] The latter carried the day.

Cuzco Rebellion

The Cuzco movement began in the capital of the province and spread quickly among indigenous peasants and villagers in the surrounding countryside before gaining support from rural and urban residents in the adjacent provinces of Arequipa, Puno, and Ayacucho (see map 4.2).[65] At the height of the movement in 1815, the rebels controlled most of the southern half of the country and had the support of more than 20,000 persons, including churchmen, indigenous peasants, villagers, lawyers, and artisans.

Cuzco's priests played a major role in this movement. According to estimates provided by Tadeo Haenke in the 1790s, the ratio of priests to residents in Cuzco was about 1 to 787, considerably lower than in Trujillo (1 per 500) and Arequipa (1 per 358).[66] However, Cuzco's clerics, in contrast to those elsewhere, were committed "probabilists" and favored

63. "Proclama de D. José de San Martín," *Gaceta Extraordinario de Lima*, 11 March 1819, 142.

64. Radicals, nationalists, and neo-indigenists have interpreted Peruvian independence in different ways. For radicals such as Heraclio Bonilla and Karen Spalding, *La independencia en el Perú* (Lima: Instituto de Estudios Peruanos, 1972), and Julio Cótler, *Clases, estado y nación en el Perú* (Lima: Instituto de Estudios Peruanos, 1978), the national bourgeoisie was, like the country itself, backward and incapable of emancipating the nation. According to José A. de la Puente, *Notas sobre la causa de la independencia del Perú* (Lima: Librería Studium, 1970), Luis Durand Flores, *Criollos en conflicto* (Lima: Universidad de Lima, 1985) and other nationalists, the Spanish army in Peru was stronger than in any other country, making it difficult for the urban elite to lead an anticolonial struggle. Finally, according to Alberto Flores Galindo, *Buscando un Inca* (Lima: Editorial Horizonte, 1988), Manuel Burga, *Nacimiento de una utopía: Muerte y resurreción de los Incas* (Lima: Instituto de Apoyo Agrario, 1988), and other neo-indigenists, Quechua and Aymara-speaking peoples across the Andes led and organized these movements with the goal of reestablishing an Incan empire (*Tawantisuyu*) in Peru.

65. See Magnus Morner, *Perfil de la sociedad rural de Cuzco a fines de la colonia* (Lima: Universidad del Pacífico, 1978) for a study of socioeconomic life in the area.

66. Tadeo Haenke, *Descripción del Perú* (Lima: Imprenta de "El Lucero," 1901), 287–302. Christine Hunefeldt, *Lucha por la tierra y protesta indígena: Las comunidades indígenas del Perú entre colonia y república, 1800–1830* (Bonn: Bonner Amerikanische Studien, 1982), 67 gives a slightly higher estimate.

Map 4.2 Popular Movements, 1814–1825

home rule.[67] They also had an extensive and complex set of networks in the area that enabled them to propagate their views in public life. The

67. René Millar Carvacho, "El Obispo Alday y el Probabilismo," *Historia* [Santiago] 22 (1987): 198, and his "La controversia sobre el probabilismo entre los obispos chilenos durante el reinado de Carlos III," in *Estudios sobre la época de Carlos III en el reino de Chile,* ed. Fernando Campos Harriet, Juan Benavide Courtois, and Alamiro de Ávila Martel (Santiago: Ediciones de la Universidad de Chile, 1989), 231–32.

monasteries of "La Merced" and "San Francisco" in the center of the city of Cuzco housed between 170 and 200 priests and half as many nuns. According to colonial officials, these monasteries had become hotbeds of constitutionalism.[68]

Churchmen from La Merced and San Francisco had close ties to Cuzco's professional middle classes—lawyers, merchants, medical doctors, artisans, and teachers—as well as to the plebeian sector. The ties to the first had been forged within the family:

> All the families in Cuzco have a spiritual director. . . . After morning mass, priests visited the home of all the families in their jurisdiction. . . . They normally ate breakfast and lunch with them . . . and would not return to their monastery until late at night. . . . The residents in humble neighborhoods were visited by parish priests, their vicars, and altar boys.[69]

The ties to the non-elite were rooted in parish life. Commoners and indigenous peoples attended mass on Sunday and on religious holidays and had close ties to the parish priest through their participation in confraternities. In Cuzco, priests maintained individual, private ties to elite families and public and collective ties to plebeian and indigenous peoples, enabling churchmen to serve as a bridge between the two.

Church service also contributed to blurring the color line among the elite and non-elite. The most inspired orators—José Díaz Feijoo, Juan Becerra, and Ildefonso Muñecas—were bilingual and often delivered their sermon in Sunday mass in Quechua and Spanish. Cuzco's elite were fluent in both, having learned Quechua as children from their nannies and housemaids.[70] Public life in Cuzco remained socio-ethnically divided, but parish life provided local residents, even in such strictly segregated parishes as "Españoles" and "Catedral," a place to mingle.

Schooling reinforced social ties between churchmen and the city's middle class. Most of them had graduated from the University of San Antonio and sent their sons to study law, theology, and medicine with their own teachers at their alma mater. During his thirty-year tenure as dean of the University, José Pérez Armendáriz had overhauled its entire curriculum, introducing notions of natural rights and probabilism. Law students

68. José M. Goyeneche, *Memorias apócrifas del General*, ed. Emilio Romero (Lima: Editorial Minerva, 1971), 55.

69. Goyeneche, *Memorias apócrifas*, 27.

70. Concolorcorvo (Carlos Calixto), *El lazarillo de ciegas caminantes desde Buenos Aires hasta Lima* (1776; Buenos Aires, 1942), 96; Ignacio de Castro, *Relación de Cuzco* (Lima: n.p., 1978), 44; and Manuel Aparicio Vega, *El clero patriota en la revolución de 1814* (Cuzco: ?????, 1974), 110, 121–23, 162.

began each day reciting maxims such as: "Justice comes before Kinship," "Unjust laws must be disobeyed," and "If the King undermines our liberty, then he is not our ruler."[71] Although in the 1780s the bishop of Lima had banned probabilism from all the schools in the kingdom, it continued to be taught in San Antonio.[72] Nearly all the lawyers who went on to participate in the Cuzco movement were graduates of San Antonio and confirmed probabilists.

Church-centered networks were also extensive and reached deep into the countryside. Parish priests who had graduated from San Antonio now served in indigenous villages. These priests corresponded and visited each other and their other classmates, including lawyers and other priests, who lived in the city of Cuzco. The parish priest of Ocongate, Yaurisque, Capri, Lares, Quispicanchis, and several other villages, along with the schoolteachers they had trained, joined and recruited residents to the rebel movement. Whether they followed or not depended on the social and moral relations with the priest and teacher in their community.[73]

Indigenous leaders also played an important role in the Cuzco rebellion. There were roughly 210 noble chiefs in the province. Most of them had studied in San Francisco de Borja and had forged close ties with churchmen.[74] Most of these chiefs now lived in villages deep in the countryside and, in contrast to those who resided in the city, had little contact with each other. In the city of Cuzco, the chiefs had their own association, the "Electors." Composed of twenty-four members, this group represented the original twelve royal Incan families and members of their extended clans. In addition to discussing common concerns, the Electors organized ritual dances in the central plaza in honor of their Incan lords and marched alongside the urban elite in their regal outfits carrying banners with Incan symbols emblazoned on them. In recognition of their noble status, Incan aristocrats did not have to pay a head tax to the colonial state.[75] The Incan aristocracy's influence on public life was stronger in the city of Cuzco than in the countryside, where many of them had been

71. Aparicio Vega, *El clero patriota,* 62–63, 83.

72. Luis Macera, "El probabilismo en el Perú durante el siglo XVIII," in his *Trabajos de Historia,* vol. 2 (Lima: Instituto Nacional de Cultura, 1977), 79–137.

73. David Cahill and Scarlett O'Phelan Godoy, "Forging Their Own History: Indian Insurgency in the Southern Peruvian Sierra, 1815," *Bulletin of Latin American Research* 2, no. 1 (1992): 21. Also see Aparicio Vega, *El clero patriota,* 60–63, 254, 280–81; and Urbina, "Ilustre Ayuntamiento (3 October 1814)," in *Conspiraciones y rebeliones en el siglo XIX,* ed. Horacio Villanueva Urteaga (Lima: Comisión Nacional del Sesquicentenario de la Independencia del Perú, 1971), 77–78.

74. Castro, *Relación de Cuzco,* 56.

75. Nuria Sala i Vila, "De Inca a indígena: Cambio en la simbología del sol a principios del siglo XIX," *Allpanchis* [Cuzco] 35–36 (1990): 599–633.

or were about to be displaced from the post of village chief by commoners (*varayocs*).[76] Despite their rivalry, the native gentry and commoners joined the rebellion. Whether or not they succeeded in winning over the rest of the villagers depended less on their social status than on their reputation in the community for justice, as demonstrated by how they practiced forced consumption, collected taxes, and distributed communal lands and chores among residents. The villages of Oropesa and Chinchero were ruled by Incan aristocrats; in contrast, Ocongate, Marcapata, Conquepata, Ceatca, and Quiquijana were ruled by commoners. Both sets of communities joined the rebellion.

Nearly all thirty-five members of the newly organized "Constitutional Lawyers" were graduates of San Antonio. The Lawyers were responsible for leading the campaign to hold free municipal elections in Cuzco, as stipulated by the Cadiz Constitution. The Lawyers presented their case in support of "sovereignty of the people" before the supreme court, which remained committed to absolutism, and although the magistrates agreed to hold elections, they arrested the leaders of the group in December 1813, effectively ending their campaign.[77] The other members of the Lawyers campaigned on their behalf and spent the next few weeks visiting all eight parishes. In the largest indigenous and plebeian parish, San Jerónimo and San Sebastián, they distributed two thousand copies of the Constitution, although the vast majority of residents were illiterate and could not vote.[78] In the words of one of the Lawyers, "we did not have enough copies of the constitution, so the ignorant pleb divided it and took small pieces (of the document) with them."[79] For indigenous peoples, the Constitution had spiritual-magical powers; each piece was a talisman to be used to protect them against evil spirits. Social relations made it possible for Cuzco's lawyers, priest, merchants, artisans, indigenous peoples, and plebeian

76. Charles Walker, "Peasants, Caudillos and the State in Peru: Cuzco in the Transition from Colony to Republic: 1780–1840" (Ph.D. dissertation, University of Chicago, 1992), 74–85 on the rivalry between Incan aristocrats and commoners. Also see David Cahill, "Una visión andina: El levantamiento de Ocongate de 1815," *Histórica* [Lima] 7, no. 2 (December 1988): 133–60.

77. Rafael Ramírez, "Los verdaderos hijos de la nación, son los amigos de la constitución (17 January 1813)," and "Pedro López de Segovia y Martín Valer, "Informe que hacen los electores (7 February 1813)," in *Conspiraciones y rebeliones en el siglo XIX: La Revolución del Cuzco*, ed. Manuel Aparicio Vega (Lima: Comisión Nacional del Sesquicentenario de la Independencia del Perú, 1974), 24–28, 40–45.

78. Martín Valer, Mariano Lechuga, and Juan José de Olañeta, "Los Señores Electores de las parroquias del Distrito de esta Ciudad (14 February 1813)," in *Conspiraciones y rebeliones* (1971), ed. H. Villanueva Urteaga, 23–27.

79. Sala Consistorial, "Notas al Virrey (13 May 1813)," in *Conspiraciones y rebeliones,* ed. H. Villanueva Urteaga, 183.

groups to overcome their cultural differences and become part of the same movement.

On election day, the constitutionalists marched in the main plaza, one thousand strong in support of free elections. Afterward, they stormed the jail, freed the lawyers, and arrested the magistrates, who accused them of "lacking discipline and rationality."[80] Then they proceeded to remove all the colonial emblems and insignia from public buildings and took an oath in public to defend the constitution; according to the oath, "sovereignty resides in the nation itself."[81] Months later, the newly elected township officials met with churchmen and representatives of the elite and voted to establish a rebel government in Cuzco. After dissolving the supreme court and the municipal township, the new government—which included José Angulo, a merchant; Pumacahua, an indigenous noble; and José Armendáriz, the bishop of Cuzco—sent the viceroy in Lima a letter explaining that the people of the area had "responded to the call of nature, reason and law" and that the rest of Peru should now follow them.[82]

After dissolving the supreme court, the municipal township, and the local militia, the rebel government divided itself into a civil and a military wing, thereby overriding the secular-religious dichotomy that had prevailed in public life throughout the late colonial period.[83] The members of the civilian wing established themselves in the monastery of La Merced and San Francisco and from there tried to provide justice and administer rebel-held areas. They appointed judges and made them responsible for evaluating and resolving land disputes among residents and for punishing rebel soldiers accused of raping women or stealing horses and crops. They also protected colonial officials from the threat of mob violence by moving them from Cuzco to a stockade in the town of Paucartambo. In addition to collecting taxes from residents and rent from merchants with stores or stalls in Cuzco's main plaza, rebel administrators organized work parties to clear and repair roads and bridges, to provide children with schooling, to keep local markets supplied with meat, vegetables, and potatoes, and to control the price of these staples according to the norms of the "moral economy." They published pamphlets in Spanish and Quechua

80. Pedro López de Segovia y Martín Valer, "Informe que hacen los electores (7 February 1813)," in *Conspiraciones y rebeliones,* ed. M. Aparicio Vega, 41.

81. Mateo García Pumacahua, Martín Valer, and Antonio Ochoa, "Ilustre Ayuntamiento (1 March 1813)," in *Conspiraciones y rebeliones,* ed. H. Urteaga Villanueva, 32–34.

82. Dr. Corbacho Lechuga, Martín Valer, Narciso López de Neyra et al., "Ilustre Ayuntamiento (3 August 1814)" and "Mensaje de la ciudad del Cuzco al Virrey (17 September 1813)," in *Conspiraciones y rebeliones,* ed. H. Urteaga Villanueva, 56–59 and 216–20.

83. José Angulo, Juan Moscoso, Jacinto Ferrándiz et al., "Ilustre Ayuntamiento (5 October 1814)," in *Conspiraciones y rebeliones,* ed. H. Urteaga Villanueva, pp. 78–80.

and circulated them among creoles and indigenous villagers within and outside the area urging them to support the Cuzco rebellion.[84]

The movement's military wing, which called itself the "army of public opinion," had at its peak in late September 1814 roughly 50,000 men.[85] The largest force remained in Cuzco defending the rebel capital. Three other units marched into and gained control of large parts of Arequipa, Puno, and Ayacucho, and along the way they picked up local supporters in rural and urban areas. By the end of the month, the rebel movement controlled the southern part of the country, and was preparing to attack Lima. In Arequipa, the only "white city" in the south, fair-skinned peoples remained frightened of the "Indian hordes" who now roamed the streets and stood guard in all the public buildings. The rebels behaved in an orderly and disciplined manner.[86] Even the viceroy recognized that they had been "benevolent" in their treatment of captured soldiers; they acted as if they were "grateful guests" rather than a "victorious army."[87] Their conduct convinced a small number of fair-skinned creoles in Arequipa and Lima, the most racist cities in Peru, that some indigenous peoples had succeeded in restraining their passions and transforming themselves into rational adults. These creoles supported home rule.

By April 1815, the Spanish army had regained control of Puno, Arequipa, and Ayacucho and had recaptured the rebel capital of Cuzco.[88] The rebels retreated into the countryside and spent the next year waging a guerrilla war against the Spanish.[89] During this last phase, the movement lost its multi-ethnic character and came to be dominated by indigenous groups who relied mainly on Incan notions to make sense of themselves. In their first proclamation, the leaders of the movement used the colonial Catholic terminology to explain their objectives:

84. José Angulo, Juan Moscoso, and Miguel Vargas, "Habiéndose congregado las tres corporaciones (22 October 1814)" and "Ilustre Ayuntamiento (15 November 1814)," in *Conspiraciones y rebeliones,* ed. H. Urteaga Villanueva, 82–85 and 161–300.

85. José Mariano de Ugarte, Narciso López de Neyra, Francisco Villacorta et al., "Ilustre Ayuntamiento de la Capital (18 March 1815)," in *Conspiraciones y rebeliones,* ed. H. Urteaga Villanueva, 138.

86. José Angulo, "Instrucción militar y económica para el ejército auxiliar (11 October 1813)," in *Conspiraciones y rebeliones,* ed. H. Urteaga Villaneuva, 275–76.

87. Abascal, "Avisa del arresto del Conde de la Vega del Ren," in *Documentacion Oficial Española,* vol. 1, ed. Guillermo Lohman Villena (Lima: Comisión Nacional del Sesquicentenario de la Independencia del Perú, 1972), 356–65.

88. Juan Ramírez, "Diario de la expedición sobre las provincias interiores de la Paz, Puno, Arequipa y Cuzco," in *Conspiraciones y rebeliones,* ed. H. Urteaga Villanueva, 221–55.

89. David Cahill and Scarlett O'Phelan Godoy, "Forging Their Own History," and Nuria Sala i Vila, "La pariticipación indígena en la rebelión de los Angulo y Pumacahua, 1814–1816," in Pilar García Jordán and Miquel Izard, *Conquista y Resistencia en la Historia de América* (Barcelona: Universidad de Barcelona, 1992), 1–61 and 273–88.

our America has grown and moved away from its infancy, which is typical of nations not enslaved by stronger, more astute ones. The development of social relations has enabled us to know each other. Although we remain economically backward, we now have a greater political understanding of natural rights . . . and know that it is better to live with wild beasts than to [continue to live under] rational despotism.[90]

During the last phase of the movement, Incan symbols eclipsed colonial Catholicism. In March 1815, after colonial troops had retaken Cuzco, military officers interrogated the city's postmaster and three rebel commanders and asked them whether Pumacahua, an Inca chief and rebel leader, had worn his royal tunic and headdress (*Mascaypacha*) during the uprising and whether he sought to reestablish Inca rule. They responded in the affirmative to both questions.[91] A muleteer from an indigenous community (Laqueque, Sandia) in a remote region in the highlands of Puno also commented that "Pumacahua was to be crowned as king."[92]

Most fair-skinned creoles in Lima and other cities on the coast who had favored home rule came to regard Cuzco's rebels as irrational and were driven to support colonial rule.[93] In the 1820s, a lawyer defended an indigenous person accused of murder in this way:

> Indians are lacking in reason . . . and enlightenment, and this is what makes it impossible for them to correctly appraise even their own situation. . . . They are not responsible for whatever mischief and malice they cause; all our laws and municipal ordinances consider Indians even more leniently than they would a child.[94]

In a letter to a friend, Manuel Lorenzo de Vidaurre, a court judge who had served in Cuzco and knew Pumacahua, described the Inca leader as "passionate . . . devoid of any reason and driven only by his sensations."[95] Twenty years after the rebellion, the public intellectual Bartolome Herrero, who had lived as a young boy with his family in Cuzco during the great rebellion, recalled:

90. José Angulo, "Manifiesto . . . al pueblo de Cuzco (16 August 1814)," in *Conspiraciones y rebeliones* (1974), ed. M. Aparicio Vega, 211–15.

91. "Proceso de Pumacahua (March 1815)," in *Conspiraciones y rebeliones*, ed H. Villanueva Urteaga, 306–9.

92. Christine Hunefeldt, "Los indios y la constitución de 1812," *Allpanchis* [Cuzco] 11–12 (1978): 33–52.

93. Timothy Anna, *The Fall of the Royal Government in Peru* (Lincoln: University of Nebraska Press, 1979), 86–98; and César Pacheco Vélez, "Las conspiraciones del Conde de la Vega del Ren," *Revista Histórica* [Lima] 21 (1954): 355–425.

94. Quoted in Walker, "Peasants, Caudillos and the State," 98.

95. Manuel Lorenzo de Viadurre, "Carácter del General Pumacahua," in *Cartas Americanas*, ed. Alberto Tauro (Lima: Universidad Nacional de San Marcos, 1971), 191–92.

I don't know if the movement was an act of poetic inspiration or . . . an irrational act. . . . The [rebels] conceived Peruvian independence and the return of the Incan empire as one and the same. . . .[96]

By the mid-nineteenth century, most public intellectuals were in favor of Peruvian independence, but they remained convinced that indigenous peoples were still incapable of acting as rational adults and would have to be disciplined by an authoritarian state.

Huanta Rebellion

The Huanta movement began in late 1825 in a remote, poor area in the highlands of Ayacucho that was populated by indigenous villagers, farmers, estate owners, and muleteers. Unlike their counterparts in Cuzco, the Huanta rebels wanted to nullify independence and restore colonial ties between Peru and Spain. Like Cuzco's rebels, the insurgents in Huanta also used Catholic terminology and were committed to blurring ethnic and class distinctions among members. The Huanta movement, however, never gained broad support beyond a small area in the highlands.[97]

The Huanta uprising was led by muleteers rather than by priests and indigenous chiefs. Farmers and planters in Paraíso, Laupay, Choimacota, and other areas in the tropical lowlands cultivated coca bushes and relied on muleteers to sell their crop and buy potatoes, wheat, sheep, and other foodstuffs from indigenous villagers in the cold highlands in and around Sec Sec, Huaillay, Caruahuran, and Uchuraccay. Muleteers shuttled back and forth and often spent weeks at a time on the trail. In the evening they would rest in lodging houses (*tambo*) along the way in the company of other muleteers and seasonal workers on their way to or from the coca estates. Muleteers developed close ties with each other and with seasonal workers, coca growers, and indigenous villagers, all of whom depended on them for their livelihood and for news from their families while they were away. The most influential leaders of the rebellion—Antonio Navala Huachaca, Manuel Leandro, Manuel Meneses, Andrés Hacha, and Antonio Huamán—were all muleteers.[98]

Estate owners and indigenous chiefs also played a major role in the civil wing of the movement as tax collectors and local justices of the peace.

---

96. Bartolomé Herrera, *Escritos y Discursos,* vol. 1 (Lima: F. and E. Rosay, 1929), 89.

97. S. Cecilia Méndez, "Rebellion without Resistance: Huanta's Monarchist Peasants in the Making of the Peruvian State" (Ph.D. dissertation, State University of New York-Stony Brook, 1996).

98. Méndez, "Rebellion without Resistance," 57, 187, 193–97, 211–19. Also see Miriam Salas de Coloma, "Arrieraje y producción mercantil en el centro-sur-este del Perú colonial," *Historia y Cultura* [Lima] 16 (1983): 51–66, in which the author estimates the number of mules in the area at 410, and infers that there were roughly 80 drivers (estimating 5 mules per train) in the area.

Coca planters organized into a "Council of Estate Owners" in order to support the rebellion. The council negotiated with rebel leaders and agreed to pay taxes, but in return they demanded that the amount and method of collecting the taxes be changed. Taxes were to be assessed only on the amount of profit, that is, the amount earned after all the expenses had been deducted (salaries, supplies, maintenance). In order to prevent fraud, rebel collectors, many of whom were themselves coca owners, would require workers to provide them with a voucher indicating the amount of salary paid to them, the one expense that was most difficult to monitor. All three groups considered this new system to be fair, as indicated by the amount of revenue generated and the relatively high level of compliance.[99] Prior to the rebellion, the 230 or so growers who lived in this area had for year after year refused to pay any taxes to state officials.

Indigenous chiefs, most of whom were commoners rather than (as in Cuzco) Incan aristocrats, played a key role in administering justice in rebel-held areas. Huanta's village chiefs, including Manuel Yngo and Manuel Leandro, considered themselves first and foremost as colonial subjects of Spain rather than as Incans. Fair-skinned creoles and mixed bloods in the area who participated in the movement also viewed them in this way. Village chiefs were responsible for administering civil and criminal justice and maintaining public order in rebel-held territory. Unlike their counterparts in Cuzco, rebel judges in Huanta were responsible for hearing cases and rendering justice in cases involving creoles, mixed bloods, priests, and indigenous peoples. The converse was also the case; non-indigenous judges often served in villages.[100] Judicial practices served to blur the ethnic barriers that continued to divide Peruvians from each other.

The military wing of the movement was as ethnically integrated as the civil wing. Huanta's rebel leaders, including Antonio Huachaca, Tadeo Choque, Martín Ccente, and Huamán Arancibia, identified themselves as colonial subjects rather than as indigenous peoples or citizens of Peru. Their officers included men of different ethnic backgrounds. Four of the rebel camps were established in coca-growing estates owned by fair-skinned creoles; the other three were established in indigenous villages. The rank and file in all seven camps was also far more ethnically and socially integrated than in Cuzco. This movement, ironically, "managed to undermine the bases of the colonial order in ways that the republic itself had not."[101]

99. Méndez, "Rebellion without Resistance," 247–54.
100. Méndez, "Rebellion without Resistance," 258, 275–83, 324–27.
101. Méndez, "Rebellion without Resistance," 327–28.

Huanta's churchmen played a secondary role in this movement, but they had a strong if indirect influence on it. The bishop of Huanta and his priests had propagated probabilism among the faithful of the region, and they refused to ban the teaching of it even after the Bishop of Lima had instructed them to do so.[102] The Huanta rebels considered themselves rational adults, and they were even willing to defy the Church's hierarchy and defend their cause. In a letter responding to an offer made by the bishop of Lima to serve as mediator between the rebels and the Peruvian army, the insurgents wrote:

> you are responsible for undermining our Holy Religion and King Ferdinand's throne. . . . If you dare to set foot in our region, we will escort you to the shore of the Marañon [River] and send you off to conquer infidels, for it is they, not us, who truly need you. We are C.A.R. [Catholic, Apostolic, and Roman].[103]

Huanta's rebels considered themselves rational adults because they had suppressed their passions and remained loyal to colonial Spain. In his private correspondence with the insurgents, Domingo Tristán, prefect of Ayacucho, described them as "naive children" and portrayed himself as a "compassionate and benevolent father."[104]

Government officials, army commanders, parish priests, provincial elite, and insurgent rebels in Cuzco and Huanta described each other in colonial Catholic terms. This had practical consequences for rebels who had been captured, and it shows the enormous influence "speech acts" had even under conditions of war. Because indigenous peoples were said to be irrational, colonial and Peruvian state officials granted them pardons; however, because mixed bloods and fair-skinned creoles were considered rational adults they were sent to the firing squad. Whether a rebel prisoner lived or died in Peru (and in Mexico) depended on the type of narrative resources used to portray him. In contrast to Mexicans, the majority of Peruvians were not yet convinced that they had achieved adulthood and become rational, disciplined persons.

During the postcolonial period, Latin Americans continued to use Catholic terminology to transform their passions into rational faith in the same way that French Jacobins, New Englanders, and English Puritans relied on their own idiom based on notions of "particular interests vs. the general will," "private vice vs. public virtue," and "damned vs. elect" in or-

---

102. Carvacho, "La controversia sobre el probabilismo," 231–32 notes that the bishop of Huamanga, along with the bishop of Cuzco, supported probabilism. The Jesuits, who were the leading champions of probabilism, had a school in Huamanga until the late 1770s.
103. Quoted in Méndez, "Rebellion without Resistance," 359, 348–58.
104. Quoted in Méndez, "Rebellion without Resistance," 363.

der to accomplish the same. Each vocabulary formed part of a unique way of life and was in part an expression of alternative conceptions of selfhood and public life. Throughout the postcolonial period, Latin Americans were inclined to migrate toward civil society and to practice solidarity in order to tame each other's passions. The French, in contrast, gravitated toward political society and relied on the state to ensure law and order. The Anglo-Americans and British took a different route, congregating in economic society and counting on "sweet commerce" to domesticate their passions.[105]

Postcolonial Mexicans and Peruvians practiced democracy and nationalism in civil society far more readily than in any of the other terrains (economic society, political society, the public sphere). Now that they had become rational adults, Mexicans and Peruvians assumed that the most effective way of disciplining their passions was by organizing voluntary associations. The center of gravity of democratic life during the postcolonial period in Mexico and Peru shifted downward to these groups and became dispersed across civil society, economic society, political society, and the public sphere. It was from these terrains that citizens were able to generate new sources of social power and to use them to democratize public life. During the postcolonial period, the number and significance of rebel movements declined dramatically in Mexico and Peru, suggesting that citizens in both countries were able to develop a new set of practices based on nonviolence and everyday forms of resistance.[106]

Public life in Latin America bears an uncanny resemblance to Bali's Negara polity, but the two differed in four ways.[107] Public life in postcolonial Mexico and Peru, as I noted in the preface and will elaborate in the concluding chapter, was radically lopsided, with citizens inclined to practice democracy in civil society more than in any other terrain; it was radically fragmented, with citizens unable to blur racial and ethnic differences; it was radically bifurcated, with citizens depositing their sovereignty on each other rather than in government institutions; and its vocabulary was based on Civic Catholic notions of selfhood.

---

105. Albert O. Hirschman, *The Passions and the Interests: Political Arguments for Capitalism before Its Triumph* (Princeton, N.J.: Princeton University Press, 1977).

106. John H. Coatsworth, "Patterns of Rural Rebellion in Latin America," in *Riot, Rebellion and Revolution: Rural Conflict in Mexico* (Princeton, N.J.: Princeton University Press, 1988), 21–62.

107. Clifford Geertz, *Negara: The Theater State in Nineteenth Century Bali* (Princeton, N.J.: Princeton University Press, 1980).

PART THREE

THE EMERGENCE OF
CIVIC DEMOCRACY:
BREAKING OLD HABITS

CHAPTER 5

Crafting Citizens: Mexican Civil and Economic Society

During the first half of the nineteenth century, Mexicans broke with their old habits and organized hundreds of civic and economic associations. The various anticolonial movements that had spread out across the country during the wars of independence enabled Mexicans to construe themselves as rational adults. By the mid-1820s, these movements had vanished from the landscape, but their influence lingered on, encouraging Mexicans to practice democracy and nationalism in civil and economic society even though authoritarianism remained dominant throughout political society. The movements that broke out in Peru, in contrast, failed to convince the Peruvian people that they had achieved adulthood; the vast majority remained attached to their colonial habits and did not develop civic and associative forms of life (see chapter 6).

Socio-institutional Structures

Between 1826 and 1856, Mexicans from all walks of life and parts of the country came together and organized no fewer than 400 civic and economic associations (fig. 5.1).[1] Associative practices developed steadily from 1840 to 1846, and then plummeted during the U.S. invasion and occupation of Mexico (1846–1848). After the war, citizens regained their civic momentum and went on to organize hundreds of new associations, until in 1855 the "War of Reform" signaled a turning point in Mexican public life.

1. Unless indicated otherwise, the data in all the tables and maps in this chapter are from Carlos A. Forment, "Databank on Associative Life in Nineteenth Century Mexico" (Unpublished working document, Princeton University, 1997). In order to show clearly how the number of new associations created in the country changed over time, I grouped them into five-year periods, as indicated on the Y-axis in figure 5.1.

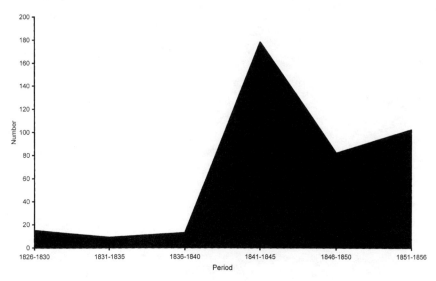

Figure 5.1   New Civic and Economic Associations, 1826–1856

Records indicate that Mexicans created approximately forty civic and economic associations between 1826 and 1840, although I suspect that many more were established than were reported in the tabloids and pamphlets I consulted. These sources were published mostly by one or another partisan group, and they concerned themselves primarily with political factionalism rather than associative life.[2] The decline of partisan politics in the early 1840s altered journalistic practices, as signaled by the appearance of *Siglo XIX,* the country's first semiprofessional daily. From 1841 to 1845, this and other newspapers regularly published stories on civic and economic groups. For this five-year period, I was able to locate no fewer than 178 civic and economic associations.

Associative life declined from 1846 to 1848 after U.S. troops invaded Mexico. Public life remained moribund during the occupation after the fighting had ended, even in Mexico City, which prior to the war had had a great many civic and economic associations. A U.S. officer complained to Guillermo Prieto, an influential public intellectual:

> we look forward to restoring social trust (*confianza*) in the city, and for the stores, warehouses and commerce to reopen. It is silly for [Mexicans] to remain indoors for fear that the soldiers will bother and harass

2. Michael Costeloe, *La Primera República Federal de México: 1824–1835* (Mexico City: Fondo de Cultura Económica, 1975), 68–70; and María del Carmen Reyna, *La prensa censurada, durante el Siglo XIX* (Mexico City: Secretaría de Educación Pública, 1976), 7–109.

Table 5.1   Duration of Civic and Economic
Associations, 1826–1856

Duration in Years	Percentage of Associations
1–3	53
4–6	27
7–9	0
0–12	0
3–15	0
16 or more	20

Table 5.2   Membership in Civic and Economic
Associations, 1826–1856

Number of Members	Percentage of Associations
1–15	32
16–30	12
31–45	19
46–60	7
61 or more	30

them. . . . By keeping their workshops and offices closed, they are hurting themselves more than anyone else.[3]

Associative life throughout the Central Valley and in Puebla, Veracruz, and other important cities also remained moribund throughout the occupation.

Immediately after the war, Mexicans regained their civic momentum and repopulated public life with all sorts of voluntary groups. Between 1848 and 1850 they organized 96 new associations, and from 1851 to 1855 they organized another 102 civic and economic groups.

The duration and size of voluntary groups varied considerably. Eighty percent of all associations lasted six years or less, with nearly all of these dissolving before the third year.[4] The remaining 27 percent lasted for twenty or more years (table 5.1). The majority of associations were short-lived, making it difficult for members to forge stable ties with each other. As table 5.2 indicates, 70 percent of all voluntary groups had sixty or fewer members, with about half of these having fifteen or less; even the largest associations had less than eighty members.[5] The socio-organizational

3. Guillermo Prieto, *Memorias de mis tiempos* (Puebla: J. M. Cájica, 1970), 425–28.
4. I found data on only 4 percent of the groups.
5. These data are based on a sample of 15 percent of the associations.

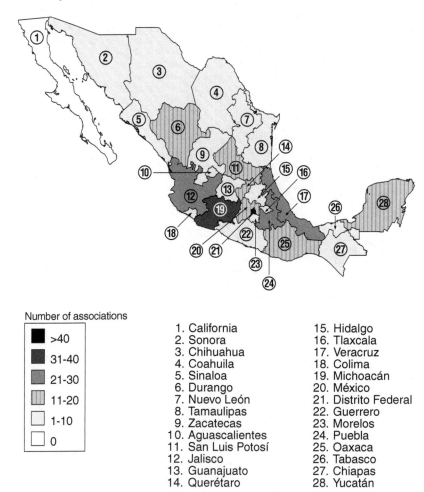

Number of associations

- ■ >40
- ▨ 31-40
- ▨ 21-30
- ▦ 11-20
- ☐ 1-10
- ☐ 0

1. California
2. Sonora
3. Chihuahua
4. Coahuila
5. Sinaloa
6. Durango
7. Nuevo León
8. Tamaulipas
9. Zacatecas
10. Aguascalientes
11. San Luis Potosí
12. Jalisco
13. Guanajuato
14. Querétaro

15. Hidalgo
16. Tlaxcala
17. Veracruz
18. Colima
19. Michoacán
20. México
21. Distrito Federal
22. Guerrero
23. Morelos
24. Puebla
25. Oaxaca
26. Tabasco
27. Chiapas
28. Yucatán

Map 5.1   Geography of Civic and Economic Life, 1826–1856

structure of associative life in civil and economic society remained relatively frail.

By mid-century, associative forms of life had become widespread and rooted in most states. Map 5.1 shows the extent and depth of civic activity in early nineteenth-century Mexico. The nation's capital ("Distrito Federal"), highlighted in the center of the map, accounted for 30 percent of all associations; Michoacán had 8 percent; Veracruz and Puebla, on the Gulf Coast, each claimed 7 percent; the state of Mexico (minus the capital) had 5 percent; and Oaxaca (in the far south), the Yucatan peninsula, and San Luis Potosi (in the north) had 4 percent each. Durango (in the far

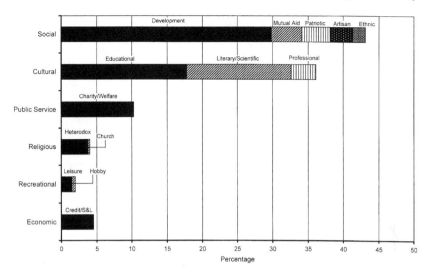

Figure 5.2   Civil and Economic Terrains, Fields, and Subfields, 1826–1856

north) had 3 percent; and all the other states claimed no more than 2 percent each, together accounting for 32 percent of the total. Associative life had become rooted throughout the country, although it was distributed unevenly.[6]

Civil society accounted for 96 percent of all associations in the country; economic society accounted for the remaining 4 percent. Figure 5.2 shows the percentage and type of associations in each of these terrains, as well as their respective fields and subfields. In civil society, the social field had the largest number of associations (45 percent), followed by the cultural field (36 percent), the public service field (11 percent), the religious field (4 percent), and the recreational field (2 percent). Associative life in economic society remained relatively undeveloped; the ratio of civic to economic associations was 24 to 1, making public life in Mexico radically lopsided.

The next section provides a detailed discussion of associative and storytelling practices across civil society, as an aid to understanding how such practices shaped and were shaped by the institutional structures of public life.

6. Alejandra Moreno Toscano, *Ciudad de México: Ensayo de construcción de una Historia* (Mexico City: Secretaría de Educación Pública, 1978); and Sonia Pérez Toledo, *Los hijos del trabajo* (Mexico City: El Colegio de México, 1996), 150–58 for estimates on the number of rural immigrants in Mexico City.

Associative Practices in Civil Society

In terms of organizational structure, civil society in Mexico was varied and complex, with citizens practicing democracy in all five fields—social, cultural, public service, religious, and recreational—as well as in the different subfields within each.

Social Field

The social field, comprising community development groups, mutual-aid societies, and patriotic, ethnic, and artisan associations, was the most populous and democratic field, and non-elite groups played a central role in shaping its everyday practices.

Community Development Groups

These associations, either alone or in partnership with local township officials, brought citizens together to build bridges, clear roads, dredge irrigation canals, construct schools, repair hospitals, and offer welfare and medical relief to the poor and sick. Small farmers living in provincial areas played a leading role in these groups.

The Sociedad de Jardinería (1855), composed of mixed-bloods and indigenous peoples from Izquimilpan (Mexico) and half a dozen nearby towns in the Central Valley, enabled members to improve their bargaining capacity in the central market in Mexico City where they sold their fruits and vegetables. Before hauling their crops to market, members from each community met and agreed on a ceiling and floor price for their produce, in order to prevent the "laws of supply and demand" from wreaking havoc with their "moral economy."[7]

Farmers from Tacubaya (Mexico) active in the Sociedad de Fomento (1850) took turns digging wells, clearing canals, hauling water, and irrigating each other's fields.[8] They also met weekly to discuss common concerns and resolve whatever differences arose pertaining to water allotment, an issue that had in the past generated much rancor and bad blood among them.

Elite owner/operators of pulque estates around Apam (Mexico), north of the country's capital, organized the Sociedad Mexicana de Agricultura (1845), the most ambitious group of its kind. Initially, this association limited itself to problems pertaining to the planting, harvesting, and marketing of pulque. But soon its bulletin, *Memorias de la Sociedad Mexicana*

---

7. "Ixquimilpan," *Siglo XIX*, 16 December 1855, 4.

8. "Junta," *Siglo XIX*, 9 September 1851, 3; "Junta," *Siglo XIX*, 4 May 1850, 4; "Junta," *Siglo XIX*, 3 July 1850; 4.

de Agricultura, was publishing broad and general articles on "scientific" farming, generating interest among non-pulque growers in the Central Valley and beyond. Estate owners, ranchers, and small farmers read the *Memorias* and wrote countless letters to the editors, initiating the first nationwide discussion on the need to "organize all the agriculturalists in the country."[9] The Sociedad enabled rural producers to overcome their social isolation and sense of mutual mistrust.

In the 1840s, citizens organized scores of "Juntas de Progreso" to encourage citizens to boycott foreign imports and instead purchase domestic-made products. These Juntas surfaced in small- and medium-sized towns across the country: in Victoria (Tamaulipas); in Cedral, Matehuala, and Catorce (San Luís Potosí); in Aguascalientes (Aguascalientes); in Zacapu, Zinapecuaro, Jiquilpam, and Morelia (Michoacán); in Tehuantepec (Veracruz); and in San Juan del Río (Querétaro).[10] A member from the Tamaulipas chapter outlined the aims of his Junta:

> A nationalist spirit is spreading across many states in our republic, and is making itself felt by supporting our domestic products and demanding protection for our artisan class. Our associations are leading the way and fomenting this (nationalist) spirit by encouraging consumers to boycott foreign-made goods.[11]

These associations also established a few vocational schools in order to retrain workers so that they might be able to compete more effectively in the marketplace, and created a common fund to provide the unemployed with financial relief. They organized mass rallies and public meetings and instructed citizens,

> when attending a civic or religious event, [to] wear at least two pieces of domestic-made clothing, and make sure that one of them is an outer garment, such as a vest or overcoat . . . something that is visible to others. . . . Do the same when attending to your daily chores. . . .[12]

These associations encouraged citizens to deposit the sovereignty of the people in the nation itself rather than in the central state, which had "denationalized" the Mexican economy and undermined their self-rule.

9. "Introducción," in *Memorias de la Sociedad Mexicana de Agricultura* (Mexico City, 1846), I–III; "Informe," in *Memorias de la Sociedad Mexicana de Agricultura* (Mexico City, 1847), 38–41.
10. "Junta de Amigos del Progreso de las Manufacturas de Acapulco," *Siglo XIX,* 17 February 1844, 2–4; "Departamento de Michoacán," *Semanario Artístico,* 7 September 1844, 3–4.
11. "Departamento de Tamaulipas," *Semanario Artístico,* 15 June 1844, 3.
12. "Departamento de San Luis Potosí," *Semanario Artístico,* 29 June 1844, 3–4; "Sociedad," *Siglo XIX,* 15 October 1850, 3; "La sociedad," *Siglo XIX,* 15 October 1859, 3; "Sociedad," *Siglo XIX,* 27 December 1857, 3.

Mutual-Aid Societies

The majority of mutual-aid societies were organized locally and sustained by the social ties among members, which were rooted in daily life in neighborhoods, parishes, work, and extended kinship networks.[13] These societies provided unemployment and medical insurance to members in distress, and when members died provided burial costs and a monthly stipend to widows and surviving children .

The Sociedad de la Caridad (1845), a mutual-aid society in the town of Maravatio (Michoacán), provided relief to local residents in distress. Despite its name, the Sociedad was part of the larger associative movement and was committed to providing citizens with welfare relief rather than Christian charity. In the words of one of its members:

> the associative spirit is spreading in our state, and beginning to bear fruits, bringing us closer to our dreams. . . . These societies are enabling citizens to overcome their egoism although they, like any one else, are also suffering from economic hardship.[14]

Governance in these societies, even in the eighty-five-member Sociedad Artística de Protección Mutua (1849), was based on self-rule. The civic terminology members used to describe their group is indicative of how they imagined themselves:

> ours is a free and independent society, the same way that our nation is sovereign of all others. Our members are committed to representative, republican, federalist and democratic governance.[15]

Citizens in these associations practiced sovereignty of the people in a horizontal manner, although they were discouraged from doing so in the political domain. A member of the Compañía de Artesano (1850) explained why Mexicans practiced the "politics of antipolitics":

> Politics has never improved our situation, although a tiny minority has always profited from the business of rulership. . . . This is why we are of the opinion that politics, by itself, has little to contribute to the life of ordinary working people. Whatever improvements occur will come about through social means. The countries which have flourished have done so by reorganizing their societies, not because of their political system.[16]

---

13. "Sociedad Mexicana Protectora de Artes y Oficios," *Siglo XIX,* 17 January 1844, 2; "Asociación de Sombreros," *Siglo XIX,* 29 May 1854, 1–2.

14. "Socios de la Caridad," *Semanario Artístico,* 13 December 1845, 3.

15. Sociedad Artística de Protección Mutua para la Juventud y los Adultos, *Reglamento de la sociedad* (Mexico City, 1849), 2.

16. Vicente Ortigoso, *Junta general de artesanos* (Guadalajara, 1850), 4–5.

Mutual-aid societies encouraged members to practice a form of antipolitics in order to preserve and protect democratic sovereignty from abridgement by state officials.

Patriotic Associations

Mexico City's Junta Patriótica (1826) was the most active and important among groups of this type, although it was similar to the other such groups that existed throughout the provinces. The patriotic calendar determined the organizational life of the Junta, which became especially active in late summer and early winter in preparation for the patriotic celebrations on September 15 and 20 and was relatively inactive throughout the rest of the year. During the off season, a standing committee attended to the affairs of the group. Despite its cyclical character, membership in the group grew steadily from year to year until, in the early 1840s, just prior to its demise, its average membership was 500.[17]

The Junta was socially inclusive and its systems of governance were based on democratic practices. The bylaws of the group stated as much:

> Any Mexican, by birth or naturalization, without any exception, regardless of class, age, sex or other distinction, is eligible for membership in the group. The tasks and duties assumed by any of our members will be done on a voluntary basis, and they are free to accept or decline any of them, without having to provide any justification for their decision.[18]

Women played a prominent part in Juntas and held positions of authority in important subcommittees such as fundraising.[19] Elections were very competitive and at times somewhat factionalized, which is why in 1843 Mr. Carvajal, the leader of one Junta, called for a truce. In making his case, he employed the same democratic rhetoric members customarily used to discuss other common concerns in the group:

> Elections are the only means we have to evaluate and compare candidates, and for selecting the best qualified among them, for determining the one who is most committed to advancing the public good, which is, after all, the aim of democracy. . . . Our republic cannot exist without patriotism, and patriotism cannot endure without public spirit. . . .[20]

17. "Festividades nacionales," *Siglo XIX,* 15 October 1844, 2.
18. Sociedad Artística, *Reglamento,* 4.
19. "Editorial," *Siglo XIX,* 13 July 1843, 2. Also see: Michael Costeloe, "The Junta Patriótica and the Celebration of Independence in Mexico City, 1825–1855," *Mexican Studies* (winter 1997): 23–24.
20. "Junta Patriótica para celebrar el Aniversario de la Independencia," *Siglo XIX,* 28 July 1843, 2.

The Junta and all the other civic and economic associations studied in this chapter kept alive the memory and practice of democratic elections authoritarian officials had abolished in the political realm.[21]

The Junta dissolved itself in the early 1850s rather than lose its autonomy to state officials, who had been trying for some time to gain control over the group. Prior to disbanding, the Junta published a newspaper article accusing the "government of corrupting our democratic elections in order to undermine our sovereignty . . . our independence and our commitment to republicanism."[22] State officials responded by accusing the Junta of having become a "center of seditious thought."[23]

Artisan Guilds

The Junta de Fomento de Artesanos (1843), composed of artisans and factory workers, was an umbrella organization made up of three dozen semi-independent, loosely affiliated groups nationwide, many of them in the Central Valley. Of the 2,200 members, nearly 1,700 came from this area.[24]

The Junta's system of governance was layered and complex. It was designed to prevent state officials, with whom the group shared close ties, from taking over the association. Government authorities were heavily represented at the top of the organization, commoners at the bottom. The influence, authority, and information in the Junta flowed in both directions, and when it did not activities and policies in the group came to a halt. Government officials selected half of the board of directors from the rank and file, although their colleagues at the bottom had considerable influence over the appointments, and monitored appointees closely once they took office to ensure that they remained loyal to their proletarian roots rather than to the state. Board members usually made decisions arbitrarily and without consultation, but among the rank and file the process was more democratic, with members sometimes taking an opposite view and refusing to implement policy directives from the top. The Junta's two-tiered system was cumbersome, but it provided those at the bottom a means of subverting Roberto Michel's "iron law of oligarchy."[25]

Admission and monthly dues in the Junta were within reach of most members, in the provinces and in the Central Valley, and local chapters encouraged members to overcome their hatred of foreign-born artisans.

21. "El Gobierno y la Junta Patriótica," *Siglo XIX,* 23 July 1851, 2–3.
22. "La Junta Patriótica de México a la nación," *Siglo XIX,* 18 July 1851, 3.
23. *Una cuestión vergonzosa sobre la Junta Patriótica* (Mexico City, 1851), 12.
24. Pérez Toledo, *Los hijos del Trabajo* is the best study on the Junta. I am indebted to her work, but I disagree with her "corporatist" interpretation.
25. Roberto Michels, *Political Parties: A Sociological Study of the Oligarchical Tendency of Modern Democracy* (Glencoe, Ill.: The Free Press, 1958).

Members of the Junta learned to judge their worth in terms of moral and technical skills rather than of national origin.[26] In 1844, the country's wealthiest merchants and moneylenders in the capital began to purchase artisan workshops and tried to take control of the Junta in order to gain additional leverage. The rank and file rallied together and issued a statement in their tabloid, *Semanario Artístico,* explaining the consequences for public life of this hostile takeover:

> these new owners have generated mistrust in all the workshops . . . and undermined our civic education. . . . They have a deficient understanding of their duties to God; our fatherland; our members and our compatriots. They are responsible for the impoverishment of public spirit in the country today.[27]

The Junta employed a civic vernacular, the same one they were accustomed to using in daily life, to defend their association.[28]

Although the Junta bore a vague resemblance to colonial guilds, the differences between the two need to be underscored. Membership in the Junta was voluntary, not compulsory; admission was open to journeymen, apprentices, and even factory workers, not just master artisans; and the Junta inculcated members with a sense of loyalty to the nation rather than to their own corporate group. Above all, the Junta, in contrast to guilds, challenged the government's economic policy and was a source of concern to the elite:

> These ridiculous associations are good only for generating public disturbances, as we can now see from what is occurring in numerous places, including Azcapotzalco, Jilhu and Guadalajara, to mention only those towns where the groups have rebelled.[29]

The Junta was, clearly, a civic-oriented rather than a state-contolled voluntary association.

Ethnic Associations

The Sociedad de Beneficencia de Españoles in Mexico City and the Sociedad Francesa de Beneficencia (1849), with a chapter in the capital and another in Veracruz, provided welfare relief to all their members. Admis-

---

26. "Bases generales para la formación de los estatutos de la Junta de Fomento de Artesanos," *Semanario Artístico,* 17 February 1844, 7–8.
27. "Discurso de los encargados de la Junta de Fomento de Artesanos," *Semanario Artístico,* 9 February 1844, 6–7.
28. Severo Rocha, "Respuesta a los comerciantes," *Semanario Artístico,* 20 April 1844, 4.
29. "Documentos disolventes," *El Universal,* 1 May 1850, 4.

sion was based on national origin, although the Spanish interpreted this requirement somewhat loosely, extending membership to anyone born in Mexico of Spanish descent.[30] The French had even fewer ties with Mexicans, which is perhaps why the group never flourished.[31]

The Sociedad Española became active in public life for the first time after "bandits" killed the Spanish-born owners and staff of several large estates in the Chinconcuac and San Vicente areas of the Central Valley. The Sociedad launched a newspaper campaign denouncing the incident, demanding indemnification for the families of the victims, and reminding Mexicans of the dangers of xenophobia in a country that was overwhelmingly nonwhite.[32] Creole Mexicans had as much to lose from ethnic cleansing as did fair-skinned foreigners. These associations did not play a major role in public life.

Cultural Field

The cultural field had the second largest number of associations, and comprised the following subfields: educational groups, learned societies, and professional bodies. With the exception of professional groups, these associations provided Mexicans a place to practice democracy in daily life.

Educational Groups

The Compañía Lancasteriana (1830) had hundreds of local chapters in the Central Valley and in the provinces, each committed to providing citizens from all social and ethnic backgrounds with primary schooling despite the low level of support from the central state.[33] From 1830 to 1840, 85 percent of all students in Mexico City who attended Lancasterian schools came from poor families.[34] For these children schooling was the first step on the way to improving their life chances and assuming a place in public life. Learning reading, writing, and arithmetic was a prerequisite for employment as an artisan, a parish priest, a factory worker, or even a

---

30. "Sociedad de Beneficencia Española," *Siglo XIX*, 11 October 1842, 2; *Reglamento de la Sociedad de Beneficencia Española* (Mexico City, 1842); Alberto María Carreño, *Los Españoles en el México Independiente* (Mexico City: Ediciones Botas, 1942), 79–112.

31. Juan de Dios Peza, *La Beneficencia en México* (Mexico City, 1881), 154–61; Nancy Nichols Barker, *The French Experience in Mexico: 1821–1861* (Chapel Hill: University of North Carolina Press, 1979), 129–30.

32. Pablo Lorenzo Laguarta, *Historia de la Beneficencia Española en México* (Mexico City: Editorial España en America, 1955), 229–31.

33. Dorothy Tanck de Estrada, "Las escuelas Lancasterianas en la Ciudad de México: 1822–1842," *Historia Mexicana* 22, no. 4 (April-June 1973): 494–513; Angela Thompson, "Children and Schooling in Guanajuato, Mexico: 1790–1840," in *Molding the Hearts and Minds,* ed. John A. Britton (Wilmington, Del.: Scholarly Resources, 1994), 19–36.

34. Estrada, "Escuelas Lancasterianas," 508.

chambermaid, butler, maid, or cook for a wealthy family. Although each school was administered by a different Lancasterian group and remained autonomous from the rest, the internal practices were remarkably similar from school to school.[35]

Lancasterian groups attracted elite and non-elite members alike, and charged members a modest monthly fee that was within their reach. Single mothers, widowed wives, and unemployed fathers paid a lower rate until they were solvent and able to contribute the full amount.[36] Members participated in weekly meetings and took an active role in governing the group, electing officers to the board of directors and holding the officers accountable by requiring monthly reports on all financial and administrative affairs of the association. Their commitment to self-rule is evident in the way they referred to their associations as "small republics."[37]

Each association provided members an opportunity to acquire a number of skills they needed to become active, responsible citizens in public life. Affiliates from poor backgrounds lacked deliberative skills and found it difficult to participate fully in the discussions in the group. Some associations, including the Sociedad Amigo de los Niños (Oaxaca, 1826), encouraged members to deliberate in public and gave them guidelines on how to do so:

> speak in the same order in which your are called, and do not wander off the topic; if you do, you will be interrupted. No one can speak more than twice on the same point unless they initiated the discussion, in which case they have the right to respond to any criticism as often as they like.[38]

Deliberating in public improved members' social standing in the group and gave them the confidence and moral authority to challenge local notables in the community, including parish priests and estate owners, who previously had controlled all public discussions. Members were also encouraged to be tolerant in their outlook. A member explained that his association was

---

35. "La instrucción pública en Guanajuato," *Siglo XIX*, 30 September 1843, 3–4; "Academia de Literatura de Puebla," *Siglo XIX*, 12 April 1850, 3; "Compañía Lancasteriana en México y dirección general de la instrucción primaria de la República," *Siglo XIX*, 18 May 1843, 1–3.

36. Manuel Dublán and José Lozano, in *Legislación Mexicana*, vol. 4 (Mexico City, 1876), 524–31.

37. Manuel Codorniú y Ferrera, *Discurso inaugural que en la abertura de las escuelas mutuas de la filantropía* (Mexico City, 1823), 9; "Reglamento de las compañías Lancasterianas de los partidos del Departamento de México," *Siglo XIX*, 26 March 1843, 2–4; "Sociedad Filantrópica de México," *El Eco de México*, 16 May 1848, 2.

38. Aurelio Bolaños and José Antonio Silva, *Reglamento para el gobierno interior de la Sociedad Amigo de los Niños* (Oaxaca, 1835), 19–20.

one of the few places where men with competing political outlooks can come together, if only for a moment. Our common concern for education stills our passions and makes it possible for us to look beyond our differences.[39]

Lancasterians instilled Mexicans with a sense of citizenship at a time when authoritarian officials remained in control of the central state and local governments.

Lancasterian schools inculcated democratic habits in their students, who in turn propagated those habits among family members. In 1842, Manuel Payno, the great Mexican novelist, visited a Lancasterian school in the small town of Azcapotzalco in the Central Valley, and noted:

> The majority of students in these schools are of indigenous descent; they are dressed in rags and without shoes, and this is how I saw them; but in their hands . . . they held copies of the *Manual de Urbanidad*. . . . [These] students take home the lessons they have learned in school, bringing about changes in the backward customs of their ignorant families.[40]

Fathers were often opposed to sending their children to school for fear that, having acquired an education (a source of public prestige at the time), the children would lose respect for their authority at home. Teachers persuaded such protesting fathers otherwise by agreeing to provide breakfast to students who attended regularly. The association paid for them, transferring the burden of feeding poor students to the community, undermining patriarchal authority in these families to the benefit of children, and setting a precedent for wives, especially abused wives, who began to consider inviting outsiders to intervene in domestic affairs.

Lancasterian groups opposed corporal punishment, which they considered a violation of democratic notions of self-rule and individual autonomy. When teachers failed to live up to these civic ideals, parents took it upon themselves to enforce them. In 1828, the father of one Tomás gave his son's teacher a stern warning, using civic terminology to demand that he rid himself of his authoritarian habits at once:

> My dear teacher: neither politics nor the law allows anyone, including yourself, to punish my son. . . . Your despotic treatment of him was caused by your loss of judgment, but I am now warning you: this must never happen again.[41]

---

39. Juan M. Govantes, *Memoria leída por el secretario de la compañía Lancasteriana* (Mexico City, 1850), 13.

40. Manuel Payno, "Ni yo sé qué escribiré," *Siglo XIX*, 18 February 1842, 2–3. José Gómez de la Cortina, *Cartilla social: Deberes del ciudadano con la sociedad civil* (Mexico City, 1849) and the *Catecismo de moral, virtud y urbanidad* (Mexico City, 1855) were reprinted many times.

41. Estrada, "Escuelas Lancasterianas," 512.

Corporal punishment was associated with excessive passion and loss of reason, to recall the old colonial dichotomy. In 1855, graduates of Mexico City's San Gregorio, a school for indigenous boys, staged a protest to denounce the newly appointed headmaster, a priest famous for his "rigorous treatment" of students.[42] Physical punishment had come to be seen as a violation of self-rule.

Lancasterian groups spent a large portion of their meager budgets on shoes, clothes, and other prizes to reward outstanding students. They distributed these awards at the end of each academic year in public ceremonies held in the main plaza, in front of an audience ranging from a hundred to a thousand, including parents and public officials. Students were invited to the podium to recite poems and deliberate on subjects such as civicness in public life and the detrimental effects of corporal punishment on the moral development of children. Whether or not these rituals also contributed to the demilitarization of public life is worth studying.[43]

Learned and Scientific Societies

Mexicans organized numerous literary-scientific societies throughout the country, relying on meritocratic principles to admit candidates and to reward their most outstanding members. The Liceo, one of the most prestigious societies of this type, charged members a modest fee. The Academia Letrán (1836) and the Sociedad Filantrópica (1840) were more egalitarian and invited candidates to submit an original essay on a topic of their choice to a blind jury. This enabled writers from the provinces to compete with "cultural insiders" who had patronage ties to the country's most influential writers. The competitions were far from perfect, but still they were much more meritocratic than ever before. A member of the Academia noted:

> the Academia bestowed prizes on anyone who displayed excellence in their work, without any regard for their social status, age or wealth, and this has democratized literary life.[44]

Members who entered the group without patronage ties were often among the most respected.

In 1837, Ignacio Ramírez, a mixed-blood from the small town of San Miguel El Grande (Guanajuato), was admitted to the Academia. As part of his induction into the association, he was invited to deliver a "disserta-

42. "Colegio de San Gregorio," *El Monitor Republicano,* 19 November 1855, 12.
43. David Hogan, "Market Revolution and Disciplinary Power: Joseph Lancaster and the Psychology of the Early Classroom System," *History of Education Quarterly* 29, no. 3 (fall 1989): 381–417 on "disciplinary" practices in classrooms.
44. Prieto, *Memorias,* 181.

tion" in public to all the members. The hall was packed with the country's leading public intellectuals, radicals and conservatives alike. A witness described what happened next:

> Ramírez walked up to the podium, reached into his pocket and took out a handful of crumpled pieces of paper of different colors and sizes. . . . Then he announced the title of his work: "God does not Exist." It hit us like a bomb. . . . We stood up immediately and began to yell (some in favor and others against him). . . . The Academia's president intervened and restored order, and forbade Ignacio from delivering his dissertation. The majority of members challenged his decision in public, and demanded that a vote be taken.[45]

Mr. Ramírez's supporters won, and after he finished his speech they welcomed him into the group, despite stiff opposition from conservatives. Heterodox-minded intellectuals were able to join these groups because admission was somewhat meritocratic. Their presence expanded the boundaries of public debate, and this, in turn, made for controversy, compelling members to become tolerant of their differences. In the words of a contemporary:

> The Ateneo is a neutral terrain, and although its members belong to rival parties, this does not stop us from meeting and learning from each other. . . . The hatred we once felt toward each other has been silenced. . . .[46]

Learned and scientific associations instilled members with a sense of moderation at a time when political society remained polarized.[47] In these meetings, members reconstrued each other as "rivals" instead of "enemies," to invert Carl Schmitt's argument, thereby contributing to deradicalizing and decompressing public debates.[48]

Cultural associations provided disaffected writers and artists the social and moral support they needed to break with "neocolonial" models of literature and art, as propagated by government-sponsored academies, including the Academia de Lengua (1835) and the Academia de Bellas Artes (1843). Guillermo Prieto, a member of the Ateneo, encouraged writers to develop a creole style that reflected the reality of Mexican life:

45. Prieto, *Memorias,* 165.
46. Prieto, *Memorias,* 322–23.
47. "Presentación," in *El Atenéo de México,* vol. 1 (Mexico City, 1844), 263; *Bases generales para la organización del Licéo Hidalgo* (Mexico City, 1850); Enrique de Olavarría y Ferrari, *La Sociedad Mexicana de Geografía y Estadística: Reseña histórica* (Mexico City, 1901), 38–41.
48. Carl Schmitt, *Political Theology* (Cambridge, Mass.: MIT Press, 1989).

rather than borrowing foreign phrases such as "nectar of the liquor
goddess" use the term pulque; and, in your stories . . . do [not shy away]
from . . . placing jugs of pulque next to champagne bottles or . . . plat-
ters of turkey in "mole" sauce [of chocolate, nuts, and chiles] . . . next
to the roast beef. And instead of intoning the "Marseillaise" or "God
Save the Queen," have your characters in your stories singing our own
patriotic songs. . . . It is shameful that our government has not yet been
able to forge a nation. . . .[49]

The situation was even worse in the world of art. The curriculum at the
prestigious Academia de Bellas Artes was "classical." Students were
trained to paint in the "Spanish" style, and they limited themselves to
religious themes or family portraits. The director and staff of the school,
in the words of a contemporary, had "disdain for all art that is Mexican,
although in fact they know nothing about it . . . and refuse to exhibit the
works of our most talented painters."[50] In any case, the eight hundred or
so patrons who subsidized the school and were the only ones who bought
paintings shared a similar taste. The market for heterodox art was nonexistent, which made it difficult for artists to develop a "national" style.[51]
The curriculum, staff, and patronage system at the Academia was authoritarian, but the social composition of its student body was democratic. A
visitor noted:

> numerous students are taught free of charge . . . at this school. Equality
> is visible everywhere, and this is very refreshing. [In the Academia], the
> child of the peon and aristocrat sit side by side, and on the days when
> there are public exhibitions, the audience . . . who attend is just as var-
> ied as the pupils who study there.[52]

Artisans and other civic-minded citizens maintained pressure on the Academia to keep its doors open to commoners.[53]

In Mexico City, families of modest means, those who rented small
apartments, began to decorate their living rooms with creole art. A visi-

49. Guillermo Prieto, "Cuadro de costumbres," in *Revista Científica y Literaria de
México*, vol. 1 (Mexico City, 1845), 27–29. Francisco Zarco, "Estado de la Literatura en
México," in *La ilustración Méxicana*, vol. 2 (Mexico City, 1852), 5–8.
50. "Academia de San Carlos," *El Siglo XIX*, 2 August 1849, 2.
51. "Adelanto de las bellas artes en México," *El Universal*, 16 January 1854, 2; "Exposición de 1854," *La ilustración Mexicana* (Mexico City, 1854, 3; Esther Acevedo, Rosa
Casanova, and María E. Eguiarte, "Modos de decir: La pintura y los conservadores," *Historias* 6 (April-July 1984): 71–84.
52. Robert Wilson, *Mexico: Its Peasants and Its Priests* (New York, 1856), 210.
53. "Academia de San Carlos," *El Semanario Artístico*, 8 February 1845, 4. The Academia had been meritocratic in the colonial period, but after independence it was artisans
who were responsible for keeping it so.

tor recorded this description of the paintings that adorned the walls in one of these homes:

> It is common to see frescos of the Chapultepec castle and forest; of the Viga Promenade and its canals with [Indian] musicians and singers on canoes; and of ranchers [wrestling] bulls and pulling their tail. Although some of these paintings are of poor quality and lacking in good taste, others are appealing. . . .[54]

Religious and creole paintings depicting "historical and mythological scenes" now hung side by side.[55] Taverns also provided artists a market for and a place to exhibit such work. Mexico City's taverns were decorated with gaudily colored "frescos of cowboys on horses, brawling plebeians, bullfighters, and caricatures of government officials."[56]

"Mr. Poison" was without doubt the most successful of the rebel artists. Visitors trekked from the center of the city to the outskirts, where he had his workshop, to admire his famous painting, "The Grand Promenade of Retama," an "underground" classic among aficionados even though no gallery had ever exhibited it. This mural-sized work depicted commoners and aristocrats strolling on opposite sides of a public park, in opposite directions, the former under a portico labeled "Sovereignty of the People" and the latter under one labeled "Elegant People."[57] Creole painters, like their literary counterparts, identified commoners with nationhood and the privileged elite with the colonial past, inverting the symbolic worth of the two groups.

Cultural life in the provinces became animated as well, which did much to change the circulation of "symbolic capital" in the country. A contemporary noted:

> An enthusiasm for literature has spread across our states; in Jalapa, the Falange de Estudios was organized; in Puebla, the Academia de Bellas Artes; in Yucatán, the Sociedad Literaria is now a reality. . . . The [associative] spirit continues to spread, judging from the efforts underway to create new groups in the states of Zacatecas, Querétaro, Morelia, and Oaxaca. [These associations] have benefited from the support that

54. Prieto, *Memorias*, 222.

55. Otto Ferdinand Geger, *Panorama of Mexico, Comprising a Complete and Adequate Description* (London, 1835), 5.

56. Prieto, *Memorias*, 85; and Edward Burnett Tylor, *Anahuac; or, Mexico and the Mexicans* (London, 1861), 63–64. Also see: Manuel Alvarez, "Las pinturas de la Academia Nacional de Bellas Artes; su merito artistico y su valor comercial," *Cuadernos de arquitectura y conservación del patrimonio artístico* 18–19 (November-December 1981 and January-February 1982): 103–56.

57. Prieto, *Memorias*, 398–99.

township officials and individual patrons have given to them, while those in the capital remain inactive due to lack of support from local municipal authorities.[58]

In the provinces, citizens and township officials forged partnerships with the aim of improving cultural life, contributing to a resurgence of public life at the municipal level. Associations decentralized the production and consumption of art, literature, and science from the capital to the provinces and "creolized" aesthetic taste.

Associations with links to local townships were more successful in retaining their autonomy than those in the capital with connections to the central state. The Sociedad Mexicana de Geografía y Estadística (1833), however, is an exceptionto the rule. In 1839, prior to the war with the United States, the Ministry of Defense called on the Sociedad for assistance in surveying the disputed region on both sides of the Río Grande. The members agreed to place their expertise at the service of the nation, but on the condition that the state not intrude into their affairs—a demand they had no difficulty enforcing, since the government officials overseeing their work did not have any scientific training. If anything, the latter became dependent on the former for information on a host of public issues, including those of the border:

> since gaining our independence, our government officials have erred many times [and implemented mistaken policies] due to the lack of information they have about our country. . . . The Mexican nation will begin to know its real strengths, its resources and the means to augment both and overcome their shortcomings when the government has the knowledge it needs to devise enlightened policies.[59]

As the wording above suggests, the members of the Sociedad identified themselves first and foremost as patriotic citizens devoted to the nation, not dutiful servants of the central state. In 1849, after the war, the Sociedad transferred itself to the Ministry of the Interior, gaining even more autonomy.[60]

---

58. Francisco Granados Maldonado, "Discurso," in *Composiciones leídas en sesión pública del Liceo Hidalgo* (Mexico City, 1850), 10–11.

59. "Introducción," in *Boletín del Instituto Nacional de Geografía y Estadística de la República Mexicana*, vol. 1 (Mexico City, 1839), 5–8.

60. *Memoria de la Secretaría de Estado y del Despacho de Guerra y Marina* (Mexico City, 1849), 17; Ferrari, *Sociedad Mexicana*, 38–41, 47–48; María Lozano Meza, "La Sociedad Mexicana de Geografía y Estadística y su relación con el Estado," in *Memorias del Primer Congreso Mexicano de Historia de la Ciencia y de la Tecnología*, vol. 1 (Mexico City: Universidad Nacional Autónoma de México, 1989), 833–40.

Professional Bodies

Professional life remained undeveloped throughout the first half of the century, and the associations of medical doctors and lawyers that existed in the country remained relatively uncivic.

The Sociedad Médica (1831), composed of medical doctors, was factionalized from the outset, and because its members lacked civic predispositions, they were also unable to resolve their differences in a consensual manner. Rivalry in the association escalated, and the two sides sought support from government officials, increasing the level of rancor in the group and turning the squabble into a state problem rather than a civic affair. The democratic-minded faction was especially effective at enlisting the aid of like-minded officials in reforming the Sociedad. Together they abolished honorific posts, granted membership to midwives, sponsored elections for officers, and granted licensed doctors the legal right to practice medicine in any state, putting an end to the old corporate restrictions.[61] They also began publishing a tabloid with articles on issues pertaining to medical reform in other countries and on the latest scientific findings. Conservative members resigned in protest, and because they were in the majority, the Sociedad did not recover.[62]

The Colegio de Abogados (1829) also tried to transform itself from an old corporate into a "modern" professional group in the service of the nation at large. Unlike the doctors, the Colegio's lawyers used collegial means to reform their association. Membership in the group was made voluntary, and racial-religious purity was abolished as a requirement for admission.[63] The conservative wing in the group agreed to these changes, knowing full well that Mexico's new constitution mandated them. The conservative wing in the Colegio, however, was in the majority in the group, and because decisions were reached by consensus, they blocked all other reforms. In 1833, they voted in favor of retaining the old colonial legal code and against adopting a republican one. They were also adamantly opposed to including the latter in the curriculum in any of the law schools.[64] In addition, the members of the Colegio continued to define

61. Sociedad Médica, *Reglamento de la Sociedad Médica* (Mexico City, 1831), 4; "Escuelas para parteras," *El Fénix*, 13 February 1834, 4; Anne Staples, "Medicina," in *Historia de las Profesiones en México* (Mexico City: Secretaría de Educación Pública, 1987), 105–6.

62. L. Blaquiere, "Prospecto," *Periódico de la Academia de Medicina*, 15 July 1836, 3–8

63. Colegio de Abogados, *Estatutos del Nacional Colegio de Abogados* (Mexico City, 1830), 16–17; José Bernardo Conto, *Discurso en la elección de oficios del ilustre y Nacional Colegio de Abogados de México* (Mexico City, 1860), 10; Anne Staples, "La Constitución del Estado Nacional," in *Historia de las Profesiones*, 79–82.

64. María del Refugio González, "La Academia de Jurisprudencia Teórica-Práctica de

their professional duty in an authoritarian way, as advisors to government officials rather than as defenders of the public at large.[65]

Public Service Field

Mexicans organized scores of charitable and welfare associations to provide for the needy, the poor, and the infirm. Neither the state nor local townships had the financial or administrative capacity to care for the destitute, which is why the Catholic Church, sometimes alone and sometimes in partnership with them, continued to play a significant role in this field.[66] Mexicans regarded welfare as their birthright by virtue of their status as citizens, and not just an expression of religious piety and Christian mercy, as the Church maintained.

The Catholic Church and local townships created partnerships to provide local residents with welfare relief. In Querétaro, Mexico City, and other places, the Church took a leading role in providing the poor sectors of society with schooling, job training, and two meals a day in public kitchens, staffing and subsidizing the local Beneficencias (1843).[67] These charitable groups also held public forums to discuss civic and moral issues pertaining to the impact of welfare relief and public confinement on citizens.[68]

Religious Field

In those areas where parish priests had led parishioners into battle under the banner of the Virgin of Guadalupe, they exerted a civic influence on local residents during the postcolonial period, as Guillermo Prieto noted during his travels through the Central Valley. In a small town, he noticed that the local priest

> had persuaded residents to organize themselves into a band and play concerts for church benefits. . . . These [feuding] families eventually became friends and this motivated them, in turn, to undertake ambitious projects related to public welfare and urban beautification. Similar scenes are common elsewhere as well.[69]

México: 1811–1835," *Revista de Investigaciones Jurídicas* 6, no. 6 (1982): 301–17; Jaime del Arenal Fenochio, "Los abogados en México y una polémica centenaria: 1784–1847," *Revista de Investigaciones Jurídicas* 4, no. 4 (1980): 521–56.

65. González, " Academia de Jurisprudencia," 301–17.
66. Silvia Marina Arrom, "De la caridad a la beneficencia" (Unpublished typescript, Brandeis University, 1995).
67. *Noticia de la distribución de premios hecha en la Escuela Patriótica del Hospicio de Pobres* (Mexico City, 1854).
68. "Casa de Beneficencia de Mérida: Reglamento," *Siglo XIX*, 15 March 1855, 1, 3.
69. Guillermo Prieto, "El Cura del Pueblo," in *El Álbum Mexicano*, vol. 2 (Mexico City, 1849), 271–73.

Parish priests propagated civicness in some communities. The Nueva Sociedad (1848), composed of indigenes and artisans, had fifteen branches scattered across the northern half of the state of Mexico, most of them in and around Acambay. The Sociedad denounced corrupt clerics and launched a campaign of moral regeneration. Candidates who joined the group took an oath of loyalty in the main plaza, in plain view of other residents, to uphold the "teachings of the gospel," "republican federalism," and "communal sovereignty," and to behave at all times in a "dignified" manner.[70] They also vowed to turn their backs on state-centered politics:

> The evils besetting us cannot be corrected through political means; we must penetrate society, and deposit a religious sentiment in the conscience of each person, so that they can follow the moral path and avoid the immoral one. . . . [Our] aim is social, not political, and this is why our association admits only persons of integrity.[71]

In 1849, during a cholera epidemic, the Sociedad became very active in public health, campaigned against church burials and alcoholism, and demanded that government officials improve the sanitation system, water supply, and housing of residents.[72] The local priest and government official closed ranks and mobilized 4,000 residents from Azcapotzalco and 200 more from Acambay against members of the Sociedad. They were accused of "heresy" and their houses were burned, putting an end to the Sociedad but not to the civic practices they had instilled in members.[73]

Recreational Field

Mexicans organized few social and recreational clubs. The elite gathered in social clubs. They also attended concerts in public parks alongside the non-elite, which had consequences for democratic life.

Mexico City's declining aristocratic and upwardly mobile, nouveau riche families organized the Liceo Artístico (1854), enabling them to blur old and new distinctions based on family pedigree and wealth. Members who went to the club or to any event sponsored by the Liceo were, in the words of a member, "prohibited from wearing extravagant jewelry, as this would inhibit families of modest means from attending."[74]

70. Mariano Torres Aranda, "Discurso: La nueva sociedad," *Siglo XIX*, 31 July 1848, 2; Sr. Portugal, "Discurso: Nueva sociedad," *Siglo XIX*, 7 August 1848, 3.
71. Mariano Torres Aranda, "La nueva sociedad: Discurso pronunciado el 16 de Julio de 1848," *Siglo XIX*, 21 July 1848, 3.
72. "Remitidos," *Siglo XIX*, 12 January 1845, 3; and "Sección fundadora de la nueva sociedad," *Siglo XIX*, 8 January 1849, 4.
73. "La nueva sociedad," *Siglo XIX*, 12 January 1849, 2.
74. "Bases para un Liceo Mexicano," *Siglo XIX*, 23 January 1854, 3–4.

The elite also organized hobby-oriented and businessmen's clubs. Horse racing enthusiasts organized the Sociedad para Caballar (1851), which lasted only a year or so. Mexico City and Veracruz merchants and businessmen met at the Sociedad del Comercio (1850) and Lonja (1852), where they played pool, read newspapers, and shared late-breaking news about business opportunities, enabling them to compete on better terms against moneylenders with access to "insider" information provided by government officials.[75]

The Sociedad Filarmónica (1844) of Mexico City, and La Unión (1852) of Tampico (Tamaulipas), composed of amateur musicians, mainly dark-skinned peoples, held open-air concerts in the park every other Sunday. Elite and non-elite families flocked to these events to enjoy the same "sober" and "sedate" tunes, eroding the distinction between "popular" and "elite" music. Bawdy tunes and pulsating rhythms were still heard in neighborhood taverns, but musical associations altered musical tastes and the social relations that accompanied them: "music is no longer the pastime only of the rabble; our most distinguished families have acquired an appreciation for it."[76] Members in musical associations described their concerts as contributing to the "common good" and the "enlargement of the nation."[77]

Associative Practices in Economic Society

Bribery and fraud were a customary part of business life throughout Mexico, although distributed unevenly in economic society. Corruption predominated in the export sector, and was somewhat less influential in the domestic sector.

Export Sector: Booty Capitalism

Foreign merchant houses, such as the British-owned Barclay and Co. and the French-owned Jecker and Co., two of the most influential of this type, controlled the country's export sector. The number of British establishments in Mexico jumped from 16 in 1826 to 32 in 1835, about twice as many as the French. Foreign houses established their main warehouses in

75. David Walker, *Kinship, Business and Politics: The Martinez del Rio Family in Mexico* (Austin: University of Texas Press, 1986), 80.
76. "Instalación de la Sección Artística de Música," *Semanario Artístico*, 23 November 1844, 1.
77. "Instalación," 1; *Prospecto y reglamento de la Gran Sociedad Filarmónica* (Mexico City, 1839); "Bases reglamentarias de la Sociedad Filarmónica," *Siglo XIX*, 3 December 1845, 3; "Academia de Música," *Siglo XIX*, 19 March 1852, 4.

all the major ports on the Gulf (Matamoros, Tampico, Veracruz, Tabasco, Campeche) and Pacific coasts (Mazatlan, San Blas, Acapulco); they were the links between Mexico and the world economy. Each region had its own supplier; French firms, for example, were stationed in San Blas and from there pumped goods throughout the region, especially into Guadalajara. Foreign houses imported goods of all types (champagne, carriages, cottons, machinery, farm tools) into Mexico, and paid for it in silver specie, which was then exported back to Europe (causing a chronic shortage of currency in the country). Mexican wholesalers then resold their stock to local retailers, who then resold it to hawkers who peddled their wares from one hamlet to another throughout the hinterlands.[78] A business cycle, counting from the time the merchandise was unloaded on the docks to the time it was sold and a new shipment received, took two and a half years to complete. Foreign houses staggered the arrival of goods into the country to prevent a glut and a consequent decline in prices.[79]

Business relations between foreign importers and Mexico's wealthy wholesalers were characterized by mistrust. Most importers were "booty capitalists," to use Max Weber's phrase; they were devoid of a "vocational calling," driven by greed, and reckless in the way they transacted business.[80] After independence, the British firms Barclay and Co. and Goldschmitt and Co. rushed headlong and invested heavily in the mining sector, having been dazzled by fanciful stories of "El Dorado." They lost 32 million pesos in a decade. Despite the debacle, the number of British firms in Mexico rose throughout the 1830s, as I noted above. The later entrants were as foolish as their predecessors, although they adopted a different business strategy:

> they [now had a marked] preference for short-term investments, which meant that capital would not be tied up in any long-term project and that withdrawal from the country could be done relatively quick and painless. British interests and capital sought to profit from the country's financial crisis. . . .[81]

---

78. Hilarie J. Heath, "British Merchants in Mexico, 1821–1860," *Hispanic American Historical Review* 73, no. 2 (May 1993): 261–90; Nancy Nichols Barker, *The French Experience in Mexico: 1821 to 1861* (Chapel Hill: University of North Carolina Press, 1979), 44, 128–29.

79. Heath, "British Merchants," 262–67; Hilarie J. Heath, "Los primeros escarceos del imperialismo en México," *Historias* 22 (April-September 1989): 77–90; John Mayo, "Imperialismo de libre comercio e imperio informal en la costa oeste de México durante la época de Santa Anna," *Historia Mexicana* 40, no. 4 (April-June 1991): 673–96.

80. Max Weber, *The Protestant Ethic* and *Economy and Society: An Outline of Interpretive Sociology*, ed. Guenter Roth and Claus Witich (Berkeley: University of California Press, 1978).

81. Heath, "British Merchants," 290.

This strategy failed as well. By the 1850s, most British- and French-owned houses had abandoned the country.

Mexican wholesalers were just as corrupt and had the advantage of "local knowledge." The Spanish wholesaler, Ventura de la Cruz, a worldly man and a product of "Hispanic" culture, bemoaned the lack of business ethics among Mexican wholesalers:

> Everything here is in a state of uncertainty. . . . We are at the mercy of mandarins, rogues and reprobates, all of whom extort from those with whom they transact business. . . . [Businessmen in Mexico] will do anything, including rob, in order to become rich.[82]

Other foreign investors expressed similar complaints and were dismayed to find that Mexican wholesalers seldom paid back their loans, nor would they return the goods they had gotten on credit. And because they had influence over the local magistrate, it was impossible to bring them to justice.[83]

In the mid-1830s, business practices between foreign importers and wholesalers began to change as a result of the emergence of a new type of professional group: brokers (*corredores*). They arranged and monitored all business transactions, which, according to the *Cuadro Sinóptico* of 1850, the most reliable census to date, amounted to between 30 and 40 million pesos annually, nearly all of it in drafts or bills of exchange.[84] Agents depended on their reputation to secure clients. But their ability to transact business in an honest and efficient way depended in large measure on the agents with whom they were in negotiation; they therefore tried to work with only those who had a reputation similar to their own. Brokers dealt with each other and their clients in a professional and responsible manner and so contributed to altering business practices in the export sector:

> Most business is done by these brokers. . . . Generally, there is much good faith and confidence in doing business, important transactions are frequently arranged without witnesses, and considerable sums change hands.[85]

82. Quoted in Walker, *Kinship, Business and Politics,* 81.

83. "Tayleur, Jamieson and Co. to Pakenham (14 April 1837)," in Heath, "British Merchants," 271–72.

84. Miguel Lerdo de Tejada, *Cuadro sinóptico de la República de México* (Mexico City, 1856), 63–64; Charles Lempriere, *Notes in Mexico in 1861 and 1862* (London, 1862), 203.

85. Carl Sartorius, *Mexico about 1850* (Stuttgart: Brockhaus, 1961), 123. Recent studies concur with Sartorius's obsevations: see Leonor Ludlow, "La formación de las casas bancarias de la ciudad de México durante el periodo independendiente," *Sociológica* 9, no. 26 (September-December 1994): 117–34; and Anne Staples, "La Constitución del Estado Nacional," in *Historia de las profesiones en México,* 87–90.

Agents created social and economic distance between foreign importers and Mexican businessmen, which helped make business life in the export sector slightly less predatory than had been the case.[86]

Bills of exchange were commonly used in the export sector, but rarely in the domestic sector. In 1861, Charles Lempriere, an Oxford-trained lawyer interested in investing in Mexico, noted:

> exchanges by drafts, although not generally understood or adopted throughout the Republic, are used . . . between the capital and such points . . . open to foreign commerce and in other principal cities.[87]

In the domestic sector, retailers and peddlers did business only with those they knew. Although this greatly limited the number of persons with whom they transacted business and kept the size of local markets very small, it also served to protect the moral economy from whatever un-civic influences surrounded it.

Domestic Sector: Credit Networks and Associations

Mexican wholesalers diversified their portfolios and transferred large amounts of their wealth from the export to the domestic sector between 1830 and 1842, in response to socioeconomic conditions in both. This sudden influx of cash and credit benefited farmers and artisans, but it also posed a grave threat to their moral economy.[88]

Paper Money and Credit Relations

The central state tried several times in the 1840s to introduce paper money in order to restore public confidence in the economy. The government printed bills and minted copper coins of small denominations, and decreed that one-third of all transactions had to be done in cash. Most Mexicans, including those who worked in state-owned cigarette factories in Mexico and Puebla, boycotted the law and refused to accept government-printed money for their wages. In rejecting the national currency, factory workers and other plebeian groups were in effect expressing their opposition to the economic policy of the government.[89] According to them,

---

86. The number of notaries in each region was itself an indication of the amount of business transacted. Mexico City had 80; Puruandiro (Michoacán) had 25, and Morelia (Michoacán) had 20.

87. Lempriere, *Notes in Mexico,* 203.

88. Barbara Tenenbaum, "Banqueros sin bancos: El papel del los agiotistas en México: 1826–1854," in *Banca y poder en México: 1800–1925,* ed. Leonor Ludlow and Carlos Marichal (Mexico City: Grijalbo, 1986), 81–89.

89. Carlos María de Bustamante, *Apuntes para la historia del gobierno del General don Antonio López de Santa Anna* (Mexico City, 1945), 9, 24–26; and "Protesta," *El Monitor Republicano,* 9 August 1849, 3.

the government's monetary policy had been adopted under pressure from moneylenders and served only to advance their private interests at the expense of Mexico's working people.

During the independence wars, rebel movements in Michoacán and other parts of the country, had wreaked havoc throughout the region, causing enormous material losses. But by the 1840s, rural production in this area had more than recovered; it had surpassed previous levels and the area had become Mexico's bread-basket. As Margaret Chowning's work suggests, the resurgence of economic life across Michoacán was the result of a host of natural and economic factors—type of crop, climatic conditions, access to markets, credit, land tenure patterns, and so on.[90] In my view, civic relations played an equally pivotal role in the region's success. The rebel movements that had swept the area during the anticolonial struggle left behind a residue of civic commitment that rural producers used throughout the postcolonial period to jump-start the economy and to prevent wholesalers from corrupting it.

Chowning has done more than any other scholar to shift our focus of attention from national markets to regional production, although she has not been alone in this effort.[91] Heriberto Moreno García's micro-study of credit relations in the area of Puruandiro (Michoacán) is also important: "farmers had the same access to credit as large estate owners; relations between them were not as divisive nor as oppressive as we had assumed."[92] Civic reciprocity played a major role in reviving economic life at the local and regional levels. In and around the cities of Veracruz and Córdoba on the Gulf Coast, a tobacco, sugar, and coffee growing area, credit relations cut across socioeconomic differences as a manifestation of civic unity. According to Eugene L. Wiemers:

> large and small landowners differed little from one another in their ability to get credit . . . although credit relationships [between them] followed broader social hierarchies. . . . For borrowers high in status, access to credit from merchants and hacendados was direct and routine; for borrowers at the bottom, access was often through some intermedi-

90. Margaret Chowning, *Wealth and Power in Provincial Mexico: Michoacan from the Late Colony to the Revolution* (Stanford, Calif.: Stanford University Press, 1999).

91. Margaret Chowning, "Reassessing the Prospects for Profit in Nineteenth Century Mexican Agriculture from a Regional Perspective: Michoacan, 1810–1860," in *How Latin America Fell Behind: Essays on the Economic Histories of Brazil and Mexico: 1810–1914,* ed. Stephen Haber (Stanford, Calif.: Stanford University Press, 1997).

92. Heriberto Moreno García, "Los beneficiarios del crédito agrario en Puruandiro, Michoacán," in *Los negocios y las ganancias de la colonia a México Moderno,* ed. Leonor Ludlow and Jorge Silva Riquer (Mexico City: Instituto de Investigaciones Dr. José María Luis Mora, 1993), 255.

ary or, if direct, from merchants, and for limited sums and purposes. At all levels, credit was a mixture of business and trust.[93]

Interest rates were about 8 percent, roughly 80 percentage points less than what was moneylenders charged in Mexico City. Most borrowers (96 percent) in Veracruz and Córdoba, the two most economically active cities in the region, repaid their debt in a timely manner, which helped to make economic life in the area civic and stable.

Credit relations in most cities, in contrast, were controlled by moneylenders and were extremely exploitive. Master artisans were locked in struggle against moneylenders over interest rates, payment schedules, and even bookkeeping practices. In the 1850s, artisans began to demand that creditors make public the money they were owed in order to keep them from inflating the amount every few months. In Guadalajara, the Compañía de Artesanos demanded that

> merchants post on their doors what each person owes, instead of relying on their memory and ledger books to keep track of our debts.[94]

This demand for accountability reframed the problem of credit as a public rather than a purely private matter.[95] Credit relations between master artisans and moneylenders were even more strained in Mexico City, in part because of the large number and amount of wealth owned by the latter. In contrast, in Puebla, credit ties between the two groups were civic, a legacy of the alliances and coalitions that artisans and businessmen had forged in the 1830s in protest against the government's effort to liberalize the economy by lifting tariffs.[96]

The savings and loan movement attracted water-carriers, army veterans, and public employees in Mexico City; tobacco farmers and artisans in Orizaba; indigenous peoples working in the mining camps in and around Regla (Mexico); and artisans and factory workers in several small towns in the states of Aguascalientes and Jalisco, to mention only the most important groups.[97] The members themselves owned and operated these

93. Eugene L. Wiemers, "Agriculture and Credit in Nineteenth Century Mexico: Orizaba and Cordoba, 1822 to 1871," *Hispanic American Historical Review* 42, no. 2 (1985): 530, 536–37.

94. Vicente Ortigoso, *Junta General de Artesanos* (Guadalajara, 1850), 13.

95. "Comisión de la Junta de Fomento de Artesanos," *Semanario Artístico*, 23 March 1844, 3; Frederick Shaw, *Poverty and Politics in Mexico City, 1824–1854* (Ph.D. dissertation, University of Florida, 1975), 78.

96. Guy P. C. Thomson, *Puebla de los Angeles: Industry and Society in a Mexican City; 1700–1850,* (Boulder, Colo.: Westview Press, 1989), 330, 428–43.

97. "Sección de Policía Civil," *Siglo XIX,* 21 June 1852, 3; "Caja de ahorros," *Siglo XIX,* 18 August 1851, 3; Luis Riquelme, *Proyecto de suscripciones voluntarias por los empleados civiles de la república Mejicana* (Arizpe, 1837); El Republicano Jaliciense, "El Estado de Jalisco: Cajas de ahorro," *El Eco del Comercio,* 30 May 1848, 2; "Establecimiento

banks and met regularly to discuss policy and find ways of preventing moneylenders from taking them over. They also formed part of a campaign to prevent citizens from squandering their money and running the risk of losing their place in public life. A member summarized the mission of savings and loans in these terms: "they are the principal source of morality for working people; they instill us with virtue, teach us to be orderly and . . . to rely on our selves."[98] Depositors were encouraged to save money and keep a ledger book. They were also "moralized" on the dangers of drinking and gambling and of ending up in jail or worse.

In 1852, 2,500 water-carriers and haulers met in Mexico City's Mizcalco plaza and organized a savings and loan. Each neighborhood elected its own "captain" whose duties included collecting the money from members and depositing it in a central treasury.[99] This bank, in the words of one member, had broader implications for public life:

> Our capitalists are . . . responsible for the credit crisis that is now afflicting our country. . . . Although our bank cannot resolve this problem, it can alleviate it. By pooling our savings and investing them, we will be also contributing to republican rule in our country.[100]

Savings and loans taught working people to become, in the words of one member, "self-reliant"; this was the only way of acquiring a place in public life. Throughout the 1830s, Orizaba's moneylenders launched an attack against local savings and loans. They discouraged residents from depositing money in such institutions by claiming that the bank was nothing more than a scheme to steal money from customers. The bank's directors challenged the moneylenders to a public debate, with the parish priest invited to serve as moderator. After explaining how the bank worked, the directors accused Orizaba's moneylenders of charging usurious rates on loans in violation of Church doctrine and of behaving like "philistines."[101]

---

de Beneficencia de empleados del Departamento de Puebla," *Siglo XIX*, 23 December 1842, 3; *Escritura de la Sociedad de Cajas de Ahorros de Orizaba* (Orizaba, 1840); "Cajas de Ahorro," *Siglo XIX*, 6 January 1842, 3; "Cajas de Ahorro," *Siglo XIX*, 18 September 1851, 3; "Importante Caja de Ahorros," *Siglo XIX*, 28 July 1851, 3; "Cajas de Ahorro en los Minerales," *Siglo XIX*, 18 June 1843, 2.

98. Republicano Jaliciense, " Cajas de Ahorro," 2. Also see: "Cajas de Ahorro," *Siglo XIX*, 6 January 1842, 3; "Cajas de Ahorro en los Minerales," *Siglo XIX*, 18 June 1843, 2; and "Sección de Policía Civil," *Siglo XIX*, 21 January 1852, 3.

99. "Sección de Policía Civil," 3.

100. "Sección de Policía Civil," 3; "Estado de Jalisco," *El Eco del Comercio*, 30 May 1848, 2.

101. Félix Mendarte, *Invitación a una polémica entre los que juzgan ilícitos los jiros que la Sociedad Mercantil de la Caja de Ahorro de esta Ciudad* (Orizaba, 1840), and his *Resultado de la invitación que hice en el número 1 a una polémica* (Orizaba, 1841); "Cajas de Ahorro," *Siglo XIX*, 9 June 1848, 4.

The director spoke to his audience in the same civic and religious terms they used in daily life.

Regional Fairs

Nearly all of Mexico's fourteen regional fairs were celebrated between late September and early February; each lasted for a week. The one in held in San Juan de Lagos (Jalisco) in mid-December was the largest, attracting some 40,000 buyers and sellers. Smaller fairs such as the one held in the town of Amecameca (Mexico) drew about 10,000 persons. Peddlers, itinerant salesmen, and retailers from each region flocked to these fairs to buy foreign imports, almost all of them contraband goods, at reduced prices; foreign wholesalers "dumped" their unsold stock at these fairs.[102] Domestic producers also attended these fairs with their goods, including rough woolens, vegetable dyes, livestock, and so on:

> From Chihuahua came wagons large as houses, carrying cotton, leather and silver bars; they were so heavy that each one was pulled by ten or twelve mules. Walking alongside them were the drivers . . . all of them looked alike: bearded faces; thigh-high leather boots; and waists covered with big cartridge belts, guns and knives. . . . The wagons from New Mexico were surrounded by herds of white-fleeced, black-headed sheep. From Texas came wagons loaded with tile, tools and farm implements; and from Tamaulipas came mules . . . to be sold [at the fair]. . . .[103]

According to the most reliable estimates, a single wholesaler in the 1840s at the San Juan Fair transacted a total of 300,000 pesos worth in goods and credit.[104]

Nearly 40 percent of all foreign goods sold in fairs had been smuggled into Mexico as contraband (with no import taxes) and circulated in the "underground economy." The country's small businessmen relied on the black market, and fairs were its central institution:

> In large towns there are merchants of ample means, who can visit the capital of each district or ports on the coast and purchase whatever they need for their stores; but not everyone has the money to finance or the local contacts needed to undertake these long, costly trips. . . . Whole-

102. Juan Nepomuceno Almonte, *Guía de forasteros y repertorio de conocimientos útiles* (Mexico City, 1852), 409; J. M. Lares, "Ferias Anuales," *Calendario para 1844* (Mexico City, 1844), 71–72; Moisés González Navarro, *Anatomía del Poder en México* (Mexico City: El Colegio de México, 1977), 322–23.

103. Manuel Payno, *Artículos y narraciones* (Mexico City: Universidad Nacional Autónoma de México, 1945), 178–79.

104. Anonymous [Barrister Forbes], *A Trip to Mexico or Recollections on a Ten-Month's Ramble in 1849–1850* (London, 1851), 110.

salers, artisans and agriculturalists also need these fairs to sell whatever merchandise they have not been able to sell in their own region. The feria . . . is today the one place where they all go to bid on these goods. . . .[105]

These fairs generated as much, if not more, wealth than the economic sectors that were "taxed" by the state. Government officials tried to tax these fairs by relocating them to towns where they could monitor business transactions; during the 1840s they tried to move the San Lagos fair from Jalisco to Veracruz, where the state had a large and well-trained force of customs officials. Jalisco's residents and business community resisted and prevented the move.

In contrast to other types of underground economies, regional fairs attracted more or less the same buyers and sellers year after year, permitting the development of a loosely structured network among them. Merchants spent the first few days of the fair exchanging information on each other's business practices.[106] Anyone who had violated business norms during the previous fair was approached with caution or, in the case of repeated offenders, ostracized. At the end of each day, buyers and sellers spent the evening drinking, gambling, dancing, and promenading with their families and in each other's company:[107]

These gatherings provide citizens an opportunity . . . to make new acquaintances and renew old friendships. The polite and uncouth come together here and in doing so expose each other's virtues and vices. . . . The haughty acquires modesty, the greedy scoundrel become generous. These fairs are lifting the barriers that had led us to focus on appearances rather than on our true selves.[108]

During the off season, business partners often visited each other on the way to or from selling stock. Hawkers, peddlers, and shopkeepers were linked together in a loose and extensive network, enabling them to practice civic-mindedness at a time when the economic field remained very corrupt and unstable. These ties prepared the way for the development of regional and larger markets.

---

105. "Feria de San Juan," *Siglo XIX*, 23 November 1843, 2.
106. Heath, "British Merchants," 261–90; and John Mayo, "English Commercial Houses on Mexico's West Coast, 1821–1867," *Ibero-Amerikanisches Archiv* 22, no. 1 (1966): 173–90.
107. "Feria de San Juan," *Siglo XIX*, 23 November 1843, 3; "Feria en León," *Siglo XIX*, 8 February 1852, 4; "Feria en Huejutla," *Siglo XIX*, 1 November 1850, 4; "Gran Feria en la Ciudad de Iguala de Iturbide," *Siglo XIX*, 18 November 1851, 3; "La Feria de Linares," *Siglo XIX*, 6 January 1854, 3; and R. H. Mason, *Pictures of Life in Mexico*, vol. 2 (London, 1852), 18–20.
108. "San Agustín de las Cuevas," *Siglo XIX*, 14 May 1842, 2.

CHAPTER 6

Republic without Citizens: Peruvian Civil and Economic Society

During the first half of the nineteenth century, Peruvian civil and economic society remained relatively flat and barren. In contrast to Mexico, the anticolonial movements that had swept Peru in the 1820s had failed to convince citizens that they were rational adults capable of organizing associations, leaving them without civic and democratic traditions on which to build. In contrast to Mexicans, the overwhelming majority of Peruvians remained attached to their old authoritarian habits. Peruvians had achieved independence, but the majority of them continued to conceive of each other as colonial subjects rather than democratic citizens.

Socio-institutional Structures

The public landscape in Peru during the first half of the century saw the creation of about two dozen new associations, the majority appearing toward mid-century, as indicated in figure 6.1—relatively late in comparison to the Mexican case.[1]

Public life in Peru was not only feeble. The few associations that existed were thinly distributed across public life, making each field relatively weak and vulnerable to outside influences from the state (including the army), the Catholic Church, and the market.[2] The most important forms of asso-

1. The data in all the tables and maps in this chapter are from Carlos A. Forment, "Databank on Associative Life in Nineteenth-Century Peru" (Unpublished working document, Princeton University, 1997). The fifty-eight charitable-welfare groups listed in Juan Manuel Pasquel, *Exposición que hace la Junta Permanente a los Señores de la Sociedad de Beneficencia* (Lima, 1847) and the Sociedad de Beneficencia Pública, *Razón que da al Público la Sociedad . . .* (Lima, 1828) were in fact nonexistent.

2. There were a total of 5 mutual-aid societies, 4 community development groups, 4 literary associations, and 3 professional associations.

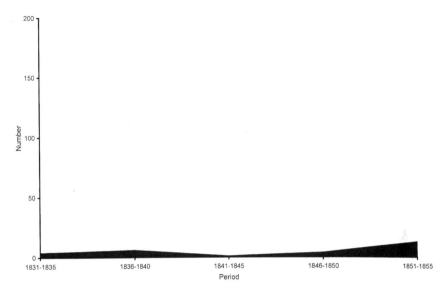

Figure 6.1 New Civic and Economic Associations, 1831–1855

ciative life in Peru were vestiges from the colonial past. Guilds of artisans and merchants, along with religious confraternities, continued to occupy a central place in public life, having survived the social chaos, economic debacle, and military violence brought on by the wars of independence.

Public life in postcolonial Peru was moribund from the outset and would remain so throughout this period because of the countless civil wars and foreign invasions that ravaged the country. Regional commanders in the state's factionalized army, sometimes alone and other times in alliance with roving bands of semi-bandit–guerrilla groups, would often leave their barracks and march their troops across the country, pillaging and capturing one provincial town after another before finally encircling and laying siege to Lima, the capital. The Bolivian and Chilean armies invaded and occupied Peru at different times between 1836 and 1841, causing further damage to public life.

Decades of civil and international warfare compelled the majority of Peruvians to retreat indoors and seek refuge in the privacy of their homes among family members and friends. In 1850, the editors of *El Progreso,* one of Lima's leading daily newspapers, described public life in the country in these terms:

> our nation remains to this day averse to becoming involved in public affairs, on account of the bitter betrayals it has suffered over the years due to the many outbreaks of revolutionary [violence] that have swept our

country. Our current aversion [to public affairs] is compounded by our habits dating back to the *ancien regime* [when we were not allowed to participate in managing our affairs]. The needs of modern society, however, will remain unmet if we continue to be divided; we must unite and attend to the public good. . . .[3]

Military violence made it increasingly difficult for associative life to emerge anywhere prior to mid-century. Furthermore, because the public landscape remained relatively barren and devoid of voluntary groups, the boundaries between civilian and military life remained blurry. Citizens and soldiers intruded in each other's affairs, making daily life nasty, brutish, and short.

Associative Practices in Civil Society

Civil society was populated mainly by associations from the colonial past, with artisans guilds and religious confraternities playing a major role in daily life in the country's capital, Lima, and in the provinces.

Artisan Guilds and Plebeian Sociability

Artisan guilds were socio-institutional remnants from the colonial past, and although they had successfully transplanted themselves into republican soil, they did not adapt well to postcolonial society.

In the mid-1830s, Lima had the largest number of guilds (45), followed by Huancayo (34), Arequipa (27), and Cuzco (16). The guilds provided employment to a significant number of artisans and plebeian groups in these major cities.[4] In contrast to those in western Europe, Lima's guilds employed artisans and nonskilled workers, and even petty thieves and hardened criminals. Instead of closed corporate bodies composed of skilled craftsmen, Peruvian guilds were socially inclusive and were used by marginalized groups to gain entry into civil society. Peru-

3. "Gobierno Civil," *El Progreso,* 2 November 1850, 5–6. Also see "Gobierno Civil," *El Progreso,* 13 November 1850, 5–6.
4. Raúl Rivera Serna, "Aspectos de la economía durante el primer gobierno del Mariscal Don Agustín Gamarra," *Revista Histórica* 24 (1959): 400–439; Paul Gootenberg, "Artisans and Merchants: The Making of an Open Economy in Lima, Peru, 1830–1860," (Master's thesis, Oxford University, 1981), 230–31; Paul Gootenberg, *Imagining Development: Economic Ideas in Peru's "Fictitious Prosperity of Guano," 1840–1880* (Berkeley: University of California Press, 1992), 67, 338; Thomas Kruggeler, "Unreliable Drunkards or Honorable Citizens: Artisans in Search of Their Place in Cuzco Society, 1825–1930" (Ph.D. dissertation, University of Illinois, 1993), 29, 41–45; Sarah Chambers, "The Many Shades of the White City: Urban Culture and Society in Arequipa, Peru: 1780–1854" (Ph.D. dissertation, University of Wisconsin-Madison, 1992), 99, 121, 125. Lima and Arequipa's workshops employed 11 percent and 20 percent of the local population, respectively; Cuzco and Puno's guilds included 5 percent and 3percent of all skilled workers, respectively.

vian artisans, in contrast to the French, as studied by William Sewell Jr., did not develop strong ties, a common identity, or a shared vocabulary.[5] Peruvian artisans were identified less with their guilds than with their neighborhoods.

Guilds were one of the few arenas were interethnic and interracial friendships were forged with any degree of regularity; in this way they contributed to the desegregation of public life. In Lima, a small percentage of slaves worked in guilds, which enabled them to earn a "daily wage"; they would turn a portion of their earnings over to their masters and use the rest to buy their freedom and the manumission of family members.[6] The opportunity of earning a salary, learning a skill, working far away from their master, and having daily contact with citizens had a transformative effect on the slaves, their family members, and other slaves living in the same barracks. Once the slaves had gained freedom, workshop owners sometimes retained them, increasing the ranks of blacks in the artisan sector, especially among coachmakers, where they became the majority.[7]

The same was true in other cities throughout the country. In Cuzco, mixed-bloods accounted for 74 percent of all skilled workers; indigenous peoples (22 percent) and whites (4 percent) worked alongside them, making these workshops racially and ethnically mixed, even if not in proportion to the social composition of the town. Arequipa's guilds were also integrated, with mixed-bloods the overwhelming majority, a reflection of the socio-ethnic composition of the city.[8] Civic ties in these guilds softened racial, ethnic, and national differences among plebeians, by far the most divided group in the country, providing them a place in which to meet as social equals.[9]

Artisan guilds in Lima and elsewhere were socially inclusive and egalitarian, but their governance structure was not. Master artisans made all decisions in an arbitrary and unilateral manner, without consulting even their most skilled workers, domestic or foreign. This pattern of governance reproduced the same "command-obedience" model that prevailed

---

5. William H. Sewell Jr., *Work and Revolution in France: The Language of Labor from the Old Regime to 1848* (New York: Cambridge University Press, 1981).

6. Carlos Aguirre, *Agentes de su propia libertad: Los esclavos de Lima y la desintegración de la esclavitud* (Lima: Pontífica Unviersidad Católica del Perú, 1993), 37–39, 76–80, 127–30, 138–48 estimates that between 5 and 8 percent of Lima's slaves labored in guilds. Also see Christine Hunefeldt, *Paying the Price of Freedom: Family and Labor among Lima's Slaves, 1800–1854* (Berkeley: University of California Press, 1994), 37–39, 63–65, 68–69.

7. Hunefeldt, *Price of Freedom*, 108.

8. Kruggeler, "Unreliable Drunkards," 45–46; Chambers, "Many Shades," 99, 141–42, 181, 189–90, 196.

9. Alberto Flores Galindo, "Los rostros de la plebe," *Revista Andina* 1, no. 2 (December 1983): 338; Hunefeldt, *Price of Freedom*, 18, 187–89; Aguirre, *Agentes*, 163; Jorge Basadre, *Historia de la República del Perú*, vol. 2 (Lima: Ediciones Historia, 1961), 563.

during the colonial period between the elite and non-elite, and it also made
it even more difficult for master artisans to negotiate among themselves.
They had become accustomed to imposing their will on those around them
and this was reflected in the way they made and broke agreements with
each other. In the late 1840s, when government officials began dissolving
guilds, the bakers were unable to put up any resistance. The owners were
too factionalized and unaccustomed to negotiating with each other to be
able to organize a coalition to defend themselves against the state.[10]

Artisan guilds played a major role in disciplining plebeian groups and
protecting property rights.[11] Peruvian artisans were "sandwiched between
a white elite and a frightfully dark-skinned populace whom they helped
to contain . . . through work routines and regulations."[12] More than half
of all breadmakers in Lima, for example, were convicted criminals. Petty
thieves, hardened criminals, and skilled artisans worked side by side, a
mixture that had a corrosive effect on the social and moral life of the
artisans:

> A chaotic and unregulated relationship developed between master arti-
> sans and their journeyman, apprentices and peons, [a problem that was]
> continuously alluded to by the artisans and political elite alike as [one
> of the] . . . major reasons for the [decline] . . . in local manufacturing.
> This crisis of excessive democratization led to several attempts to recre-
> ate the colonial hierarchical order within workshops.[13]

Social inclusion undermined authority, making the guilds ever more egalitarian but also undermining their own socio-institutional foundations,
making them ever more fragile and consequently vulnerable to the recurrent downturns that afflicted the domestic sector of the economy. Their
disappearance from public life deprived citizens from various racial and
ethnic backgrounds of a point of entry into public life.

Lima's guilds were devastated by downturns in the economy, but those
in Cuzco and Arequipa were unaffected. Between 1837 and 1847, Lima's
guilds lost control of 30 percent of their share of the market and were
forced to cut back radically the number of entry-level positions, leaving
workshops without many apprentices, turning away the next generation

10. "Monopolio del pan," *El Comercio*, 13 July 1842, 2; "Panaderos," *El Comercio*,
21 July 1842, 2; "Panaderos en contienda," *El Comercio*, 18 March 1842, 2; "Señores Editores," *El Comercio*, 28 June 1842, 2; "Los artesanos," *El Comercio*, 20 October 1849, 2.
11. Gootenberg, *Imagining Development*, 67, 338; Gootenberg, "Merchants, Foreigners and the State" (Ph.D. dissertation, University of Chicago, 1985), 142, 168.
12. Gootenberg, *Imagining Development*, 32, 338.
13. Gootenberg, "Artisans and Merchants," 183.

of aspiring artisans and forcing them to work in unskilled, menial jobs, as water-carriers, street cleaners, domestics, and the like. But the majority were not so fortunate: many were left unemployed and made a living as bandits or thieves.[14] According to Manuel Atanasio Fuentes, the country's first census taker, in the mid-1850s one out of every fifteen adult males in Lima was without a job.[15] The decline of guilds transformed Lima's artisans into outcasts. The majority of them migrated from guilds to neighborhood taverns, urban promenades, and plazas, turning them into centers of plebeian life.

Cuzco and Arequipa's guilds survived the crisis. Workshops in these cities were family-run, with the head of each household serving as master and his children and wife, plus one or two apprentices, laboring as journeymen. The exact number and social composition of each workshop depended on economic conditions. During downturns, the master cut back on the number of apprentices and worked only with family members; in boom times he rehired them. More than half of those who worked in workshops continued to work their family plots, enabling them to buffer themselves even during hard times.[16] In Arequipa too artisans fused family and work, and labored in both workshops and farms. In addition, the artisans in Arequipa, unlike artisans elsewhere, were jacks-of-all-trades and refused to specialize in any one task, thereby increasing their chances of finding employment during lean periods.[17] Artisan life in Cuzco and Arequipa was far more flexible than in Lima, enabling local residents to occupy a place in civil society at a time when their counterparts in the capital were losing theirs.

Peruvian guilds democratized civic ties and provided outcast groups with a stable niche in civic life, making public life much more racially and ethnically integrated, but in the process the plebeian groups that were forming were also undermining the moral authority inside these associa-

---

14. Manuel Atanasio Fuentes, *Estadística general de Lima* (Lima, 1866), 153, 164–68, 209–11, 609–11, 66. Paul Gootenberg (*Imagining Development*, 32–33, 35, 67; and *Between Silver and Guano: Commercial Policy and the State in Postindependence Peru* (Princeton, N.J.: Princeton University Press, 1989), 49–50 argues that real production grew but only slightly.

15. Fuentes, *Estadística general de Lima*, 164–68; 209–11; 609–11. Gootenberg, *Between Silver and Guano*, 165, and Aguirre, *Agentes*, 30–31, 55–60, 135–48 discuss these figures.

16. Kruggeler, "Unreliable Drunkards," 15–17, 70–111. Cuzco's guilds had been organized after independence, but they were weak and incapable of regulating production.

17. Betford Betalleluz, "Fiscalidad, tierra y mercado: Las comunidades indígenas de Arequipa, 1825–1850," in *Tradición y Modernidad en los Andes*, ed. Henrique Urbano (Cuzco, 1992), 154; Chambers, "Many Shades," 125–35, 155.

tions.[18] When they finally disappeared from the public landscape, these colonial associations left civil society all the more barren.

Religious Field

Religious confraternities provided urban blacks and indigenous peoples in the countryside a degree of civic autonomy and social recognition in public life.

Confraternities and Urban Blacks

In the early 1840s, Lima had about twenty confraternities, a small fraction of the number that existed during the late colonial period, and although they were by now in crisis and on the decline, they continued to play a role, even if a subsidiary one, in the emancipation of slaves.[19] Eyewitness accounts from this period confirm the importance these associations had for blacks:

> In the suburbs of San Lázaro, the confraternities or clubs belonging to different . . . African nations . . . assemble in an orderly manner, usually on Sunday afternoons; and if any member of one of their royal families happen to be in the city, they are dubbed King and Queen by whichever confraternity is holding its meeting on that particular day. . . . The walls of these places . . . are decorated with pictures of members from their royal family.[20]

On Sundays, the day of rest in the Catholic calendar, slaves were granted permission by their masters to visit the district of San Lázaro in Lima, to attend the meetings and events sponsored by their own confraternities. These associations had their own club house, which they owned or rented and paid for from their common fund, with membership dues.

These associations seldom practiced self-rule, nor did they promote social equality. In fact, nearly all of them adhered to monarchical principles, complete with a crowned king and queen and their "royal court," all of whom were themselves slaves. Peruvian blacks had lost whatever faith they had in democratic rule. None of the presidents who came to power prior to mid-century had kept his promise of emancipating slaves who had served in the military. Blacks continued to be considered "pri-

18. Manuel Atanasio Fuentes, *Guía descriptiva, administrativa, judicial y de domicilio de Lima* (Lima, 1861), 227–28; Galindo, "Los rostros de la plebe," 336–37.

19. José María Córdova y Urrutia, *Estadística histórica, geográfica, industrial y comercial de los pueblos que componen las provincias del departamento de Lima* (Lima, 1839), 161; Fuentes, *Estadística general*, 83, 397–430; "Cofradías," *El Comercio*, 26 March 1845, 2; "Cofradías," *El Comercio*, 3 September 1845, 2.

20. William Bennett Stevenson, "Memorias de . . . sobre las campañas de San Martín y Cochrane en el Perú," in *Colección Documental de la Independencia del Perú* 27, no. 3 (1971): 168–70.

vate property" even though Peru was now a sovereign republic composed of citizens.[21] For blacks, one reason monarchy remained an attractive form of life was that it provided them an opportunity to regain their sense of self-worth and act with dignity and decorum. Meetings were extremely ritualized. Members were required to adhere to local etiquette, although outside the group, especially in the presence of their white masters, they often smoked, carried on, and were impolite in other ways.

Disgruntled slaves and masters relied on confraternities to mediate and resolve their differences, since this was a cheaper and quicker way than by presenting formal charges against each other in front of a local judge in his courtroom.[22] In order to continue serving this function, the confraternities had to be trusted by both master and slave, which is why the officers in charge of resolving disputes had to be somewhat balanced and impartial in their judgments. Cases were discussed thoroughly, with the two sides presenting whatever evidence they had in support of their claim. If neither side could persuade the other or if the official in charge of the case remained undecided, then he encouraged them to part ways and assisted them by getting master and slave to agree on the price of the latter.[23] Confraternities used funds from their own treasury to buy the slave's freedom in such cases. Slaves who were manumitted in this way remained bonded to the confraternity until they had repaid their debt.[24] Confraternities were one of the few places where masters and slaves encountered each other as "near equals," and contributed to rearranging authority relations between them in other domains of public life. Once a slave had accused his master of acting arbitrarily and brought him to be judged before a confraternity official, the experience marked them and all those who heard about it, making everyone aware of the power of words. These exchanges were not, clearly, "ideal speech situations," but they provided slaves with a sense of justice.[25]

Confraternities provided slaves with loans and credit in order to purchase their freedom, but if the slaves were unable to repay their debt, then they worked for the group until they had done so. At first glance this arrangement may seem overly commercial and based on market principles,

21. Peter Blanchard, *Slavery and Abolition in Early Republican Peru* (Wilmington, Del.: Scholarly Resources, 1992), 8–9; Aguirre, *Agentes,* 10–40; *El Comercio,* 25 April 1844, 2; *El Comercio,* 17 February 1844, 2; Basadre, *Historia de la República del Perú,* 2.554–56.
22. Slave owners preferred presenting their complaints in front of confraternities rather than in the state's court system, the "Defensores de Menores," who usually ruled on behalf of slaves.
23. Hunefeldt, *Price of Freedom,* 20, 170–79.
24. Max Radiquet, *Lima y la sociedad Peruana,* trans. Catalina Recavarrón (Lima: Biblioteca Nacional del Perú, 1971), 77.
25. Aguirre, *Agentes,* 197.

but in fact it was driven mainly by social honor.[26] Lending and borrowing money was for them an issue of personal dignity and pride, and not
just a market transaction. Blacks in the confraternity relied on each other
to find lenient masters, marriage partners, and, after they were free, affordable housing and stable employment. Confraternities served as a bridge
between the world of slavery and that of freedom; they constituted one of
the most important routes blacks used to enter civil society. Most of the
surgeons, barbers, phlebotomists, and dentists in Lima had been slaves.[27]
Confraternities contributed to improving the civic status of blacks, with
women playing a key role in securing the money and buying manumission
for their kinsmen.[28] These groups were so successful at emancipating
blacks that once the majority had been emancipated, there was little reason for confraternities to remain. Their disappearance was in part provoked by manumission. In contrast to Cuba and Argentina, where free
blacks went on to create a new set of groups, Afro-Peruvians did not develop alternate forms of associative life during the second half of the nineteenth century.

Confraternities and Rural Peoples

Across the hinterlands, religious confraternities were the most vital form
of associative life, especially among indigenous peoples. They fulfilled a
variety of needs, from religious to financial, and contributed to the creation and expansion of civic ties. The number of confraternities across the
countryside probably had changed very little since the colonial period,
judging from a large region in the state of Piura in the far north, the only
place for which reliable estimates are available. The area studied had a
total of seventeen communities, each of which had an average number of
2,000 residents, and a total of 105 confraternities. According to my calculations, the number of members in each confraternity varied considerably,
with 65 percent of them having at least 300 affiliates, and the remaining
35 percent no fewer than 200.[29] These averages cannot be generalized to

26. Hunefeldt, *Price of Freedom,* 102–3; William Bennett Stevenson, *Historical and
Descriptive Narrative of Twenty Years in South America,* vol. 1 (London, 1829), 306–7;
Aguirre, *Agentes,* 178.

27. Fuentes, *Estadística general,* 183; Pablo E. Pérez Mallain, "Profesiones y Oficios de
Lima en 1850," *Anuario de estudios americanos* 37 (1980): 191–233, includes an official
report by the French consul, Félix Lettelier, in which he notes the role of blacks as health
professionals. Also see Juan Jacobo de Tschudi, *Testimonio del Perú, 1838–1842,* trans.
Elsa de Sagasti (Lima: n.p., 1966), 118; and Archibald Smith, *Peru as It Is: A Residence in
Lima and Other Parts of the Peruvian Republic,* vol. 1 (London, 1839), 178–80.

28. Aguirre (*Agentes,* 214–19, 230–34) and Hunefeldt (*Price of Freedom,* 102, 169–
70) concur.

29. Olinda Celestino, "Cofradía: Continuidad y transformación de la sociedad andina,"
Allpanchis 17, no. 20 (1982): 147–66, provides a list of confraternities for the year 1795,
the last time a census was taken. Florencia Mallón, *The Defense of Community in Peru's*

any other part of the country; however, it is safe to say that associative life in the Central Highlands, around Junín, and in the state of Arequipa in the south was relatively well-developed.

The principal aim of these confraternities was to bring people together to celebrate the Catholic liturgical and ritual calendar, to venerate its "patron saints," and to finance all related activities, including the fees charged by parish priests for performing these and other religious services. Confraternities drew their income from a variety of sources: the sale and/or rental of single rooms or family-sized dwellings; the operation of *pulpería* stores, warehouses, and milling stations; cultivation of plots of farmland; and breeding and sale of livestock; in addition to water and grazing rights. Collective ownership of these properties and trusteeship over the income generated by them made it possible for these associations to become financially solvent, in spite of the commercial crisis and economic depression that still afflicted much of the countryside.[30] Moreover, because members donated their labor, taking turns working for the association and attending to its rural and urban properties, the expenses for the various enterprises were low, and the profit earned on them was consequently high. In return, confraternities made available a portion of their capital to their most loyal members in the form of property, loans, and credit, thereby improving their life chances.[31]

Governance in these confraternities was not too different from the colonial past, although many of them had become autonomous and independent from the church, undermining the spiritual and social authority of priests and thereby contributing to the spread of civic egalitarianism across the countryside. Members still paid annual dues to the association, entitling the head of each family to nominate, vote, and run for office; nearly all male members held office two or three times in their adult life. Elections were competitive and often accompanied by petty graft and corruption, itself an indication that members were indeed interested in matters of governance. Most elections were decided on a candidate's capacity to forge broad-based alliances between families from different ethnic, racial, and occupational backgrounds, to venerate and service the same

Central Highlands (Princeton, N.J.: Princeton University Press, 1983), 34, has data on a few other confraternities. See George Kubler, *The Indian Caste of Peru, 1795–1940: A Population Study Based upon Tax Records and Census Reports* (Washington, D.C.: U.S. Government Printing Office, 1952) for size of population for these districts.

30. Celestino, "Cofradía," 149–53, 156–63; and Mallón, *Defense of Community*, 34, provide an inventory of the wealth and resources owned by more than 50 confraternities.

31. Olinda Celestino and Albert Meyers, *Las cofradías en el Perú: Región central* (Frankfurt: K. D. Vervvert, 1981), 184–87; Celestino, "Cofradías," 154–61; Alejandro Diez Hurtado, *Fiestas y cofradías: Asociaciones religiosas e integración en la historia de la comunidad de Sechura* (Piura: Centro de Investigación y Promoción del Campesinado, 1992), 184.

set of patron saints. Saint worship, in other words, encouraged the development of civic relations among rural peoples.[32] These associations were also becoming increasingly autonomous from the church. For example, many of the confraternities of Sechura (Piura), in the far north, had severed their institutional ties to the church, making it impossible for priests to play a decisive role in elections and to control their financial records. Members also erected "devotional shrines" (*capillas*) outside the church, further undermining the religious authority of priests.[33] Popular religiosity flourished in these communities, making social relations between churchmen and rural peoples increasingly egalitarian and civic. Confraternities were rooted in local forms of life, strengthening subnational identities in defiance against those imposed on them by the Catholic church and the national government.

In rural areas, associations with the most developed civic ties were the most financially successful and the most socially cohesive; those with weaker civic ties were also weaker financially and socially. Confraternities that were ethnically and racially pluralistic tended also to be economically diversified (with investments in urban real estate, agriculture, commerce, and so on); those that were homogeneous tended to invest most of their money in a single economic sector. One of the advantages of drawing income from different sources was that the association was consequently able to shift its investment from one sector to another to insulate itself from economic downturns. In this part of Peru, ethnic diversity, economic diversification, and financial stability went together and contributed to the success of religious confraternities. Geographical location was one of the factors that shaped this relationship. The most ethnically diverse groups were located midway between indigenous and mestizo communities and drew members from both. But income was not the only resource accruing to these ethnically mixed associations; they were also the most cohesive. Because each ethnic group venerated its own patron saint, the most diverse association had to render homage to a great many saints, providing members an opportunity to mingle. In Sechura, the confraternities sponsored no fewer than forty-five celebrations in 1846:

> confraternities . . . composed of indigenes and mestizos . . . were generally egalitarian. [In these confraternities, in spite of the racial domination that exists in the region], mestizos did not monopolize the representation [of saints]. It might very well be that the strong showing of indigenous peoples in these symbolic representations, along with the

32. Hurtado, *Fiestas y cofradías*, 154, 160–68, 176.
33. Hurtado, *Fiestas y cofradías*, 153, 166, 169, 175–76; Celestino, "Cofradías," 151.

sizeable patrimony they had turned over to the confraternity . . . [might have influenced matters].[34]

Partaking in each other's celebrations enabled them to blur socio-ethnic boundaries and to become more tolerant.[35]

In the countryside, geographical dispersion and social isolation made it difficult for families to forge stable and lasting relationships with each other. Rural life, inside indigenous villages (*ayllus*) and outside of them, among small farmers as well as tenant workers, was organized around the family. Religious confraternities brought families together, enabling them to forge ties with each other. By the mid-1850s, the term *ayllu,* Quechua for kinship, which indigenous villagers used to describe social life, was displaced by the term *cofradía,* according to the historical anthropologist Alejandro Diez Hurtado. Associative relations eclipsed familial ties even within communal villages where the latter had been strongest.[36] Confraternities provided rural peoples a place to forge "fictive kinship" with each other, paving the way for the spread of civic relations, especially in rural Arequipa and in the Central Highlands, around Junín. Rural peoples used these fictive relations to shuttle to and from nearby urban centers but without losing their social place in their own communities, blurring the age-old distinction between "resident" (*originario*) and "foreigner" (*forastero*).

Social ties based on fictive kinship were relaxed and stretched by those who formed part of these networks, paving the way for the rise of civic relations across much of the countryside. In certain parts of the country, confraternities uncoupled kinship ties from community relations, paving the way for the proliferation of individual farming plots in the region. Changes in land-tenure patterns altered the character of moral authority in the countryside. Manuel Burga, a leading scholar of rural life, has summarized the change in this way: "by the mid-nineteenth century, a new type of rural community had emerged, based on voluntary associations among peasant families." [37] Confraternities competed against and in many places won over the very indigenous villages that had originally given them life, preparing the way for the spread of civic forms of life.

Confraternities enlarged the social horizon of families and enriched civic life in important ways, but the associative ties resulting from them often had the opposite effect. Instead of decompressing and pacifying

34. Celestino, "Cofradías," 152.

35. Celestino, "Cofradías," 150–52; Hurtado, *Fiestas y cofradías,* 172–83; 187–89.

36. Hurtado, *Fiestas y cofradías,* 184; Celestino and Meyers, *Cofradías en el Perú,* 186; Carlos Contreras, "Estado republicano y tributo en la Sierra Central en la post-independencia," *Histórica* 13, no. 1 (July 1989): 24.

37. Manuel Burga, "Rasgos fundamentales de la historia agraria Peruana," in *La historia agraria,* ed. M. Burga (Chiclayo: Universidad de Chiclayo, 1995), 32–34.

social life, it often produced anti-civic practices. In the words of Luis Miguel Glave,

> the ire was all the worse and the arguments impossible to resolve when families were pitted against each other [in disputes over property boundaries and the like] than when they were among individuals who only had commercial ties with each other.[38]

Confraternities generated civic ties among rural peoples, but they also escalated petty struggles into bloody, hateful, and longstanding feuds, drawing in extended families and their friends, contributing to the spread of anti-civic forms of life. Florencia Mallón, a scholar who has done much work on the Central Highlands around Junín, provides a fine analysis of how this happened:

> Channeling conflict through community struggles was a double-edged sword . . . for it could transform individual problems between *comuneros* (villagers) into community issues. Thus the inevitable disagreements between villagers—land boundaries, overlapping rights to common pastures, access to water, the trampling of one community's fields by another's animals—fed into the innumerable petty rivalries between individuals, creating violent, endemic competition. And the tales of struggles between neighboring communities were a common thread woven into the very fabric of village history.[39]

These practices shaped the development of civil society across the countryside in complex and contradictory ways.

Confraternities democratized social and property relations in the countryside, although by the mid-1850s they began unraveling under pressure from external and internal factors. Decades of civil warfare disrupted economic life in the countryside, with all the typical indicators—land values, property rent, commodity prices—pointing downward, even in Jauja, the country's most productive region.[40] This is how George Kubler summarized the results of his decade-long study of tax records:

> Provincial tax collectors in 1842 . . . lamented the disintegration of economic life in the provinces, the moral decay of the citizenry, and the alarming degeneration of the standard of living since 1800. . . . [They] also bemoaned the devastation of the provinces [caused] by republican

---

38. Luis Miguel Glave, *Vida, símbolos y batallas* (Mexico City: Fondo de Cultura Económica, 1992), 206–7.

39. Mallón, *Defense of Community*, 32–33.

40. *El Comercio*, 18 June 1855, 2; Burga, "Rasgos fundamentales," 32–33; Nils Jacobsen, "Liberal Indian Communities" (Unpublished typescript, University of Illinois, 1996), 18–19.

troops, and the decay of domestic markets for provincial produce owing to the flooding of the economy by foreign imports.[41]

Confraternity members no longer had the financial means to contribute to the group's communal celebrations. The wealthiest families paid for them and in doing so undermined their egalitarian character. Rather than having a "leveling" effect and contributing to the redistribution of income, rural confraternities became another way for the privileged elite to reaffirm their economic standing and social status in the community.[42] In the 1860s, the central state ordered the newly organized municipal townships to "nationalize" the wealth of religious confraternities, and to invest this money in building local public schools, hospitals, and roads.[43] Both sets of pressures undermined religious confraternities in both rural and urban areas, depriving the country's most marginalized groups of an important channel for entry into civil society.

Associative Practices in Economic Society

During the first half of the century, Peruvian businessmen often quarreled about protectionism and free trade, but none of them ever considered turning Peru into a market-centered society. In the words of Fernando de Trazegnies,

> The major difference between liberals and conservatives is to be found in the political field. . . . Neither of them could even imagine a market-based, commercialized society devoid of traditional ties, one in which social hierarchies would have been forced to yield to . . . competitive forms of equality. . . . [In] any case, the cultural and economic distance that existed between the indigenous peoples and the elite was simply too great to enable them to consider market forms of egalitarianism [as a viable alternative].[44]

Even Peru's most aggressive businessmen assumed that economic society was embedded in sociopolitical life. They would not have been able to make sense of the work of contemporary economic historians who have imposed on the past an anachronistic conception of markets based on our own experience of them.

41. Kubler, *Indian Caste of Peru*, 40.
42. Hurtado, *Fiestas y cofradías*, 185–86, 192–93.
43. Celestino and Meyers, *Cofradías en el Perú*, 191–97, 200–205; Celestino, "Cofradías," 147–66, suggests that the most successful confraternities transformed themselves into "artisan clubs and cooperatives" rather than waiting passively to become extinguished.
44. Fernando de Trazegnies, *La idea del derecho en el Perú republicano del siglo XIX* (Lima: Pontífica Universidad Católica del Perú, 1980), 46–47.

Associative life in economic society was as flat and barren as it was across civil society. The Merchants' Guild, the only association of importance, continued to exert a powerful influence on business life in the export and domestic sector, although even it was now coming undone.

The Export Sector: Merchants' Guilds and Business Networks

The Merchants' Guild, the most influential association of this period, dating back to the colonial era, played a pivotal role in shaping the practices of just about anyone involved in economic life, from the hundred or so wealthy wholesalers linked to the export sector to the thousands of street hawkers and rural traders in the domestic sector who sold their wares door to door, either on foot or on muleback. Based in Lima, the Guild also had several smaller branches in provincial towns such as Arequipa in the far south, and Trujillo in the far north. To call them branches may in fact be an exaggeration; each was only a two-person operation.

Lima's Guild, comprising between 175 and 200 merchants, included both wealthy wholesalers engaged in the import/export trade and small-scale retailers who focused mostly on domestic trade, with the former twice as wealthy as the latter but not nearly as well-represented in the association. Domestic retailers were in the clear majority, accounting for 80 percent (160) of Guild membership. Wholesalers bought imported merchandise and resold it on credit to retailers, who in turn resold it to street hawkers and peddlers throughout the country, in urban and rural areas.[45] Despite their differences in income and business interests, wholesalers and retailers were not nearly as divided as it might seem. They relied on each other for supplies, customers, and credit, practicing a type of "flexible specialization." The two groups collaborated with each other and often even fused and integrated their firms horizontally and vertically in order to reduce the level of uncertainty and the cost of transacting business between them.[46] Guild members were a socially cohesive group, with the life chances of any one merchant partly dependent on the success or failure of his associates. This is one of the main reasons why the Guild endured for as long as it did, surviving the chaos and devastation brought on by the wars of independence and by decades of incessant civil warfare during the early republic.

Governance in the Guild was not a textbook model of civic democracy, but it was quite egalitarian and participatory, judging from the numerous documents they left behind. Each year the members of the Guild elected a

---

45. Gootenberg, "Merchants, Foreigners and the State," 168–70.
46. Mark Granovetter, "Business Groups," in *The Handbook of Economic Sociology,* ed. Neil Smelser and Richard Swedberg (Princeton, N.J.: Princeton University Press, 1994), 453–75, on flexible specialization, firm integration, and social trust.

board of directors, composed of thirty of the most experienced and committed members, those who had proven to be among the most civic-minded and the most involved in the affairs of the association. Board members selected the association's executive officers. Given the large number of board members, the frequency of elections, and the system of rotating executive officers, most Guild members had an opportunity to experience the duties required of those in office and the demands placed on the rank and file, who were responsible for monitoring their representatives and holding them accountable for their decisions. Judging from the documents left behind by this association, annual elections were somewhat competitive; members circulated petitions, organized protests, and pressured candidates for or against one or another issue. Power and influence were decentralized and distributed more or less evenly, with wholesalers and retailers usually equally represented in the board of directors, the balance changing slightly but not dramatically over time. Guilds' members, admittedly, were divided on a number of issues, but these had less to do with income and specialization than with changes in business opportunities and access to the state—differences which, however important, were kept under control by the civic cohesion among the members of the association.

The various Guilds enrolled only a small percentage of the country's merchants, but because they controlled many of the most important business and credit networks throughout country, their practices had a profound impact on economic life. Their networks originated and were also best developed in Lima, the country's capital and commercial entrepot; in Trujillo, to the north; and in Arequipa, to the south. Commercial ties extended outward to the rest of the country from these three points, along the way linking small and large towns, including Cuzco, a manufacturing center in the Andean highlands, and Junín, an agricultural producing region in the Central highlands, along with mining towns like Cerro del Pasco and Yauli, even further out. Credit and goods circulated between urban-based Guild members and rural nonmembers, producing one long, continuous, and uninterrupted set of transactions, drawing in thousands of businessmen, each of whom was dependent, financially and otherwise, on those adjacent to him in the chain.[47] Conceptually, these networks were pyramid-shaped, with the country's two or three hundred Guild members at the apex, followed by a few thousand regional traders around the trunk, and with twice as many peddlers and hawkers forming the broad base. Social and commercial ties linking Guild members to nonmembers were

---

47. Alberto Flores Galindo, *Aristocracia y Plebe* (San Isidro, Peru: Mosca Azul Editores, 1984), 63, 64–68; Gootenberg, "Merchants, Foreigners and the State," 168–69, 187; and Kruggeler, "Unreliable Drunkards," 53, 78.

almost as dense and complex as those that existed within the association, but the character of these relations was distinctly different. Within the association, Guild members forged intensely civic ties with each other; relationships that extended outside their association, however, were characterized by opportunism and predatory practices, which shaped the economic domain in basic ways.

Non-Guild members—that is, most businessmen situated somewhere across the trunk of the pyramid—closely monitored their business dealings with Guild members, as this was one of the few ways of gaining information and insight about the rapidly changing "business climate" in the economic sector and geographical region in which they operated. In the absence of a banking system and due to the extreme scarcity of liquid capital (currency), the overwhelming majority of business transactions were based on credit and transacted with bills of exchange, backed by personal trust and little more.[48] Goods were exchanged between buyers and sellers on the promise that they would be repaid at a later date; credit, the promise of repayment, is what made this possible. Social trust enabled buyers and sellers to reduce the extremely high levels of uncertainty that existed during the months, sometimes years, between the moment the transaction took place and the time the debt was finally discharged.[49] In this context, suppliers, sellers, and buyers were driven to study carefully the "signaling" practices that took place among them along the length of these networks, as this was the only way of developing effective strategies for maneuvering across the economic terrain, which was deeply marked by decades of crisis and uncertainty.[50]

The Merchants' Guild had "donated" millions of pesos to the colonial and, after independence, the postcolonial state in order to finance its war effort; the Guild lost several more millions to the civil warfare that ravaged Peru from the 1830s to the 1850s. The Guild and its members lost whatever social trust they had in their own government, and also in each other. If institutions refused to discharge their financial obligations, how could one expect individuals to repay their debt?[51] Guild members turned the predatory habits they had acquired from dealing with the Peruvian government on others throughout economic society, contaminating each

48. Alfonso Quiroz, *Domestic and Foreign Finance in Modern Peru, 1850–1950* (Pittsburgh: University of Pittsburgh Press, 1993), and his *Deudas Olvidadas: Instrumentos de crédito en la economía colonial Peruana, 1750–1820* (Lima: Pontífica Universidad Católica del Perú, 1993); Gootenberg, *Between Silver and Guano*. I disagree with their interpretation.

49. Granovetter, "Business Groups," 453–75.

50. Michael Spence, *Market Signaling: Informational Transfers in Hiring and Related Screening Processes* (Cambridge: Harvard University Press, 1974).

51. Quiroz, *Domestic and Foreign Finance*, 16, 20–30.

and every one of their business transactions. Booty capitalism became a way of life for all. In 1858, Manuel Argumaniz Muñoz, a stalwart member of the Guild and a business partner of Zaracondegui and Pedro Gonzales Candamo, two of Lima's most influential merchants, described in detail how his closest associates transacted business with each other:

> Don Pedro Gonzales Candamo had a well-known tactic in Lima's commerce of obtaining all possible gains and guarantees without [expending any] labor or responsibility in capital concerns. . . . Don Julián Zaracondegui . . . wanted absolute control and had no scruples in the managing [of] matters related to his business. . . . [This] is why Señor Candamo usually took a revolver with him on his rare visits to Zaracondegui's office, and Señor Zaracondegui had his always ready; this was the measure of understanding and harmony in which my two partners lived . . . two of the leading persons in Lima's world of trade.[52]

Under conditions of social mistrust, Peruvian entrepreneurs found it reasonable to adopt predatory practices.

Foreign merchants also played an important role in spreading predatory practices throughout the economy. Between the mid-1820s and the late 1840s, there were between twelve and twenty foreign merchant houses in Lima—mostly British, but also French and American—pumping millions of dollars into the country each year in merchandise and credit, mainly through the port of Callao and Lima, and from there across the hinterlands. Smitten by the bug of greed and speculation, foreign merchants were bent on making a quick profit; these merchants were not the type of sober, methodical, austere entrepreneurs who had contributed to the rise of capitalism in the West, the type studied by Max Weber. In the words of the Consul, British investors in Peru were suffering from an excessive

> spirit of speculation . . . the exaggerated descriptions of riches [to be made in this country] . . . has made them import more than what the public needs and is capable of paying.[53]

The spirit of predatory capitalism, not the Protestant ethic, is what motivated and stirred foreign investors. Mesmerized by fanciful, imaginary accounts of fabulous wealth, these businessmen became impulsive, reckless, and prone to commit all types of excesses. Expectations based on symbolic constructions, not supply and demand schedules, drove these entre-

52. Manuel Argumaniz Muñoz, "Memorias inéditas," vol. 3 (Personal Papers, 1858–1868), 5 and 15, quoted in Quiroz, *Domestic and Foreign Finance,* 28.

53. "De Charles Milner Ricketts a George Canning (1826)," in *Gran Bretaña y el Perú: 1826–1919: Informe de los Cónsules Británicos,* vol. 1, ed. Heraclio Bonilla (Lima: Instituto de Estudios Peruanos, 1977), 23.

preneurs to do business in a country they knew very little about.[54] In the words of Belford Hinton Wilson, another British Consul in Peru,

> oversupply produced a necessity of trusting Peruvians without due caution and to such an extent was this system carried on that hardly any other qualification but that of being a native of the interior was demanded . . . [as a result] the goods thus impudently sold on trust were never paid, and no returns could be made them to England.[55]

British houses in Peru, the single largest contingent of foreign investors, lost in a single year no less than 5 million dollars. Instead of investing in legally regulated and crowded markets at home, these foreign merchants invested in Peru because they wanted to be able to make enormous profit in a short time without having to compete with other businessmen and adhere to the laws of the land. Although markets in Peru were relatively open, they were also extremely risky.

Guild members, who were as corrupt as foreign merchants, had their own way of dealing with the foreigners. Charles Milner Ricketts, of the British Consulate, described relations between Peruvian retailers and foreign merchants like this:

> Retailers are provided with a quantity of stock in advance, whose price is fixed in proportion to the risk entailed [in distributing and selling it], paying for it in return only a small fraction of its worth, with the remainder charged to their account. Often, the retailer will sell the first installment of goods for a loss, and with the money made they will then buy additional merchandise but from another foreign house, who offers him a better deal and under improved terms. . . . When they are forced to pay, what they generally do is to "borrow from Peter to pay Paul," or else declare . . . that they simply cannot fulfill their financial obligations, nor is there any law to oblige them to do so. . . . The logical precaution is to not offer a second credit to anyone who has not discharged his debt the first time around . . . but in Peru . . . there is such an inability to honor commitments . . . to deal with each other in good faith, prudence never prevails. . . .[56]

Foreign merchant houses paid dearly for their greed, but they also learned how to read these signals and devise their own set of predatory practices.

Property rights in Peru were rarely protected. In 1850, the French consul in Lima, Félix Lettelier, sent the Ministry of Foreign Affairs in Paris a

---

54. Frank Knight, *Risk, Uncertainty and Profit* (Chicago: University of Chicago Press, 1971).

55. "British Consular Report, 1834," quoted in Gootenberg, "Merchants, Foreigners and the State," 180.

56. "De Charles Milner Ricketts a George Canning, (1826)," 32.

detailed report on job opportunities in Peru; the section on debt collectors included this passage:

> I have no idea how members of this profession make a living. . . . For the past two years, I have not seen a single person arrested for defaulting on their debt. The legislation makes it difficult, if not impossible, for creditors to press charges against debtors.[57]

In the absence of any legal protection, foreign merchants seeking to recover money or merchandise sought assistance from their country's consul in Lima, turning uncollected debts between local retailers and foreign merchants into major diplomatic incidents between the Foreign Minister of Peru; his counterparts in London, Paris, and Madrid; and their local consuls in Lima. In the late 1840s the Peruvian government, under pressure from the British consul, lifted the ban prohibiting foreign merchants from joining the Guild, but in return required them to renounce their citizenship and become Peruvian nationals, a measure designed to prevent foreign consuls from intervening ever again in the domestic affairs of the country.[58] By the early 1850s, foreign merchants controlled the Guild, signaling the beginning of the end for Peru's most important economic association.[59]

The Domestic Sector: Credit Networks

Credit networks among plebeian and rural groups formed a vital part of economic life, and because Peru still did not have a single government-sponsored pawn shop from which individuals could borrow money at affordable rates, as they could in Mexico, they relied on the merchant community and, more importantly, on each other for loans. Lima's peddlers borrowed small sums from Guild members; according to an observer, indigenous peoples were

> active [in commercial pursuits]. . . . Many of them have stores and enjoy credit with the big commercial houses due to their honesty. Most street hawkers who sell staircase railings in the Portal de Botoneros are indians; many of them also work with leather and silver. . . .[60]

Lima's indigenous peoples, along with slaves, often borrowed small sums of money and merchandise on credit from wealthy merchants and estate

57. Mallain, "Profesiones y Oficios," 28–29.
58. Basadre, *Historia de la República del Perú*, 2.546, 835–36, and his "La riqueza territorial y las actividades comerciales e industriales en los primeros años de la República," *Mercurio Peruano* 115 (January 1928): 15–31.
59. Gootenberg, "Merchants, Foreigners and the State," 172.
60. Tschudi, *Testimonio del Perú*, 114.

owners, with the understanding that if they did not discharge their debts in a timely manner they would lose their civic freedom. Plebeian and indigenous peoples were frequently forced by creditors into servitude and peonage.[61] Credit practices were racially coded, compelling non-elite groups to exercise care in their financial dealings, which experience made them increasingly aware of the limits civic life and the meaning of civility. In Arequipa, where commercial life was more egalitarian, plebeians borrowed small sums from various individuals, usually their own peers, rather than from a single wealthy patron, thereby avoiding the risk of becoming indebted and losing their civic freedom. About 43 percent of all outstanding loans registered in Arequipa's notarial archives during the 1840s were for less than 25 pesos; more than 73 percent were for less than 100 pesos.[62] An unpaid debt took on a different meaning when the borrower was a copper-colored plebeian than when he was a fair-skinned elite, reminding both that the economic domain, under the control of Guild members, remained hierarchical and anti-civic.

Decades of civil warfare radicalized economic practices, provoking some of the most successful regional entrepreneurs into subsidizing rival commanders, and contributing (unintentionally) to increasing the social and economic uncertainty that undermined their own business practices. In 1835, the prefect of Arequipa forced the elite to "donate" between 2,000 and 6,000 pesos, money he used to pay for the cost of defending the town; those who refused were accused of sympathizing with the enemy. General Salaverry captured the city despite the "donation," and again extracted money from the elite, this time as retribution for having financed the defeated army. Salaverry's troops pillaged and looted the homes of anyone who resisted.[63] These extreme conditions often led entrepreneurs to adopt the most reasonable course of action, supporting one of the factions in the expectation that they would have to pay commanders only once. Admittedly, there were some entrepreneurs, for example, Cuzco's textile factory owners, who were able to bargain with army generals, supplying them with army uniforms and other basic necessities and demanding in return that neither their factories nor their workers would be attacked or threatened.[64] These alliances permitted Andean mill owners to

61. Hunefeldt, *Price of Freedom,* 170–71.

62. Chambers, "Many Shades," 140–41, 393–97.

63. John Frederick Wibel, "The Evolution of a Regional Community within the Spanish Empire and Peruvian Nation: Arequipa, 1780–1845" (Ph.D. dissertation, Stanford University, 1975), 401–2; Flora Tristán, *Peregrinaciones de una Paria* (Lima: Editorial Cultura Antártida, 1946), 242–57. The urban and rural elite kept its wealth hidden at home in safe boxes, a system that worked reasonably well except during periods of civil war.

64. Charles Walker, "Peasants, Caudillos and the State in Peru: Cuzco in the Transition from Colony to Republic, 1740–1840" (Ph.D. dissertation, University of Chicago, 1992),

transform Cuzco, in the heartland of Quechua-speaking peoples, into one of the country's most dynamic "growth poles," with aspirations of eventually surpassing Lima and Arequipa as a manufacturing center and becoming the center of national life.[65] The demands and exigencies of economic production made the war effort possible, but it also, paradoxically, contributed to taming even the most unruly generals.

Decades of civil warfare left the merchant community in financial ruins and without much sense of civicness among themselves. Arequipa's businessmen, wrote Flora Tristán during her long stay at the home of her uncle, a leading entrepreneur, have "had their fortune taken away from them so many times that they can no longer afford to extend sympathy to anyone, even those in a similar situation."[66] Decades of civil warfare had depleted the reservoir of "sympathy" that had once existed in the business community, transforming the vast majority of its members into egoistic, self-absorbed persons who displayed little concern for public affairs.[67]

Regional Fairs, Business Ethics, and "Jew-Killing"

Market fairs, along with the credit and business networks organized by the Merchants' Guild and reviewed above, influenced economic practices across the hinterlands, but because the buyers and sellers attending these fairs adhered to notions of social reciprocity rather than to less civic ideals, as propagated by the Guild, these regional markets contributed greatly to strengthening local forms of life.

The most important weekly fairs took place in the central highland region and attracted mainly local residents. In the mid-1860s, Antonio Raimondi, a natural scientist, visited Huancayo's fair in the province of Junín and described it like this:

> Huancayo's singularly unique custom is its fair, held each Sunday in the central plaza and the principal thoroughfare, which is attended by almost all the inhabitants from the surrounding region, with some coming as far away as the mountains. At fair-time, Huancayo [sheds its tranquil routine] and becomes surprisingly animated; there is such a congestion of people that . . . the population increases by threefold. . . .[68]

185–87. In Cuzco the owners of the two most important mills, Amancay in the town of Paruro and Lucre in the town of Quispicanchis, provided General Gamarra 84,000 meters of woolen cloth each year, which he desperately needed for his men.

65. Paul Gootenberg, "Origins of Protectionism and Free Trade in Nineteenth-Century Lima," *Journal of Latin American Studies* 14, no. 2 (1982): 329–58.

66. Tristán, *Peregrinaciones de un paria*, 237.

67. Adam Smith, *The Theory of Moral Sentiments* (Indianapolis: Liberty Classics, 1982).

68. Antonio Raimondi, *El Perú: Itinerarios de viajes* (Lima: Imprenta Torres Aguirre, 1929), 10.

Social relations at these fairs between rural peoples and townsmen were short-lived and local in nature, but they were also recurrent and contributed to softening racial and ethnic boundaries in the region and to the development of a distinct regional identity.[69]

Annual fairs were especially important in the Andean south, in the area of Cuzco and Puno, the cultural and social heartland of Peru's indigenous peoples. The Vilque fair, near Lake Titicaca, was perhaps the most important of these. In the 1840s, France's vice consul attended it and left this account:

> they attend from all the nearby communities as well as those from Arequipa, Moquegua and Cuzco, as well as Bolivia and Argentina, in particular from Tucuman. For fifteen days, the population of Vilque, which is only a few hundreds, swells to between ten and twelve thousand.[70]

Artisans, pastoralists, agriculturalists, and merchants from southern Peru, northern Argentina, and southwestern Bolivia attended, speaking Quechua, Aymara, Spanish, or a combination of all three. The Guadalupe fair, also an annual event, attracted more than 20,000 persons, with buyers and sellers transacting no less than 1 million pesos in merchandise, most of the exchanges taking place without paper money.[71] In the course of exchanging goods and extending credit to one another, buyers and sellers forged civic ties that also served to reaffirm their commitment to local forms of life unrelated to those emanating from the coast, which they identified with the predatory practices of fair-skinned creole groups. Contemporary and secondary accounts concur that social relations in regional fairs were relatively civic, although they also served to reaffirm regional and subnational identities and contributed to the further fragmentation of public life.[72]

Plebeian and indigenous groups in urban and rural areas attacked foreign merchants, referring to them as "Jewish" even though the majority were Protestant. A longtime resident of Lima noted that there was widespread

69. See Thomas J. Hutchinson, *Two Years in Peru*, vol. 2 (London, 1873), 191, for a description of Cajamarca's Guadalupe Fair.
70. Eugene de Sartièges and Adolfo de Botmiliau, *Dos viajeros franceses en el Perú republicano* (Lima: Editorial Cultura Antártida), 204.
71. Manuel Burga, *De la encomienda a la hacienda campesina* (Lima: Instituto de Estudios Peruanos, 1976), 200.
72. Sartièges and Botmiliau, *Dos viajeros franceses*, 205–6; Alberto Flores Galindo, *Arequipa y el Sur Andino* (Lima: Editorial Horizonte, 1977), 74; Basadre, *Historia de la República del Perú*, 2.585; Nelson Manrique, *Las guerrillas indígenas en la guerra con Chile* (Lima: Editorial Ital, 1981), 19–22.

fanaticism [in this city] against foreigners . . . especially among the lower classes, specifically, among Blacks and zambos, endangering the personal security of foreigners . . . mainly Englishmen and Frenchmen. . . .[73]

The situation in the provinces was worse. Foreign houses sent their agents to small towns to sell imported goods, but the agents were forced to flee. An English merchant, alarmed at the spread of xenophobia in the provinces, wrote that indigenous peoples are concerned "that if they do not abolish our neighborhoods, then other Englishmen, that is, Jews, will settle [here] after us." [74] In 1842, in the town of San Marcos (Huari), during the Corpus Christi celebration, one of the holiest days in the Catholic calendar, indigenous peoples staged a ritual killing of "a Jew" who had recently moved there, identifying him as an "Anti-Christ" and a spiritual menace to the survival of the community. Foreign businessmen panicked and fled the area on hearing about this incident. By 1845, there were few foreign merchants doing business in the countryside.[75] In the absence of patriotic sentiment, popular religiosity reaffirmed subnational identities and local forms of life.[76]

By the early 1850s, most civil and economic groups in the country were fast unraveling and well on their way to disappearing from the public landscape altogether.

73. Tschudi, *Testimonio del Perú*, 71, 121.
74. Smith, *Peru as It Is*, 1.163.
75. Heinrich Witt, *Diario y Observaciones, 1824–1890* (Lima: Banco Mercantil, 1992), 155.
76. Gootenberg, "Merchants, Foreigners and the State," 220–22.

CHAPTER 7

Losing and Reclaiming Liberty:
Mexican Political Society

The majority of Mexicans who were active in public life were far more inclined to practice democracy in civil than in political society. Citizens continued to live with their backs to the state, a tendency that became even more pronounced after the 1830s with the consolidation of authoritarian rule:

> How can a handful of mean-spirited and capricious politicians rule over 7 million citizens? We complain continuously that they have undermined our government and economy. . . . But as long as we remain inactive in public affairs these officials will continue to rule over us. The majority of citizens despise elections and express contempt for anyone who partakes in them.[1]

The small number of Mexicans who participated in government-centered politics did so by becoming active in voting clubs, municipal life, and rebellions. Although significant, these practices were too short-lived and sporadic to enable citizens to alter their habits in any permanent way. Political life in Mexico remained authoritarian and relatively stunted throughout this period, but even so it was far more developed and dynamic than in Peru, the subject of the next chapter.

Socio-institutional Structures

Between 1826 and 1856, Mexicans organized approximately 123 new political clubs.[2] Eighty percent of them (98) appeared in preparation for the

---

1. "La Mayoría," *Siglo XIX*, 16 October 1848, 3.
2. Unless otherwise indicated, the data in the figures and maps in this chapter are from Carlos A. Forment, "Databank on Associative Life in Nineteenth Century Mexico" (Unpublished working document, Princeton University, 1997).

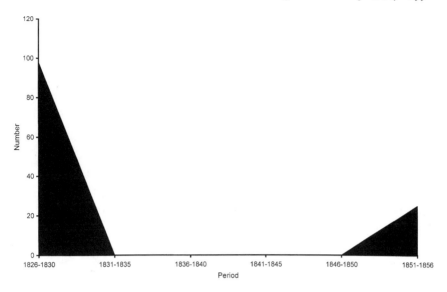

Figure 7.1 New Political Clubs, 1826–1856

1828 presidential election. Between 1830 and the mid-1850s, the author-itarian governments that ruled the country banned all political clubs. The Ayutla Revolution (1854) that toppled President Antonio López de Santa Anna's authoritarian government paved the way for the resurgence of as-sociative life in political society. From 1854 to 1855, Mexicans organized 25 new clubs (fig. 7.1). Newspaper writers from across the ideological spectrum expressed support for them:

> Clubs have enabled us to replace tyranny with liberty. They have pro-vided the government with a way to become acquainted with public opinion, and this is the reason we support them.[3]

In a departure from the practice of the late 1820s, public intellectuals now used neutral terms such as "club" or "association" to describe these groups, rather than "faction" or "secret society."[4] The resurgence of as-sociative life was significant; however, as shown in figure 7.1, the number of clubs remained so small that they did not alter political practices in any lasting way.[5]

Associative life was distributed unevenly in Mexico. Residents of the

3. "Clubs," *El Republicano*, 29 October 1855, 1.
4. "Editorial," *El "mnibus,* 21 November 1855, 2; and "Crónica electoral," *Siglo XIX,* 1 April 1857, 1.
5. I did not find reliable data on the size of these clubs and societies.

Number of clubs

▓	21-30
▥	11-20
☐	1-10
☐	0

1. California
2. Sonora
3. Chihuahua
4. Coahuila
5. Sinaloa
6. Durango
7. Nuevo León
8. Tamaulipas
9. Zacatecas
10. Aguascalientes
11. San Luis Potosí
12. Jalisco
13. Guanajuato
14. Querétaro

15. Hidalgo
16. Tlaxcala
17. Veracruz
18. Colima
19. Michoacán
20. México
21. Distrito Federal
22. Guerrero
23. Morelos
24. Puebla
25. Oaxaca
26. Tabasco
27. Chiapas
28. Yucatán

Map 7.1   Geography of Political Life, 1826–1856

nation's capital accounted for 20 percent of the clubs, the state of Veracruz another 11 percent (map 7.1). Associative life in Guerrero, San Luis Potosí, Querétaro, and other states remained embryonic, although together they accounted for 69 percent of the total. Clubs had not yet surfaced in Aguascalientes, Tlaxcala, and several other states.

Associative Practices in Political Society

Mexicans practiced democratic politics both within and outside the legal channels provided by the regime. From the 1820s to the 1840s, they practiced politics in voting clubs, electoral colleges, and municipal townships.

The authoritarian state then outlawed all three, provoking several major rebellions. In preparation for the war against the United States (1846), residents created local militias, which they used after the war to topple Santa Anna's government in the Ayutla Revolution. Clubs reemerged soon after that.

Voting Clubs and Presidential Elections

The presidential election of 1828, the first in the history of Mexico, was far more inclusive than those held in the United States and England at the time. Almost 70 percent of Mexicans were eligible to vote, including the poor and illiterate.[6] Electoral laws were so inclusive that voting clubs, even those that were against mass suffrage, were compelled to "mobilize large numbers of people from the lower strata of society."[7]

Most voting clubs began as Masonic lodges, but by 1828 they had lost their "patent" and become political associations.[8] The Scots and Yorks, as the two political "parties" were called, had local chapters throughout the country. The latter had twice as many chapters as the former and were also more evenly distributed across the provinces. The Yorks were especially strong in Veracruz and Guerrero; the Scots were strongest in the state of Mexico. The British consul in Mexico City, in a confidential memo written to the Foreign Office in January 1829, reported:

> There is I believe not a town nor village throughout the republic that does not now possess one or more York lodges, according to the size of the population.[9]

The consul's assessment seems inflated, but it is important to recall that there were only a dozen or so cities in the country with populations of 5,000 or more residents.

The Yorks and Scots differed in their social base and political program. Yorks were in favor of decentralizing power, making the legislative branch stronger than the executive, autonomous townships, citizen militias, inclusive suffrage laws, and economic protectionism—stances that defined federalists. The conservative Scots, in contrast, were in favor of centralizing power, granting the executive power over the legislative branch, subordinating local and state governments to the central state, making suffrage laws exclusionary, and opening the economy to foreign investors.

6. Richard Warren, "Vagrants and Citizens: Politics and the Poor in Mexico City, 1830–1836 (Ph.D. dissertation, University of Chicago, 1994), 110–56, 179–80, 186–87.
7. Stanley Green, *The Mexican Republic* (Pittsburgh: University of Pittsburgh Press, 1987), 91.
8. Luis J. Zalce y Rodríguez, *Apuntes para la historia de la masonería en México*, vol. 1 (Mexico City: Editorial Botas, 1950), 63–70.
9. Richard Pakenham, "Letter (13 January 1829)," in Green, *Mexican Republic*, 91.

Although they differed in political outlook, the Yorks and Scots were similar in the way they practiced politics. Monthly dues (1 peso) in most clubs in Mexico and other cities were beyond the reach of most citizens; in the provinces, in contrast, the dues were affordable (5 reales) and the working poor paid based on a "sliding scale." In their meetings, radical Yorks addressed each other as "Indian" and prohibited the use of honorific titles such as "don and "excelencia." [10] Their sense of egalitarianism came across in other ways as well:

> as long as we remain attached to our old habits and continue behaving as if we are either masters or slaves we will never succeed in forging a nation.[11]

Despite all these examples, clientelism remained strong even among the radical Yorks. In the farming community of Santiago de Ocuilan, a town of about five hundred in the countryside of the state of Mexico, the local York club was composed of indigenous villagers and mixed-blood farmers. They met two or three times a week in Ferreira's tavern; according to the parish priest, the tavern owner was considered an "oracular figure" by the indigenous peoples of the area, and "this is why they are always seeking his advice." In his letter to a local official, the priest went on to denounce all the club members for having

> undermined the authority of my pulpit and for propagating all sorts of perverse maxims among my own parishioners. . . . These libertines used to ridicule me in private, but now they have the audacity to also do it in public. . . . They have even gone door to door . . . instructing residents not to give alms to the Church, claiming that this is a form of tyranny, whose only purpose is to fatten churchmen. . . . Last Sunday, as I was walking in front of the tavern on my way to celebrate mass, [club members] . . . inside insulted me and had their dog chase me down the street. I could hear them laugh as I ran away.[12]

Social relations in most clubs remained cliquish; however, it is also clear from the remarks above that the content of these ties was somewhat egalitarian. Club members fused democratic and clientelistic practices in ways that were strikingly similar to what Maurice Agulhon found among Jacobin clubs in the Var region of southern France during the 1840s.[13]

10. *Reglamentos generales del Rito de los YY. FF.* (New York, 1834), 16.

11. "Editorial," *Correo de la Federación,* 5 December 1826, 1.

12. Archivo General de la Nación, "Relación de cura, 1837," Bienes Nacionales, leg. 1286, exp. 2.

13. Maurice Agulhon, *The Republic in the Village: The People of the Var from the French Revolution to the Second Republic* (Cambridge: Cambridge University Press, 1982), 124–50.

Despite their conservatism, the Scots contributed as much as the Yorks to democratizing social relations by blurring socio-ethnic boundaries between members. In Antequera (Oaxaca), a multiethnic city of 20,000 composed of Zapotec Indians (75 percent), mixed-bloods (20 percent), and a small number of fair-skinned peoples (5 percent), the "Oils" and "Vinegars" (as the local Scots and Yorks called themselves) recruited voters from all three of these groups. At night, they would organize rallies and lead marches through the city's neighborhoods inviting local residents to join. The Oils, according to a contemporary source,

> went each night to preach in certain neighborhoods, stopping at the homes of pious families where residents had gathered. They marched 50 or 60 strong down the main thoroughfare, with banner flying overhead, a lantern illuminating the path, and everyone praying the rosary and singing "Ave María." The march ended at 8:30, at which time each group returned to the same house from where they had started, and spent the remainder of the night drinking and carousing. [Since the beginning of the campaign], residents have marched 25 or 30 times.[14]

Conservative clubs were as skillful as Yorks in combining clientelism with democratic practices, which suggests that this had become a common pattern in political life.

Elections were extremely corrupt, and Yorks and Scots encouraged members in their fraudulent practices. They often stole and stuffed ballot boxes; attacked citizens on their way to and from the voting booth; bribed voters with chocolate, liquor, and money; and tampered with the electoral rolls.[15] In the town of San Juan (Querétaro), where most of the voters were textile workers, and in Mexico City's plebeian quarter of "Salto de Agua," the local Yorks deposited six ballots for every registered voter on the roll.[16] Elections in Mexico were as corrupt as in any other country at this time. What makes the Mexican case distinct is that they remained somewhat competitive. According to Michael Costeloe, in the most important states the opposition was as likely to win the election as the official candidate.[17]

14. Pablo Villavicencio, *Ya tenemos en Oaxaca parte de la Liga Santa* (Mexico City, 1826), 600–605; Peter Guardino, "Total Liberty in Casting Our Ballots: Plebes, Peasants and Elections in Oaxaca, 1808–1850" (Unpublished typescript, Indiana University, 1998).

15. *Apuntes para la historia o sean maldades cometidas por la facción de los jacobinos del pueblo de San Juan del Pablo del Río* (Mexico City, 1829), 8–12.

16. *Apuntes para la historia*, 8–12.

17. Michael Costeloe, "Generals vs. Presidents: Santa Anna and the 1842 Congressional Elections in Mexico," *Bulletin of Latin American Research* 8, no. 2 (1989): 259–71, and his "Mariano Arista and the 1850 Presidential Election in Mexico," *Bulletin of Latin American Research* 18, no. 1 (1999): 51–70.

During the 1826 elections for state congressmen, York clubs won nearly all the contested seats in the country's eighteen state legislatures.[18] The terms of those occupying the other seats would not expire for another two years; most of them were monarchists who had been appointed to office by Agustín de Iturbide and remained opposed to republican rule.[19] The system they had designed gave conservative states far more electoral colleges and voting districts than liberal ones.

The political consequences of this institutional lag became apparent in the presidential election of 1828. The York candidate, Vicente Guerrero, won nine states (48 percent of the votes cast by state-level congressmen); the Scot candidate, Manuel Gómez Pedraza, won eleven states (52 percent of the votes).[20] In the words of Lorenzo Zavala, "the numerical majority of the nation will be sacrificed to the numerical majority of the states."[21] The Yorks challenged the legality of these elections. They described Gomez Pedraza's electoral base as made up of

> generals . . . colonels, clerics . . . landlords and other so-called civilized and cultivated persons . . . who consider [Guerrero] our president an abomination because he is dark-skinned and without social graces.[22]

York chapters across the country organized mass demonstrations in support of Guerrero. The largest one took place in Mexico City's central plaza in late November and early December. The first rally was attended by 15,000; the second was attended by 5,000 supporters, mainly dark-skinned plebeians from the city's poorest neighborhoods. They had broken into the national armory and stolen a large quantity of weapons and munitions.[23] This might explain why attendance at the second rally dropped dramatically—everyone expected the worst to happen. It did. The rally turned into a day-long riot. Guerrero's supporters looted and

---

18. Joseph Palombara and Myron Weiner, *Political Parties and Political Development* (Princeton, N.J.: Princeton University Press, 1966). Like those in the United States and England, Mexican elections were based on indirect voting. Citizens voted only for representatives to the 137 district-level electoral colleges. Every two years, these colleges gathered in the capital of each state and selected from their own ranks the members of the state legislature. Electoral college members appointed each other to serve in the National Congress. Congressmen were the only ones who voted directly for the president.

19. Michael Costeloe, *La Primera República Federal de México: 1824–1835* (Mexico City: Fondo de Cultura Económica, 1975), 14–40; and Green, *Mexican Republic*, 30–60.

20. Costeloe, *Primera República*, 49, 57–60; and Green, *Mexican Republic*, 91–93.

21. Lorenzo Zavala, *Ensayo histórico de las revoluciones de México desde 1808 hasta 1830* (Mexico City, 1969), 498.

22. Lorenzo Zavala, *Ensayo histórico*, 353.

23. Silvia Arrom, "Popular Politics in Mexico City: The Parian Riot in 1828," *Hispanic American Historical Review* 68, no. 2 (May 1988): 245–68. The fact that they plundered Mexican as well as Spanish shops suggests that this was not an "ethnic"-based riot.

burned scores of boutiques owned by Scot sympathizers and supporters of Gómez Pedraza. Total damages exceeded 25 million pesos in less than twenty-four hours.[24] The York tabloid, *El Correo de la Federación,* in an editorial published several days after the riot, explained the reasons for the unrest without quite condoning it:

> society rests on the notion of sovereignty of the people; since September society has been expressing its views against Gómez Pedraza [in mass demonstrations] even in states where congress voted for him. . . .[25]

The York-dominated Congress in Mexico City forced Gómez Pedraza to resign and awarded the presidency to Vicente Guerrero. Soon after taking office, Guerrero approved a series of laws that led to the expulsion of 10,000 or so Spaniards from Mexico between December 1827 and 1828. Most of them came from Scot-controlled cities such as Mexico, Puebla, Jalisco, and Veracruz. More than 50 percent of those expelled were merchants; 20 percent were clergymen; 10 percent were estate owners; 7 percent were artisans. There is no information on the remaining 13 percent.[26] Guerrero and his York supporters thus destroyed the social base of the Scot party in Mexico.

Even Lorenzo Zavala, the radical York, was pessimistic about the political situation: the Scot party is "driving . . . [the country] toward military tyranny, while the [Yorks are driving it] . . . toward despotism of the masses."[27] A year after taking office, a congressional committee composed of moderate Scots and Yorks advised that Guerrero be removed from office. According to them, the president is like a "child, he is mentally and morally unfit to govern."[28] In their report to congress, the members of the committee had used the same old colonial Catholic rhetoric; however, they used it in a radically new context and with an entirely new goal: removal of the executive. The congress accepted the recommendation. After deposing Guerrero, they proceeded to outlaw all voting clubs and increase income and literacy requirements for voters. Between 40 and 55 percent of voters in Mexico City and Oaxaca were eliminated from the rolls.[29] From the 1840s onward, elections were described in newspapers

24. Manuel Flores and Ramón Gamboa, *Voto particular leído ante el Ayuntamiento sobre la destrucción del Parián* (Mexico City, 1829), 5.

25. "Editorial," *Correo de la Federación,* 1 December 1828, 1.

26. Harold Sims, *The Expulsion of Mexico's Spaniards: 1821–1836* (Pittsburgh: University of Pittsburgh Press, 1990), 43–78.

27. Quoted in Luis Chávez Orozco, *Historia de México* (Mexico City, 1978), 31.

28. *Registro Oficial,* 2 February 1830, 1–2.

29. Warren, "Vagrants and Citizens," 179–87; "Oaxaca," *Siglo XIX,* 29 January 1849, 4.

as "orderly," "peaceful," and "tranquil," an indication that they were no longer competitive.[30]

The dissolution of voting clubs had a mixed effect on political life. On the one hand, it encouraged regional elites to overcome their parochialism. In preparation for the 1842 election, Nicolás Bravo and other local elites from Guerrero and Mariano Riva Palacio and others from his circle in Mexico City developed close ties to each other and to their counterparts in other states.[31] The demise of clubs weakened patronage ties between the elite and non-elite and in this respect contributed to the democratization of political life. However, it also had the opposite effect—without backing from commoners, the regional elite were unable to compete effectively against state officials and their candidates.

Electoral Colleges, Municipal Townships, and the Demise of Liberty

Beginning in the late 1830s, the center of democratic politics shifted from nationwide voting clubs to state-level electoral colleges and municipal townships. The opposition remained in control of nearly all 137 electoral colleges in the country and relied on them to prevent the government-backed candidate from winning a seat in these electoral colleges or in the state legislature, making it difficult for President Santa Anna to centralize power.[32] In the 1840s, the president and congress replaced the colleges with the Junta de Notables and the Junta de Representantes, the two most important representative bodies of this period.[33] Few Mexicans were willing to invest any sovereignty in them:

> Juntas have never been nor can they ever be a repository of popular sovereignty. If we were to have a discussion about them and confront the basic issue underlying them, we would discover that they do not repre-

30. See the following articles in *Siglo XIX:* "Elecciones," 30 August 1843, 4; "Elecciones," 4 September 1843, 3; "Elecciones," 19 October 1843, 3; "Impresos de Querétaro," 14 November 1843, 3; "Elecciones," 16 June 1842, 1; "Elecciones," 16 August 1843, 3; "Elecciones," 1 August 1843, 3. Elections in Guadalajara remained unruly: "Elecciones," 3 September 1843, 3.

31. Costeloe, "Generals vs. Presidents," 263.

32. Costeloe, "Generals vs. Presidents," 259–71, and his "Mariano Arista," 51–70. The opposition was in control of all the colleges except those in Mexico, Querétaro, Puebla, and Guerrero. On the social composition of all the colleges in Querétaro, see Marcello Carmagnani and Alicia Hernández Chávez, "Dimensiones de la ciudadanía orgánica Mexicana: 1850–1910," in *Ciudadanía política y formación de las naciones,* ed. Hilda Sábato (Mexico City: Fondo de Cultura Económica, 1999), 376–77.

33. Cecilia Noriega Elio, *El constituyente de 1842* (Mexico City: El Colegio de México, 1842), 94–99, 111–13, 115–16; and Lucina Moreno Valle, "La Junta de Representantes o Consejo de Departamentos," *Estudios de historia moderna y contemporánea de México* 4, no. 6 (1977): 105–26, for a detailed study of them.

sent our nation. Our political system, as everyone knows, is based on popular and representative rule.[34]

Citizens turned their backs on these juntas and became active in local municipal life.[35]

Beginning in the mid-1830s, the central government undermined municipal liberty by replacing local officials with state-appointed ones; abolishing militias; increasing federal taxes by 40 percent and thereby driving many townships into bankruptcy; and by increasing the socioeconomic and demographic requirements to become a legally recognized township.[36] The number of townships in Mexico, the state in which they were most concentrated, dropped from 80 in 1843, to 26 in 1850, to 4 in 1855.[37] Manuel C. Rejón, an ardent defender of municipal life, summarized the damage done to townships:

> We have centralized public life and have been forced to deposit our sovereignty in a single place without allowing citizens to divide it among different locales. . . . This has left the nation cold, inert and in a state of complete paralysis. Our country is vast. The state cannot attend to our interests without also extinguishing all our energies. In any case, the administrators they have sent to manage our local affairs are uninterested in them. This is the cause for all the rebellions that have taken place in the country. Citizens now regard the government as a foreign power.[38]

The demise of voting clubs, electoral colleges, and municipal townships left Mexicans without a place to practice democracy in political life and drove rural peoples to challenge the regime.

Rebellions, Militias, and the Ruralization of Liberty

The epicenter of democratic life migrated to the countryside and remained there throughout the 1840s. Rural peoples organized several major rebel-

34. "Las Juntas Departamentales," *Siglo XIX*, 15 January 1842, 3.

35. María del Carmen Salinas Sandoval, "Transformación o permanencia del gobierno municipal del estado de México: 1760–1880" (Ph.D. dissertation, El Colegio de México, 1993), 50–63, 93–107, estimates that 20–25 percent of residents in the farming town of Cuapixtla continued to participate in township elections in violation of the new suffrage laws. Also see Michael T. Ducey, "From Village Riot to Regional Rebellion: Social Protest in the Huasteca, Mexico, 1760–1870" (Ph.D. dissertation, University of Chicago), 205–55; and T. G. Powell, *El liberalismo y el campesinado en el centro del país* (Mexico City: Secretaría de Educación Pública, 1974), 27, 53–56.

36. Pedro Santoni, *Mexicans at War: Puro Federalists and the Politics of War, 1845–1848* (Fort Worth: Texas Christian University Press, 1996), 63–68. Militias had been dissolved in 1835 in order to prevent ex-York members from infiltrating them.

37. Sandoval, "Transformación o permanencia," 50, 65–66, 109.

38. Manuel Cresencio Rejón, *Programa de la mayoría de los diputados del Distrito Federal* (Mexico City, 1846), 3–4.

lions against the regime and then refused to fight against U.S. troops during the war. After the war, they relied on the militias they had created for the country's defense to topple the government during the Ayutla revolution.

The demise of municipal liberty generated regional rebellions throughout the country, with the two most significant surfacing in northern Veracruz from 1836 to 1838, and in the Pacific Hotlands in the state of Guerrero from 1840 to 1843. Both movements sprouted from local networks that had been left behind by York clubs after they had been banned.[39] These networks brought together residents from medium-sized and small towns and hamlets. Those in Veracruz connected no fewer than twenty-two communities; those in Guerrero linked thirteen communities. The people who made up these networks came from different ethnic and racial backgrounds—indigenous peoples, mixed-bloods, blacks, and fair-skinned creoles—and from different sectors of the economy—farmers, tenants, muleteers, itinerant traders, and the like. According to amnesty records, most fair-skinned creoles came from medium-sized towns, and most indigenous peoples came from hamlets deep in the countryside. Activity in these networks followed the agricultural cycle; members flocked to them during the off season and returned to their communities during harvest and planting season. Rebel militants at the core of these networks were provided with food, medicine, shelter, and intelligence information by local supporters at the edges. According to Michael Ducey and Peter Guardino, the demands made by both movements included electoral reforms, township autonomy, lower taxes, fair and equal enforcement of the laws by justices of the peace, and so on; this makes clear that the members were committed federalists rather than simply disgruntled peasants seeking communal land. These movements kept the authoritarian regime off balance, but they were not strong enough to topple it.[40]

Mexicans organized countless rebellions during the late 1830s and early 1840s, but the majority of them refused to fight U.S. troops during the invasion and occupation of the country in 1846. The U.S. army invaded with only 12,000 men and took less than two weeks to march all the way from Monterrey and Veracruz to Mexico City. The troops encountered little resistance along the way; desertion by Mexican soldiers was common.[41] According to Charles Gagern, a Prussian colonel who had

---

39. Ducey, "Village Riot," 239–70; and Peter Guardino, *Peasants, Politics and the Nation* (Stanford, Calif.: Stanford University Press, 1996), 210–70. My discussion of both movements derives entirely from their work.

40. Ducey, "Village Riot," 239–70; and Guardino, *Peasants,* 210–70.

41. José María Roa Bárcena, *Recuerdos de la invasión norteamericana* (1883; Mexico City: Editorial Porrúa, 1947), 2.64–66, 102–6, 121–22; and 3.140–41; Mariano Otero,

been commissioned by the defense minister to study the debacle, Mexican soldiers were competent and well-paid; what they lacked was "patriotism."[42] Civilians had also turned their backs on the Mexican state. Landowners and small farmers had refused to sell food and horses to soldiers, which they were required to do by law.[43] Following the war, José M. Roa Bárcena wrote a three-volume history of the U.S.-Mexican War in which he offered the following explanation for the lack of patriotism among the elite and non-elite:

> it is time that our politicians realize that patriotism is not some abstract notion that they can use as pretext to disguise their own petty intrigues and ambitions. For the majority of us, patriotism is our family, our homes, our temples, our workshops, and the natural beauty that surrounds us, in addition to our own sense of individual liberty and civic rights. . . .[44]

Mexicans distributed their sense of sovereignty horizontally, on other citizens in daily life, rather than in the government.

In preparation for the war, President Santa Anna ordered local townships to reestablish their militias (National Guard).[45] By 1847, most towns and cities along the Gulf Coast and in the Central Valley had their own militia units; for example, the state of Veracruz had a total of 14,000 citizen-soldiers on active duty.[46] In military terms, militias, as I indicated earlier, were a failure; however, in sociopolitical terms they were a resounding success. Militias rekindled democratic practices in several ways. Within each unit, militiamen voted for their commander. For many commoners, these were the first elections they had participated in since 1830,

Consideraciones sobre la situación política y social de la República Mexicana en el año 1847 (Mexico City, 1848), 3–7; Francisco Suárez Iriarte, *Comparencia ante la Cámara de Diputados* (Mexico City, 1850), 4; Abraham López, "La revolución de los polkos o la Cruzada de México en el Siglo XIX," *Décima calendario de López* (Mexico City, 1852), 56–61. Eight thousand Mexicans deserted during the battle at Molino del Rey and Churubusco outside the nation's capital. In the capital, plebeians from San Pedro and Salto de Agua spent an entire afternoon attacking U.S. troops. Each time they charged, the Mexicans shouted "Death to the Yankees" and "Death to Santa Anna," as if they were one and the same enemy.

42. Charles Gagern, "Rasgos característicos de la raza India en México," *Boletín de la Sociedad Mexicana de Geografía y Estadística* 2, no. 1 (Mexico City, 1869), 809–12.

43. Edward B. Tylor, *Anahuac; or, Mexico and the Mexicans* (London, 1861), 199; F. von Tempsky, *Mitla: A Narrative of Incidents and Personal Adventures on a Journey in Mexico, Guatemala and Salvador in the Years 1853 to 1855* (London, 1858), 257–58, T. G. Powell, *El Liberalismo y el Campesinado en el centro de México,* trans. Roberto Gómez Ciria (Mexico City: Secretaría de Educación Pública, 1979), 23–25.

44. Bárcena, *Recuerdos de la invasión norteamericana,* 2.146–47.

45. Santoni, *Mexicans at War,* 63–68. In 1835 militias had been dissolved by President Antonio Bustamante as part of the campaign to centralize power.

46. Alicia Hernández Chávez, "La Guardia Nacional y la movilización política de los pueblos," in *Patterns of Contention in Mexican History,* ed. Jaime Rodríguez (Wilmington, Del.: Scholarly Resources, 1992), 215–16.

when voting clubs were abolished and suffrage requirements increased. Elections in militia units were, as they had been in voting clubs, a mixture of patronage and egalitarianism, the exact balance between the two determined in large measure by recruitment practices. The most civic militias were those whose

> members had been recruited in the district block by block. . . . This enabled commoners to become influential in each battalion and company, while at the same time it prevented office clerks, industrialists, merchants and aristocrats from predominating in them. Militia units provided artisans, workers, literate persons and property owners a place to experience republican fraternity. . . .[47]

Militias provided elites and commoners in each community a stable place to mingle and rebuild their sociopolitical ties.

Militia members also challenged authoritarian-minded citizens prior to and in the years immediately after the war. While U.S. troops were marching inland toward Mexico City, militia units in the nation's capital held patriotic rallies daily in neighborhoods. Some of them, however, turned into anti-government demonstrations:

> instead of arming the people and calling them into the barracks, the [leaders] assembled them into groups and explained to them their [political] rights and the nefarious influence that the wealthy elite and the priests have had on our country. Rather than defending the city against the enemy, they trained their weapons against these groups.[48]

The government became alarmed but could do nothing to stop them, since it was preparing for battle itself. After the war, militia units across the countryside in the states of Veracruz, Morelos, and Guerrero assisted indigenous peoples and farmers in invading large estates and dividing them into small plots. The average number of land-related conflicts rose from 6 in the period from 1842 to 1846, prior to the war, to 16 in the period from 1847 to 1851, after the war.[49] Militiamen also encouraged rural peoples not to pay tithe to the Church and to refuse to pay parish priests for administering the Holy Sacraments. In many places, the priest was left without an income and was forced to abandon the community, thereby eroding the authoritarian government's social base of support in the countryside.[50]

47. "Guardia Nacional," *Siglo XIX,* 7 November 1855, 1.
48. "Juntas Populares," *Siglo XIX,* 23 October 1846, 3; "Editorial," *Siglo XIX,* 13 September 1846, 3; Bárcena, *Recuerdos de la invasión norteamericana,* 1.137.
49. Leticia Reina, *Las luchas populares en México en el siglo XIX* (Mexico City: Secretaría de Educación Pública, 1983), 13–172.
50. Michael Costeloe, *The Central Republic in Mexico: 1835–1846* (Cambridge: Cambridge University Press, 1993), 303.

Militia units prepared the way for the Ayutla Revolution (1855), which toppled the authoritarian regime and ushered in an era of democratization.[51] Important as this uprising was, what ultimately brought down the government, according to its finance minister, Lucas Alamán, was the "force of public opinion rather than military power." [52] The uprising lasted from March 1854 to August 1855; Guy Thomson describes it like this:

> in military terms, [Ayutla] was an undramatic series of battles and skirmishes between the National Guard forces of the rebels, against Santa Anna's regular army. . . .[53]

The Ayutla movement had its base of support in small and medium-sized towns and village hamlets throughout the countryside.[54] This explains why public opinion was far more important than military violence in toppling the regime. Ayutla had broad support in southern Jalisco, in the Pacific Hotlands of Guerrero, across the state of Veracruz, in the sugar-growing areas of Morelos, and in the highlands of Puebla and large parts of Hidalgo. Ayutla also had strong support in communities around Tehuantepec, in the far south, in the northern states of Durango, Tamaulipas, Nuevo Leon, and San Luis Potosi, and in the western states of Zacatecas and Colima.

The movement flourished wherever federalists remained in control of militia units.[55] Each community expressed its support for federalism in its own way. Indigenous peoples and mixed-bloods from the small town of Zacoalco and the hamlet of San Cristobal in southern Jalisco published their own "Proclama de los pueblos de San Cristóbal y Zacoalco." It read in part:

> we and the other [nearby] villages do not recognize any other form of government than the popular, federal and representative one, and . . . do hereby protest solemnly against all other forms of government as a violation of the wishes of the entire nation.[56]

Soon after this proclamation was published, the government marched troops there, arrested a great many residents, and shot the governor, an

51. Richard Johnson, *The Mexican Revolution of Ayutla: 1854–1855* (Rock Island, Ill.: Augustana College Library Press, 1939).

52. Lucas Alamán, *El partido conservador* (Mexico City, 1855), 3; "Ecisiones," *Siglo XIX,* 15 November 1855, 3.

53. Guy Thomson, "Popular Aspects of Liberalism in Mexico: 1848–1888," *Bulletin of Latin American Research* 10, no. 3 (1991): 274.

54. Thomson, "Popular Aspects of Liberalism," 274–76.

55. Florencia Mallon, "Peasants and State Formation in Nineteenth-Century Mexico: Morelos, 1848 to 1858," in *Political Power and Social Theory,* vol. 3, ed. Maurice Zeitlin (Greenwich, Conn.: JAI Press, 1988), 19–21.

56. Leticia Reina, *Las rebeliones campesinas en México* (Mexico City: Siglo Veintiuno, 1980), 149.

indigenous person named Lugardo Onofre. In Morelos, Ayutla supporters continued doing what the militias had done before: invading and dividing landed estates.[57] This prompted the country's elite to portray the
rebellion as a "caste war" rather than a pro-federalist movement. When
the Ayutla rebels entered Mexico City, residents expected the worst. Robert Wilson, a circuit court judge from California, who had been living
there for several months, left this description:

> All classes at the capital now had forebodings of what would soon take
> place; for the Pintos [darkies] are as much considered foreigners at the
> city of Mexico as were the Americans; with this difference: Americans
> were considered men of good caste, while Pintos are looked upon as a
> servile race. . . . At length the advent of Alvarez, so long expected, with
> his 5,000 Pintos, took place. . . . A strange army was this of the Pin-
> tos. . . . An old straw hat—a stripped blanket, with a slit for the head
> to pass through, serving as covering by night and coat by day—together
> with a pair of ragged cotton drawers, constituted their uniform. Now
> and then one rejoiced in the luxury of shoes, but the majority contented
> themselves with sandals. They strode along like persons unaccustomed
> to military exercise, but with a self-possession which showed that they
> saw nothing to fear in the elegant city they had captured.[58]

Political life remained racially fissured and was one of the most important
sources of support for authoritarian rule among elite and non-elite groups
alike.[59]

Debating Societies and Public Opinion

After two and a half decades of authoritarian rule, Mexicans regained
their civic momentum and organized "debating societies" across the country. According to the conservative daily, *El Omnibus,* these societies

> replaced the dead letter of newspapers with lively discussions. The meet-
> ings that they organize have inspired citizens, rich and poor alike, to
> support our new [political] system.[60]

Debating societies introduced two new practices to political life in Mexico. First, they undermined clientelism by encouraging members to evaluate candidates in political rather than personal terms. Mexico City's Elec-

---

57. Mallon, "Peasants and State Formation," 19–22.
58. Robert A. Wilson, *Mexico: Its Peasants and Its Priests* (New York, 1856), 401.
59. Nelson Reed, *The Caste War of Yucatan* (Stanford, Calif.: Stanford University Press,
1964); Robert Wasserstrom, "A Caste War that Never Was: The Tzeltal Conspiracy of
1848," *Peasant Studies* 7, no. 2 (spring 1978), 73–85. In contrast to Peru, ethnic rebellions
in Mexico erupted on the fringes of the political system. More on this later in the chapter.
60. "Clubs," *El "mnibus,* 21 November 1855, 2.

toral Progresita (1856) criticized their candidate for president, Miguel Lerdo de Tejada, for refusing to debate his ideas in public:

> It is not the names or persons that interest us, but the ideas and principles which have to be discussed in front of the electorate. . . . We cannot simply change names, we must alter the nature of politics.[61]

Debating societies also contributed to expanding the public agenda by introducing into it issues that had never been discussed. In their weekly meetings, miners in the Club de Angangueo (1857) in the town of the same name in Michoacán discussed ways of "improving the working and living conditions of laborers."[62] Indigenous peoples and mixed-bloods who joined Tixtla's Club de Progreso (1856) discussed ways of "fusing all the castes" in the country as a way of strengthening democratic life.[63] The Sociedad Democrática (1855) of Cuautitlán (Mexico) and the Club de Morelos (1855) of Jalapa (Veracruz) sent members to monitor primary schools in order to ensure that its "youth was getting proper religious and civic education . . . and understanding the full meaning of democracy as outlined in the 'Social Catechism' [the textbook used in most classrooms]."[64] Discussions in Mexico City's Club de Reforma (1855), which was the most broad-minded of all the debating societies in the country, also "became increasingly animated as a result of the debates that we now have on social and political issues that affect all the different sectors of society."[65]

For most of the first half of the century, political life in Mexico was authoritarian. Despite the inhospitable conditions in the country, citizens, elite and commoner alike, found a variety of ways to practice democracy. In contrast, political life in Peru was despotic, with the army in control of the state and soldiers in charge of administrative and government affairs at the local level. Power in Peru was militarized and centralized, offering citizens few places to practice democracy in public life.[66]

61. "Crónica Electoral," *Siglo XIX*, 21 December 1854, 4; "Necesidad de un programa del ministerio," *Siglo XIX*, 14 November 185, 1; and "Clubs," *La República*, 20 October 1855, 1.

62. "Club de Progreso," *Siglo XIX*, 1 April 1855, 3.

63. "Club de Progreso," 3.

64. "Sociedad Democrática de Cuautitlán," *Siglo XIX*, 9 November 1855, 1; and "Mediante un remitido," *Siglo XIX*, 19 January 1858, 4.

65. "Club de la Reforma," *El Republicano*, 26 November 1855, 2.

66. Brian Hamnett, "Partidos políticos Mexicanos e intervención militar," in *America Latina dallo stato coloniale allo stato-nazione*, vol. 1, ed. Antonio Annino and Marcello Carmagnani (Milan: F. Angeli, 1987), 574.

CHAPTER 8

Militarizing Sovereignty of the People: Peruvian Political Society

Political life in early nineteenth-century Peru was militaristic and centralized, which discouraged the vast majority of Peruvians, elite and non-elite alike, from practicing democracy. Regional commanders in the country's factionalized army assigned their high-ranking officers to staff all the positions in the executive and legislative branches of the central government and in local administrative life throughout the provinces. José Casimiro Ulloa, a civic-minded publicist, described the situation:

> Our army generals . . . have taken charge of all government positions: in the administration, senate, chamber of deputies, and at the provincial level as well, degrading each of them with the type of ignorance and immorality that can only be acquired from years of living in an army barrack.[1]

When the military abolished municipal townships and state legislatures, the citizenry did not resist.[2]

> administrative centralization has drained vitality from our social body, extinguished our public spirit, and left our [Indian] communities in a state of stupor bordering on idiocy.[3]

Peruvians considered government institutions as foreign to the nation, and they seldom participated in government-centered politics:

> military intrusion into political life has made it difficult for us to attain liberty. . . . The government will only become genuinely representative

1. José Casimiro Ulloa, *El Perú en 1853* (Lima, 1854), 17.
2. Raúl Rivera Serna, "Las juntas departamentales durante el primer gobierno del Mariscal don Agustín Gamarra," *Boletín de la Nacional* (Lima, 1964), 3–18; Jorge Basadre, *Historia de la República del Perú* (Lima: Ediciones Historia, 1961), 1.348, 443.
3. "Municipalidades," *El Progreso*, 27 October 1849, 2; and "Municipalidades," *El Progreso*, 3 November 1849, 1–2.

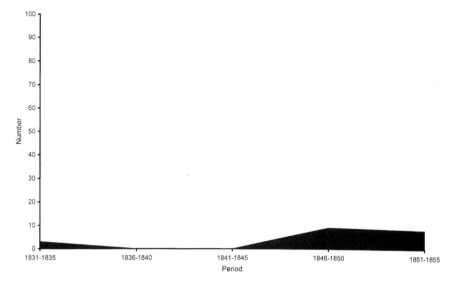

Figure 8.1 New Political Clubs, 1831–1855

the day civilians . . . acquire control of [our public institutions]. . . . The military has undermined democracy and has centralized authority in itself . . . transforming most Peruvians into passive moles waiting for orders from above. . . .[4]

The Peruvian military was convinced that its officers were the only individuals in the country imbued with "rationality" and capable of representing the nation. Military notions of citizenship bore a vague resemblance to the French Jacobin notion of the "nation in arms," except that in the Peruvian version citizenship was based on hierarchy, domination, and xenophobia rather than on equality, liberty, and fraternity.[5]

Socio-institutional Structures

During the two and a half decades under study, Peruvians organized a total of twenty-one political associations (see fig. 8.1). The majority of voting clubs (14) appeared in preparation for the 1851 presidential election.[6] These clubs were insignificant in numerical terms, but they were impor-

4. Francisco Quiroz, *A la Nación* (Lima, 1851), 5.
5. Cristóbal Aljovín, "Representative Government in Peru: Fiction and Reality, 1821–1845" (Ph.D. dissertation, University of Chicago, 1996), 358–62.
6. Carlos A. Forment, "Databank on Associative Life in Nineteenth-Century Peru" (Unpublished working document, Princeton University, 1997).

tant in symbolic terms, providing citizens an opportunity to express their opposition to military rule.[7]

Associative Practices in Political Society

Associative life was as undeveloped in political society as it was across civil and economic society, making it necessary for democratic-minded citizens to practice politics outside the institutional channels established by the military regime. I discuss this here in three parts: (1) the relationship between soldiering and civic life; (2) voting clubs during presidential elections and their role in demilitarizing political life; and (3) the impact the 1855 popular movement, the first of its kind, had on ushering in civilian rule.

Soldiering, Militia Service, and Citizenship

Soldiering and warmaking did not, as some scholars assume, exert a positive and beneficial influence on the development of democracy and citizenship in Peru. If anything, it can be said to have stunted both.[8] Citizens' militias, in contrast, did propagate democratic habits among their members, but so few units existed in the country that their influence on political life was extremely limited.

Soldiering touched the lives of a great many citizens, especially urban plebeian groups and indigenous people. Estimates place the total number of men in the regular army at 3,000 or so in the 1830s, at its lowest point, and 12,000 when it was at its highest.[9] Service in the military, claims Basadre, a distinguished historian, eroded ethnic and racial boundaries among citizens: "The army took in people from varied racial and socio-economic groups and in this way undermined the differences and inequalities that existed among them, and had a democratic influence on public life."[10] In the process of mingling with other recruits, soldiers gradually discovered that they were part of a much larger "nation," an imagined community that went beyond the narrow confines of their hamlet or village. Because the majority of these conscripts came from the very bottom of the social ladder, military training provided them with an opportunity to learn how to read and write and, in the case of Quechua-

7. Vincent Peloso, "Liberals, Electoral Reforms and the Popular Vote in Mid-Nineteenth Century Peru," in *Liberals, Politics and Power: State Formation in Nineteenth-Century Latin America*, ed. Vincent C. Peloso and Barbara A. Tennenbaum (Athens: University of Georgia Press, 1996), 195–97.

8. Basadre, *Historia*, 2.552, makes the opposite argument.

9. Basadre, *Historia*, 2.551–52. These estimates do not include the many guerrilla groups and "montonera" bands that were part of the national army.

10. Basadre, *Historia*, 2.552.

speaking peoples, acquire a basic understanding of Spanish. As part of their curriculum, recruits were also taught elementary notions of patriotism, citizenship, and democratic rights, expanding their political horizons beyond heterodox notions rooted in popular religiosity, kinship loyalty, and village communalism.[11] Once these bicultural recruits were released from military service, those who went back to their communities became sociocultural bridges between the creole and indigenous worlds, infused democratic habits among their families, friends, and acquaintances, and contributed, in their own way, to the political and cultural unification of the nation.[12]

The experience of battle instilled combatants with notions of democratic patriotism. In the words of Juan Bustamante, a mixed-blood from Puno and one of the country's most committed defenders of indigenous peoples, the women of Pucará (Puno), four years after the Battle of Motoni (1841), would gather in their homes to commemorate

> the heroism displayed by their husbands and sons in battle, recounting their stories lovingly, nay, with . . . delirium . . . and this is to be expected since they, too, actively participated [in fighting the Bolivian army] . . . making cartridges, carrying arms and transporting munitions to the battlefield. . . .[13]

Even in this remote Andean village, near the Bolivian border, where residents remained committed to their own forms of life, their experience and, perhaps more importantly, their communal memory and retelling of wartime feats had a transformative effect on their sensibilities. Soldiering and warmaking infused soldiers with democratic sensibilities, contributing to the spread of the ideas of popular sovereignty and nationhood among rural groups at a time when there were few other ways of reaching them.

But military service also impeded the development of democratic citizenship and nationalism. Army service was brutal and despotic, transforming conscripts into docile, disciplined, and fearful citizens, making them terrified of government officials, leading many of them to reject the central government's notion of nationhood and patriotism. Recruits were hunted down, savagely beaten, and incarcerated for days in makeshift stockades, then marched off to the nearest army garrison, where they were brutalized all over again by the camp commander, who would "cut their hair and mark their ears so they could be clearly recognized and shot

11. Agustín Gamarra, "Excmo. Sr. Vice Presidente de la República," 156–57 and "Sr. Secretario General de S. E. el Presidente," 152–53 in *Epistolario*, ed. Alberto Tauro (Lima: Universidad Nacional Mayor de San Marcos, 1952).

12. Manuel Atanasio Fuentes, *Lima: Apuntes históricos, descriptivos, estadísticos y de costumbre* (Lima, 1867), 171–72.

13. Juan Bustamante, *Viaje al Viejo Mundo* (Lima, 1845), 18; Basadre, *Historia*, 2.497.

in case of desertion."[14] For many indigenous groups, wearing long hair was linked to social honor and had other symbolic significance. For Andean peoples, cutting hair forcibly was a form of ritualized degradation intended to cast public humiliation and shame on the person. For indigenous peoples, military service was a kind of serfdom, like what they often endured working on the estates of the landed elite, rather than an experience that imbued them with patriotic citizenship.

In the countryside, rural peoples evaded conscription by finding influential patrons and becoming socially dependent on them; in 1841, the British consul, John McGregor, toured the countryside and noted:

> In each of the villages across the valleys between the mountains, whites and mestizos have "godfathers" or protectors, individuals of their own caste, who have an official position, such as militia captain, governor or mayor. . . . But the Peruvian or native Inca, which cultivates his own parcel of land . . . to maintain his own family, are exposed continuously and suffer countless abuses. . . . [These] natives are . . . torn from their homes and dragged from caves [where they were hiding]. . . .[15]

In exchange for protection, mixed-bloods paid their patrons with labor services and personal loyalty, making rural sociability ever more clientelistic. Moreover, because these networks were often ethnically divided, they contributed to the further fragmentation of public life. During his travels through the Andean highlands, Monsieur Sartiège, the French consul, visited Lampa, and witnessed how Colonel Miguel San Román, on the way to and from battle, forced citizens to turn over to his troops their homes, livestock, and grains, "claiming it all in the name of the patria."[16] Citizens regarded soldiers as mercenaries rather than as the embodiment of the "nation in arms." Once they were released from military service, soldiers returned to civilian life with their bodies marked and permanently deformed by the brutal treatment they had suffered in the army. That abusive treatment led many of them to become extremely violent in their own personal dealings with other citizens. The majority of forced conscripts came from the very bottom of the social ladder; contrary to what scholars assume, military service did little to undermine racial and ethnic differences among them. Blacks and Indians served in different

14. Aljovín, *Representative Government*, 203. Local officials were responsible for organizing mass levies and conscripting about two hundred men annually from each state. Cuzco was the most populous province, with the highest proportion of indigenous peoples, and sent twice as many recruits.

15. John McGregor, "Bosquejo general del Perú, 1847," in *Gran Bretaña y el Perú: 1826–1919: Informe de los Cónsules Británicos*, vol. 1, ed. Heraclio Bonilla (Lima: Instituto de Estudios Peruanos, 1975), 150.

16. Emilio de Sartiège and Adolfo de Botmiliau, *Dos viajeros franceses en el Perú republicano* (Lima: Editorial Antártida, 1947), 53, 55.

troops and were assigned to different duties. In the words of a contemporary observer:

> The Peruvian army is made up almost exclusively of Indians and Negroes or zambos [mixed-bloods]. The Indians constitute the infantry and being accustomed to the mountainous interior [are sent there]. . . . The Negroes are confined to the plains of the coast, and are accustomed to riding. . . . Hence the peculiar distribution.[17]

The racial and ethnic composition of each army unit reflected the composition of each province, reproducing the same social fragmentation that existed throughout public life. Moreover, Indians and blacks were assigned different duties, the former serving as infantry and the latter as cavalry, thereby deepening the split between the two, although inverting the status ranking that prevailed in civilian life, assigning blacks the superior position.[18] Indigenous peoples, in any case, seldom knew why they were fighting, which is why they often deserted.[19] In 1835, during the "Battle of Ingavi" (Cuzco), which made it possible for the Bolivian army to invade and occupy Peru for almost a decade, more than 8,000 troops abandoned the battlefield, despite the fact that their commanders had provided them with thousands of sacks of coca leaves, a form of ritual gift-giving among the indigenous peoples of this region.[20]

Authority relations among commanders and between commanders and their soldiers were arbitrary and lax, inadequate to inculcate in conscripts the orderly, methodical, and "rationalized" habits normally associated with military life and necessary for political citizenship. Regional commanders were often disloyal to each other and frequently changed their allegiances on the way to battle, exposing their own officers and soldiers to additional risks, and driving others to behave in an equally opportunistic manner. Moreover, each unit had its own pack of female *rabonas* to cook, mend uniforms, and care for the men. Their presence also undermined civic relations across public life and authority relations within each battalion. After battle, these *rabonas* would plunder and prey on the civilian population, stealing as much booty as they could and distributing

---

17. E. George Squier, *Peru: Incidents of Travel and Exploration in the Land of the Incas* (New York, 1877), 46; Fuentes, *Lima*, 177.

18. Alberto Flores Galindo, *Aristocracia y plebe: Lima, 1760–1830* (Lima: Editorial Mosca Azul, 1984), 111–18. Montenegro's bands operated along the coast. They were multi-ethnic, but members joined and deserted their units at will without any sense of personal solidarity or political loyalty to any cause.

19. Carlos Prince, "El soldado de infantería y de caballería," *Lima Antigua* (Lima, 1890), 17–20.

20. Charles Walker, "Peasants, Caudillos and the State in Peru: Cuzco in the Transition from Colony to Republic, 1780–1840" (Ph.D. dissertation, University of Chicago, 1992), 288–93.

it among themselves. Most commanders did not dare expel them from their camps, knowing that in the past this had provoked mass desertions and riots among the men.[21]

Scholars have failed to examine the repercussions of ethnic fragmentation in public life on military factionalism in early nineteenth-century Peru, although contemporaries of the period often noted the links between them. The French consul's remarks are instructive in this regard:

> Ever since [independence], racial rivalry has been spreading and it is not about to end any time soon. The majority of civil wars which have broken out in this country during the last several years have no other source but this invincible antipathy which White, Indian and Black races have toward each other, a problem which in Peru had been accentuated . . . by proclamations of social equality.[22]

Race and ethnicity played a major role in the socio-military and political alliances that were forged among regional chieftains. Lima and Arequipa's fair-skinned troops closed ranks when threatened by the indigenous army of General Agustín Gamarra from Cuzco, who was seeking to transform Peru into a neo-Incan nation-state.[23] In the course of a conversation with another military officer, Arequipa's General Valdivia expressed his opposition to Gamarra's plan to "redelineate Peru's boundary, [and make them] . . . the same as during the ancient empire."[24]

Authoritarian groups tried to transform southern Peru into the epicenter of this Incan-centered vision of nationhood, according to one of its sworn enemies, General José Rufino Echenique: "the idea of federation was very well received by the people of the south, mainly in Cuzco . . . who were looking forward to having their own government . . . and to be able to return to their previous state of grandeur."[25] Pro-Incan publicists stripped the "Tawantisuyo" project of its "antimodern" baggage in order to convince regional elites throughout the country that the only way of

21. Flora Tristán, *Peregrinaciones de una paria,* trans. Emilia Romero (Lima: Editorial Cultura Antártida, 1946), 279–80.

22. Sartiège and Botmiliau, *Dos viajeros franceses,* 123. Also see: Max Radiguet, *Lima y la sociedad Peruana,* trans. Catalina Recavarren Ulloa (Lima: Biblioteca Nacional del Perú, 1971), 68.

23. Paul Gootenberg, "North-South: Trade Policy, Regionalism and Caudillismo in Post-Independence Peru," *Journal of Latin American Studies* 23, no. 2 (1991): 294. Cuzco's elite transformed this city into a "genuine center of nationalist agitation . . . an industrial Tawantinsuyo," and tried to convince other regional elites in the country that national integration was possible only by instilling citizens with a respect for social hierarchy, an appreciation for economic autonomy, and a sense of loyalty to an authoritarian state.

24. Juan Gualberto Valdivia, *Memorias sobre las revoluciones de Arequipa: 1834–1866,* vol. 1 (Lima, 1874), 40.

25. José Rufino Echenique, *Memorias para la historia del Perú,* vol. 1 (Lima: Editorial Huascarán, 1952), 73.

turning Peru into a nation-state was to instill citizens with respect for social hierarchy, a commitment to economic independence, and loyalty to
the authoritarian state.

Cuzco's regional elite put forward an alternative vision of nationhood
and citizenship, one that was every bit as "modern" (albeit antidemocratic) as the creole-centered vision current in Lima. The Andean elite began
the campaign by demanding that the country's capital be transferred to
Cuzco, and used their newspaper to publicize their view:

> In colonial days . . . it made sense for the capital of what was once the
> Peruvian Viceroyalty to be in Lima; but today Peru is a sovereign state
> . . . and [that is why] the country's capital should reside in one of the
> provinces.[26]

According to neo-Incans, Cuzco was the symbolic and geographical center of Peruvian nationhood; Lima, in contrast, was nothing more than
a colonial artifact propagated by fair-skinned creole upstarts from the
coast.[27] General Gamarra's government invested heavily in the region and
transformed Cuzco into "an industrial Tawantinsuyo."[28] Like so many
other "invented traditions," pro-Incan elites from Cuzco invoked the
mythical past while remaining rooted in the present.

The Peruvian army was too politically factionalized, too racially segregated, too lacking in organizational discipline to instill in recruits any
civic habits or democratic sensibilities. If anything, it contributed to the
erosion of whatever faint traces of social equality and political liberty existed in the country. Civic militias, in contrast, imbued citizens with notions of nationhood and civic democracy and played a pivotal rule in driving the army back into their barracks and demilitarizing political society,
thus paving the way for civilians to practice politics.

In July 1845, after nearly a decade and a half of authoritarian rule,
Lima's citizenry, with the aid of several militia units from nearby towns,
successfully defended the capital against an attack from General Echenique's army, signaling a decline in militarism and the rise of civilian rule.
When news reached Lima's residents that General Echenique was marching on the capital, more than 2,500 citizens gathered in the central plaza
and had a public debate to decide whether or not to surrender the city.
They decided to defend it and agreed to organize themselves into civic
militias, with residents from each neighborhood taking responsibility for
defense of their home territory. According to a contemporary, the mili-

26. Quoted in Walker, "Peasants, Caudillos and the State," 190.
27. Echenique, *Memorias*, 1.73.
28. Gootenberg, "North-South," 294, does not discuss the broader socio-moral and political implications of neo-Incan nationhood.

tia commander, Domingo Elías, toured the various neighborhoods and stopped in each one; "he knew how to harangue Lima's rabble, and they promised him they would not surrender . . . they [spent the rest of the day] erecting barricades, digging trenches and lifting each other's fighting spirit."[29]

The "Semana Magna," as contemporaries came to call the eventful week, was not nearly as heroic as its name suggests; nevertheless, its significance to political life is undeniable, as it represents the first time in the country's history that citizens defeated the national army. The Semana Magna demilitarized public life and initiated a period of relative political stability that was to last for two years. Even more importantly, it shattered forever the notion that the soldiers rather than the citizens were the embodiment of democratic notions of sovereignty of the people. This uprising was, admittedly, unimpressive in military terms, but it altered the symbolic landscape. From here on, civilians, not soldiers, were said to be the embodiment of nationhood, a subtle change in mentality that is reflected in newspaper articles from this period:

> it is still not too late, even after 22 years of unruly liberty, to renew Peru by challenging the military oligarchy which has always proclaimed itself . . . guarantors of patriotism, enlightenment, morality and all the other civic virtues which we still lack . . . [but] now that the nation is armed, the selfish efforts [of our generals] to control our nation will have to cease.[30]

Democrats had their own citizen militias to protect the sovereignty of the people and nationhood. In the words of a contemporary, militias are "the corollary of and expression of our republican spirit."[31] Although Lima's militia came to be identified with civilian rule, most of the other militias remained committed to military authoritarianism.

Blacks and Indigenous Communities: Taxation and Judicial Protection

Indigenous peoples paid taxes in order to remain outside the political domain, as a way of not becoming citizens. Forty percent of the state's annual income came from village communities, and any attempt to change or intrude in the internal affairs of those communities was likely to undermine the state's own fiscal foundations:

> During the first half century of republican rule in Peru, neither liberal decrees nor tributary status significantly affected the Indian communi-

29. Heinrich Witt, *Diario y observaciones sobre el Perú del siglo XIX*, trans. Gladys Flórez-Estrada, vol. 1 (Lima: Banco Mercantil, 1992), 246.

30. XZ, "Honor y gloria a los nacionales de Ica," *El Comercio*, 24 December 1843, 3.

31. "Honor y gloria a los nacionales de Ica," *El Comercio*, 25 December 1843, 2; Domingo Elías, *Manifiesto a la nación* (Lima, 1844), 3.

ties. Naturally isolated and sheltered by the breakdown in national politics, communications and markets . . . indigenous communities were left mainly to themselves. No army of local officials entered their hamlets, and the local *hacendados* was reduced to first among equals. . . . During this period, many quietly resisted encroachments from . . . Hispanic society, and few stopped or cared to stop being Indians.[32]

In exchange for paying a head tax, indigenous peoples were allowed to live in a sort of socio-legal bubble, one that was neither colonial nor postcolonial, authoritarian nor democratic, civilian nor militaristic, national nor ethnic, only communal. In contrast to their function in western Europe, taxation practices in Peru contributed to the fragmentation of democratic nationhood and the spread of non-citizenship.

Afro-Peruvians relied heavily on the judicial system to gain manumission and to balance power relations between themselves and their masters, rarely if ever adopting collective solutions to their common plight. Slaves were interested in social and civic freedom, but they were not interested in practicing politics. Masters and slaves were locked in judicial struggle, with accuser and accused presenting their case in front of the "Defensor de Menores," with surprising results; in the words of a landlord, the Defensor was our "greatest enemy and most terrible obstacle. The smallest detail reported to him by any slave is usually taken as evidence . . . against an owner. . . . There is not one *hacendado* who, if asked, would disagree with this statement."[33] Slaves had a different view of the Defensor, regarding his court chamber, in the words of one of them, as "their only refuge . . . [from which] to escape . . . oppression."[34] The Defensor played an especially important role after 1839, during the worst period of authoritarian rule, when the government was trying to repair authority relations and restore social discipline across public life.[35] Judicial cases were organized on an "individual" basis, with the Defensor reviewing the evidence in the privacy of his chamber and making a judgment based on it, a method that was relatively effective in protecting the individual rights of slaves while at the same time depoliticizing and disaggregating them as a group.[36]

32. Paul Gootenberg, *Población y etnicidad en el Perú republicano* (Lima: Instituto de Estudios Peruanos, 1995).

33. Quoted in Carlos Aguirre, *Agentes de su propia libertad* (Lima: Pontífica Universidad Católica del Perú, 1993), 65; Basadre, *Historia*, 2.833–34 for a history of the institution of Public Defender.

34. Quoted in Aguirre, *Agentes*, 190.

35. Santiago Tavara, *Abolición de la esclavitud en el Perú* (Lima, 1855), 19.

36. Aguirre, *Agentes*, 107, 190–97, notes that in 1841, a group of twenty-one slaves organized a "class" action suit against Juan Calorio, a tenant farmer. The case was unique and this is why it caught the attention of other slave owners.

Elections, Mass Movements, and Voting Clubs

During the first half of the century, Peruvians had two elections—in 1831 and 1851.[37] Each one of them generated new forms of political life. During the first, democratic-minded citizens organized a political rebellion to prevent the army from annulling the election. Because they were unable to defeat the military, President Luis de Orbegoso and his civilian supporters requested that Bolivia's government invade, occupy, and annex Peru. The Peruvian-Bolivian Confederation lasted from 1836 to 1839, and served to further discredit civic democracy among the Peruvian elite and non-elite. During the 1852 presidential election, Peruvians organized voting clubs in the nation's capital in order to challenge the army's control of electoral life.

Voting requirements for the 1831 and 1850 presidential elections were, in contrast to Mexico, very exclusionary and restrictive and were based on a complex set of requirements related to income, literacy, residency, and moral character. More than 95 percent of Peruvians were disqualified from participating in elections as a result of the rules.[38] Voting in Peru was multi-stage and indirect, with the first stage taking place in the neighborhood parish and lasting for a week or so. At this stage eligible voters elected their "representative" to the electoral college. The second stage, which lasted another week, took place in the state's capital, with electors from each district gathered together in the college to vote for members of the national congress. The third and final stage, relatively brief and simple, was held in Lima in the congressional chamber, with deputies and senators voting for the president.

The few citizens who voted in Peruvian elections did so at the local parish, the one place where sovereignty of the people had any meaning for them.[39] Although participation in these elections was restricted to only a very few, as I noted earlier, they attracted voters and nonvoters alike, with the latter serving as human shields for candidates and their supporters and assaulting the opposition near the voting booth.

The 1831 elections proceeded as planned, moving from the parish to the provincial college and from there to the halls of congress, with gov-

---

37. Basadre, *Historia*, 2.753, 911–13, 920–27.

38. Convención Nacional, *Colección de las leyes reglamentarias de elecciones municipalidades y jueces de paz* (Lima, 1834). Also see Jorge Basadre, *Elecciones y centralismo en el Perú* (Lima: Universidad del Pacífico, 1980), 6–32.

39. Archivo Histórico Municipal (Lima, Peru), "Cabildo: Junta Municipal; Registros Cívicos y Elecciones," C-3 to D-37, 38, 39, 40, 42, 45; and C-4 to D-53. Elections were exclusionary, but participation was relatively high among the small number of citizens who actually qualified to vote. The electoral turnout for several of Lima's parishes: Santa Ana (85 percent), San Sebastián (68 percent) Sagrario (67 percent), and San Marcelo (54 percent).

ernment officials intervening at each step of the way and making the entire process fraudulent and corrupt.[40] But in the last stage congressional deputies withdrew their support from the official candidate and voted for the opposing candidate, Luis de Orbegoso. The president, Agustín Gamarra, called out the army and annulled the elections, and the citizenry reacted by organizing rebellions throughout the country.[41] Although this election was no more fraudulent than any other, it was the only one that stirred citizens to action, which suggests that they had imbued it with special significance, having invested the voting process with their own sense of democratic sovereignty.

Civilians organized local rebellions in Lima, Ayacucho, Cuzco, Arequipa, and several smaller towns and villages across southern Peru between January and August 1833. The first erupted in Lima when members of the municipal council, along with the "lazies, slaves, and . . . the most depraved members of society . . . filled the central plaza and streets of the capital, and began exchanging gunfire with soldiers." The fighting continued throughout the night, forcing the army and the president to flee the city at dawn. The "rabble" moved in and attacked the main visible symbols of military rule, "forcing their way into the Presidential Palace, and looting the homes of known Gamarristas . . . [and] also the Military Academy."[42] The plebeians who selected and attacked these targets seem to have been much more politically conscious, disciplined, and deliberate than is often assumed.[43] Similar rebellions broke out in the provinces. General Echenique, a Gamarra loyalist, noted during his march from Lima to the Andean highlands that residents from the Valley of Canta, near the capital, were "in arms against us . . . to such an extent that it was impossible to [obtain food and supplies] even from the children

40. A dispute broke out between the president and the deputies. Congress was in recess, and this is why the members of the Constituent Assembly were given the responsibility of selecting the country's president, voting for Orbegoso over Bermúdez, the official candidate, and provoking General/President Gamarra and his followers to rebel.

41. José María Blanco, *Diario del viaje del Presidente Orbegoso al sur del Perú* (Lima: Pontífica Universidad Católica del Perú, 1974), 124, 222; Modesto Basadre y Chocano, *Diez años de historia política del Perú, 1834–1844* (Lima: Editorial Huascarán, 1953), 1–2; "Comunicados," *El Genio del Rímac*, 26 November 1834, 2; "Cuadernos Primero," *El Genio del Rímac*, 30 November 1833, 2; "Cuaderno Tercero," *El Genio del Rímac*, 2 December 1833, 2; "El Genio," *El Genio del Rímac*, 24 December 1834, 2; "Interesante," *El Genio del Rímac*, 19 December 1834,2; Doce Ciudadanos de Chincha-Abajos, "Elecciones de Chincha-Abajo," *El Genio del Rímac*, 23 December 1833, 2; Juan Bautista Bolívar, "Alcance," *El Genio del Rímac*, 30 December 1833, 2; "Señores Editores," *El Telégrafo de Lima*, 4 July 1833, 2; "Pillografía," *El Telégrafo de Lima*, 9 July 1833, 2; Valdivia, *Memorias*, 1.19–20.

42. Basadre, *Historia*, 1.336. For contemporary accounts: Echenique, *Memorias*, 1.17, 46–55; and *El Limeno*, 15 April 1834, 1.

43. Basadre, *Historia*, 1.336.

and women." Further inland, in the mining town of Pasco, more than
1,000 men armed with rifles and slings blocked the entrance to the city,
preventing Echenique's army from entering it. In Ayacucho, in July of the
same year, indigenous people and mixed-bloods joined together and expelled the local prefect, an ally of President Gamarra.[44] Anti-authoritarian
practices were even surfacing in Cuzco, Gamarra's hometown; in August
1830 a coalition composed of artisans, lawyers, churchmen, and (sur-
prisingly enough) landowners, traditionally bulwarks of authoritarianism
in this region, expelled Gamarrista officials from their posts.[45] There was
"a great deal of ferment" across the southern half of the country, with
"groups from all sectors of society" criticizing and attacking them and
distributing pamphlets and flyers among the militia of each region, inviting them to join the rebellion.[46] In the absence of an organized, unified,
and hierarchical political party, these rebellions remained locally rooted
and disconnected from each other. Each one was nourished and sustained
by preexisting civic ties and democratic institutions and practices among
the residents of these towns, villages, and hamlets.

President Orbegoso's civilian government triumphed because of these
citizen-led movements and they remained his principal base of support
throughout his brief tenure. Soon after gaining power, Orbegoso and
members of his government organized a "political pilgrimage" across
southern Peru, taking several months to travel from Lima to Cuzco, stop-
ping along the way to meet with their supporters and using the opportunity to build a nationwide network of support for civilianism. Wherever
it went, the president's entourage was greeted by groups of dancing Indians dressed in regional costume who would escort them to the central plaza, where local residents, mostly mixed-bloods and indigenous
peoples, were gathered and ready to partake in a public banquet. Between
patriotic speeches and toasts, local residents and government officials discussed ways the central government could assist them. This was the first
time these residents had any direct contact with government officials.[47]
Citizens and officials mingled, eroding some of the social, institutional,
and regional differences between ruler and ruled, contributing to the "cre-
olization" of civic democracy, transforming the sensibilities of both groups
and making them responsive to each other's needs. Popular rebellions,
public celebrations, and political pilgrimages were the primary vehicles

44. Echenique, *Memorias*, 1.51–55; "El Genio del Rímac," *El Genio del Rímac*, 27 November 1833, 2; "Ayacucho," *El Genio del Rímac*, 25 November 1833, 2.
45. Walker, "Peasants, Caudillo and the State," 201–3.
46. "El Genio del Rímac," *El Genio del Rímac*, 20 November 1834, 2.
47. Blanco, *Diario del viaje*, 70–218.

available to civic liberals at this time, but because none of the groups in the coalition were capable of forging lasting ties, democratic practices remained weak, scattered, and limited to a few isolated enclaves in a sea of authoritarianism. In 1834, when the army deposed President Orbegoso, he invited the Bolivian government under President Santa Cruz to occupy the country. Bolivia annexed Peru and ruled over it as part of a confederation until 1839. From then until the mid-1840s, civilian rule in Peru was associated with anti-nationalism.

The presidential election of 1850–1851 was the second time since independence was declared that citizens used electoral means to transfer power from one government to the next. More importantly, it was the first time citizens organized electoral clubs, which they used to undermine government control of the voting process at the parish level. The emergence of clubs expressed a subtle change in the political subjectivity of people who imagined themselves as democratic citizens rather than as junior allies of congressional elites. In the citizen-led rebellion of 1831, democratic-minded Peruvians revolted to express their support for congress and their choice for president; citizens became involved in these elections only at the last stage of the process. Electoral clubs, in contrast, were organized at the outset; were focused on parish elections, the first stage of the electoral process; and aimed at increasing voter participation. Electoral clubs marked an important change in political life.

The presidential election of 1850–1851 was the most closely contested to date, and also had the highest voter turnout. Citizens at the parish level were active in the campaign from the outset. Among Lima's citizens,

> newspaper discussions . . . have turned into shouting matches . . . private letters are exchanged constantly, and parish residents are always organizing meetings . . . in support of one or another candidate. . . .[48]

This election was also more violent and corrupt than any previous one; the opposition was organized and prepared to challenge state officials' continued control of voting booths. The competition was fierce at the parish level, the one place where the abstract phrase "sovereignty of the people" was most palpable.[49] This was the first election in which citizens organized electoral clubs across the country to challenge the army's control of political life. Parishes with the most active clubs were the most civic; ironically, they were also the most violent. Electoral practices in the

48. *Relación suscinta de los principales hechos ocurridos en algunos pueblos del Perú, con motivo de la ingerencia de los funcionarios políticos en la renovación de los colegios electorales* (Lima, 1850), 5–6.
49. "Revista," *El Progreso*, 2 March 1850, 2.

political domain were as hybrid as in all the other terrains, with citizens fusing civic and uncivic tendencies and practices in order to undermine authoritarian rule and usher in democratic life.

Political citizenship had begun to stir, although it had only surfaced in a few places across the landscape and was sustained by only a small number of Peruvians. The majority of electoral clubs (fourteen, or 66 percent) appeared between 1849 and 1853; most of them emerged in the months prior to the election and dissolved soon after. The Club Progresista was the most important electoral club, with branches in Lima and the capitals and major towns in several provinces, including Cajamarca, Arequipa, Cuzco, Huaraz, Puno, and Trujillo.[50] The formation of clubs in some of these places spawned yet more new clubs, making parish elections dynamic and competitive. Cajamarca is typical in this regard. Citizens had "divided into four camps . . . before the gendarmes attacked them, [then] they united themselves into one single party to put an end to the government's abuse."[51] Clubs provided citizens an opportunity to forge horizontal alliances between rival political groups in order to challenge the military, which lorded over them. Despite their significance, there were only a few clubs, mostly concentrated in Lima—not enough to challenge authoritarian rule in the country.

Social relations in electoral clubs were intensely personal and somewhat clientelistic, causing dismay among their leaders. The editors of *El Progreso,* a supporter of the Club, attributed this shortcoming to the citizenry's lack of political experience and encouraged rank-and-file members to change their ways:

> The Club . . . is not motivated by or attached to individuals . . . and is independent of all personal interests. Our only reason for existing is to participate in elections, and we will endure only as long as they are in effect. . . . Our only means of making our case is by using newspapers and by relying on participation.[52]

Political ties among citizens, according to the editors, were different from social relations. The former were based on ideological principles, whereas the latter were based on personal gain and loyalty:

> the other parties deliberately focus on . . . personalities . . . the names of Echenique and Vivancos reverberate on either side, with each side waving its banner and burning incense in front of their leader. . . . But

50. Basadre, *Historia,* 2.918; Juan Luis Orrego, "Domingo Elías y el Club Progresista," (B.A. thesis, Pontífica Universidad Católica del Perú, 1989).
51. "Elecciones en Cajamarca," *El Comercio,* 27 February 1850, 2.
52. "Principios políticos del Club," *El Progreso,* 8 December 1849, 1–2

what are the principles of each party; what is the program that they are offering to the nation? This is what we never get from them, and this is precisely what the fatherland demands of us. . . .[53]

Although the Progressive Clubs accused their rivals of relying mainly on "individual ties, promises, friendships, and family relations to enlarge their circle [of members]," they did the same thing, according to the Chilean publicist José Victoriano Lastarria:

> personal affections and factional interests. . . . The [Progresista Club] which sustains Elias' candidacy has already publicized its program and while I have no doubt that they have every intention of delivering on it, I remain skeptical that it expresses the . . . opinions of its affiliates. . . . [In any case),] there are no political parties [in Peru]. And what I have said here also applies to Vivanco and Echenique's parties.[54]

The Progressives employed a "universalistic" argument based on "general" principles in order to distinguish themselves from their rivals although in fact both of them relied on clientelism and patronage to recruit members and advance their cause.

Voting practices at the local level were extremely corrupt. In Lima, for example, where the opposition and government-sponsored clubs were most numerous and active, members from the latter deprived "hundreds of voters . . . [of] their right to suffrage," tampered with the voting rolls, and gave "vagabonds and thieves" marked ballots to deposit in the electoral urn.[55] On voting day, rival clubs partitioned the city and took over different areas, seizing control of all the cafes and taverns, standing guard in all major thoroughfares, and defending their turf by attacking opposition members with knives and clubs. Street brawls broke out in every neighborhood, with rival groups competing for control of the voting urn in which all the ballots had been deposited. The winning side, once it had seized the urn, would throw away any ballots marked for the opposing candidate.[56] In outlying towns in Ayacucho and Cajamarca where associative life remained undeveloped, soldiers assaulted and incarcerated anti-government voters and paid plebeian groups to do the same.[57] Club

53. "Programa político," *El Progreso,* 29 December 1849, 2; "Política del Club," *El Progreso,* 15 December 1850, 2.

54. "Principios políticos del Club," *El Progreso,* 8 December 1849, 1–2; and José Victorino Lastarria, "Lima en 1850," in *Viajeros en el Perú republicano,* ed. Alberto Tauro (Lima: Universidad Nacional Mayor de San Marcos, 1967), 108–9.

55. *Relación suscinta de los principales hechos,* 6, 10.

56. *Relación suscinta de los principales hechos,* 10–16, 18. Some of these battles lasted for two hours and were quite bloody: "200 negroes [remained outside the plaza] armed with carbines, pistols, clubs and rocks" ready to "finish off the injured and those in retreat."

57. *Relación suscinta de los principales hechos,* 18–33, 36–39, 47–54, 63–69.

life in Tacna, Ayacucho, and Huancavelica remained weak, allowing local officials to bribe a thousand or so indigenous peoples with money and
drinks in exchange for their votes.

Electoral fraud was common and widespread, but in some places the
voting process was orderly and peaceful, in part because of the balance of
power that existed between electoral clubs and state officials. In Huancavelica and Jauja, the voting process was imperfect but more or less tranquil, with citizens organizing street marches of some six hundred strong
to express support for their candidate and to protest irregularities in the
procedure. And in some of Lima's most important parishes, including San
Sebastian, the electoral process was quite fair. The same was true in several provincial towns, including Moquegua, Yauyos, Huarochirí, Piura,
and Jauja. Electoral clubs contributed to the spread of civic democracy in
these places, although it would take another half century or so for democratic tendencies and practices to become fully integrated into public life.

This street-level analysis of voting practices will give us a clearer and
more nuanced view of the 1851 presidential elections and will enable us
to establish where electoral clubs where strongest—in other words, where
democracy was most rooted.[58] In the 1851 election, the official candidate (Echenique) won 63 percent of the votes; the remaining 37 percent
were distributed unevenly among his four opponents (Elías, Vivanco, San
Román, and Bermúdez). The skewed distribution reflects the fraudulent
character of these elections. Corruption was rooted more deeply in some
regions than in others. Echenique won handily in Huancayo (100 percent), Tacna (99 percent), Ayacucho (90 percent), Cuzco (82 percent),
Puno (70 percent), and Junín (68 percent). He obtained a narrower victory in Lima (59 percent) and Arequipa (52 percent), and lost in Huaraz
(28 percent) and La Libertad (46 percent).[59] Echenique was strongest in
those places where the opposition did not have electoral clubs and in areas where local officials were able to deny opposition voters access to the
voting stations. In those provinces where the opposition had its most active electoral clubs, the official candidate did poorly or only moderately
well. The opposition, however, also lost in some places where they had

58. Basadre, *Historia*, 3.295.
59. My estimates are based on the following: "Elecciones," *El Comercio*, 9 January
1851, 2; "Crónica electoral," *El Comercio*, 5 January 1851, 2; "Extractos," *El Comercio*,
6 January 1851, 3. According to the most reliable data available, the electoral colleges
turned in a total of 3,804 marked ballots, which broke down as follows: Echenique (2,392),
Elías (609), and Vivanco (326). The remaining 295 votes went to minor candidates: San
Román (242), Bermúdez (52), and Iguain (1). The Progresistas were also strong in La Libertad and Huaraz, while Vivanquista clubs were strongest in the candidate's hometown
of Arequipa (46 percent) and in Junín (17 percent), with a small following in several other
areas.

very active clubs, including Lima, because the electoral field was crowded by anti-government candidates. Echenique secured only 20 percent of the vote in the state that included Lima, but the official candidate won by a slight margin; the remainder of the votes were distributed evenly among several candidates.[60]

Associative life in political society remained undeveloped and the notion of citizenship remained poorly understood; however, it had by now surfaced in Junín, Lima, La Libertad, and Arequipa. Members of the Club launched a campaign to persuade citizens that the "nation," by partaking in presidential elections, was seeking to transfer sovereignty from the national army to the country's voters, contrary to what had been claimed to that point. In other words, elections formed part of a broader symbolic struggle between civilians and authoritarians over the meaning of the phrase "sovereignty of the people." Democratic-minded voters changed strategy from leading mass rebellions to organizing voting clubs.

This change was especially evident among Lima's artisans. Many of them transformed their guilds into political associations:

> [Master artisans] under pressure from [followers] became eloquent spokesmen for artisan interest. . . . Guild organization provided craftsmen with a ready-made structure for mobilization [as] seen clearly in the way artisan demands were framed, meetings [were] organized, and electoral pressures handled during the 1849–1851 agitation over the tariff question.[61]

Artisans in the city's most politicized guilds also circulated petitions and organized mass demonstrations to protest the state's lifting of tariff barriers. In addition, they published countless pamphlets and newspaper articles in *El Comercio* reminding politicians that they were now a political force to be reckoned with: "we have defended . . . you with our votes [and] chosen your as our representatives."[62] Lima's artisans used the slogan "We are the majority," a phrase that suggests the extent to which they had already assimilated the notion of democratic sovereignty. In October 1854, they sent a cigar maker, José María García, to argue their case before the members of the national congress, and although the government did not change its policy, his appearance before the country's deputies, president, and ministers signaled a shift in the symbolic landscape of political life.

---

60. See note 59 for the sources of these data. I eliminated all "annulled" and "dual" votes from my calculations.

61. Paul Gootenberg, "Artisans and Merchants: The Making of an Open Economy in Lima, Peru, 1830–1860" (Master's thesis, Oxford University, 1981), 139.

62. "Clamor a los padres de la patria," *El Comercio,* 4 August 1849, 2.

Public Morality, Political Revolution, and Decentralization of Power

In the 1850s, the sale of guano provided the national treasury with about three times as much annual income as had been available previously, providing government officials the wherewithal to modernize the state and to pacify military chieftains throughout the country. As part of these reforms, officials replaced old colonial statutes and legal codes with liberal, republican laws that protected property and personal rights, enshrining these in the country's first Civil and Commercial Code in the early 1850s. The legal historian Fernando Trazegnies has clarified the meaning of these codes for public life:

> the main concern was not with creating a juridical framework for ushering in a liberal economy. Instead, the basic priority was to organize a state . . . and this is why the legal order which emerged, although inspired by liberal premises, pursued aims entirely foreign to it.[63]

In Peru, these codes paved the way for the formation of a national state rather than the development of economic markets, as in western Europe and the United States.

These codes provided a legal framework for property rights, enabling wealthy merchants and landowners to demand monetary indemnification from the national treasury for the losses they had incurred in 1854 when the government abolished slavery. In less than a year, treasury officials paid out nearly 7 million pesos to almost two thousand former slave owners, the majority of whom resided in the state of Lima. The terms of the agreement were exceeedingly generous, with the treasury paying up to 300 pesos for each slave, regardless of their real market worth or their physical condition. The process was fraught with other irregularities, with owners often listing many more slaves than they had ever owned and claiming payment for slaves who had in fact paid for their own manumission.[64] This code increased the economic power of Lima's landlords, who were among the most important supporters of authoritarian rule, and thereby ironically further undermined the liberal and democratic foundations of political society in Peru.

The government also indemnified the elite for the losses they had incurred during the independence wars and civil wars. Fernando Casos, an

---

63. Fernando Trazegnies, *La idea de derecho en el Perú republicano del siglo XIX* (Lima: Pontífica Universidad Católica del Perú, 1992), 47–48, 201–2, 325–35.

64. Alfonso Quiroz, *La deuda defraudada: Consolidación de 1850 y dominio económico del Perú* (Lima: Instituto Nacional de Cultura, 1987), 159. Masters often received much more than their slaves were actually worth in the "market" and were even paid for slaves who had already bought their own freedom through manumission.

influential publicist, argued vigorously against both, but most especially the first:

> Wasn't it the duty of the entire [Peruvian nation] ... to gain our liberty? We were all involved in this ... with each one contributing his share ... the rich with his fortune, because he did not want to run personal risks, and the poor with his own blood because that is all he had to give.[65]

The government ignored his argument and distributed approximately 24 million pesos among nearly 2,900 citizens, with the majority of the funds going to the same Lima merchants and landlords who had benefited previously. According to Alfonso Quiroz, the leading scholar on this topic, the process by which the claims were made and funds transferred was riddled with corruption:

> Government officials and their merchant partners obtained large sums through forgery, fake recognition of claims, and other illegal means, and rapidly sold their tainted bonds to avoid prosecution. ... Beneath the surface, the corruption of the Consolidation was an expression of the political struggle between the opposing supporters of military [and civilian rule].[66]

These policies reinforced the widely held view that public institutions were the patrimony of the elite rather than the embodiment of the nation.

The central government and state had become more stable, but citizens still refused to invest sovereignty of the people in any of its institutions, considering them corrupt and unworthy of the honor. An influential pamphlet, written by one Timoleón, explained:

> In the eyes of the nation, our government ceased to be the just and fair administrator of national treasury, and became, instead, beholden to a band of favorites ... whose aspirations came at the price of our treasury and constitution.[67]

The Consolidation scheme, as it came to be known, was part of a symbolic and moral struggle over the meaning of nationhood and citizenship in the country, a struggle made all the more complicated by public accusations of graft and corruption leveled against government officials. The citizenry remained firm in their anti-militarism but became critical of civilian officials who used public monies for private gain. And they regis-

---

65. Fernando Casos, *Para la historia de Perú* (Cuzco, 1854), 26–27; Quiroz, *Deuda defraudada*, 49.

66. Alfonso Quiroz, *Domestic and Foreign Finance in Modern Peru, 1850–1950* (Pittsburgh, Pa.: University of Pittsburgh Press, 1993), 25.

67. Timoleón, *El Perú y los gobiernos del General Echenique y de la Revolución* (Lima, 1855), 15–16.

tered their disapproval in the only way they could, by organizing a mass rebellion, the largest to date, winning over the support of elite and non-elite groups throughout the country.

Citizens in Lima and a dozen or so towns across the provinces rebelled in protest against public corruption. In the country's capital, artisans, blacks, and elite groups joined together and rebelled, much as they had done in the 1830s in support of the presidential candidate selected by Congress. But this rebellion was different, according to Jorge Basadre:

> it came from below, it was general, uncontainable, much more extensive and thorough than the one in 1834 . . . it was a plebiscite against a regime accused of thievery. . . . Moreover, the [recent] abolition of slavery and the suppression of the indigenous head tax infused a social content into this civil war, making it the first of its kind. The entire country was shaken, from one end to the other. . . .[68]

The rebellion in the capital was spontaneous and based in the masses, with plebeian groups choosing their political targets with considerable precision. In Lima, Manuel Mendiburru, a target of the uprising, described the rebellion from the window of his home:

> bands of blacks . . . crossing the streets and mingling with the vulgar rabble . . . hurling epithets . . . and denouncing their [opponents] with the terms thief and "consolidado." . . . [Artisans] joined them and brought along a cannon from . . . the military school, and were aiming it at the doors of [several homes]. . . . The homes of [President] Echenique, his supporters, and his public officials suffered cruel attacks, as well as the presidential palace, which was sacked and destroyed, also spreading to [adjacent] ministries, public offices and archives. The vice-president's home was also completely destroyed.[69]

Citizens attacked government officials and the economic elite for stealing public monies, calling them "thieves" and "consolidators," which indicates that they knew very well why they were rebelling; these were no "primitive rebels," to use Eric Hobsbawn's phrase. They rebelled in order to protect public norms and to prevent the economic elite from privatizing the state, which they now identified with the nation at large.

Throughout the countryside, many of those who had joined voting clubs and participated in the previous election now rebelled. More than fourteen towns joined the uprising, with local notables playing leading

---

68. Basadre, *Historia*, 1.312. This was the most important mass movement of the period, but we still lack any study of it.
69. Quoted in Quiroz, *Deuda defraudada*, 134–35.

roles.[70] In order to coordinate their efforts, leaders reorganized municipal life, relying on townships to recruit rebels, collect funds from local residents, and provide citizens a place to debate common concerns. Township delegates visited each other and negotiated demands throughout the uprising, to the dismay of Lima's rebels, who wanted to remain in control of the movement. They were unable to do so, and were for the first time in the country's history forced to yield to the demands of the provincial elite. In exchange for continued support, Lima's elite agreed to decentralize power, revive municipal townships, and replace all the old centralist political institutions with federalist ones, supported by a new constitution.[71]

The movements that erupted in the capital and in the provinces were committed to the same goal, although the demands they made were slightly different because of their different interpretations of the recent fiasco. According to the provincial elite, the only way of preventing government corruption and insuring accountability of public officials was by decentralizing power; Lima's rebels claimed that changing the government would be enough to alter public morality.[72] The revolution triumphed and President Castilla's new government delivered on the promise made earlier to the rebels throughout the province, resurrecting the regional councils and municipal townships that had been abolished in the 1830s.

In Peru, military despotism denied citizens a place to practice politics, thereby reaffirming their own strong disposition to live with their backs to the state.

70. Carmen McEvoy, *Un proyecto nacional en el siglo XIX* (Lima: Pontífica Universidad Católica del Perú, 1994), 57–58.

71. Frederick Pike, *The Modern History of Peru* (New York: Praeger, 1967), 100–103.

72. The residents of Cajamarca, in the north, were among the most committed to federalism. They seceded from La Libertad and created their own province, a precedent that was soon followed by other provinces.

CHAPTER 9

Learning a Language:
The Mexican Public Sphere

Prior to mid-century, the overwhelming majority of Mexicans did not participate in the public sphere. Illiteracy rates were extremely high, and linguistic differences and government censorship of the press made it difficult for citizens to deliberate publicly about common concerns. In addition to newspapers, which were relatively expensive and had a limited readership, Mexicans relied on gossip networks and other informal communicative practices to criticize the authoritarian regime. Mexicans created a new vernacular, Civic Catholicism, and used it in their public discussions. Central to it was the notion of associative life. Associations were designed to reconcile the age-old Catholic concern for socio-moral order with the new democratic concern for self-rule.

This chapter is divided into three parts. The first analyzes the production and circulation of newspapers; the second discusses communicative practices and networks among the elite and non-elite; and the last examines the ways public writers and intellectuals used Civic Catholicism.[1] Critical deliberation and public opinion in Mexico, limited as it was, was far more developed than in Peru, which I discuss in chapter 10.

Socio-institutional Structures

Mexicans published no fewer than 358 newspapers and tabloids between 1826 and 1856. The number of publications varied significantly from one five-year period to the next and also by region (fig. 9.1).[2] From 1826–

---

1. Jacqueline Covo, "La prensa en la historiografía mexicana," *Historia Mexicana* 42, no. 3 (1993): 699, on the role of public intellectuals in Mexico.

2. Data compiled from the following sources: Enrique Dávila Diez and Silvia Soledad Jiménez, *La prensa en México del siglo XIX al periodo revolucionario* (Mexico City: Universidad Nacional Autónoma de México, n.d.); Archivo General de la Nación, *Catálogo de*

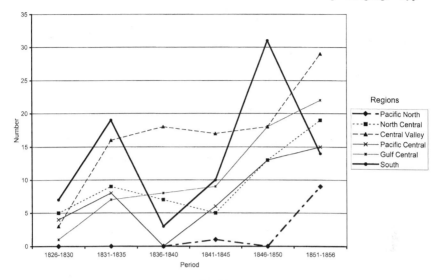

Figure 9.1   Newspaper Production and Public Opinion, 1826–1856

1830 to 1831–1835, the number of publications in the country rose from 20 to 53 primarily because of the political unrest following the 1828 presidential election. The number then dropped to 38 in 1836–1840 with the coming to power of the authoritarian regime. Newspaper production rose, ironically, after the regime became consolidated; in order to avoid censorship, public writers restrained themselves (see below), leading state officials to relax their control of the press. The number of publications climbed during this period, from 48 in 1841–1845, to 93 in 1846–1850, to 108 in 1851–1855 when the regime was finally toppled. Most publications produced during the first half of the century were short-lived (less than three years), but because production was relatively constant, the public sphere remained well-stocked.

In regional terms, the Central Valley accounted for 40 percent of all new publications in the country.[3] The southern region was home to 21 per-

---

la Hemeroteca (Mexico City: n.p., n.d.); Biblioteca Nacional, *Catálogo de la Hemeroteca* (Mexico City: n.p., n.d.); Fernando Castañón Gamboa, *La imprenta y el periodismo en Chiapas* (Tuxtla: Universidad Autónoma de Chiapas, 1983); José Lama, *La imprenta y el periodismo en el estado de Veracruz* (Veracruz: Universidad Autónoma de Veracruz, 1987); Francisco Madrid and Carlos Sánchez, *Un siglo de prensa en Oaxaca: 1835–1943* (Oaxaca: Universidad Autónoma "Benito Juarez" de Oaxáca, 1987); and Margarita Luna García, *La prensa en el estado de México en el siglo XIX* (Mexico City: Secretaría de Educación Pública, 1986).

3. The six regions are: (1) Central Valley (Mexico City, Mexico, Tlaxcala); (2) South (Yucatán, Campeche, Chiapas, Tabasco, Oaxaca); (3) Gulf Central (Puebla, Veracruz, Hidalgo, Querétaro, Guanajuato); (4) North Central (Chihuahua, Coahuila, Durango, Nuevo León, Tamaulipas, San Luis Potosí, Aguascalientes, Zacatecas); (5) Pacific Central (Jalisco, Gue-

cent, followed by the Gulf central with 18 percent, the north central with 16 percent, and the Pacific central with 13 percent. Newspapers did not appear in the Pacific north until the mid-1850s.

Newspaper production was limited due to a host of sociocultural and political factors. Illiteracy was widespread. In the late 1830s, José Gómez de la Cortina, a member of the Sociedad Geográfica, visited Mexico City's National Prison and analyzed the arrest sheets of 202 male and female inmates. Forty-eight percent of them could sign their names. Cortina also visited the city's main military barracks and examined the service sheets of 556 recruits. Forty-five percent of them were literate. Cortina's figures are, clearly, too high, the result of having relied on name-signing as the main criterion, a method that remains widely used even by cultural historians today.[4] Literacy among groups slightly higher in the social scale, such as farmers, mule-pack drivers, and tavern owners, has been estimated to be 45 percent, reaffirming our judgment about Cortina's figures.[5] In general, men at the very bottom and middle of the social ladder were three times as likely as women to have reading and writing skills.[6]

Mexico was a multilingual country. In his study of language use in 73 towns and hamlets in the Central Valley, Thomas Powell found that in 33 percent of these communities, most residents were fully bilingual; in another 56 percent, the majority spoke only Spanish; and in the remaining 11 percent they spoke only their native tongue.[7] Indigenous peoples who lived in or near urban areas were far more likely to be bilingual than those who lived in isolated and remote communities in the countryside. Litigation played a key role in the spread of Spanish, according to Edward Tylor, the great English anthropologist:

> [Indians] are excessively litigious, and their continual law-suits take them into large towns [to] courts of justice. . . . There is a natural connexion between farming and lawsuits . . . writs and hard swearing is as

rrero, Michoacán, Morelos, Colima); and (6) the Pacific North (Sonora, Sinaloa, California, Nayarit).

4. José Gómez de la Cortina, "Población," *Boletín del Instituto Nacional de Geografía y Estadística* (Mexico City, 1839), 28–29.

5. Estela Villalba, "El analfabetismo en los instrumentos notariales de la Ciudad de México, 1836–1837," *Historia Mexicana* 30, no. 3 (January–March 1986): 447–60. She sampled 173 notarized documents of all types, including rental contracts, marriage licenses, divorce agreements, and adoption papers.

6. R. S. Schofield, "The Measurement of Literacy in Pre-Industrial England," in *Literacy in Traditional Societies,* ed. J. R. Goody (Cambridge: Cambridge University Press, 1968), 311–25, discusses the problem.

7. T. G. Powell, *El liberalismo y el campesinado en el centro de México,* trans. Roberto Gómez Ciriza (Mexico City: Secretaría de Educación Pública, 1974), 41–72. Because the data he found on the remaining thirty-two communities are inconclusive, I have omitted the communities from my discussion.

remarkable among this agricultural people as it is among our own small farmers in England.[8]

Indigenous peoples who worked in large estates as salaried peons or as sharecroppers were also bilingual. Collective identity also played a key role in what linguists call "code-switching":

> A great many indigenes speak Spanish, however, they do so with a certain repugnance. For them, their language is a repository of feelings and yearnings, and they are fearful of losing their own native tongue. Each time they speak it, they are regaining their sense of nationhood.[9]

A large number of indigenous families who had migrated to or were born in Mexico City remained fluent in their own native tongue because they found Spanish morally repugnant.

Economic factors also shaped newspaper production and contributed to undermining the public sphere. Mexico had to import all its newsprint, which put the price of newspapers out of reach of most citizens. In Mexico City, where newspapers were cheapest, the price of an issue was between ten and twenty reales, roughly twice the price of a kilo of corn. Newspapers were not an item for mass consumption. In the mid-1840s, *Siglo XIX,* Mexico's leading daily, had 2,200 subscribers; the *New York Daily News,* its counterpart in the United States, had eleven times that number.[10]

The market for readers in Mexico City, which had the largest number of readers in the country, remained so limited that the government had to subsidize most newspapers. This undermined critical deliberation and the spread of public opinion:

> the press, with a few notable exceptions has lived . . . off the government and is beholden to it. In return for monies from the national treasury, newspaper writers applaud the government's policies.[11]

The *Siglo* was one of the few newspapers not subsidized.[12] Although the *Monitor* was financed by the state, it remained politically independent and was censored as often as the *Siglo.* The situation throughout the provinces was far worse. The editor of the *Siglo* explains:

8. Edward Burnett Tylor, *Anahuac; or, Mexico and the Mexicans* (London, 1861), 300–301.
9. "Guerra de castas," *Siglo XIX,* 1 August 1848, 3.
10. "Editorial," *Siglo XIX,* 17 April 1845, 3.
11. "La prensa ministerial," *Siglo XIX,* 19 June 1852, 1.
12. Michael Costeloe, "Manuel Arista and the 1850 Presidential Election in Mexico," *Bulletin of Latin American Research* 18, no. 1 (1999): 62. State officials bought 20 percent of all the issues published.

Last week we received in our main office copies of 19 provincial newspapers: 7 from Veracruz, 1 from Jalisco, 2 from Puebla, 2 from Oaxaca, 1 from Matamoros, 1 from Tabasco, 2 from Michoacán, 1 from Sonora, and 1 from Chihuahua. After reading them we came to the conclusion that the majority were worthless. . . . Of the 19 dailies we reviewed, only 7 carried editorials.[13]

The *Siglo XIX, El Monitor, La Sociedad,* and other newspapers published in Mexico City also circulated in the provinces; the *Siglo,* for example, was read in roughly 125 cities and towns outside the nation's capital. Mexico City newspapers provided residents of the provinces with critical information and opinions not found in their own local tabloids.[14] However, because the cost of sending a newspaper by stagecoach from Mexico City to the provinces was relatively high, few provincial readers subscribed. In any case, during the rainy season, the newspapers arrived waterlogged and with the ink smeared across the page, making them unreadable.[15] All these factors served to undermine the public sphere in Mexico.

Communicative Networks

The public sphere in Mexico was populated by newspaper writers, their readers, and by illiterate persons who relied on oral and visual forms of communication to deliberate critically about common concerns.

Reading and Writing Practices

The *Siglo XIX* and *El Monitor Republicano,* the first privately owned dailies, appeared in the early 1840s, at the height of authoritarian rule. In order to prevent government censorship, the editors instructed their own writers to

focus on generalities. Let readers understand your argument, extract from it a specific point and then use it in order to elucidate and correct shortcomings [in our country].[16]

13. "Prensa departamental," *Siglo XIX,* 22 May 1843, 3. Also see: "El siglo XIX y la Gaceta de San Luis Potosí," *Siglo XIX,* 3 January 1842, 3; "Nuevas observaciones sobre la libertad de imprenta," *Siglo XIX,* 10 May 1843, 3; "La prensa ministerial," *Siglo XIX,* 19 June 1852, 1.

14. "Subscripción," *Siglo XIX,* 22 January 1844, 3; "Lista," *La Sociedad,* 2 December 1855, 2. According to Costeloe, "Manuel Arista," 62, during this election, 17 of 45 dailies circulated outside the city in which they were published.

15. "Imprenta y Correos," *Siglo XIX,* 18 November 1843, 2–3; Jesús Hermosa, *Manual de geografía y estadística de la República Mejicana* (Paris, 1857), 56–59.

16. "Fruto que debe sacar un gobierno de los escritores públicos," *Siglo XIX,* 9 May 1843, 3.

Because writers were paid only if their articles were published, most of them complied:

> One of the most important signs of progress in our country is related to the changes that have occurred in the press. . . . We are not referring only to the recent rise in the number of dailies, readership and profit. All three are significant, but what impresses us the most is the improvement in writing style.[17]

Newspaper writers remained critical of government officials, but they were careful not to impugn their reputations or intrude in their personal affairs. Changes in rhetoric contributed to redefining the institutional boundaries between public and private life. In the words of the *Siglo's* editor:

> The private domain of family life is sacred, and no writer has any right to allow his pen to intrude. If anyone violates this by exposing the secrets of any family, then he must be punished. . . . But this raises the question of where the boundary lies between public and private life. The private life of a citizen must be protected, but the personal life of government officials must be subjected to public scrutiny. . . .[18]

Rhetorical practices and institutional structures shaped each other and were reflected in the tone and style of newspaper articles.

In order to prevent state officials from censoring newspapers, editors and their staffs launched a campaign against letter-writers and scribblers who used radical rhetoric. The former (*evangelistas*) made a living composing letters for nonliterate persons and mailing them; the latter (*tinterillos*) were responsible for transcribing official documents such as land titles and contracts and getting them notarized. During periods of unrest, letter-writers and scribblers turned into "agitators and organizers" and became the cultural and political bridge between elite and plebeian groups.[19] Their pamphlets, handbills, and flyers circulated widely among the non-elite:

> If these liberal, fanatical flyers circulated only among the reasonable people of our country, we would not have to worry; educated people cannot be influenced by nonsense. However, these pamphlets circulate from hand to hand among simpletons, and the sophistry and shameful arguments contained in them are producing enormous confusion and infusing them with all sorts of erroneous ideas.[20]

17. "Decoro de la prensa," *Siglo XIX*, 5 March 1845, 3.
18. "Libertad de imprenta," *Siglo XIX*, 18 April 1852, 1.
19. Rafael Rojas, "Una maldición silenciada: El panfleto político en México independiente," *Historia Mexicana* 185 (July-September 1997): 39.
20. José Joaquín Fernández Lizardi, *Dentro de seis años o antes hemos de ser Tolerantes* (Mexico City, 1825), 1.

The radical rhetoric used by pamphleteers often provoked government officials to impose limits on freedom of the press or to practice strict censorship. Because pamphleteers used portable hand presses, they were able to evade state officials, who would then focus their energy on newspaper editors and their publishers, who were comparatively easy targets.[21]

In attacking pamphleteers, newspaper writers were protecting themselves from government censorship, but they were also contributing to deradicalizing public debate:

> [Newspaper writers] have attacked and discredited us for partisan reasons because we hold political views that are different from their own. By condemning our writings before they have reached our public, they have undermined our influence.[22]

Although pamphleteers remained influential in certain communities (see below), by the 1840s newspaper writers had earned the respect and admiration of readers for defending public opinion from the threat of state censorship:

> Public opinion, the capacity to deliberate and evaluate claims in a reasonable manner, belongs to the citizenry, not to the state. Our press enables citizens to discuss public affairs with each other, amongst ourselves, in a moderate manner, listening to each other's reasoning, defending our truth and attacking our own errors. In the course of these debates, the public forms its own opinion.[23]

Citizens granted public intellectuals the same social prestige they had once accorded only to churchmen. While visiting the capital of Zacatecas, Guillermo Prieto, a writer for the *Siglo,* was surprised to find himself "showered with praise and made into an object of esteem."[24] Censorship increased the status of newspaper writers while undermining that of government officials.[25]

Unlike their counterparts in western Europe, public intellectuals in Mexico, Puebla, Veracruz, and other large cities rarely met at home in

21. *Nuevo febrero Mexicano,* vol. 2 (Mexico City, 1850–1852), 766–67; Guy Thomson, *Puebla de los Ángeles: Industry and Society in a Mexican City, 1700–1850* (Boulder, Colo.: Westview Press, 1989), 199, describes how Puebla's artisans circulated pamphlets door to door.
22. José Zorrilla, *México y los Mexicanos,* ed. Andrés Henestrosa (Mexico City: Ediciones de Andrea, 1955), 79.
23. "Opinión Pública," *Siglo XIX,* 19 April 1842, 2–3; "Editorial," *El Monitor Republicano,* 21 February 1847, 2.
24. Guillermo Prieto, *Memorias de mis Tiempos* (Puebla: Editorial J. M. Cájica, 1970), 353, 370, 487, 532.
25. "Subscripción," *Siglo XIX,* 22 January 1844, 3; "Subscripción," *Siglo XIX,* 10 January 1843, 4; "Revista de los periódicos de esta Capital," *Siglo XIX,* 11 October 1842, 3.

literary salons. Instead they met in cafes and other public centers of sociability. Edward Tylor was one of the first to comment on the lack of salon life in the nation's capital, where they had once flourished:

> it must be recollected that many families here are content to live miserably enough at home, if they can manage to appear in good style at the theater and on the promenade. This is one of the reasons why so many of the Mexicans who are so friendly with you out of doors, and in the cafes, are so very shy of letting you see the inside of their houses.[26]

Salon life in the city of Veracruz on the Gulf Coast, the city of Acapulco on the Pacific, and in the state capital of Oaxaca in the far south was even less developed.[27]

The cultural elite congregated outdoors in cafes, corner grocery stores, and arcades in order to avoid having guests visit their shabby homes and running the risk of being ridiculed in public. Mexico City had approximately twenty-five cafes.[28] They were frequented by scribblers, lawyers, medical doctors, office clerks, master artisans, shopkeepers, priests, and other "middling sorts." Carl Sartorius visited several coffee houses and left this description of one:

> people are seated around marble tables, conversing, browsing at dailies, playing chess and dominoes. Congress has just resumed, and the topic of discussion is the upcoming elections and the tactics each party will use to win them.[29]

Puebla, the country's second largest and most conservative city, had three coffee houses. Churchmen still controlled the pulpit and had a captive audience each Sunday; however, according to the bishop, public writers controlled the cafes and had transformed them into centers of cultural heterodoxy: "it is common to hear citizens in our cafes . . . challenge religious truths . . . but rarely do we hear any of our theologians defend them."[30]

By the 1840s, newspaper writers had carved out a central place for themselves in public life:

26. Tylor, *Anahuac*, 64–65.
27. Carl Christian Beecher, *Cartas sobre México: 1832–1833*, trans. Juan A. Ortega (Mexico City: Universidad Nacional Autónoma de México, 1959), 75; Mathieu de Fossey, *Viaje a México* (Mexico City, 1884), 89, 193; Basil Hall, *Extracts from a Journal, Written on the Coast of Chili, Peru and Mexico in the Years 1820, 1821, and 1822*, vol. 2 (Edinburgh, 1824), 196; José María Luis Mora, "Costumbres Mexicanas," in *Calendario de Ramírez* (Mexico City, 1845), 58–63.
28. Manuel Orozco y Berra, *Historia de la Ciudad de México* (1852; Mexico City, 1987), 125–30.
29. Carl Sartorius, *Mexico about 1850* (Stuttgart: Brockhaus, 1961), 111.
30. "Informe que de la comisión de visita de colegios al Exmo. Sr. Gobernador de este departamento de Puebla," cited in Michael Costeloe, *The Central Republic in Mexico: 1835–1846* (Cambridge: Cambridge University Press, 1993), p. 135.

we waited for the postman to deliver *El Siglo;* when it arrived, we then would gather in large groups in cafes, corner stores, arcades, plazas and portals.[31]

Corner stores (*pulperías*) provided the elite and non-elite a place to congregate and discuss public affairs. These all-purpose stores sold everything from cheap liquor (*pulque*) to candles, soap, sugar, and lard. In the mid-1850s, Mexico City had about 530 of them.

Letter writers and scribblers remained influential throughout the countryside and were the first link in a communicative chain that extended from plebeian neighborhoods in the city all the way down to village hamlets. Indigenous peoples and small farmers deep in the countryside relied on them for information and to shape their own opinions about public affairs. In the 1840s, several estate owners from the Central Valley wrote a pamphlet denouncing them for spreading anti-elite propaganda:

> Public orators are denouncing the horrors of the conquest and telling Indians how much they have been wronged, and our ignorant and malevolent scribblers in this region have been spreading this message among indigenous peoples in all the towns nearby.[32]

Letter writers and scribblers also published "almanacks" with all sorts of advice and suggestion on planting, weather patterns, religion, and so on. These calendars circulated widely in plebeian neighborhoods and among rural peoples, who bought them from peddlers. Jose Zorilla, a Spanish writer who visited Mexico in the 1840s and spent some time in the countryside, noted:

> each home in most towns, ranchos and estates, each has 3 or 4 copies of [a calendar]. These calendars contain satirical remarks and diatribes against politicians. Their names appear [in each page], followed by a string of insulting epithets, as if they were nothing more than a common criminal or bandit.[33]

Newspapers circulated mainly in urban areas among the literate public, while handbills, flyers, and calendars circulated primarily among plebeians in urban areas and among rural peoples across the provinces.

---

31. Prieto, *Memorias*, 352–53; Guillermo Prieto, *Viajes de orden suprema*, vol. 1 (Mexico City: Editorial Porrúa, 1986), 99; and Antonio García Cubas, *El libro de mis recuerdos* (Mexico City: Editorial Patria, 1945), 323–24, for examples from Zacatecas, Mexico City, and Queretaro.
32. Varios Propietarios, *Respuesta de algunos propietarios de fincas a la manifestación que ha hecho al público el Sr. Lic. Don Mariano Arizcorreta* (Mexico City, 1849), 17, 23; and Juan María Flores, *Comunicación dirigida a los propietarios de fincas rústicas del estado de México* (Mexico City, 1849), 5–6.
33. Zorilla, *México y los Mexicanos*, 79–80.

Rumor and Gossip Networks

Elite and non-elite groups in the nation's capital and across the provinces also relied on gossip networks to criticize the authoritarian regime. These networks undermined the government's attempt to control public opinion and enabled public intellectuals to gather information on local affairs without having to rely on state-generated propaganda.

In Mexico, Puebla, Veracruz, and other cities, newspaper vendors turned street corners into centers of public discussion. Under President Santa Anna's authoritarian government, the police curbed participation in these discussions, accusing both literate and non-literate citizens of disturbing the peace and imposing a small fine and in some cases a jail sentence of a few days.[34] But the more these peripatetic circles were repressed, the more they flourished:

> these vendors [*voceadores*] are immoral. . . . Many men, women and most especially the young have abandoned their decent jobs and given up their trades in order to sell newspapers and other publications in arcades, streets and other public places. . . .[35]

These public discussions kept citizens informed.

Mexicans in urban areas flocked to neighborhood taverns at all hours of the day and night, but these establishments, in contrast to the East London pubs studied by E. P. Thompson, never played a major role in the formation of working-class culture in Mexico.[36] According to the 1855 census, Mexico City and Puebla, the largest cities in the country, were home to roughly 300 and 100 licensed taverns, respectively.[37] These taverns were frequented by "plebeians of both sexes, of all ages and various hues . . . and customers of a better class" as well as artisans and priests, the exact socio-ethnic composition of each clientele shaped by the makeup of the neighborhood in which they were located.[38] In Mexico City and Puebla, taverns near the central plaza were socio-ethnically mixed; those in the suburbs served the poorest of the poor.[39]

34. María del Carmen Reyna, *La prensa censurada durante el siglo XIX* (Mexico City: Secretaría de Educación Pública, 1976)), 22–33.

35. Manuel Dublán and José M. Lozano, *Legislación Mexicana*, vol. 2 (Mexico City, 1876–1893), 747.

36. E. P. Thompson, *The Making of the English Working Class* (New York: Vintage Books, 1964), 57–59, 149, 482–83, 511–12, 616–17, 740–41.

37. Orozco y Berra, *Historia de la Ciudad de México*, 126–29. Also see Thomson, *Puebla de los Ángeles*, "Appendix: Table 9.1: Padrón de Comercio, 1852."

38. R. H. Mason, *Pictures of Life in Mexico* (London, 1852), 23–24; Prieto, *Memorias*, 83–85, 113–14.

39. José Joaquín Fernández de Lizardi, *La nueva revolución que se espera en la nación* (Mexico City, 1823), 5.

In the mid-1840s, at the peak of authoritarian rule, state officials began to enforce an old law requiring that taverns remain exposed, without a wall on the side facing the street, in order to allow policemen to patrol them without having to step inside.[40] Every week, the bartender, who was now protected from customers by an iron grill, provided policemen with the names of "troublemakers," who were then conscripted into the army. Fearful that the government might revoke their business license, tavern owners took the additional measure of removing all the tables and benches in order to discourage customers from socializing.[41] The German naturalist Carl Sartorius described how these changes altered drinking practices in Mexico City:

> sitting and drinking together is entirely unknown here. Whoever wishes to drink calls out for what he chooses, and drinks it standing before the bar.[42]

During the first half of the century, neighborhood taverns in urban areas were never major sites of public deliberation.

In the provinces, taverns provided poor farmers a place to deliberate about public affairs without interference from churchmen, state officials, and local notables. In the small town of Santiago de Ocuilan (Mexico) in the Central Valley, the priest sent a private letter to the local official denouncing some of his parishioners:

> they gather at the tavern to learn perverse maxims . . . [and this has made them] defiant. The other day, as I was walking by it on my way to celebrate Sunday mass, the men inside insulted me and had their dog chase me down the street. I could hear them laugh as I ran away.[43]

In the small town of San Juan del Río (Querétaro), indigenous peoples and mixed-bloods met in the local tavern prior to the 1828 elections to exchange information on the candidates.[44]

40. William B. Taylor, *Drinking, Homicide and Rebellion in Colonial Mexican Villages* (Stanford, Calif.: Stanford University Press, 1979), 68. Colonial authorities also removed the front walls and tables from taverns, but by the postcolonial period this policy had for the most part ceased to be enforced.

41. Licenciado José María Zaldívar, "A sus habitantes" (broadsheet, 19 June 1848, Mexico City); Manuel Dublán and José María Lozano, *Legislación Mexicana o colección completa de las disposiciones legislativas*, vol. 8 (Mexico City, 1877), 137–38, 185–87; Frederick Shaw, "Poverty and Politics in Mexico City: 1824–1854" (Ph.D. dissertation, University of Florida, 1975), 254–61, 266–301.

42. Sartorius, *Mexico about 1850*, 111; Prieto, *Memorias*, 113–14; "Vagos," *Siglo XIX*, 11 July 1851, 3 for Mexico City; "Vagos," *Siglo XIX*, 18 October 1852, 3 for Oaxaca.

43. Archivo General de la Nación (Mexico City), "Relación de cura, 1837," Bienes Nacionales, leg. 1286, exp. 2.

44. *Apuntes para la historia o sea maldades cometidas por la facción de los jacobinos del pueblo de San Juan de Río* (Mexico City, 1829), 7–8.

In the countryside, estate owners and farmers were known for their hospitality and welcomed visitors from the nation's capital and other cities to spend an evening at their homes. These visitors provided them with the latest news and opinions about public life in other parts of the country:

> the respectable inhabitants of . . . estates and haciendas generally receive the passing traveler as a welcome guest, for the sake of news he may be able to communicate. . . . This information is usually several weeks old. . . .[45]

Estate owners also relied on their employees—domestics, salaried peons, carpenters, and smiths—for information about public life. All of them gathered daily at the country store, which was a center of information:

> It is in the nature of these establishments to be the bazaars for all the scandal and town talk. Every day, at 6:30 A.M. the women come to fetch bread, chocolate, coffee and sugar; and, of course, there is much related, as to what had taken place during the past evening and night, and as the same persons appear four times a day to make purchases, the chronicle is easily kept up. Here also assemble . . . the laborers, coachmen, water-bearers, and idlers. . . . Thus the materials for the news . . . are increased, and acquire an almost official character.[46]

The owners or managers of these country stores were rich sources of news from other parts of the country:

> In provincial towns . . . the proprietor of the . . . store is generally the wealthiest, and often the best-informed man in the place, and his return with his purchases from the capital, or from attending the great fairs which are held in various parts of the country, is anxiously looked for by his fellow-townsmen.[47]

Stagecoach drivers and muleteers traveling through the area stopped off at these stores and shared whatever news and opinions they had with local residents.

Visual Signaling and Bodily Movements

In semiliterate countries such as Mexico, citizens relied heavily on visual forms of communication in order to deliberate publicly and convey their opinions about the government. This section discusses some of the most

45. Mason, *Pictures of Life in Mexico*, 2.7–8; and Brantz Mayer, *México lo que fue y lo que es*, trans. Francisco A. Delpiane (Mexico City: Fondo de Cultura Económica, 1953), 271.
46. Sartorius, *Mexico bout 1850*, 123.
47. William Bullock, *Across Mexico in 1864–1865* (London: Macmillan and Co., 1866), 220.

important forms, including patriotic rituals, theater performances, paintings, and popular dancing.

In scores of cities and towns across the country, the local "Junta Patriótica," a civic association discussed in an earlier chapter, was responsible for organizing patriotic rituals. The Junta collected funds from all the residents, recruited volunteers to sweep and decorate the central plaza, and built "allegorical floats" depicting nationalist themes. During the 1828 celebration, residents of the small town of Santa Cruz Tlacotepec (Puebla) paraded

> a wonderful float, carrying on it a group of bejeweled young ladies, representing each state of our republic; toward the rear, was a platform carrying two young men, [one] dressed in the proper and particular costume [made of feathers] to represent the Republic of Anahuac, and the other garbed as America, as portrayed by our leading historians, Hernandez, Clavijero, Antón Muñoz, Chimalpani and Coacticonitzin.[48]

After the parade, citizens poured into the main plaza and gathered around large, elevated wooden platforms to hear patriotic speeches. These podiums resembled church altars; in the middle of them was a table with a large crucifix standing in the center and flanked on either side by a row of candles.[49] In their "patriotic sermons," orators were always careful to make mention of populist heroes from the independence wars, including Miguel Hidalgo and José María Morelos, as well as aristocratic ones, such as Agustín Iturbide, thereby reaffirming the bipartisan nature of the event.[50] Plebeians spent the remainder of the day drinking, eating, and dancing outdoors, while the elite in Mexico, Puebla, Veracruz, and other large cities were invited by high-ranking government officials such as the president or the state governor to a private banquet and ball.

By the early 1840s, few citizens participated in patriotic rituals of any type. The editors of *Siglo XIX* complained:

> In the years after our independence, our civic festivities were magnificent, but they have lost their brilliance and have become dark and gloomy . . . due to our lack of public spirit.[51]

48. Antonio Rojas, *Discurso que en celebridad del Aniversario del Diez y Seis de Septiembre se celebró en este pueblo de Santa Cruz Tlacotepec* (Puebla, 1828), 11.

49. Carlos María de Bustamente, *Viaje a Toluca en 1834* (Mexico City: Biblioteca Enciclopédica de Estudio de México, 1969), 51–66; Bernardo de Callejo, *Manifiesto o relación descriptiva de las demostraciones de Júbilo en el Día 16 de Septiembre* (Puebla, 1827), 2–10.

50. José María Castañeta, *Oración cívica que pronunció en la Alameda de la Ciudad Federal* (Mexico City, 1834), 8; Callejo, *Manifiesto*, 9; "Festividades nacionales," *Siglo XIX*, 15 October 1844, 2; Junta Patriótica, *Aniversario del memorable 16 de Septiembre de 1810; Solemnizado en la capital de Durango en igual día de 1838* (Durango, 1838), 5–6.

51. "Junta Patriótica," *Siglo XIX*, 7 July 1845, 4.

The editors of *El Universal,* another leading daily, also complained about them several years later: "why are Mexicans so uninterested in these celebrations?"[52] Citizens in the provinces also lost interest in them.

President Santa Anna's authoritarian government was partly to blame for the spread of public apathy. His government transformed these celebrations into partisan events and used them to generate support for his regime. In June 1844, the president unveiled a statue of himself in the Plaza del Volador, the city's main market, where decades earlier York supporters had rioted for days in protest against the imposition of authoritarian rule. The statue was paid for by wealthy merchants who supported the president's campaign to enforce "law and order" in the country. The statue was thirty feet high, a tall columnar pedestal surmounted by a larger-than-life standing figure of Santa Anna.[53] In June 1843, weeks after the president hosted a public celebration in honor of the country's new authoritarian constitution (Bases Orgánicas), hundreds of plebeians forced their way into the Plaza Volador and draped Santa Anna's statue in a white robe, the same type worn by common criminals on their way to the gallows to be hanged. Plebeians rejected the state's authoritarian conception of nationhood and used the government's own propaganda to mock and undermine it.

In the early 1840s, the owner of the National Theater, Mexico City's largest and most elegant, hosted a gala performance in honor of President Santa Anna. Fanny Calderón, wife of the British ambassador, describes how the audience greeted him:

> Señor Roca presented him with a libretto of the opera, bound in red and gold. . . . The theater was crowded to suffocation. . . . But there was no applause as he entered. One solitary voice in the pit said "Viva Santa Anna," although it was checked by a slight movement of disapprobation, scarcely amounting to a murmur.[54]

Plebeian groups gave government officials similar receptions in other public centers, including bull-rings and plazas. State officials relied on these

52. "Aniversario del Grito de Dolores," *El Universal,* 16 September 1849, 3.

53. *Diario del gobierno de la República Mexicana,* 1 January 1842, 3; "Destrucción del Parián," *Siglo XIX,* 30 June 1843, 4; "Voto particular sobre la destrucción del Parián," *Siglo XIX,* 2 July 1843, 3; "Exposición," *Siglo XIX,* 2 July 1843, 3; "Sobre la demolición del Parián," *Siglo XIX,* 4 July 1843, 4; José Guadalupe Victoria, "Noticias sobre la Antigua Plaza y el mercado del Volador de la Ciudad de México," *Anales del Instituto de Investigaciones Estéticas* [Mexico City] 16, no. 62, (1991): 69–91; Manuel Rivera Camba, *México pintoresco, artístico y monumental* (1883; Mexico City: Editora Nacional, 1957), 150–56.

54. Fanny Calderón de la Barca, *Life in Mexico* (Garden City, N.Y.: Doubleday, 1966), 444.

indirect expressions of "public opinion" to gauge support for the regime, the same way pollsters use modern surveys.

At the height of authoritarian rule when government censorship was strictest, artisans had on the walls of their workshop "hideous portraits of the mulatto general, Álvarez," even though such images had been banned by the government.[55] At the time, Álvarez and his rebel insurgents were battling government troops in the state of Guerrero. In plebeian neighborhoods, residents expressed their opposition to the regime by circulating caricatures of the president and reciting satirical verses against government officials.[56]

Swaying bodies were as important to the formation of public opinion as newspapers. Commoners had their own neighborhood parties (*fandangos*). These parties were hosted by artisans, "ragged Indians," "tradespeople," and "rustics," and they were attended by the elite.[57] Invitations were as informal as the gatherings themselves, with the host firing "a few rockets" into the air. Authoritarians considered them subversive of the moral order and enlisted the support of churchmen in an attempt to suppress them:

> These dances . . . are propagating Equality, Liberty and Fraternity. In the past, the nobility mingled only with their own kind, but today they are considered no different than commoners. Before the two sexes danced apart, separated by a line painted on the floor which served to restrain their passions. Our dances today, however, exhibit the same libertine spirit as the one displayed by our publicists in their speeches and writings.[58]

Regional dances such as the "jarabe, palomo, espinado and agualulco" predominated at these neighborhood fandangos rather than the polkas, waltzes, and quadrilles danced at fancy balls.[59]

In 1850, Robert Wilson, a district court judge from the state of California, spent a year in Mexico. A rabid anticleric, he was struck by the democratic character of churches and their positive influence on daily life:

55. Tylor, *Anahuac,* 198.

56. "Instrucción Popular," *Siglo XIX,* 13 June 1848, 4.

57. "Bailes Escandalosos," *Lira Oajaqueña,* 1 September 1852, 2; Mayer, *México,* 231–32; Mason, *Pictures of Life in Mexico,* 1.162; Sartorius, *Mexico about 1850,* 90–91; George F. Ruxton, *Adventures in Mexico and the Rocky Mountains* (Glorieta, N.M.: Rio Grande Press, 1973), 44–45; Camba, *México pintoresco,* 3.253, 271 on fandangos in Tlaltizapam and Yautepec; Torcuato di Tella, *National Popular Politics in Early Independent Mexico* (Albuquerque: University of New Mexico Press, 1996), 170–71, describes a fandango among mineworkers in Bolaños that culminated in a popular riot against the owner, an Englishman.

58. "Viaje en "mnibus," *El "mnibus,* 24 January 1852, 2–3.

59. José María Rivera, "La China," in *Los Mexicanos pintados por sí mismos,* ed. Ignacio V. Ramírez (Mexico City: n.p., 1855).

There are important truths to be learned in Mexico, even in these immense piles of buildings devoted to superstition. Among them there exist the [type of] perfect equality that should exist in a place of worship. Here the rich and the poor meet together upon a level; the well-dressed lady and the market-women are kneeling together before the very same image. . . . This equality is only for an hour . . . yet it is an hour daily, and must have its effect in this country of inequalities. . . .[60]

Churches were not equipped with benches. The elite sat on cushions while the non-elite knelt on the floor. The two worshiped together within range of each other's aromatic perfume and repugnant body odors and within sight of each other's elegant or tattered clothing. This arrangement proved too frightening and offensive for some in the elite; they stopped attending the neighborhood church and built "oratories in their homes, and [paid] for the services of a priest."[61]

In the countryside, the relationship between churchmen and rural peoples varied considerably. The majority of parish priests lived alone, unsupervised and beyond the reach of the bishop. Many of them were poor and dark-skinned like their parishioners and forged close, sometimes intimate, ties with residents, sharing their homes with their "sisters-in-law," as they called their concubines, and fathering their children. When relations between residents and priest were friendly, then they were flexible about religious fees and lax about doctrinal matters.[62] During his trek across the state of Guerrero, Robert Wilson visited several rural communities and described a religious celebration:

> Indians dressed up in whimsical attire, enacted plays, sang and danced in a . . . house dedicated to the worship of God, or, rather, in a temple consecrated to the adoration of the Virgin. . . . The dancing and singing was bad enough, but the climax was reached when the priests came down from the altar with an array of attendants holding immense candles, and moved to the side of the door, where the procession stopped to witness the discharge, at midday, of a large amount of fire-works in honor of the most blessed Virgin Mary.[63]

In these communities, sociocultural relations between residents and churchmen were relatively equal. But across the northern and western parts of Mexico where large estates predominated, landowners provided priests with room and board, in exchange for which the priests ministered to the spiritual needs of their peons. Churchmen often used confessional

60. Robert A. Wilson, *Mexico: Its Peasants and Its Priests* (New York, 1856), 268–69.
61. Barca, *Life in Mexico*, 297, 61.
62. Tylor, *Anahuac*, 210.
63. Wilson, *Mexico*, 230–31.

boxes to extract information about each other, which had the effect of discouraging all of them from discussing public affairs.

Civic Catholic Narrative

In the course of deliberating in public, Mexicans invented a new vocabulary, Civic Catholicism, which they used in daily life to make sense of each other. I found the first explicit usage of Civic Catholic terminology in 1827 among members of the Sociedad Económica, a community development group in Merida (Yucatán):

> The spirit of association is unique to man, and is the one trait which distinguishes him from God's other creatures. . . . But in our country, despotism has instilled in us contrary habits based on egoism and fanaticism. . . . We continue to care only for those in our circle while ignoring all those outside it. This is why we remain cold and indifferent to public and national affairs. We continue fleeing from each other. The associative spark has enabled other countries to build schools, machinery, libraries and contribute to agricultural and industrial development but in ours it remains moribund. . . .[64]

If Civic Catholicism was used in this remote part of Mexico, then it is safe to assume that its keywords and phrases were also circulating in other parts of the country. This indeed seems to have been the case, judging from the series of articles that appeared in the early 1840s in the *Siglo XIX* and titled "Origins of Civil Society," "Differences between Civil and Natural Society," and "Effects of Civil Society."[65] This was the first time public writers had paused to reflect on the broader significance of Civic Catholicism for postcolonial Mexicans. Civic Catholicism was fast becoming the vernacular of public life.

Central to this new narrative was the religious-colonial dichotomy of "passion-reason," and the new civic concern for "association" and "personal liberty." An article published by *El Monitor* in the mid-1840s illustrates how Mexicans fused these concerns:

> [Economic] liberalism has produced some negative effects; these must now be corrected. People have given free rein to their . . . self-interest, and this has generated conflict among us. . . . In these contests, the winner is usually the person most lacking in moral scruples—in other

---

64. *Discurso pronunciado en la instalación de la Sociedad Económica Patriótica de Amigos del País* (Merida, 1827), 4–6.

65. "Orígenes de las sociedades civiles," *Siglo XIX,* 9 March 1849, 3; "En qué se diferencian las sociedades civiles de las naturales," *Siglo XIX,* 15 March 1849, 4; "Efectos de la sociedad civil," *Siglo XIX,* 18 March 1849, 4.

words, the most vicious and passionate. This situation among individuals is now a society-wide problem. Social ties have been severed and . . . groups have surrendered to their passions. . . . Individualism must be curbed but without destroying personal liberty. . . . Associations are the best means to reconcile individual liberty with the general will of society, and this is why they have become a new sociopolitical symbol. . . .[66]

Civic democrats identified economic liberalism with unruly passions, with moral disorder and social chaos, although they did not want to return to the corporatism of the colonial period, as indicated by their support for liberty.[67] Citizens used Civic Catholicism in order to make sense of themselves and each other in civil society, economic society, political society, and the public sphere itself.

Self-Rule, Nationhood, and Civil Society

Public writers wrote countless articles discussing associative life in its relationship to the individual, nationhood, creole culture, the Catholic Church, and the central state. A member of a mutual-aid group described the spread of civic democratic practices in this way:

> Until recently, the associative spirit had not entered into our workshops; those artisans who were active in civic life prior to now had become involved in it but in an individualistic manner. . . . However, artisans no longer lead a shadowy existence in their own homeland.[68]

Citizens were encouraged to forge civic ties with each other and to organize voluntary groups. In the mid-1840s, a publicist writing from the small coastal town of Acapulco (Guerrero) explained the relationship between the development of associations and nationhood:

> In all our cities and in many of our towns, we have organized ourselves into associations under a variety of names, but always with the same aim: enlarging the nation. We will rekindle our public spirit by bringing together all the classes, doing this throughout the country, developing ties to each other.[69]

Self rule and national sovereignty reinforced each other.

According to public writers, associations contributed to critical deliberation and public opinion. In 1841, a member from the Bella Union, a

66. "Sistema liberal," *El Monitor Republicano*, 24 May 1846, 3–4.
67. "Liberal," *Siglo XIX*, 20 October 1841, 3; and "Las minorías," *Siglo XIX*, 29 June 1844, 3 for another example of this.
68. "Señores editores," *Semanario Artístico*, 11 June 1845, 1–2.
69. "Junta de Amigos del Progreso de las Manufacturas," *Siglo XIX*, 17 February 1844, 2–4. Also see: "Departamento de Aguascalientes," *Semanario Artístico*, 28 September 1844, 3.

literary group from Oaxaca, published an article in the *Siglo* whose argument he summarized thus:

> Compare those countries with literary, artistic and industrial associations to those without. Individuals in the latter work in isolation whereas in the former they communicate frequently with each other. In these countries, new ideas flourish, peaceful and rational discussions are common, and citizens have the chance to ponder issues and discover enduring truths. . . . By allowing each person to test and correct their views from various standpoints, these societies encourage citizens to develop judgements. . . . The members of these associations contribute to [public life] as much as priests and lawyers did in the recent past.[70]

In addition to contributing to the development of a national culture, associations encouraged individuals to become tolerant and open-minded.

By the mid-1840s, even conservative citizens resorted to using civic terminology to discuss public affairs. They did this not because they had abandoned their commitment to authoritarian rule but because they were now convinced that democracy had become the vernacular of daily life. Conservative Catholics used associative rhetoric to defend the Church from critics who favored secularizing the state:

> Let us focus on the issue at hand: the Church is a religious association and this is why its freedom and sovereignty must be preserved. The Church, of course, is different from any other association in that it was organized in 1521, three years before the Mexican nation was born. The former contributed to creating the latter; religion has made us sociable. . . .[71]

Civic terminology was becoming the vernacular of daily life, forcing authoritarians to defend their antidemocratic outlook in associative terms.

Democratic writers were against government officials intruding into the affairs of civil society. Publicists argued that associative life in Mexico remained undeveloped, but they were convinced that it had by now made deep inroads and would soon become rooted in public life, and they attributed the difficulties it had encountered so far to the obstacles the central government had put in its way:

> In our country . . . the government's policy has been to block development of the associative spirit from developing, and to consider any group to be a menace to itself. . . . Although this is no longer the case, the influence of the past still weighs on us. . . . The associative spirit, however, is now spreading, although some of our old habits remain in

---

70. "Interior," *Siglo XIX*, 26 December 1841, 2–3; "Educación literaria," *Semanario Artístico*, 6 July 1844, 1.

71. *Error Capital de los que profesan la tolerancia* (Mexico City, 1843), 9–10.

its way, and these cannot be altered overnight. Although some members in our associations . . . remain skeptical, we should not allow them to discourage the rest of us from propagating the [civic] spirit.[72]

Despite the many hurdles they still faced, democratic publicists were adamantly opposed to seeking assistance from the central state. For these writers, citizens knew better than anyone else how to take care of their interests:

> Our citizens know best how to administer their own professional affairs, artisan workshops and farms, and do so by consulting and seeking assistance from each other, relying mainly on associative ties rather than government intervention to get ahead. Citizens have a direct, immediate interest in their affairs. Our officials have theoretical knowledge but lack any practical experience, and although they have lots of resources . . . they cannot generate any on their own. . . . The 400,000 sovereign citizens [male electors] in this country must not lose sight of the power they have to create associations and use them to limit the state. . . . The general good can only come when our own particular interests are met.[73]

Although most publicists were adamantly opposed to any and all forms of state intervention in civic life, they were divided on the question of what role it should play in economic society.

Civic Practices in Economic Society

Public intellectuals also published numerous articles in *Siglo XIX* and other leading dailies on economic life, focusing most of them on the need for credit and joint stock companies.

In the late 1840s, the *Siglo* published a series of essays under the title "Social Science: Democratic Vocabulary," with the purpose of familiarizing citizens with the "new vocabulary that has emerged due to changes in our ideas and institutions." Each essay analyzed a different keyword, such as "taxation," "dictatorship," "aristocracy," "people," and "majority and minority." The essay on "credit" began:

> it comes from the term "confidence," which means to believe in someone. To have credit indicates that the person is committed to fulfilling their obligations. . . . Credit, for example, is the basis of lending. . . . The same is true for money. . . . To remain credible, money must not be devalued or cheapened; if you subtract ten cents from a coin or bill, you have already eroded its real value.[74]

72. "Las cosas y las personas," *Semanario Artístico*, 31 August 1844, 2.
73. El Nigromante, "Los Cuatrocientos mil soberanos," *Don Simplicio*, 14 March 1846, 3.
74. "Ciencias sociales: Vocabulario democrático," *Siglo XIX*, 25 October 1848, 3.

In business life, credit was related to personal credibility, and both were based on private and public morality as outlined above.

Publicists also commented frequently on the stunted character of associative life in economic society. Family firms remained dominant in economic society and kinship loyalty remained the primary guarantee among associates that they would not cheat each other. Corruption permeated this domain. Publicists attributed this situation to moneylenders:

> The spirit of association contributed to economic development in Europe, but among us this spirit remains moribund. No one in our country would dare pool their capital. . . . Speculators who have made all their wealth from lending money at usurious rate to the government have spread their influence into every corner of the economy; they have even contaminated the poor.[75]

Moneylenders controlled economic life and spread greed and fraud, making it difficult for producers and consumers alike to practice any form of civicness.

The lack of associative spirit among Mexicans contributed to the "denationalization" of their economy:

> Foreign entrepreneurs will continue threatening our nationhood and economy as long as we remain disorganized. To regain control of our economy, we must propagate the associative spirit amongst ourselves. . . . Organizing nationwide groups in each sector of the economy—mining, agriculture, industry, and commerce—will enable us to reconcile our differences and defend our national interests.[76]

Public writers discussed alternative ways of regaining control of the economy. Two views predominated. According to one group, the government should intervene in economic life:

> Among Mexicans the entrepreneurial spirit remains undeveloped; we lack joint stock companies, as well as industrial and commercial corporations of all types. . . . Our Ministry of Development must do whatever it can to disseminate associative practices, generate investment capital, and produce savings.[77]

---

75. "Espíritu de asociación," *Siglo XIX*, 11 August 1849, 4; "Mejoras materiales," *Siglo XIX*, 17 January 1850, 3; "Asociación mercantiles," *Siglo XIX*, 13 September 1850, 3; "Costumbres," *Siglo XIX*, 18 May 1851, 4.

76. L. E., "Sociedades industriales," in *El Museo Mexicano*, vol. 1 (Mexico City, 1843), 118–20; "Sociedades para el fomento del arte," *Semanario Artístico*, 26 October 1844, 1–2; and "Agricultura," *Siglo XIX*, 3 May 1850, 3.

77. "Asociación mercantiles," *Siglo XIX*, 13 September 1850, 3.

The second group also considered state officials of considerable importance in changing business practices but conceived their role in limited terms:

> In Mexico, there exists plenty of investment capital, but what we lack is an associative spirit and government support for it. . . . In developed countries, government invests heavily in public works, such as building roads, canals, telegraphs, and railroads, although private firms are responsible for managing and in many cases for owning them. Creating similar government-business partnerships in our country will generate the associative spirit we need.[78]

In helping to finance public works projects, these writers argued, the state would also be contributing to the spread of associative life in the economic domain.

Democratic Practices in Political Society

Public writers also used Civic Catholic phrases in their discussion of political life and its main institutions. According to them,

> the government is a type of an association like any other, with its own set of moral concerns and interests based on the general will of our people. . . . Given this fact, all the members of this association have a right to influence it . . . however, because it is impossible to gather all the inhabitants of our country in a single place, we [elect representatives].[79]

In contrast to the populist conceptions of self-rule that had been prevalent in the late 1820s, civic democrats from the 1840s onward favored representative government. Public writers advocated the creation of electoral clubs as a way of influencing government officials, but they were against establishing a "party-state":

> We support political clubs and their right to assemble and petition, but we do not believe that any of them should be allowed to manage or control the state. Clubs are entitled . . . to participate in public debates and elections, and in this way should be allowed to influence government, but they must not be allowed to control the state.[80]

---

78. "Espíritu de empresa y asociación," *Siglo XIX,* 15 July 1852, 1; and "Introducción," in *Revista mensual de mejoras materiales* (Mexico City, 1852), vi.

79. "La constitución política," *Siglo XIX,* 15 March 1842, 3; and "Unión de los Mexicanos," *Siglo XIX,* 8 October 1841, 3 for another example.

80. "Necesidad de un programa del ministerio," *Siglo XIX,* 14 November 1855, 1.

Civic democrats were also keen supporters of municipal life:

> History has proven to us that no one takes better care of the interests of
> the people than those who are know them best, that is, municipal town-
> ships. Without them, public virtue can never develop. . . . The average
> person is more willing to sacrifice himself and gain the applause of his
> neighbors and family in matters that affect them directly than in dan-
> gerous and abstract ones related to the state.[81]

Strong townships were doubly important, providing local residents with
access to the central state while preventing government officials from intruding into daily life. According to most public intellectuals, civic democracy could flourish only at the municipal level and never in the central state. Nevertheless, townships could curb the tendency of the latter to
become authoritarian.

Civic Catholicism had become the vernacular of daily life across civil,
economic, and political society; however, Mexicans continued to em-
ploy authoritarian terminology rooted in colonial Catholicism and based
on the dichotomy of unruly children/rational adults to describe indigenous peoples and fair-skinned creoles.[82] In 1824, Congress approved a
law that removed the term "Indian" from all official document [tax rolls,
voting lists, military service sheets, prison records] and replacing it with
the term "poor."[83] But this did not alter speaking habits. In the words of
Carl Sartorius,

> customs . . . which have taken root amongst people, and perpetuated
> by language cannot be obliterated by law . . . consequently, we find
> here [in Mexico] an aristocracy of colour as in European republics or
> monarchies and aristocracy of birth.[84]

Nevertheless, indigenous peoples in Mexico City and elsewhere altered
the semantic meaning of these terms. In 1849, residents of Tlatelolco,
the largest indigenous neighborhood in the nation's capital with roughly
20,000 residents, drafted a petition denouncing government officials for
all sorts of abuses:

> For years our community has been at the mercy of these low-life types.
> These so-called people of reason continue treating us as if we are irra-
> tional minors . . . as if we are . . . still a conquered nation . . . but in fact

---

81. "Cuestión municipal," *Siglo XIX*, 25 April 1844, 4.
82. Tylor, *Anahuac*, 61.
83. José Luis Mora, "Revista política," in *Obras Sueltas* (Mexico City: Editorial Porrúa,
1963), 110; Shirley Brice Heath, *Telling Tongues: Language Policy in Mexico* (New York:
Teacher's College Press, 1978), 62–65.
84. Sartorius, *Mexico about 1850*, 47.

it is they who are devoid of rationality, and it is we who are defending the public good in our assemblies.[85]

Indigenous peoples in Mexico inverted the terms of discussion in order to challenge the dominant view of them among fair-skinned creoles. Both were convinced their situation was without precedent and that they were about to venture into uncharted territory:

> Our situation is new and tragic. We cannot follow European models [since they never had indigenous peoples] nor adopt the North American one of exterminating Indians . . . having already tried it once before without any success.[86]

85. *Exposición que hacen los interesados en las parcialidades en contra de su ilegal y mal llamado administrador, D. Luis Velázquez de la Cadena* (Mexico City, 1849), 7. Also see: *Humilde representación que los indígenas del barrio de Santiago Tlatelolco han elevado a la augusta cámara del senado* (Mexico City, 1849), 3–5.

86. "Observaciones sobre la población de la República," *El Universal,* 29 December 1848, 1. Also see: "La raza indígena," *El Republicano,* 9 November 1855; "Estudios sociales: Los indios y los curas," *El Republicano,* 2 November 1855, 1–2, for criticisms of the U.S. model.

CHAPTER 10

Speaking in Tongues:
The Peruvian Public Sphere

During the first half of the nineteenth century, the overwhelming majority of Peruvians did not participate in public debates, and when they did
they rarely used Civic Catholicism—unlike Mexicans, who at the time
were using this vocabulary extensively to make sense of each other in daily
life. The few Peruvians in public life who used Civic Catholic keywords
employed them in a formal, almost mechanical manner to discuss abstract, programmatic issues rather than everyday concerns. Their lack of
fluency in this vocabulary, combined with the absence of associative life,
recurrent bouts of civil warfare, and the spread of extremist rhetoric, hindered the development of a culture of critical deliberation in Peru.

Socio-institutional Structures

Between 1831 and 1855, Peruvians published no fewer than 360 local,
regional, and national newspapers. Almost all of them lasted less than
a year, but because production was relatively continuous, readers were
never without a newspaper (fig. 10.1)[1] From 1831 to 1835, Peruvians
published 104 newspapers. From 1836 to 1840 the number declined to
52, and it remained roughly at this level (49) over the next five years
(1841–1845). For the five-year period from 1846 to 1850 the number increased to 68, and then climbed to 87 for the period 1851–1855. In general terms, newspaper production dropped in 1836 when Bolivia annexed
Peru to form the Peru-Bolivian Confederation, which lasted from 1836

---

1. All data presented in this paragraph are based on my tabulations of the data found in
Mariano Felipe Paz Soldán's *Biblioteca Peruana* (Lima, 1879). Because I am interested in
"public opinion," I have omitted from my analysis all publications linked to the government
and military authorities.

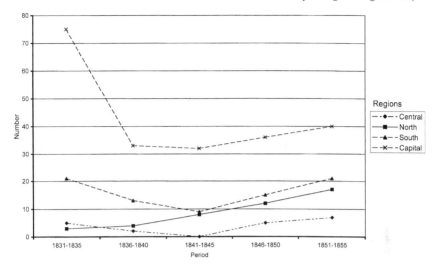

Figure 10.1 Newspaper Production and Public Opinion, 1831–1855

to 1839. The press remained stunted for the next two decades, a rather ironic consequence of the demilitarization of public life. Newspaper writers whose livelihood had depended on their links to one or another military faction had lost their support network and their readership.

Lima was the center of public opinion throughout the period. Sixty-two percent of the country's newspapers were published and circulated primarily in the capital. *El Comercio,* Lima's leading daily, had about a thousand readers. Several travelers spotted copies of *El Comercio* in small towns such as Hualgayoc (Cajamarca) and Angasmarca (La Libertad) in the northern part of the country, although most of Lima's newspapers were read only by its residents.[2] Almost all the other newspapers (27 percent) were produced in the city of Arequipa in the far south and read only by local residents. The remaining newspapers (9 percent) appeared occasionally across the northern and central parts of the country.

The overwhelming majority of Peruvians did not speak or understand Spanish, nor were they literate; these factors made it nearly impossible for them to partake in public discussions. Across the Andean highlands (Cuzco, Puno, Ayacucho) where the majority of the indigenous peoples

2. Pedro Félix Vicuña, "Imprentas," *El Comercio,* 28 February 1848, 2, and José Victoriano Lastarria, "Lima en 1850," in *Viajeros en el Perú Republicano,* ed. Alberto Tauro (Lima: Universidad Nacional Mayor de San Marcos, 1967), 88, on readership; Heinrich Witt, *Diario y observaciones sobre el Perú, 1824–1890,* trans. Kika Garland de Montero (Lima: Oficina de Asuntos Culturales, 1987), 140–41, on circulation.

lived, more than two-thirds of the population spoke only Quechua or Aymara.[3] Although there are no reliable studies of reading and writing practices in nineteenth-century Peru, in the 1830s a newspaper writer estimated literacy rates to be 30 percent in Lima, 12 percent in provincial towns, and 2 percent across the hinterlands, a figure that includes parish priests, district magistrates, soldiers, estate owners, and small merchants.[4]

In the late 1840s, Pedro Félix Vicuña, a correspondent for *El Mercurio,* Chile's leading daily, visited Lima, the center of public opinion in Peru, and noted:

> Lima is an odd, one might even say a unique place; everyone here has a passion for writing . . . and whoever writes is certain to be read. . . . Do not think that gentlemen are the only ones who read here; the people, artisans, and laborers of all types save their money in order to buy an issue of *El Comercio,* and those who are too poor to purchase their own copy borrow from others. Those who do not know how to read listen, comment and discuss with the rest. Even the women join in. . . .[5]

How did plebeians, blacks, women, and other marginal groups learn to read and write?

In an article published in *El Comercio,* an aristocrat from Lima explained how a congressmen had "given" him a *cholito* from the Sierra, and how he had sent him to school and taught him to read and write in Spanish.[6] Slaves, too, had limited access to schooling:

> Many mulattos in Lima have gained a good education simply by accompanying their young masters to primary school and then to university. It is common in public disputations in the university to hear a mulatto aid [his master] by offering him a syllogism; they are usually referred to as "palanganas," which is a local term for chatterer.[7]

A great many indigenous peoples and plebeians became fluent in Spanish and learned to read and write in the army. While stationed in Piura in the

---

3. José María Blanco, *Diario del Viaje del Presidente Orbegoso al sur del Perú* (Lima: Pontífica Universidad Católica del Perú, 1974), 283.

4. "Remitidos," *El Mercurio Peruano,* 17 November 1829, 3, and 10 November 1829, 3. In the early 1870s, the literacy rate was 9 percent in the town of Sechura, an indigenous community of about 1,500 in the northern state of Piura, according to Alejandro Díez Hurtado, *Fiestas y cofradías: Asociaciones religiosas e integración en la historia de la comunidad de Sechura; siglos XVII–XX* (Piura: Centro de Investigación y Promoción del Campesinado, 1993), 64, 102.

5. Vicuña, "Imprentas," 2.

6. "Mi Cholito," *El Comercio,* 14 November 1848, 2.

7. William Bennett Stevenson, "Memorias sobre las campañas de San Martín y Cochrane en el Perú," in *Viajeros en el Perú republicano,* ed. Alberto Tauro (Lima: Universidad Nacional Mayor de San Marcos, 1967), 170.

north, General Agustín Gamarra's troops read *El Atleta de la Libertad,* a tabloid published by the opposition:

> copies of [*El Atleta*] among my troops; it corrupted their morale, destroyed their discipline . . . and made them disobey my orders. . . .[8]

By the 1830s, indigenous peoples had their own newspaper, including *El Hijo del Montonero,* which featured the "witty verse" of Ildefonso, a political satirist whose ditties were "known in all the taverns."[9] Versification made it easier for non-literate persons to commit his writings to memory.

Women were not allowed to attend school, so they learned to read and write at home and by attending court hearings. Carmen Cubea's description is worth quoting: "I listened to [them] read the newspapers, and then tried to read . . . as many articles as possible on a variety of topics."[10]

Courtrooms also provided elite women an opportunity to learn how to read and write and deliberate publicly:

> Don't think that I am another of those charlatans who writes about legal matters without knowing anything about the subject, or that I am one of those who, as prescribed by my sex, can only mend socks, sew shirts and cook stews. Domestic life has, in fact, taught me all I need to know, and [my experiences] have confirmed what, as a young girl, I heard many times: litigation teaches women how to defend their rights. . . . By memorizing the arguments that lawyers make, we learn how to defend ourselves. . . .[11]

Slaves, too, relied on the court system to learn about their rights. The "Public Defender" became a "major figure" in the black community because he taught slaves and ex-slaves about their rights and how to protect them from abusive masters and employers.[12]

Public opinion remained stunted even in Lima. The majority of articles published in newspapers were filled with slander and extremist rhetoric:

> Reviewing our journalistic production, we find little that is of any real importance to the nation. Our newspapers are filled with disgusting,

8. Agustín Gamarra, "Excmo. Sr. Vice Presidente de la República" (Piura, 10 June 1829), 156–57 and "Sr. Secretario General de S. E. el Presidente" (Piura, 2 June 1829), 152–53, in his *Epistolario,* ed. Alberto Tauro (Lima: Universidad Nacional Mayor de San Marcos, 1952).

9. "Untitled," *El Genio de Rímac,* 19 November 1834, 1.

10. Una Mujer, "Papel en derecho escrito," *El Comercio,* 5 February 1843, 3.

11. Ibid., 2.

12. Peter Blanchard, Slavery and Abolition in Early Republican Peru (Wilmington, Del.: Scholarly Resources, 1992), 41–46, 74, 204–5; Carlos Aguirre, *Agentes de su propia libertad: Los esclavos de Lima y la desintegración de la esclavitud* (Lima, 1993), 157–58, 184–85, 194–97, 201–7, 277; Christine Hunefeldt, *Paying the Price of Freedom: Family Labor among Lima's Slaves* (Berkeley: University of California Press, 1994), 15, 65, 237.

libelous attacks and shameful polemics which our writers use simply to ruin each other's reputations. Our public debates are no better. They, too, are used to vent personal animosities. Our dailies do not live up to their main duty. . . . The lack of generosity that animates our newspaper editors . . . is an obstacle to our country rather than a factor contributing to its progress.[13]

Political fanatics inundated the public sphere with extremist newspapers such as *El Telégrafo, La Guardia Nacional,* and *La Verdad,* which were the most influential and financially successful dailies. It was usually the most intolerant and fanatical newspapers that served to define journalistic standards for the rest.[14] The few public writers who resisted were ignored:

> our new form of [democratic] life requires of us writers that we enlighten rather than inflame the passions of our readers. . . . [We must not] speak from the heart when we cannot persuade the intellect; we must not provoke fury and pity [in order to get others to act]. Instead, we should try to soothe their overheated imaginations by appealing to rational reasons.[15]

Moderate writers relied on Civic Catholic terminology to criticize and advocate for changes in journalistic practices, but without any noticeable effect. Perhaps this is why plebeians did not distinguish clearly between a newspaper article and a religious manual:

> In addition to newspapers, street peddlers hawked soap bars, religious pamphlets on the passion and crucifixion of Jesus Christ, and manuals on how to prepare for confession.[16]

Newspapers and manuals were similar in their reliance on dogma rather than deliberation to keep the reader's interest. A small number of commoners in Peru had reading and writing skills, but few of them had any deliberative skills to speak of.

---

13. "Prensa periódica del país," *El Progreso,* 5 January 1850, 7. Also see "Es fácil ilustrar la opinión pública," *El Telégrafo de Lima,* 19 July 1833, 2.

14. Felipe Pardo y Aliaga, *Poesías y escritos en prosa de Don Felipe Pardo y Aliaga* (Paris, 1869), xvii. In the 1830s, Pardo y Aliaga, the country's leading poet, transformed his literary salon into a political party; in the words of one of its members, the "conservative party was born . . . here." For additional examples, see: Santiago Távara, *Historia de los partidos* (Lima: Editorial Huascarán, 1951), 84; Jorge Basadre, *Historia de la República del Perú,* vol. 1 (Lima: Editorial Universitaria, 1968–1970), 308; Max Radiguet, *Lima y la sociedad Peruana* (Lima: Biblioteca Nacional del Perú, 1971), 55–59; and Un Vigilante, "Aviso al Prefecto y Ministro de Gobierno," *El Genio de Rímac,* 15 April 1834, 2.

15. "El Genio," *El Genio de Rímac,* 11 September 1834, 2; "Felicidad Humana," *El Genio de Rímac,* 27 June 1834, 2.

16. Lastarria, "Lima en 1850," 89.

Communicative Networks

The Peruvian elite and non-elite in urban and rural areas developed a variety of communicative practices—reading and writing, rumor and gossip, visual signaling and bodily movements—to influence each other's opinions about public affairs.

Reading and Writing Practices

In contrast to their counterparts in Mexico City, the elite in Lima did not frequent cafes. There were only five cafes in all of Lima, and, according to the French consul, Felix Lettelier, all of them were shabby and devoid of social life.[17] Because of this, and because commoners sometimes visited them, Lima's status-crazed elite avoided cafés. During his visits to Lima to purchase farm tools and supplies, a self-described rustic usually stopped at the café Bodegones, where he would "beg one of the elderly persons . . . to read . . . the advertisements" in the newspaper.[18] Lima's elite instead congregated indoors in literary salons and, later on, at family gatherings to discuss public affairs.

Public intellectuals in Lima were all active in one or another literary salon. Government officials attacked these salons frequently in order to prevent the opposition from meeting, forcing many intellectuals to shift their activity to family gatherings, which were far safer. Over time public intellectuals transformed family gatherings into centers of ideological discussion, causing alarm among state officials and the police.[19] The government tried to put an end to these "conspiratorial" groups by publishing the location of these gatherings in local dailies to encourage plebeian groups to attack them. The anti-Gamarrista daily *El Genio del Rímac* published the following list:

> The Gamarristas meet regularly in a large house on the corner of Zarate; in front of what used to be the café San Agustín; in the house just

17. Felix Letellier, "A Monsieur Theodore de Lessep," in "Profesiones, oficios de Lima en 1850," *Anuario de estudios americanos* 37 (1980): 230–33. According to Juan Antonio Pezet, *Memoria que presenta el general de Brigada . . . prefecto del departamento de Moquegua* (Lima, 1851), there were three cafes in the state of Moquegua and one in the state of Tacna.

18. Pablo Huayra-Chaqui, "Notable ingratitud," *El Comercio,* 28 November 1843, 3. Whether this account is true or not—and it seems likely that it is, given the tone and content of the letter—what needs underscoring is that the scene it portrays was quite common.

19. José Manuel Tirado, "Al público," *El Genio de Rímac,* 19 April 1834, 2; "Señores editores," *El Comercio,* 19 July 1843, 3. This letter reports on the existence of anti-Vivanquistas in "the portals and main thoroughfares, speaking loudly and with passion. . . . This is why the actual government needs to continue with its reforms [purging the streets of Lima]."

beyond the church of the Holy Spirit; in front of the Mining Tribune; in the house next door to the President of the Supreme Court; in the administrative offices of one of the ministries; and underneath the bridge.[20]

As an additional precaution, President Orbegoso's liberal government, with encouragement from *El Genio* and other like-minded dailies, organized a "Committee of Purification" to collect secret information on the opposition and used it as evidence against them in court. Those accused of subversion were expelled from the country.[21]

The politicization of family gatherings frayed kinship ties and made it difficult for members of different political factions to attend the same gatherings. During her stay in Lima, Flora Tristán, the French socialist feminist, noted

> a profound enmity among kin, even among blood brothers. The issue of Liberty never featured in these political debates; Gamarrista and Orbegosita epithets was what distinguished factions within each divided family. Distrust reigned among them and everywhere, and whenever they could the family members tried hurting each other.[22]

Political extremism damaged Lima's kinship networks, which contributed to the further radicalization of public debates. Personal ties became far more important than ideological differences. The most strong-willed and clever salon hostesses manipulated these ties in order to get rival generals to return to their barracks. In April 1834, eight of General Gamarra's most loyal generals signed a truce with their counterparts on the battlefield of Maquinhuayo.[23] Salon life radicalized family relations, but it also served to humanize political differences, and it is the reason why despite countless civil wars, Peru never experienced a "Reign of Terror" similar to the one in Jacobin France.[24]

20. Un Vigilante, "Aviso al Prefecto y Ministro de Gobierno," *El Genio de Rímac,* 15 April 1834, 2, and 16 April 1834, 2; "Los empleados honrados que morirán," *El Genio de Rímac,* 24 April 1834, 2.

21. Luis Orbegoso, "Bando," *El Genio del Rímac,* 24 February 1834, 2; "Clamor a S. E. el Presidente," *El Genio del Rímac,* 23 October 1834, 2.

22. Flora Tristán, *Peregrinaciones de una Paria,* trans. Emilio Romero (Lima: Editorial Atlántida, 1946), 346.

23. Modesto Basadre y Chocano, *Diez años de historia política del Perú: 1839–1844* (Lima: Editorial Huascarán, 1953), 16; and Manuel Bilbao, *Historia de Salaverry* (Buenos Aires, 1867), 145.

24. Santiago Tavara, *Historia de los Partidos* (Lima: Editorial Huascarán, 1951), 185–91, claims that most politically motivated killings took place in the late 1830s under Bolivian rule. José Rufino Echenique, *Memorias para la historia del Perú, 1808–1878* (Lima: Editorial Huascarán, 1952), 50.

Rumor and Gossip Networks

The transformation of family gatherings in Lima into centers of political indoctrination and agitation deprived strong-willed matriarchs of their traditional role as hostesses and drove many of them into the streets. Before leaving home, these women would put on their "sayas and mantos" and veil themselves, making it difficult for even family members to recognize them. Elite women spent part of the day roaming the streets of the city unescorted; the famous French feminist Flora Tristán said that Lima's "veiled ones" were even more emancipated than the women of Paris.[25] Plebeians took a special liking to Lima's veiled women and were only too happy to protect them: the "urban rabble punished . . . any wrongdoer" who tried to expose their identity.[26] In colonial times, the donning of a veil had been an expression of female submission to one's husband, but it was now an expression of emancipation, according to the famous Chilean writer José Victoriano Lastarria:

> The saya and manto are women's weapons of independence, they have done more for the social elevation and influence of the fair sex than all the books and congresses the French have used to achieve the same. . . . With the saya and manto, women dominate the promenades, the visitors' gallery in the Chamber of Congress, and even the temples.[27]

Women became part of a complex communicative network that stretched from the halls of congress to the parish church to the home. Beginning in the mid-1850s, the government, under pressure from the men of Lima, outlawed the use of the skirt and shawl.[28]

In the southern city of Arequipa, the second most important urban center in the country, elite ladies also undermined masculine control of public life but did so with characteristic elegance. According to a visitor, "the women . . . [of this city] make few visits, but content themselves with keeping up a verbal communication by means of their chamber women, and of perpetually exchanging flowers, fruits and sweets. . . ."[29] Chambermaids spent their mornings paying courtesy calls to each other's house-

25. Radiguet, *Lima y la sociedad Peruana*, 39; Lastarria, "Lima en 1850," 55; Tristán, *Peregrinaciones*, 401.

26. Juan Jacobo de Tschudi, *Testimonio del Perú, 1838–1842*, trans. Elsa de Sagasti (Lima, 1966), 110.

27. Lastarria, "Lima en 1850," 101.

28. C. Skogman, "Perú en 1852," in *Viajeros en el Perú Republicano*, ed. Alberto Tauro (Lima: Universidad Nacional Mayor de San Marcos, 1967), 122; Lastarria, "Lima en 1850," 101.

29. Paul Marcoy, *Travels in South America*, vol. 1 (London, 1875), 39.

holds, gathering and passing on information on the day's events and engaging in ritualized forms of gift-giving in order to consolidate the social
ties among the city's matriarchs. They also invited men to visit them at
home, relying on their guests for additional information. Although men
controlled the press, the pulpit, and other channels of public communication in Arequipa, the women succeeded in bypassing them and establishing their own network of information rooted in private life and based
on rumor and gossip.

In Lima, newspapers and pamphlets circulated "from cafés to pulperías and other places, with persons [stationed along the way and] asking always the same question: 'what's new.'"[30] Plebeians congregated
in corner stores (pulperias), in working-class eateries (chicherias), and in
neighborhood taverns (chinganas) to discuss public affairs. Almost all
these establishments were in the city's poorest and most racially mixed
neighborhoods.[31] Corner stores were frequented by "cholos, zambos
and Blacks," although not many whites.[32] Eateries, in contrast, attracted
"Congo Blacks . . . dour Spanish creoles, attractive white ladies, uppity
mulattas, monks, soldiers and merchants."[33] Women owned a quarter
of all the taverns and Blacks owned another 50 percent. Plebeians of all
racial and ethnic backgrounds were welcomed at these establishments,
and they visited them often in order to share late-breaking news about
housing, jobs, and marriage opportunities.[34] Taverns, eateries, and corner
stores were among the few places where plebeians could discuss political
and religious issues in a relaxed and convivial setting far away from the
elite.

In 1835, under General Salaverry's authoritarian government, the army
unleashed a campaign of terror against Lima's downtrodden. As part of
this campaign, state officials attacked these plebeian centers of discussion,
even though they constituted no threat to "law and order." Aldo Panfichi
explains why:

> urban plebeians developed their own specialized vocabulary (jerga),
> their own antiheroes . . . their own brand of satire that poked fun at the

30. "Editorial," El Comercio, 6 September 1842, 2.
31. Carlos A. Forment, "Map of Lima's Chinganas and Pulperías: 1830–1850" (Unpublished working document, Princeton University, 1993), provides a sociogeography of
these establishments. District I, on the northwest side of the city, had 27 percent of them;
district II accounted for 18 percent; district III, on the northeast side, accounted for 25 percent; and district IV, in the south, 20 percent. Note 34 below lists the sources I used to develop these estimates.
32. Radiquet, Lima y la sociedad Peruana, 40.
33. Tschudi, Testimonio del Perú, 144.
34. Hunefeldt, Price of Freedom, 74–76, 172–73; and Aguirre, Agentes de su propia
libertad, 81–92.

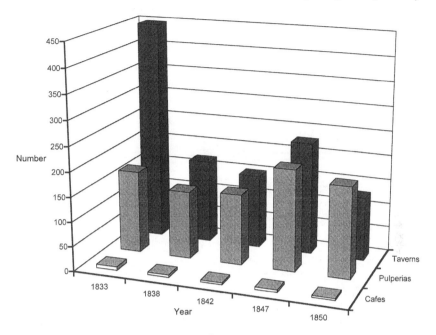

Figure 10.2   Taverns, Pulperias, and Cafés in Lima, 1833–1850

elite, scandalous dances and bawdy songs, but they were not a threat to the [political order]. . . .[35]

In attacking plebeian taverns, the government was trying to destroy a center of deliberation, a counterpublic.[36] Prior to 1834, Lima had no fewer than 447 taverns; after 1838, once the campaign was underway, only 147 of them remained standing (fig. 10.2).[37] At the height of the campaign in the late 1830s, plebeians had lost roughly 66 percent of their taverns. The number of taverns in Lima began rising again soon after that, as the plebeians began to fight back, engaging each other in continuous skirmishes. By the time the campaign ended in 1850, the number of operating taverns had risen to 71 percent of the 1834 total.

35. Aldo Panfichi H., "Urbanización temprana de Lima, 1535–1900," in *Mundos interiores: Lima 1850–1950,* ed. Aldo Panfichi H. and Felipe Portocarrero (Lima: Universidad del Pacífico, 1995), 37–38; *Aristocracia y plebe: Lima, 1760–1830* (Lima: Editorial Mosca Azul, 1984), 155–60; Luis Millones, *Tugurios: La cultura de los marginados* (Lima: Instituto Nacional de Cultura, 1978), 41–44.

36. Aguirre, *Agentes de su propia libertad,* 174.

37. All the data came from the Archivo Histórico Municipal in Lima. For data on 1833, see H4-1715; on 1838, see H4-1787; on 1842, see H4-1735; on 1847, see H4-2184; and on 1850, see H4-1961.

Visual Signaling

The Peruvian elite and non-elite also relied on visual signaling in bull-rings, in theater halls, and in patriotic and religious celebrations to express their approval or disapproval of the government. Public murals also provided them with a way of representing themselves.

State officials, like their counterparts in other countries, used "bread and circus" to distract the citizenry from the pressing problems of public life. With a seating capacity of 10,000 spectators, Lima's bullring was twice as large as the one in Pamplona, Europe's largest. According to contemporary accounts, bullfights were well attended and were one of the few places in public where the elite and non-elite mingled: "the seats are crowded . . . with beauty and rank alongside the motley and variously tinged populace"; "Whites, Europeans, Indians, Americans, Blacks, and a variety of mixed bloods" flocked to them.[38] Bullfights brought the nation together, providing the president and his staff an excellent opportunity to take a "random survey" of public opinion: "Upon entering the ring, [elite and plebeian] spectators, depending on what mood they were in and their degree of satisfaction with the administration, would greet them with enthusiasm or a cold silence."[39] Examples of both abound.

Theater halls were also an important deliberative site, although attendance at them was restricted to the elite, providing the president what contemporary pollsters would call a "focus group." In 1843, after President Vivanco defeated his rivals, he attended the theater hall and

> was greeted enthusiastically, with exultation and . . . applause. . . . The men gathered [in the audience], property owners, capitalists, merchants, those who because of their enlightenment, knowledge, and wealth can be said to constitute all that is best in society, that is, Public Opinion . . . made their views known, expressing indignation and horror against those who had organized the military revolt. . . . [This expression] was . . . based not on ceremonialism [but on] spontaneity.[40]

Theatergoers did not always give the president and his staff such a warm reception.

Theater life throughout the hinterlands was radically different from the capital and attracted mainly indigenous peoples, providing them with an

---

38. John Miller, *Memoirs of General Miller in the Service of Peru,* vol. 1 (London, 1829), 392; Radiguet, *Lima y la sociedad Peruana,* 64.

39. John McGregor, "Bosquejo general del Perú, 1847," in *Gran Bretaña y el Perú: 1826–1919: Informe de los Cónsules Británicos,* vol. 1, ed. Heraclio Bonilla (Lima: Instituto de Estudios Peruanos, 1975), 145.

40. "Supremo Director," *El Comercio,* 20 June 1843, 2.

opportunity to represent themselves onstage in public without having to portray themselves in the image and likeness of fair-skinned creoles. Indigenous peoples staged their own plays. In the 1840s, a longtime resident of Peru visited the town of Pallasca (Ancash), which had a population of two thousand, and left this description of a performance:

> An Indian with a small crown . . . and a long staff in hand, with a small mirror encrusted on the tip of it, representing Atahualpa, next to him was his friend and minister, Chimunga [*sic*], dressed in the same way, and [alongside them] members of their court, composed of a great many men and women as well as young girls.[41]

Across the hinterlands, indigenous peoples used theatrical life to revive their imagined past, one which had little to do with the rest of the Peruvian republic. Indigenous theater was especially dynamic across southern Peru, in Cuzco, Ayacucho, and Puno, where most rural peoples lived:

> Indians gather during dusk, and on certain special days, in the huts of village elders or the cacique, who narrates to them the history of the Incas, the deeds of their own descendants and those of Túpac Amaru's insurrection . . . they inculcate in them a hatred for the Pucacuncas, reassuring them that the kingdom of their rulers will soon be reestablished, placing before them effigies of past rulers.[42]

These communicative practices rooted in indigenous notions of collective memory competed with state-centered practices, although they also undermined the spread of public opinion.

Prior to mid-century, plebeian groups and indigenous peoples relied primarily on religious rather than patriotic celebrations to represent themselves in public life.[43] In 1840, *El Comercio* described the annual festivities the same way that its writers and other public intellectuals had always described them, as "a cold, ridiculous and pretentious ceremony."[44] While visiting Chile in the early 1850s, the editor of *La Semana*, José Arnaldo Márquez, was struck by the display of patriotism and enthusiasm put on by Chilean citizens. He published an article about it, and concluded with a question:

41. Witt, *Diario y observaciones*, 143.
42. McGregor, "Bosquejo general del Perú," 145.
43. Catherine Bell, *Ritual Theory, Ritual Practice* (New York: Oxford University Press, 1992), 182–96, 227–34.
44. "Fiestas," *El Comercio*, 29 July 1840, 2, and 7 December 1839, 1; *El Comercio*, 7 December 1839, 2; *El Comercio*, 28 July 1840, 2; Sartiège and Botmiliau, *Dos viajeros franceses*, 122.

Why is it that in our country the 28th of July and the victory at Ayacucho, the two most significant of battles that were waged against Spanish domination, arouse nothing but apathy?[45]

Patriotic rituals were so lifeless that in the 1850s even the president ceased
hosting a private banquet and ball for the city's elite in the National Palace.[46] They were based on passive and exclusionary notions of citizenship and nationhood, whereas religious festivities were rooted in opposite
principles.

Religious celebrations fostered socio-ethnic cohesion and political integration. The French consul, Viscount Eugene de Sartiège, described them
as follows:

> religious festivities and public solemnities are numerous in Lima, and
> they have proven very successful at momentarily dissipating the hatreds
> that divide Limeños and that reawaken with increased intensity the next
> time around.[47]

Each community choreographed its religious celebrations differently. In
urban areas, the festivities bore the imprint of plebeian influence. During
her visit to Arequipa in the south, Flora Tristán attended one of the most
important religious celebrations in honor of the patron saint of the city:

> At the head of the procession marched the musicians and the dancers,
> all of them in costume. Some of the blacks and zambos had been rented
> out to the church for this very purpose, and it was they who dressed the
> participants in gaudy, burlesque outfits . . . (such as harlequins, idiots,
> and so on). The forty or fifty dancers made the most . . . shameless ges-
> tures and contortions with their bodies and hurled the most obscene
> comments, embarrassing colored women and girls who were standing
> along the entire length of the street. After the dancers appeared the Vir-
> gin dressed in the most magnificent garments . . . in velvet and . . . pearls
> . . . and diamonds on her head, neck, and hands. Twenty or thirty
> blacks carried the Image [of the Virgin], and behind them marched the
> bishop along with all clerics . . . from all the religious houses in the
> city. . . . The [state] authorities followed . . . and directly behind them,
> in no particular order, came the masses of people, laughing and shout-
> ing every step of the way.[48]

45. Quoted in Pedro Dávalos y Lissón, *Historia republicana del Perú*, vol. 4 (Lima: Imprenta Gil, 1936), 226–27.

46. For descriptions of civic rituals, see: Lastarria, "Lima en 1850," 105; Sartiège and
Botmiliau, *Dos viajeros franceses*, 122. In the late 1840s, the president refused to invite
Lima's elite to his palace for snacks and drinks, as was customary. This snub led many of
them to lose what little interest they had had in patriotic rituals.

47. Sartiège and Botmiliau, *Dos viajeros franceses*, 122.

48. Tristán, *Peregrinaciones*, 170.

Religious celebrations in Arequipa and other major cities inverted the symbolic hierarchy established by state officials. Churchmen occupied a more prominent place in the parade than government officials.

Indigenous peoples played a central role in the religious celebrations that took place throughout the countryside. In the town of Jauja in the late 1830s, local residents celebrated the feast day of Santa Helena, their patron saint, by engaging in what anthropologist call "ritualized warfare":

> they [Indians] divided into two bands, with a few thousand on each side, placing themselves in battle formation and initiating combat with their slings. The women brought the stones, shouted and encouraged them with chicha to continue fighting, and dragged the fallen, removing them [to the side]. It was a terrible sight to behold . . . [then] they engaged in hand-to-hand combat, going after each other with clubs and knives. . . . By late afternoon, the weaker side were driven from the central plaza. . . .[49]

Across the Andes, ritualized warfare has always served to "integrate" the members of the community by providing them with a way of releasing their anger in a relatively contained and limited manner, thereby restoring the social cohesion of the group. However, it is significant to note that although Jauja had a large number of fair-skinned creoles and mixed-bloods, they rarely participated in the same celebrations. Ritualized warfare united the indigenous peoples while setting them apart from the rest of the community.[50] Religious celebrations served to reinforce racial and ethnic differences while preventing the emergence of more basic differences based on notions of democratic equality and national sovereignty.

Public opinion was also expressed in outdoor murals. In Lima, along the city wall that ran parallel to the River Rímac, alongside the Alameda de los Descalzos, the elite's favorite park, there was a mural

> representing the strangest idea imaginable. It is called "The World Upside Down," [and in it] the order of nature is . . . inverted: horses are seen riding on men's backs, dogs are hanging men by their heels, and a number of fish are depicted standing on the bank of a stream, on the tips of their tails, holding fishing rods in their mouths, with which they are catching men who are rising to the bait.[51]

49. Tschudi, *Testimonio del Perú*, 120.
50. On ritualized combat, see: Diane Hopkins, "Juego de enemigos," *Allpanchis* 17 (1982): 167–87; and Tristan Platt, "The Andean Soldiers of Christ: Confraternity Organization, the Mass of the Sun and Regenerative Warfare in Rural Potosi (18th–20th Centuries)," *Journal de la Societé des Americanistes* 72 (1987): 139–92.
51. Archibald Smith, *Peru As It Is*, vol. 1 (London, 1839), 151.

This mural served as a vivid reminder to the elite and non-elite of the brutality of the conquest and the continued racial and ethnic divisions that threatened to overwhelm public life.

Democratic Narrative

Between 1830 and 1850, Peruvians rarely employed Civic Catholicism in public discussions. In the early 1850s, a small group of elite men active in a handful of voting clubs in Lima began to use Civic Catholic terminology and phrases to discuss abstract, programmatic matters.

The first and most explicit usage of Civic Catholic keywords appeared in 1849 in an article titled "Spirit of Association," published in *El Progreso,* an organ of the Civilian Club, an electoral club discussed in an earlier chapter. The article lamented the absence of voluntary groups in Peru:

> the spirit of association, when applied to any goal, has the potential of becoming the main agent and motor of progress [but] Peru remains one of the only South American countries in which this spirit has not yet manifested itself. . . .[52]

The absence of associative life in Peru became a central and recurrent issue for members of the Civilian Club: "it is impossible to have a much sadder judgment of our society; citizens remain unable to form associations and to commit themselves to the common good."[53]

José Najora's *Cartilla del Pueblo sobre principios democráticos* circulated widely among the elite and non-elite of Lima. Written in the form of a "political catechism," the *Cartilla* employed a question-and-answer format that was typical of religious manuals. In response to the question "What is democracy?" Najora wrote:

> democracy is God's law, and because this is so it must be applied at all times and in all places; religion judges men in the afterlife, but democracy does so in this one. What makes them similar is their commitment to equality and fraternity.[54]

In rhetorical terms, the *Cartilla* performed a double maneuver: on the one hand, it brought together religion and democracy, but on the other it separated them by limiting the former to "otherworldly" and the latter to "worldly" matters. The church hierarchy rejected this interpretation, but it was already widespread even among priests and the faithful.

---

52. "Espíritu de asociación," *El Progreso,* 29 December 1849, 3–4.
53. "Política del club," *El Progreso,* 15 December 1850, 2.
54. José Miguel Najora, *Cartilla del Pueblo sobre principios democráticos* (Lima, 1855), 8, 44.

Taming Passions and Releasing Virtue

Public intellectuals were convinced that the most effective way of democratizing Peru was by altering public opinion and by promoting associative life. Although they considered both important, in their writings they usually emphasized one or the other.

The earliest and most explicit statement on the meaning of public opinion in Peru appeared in the late 1830s in an article published in *El Comercio:*

> Prior [to the emergence of public opinion in our country], it used to be necessary to probe deeply into the private conscience of each person . . . in order to find out their ideas . . . but today everything is done publicly. . . . And this is why secrecy used to be so important whereas today it is publicity that plays that role. The press has completely transformed the art and style of governing in the same way that technological inventions have altered the art of warfare.[55]

It is not coincidental that in the last sentence the author used the metaphor of warfare to describe public opinion. Like other writers of this period, the editor of *El Comercio* had a Schmittian understanding of politics ("war by other means") and was inclined to construe "military violence" as "speech acts" or, better stated, "fighting words."

Public intellectuals disagreed on how to generate public opinion and to propagate critical deliberation. Because so few citizens had any reading and writing skills and even fewer were fluent in Spanish, one group of writers proposed a statist and technocratic solution:

> the government . . . is responsible for . . . reanimating our social body and public spirit, and they can achieve this by organizing balanced and impartial discussions about common concerns. This will enable the press to become a source of public power and an ally of democracy.[56]

In this account, government officials were responsible for devising, implementing, and informing citizens of which policies had to be followed; the responsibility of citizens was to listen attentively to government. The other group put forward an associative approach to deliberation:

> In the past, we never had [any associations] and we still have great difficulty creating them due to our . . . lack of nationalism and to the fact that the public good still does not flow through the blood of the citizenry

55. "Respuesta del comercio," *El Comercio,* 15 October 1839, 2.
56. "Prensa periódica," *El Progreso,* 5 January 1850, 7. Also see: "Quién puede y quién debe rectificar la opinión pública," *El Genio de Rímac,* 21 August 1834, 2; and "Federación en el Perú," *El Nacional,* 21 October 1835,2.

which is the fire that enlivens civic life. In our clubs we will . . . find ways of combining the general good with particular concerns. They will also provide us a place to develop our discursive abilities, to learn how to reason and to exercise our judgment. . . .[57]

In this account, the role of associations was to provide citizens an opportunity to deliberate on public affairs and reconcile the common good with self-interest. Both perspectives—statist and associative—continued to be debated until late in the century.

Some public intellectuals downplayed the role of public opinion and gave far more weight to voluntary associations:

Our aim is to promote associative life . . . by bringing together [in one place] all the [social] forces currently dispersed [throughout the country]; this is the starting point for overcoming the many obstacles that face us, some of which still appear insurmountable to us because we remain isolated from each other. By [organizing associations], we will make contact with each other. This will make it possible for the honest men from the provinces to forge ties with state officials in different spheres of government.[58]

In addition to creating horizontal ties among the citizenry, associations hoped to enable Peruvians to forge vertical ties with state officials. An article published in *El Progreso* in July 1849 developed the argument further by claiming that the purpose of associations was to "fill in" all those places in public life that remained unoccupied by state officials; associations were supposed to steer citizens toward "those areas that were not accessible to the state" in order to promote civic-mindedness in them.[59] Voluntary groups, in this account, were an appendage of the state and in this respect not too different from Lenin's notion of "transmission belts."

Associative Life in Civil, Economic, and Political Society

Public intellectuals used Civic Catholicism in discussions about civil, economic, and political life, although, as I noted in a previous chapter, prior to mid-century associative life in all three terrains was stunted.

Even the most democratic-minded Peruvians adhered to a state-centered conception of civil society. In 1851, artisans published several articles in *El Comercio* defending their right to associate freely:

certain sectors of society have become alarmed by the stirring of an associative spirit among artisans. . . . Until now, we have been an inert

---

57. "Sociedad," *El Progreso*, 12 January 1850, 2.
58. "Contacto de los pueblos," *El Progreso*, 28 July 1849, 5–6.
59. "Espíritu de asociación," *El Progreso*, 29 December 1849, 3–4.

mass . . . without the benefits and advantages that democracy offers. . . . In our country, only the wealthy prosper, and this is the reason why social equality remains foreign to us. The government must intervene and extend a protective hand so that we can learn to associate amongst ourselves, which is our dream.[60]

Artisans were demanding that the government establish trade barriers and assist them in creating mutual-aid and credit associations to protect their workshops from foreign imports and moneylenders. Lima's skilled workers, too disorganized and weak to achieve anything on their own, appealed to the government for assistance. Note that their appeal was rooted not in their social and economic rights as citizens of Peru, but in clientelistic terms as workers in need of tutelage and protection.

Public writers also discussed the need for civic-mindedness in economic society. In 1849, *El Progreso* suggested as much:

Our principal need [at the moment], the one which without a doubt is of the most vital importance to us, is the preservation and consolidation of our [public] morality as it applies to commercial transactions. . . . The transformations [brought about by democracy] and based on liberty, have generated . . . profound moral dislocations, and these have had an impact on all social classes.[61]

The spread of social equality was, in this account, responsible for undermining the moral bonds that enabled merchants to transact business. Businessmen were extremely concerned with the way democratic practices had eroded social trust among them:

The founders of our independence believed we were endowed with republican virtue simply because they declared our country democratic. . . . From that moment on, under the false pretense of liberty, merchants went around transacting business with major warehouses and small stores, opening new accounts and purchasing stock on credit [without ever repaying].[62]

Democratic freedom was not, as some claimed, the complete absence of individual restraint; that led only to the tyranny of unruly passions. Self-interest properly understood had to be based on mutual reciprocity and limits on individual freedom.

Public writers also discussed the issue of civic practices and associative life in political society. Most of them focused on the role of municipal

60. "Unos artesanos," *El Comercio,* 29 November 1851, 3.
61. "Legislación mercantil," *El Progreso,* 18 August 1849, 1.
62. "Código de comercio," *El Progreso,* 20 October 1849, 3; "Prisión por deudas," *El Comercio,* 10 July 1845, 2.

townships in the development of a democratic and federalist regime. The most effective way for citizens to overcome their passions was by organizing townships:

> Citizens living in isolation and unattached to each other will succumb to their own worst impulses based on factionalism and despotism. . . . These persons invoke the public good in order to disguise their own egoistic passions. But when a man becomes active in a township, then he is transformed into a citizen and learns what are his rights and obligations. . . .[63]

Townships were important in another way: they decentralized power and in doing so provided citizens an opportunity to practice self-rule:

> sovereignty of the people remains an empty notion without the presence of townships, whose main function is to shape the public spirit. The underlying idea behind them is that each community is the best judge of its own interest, and this is doubly important in Peru, where the central government . . . is always said to be the [nation's] tutor; what type of democratic sovereignty can exist under these conditions? The way things are now, the nation has only two options: either they can appeal to Congress, which, lacking the most elementary knowledge about local conditions, often rejects their petitions, or they can appeal to the central government, which, like Congress, is also uninformed and, in any case, lacks the institutional capacity to implement whatever policy it decides. . . . The [municipalities we create] in Peru . . . will become our schools, and teach us our first lesson about politics. . . . In order for a democracy to exist, each individual has to be allowed to be the judge of his own interest.[64]

With the exception of the article published by the artisans, the problem with all these discussions is that they remained at the programmatic level and so had little relevance for most Peruvians.

Peru was a military dictatorship. The majority of public writers in the country were opposed to civic democracy and associative life and continued to use colonial Catholic terminology to make sense of themselves and each other. According to them,

> despotism is the only way we can shelter ourselves from our own political infancy . . . the army is the strong arm we need to silence our irritated passions.[65]

63. "Municipalidad," *El Progreso*, 15 September 1849, 2–3. "Comunicados," *El Telégrafo de Lima*, 19 April 1834, 2 for an earlier formulation.
64. "Municipalidades," *El Progreso*, 27 October 1849, 2.
65. "Sobre la libertad," *El Nacional*, 7 November 1835, 2.

Peruvians continued to construe themselves as unruly children. They also added a layer of gendered and racial notions to the old dichotomy of passion vs. reason. During the war between Peru and Bolivia (1829) that led to the latter's annexation of the former, Agustín Gamarra, commander of the losing army, and Rufino Macedo, one of the generals on the winning side, exchanged a series of private letters. In one of his last letters, Gamarra defended Peru's sovereignty:

> Peru has never belonged to Bolivia; instead, Bolivia has always belonged to Peru. . . . Without us, Bolivia would still be obeying and worshiping Black Colombians; we emancipated you from them. We will defend our national honor, which is really the same thing as personal honor and the honor of one's woman. We can negotiate and surrender almost everything, except our personal honor and the honor of our women.[66]

For Gamarra and like-minded authoritarians, the Peruvian nation, like its women, was honorable, whereas Bolivia had lost its dignity when it surrendered itself to libidinous Afro-Colombians. In contrast to the effeminate Bolivian army, Peruvian soldiers were manly and capable of defending the country's national honor.

---

66. Agustín Gamarra, "Letter to Sr. Colonel Rufino Macedo (27 August 1829)," in *Epistolario*, ed. Alberto Tauro (Lima: Universidad Nacional Mayor de San Marcos, 1952), 228.

PART FOUR

THE DEVELOPMENT
OF CIVIC DEMOCRACY:
CREATING NEW FORMS
OF LIFE

CHAPTER 11

Living Democracy: Mexican Civil and Economic Society

From mid-century onward, Mexicans organized a great many civic and economic associations, enabling them for the first time in their history to institutionalize democratic life.

> The associative spirit has spread across the country. . . . Until now, we had assumed that the government was responsible for rebuilding [public life]. But the patriotic groups, electoral clubs, welfare and educational societies that have appeared in all our states . . . are proof that our nation has finally become a true republic. . . . We have succeeded in changing our customs . . . but we must continue to improve the moral, intellectual, economic, and institutional foundations of society.[1]

The incorporation of indigenous peoples, mixed-bloods, women, and the working poor into civic and economic groups made public life far more egalitarian. The practices of self-governance that prevailed in these groups, based on relatively elaborate systems of electoral representation and trial by jury, contributed to the spread of democratic practices throughout the country. Associations also organized mass strikes and other nonviolent forms of protests in order to undermine everyday forms of authoritarianism. Civic and economic groups forged regional and national ties amongst themselves and established lateral contact with townships, newspapers, political clubs, and the central state. These interconnections contributed to fortifying and integrating public life.

Socio-institutional Structures

Mexicans organized a total of 1,526 civic and economic groups between 1857 and 1881. The vast majority of them appeared in the postwar period

1. F. M., "La Sociedad de Socorros Mutuos," *El Globo,* 3 November 1867, 1.

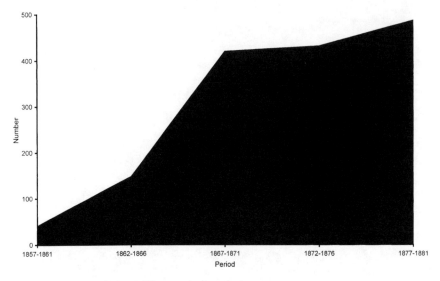

Figure 11.1 New Civic and Economic Associations, 1857–1881

after 1868 (fig. 11.1).[2] The Reform War (1857–1860), the bloodiest civil war Mexico had ever seen, and the French invasion and occupation (1862–1867) interrupted the spread of associative practices.[3] Between 1857 and 1862, citizens organized 47 associations. They organized 148 new groups between 1863 and 1866; most of these were patriotic associations. Public life remained relatively flat and one-dimensional throughout the decade.

During the postwar period, associative life grew steadily broader and deeper. In the years from 1867 to 1871 Mexicans founded 420 new civic and economic groups; for the years 1872 to 1876 the number jumped to 431, and again to 486 for the period 1877 to 1881.

Another way of gauging the institutional stability of civil and economic society in Mexico is by analyzing the duration and size of associations in

2. Unless otherwise indicated, the data in all the tables and maps in this chapter are from Carlos A. Forment, "Databank on Associative Life in Nineteenth Century Mexico" (Unpublished working document, Princeton University, 1997).

3. Richard N. Sinkin, *The Mexican Reform: 1855–1876* (Austin: University of Texas Press, 1979); and Walter Scholes, *Mexican Politics during the Juarez Regime: 1855–1872* (Columbia: University of Missouri Press, 1957). The War of Reform began when General Zuloaga's army attacked Juarez's Ayutla government. During the war, Juarez's government approved a number of laws attacking the socioeconomic and institutional power of the aristocracy, church, and military. Unable to fight back, these groups convinced Napoleon III to invade and occupy Mexico. He sent Archduke Maximilian and Carlota to establish a monarchy, thereby initiating the Franco-Mexican War. They had broad support from elite and non-elite groups in the states of Mexico, Puebla, Queretaro, Michoacan, and the nation's capital. Juarez's rebel government had broad support in all the other states.

Table 11.1 Duration of Civic and Economic
Associations, 1857–1881

Duration in Years	Percentage of Associations
1–3	47
4–6	47
7–9	0
10–12	0
13–15	6
16 or more	0

Table 11.2 Membership in Civic and Economic
Associations, 1857–1881

Number of Members	Percentage of Associations
1–15	12
16–30	15
31–45	15
46–60	11
61 or more	47

both terrains. According to table 11.1, 94 percent of the groups lasted six years or less, with the other 6 percent lasting anywhere from thirteen to fifteen years.[4] Although most associations were short-lived, the rate at which they were founded was relatively high and constant from 1866 on.

The size of the groups is also worth considering. Fifty-eight percent of all civic and economic groups had 64 or more members; almost all in this subset had between 80 and 100 members (table 11.2).[5] Membership remained low for most groups, but because most fields now had a few nationwide associations, public life remained relatively stable.

Associative life had become decentralized and widespread across the country (map 11.1). The greatest concentration of groups was in Mexico City (23 percent). The second tier included the following states: Veracruz (12 percent), Mexico minus the Federal District (11 percent) and Jalisco (10 percent). Next in line were Zacatecas, Guanajuato, Michoacán, Puebla, and Oaxaca all with 4 to 5 percent. At the bottom of the list were Sonora, Sinaloa, Durango, Chihuahua, Coahuila, Tamaulipas, Nuevo Leon, Aguascalientes, Colima, San Luis Potosí, Querétaro, Tlaxcala, Hi-

4. I was able to obtain data on only 1 percent of the associations in my bank, a sample too small to be reliable or representative.

5. This sample includes data on 22 percent of the associations in my bank.

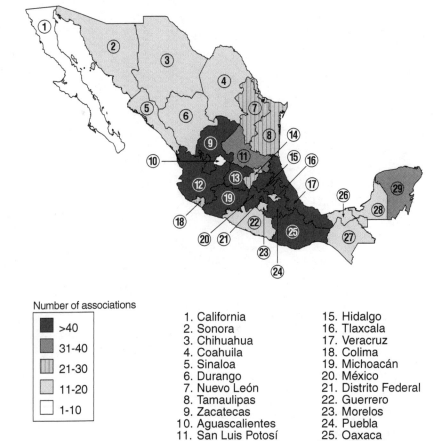

Number of associations

■	>40
▨	31-40
▥	21-30
▢	11-20
☐	1-10

1. California
2. Sonora
3. Chihuahua
4. Coahuila
5. Sinaloa
6. Durango
7. Nuevo León
8. Tamaulipas
9. Zacatecas
10. Aguascalientes
11. San Luis Potosí
12. Jalisco
13. Guanajuato
14. Querétaro

15. Hidalgo
16. Tlaxcala
17. Veracruz
18. Colima
19. Michoacán
20. México
21. Distrito Federal
22. Guerrero
23. Morelos
24. Puebla
25. Oaxaca
26. Tabasco
27. Chiapas
28. Campeche
29. Yucatán

Map 11.1   Geography of Civic and Economic Life, 1857–1881

dalgo, Guerrero, Morelos, Chiapas, Tabasco, Oaxaca, Yucatán, and Campeche, all with 3 percent or less.

Associative life remained far more developed in civil than in economic society; the former had 13 times as many groups as the latter. In civil society, the cultural field was now the largest (33 percent), followed by the social field (25 percent), the religious field (16 percent), the public service field (15 percent), and the recreational field (4 percent); a detailed breakdown may be found in figure 11.2. Economic society, at the very bottom of the figure, accounted for 7 percent of all voluntary groups.

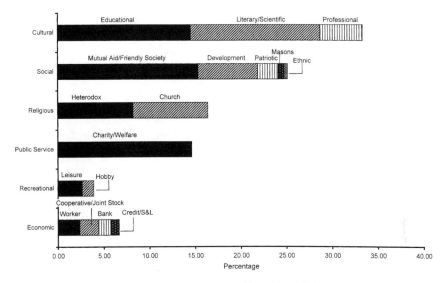

Figure 11.2 Civil and Economic Terrains, Fields, and Subfields, 1857–1881

Associative Practices in Civil Society

This section analyzes the development of democratic practices in civil society. The discussion is based on figure 11.2, and moves from the largest field (cultural) to the smallest (recreational).

The Cultural Field

The cultural field comprised educational, learned-scientific, and professional societies. All but the last type of association contributed to the spread of civic practices in this particular field.

Educational Associations

After the Franco-Mexican War, all governments that came to power in Mexico were committed to providing children and adults with a primary education.[6] However, none of them had the administrative or financial capacity to deliver on their policy. The central government was responsible for only 7 percent (603) of the nation's schools, most of them in the nation's capital.[7]

6. José Díaz Covarrubias, *La instrucción pública en México* (Mexico City, 1875), lxiii–lxxxvii. Mexico had the best ratio of schools to pupil (1:1,110) in Latin America, far better than second-place Argentina (1:1,547), but still far behind the United States, where the school-to-student ratio was 1:170.

7. Covarrubias, *Instrucción pública*, lxiii–lxxxvii. The government spent fifteen times more per student in the nation's capital than in the provinces.

Educational groups and municipal townships forged a partnership and played a central role in promoting primary schooling throughout the country. They accounted for the remaining 93 percent (7,500) of schools in the country. Religious associations were responsible for roughly 20 percent (1,581) of these schools. These "academies," as they were called, were established only in large cities and although they were supposed to meet the educational needs of children from elite backgrounds, they also accepted and provided generous scholarships for a great many children from poor families. According to José Díaz Covarrubias, the great pedagogue and Minister of Education, the curriculum in most of these academies was designed to "instill students with . . . aristocratic notions."[8] The hundreds of religious associations that were active in the educational subfield were committed to propagating authoritarian forms of life.

The remaining 70 percent (5,735) of the schools in Mexico were organized by Lancasterian and other associations, in partnership with municipal townships:

> associations have established numerous public schools across our country . . . which is itself another indication of the extent to which public spiritedness exists amongst us. . . . Moreover, the quality of education in their schools is superior to those the government provides. . . . Lancasterian groups are leading the way and filling an enormous void . . . with other associations doing their share. . . .[9]

Most of these schools were established in small towns and communities out in the provinces and were responsible for providing poor children with a basic education.[10] The division of labor between townships and educational groups was simple enough. The former collected taxes from local residents and used this money to purchase books, desks, and other supplies and to pay the schoolteacher; the latter pressured parents into paying taxes, donating money and labor for the school, and, most importantly, sending their children to school every morning instead of forcing them to work at home or in the fields.[11]

8. Covarrubias, *Instrucción pública*, lxiii–lxxxvii; and *Memoria de la Sociedad Católica* (Mexico City, 1877), 74–87, 92–93 100–104.

9. Covarrubias, *Instrucción pública*, lxxv.

10. Covarrubias, *Instrucción pública*, lxiii–lxxxvii. In his report, the minister listed separately schools financed by associations (495) and those funded by townships (5,240) for administrative and budgetary purposes, although in reality they worked together.

11. "Escuela de comondu," *Siglo XIX*, 4 April 1855, 3; "Escuela de obreros," *El Municipio Libre*, 8 June 1879, 2; "Mejoras Materiales," *El Monitor Republicano*, 3 February 1878, 3; "Chihuahua," *Siglo XIX*, 11 May 1869, 3; "Escuelas de adultos," *Siglo XIX*, 1 July 1868, 3; "Sociedad pro-escuela de adultos," *Siglo XIX*, 23 May 1868, 3; "Sociedad Minerva," *Siglo XIX*, 11 September 1874, 3; "Instrucción pública," *Siglo XIX*, 30 May 1870, 3; Compañía Lancasteriana, *Memoria que presenta la Compañía . . . de México* (Mex-

Educational groups were socially inclusive. Women played a major role in Lancasterian groups and participated in their elections both as candidates and as voters. A member noted:

> I witnessed them and can report with delight that the elections were carried out properly. This is an indication that the fair sex is now capable of participating in public affairs.[12]

Indigenous peoples organized the Sociedad Gregoriana (1866). It had local chapters in Mexico City and in the nearby towns of Texcoco and Pachuca. After the Franco-Mexican War, all three chapters invited mixed-bloods and fair-skinned creoles to join the group; many of the society's old members had perished in the war and had to be replaced.[13] A year later, the Sociedad called a plenary meeting; it was attended by

> magistrates and artisans, soldiers and parish priests from poor villages, government ministers and ex-political prisoners, the old and young, the fortunate and wretched, the descendants of the conquistadores and indigenous peoples. All classes, all viewpoints, all colors, and all social rankings were present and fraternizing with each other at the gathering.[14]

The Sociedad also allowed any student from a "poor family" to enroll in its school, not just those of indigenous descent.[15] Farmers of indigenous and mixed backgrounds from the towns of Chicoloapan, Coatepec, Acuantla, San Martín, and Texcoco (Mexico) attended the Free School of Chalco (1869), where they were encouraged by their teachers to "organize agricultural associations" and to use them to establish a "new type of social contract [in the countryside] based on respect" rather than exploitation.[16]

Educational groups encouraged members to forge vertical ties with each other. The Confederación de los Amigos de la Enseñanza (1874) was, as its very name indicates, a confederation of no fewer than fifteen different groups from across the Central Valley. The Confederación was multi-ethnic and included farmers, barbers, carpenters, and furniture-

---

ico City, 1871, 10–11; and Manuel Rivera Cambas, *México pintoresco, artístico y monumental*, vol. 3 (Mexico City, 1880), 139–40.

12. "Elecciones," *Siglo XIX*, 28 January 1870, 3; "Educación de la mujer," *Siglo XIX*, 1 June 1873, 3.

13. Sociedad Gregoriana, *Asociación Gregoriana: Primer banquete* (Mexico City, 1866), 6.

14. Sociedad Gregoriana, *Asociación Gregoriana: Tercer Banquete* (Mexico City, 1868), 70–73, 3–4.

15. "El Colegio de San Gregorio," *El Monitor Republicano*, 20 November 1868, 1.

16. Julio Chávez López, *Manifiesto a todos los oprimidos y pobres de México y del universo* (Chalco, 1869), 2.

makers as participants. Similar groups appeared in other parts of the country.[17] The Lancasterian society had more than a hundred chapters throughout the country and was the first to develop a nationwide organization. Members corresponded and visited each other, sent delegates to national conferences, and maintained contact with the central office in Mexico City.[18] Local chapters were responsible for turning this association into a nationwide organization.[19]

Educational groups inculcated democratic habits in students, their parents, and public life in several ways. The award ceremonies held several times a year after the examination period were rooted in notions of egalitarianism. Albert Evans, a member of William Seward's entourage, which stayed in Mexico for two years, attended several of these ceremonies. His description of the one held in the small town of Sayula (Guadalajara) is worth quoting:

> about one hundred and twenty five boys and two hundred girls, with the sexes being seated separately. . . . The furniture of the school-room was scant . . . and the children . . . plainly dressed; but they were . . . perfectly neat and clean. There were all colors and shades of colors among the pupils, but there was no distinction of class or condition, so far as their treatment and conduct toward each other went. . . . The distribution of prizes, silver coins with tri-colored—green, white and red—ribbons, followed. I noticed that a majority of the prizes were carried off by children of full Indian blood, and one of the highest was taken by an Indian woman of seventeen, whose scant but . . . neat apparel indicated, unmistakably, that she was the daughter of people in very poor circumstance.[20]

The award ceremony, like the curriculum in most Lancasterian schools, was meritocratic. This was true even in the nation's capital, where the socio-ethnic differences between elite and non-elite groups were far more rigid. Ignacio Altamirano, the brown-skinned publicist, attended the award ceremony held in the National Theater and noted: "whenever a poor child was awarded a prize, the public applauded especially loud." [21]

Strikes became an integral part of public life. In Mexico City, the Socie-

17. Francisco Salas, "Confederación de los amigos de la enseñanza," *Siglo XIX,* 30 September 1874, 3. Also see: "Chihuahua," *Siglo XIX,* 11 May 1969, 3; "Tehuantepec," *Siglo XIX,* 30 September 1874, 3; "Noticias varias," *El Socialista,* 16 June 1872, 4.

18. Compañía Lancasteriana, *Memoria,* 10, 47–48; Compañía Lancasteriana, *Memoria que presenta la Compañía . . . de México* (Mexico City, 1872), 34, and 9 for statistics on the number of letters exchanged among local chapters.

19. Mary Kay Vaughan, *The State, Education and Social Class in Mexico: 1880–1920* (Dekalb: Northern Illinois University Press, 1982) remains the best study of its kind.

20. Albert S. Evans, *Our Sister Republic: A Gala Trip through Tropical Mexico in 1869–1870* (Hartford, Conn., 1870), 101–2 and 194.

21. "Crónicas de la semana," *Siglo XIX,* 9 January 1869, 4.

dad de Escuelas Secundarias (1875), composed of high-school students from the provinces who were on scholarship, led a month-long strike to challenge the government's control of education.[22] In April 1875, students in the Sociedad del Porvenir (1868), the Sociedad Washington (1872), and various other associations held a public meeting in the Hidalgo Theater. They were there to protest the expulsion of several students from medical school and to demand that they be reinstated with full scholarship. During the meeting, they raised a host of other issues.[23] The government-run boarding houses for students on scholarship, they claimed, resembled "army barracks." The staff was despotic, and boarders were deprived of constitutional freedoms, including the right to speak and associate, enjoyed by other citizens. The students also called on teachers and administrators to assist in "emancipating education from the state the same way that the previous generation had emancipated it from the Catholic Church."[24] As a means of achieving this emancipation, they demanded that positivist textbooks be abolished and replaced with humanistic ones and that the country's leading scholars be allowed to design a new national curriculum.

In order to draw public sympathy for their demands, the students established a "Free University" in Mexico City and invited a number of intellectuals to teach courses. In response, the Minister of Education pressured the members of Congress into depriving strikers of their scholarships. The *Siglo XIX* and *El Monitor Republicano* launched a vigorous campaign in defense of the students:

> some people are portraying the strike as a rebellion against our government, but this is not what our nation's youth is demanding from us. If anything, they are trying to prevent the strike from becoming politicized and deformed.[25]

Newspapers swayed public opinion in favor of the need to reform the entire educational system and to guarantee it autonomy from the state.

Learned and Scientific Societies

Following the Franco-Mexican War, public writers throughout the country began a movement to revive "national culture," contributing to the

22. Charles Hale, *The Transformation of Liberalism in Late Nineteenth Century Mexico* (Princeton, N.J.: Princeton University Press, 1989), 161–68 for a detailed discussion of the strike.
23. "Sociedad Porvenir," *Siglo XIX*, 9 June 1869, 3; "Sociedad Washington," *Siglo XIX*, 27 August 1872, 3.
24. Miguel S. Macedo, "Ensayo sobre los deberes de los superiores a los que son inferiores," *Anales*, 17 July 1877, 226.
25. "Manifiesto," *Siglo XIX*, 11 May 1875, 3. Also see: "Editorial," *Siglo XIX*, 3 May 1875, 2 and "Charlas de Domingo," *El Monitor Republicano*, 3 February 1878, 3.

deradicalization of public life. The influential writer Ignacio Ramírez, a mixed-blood and a member of the Velada Literaria (1867), a literary group, noted:

> politics had dominated our lives. But now the struggle has ended, and we are once again gathering in each other's homes to discuss literary concerns. In our group, we have writers of all political orientations, and although personal and ideological differences still divide us, we are finding ways of overcoming them.[26]

Learned and scientific societies provided the country's cultural elite a place to mingle and to recognize each other as compatriots rather than political enemies. Contrary to the claims of some scholars, cultural nationalism contributed to the spread of tolerance.

The Asociación Pedro Escobedo (1860), according to one of its members, was committed to "creating a Mexican school of medicine, the same way that the French and Germans have created their schools."[27] The members of the Asociación collected and studied local plants used in "folk" medicine in order to discover their chemical and curative properties. The Sociedad Minera (1867) expressed their own sense of nationalism in similar terms:

> Mexico will become a great country the day our miners overcome their empiricism and begin using scientific methods appropriate to our own local conditions. We continue relying on the Germans for our methods and we still use their books, the same ones with which we were taught, although we already know their approach is unsuitable here because our conditions are different from those in their country.[28]

Members of these groups also learned to distinguish between public criticism and personal slander:

> Criticism has become the distinguishing characteristic of our age. All our political, philosophical, literary, and scientific models began as simple hypotheses . . . and became what they are today as a result of analysis. . . . In this age of freedom and creativity, we must continue to subject our writings to criticism . . . as we already do in the field of literary criticism. . . .[29]

Nationalism and tolerance went hand in hand.[30]

---

26. Ignacio Ramírez, "Introducción," *El Renacimiento*, vol. 1 (Mexico City, 1868), 3.
27. José Galindo, "Discurso pronunciado en la Asociación," *El Observador Médico,* 1 August 1874, 90 and his "Discurso leído en el séptimo aniversario de la Asociación," *El Observador Médico,* 1 August 1875, 257.
28. "El Minero Mexicano," *El Minero Mexicano,* 25 December 1873, 1–3.
29. "La literatura en México y otras cosas," *El Mensajero,* 28 January 1871, 2.
30. Dr. D. Francisco Becerril, "Discurso pronunciado en el Quinto Aniversario," *El Observador Médico,* 12 July 1873, 293.

The Sociedades Científicas de México (1877), composed of fourteen learned and scientific groups from different parts of the country, was the first nationwide group of its type. The Sociedades hosted regional and national conferences, providing men and women a place to transform their own professional identity into a national one rooted in notions of patriotism.[31]

Professional Groups

Mexico had very few professionals (doctors, lawyers, engineers). The majority of them lived in Mexico City, Puebla, and Guadalajara, and it was in these cities that their influence on public life was most palpable. According to a contemporary, "professional titles are the only honorific titles that are now recognized as valid in our country."[32]

Medical associations encouraged doctors to consider health care the same way priests considered religion:

> Medical secrets are no different than the secrets priests hear in the confessional box. Doctors must attend to the moral disorders of their patients the same way they minister to their physical ailments.[33]

Doctors campaigned to lower the cost of drugs and pressured congress and township officials to approve legislation protecting patients from unscrupulous pharmacists. In some cities, doctors organized a system of neighborhood clinics to provide health care for the poor and needy. They also created a special degree-granting program in medical school for paramedics that could be completed in two years—half the time required for a medical degree. These measures improved public health care and democratized the medical profession.[34]

Civic-minded lawyers organized the Colegio de Abogados (1863), a nationwide association, after Benito Juarez's government dissolved the "Lawyer's Guild," a corporation that dated back to the colonial period. Membership in the Colegio was voluntary rather than mandatory, and open to any lawyer—not just those who had been licensed in one or another state. The Colegio reformed the legal curriculum in all the law

31. Leopoldo Río de la Loza, *Composiciones Literarias* (Mexico City, 1877).

32. *Diario Oficial*, 20 January 1868, 1. quoted in Rosa Casanova, "1861–1876," in *Y todo . . . por una nación: Historia social de la producción plástica de la ciudad de México*, ed. Eloisa Uribe (Mexico City: Instituto Nacional de Antropología e Historia, 1987), 157. For the number of professionals in each state, see Juan E. Pérez, *Almanaque estadístico de las oficinas y guía de forasteros y comercio de la República para 1876* (Mexico City, 1877); Milada Bazant, "La República restaurada y el porfiriato," in *Historia de las profesiones en México*, ed. Francisco Arce Garza and Milada Bazant (Mexico City: Secretaría de Educación Pública, 1982), 149–92 for a detailed history of professional life.

33. "Secreto Médico," *El Observador Médico*, 1 August 1871, 25–30.

34. Bazant, "República restaurada," 166.

schools by introducing courses in political economy and abolishing the study of canon law and colonial jurisprudence. In Mexico City and other state capitals, local chapters of the Colegio hosted public forums to debate controversial issues such as the "legal relationship between civil society . . . and state" and "the legality of strikes."[35] In Oaxaca and Michoacan, they also provided indigenous peoples with legal counsel.[36] The Colegio contributed to making urban and rural citizens aware of their civil and political rights.

The Sociedad de Agricultura (1871), composed of wealthy estate owners, stockmen, and small farmers, had a dozen or so chapters across the country. The urban chapters attracted the rural elite (absentee landlords) and charged monthly dues that were four times higher than the amount charged by town-based groups, which were made up mainly of farmers.[37] Members of both groups attended regional meetings and had an equal voice in shaping the policies of the Sociedad. Like the majority of professional groups, the Sociedad published its own *Boletín,* in which appeared countless articles by members critical of the government and demanding the creation of a "Department of Agriculture." The government created such a department in 1879, and it quickly became one of the most innovative and responsive government agencies of this period. The Sociedad and the Department of Agriculture collaborated on a host of projects, including the creation of agricultural schools in different parts of the country. Hundreds of small farmers enrolled in the schools and learned the latest scientific techniques. When they returned to their communities they disseminated these techniques, thereby contributing to the modernization of rural life.[38] The Sociedad contributed to the formation of the Mexican state and to the development of public life.

The Social Field

The social field was populated by mutual-aid, community development, patriotic, masonic, and ethnic associations. All but the last of these groups contributed to democratizing daily life.

35. Guillermo Prieto, "Huelga de los sombrereros," *Revista Universal,* 4 June 1875 and 10 June 1875, 1–2. Also see G. Prieto, "El Colegio de Abogados, El Liceo Hidalgo y la Cuestión de las Huelgas," *Revista Universal,* 18 August 1875, 1–2.

36. "Conferencia en el Colegio de Abogados," *Siglo XIX,* 5 July 1875, 3.

37. "Sociedad de Agricultura," *Siglo XIX,* 5 March 1871, 3; "Sociedad de Agricultura," in *Estatutos de la Sociedad . . .* (Toluca, 1871), 5–13.

38. *Boletín de la Sociedad de Agricultura,* vol. 1 (Mexico City, 1879), 4–6. Also see: William H. Dusenberry, "The Mexican Agricultural Society, 1879–1914," *The Americas* 12, no. 4 (April 1956): 385–98.

Mutual-Aid and Friendly Societies

Mutual-aid societies were among the most egalitarian groups in the country. The Hermandad Cosmopolita (1871) was typical in this respect:

> We do not exclude anyone on the basis of their sex, whether they are married or not, nor on the basis of nationality, religion, political principles, nor even their reputation in public or private life. Even criminals who committed a mistake in the past are given in our group another opportunity to correct their errors and find their way along the straight and narrow path. The magistrate, the poor, the unemployed and the delinquent are admitted without distinction into our association. How many of our wayward citizens became this way because of upright citizens who shunned and rejected them.[39]

Mutual-aid societies provided marginalized citizens an opportunity to enter public life and gain recognition from their own compatriots. These groups also established horizontal ties with educational associations and townships. The Mutual de Obreros (1871) in Celaya (Querétaro), composed of textile workers, taxed themselves and turned the money over to the local school, which was attended by 88 boys, 63 girls, and 52 adults.[40] Any child could attend the school, regardless of whether their parents were dues-paying members of the association; adults could attend only if they had contributed to the group. The Asociación described themselves in civic terms:

> The associative spirit is incredibly powerful among the working class of our country, and it has enabled us to learn about our rights and has given us a sense of dignity. . . . We have known for some time that our problems cannot be solved by political means alone; we also need to use socioeconomic means. And we have known that the spirit of association . . . is what we need most to accomplish this. . . . In fact, it was the associative spirit that brought down the old political order and it is what will now enable us to develop a new society.[41]

39. Hermandad Cosmopolita, *Estatutos generales de la Hermandad* (Mexico City, 1871), 17–18. Also see Sociedad Paz y Union, *Reglamento de la Sociedad Paz y Unión* (Mexico City, 1875), 3–4.

40. "Fábrica de Zempoala," *El Socialista*, 8 December 1872, 3. Also see: "Asociación de Artesanos," *Siglo XIX*, 17 January 1857, 3; "Club Popular de Artesanos," *Siglo XIX*, 7 April 1869, 3; "Sociedad de Artesanos," *El Mexicano*, 11 July 1866, 2; "Sociedad de Comerciantes en Carnes del Rastro," *Siglo XIX*, 17 January 1872, 3; "El Domingo se inaguró la escuela," *Siglo XIX*, 18 January 1872, 3; "Sociedad de Constructores Prácticos," *Siglo XIX*, 11 January 1872, 3; "Sociedad de Constructores," *El Socialista*, 14 January 1872, 3; "Sociedad de Socorros," *Siglo XIX*, 6 February 1874, 3.

41. Gerardo Silva, "Una asociación de obreros," *El Socialista*, 5 May 1873, 2.

Mutual-aid groups contributed to the spread of civic reciprocity in daily life, and in doing so made citizens increasingly aware of their own capacity for generating social power.

Mutual-aid groups developed a new system of governance based on elections and trial by jury. Membership in some of the associations, including the Sociedad de Sastres (1864), the Sociedad Protectora de Dependientes (1873), and the Sociedad Mutuos de Impresores (1872), had grown significantly, making it impractical for members to decide on every issue or administrative matter by direct democratic vote. Although they continued to participate in the internal affairs of the group, members also elected representatives (one per every 20 members) and made them responsible for the day-to-day affairs of the association. Representatives met weekly and reported monthly to their constituents at the association's plenary meeting. Elections for representatives, like those for officers, were organized and monitored. A committee composed of rank-and-file members and officers was chosen by all dues-paying affiliates.[42] They, in turn, compiled a list of eligible voters; distributed, collected, and tabulated the marked ballots; and made sure that the elections had been fair; in cases of fraud, they had the power to annul the results and call for new elections.[43] Mutual-aid groups also developed a judicial system. Members accused of violating the statutes and rules of the association presented their case to a jury of their peers, who decided their case and determined whether a penalty was in order.[44]

Mutual-aid groups began to appear even within the military and administrative wings of the state. The Asociación Político-Militar (1871), made up of low-ranking soldiers and officers, was committed to democratizing life in the barracks. The Asociación demanded an end to corporal punishment, established a grievance system, and mediated in disputes between soldiers and officers. The group also invited public intellectuals to lecture recruits on the dangers of militarism. State employees in Mexico City's National Archive, Treasury Department, and Central Post Office

---

42. Epifanio Romero, "Reglamento general de la Sociedad del Ramo de Sastrería," *El Socialista*, 12 September 1875, 1–4; Ambrosio Quiroz, *Estatutos de la Sociedad Protectora de Dependientes* (Puebla, 1873), 10–11; Jose Woldenberg, "Asociaciones artesanas del siglo XIX," *Revista Mexicana de Ciencias Políticas y Sociales* 21, no. 83 (January–March 1976): 71–112. Also see Carlos Illades, *Hacia la república del trabajo: La organización artesanal en la Ciudad de México; 1853–1876* (Mexico City: El Colegio de México, 1996), 10–13, 94.

43. "Fraternidad y constancia," *El Socialista*, 24 January 1871, 1; "Sociedad de Socorros Mutuos," *La Firmeza*, 2 December 1874, 1; "Ramo de Sastrería," *El Socialista*, 12 September 1875, 2–3.

44. "Boletín," *La Firmeza*, 20 May 1874, 1; "Un hecho censurable," *La Firmeza*, 17 April 1875, 1–2.

organized the Asociación de Empleados (1875) in order to prevent the government from misusing money from their pension fund.[45]

Mutual-aid societies developed vertical and horizontal relations with other groups, paving the way for the creation of regional and nationwide organizations. The process was often initiated from below by members themselves in response to their own needs. When members of Oaxaca's Sociedad de Artesanos (1873) went to live in Mexico City, they requested that they be admitted by other mutual-aid groups in the capital and that they be granted the same rights and privileges as any other member.[46] After a series of bad harvests, small farmers from the area of San Luis, San José, San Felipe, San Miguel, Dolores Hidalgo, and San Diego overcame their sense of mistrust and recognized that they could improve their life chances by pooling their resources. The Sociedad Filantrópica de Agricultores y Labradores (1875) they organized was one of the few groups composed of farmers and peons from different communities.[47] The Gran Familia Artística, Mecánica y Agrícola (1861) was made up of artisans, workers, and farmers from Mexico City and surrounding communities. It was one of the few that succeeded in cutting across occupational and regional boundaries.[48] The miners, shoemakers, and farmers from Dolores and the Valle de Santiago accomplished the same thing when they created the Sociedad Filantrópica de Artesanos (1873).[49]

These regional initiatives prepared the way for the creation of the Gran Círculo de Obreros (1872), the first nationwide association of workers. The Círculo had about ninety affiliates, mainly mutual-aid groups, and approximately 8,000 members.[50] The leaders of the Círculo explained the purpose of the group:

> it is time for the republic of labor to have its own national constitution and institutions, just as the Government and Church have theirs.[51]

The mutual-aid groups who formed part of the Gran Círculo maintained horizontal ties amongst themselves; they attended each other's events and

45. "Asociación de empleados," *Siglo XIX,* 25 February 1875, 3.
46. "Sección oficial," *El Socialista,* 3 August 1873, 1.
47. "La Sociedad Filantrópica de Agricultores," *Siglo XIX,* 19 August 1875, 3; "Sociedad Mutualista de Labradores," *Siglo XIX,* 30 July 1875, 2; and "Sociedad de Labradores," *Siglo XIX,* 19 August 1875, 3.
48. La Gran Familia Artística, Mecánica y Agrícola, *Reglamento de la Sociedad* (Mexico City, 1861), 2–4.
49. "Composición social," *Siglo XIX,* 10 December 1873, 3.
50. "Lista de los ciudadanos diputados al Congreso Obrero Constituyente cuyas credenciales han sido aprobadas," *El Socialista,* 11 June 1876, 1.
51. "Las clases productoras," *El Socialista,* 25 January 1874, 1.

exchanged private documents.[52] They also maintained vertical ties with the Gran Congreso, the main branch in Mexico City. The Círculo and Congreso hosted two national congresses, one in February 1876 and the other December 1879. During the first Congress, the credentials committee denied female delegates the right to represent their group, even if they had been elected by their own rank and file. According to the committee, "the law of the land considers [women] to be minors, and as such unfit to represent anyone."[53] After a spirited debate, the members voted 37 to 26 in favor of granting all women the right to represent their group.[54]

Community Development Groups

After the Franco-Mexican War, local residents in major cities and small towns organized development groups to beautify public spaces in their communities.

Perched high in the Sierra Madre of Veracruz, tobacco farmers of indigenous and mixed background from the area organized the Club de la Montaña (1873). The club built and maintained the primary school and built a network of roads in order to make it easier for them to transport their tobacco crop to nearby markets. Indigenous peoples in the remote towns of Juchitán and Villa Álvarez in the state of Oaxaca on the opposite coast created the Sociedad de Progreso (1875) and the Junta de Vecinos (1877) to dredge and maintain irrigation canals in the area. Similar groups were organized in Rincón de Ramos (Aguascalientes), Tequisquiapan (Querétaro), and scores of other rural and poor communities by mixed-bloods and indigenous farmer.[55]

Development groups instilled in residents a sense of civic pride. In the mid-1870s, while traveling from Veracruz to Mexico City, John Geiger, an investor from the United States, visited and stayed in several towns along the way—relatively affluent ones such as Orizaba, which he described as

52. "Boletín," *La Firmeza,* 17 June 1874; "Junta general," *La Firmeza,* 7 October 1874); "La Sociedad Mutuos de Meseros," *La Firmeza,* 28 October 1874, 2; "Décimo aniversario de la Sociedad de Sastres," *La Firmeza,* 25 November 1874, 1.

53. "Un debate interesante," *El Socialista,* 14 May 1876, 1.

54. "La social," *El Hijo del Trabajo,* 15 May 1875, 3; "El Congreso Obrero," *El Hijo del Trabajo,* 22 May 1876, 3.

55. "Mejoras materiales," *La Unión Democrática,* 16 May 1873, 4; "Sociedad Promovedera de Mejoras Materiales," *Siglo XIX,* 12 November 1872, 3; "Sociedad de Mejoras Materiales," *Siglo XIX,* 5 August 1873, 3; "Mejoras Materiales en Tequisquiapán," *Siglo XIX,* 2 September 1868, 3; "Villa Álvarez," *El Defensor de la Ley,* [Oaxaca], 1 February 1877, 4; "Sociedad de Progreso," *Siglo XIX,* 18 May 1875, 3; "Club de las Montañas," *Siglo XIX,* 11 December 1870, 3; "Junta de Vecinos," *Siglo XIX,* 1856; "Sociedad de Mejoras Materiales, Morales, de Beneficencia y Socorros Mutuos de Texcoco," *Documentos Relativos al Primer Aniversario* (Mexico City, 1865), 4, 8; "Mejoras en Toluca," *Siglo XIX,* 26 March 1869, 2.

"shabby," and poor ones like San Juan del Rio, which he described in this way:

> We crossed the river over a good stone bridge, drove up the main street, and halted before a modest fonda. This main street is a very wide, tolerably well-paved road, overarched on both sides by rows of beautiful tress, under the shade of which the people were comfortably installed in numerous benches. The houses are gaily painted, perhaps to excess in many instances, but rendering the town peculiarly pleasing.[56]

In the early 1880s, Manuel Rivera Cambas, an engineer with an eye for ethnographic detail, visited a number of mining camps in the state of Hidalgo, an area he knew well, having traveled through it several times before. He was surprised to find that the villagers from Xochicoatlan and Tianguistengo had overcome their ancestral hatred and built a road between their communities.[57]

The Junta de Vecinos (1873) from Cerritos and Carbonera (San Luis Potosí), in partnership with township officials, cleared a road between these two towns. It took them five months to collect 1,500 pesos from residents and another three months to complete the road. Manzanillo's Junta de Vecinos (1878) took three years and received 11,000 pesos from the government to complete the Tuxpan Bridge.[58] Although corruption and fraud were common, I did not find evidence of it in either of these cases. Civic groups and government officials monitored each other and made certain that the money was used to improve public life rather than for private gain. Associations contributed to delineating the ethical and economic boundaries between public and private life.

Patriotic Clubs

The overwhelming majority of "Juntas Patrióticas" were organized during the Franco-Mexican War by citizens living in rebel-controlled areas. Juntas were responsible for collecting money and jewelry from residents and using this money to buy medicine, armaments, and uniforms for local militia units. They were also responsible for the defense of the community. Members organized work brigades to dig trenches, erect parapets, and collect blood from local residents. During the French occupation, they also provided for the families of soldiers who had been killed or captured, discouraged residents from fraternizing with the enemy, and kept a

56. John Lewis Geiger, *A Peep at Mexico* (London, 1874), 228, 336–37.
57. Cambas, *México Pintoresco*, 3.120–21, 130, 139, 583, 607.
58. Cambas, *México Pintoresco*, 3.120–21, 130, 139, 583, 607.

list of those who did.[59] In the words of a contemporary, the Juntas "rekindled public spirit" at a time when the nation had lost its sovereignty.[60]

The Juntas remained active after the war and were responsible for organizing patriotic celebrations. But by the early 1870s, they were being criticized by public writers for having become oligarchic in the way they conducted their affairs. Officers were appointed rather than elected, and commoners were discouraged from joining.[61] Their antidemocratic tendency was also expressed in the way they choreographed patriotic celebrations. Instead of hosting them outdoors and offering citizens popular dances and fireworks, the Juntas held such celebrations in the National Palace and only the elite were invited to attend the elegant balls. In the mid-1870s, public writers demanded that they be abolished:

> After each holiday, our newspapers, the voice of public opinion, criticize these celebrations for lacking any popular support and having become cold, official events. . . . Organizers are reproached and held responsible for stripping them of meaning and forcing citizens to become mere spectators. . . . The Junta . . . has succeeded in erasing our [patriotic] memory, and this is why they should now step aside and allow other associations to organize all future celebrations. . . .[62]

Artisans rarely observed these holidays, unless the gendarmes forced them to do so.[63]

---

59. "Asociación Filantrópica," *Siglo XIX*, 17 March 1863, 3; "Junta," *Siglo XIX*, 4 June 1862, 4; "Zacatecas," *Siglo XIX*, 13 December 1862, 2; "Junta Filantrópica," *Siglo XIX*, 16 January 1863), 3.

60. "Junta Patriótica," *Siglo XIX*, 16 July 1862, 4; "Junta Promovedora de Recursos," *Siglo XIX*, 31 December 1862, 3; "A trabajar en fortificaciones," *Siglo XIX*, 16 September 1862, 3; "Bomberos," *Siglo XIX*, 23 November 1862, 4; "Reunión patriótica," *Siglo XIX*, 22 July 1862, 3; "Hospitales de sangre," *El Monitor Republicano*, 2 January 1863, 3; "Hotel de Inválidos," *Siglo XIX*, 25 March 1863, 4; "Lotes del Ex–Convento del Carmen," *El Monitor Republicano*, 9 January 1863, 4; "El traidor Almonte borrado del registro," *Siglo XIX*, 2 May 1862, 3; "Gran subscripción," *La Independencia Mexicana*, 4 October 1863, 4; "Junta Patriótica," *Siglo XIX*, 14 March 1863, 3.

61. "Aniversario de la Independencia," *Siglo XIX*, 15 September 1868, 3; "Junta Patriótica de la Capital," *Siglo XIX*, 20 January 1869, 4; "El Cinco de Mayo," *El Monitor Republicano*, 4 May 1873, 2; Ignacio M. Altamirano, *Crónicas de las Fiestas de Septiembre en México y Puebla en 1869* (1869; Puebla: Universidad Autónoma de Puebla, 1987), 7–8; "Día 15 de Septiembre," *Siglo XIX*, 15 September 1862, 3. For the provinces, see: Laura E. Gutiérrez Talamas, "Fiestas cívicas y cultura política: Elaboración de la nación desde un ámbito local; Saltillo Coahuila en el siglo XIX" (Master's thesis, Universidad Iberoamericana, 1996), 220–60.

62. "Las Fiestas de la República," *Siglo XIX*, 21 September 1875, 2; and "Las fiestas nacionales," *Siglo XIX*, 18 September 1871, 3.

63. "Las fiestas cívicas," *Siglo XIX*, 7 February 1869, 3; "El 5 de Mayo," *Siglo XIX*, 6 May 1870, 3; "Cinco de Febrero," *Siglo XIX*, 5 February 1872, 3; Talamas, "Fiestas Cívicas," 250–75.

Masonic Lodges

The twenty or so lodges that appeared during the postwar period surfaced in Mexico City, Veracruz, and San Luis Potosí.[64] In all three cities, masons tried "to persuade citizens that they were just like any other civic group" rather than a "secret sect" like the Jesuits.[65] In keeping with this new image, nonmembers were invited to attend their public forums and were given pamphlets explaining the aims of the group and describing their rituals. In addition to making the group more open, masons also recruited heavily among commoners and even established a chapter for women.

The masons were successful in reentering public life in Mexico City and Veracruz, but not in San Luis Potosí. In 1868, the lodges in the capital hosted a banquet in a public park, and 350 people attended; women and artisans were well represented. In Veracruz, local lodges established a primary school for poor children with the support of local residents and the municipal township.[66] However, in San Luis Potosí, several Catholic groups pressured the state governor to prohibit the masons from distributing flyers and hanging banners in any public area. They claimed that masons, like the Church, were now a "private" group and as such had no right to impose their views on the general public. Even conservative Catholics now used civic terminology to attack their rivals. The governor, who was himself a mason, agreed with them.[67]

Church bishops instructed parish priests in all three states to mobilize the faithful against masonic lodges:

> From the four corners of our country, from every pulpit in every church, and all our Catholic newspapers, a call to arms has been sent out by priests, instructing the faithful to combat masonic lodges, threatening anyone who joins them with excommunication, eternal damnation and all the rest.[68]

Newspapers came to the masons' defense:

> masons are like any other association in the country, the only difference being that they are dedicated to self-improvement. . . . Anyone can

64. Jean-Pierre Bastian, "Una ausencia notoria," *Historia Mexicana* 46, no. 3 (January–March 1995): 439–60, on the lack of primary sources for studying the masons after mid-century; José M. Mateos, *Historia de la Masonería en México* (1884; Mexico City: Editorial Herbasa, 1994), 150–289, 298–329, 349–55 is useful.

65. "Banquete Masón," *Siglo XIX,* 25 December 1868, 3. "Bibliografía," *Boletín de la Sociedad Mexicana de Geografía y Estadística* 2, no. 1 (1869): 69–72.

66. "Los Masones en Veracruz," *Siglo XIX,* 9 August 1876, 3.

67. "Intolerancia," *El Monitor Republicano,* 18 February 1875, 3.

68. "Cruzada contra los Francomasones," *El Monitor Republicano,* 20 November 1872, 3.

become a mason irrespective of their social standing, nationality, skin-color, religion, or political orientation.[69]

Public opinion provided masons the additional support they needed to reenter public life at a time when they were too weak to achieve this on their own.

Ethnic Associations

Unlike the immigrant families who settled in Argentina and Cuba, the majority of foreigners in Mexico were wealthy investors there to make their fortunes as quickly as possible and then to return home to enjoy their wealth.[70] Charles Gagern, a Prussian expatriate who arrived in Mexico in the early 1860s, described foreign investors:

> they are greedy, interested only in getting rich and returning to Europe, and caring nothing for the country that made all this possible. . . . Like the Spanish before them, all they want is to exploit those around them. . . .[71]

Influenced by racist notions prevalent in Europe at the time, foreign businessmen regarded Mexicans as biologically and morally inferior and seldom socialized even with their own partners.[72]

Foreign businessmen organized a dozen associations, including the International Club (1864), the Círculo Mercantil y Industrial (1873), the Casino Español (1870), and the Sociedad Alemana (1867), in Veracruz and other major ports and in Mexico City.[73] Membership was open to any European, but Mexicans were not allowed to join. In other words, membership was based on racial and ethnic criteria rather than nationality. Strange as it sounds, racism enabled British, French, German, and, to a lesser extent, Spanish merchants to overcome their own nationalism and become "cosmopolitan."

---

69. "Los detractores de la Masonería," *El Monitor Republicano,* 8 November 1872, 3; "Tolerancia religiosa," *El Monitor Republicano,* 11 January 1874, 2.

70. Antonio García y Cubas, *Noticias geográficas y estadísticas de la República Mexicana* (Mexico City, 1857), 15, for number of foreigners in each state.

71. Carlos Gagern, *Apelación de los Mexicanos a la Europa bien informada de la Europa mal informada* (Mexico City, 1862), 2–3.

72. Corinne A. Krause, *Los Judíos en México* (Mexico City: Universidad Iberoamericana, 1987), 48–49; Nancy Barker, "The Factor of Race in the French Experience in Mexico: 1820–1861," *Hispanic American Historial Review* 59, no. 1 (1979): 64–80; Moisés González Navarro, *Los extranjeros en México y los Mexicanos en el extranjero: 1821–1970,* vol. 2 (Mexico City: El Colegio de México, 1994), 9–50, 73–150; Walther Bernecker, "Los Alemanes en el México decimonónico," in *Jahrbuch fur Geschichte von Staat, Wirthschaft und Gesellschaft Lateinamerikas,* vol. 25 (Cologne, 1988), 385–414.

73. "Sociedad Alemana," *Siglo XIX,* 30 November 1867, 3; "Casino Español," *Siglo XIX,* 22 February 1870, 3; "Círculo Mercantil e Industrial," *Siglo XIX,* 13 April 1873, 3; "Club Internacional," *La Razón de México,* 20 October 1864, 3.

The Public Service Field

Municipal townships collaborated closely with civic associations and church-sponsored groups to provide public relief to the country's indigent, to the poorest of the poor.[74]

Charity and Welfare Groups

During the postwar period, religious and nonreligious groups, in partnership with municipal townships, provided charitable and welfare relief to the poor and needy.

In Mexico City, the Junta Menor Municipal (1867), composed of elite women and men, served 1,000 indigents daily. In exchange for public relief, recipients donated two hours of labor daily, blurring the distinction between donor and recipient:

> we are against distributing [assistance] in a blind, impulsive manner straight from the heart. We are committed to providing enlightened charity . . . since we know from experience that the other way always leads to disaster.[75]

Junta members also went door to door collecting money from residents. Roughly 20 percent of all households contributed daily an average of 5 cents, suggesting that the Catholic tradition of alms-giving remained strong. The Junta relied on Christian notions of charity in order to propagate civic notions of welfare based on the republican idea of social rights and citizenship.[76]

The Sociedad Ruth (1875) was composed of elite ladies from the town of Guadalupe Hidalgo (Mexico). It ran a hospice-vocational school for indigenous and orphaned girls where they taught the "domestic arts" (sewing, cooking, laundering), trained as maids, and placed in homes of influential families in Mexico City. The Sociedad saved many of these girls from becoming prostitutes and petty thieves. In training these girls, the Sociedad emphasized "personal dignity," with the unintended result that the elite families they worked for complained continuously of the decline in the quality of domestics, the "brash" and "insolent" nature of maids, and the threat they represented to the tranquility of domestic life.[77]

74. Joaquín García Icazbalceta, *Informe sobre los establecimientos de beneficencia y corrección de esta capital* (1864; Mexico City: n.p., 1907), 82–101, 140–41.

75. Junta Menor Municipal, *Reglamento de la Junta de Caridad de México* (Mexico City, 1867), 4.

76. Junta Menor, *Reglamento*, 5.

77. Sociedad Ruth, *Reglamento del Asilo de Criadas* (Mexico City, 1875); "En favor de los indios," *El Federalista*, 21 September 1875, 3; "La Sociedad Ruth," *El Monitor Republicano*, 15 October 1878, 3. Also see "Fiesta," *Siglo XIX*, 4 May 1876, 3.

Religious groups such as the Señoras de la Caridad' (1865) and the Sociedad de San Vicente de Paul (1870), in collaboration with local townships throughout the country, also provided charity to the needy. The Senoras and the Sociedad had a total of 3,000 members between them, distributed among ninety or so chapters throughout the country, the majority of them in the states of Puebla, Mexico, and Guanajuato, where the Church remained strongest.[78] Governance in both groups was authoritarian. The central branch of the Senoras and the Sociedad in Mexico City made all policy and personnel decisions; it also published a bulletin, which it used to control the flow of information among local chapters.[79]

The Señoras and the Sociedad collected and distributed food, shoes, medicine, and clothing, and sent teams of doctors, midwives, druggists, and phlebotomists into the poorest neighborhoods in cities, towns, and rural communities across the country. Nearly 80 percent of the budget of both groups was spent on public relief.[80] The Señoras and the Sociedad mixed charity with proselytizing, providing the poor with moral advice and distributing religious objects (such as rosaries and icons) among them. These groups contributed to the resurgent popularity of religiosity in public life, although during this period state officials were opposed and churchmen disapproved of it.[81] After Sunday service, the members of both associations "invaded" public parks and main plazas collecting alms from pedestrians, without realizing that in doing so they had shifted the material and symbolic center of Christian charity from the Church to public life.[82]

Charitable and welfare practices were based on a fusion of civic and religious notions, although government officials tried to convince the poor that only the state was providing them with relief, and that they, in turn, should be loyal to the state rather than the Church.[83]

The Religious Field

Catholic and Protestant groups now populated the religious field, making it one of the most disputed and pluralistic. The secularization of the Mexican state by President Benito Juarez and his successors undermined the

78. Asociación de Señoras de la Caridad, *Memoria que el Consejo Superior de las Asociaciones de Señoras . . . dirige al Congreso de París* (Mexico City, 1867),25, 80; Sociedad de San Vicente de Paul, *Noticias sobre las conferencias de la Sociedad* (Mexico City, 1871), 23.
79. Sociedad de San Vicente, *Noticias,* 20–21.
80. Cambas, *México Pintoresco,* 193, 274.
81. Señoras de la Caridad, *Memoria;* Sociedad de San Vicente, *Noticias.*
82. "Función lírica a beneficios de los pobres," *La Razón de México,* 30 October 1864, 3; "Aviso importante a los Pobres," *La Firmeza,* 16 January 1875, 1–2; and "Sección oficial," *La Firmeza,* 16 January 1875, 1–2.
83. Juan D. Peza, *La beneficencia en México* (Mexico City, 1881), 147–48.

Catholic Church's influence in public life, but it contributed, ironically, to the spread of religious associations throughout the country.

Catholic Groups

The Sociedad Católica (1868) was the first conservative "mass organization" to appear in postwar Mexico. By 1877, the Sociedad had roughly 2,000 dues-paying members and no fewer than ninety chapters across the country, with the most active chapters in the states of Puebla, Mexico, and Querétaro.[84] Like other associations, the members of the Sociedad used civic terminology to describe themselves:

> The 9th article of our Constitution grants all Mexicans the right to free assembly and to associate with each other. The Sociedad we have organized is composed of Catholics, and is in keeping with the laws [of the land]. . . .[85]

In May 1875, in the largest civic parade Mexico City would see in this period, the members of the Sociedad marched directly in front of and behind several Protestant and Masonic groups whose members they considered to be the devil incarnate. The spread and pluralization of associative life made conservative Catholics more tolerant than even they themselves realized.[86]

The Sociedad, although authoritarian in its system of governance and centralist in its organizational structure, was egalitarian in its recruitment and admission policy. In Mexico City, the central board of directors, in consultation with the Church's hierarchy, formulated all policy and played a key role in selecting the officers in each of the local chapters across the country, in private meetings with the advice and consent of the outgoing officers. Monthly dues were affordable, about 10 cents per month.[87] Members volunteered or were sometimes assigned to work on one of five subcommittees, with the "prison" task force among the most active.

The Sociedad worked in the country's largest prisons, including Mexico City's Belem and National Prison. The Sociedad visited inmates and provided them with food, shoes, clothes, and blankets; served as couriers between them and their families; taught them reading, writing, and skills in order to help them find jobs on their release; and instructed them in religious dogma. The group also established legal clinics in each prison. Lawyers interviewed each prisoner in order to find out if they had been

84. *Memoria de la Sociedad Católica de la Nación Mexicana* (Mexico City, 1877), 155.
85. *Reglamento de la Sociedad Católica de Aguascalientes* (Aguascalientes, 1875), 3.
86. "Gran Círculo de Obreros Mexicanos," *El Socialista*, 2 May 1875, 2.
87. Jorge Adame Goddard, *El pensamiento político y social de los Católicos Mexicanos: 1867–1914* (Mexico City: Universidad Nacional Autónoma de México, 1981), 97–99.

falsely charged and gathered all the evidence necessary to gain their release. The Sociedad secured the release of 200 inmates from Belém Prison in an eighteen-month period.[88] The members of this group were revered by all the prisoners and their families, many of whom were led to fuse notions of civility and religiosity in complex ways and to make them part of popular culture. The Sociedad provided the Church a new entry point into civil society and had a moderating influence on the bishops and high clergy, who now felt they were making a comeback and had something to lose if they acted intolerantly or violated public norms.[89]

Protestant Groups

After the Reform War, parish priests across the Central Valley organized an association, the Constitutionalist Priests (1858), to discuss ways of democratizing the Church from within.[90] They controlled twenty-five parishes and the seminary where the next generation of priests were getting trained. The bishops excommunicated them from the Church. Most of them converted to Protestantism, established their own congregations, and recruited additional pastors in order to spread the "Good News" and gain converts. Protestantism spread like wildfire. By the 1880s there were 39,000 Protestants and 125 congregations in the country. The majority of them were found in the Valley between Chalco and Tlaxcala, on the Gulf Coast between Tampico and Veracruz, and in the Huasteca region along the border between the states of Hidalgo and San Luis Potosí.[91]

Protestant congregations were egalitarian in their composition and democratic in their governance. Most pastors were of mixed descent and from humble backgrounds: artisan (24 percent), priest (20 percent), scribbler (14 percent), local official (6 percent), and factory worker/miner/ peon/farmer (6 percent).[92] North American Protestants who visited these congregations often commented on the fact that services were "officiated

88. *Memoria de la Sociedad Católica,* 29–32, 74–79, 96–97, 105 on prisons.
89. "Las cartas pastorales," *Siglo XIX,* 15 April 1875, 2.
90. "Iglesia Mexicana," *El Monitor Republicano,* 15 June 1861, 3; Abraham Télez, "Una iglesia cismática Mexicana en el siglo XIX," in *Estudios de historia moderna y contemporánea de México,* vol. 3 (Mexico City, 1990), 253–56.
91. Jean-Pierre Bastian, *Los disidentes: Sociedades Protestantes y revolución en México: 1872–1911* (Mexico City: Fondo de Cultura Económica, 1989), is the best work on the subject. Contrary to what Bastian claims, Protestantism surfaced within the country and was not simply implanted there by British and U.S. missionaries. In any case, most Protestants in Mexico at this time were really "heterodox" Catholics. They had drifted from the Church because it had supported the French against Juarez's patriotic army, in which they had served. And this brings me to my last point. As committed nationalists, heterodox Catholics would not have embraced Protestantism because it remained closely identified with U.S. expansionism. In my judgment, Protestantism was a political "label" that bishops and members of the Church's hierarchy used against democratic-minded Catholics.
92. Bastian, *Los disidentes,* 28–55, 71–72, 78–137.

[jointly by] a white and an Indian [minister] . . . that "Indians, artisans, soldiers and workers" "sat promiscuously"; and that they addressed each other as "brother" and "sister."[93] Presbyterian groups practiced direct democracy and invited members to participate in all decisions related to the congregation. Methodists practiced indirect democracy; members elected representatives and they, together with the Synod of Bishops, were responsible for deciding doctrinal and policy matters.[94]

Municipal townships and newspapers protected Protestant groups from mob violence led by parish priests. Townships sent militiamen to guard and prevent Catholics from vandalizing and torching Protestant temples and the homes of ministers and of members of the congregations.[95] *El Siglo, El Monitor,* and other influential dailies published articles and editorials demanding protection for Protestants and denouncing the Church for promoting intolerance.[96] Townships and newspapers provided Protestants a niche in public life at a time when they themselves were too weak to secure it on their own.

The Recreational Field

Daily practices in the recreational field, as in the religious field, had become dynamic and pluralistic due to a significant increase from the 1870s onward in the number and variety of hobby-oriented groups and social clubs in the country.

Hobby-Oriented Groups

Mexicans organized hundreds of "Sociedades Filarmónicas" across the country; many of them had learned to play an instrument during the war as part of their military training. These Filarmónicas appeared in rural communities such as Totontepec (Oaxaca) and Tlatlaqui (Puebla), in remote towns such as Acapulco (Guerrero) and Matehuala (San Luis Potosí), and in cities such as Mexico and Guadalajara.

By the mid-1870s, village bands "had become a central feature of cul-

93. Melinda Rankin, *Twenty Years among the Mexicans: A Narrative of Missionary Labor* (Cincinnati, 1881), 156; Frederick A. Ober, *Travels in Mexico* (Boston, 1883), 401; Gilbert Haven, *Our Next Door Neighbor* (New York, 1875), 92–93.

94. Bastian, *Los disidentes.*

95. "Combate apostólico," *El Monitor Republicano,* 22 April 1870, 2; Rankin, *Twenty Years,* 170–72; Haven, *Our Next Door Neighbor,* 346–47; Thomas Unett Brockelhurst, *Mexico Today: A Country with a Great Future* (London, 1883), 69–70.

96. "Tolerancia de cultos," *Siglo XIX,* 25 march 1874, 1; "El fanatismo," *Siglo XIX,* 7 April 1874, 2; "Los Protestantes de Xalostoc," *Siglo XIX,* 27 March 1870, 1–2; "Asesinatos," *El Monitor Republicano,* 11 February 1875); "Protestantes de Tepeji del Río," *El Monitor Republicano,* 14 November 1876, 1; "Horribles Asesinatos," *El Monitor Republicano,* 30 January 1875, 3. "A los Protestantes de Tizayuca," *El Federalista,* 18 October 1871, 2.

tural life throughout the republic, and an indication of a community's commitment to urbanity."[97] Band members made a living from teaching music and giving performances. They also hosted free concerts on Sundays and civic holidays in the village or town plaza as a public service to the community.[98] Nabor Vázquez, the John Phillip Sousa of Mexico, noted the significance these groups had for public life:

> These groups . . . serve to disseminate music of all types among our lower classes, although often it is beyond their own economic and technical means. Bands are found in all civic, religious, and secular celebrations, and although they are poorly equipped, the members display great enthusiasm and make the most of their talent. . . . The musicians, mainly workmen, peasants, and mule-pack drivers, consider themselves "aficionados" and feel a great deal of affection for music. . . .[99]

Bands provided citizens of different socio-ethnic backgrounds a place to mingle in public and instilled in them a sense of civic pride in their community by encouraging them to appreciate local and regional melodies, such as "mariachi" tunes in Jalisco and the "son jarocho" in Veracruz. Over time, some of the village bands petitioned the township authorities to be exempted from paying municipal taxes and performing communal labor in recognition of the public service they were providing to the community.

Mexico City's Sociedad Filarmónica had about four hundred members, mainly artisans and women, and was the most important groups of its kind. It had contributed greatly to deradicalizing daily life in the city after a decade of civil strife. In the words of a contemporary, the Sociedad compelled members to "put aside their political differences for the sake of music."[100] The Sociedad had so many members that it had to alter its governance structure, shifting, like other groups of its size, from direct democracy to a relatively formal system of electoral representation.[101] According to contemporaries, this system weakened whatever ties of patronage may have existed in the group between elite and non-elite. As in the case of village bands, the Sociedad in Mexico and other cities held

---

97. Guy P. C. Thomson, "The Ceremonial and Political Roles of Village Bands, 1846–1974," in *Rituals of Rule and Rituals of Resistance: Public Celebrations and Popular Culture in Mexico,* ed. William H. Beezley, Cheryl Martin, and William E. French (Wilmington, Del.: Scholarly Resources, 1994), 308, 316–17. Also see Frederick Starr, *In Indian Mexico: A Narrative of Travel and Labor* (Chicago, 1908), 124–25, 237.

98. Cambas, *México Pintoresco,* 3.193, 583, 338. Also see Thomson, "Village Bands".

99. Nabor Vázquez, *Orientación Musical,* vol. 3 (Mexico City: Editorial Jus, 1943), 14.

100. *Memoria en que el Secretario de la Sociedad . . . da cuentas de los trabajos de la Junta Directiva* (Mexico City, 1873), 6–11; "Sociedad Filarmónica Mexicana," *Siglo XIX,* 23 January 1869, 3.

101. "Sociedad Filarmónica," *Siglo XIX,* 8 January 1869, 3.

weekly public concerts that were attended by fair-skinned and dark-skinned peoples, blurring the color line.[102]

The Sociedad also considered its concerts a public service, and in the early 1880s the Minister of Justice invited it to become part of his agency. The negotiations between the Sociedad and the government, noted a contemporary, were "legal and contractual; the [Sociedad] was properly remunerated; and no one can accuse the state of acting arbitrarily."[103] The Sociedad became the "National Conservatory," and is another example of an association contributing to the formation of the Mexican state. The Conservatory provided generous scholarships to talented students from Mexico City and the provinces regardless of their socio-ethnic background, contributing to the democratization of "classical" and other forms of "elite" music. The Conservatory also encouraged its teaching staff and students to compose patriotic tunes:

> these bands have inspired native composers, stimulating them to write nationalist tunes that express the real feelings of our people. . . . These songs are getting played in our grammar schools, churches, and battlefields.[104]

Patriotic songs restructured the musical field and were especially important for imbuing nonliterate peoples in rural and urban areas with a sense of nationhood. In addition, the Conservatory established an extramural program to "offer technical and logistical support to village bands [in the provinces] so that they might be able to fulfill their duty to society."[105] Judging from the limited evidence available, the spread of "nationalist" music did not undermine the development of "folk" music in the nineteenth century.

The Sociedad Protectora de Animales (1872) launched a campaign to ban bullfighting in the states of Mexico, Puebla, Jalisco, Veracruz, Querétaro, and Zacatecas. Composed of "middle-class types," the Sociedad published newspaper articles, organized street marches, and distributed flyers in neighborhoods in an effort to convince citizens that Mexico's national sport was in fact a barbaric holdover from the colonial period and therefore an affront to the entire country. The Sociedad succeeded in getting municipal and state officials in several states to ban bullfights. Bullfighting declined in popularity even in states where it was not outlawed, leaving Mexicans without a national sport.[106]

---

102. "Crónica del teatro," *Siglo XIX*, 28 June 1868, 138.
103. Cambas, *México Pintoresco*, 1.141–43.
104. "Confidencias," *Siglo XIX*, 1 December 1875, 1–2.
105. Vázquez, "Breves historias de las bandas," in *Orientación Musical*, 14.
106. "Sociedad Protectora," *Siglo XIX*, 30 August 1873, 3; "Sociedad," in *Gaceta Agrícola Veterinaria de la Sociedad Ignacio Alvarado* (Mexico City, 1878, 29.

"Jockey clubs" (1872) made a bid to turn horse racing into the new national sport. Clubs were organized in Mexico City, Matamoros, Chihuahua, and several other state capitals. These clubs charged very steep fees; even wealthy families in Mexico City could not pay 1,000 pesos in membership dues. The national hippodrome was built in one of the poorest neighborhoods, Peralvillo, where the city's water carriers and sewage cleaners lived and the price of real estate was relatively low. The hippodrome looked like a fortification; it was walled on all four sides in order to keep the poor from entering. During the racing season, the 4,720 seats were filled with

> young, elegant ladies and eligible bachelors, all dressed in their very finest clothes and wearing gloves. . . . The audience was also full of government ministers, bankers, and real estate magnates, as well as a few writers. . . . All those [citizens] who have contributed so much to the social development of our country are present, [which] is additional proof that horse riding . . . is essential to our sense of nationhood.[107]

The audience gambled away 6,000 pesos per race, money that was used to maintain the hippodrome and to purchase thoroughbreds from Europe and the United States. The shift from bullfighting to horse-racing became part of a broader cultural movement by the elite to identify nationhood in exclusionary terms based on wealth and privilege rather than in the way commoners construed it, based on patriotism during the war and popular culture.

"Charro" groups appeared in Jalisco and several other western states as an effort to defend "authentic" cowboy culture and rural life from the jockey clubs. The charros accused the jockeys of corrupting public morals with their laxity toward gambling, and of undermining nationhood by preferring foreign to domestic thoroughbreds.[108] The most important charro associations surfaced in small and medium-sized towns in the western, near-northern, and far-northern states, whereas jockey clubs were strongest in the Central Valley and state capitals. Manuel Rivera Cambas, the ethnographer-engineer, and John Geiger, who spent a year traveling through Mexico, noted:

> the charro costume is rarely worn [in Mexico City], although it continues to be worn in promenades elsewhere. . . .

---

107. Cambas, *México Pintoresco*, 2.88–89.

108. Cambas, *México Pintoresco*, 2.88–90; José Álvarez del Villar, *Historia de la Charrería* (Mexico City: Imprenta Londres, 1941), 21–23; William H. Beezley, *Judas at the Jockey Club and other Episodes of Porfirian Mexico* (Lincoln: University of Nebraska Press, 1987), 26–31.

The charro is . . . fast disappearing, and the nearer the capital, where European influence is most powerful, the scarcer the national costume.[109]

Cowboy associations and jockey clubs continued to challenge each other over the rest of the century.

Social Clubs

Artisans, factory workers, businessmen, soldiers, teachers, lawyers, doctors, Catholics, and other groups organized social clubs and casinos in cities and towns throughout the country, providing elite and non-elite families a place to mingle and socialize outside their own homes.[110]

Casinos and clubs became one place were families forged social ties with each other. Some of them intensified and formalized these ties by serving as godparents to each other's newborn children. The great English anthropologist Edward Tylor described the nature of fictive kinship in Mexico:

> The godfather and godmother . . . become by their participation in the ceremony [of Holy Baptism] relations to one another. . . . In Mexico, this connexion obliges the compadre and comadre to hospitality and honesty and all sorts of good offices toward one another; it is wonderful how conscientiously this obligation is kept, even by people who have no conscience at all for the rest of the world. A man who will cheat his own father or his own son will keep faith with his compadre.[111]

During family conflicts, godparents intervened, mediating between husbands, wives, and children. When all else failed, battered women and their abused children sought shelter from their "comadres" and "compadres." Clubs contributed indirectly to eroding patriarchal authority in these families.[112]

Salons and casinos replaced family salons. In the years prior to and immediately after the war, flirting, courting, and marriage among the regional and national elite had taken place in salons. Matriarchs and priests

109. Cambas, *México Pintoresco*, 1.261–62; Geiger, *A Peep At Mexico*, 200.
110. "Casino Oaxaqueño," *Siglo XIX*, 8 August 1874, 3; "Club Obreros," *El Socialista*, 12 December 1875, 3; "Club Comunero," *La Comuna*, 10 July 1874, 2; "Casino," *Siglo XIX*, 21 November 1874, 3; "Casino Militar," *Siglo XIX*, 6 December 1873, 3; "Casino Militar," *Siglo XIX*, 21 May 1874, 3. "Tertulia musical," *Siglo XIX*, 18 June 1870, 3; "Centro Mercantil de Veracruz," *El Centro Mercantil*, 7 March 1875, 2; "Colegio de Abogados," *Siglo XIX*, 28 January 1874, 3; Laura Elena Gutiérrez and María Rodríguez García, "El Casino de Saltillo" (Unpublished typescript, Coahuila, 1994), 1–3.
111. Edward Burnett Tylor, *Anahuac; or, Mexico and the Mexicans* (London, 1861), 250.
112. Tylor, *Anahuac*, 250.

closed ranks in order to prevent democratic manners and morals from entering these families. They became excessively partisan and selective in whom they invited to their parlors, transforming them into private gatherings.[113] Salons came to resemble medieval castles transplanted into the midst of a democratic landscape, and the elites who patronized them discouraged social equality and romantic love from entering into family life. The same divisions that had plunged the country into civil war became visible in private life:

> Women remain opposed to the [Ayutla] Reform and have kept it from spreading its influence among members of their families. . . . While their husbands and sons defend the principles of the French Revolution . . . wives, mothers, sisters, and daughters continue to defend religious fanaticism. . . . Children raised in these families suffer from spiritual Pandemonium; they are torn by the tender feelings they have for their mothers . . . and the admiration they feel for their fathers. . . . This anomalous situation is the direct result of the way marriage operates. In our country partners do not marry because of shared ideals or mutual sympathy [as is the case in other democracies]. . . .[114]

Matriarchs relied on family parlors to maintain ideological and social control of the marriage market.

However, a decade of civil strife had killed off thousands upon thousands of young men, making it difficult for the matriarchs to find suitable mates for their children and cousins:

> Mexico is full of young women . . . [who] have no prospect of being sought in marriage. Years of war and revolution have forced into the army and killed off, or rendered unfit for marriage, a large portion of the young men of Mexico. There are now in the capital from four to seven unmarried and marriageable young ladies to every young man of marriageable age. . . . The future of a young widow or an orphaned girl with no immediate relations to care for her is dark and doubtful. . . . Without a husband or father, these women live completely dependent on families who themselves cannot afford to maintain them.[115]

Even the most recalcitrant matriarchs were forced to become slightly more flexible and to join clubs and casinos, which now offered them the best possibility of finding a suitable mate. By the early 1880s, only a few salons

---

113. Geiger, *A Peep at Mexico,* 160.
114. Jorge Hammeken y Mejía, "La instrucción obligatoria para las mujeres," *La Tribuna,* 10 January 1874, 1.
115. Albert S. Evans, *Our Sister Republic: A Gala Trip through Tropical Mexico, in 1869–1870* (Hartford, 1870), 386, 367.

remained active in Mexico City, Guadalajara, and Puebla, where they had once flourished.[116] The *Revista Universal,* the country's leading conservative magazine, published satirical articles on salons in an effort to encourage matriarchs to change their ways:

> her house has furnishings from a bygone period. . . . The table shakes . . . and the cushion stuffing hangs over the side as if they are poking fun at us. . . . At the gathering was a priest, [Agustina's] poor sister, a retired musician, an unwed mother . . . an ex-politician, and a few medical and law students, who were answering questions about divorce, inheritance laws, and nervous fever. . . .[117]

The spread of clubs and casinos democratized marriage among the elite, but it also undermined the role of women and strengthened the role of men in family life.

Associative Practices in Economic Society

This section examines the development of associative life and civic practices in the domestic sector of the Mexican economy, focusing in particular on five fields: Worker's Resistance Societies; Producer and Consumer Cooperatives; Agricultural Societies and Commercial Banks; Savings and Loans; and Family Businesses.

Resistance Societies and Factory Workers

The number of factories (textile and cigarette) in Mexico climbed from forty to ninety-seven between 1857 and 1880. The majority of them were in the nation's capital and the states of Mexico and Puebla.[118] In keeping with liberal conceptions of public life, government officials considered factories part of the private realm; however, because the government was also responsible for maintaining public order, the Penal Code of 1872, the first of its kind, classified strikes as a criminal offence. Workers who struck were imprisoned for up to three months and/or assessed fines of 25 to 500 pesos.[119] Prior to the Code, Mexican workers had struck only five times between 1863 and 1867 and four times between 1868 and 1872. After the

116. Cambas, *México Pintoresco*1.125. Also see Geiger, *A Peep at Mexico*, 160.
117. Fidel, "11 de Abril de 1875," *Revista Universal*, 11 April 1875, 1–2.
118. Moisés González Navarro, *Las Huelgas textiles en el Porfiriato* (Puebla: Editorial J. M. Cájica Jr., 1970), tables 1 and 2.
119. Alberto Trueba Urbina, *Evolución de la Huelga* (Mexico City: Ediciones Botas, 1950), 35–56; María del Refugio González, "Introducción," *Historia Obrera* 3, no. 12 (April 1974): 14–19.

Code they struck twenty-nine times, when the "opportunity structure" was least favorable.[120]

Public opinion and the formation of "resistance societies" inside the factory go far in accounting for the increase in the number of strikes. In his study of factory life, Luis Chávez Orozco documents the importance of working-class tabloids—*La Comuna, La Huelga, El Obrero,* and others—in winning over the general public to the side of workers. These tabloids argued that strikes were protected by the Constitution, which stated that any citizen had the right to associate freely:

> The right to associate is granted to citizens . . . why shouldn't we use it in order to organize strikes? This is the main tool that we workers have to secure equity and parity in our dealings with capital.[121]

By redefining strikes in this way, newspapers convinced the citizenry at large that they were perfectly legal and not at all criminal, as factory owners and state officials had claimed. Working-class tabloids led the debate, but nationwide dailies such as the *Siglo* and the *Monitor* also took up their cause, as did several civic associations, such as the Colegio de Abogados, which hosted public forums on the subject of strikes.[122] Without their support, factory strikes would have remained outlawed.

Most strikes were organized by "resistance societies." Nearly all such societies were created in the early 1870s, and although most of them were an outgrowth of mutual-aid groups and retained those ties, they were different from the societies in which they originated. Membership in resistance societies was limited to the workforce of a particular factory.[123] Resistance societies were also engaged in fighting for the rights of workers and were committed to shortening the working day, changing methods of payment, and establishing self-rule in the factory. Strikers demanded that overtime work at night (*veladas*) be optional, that the working day be reduced to no more than twelve hours, and that those hours be measured in "clock-time" rather than "social time"—although they favored the opposite when it might benefit them.[124] Strikers demanded to be paid in cash

120. Cuauhtémoc Camareña Ocampo, "Las luchas de los trabajadores textiles: 1850–1907," in *Las luchas populares en México en el siglo XIX,* ed. Leticia Reina (Mexico City: Secretaría de Educación Pública, 1983), 173–310.

121. Gonzalo A. Lujo, "Al pueblo obrero," *La Huelga,* 29 August 1875, 1.

122. G. Prieto, "El Colegio de Abogados, El Liceo Hidalgo y la cuestión de las Huelgas," *Revista Universal,* 18 August 1875, 1–2.

123. Manuel Huerta, "Gran Círculo de Obreros," *El Socialista,* 4 October 1874, 2; I. Sastre, "Las Huelgas," *El Socialista,* 31 August 1873, 1; Amanda Rosales, Sergio Chávez, and Mario Gijon, "La Huelga en México: 1857–1880," *Historia Obrera* 3, no. 12 (April 1974): 2–13.

124. "Tlalpan," *El Socialista,* 20 December 1876, 2; José Guerrero, "Abolición de las Veladas en las fábricas," *El Socialista,* 6 December 1874, 1.

rather than in vouchers redeemable only in the factory stores, where most goods were above market prices. Resistance societies also demanded that guards cease policing the shop floor and intruding into their homes. According to a contemporary account, any worker who read "anti-Church tracts and *El Socialista,* was member of an society that supported strikes, and discussed subversive ideas" was fined for the first offense and then fired from the job and expelled from their home for subsequent offenses.[125]

Resistance societies also demanded that factory owners recognize them as an association like any other, with the authority to represent and negotiate on behalf of members. After years of strikes, they were able to achieve their goal. Resistance societies encouraged workers to construe themselves as citizens rather than producers, as indicated by the civic terminology they used to describe factory life. In the state capital of Querétaro, resistance societies struck because, in their own words, "Mr. Rubio has turned the Hercules factory into his own republic, relying on guards to enforce his own personal law and to punish defiant workers."[126] In the town of Rio Hondo (Mexico), textile workers at the Contreras factory, among the largest in the country, used the terms "tyrant" and "despot" to refer to the owner.[127] According to factory workers, "the Constitution protects our political and civic freedoms [in public life], in the same way that strikes enable us to break free from slavery [inside factories] . . . defend our rights . . . and achieve sovereignty."[128] Resistance societies focused all their efforts on changing daily life inside the factory, but as a byproduct, they also redefined the boundary between public and private life in the economic domain. Factories came to be seen as a semipublic institution rather than simply as private property.

Resistance societies collected money, food, and clothes from their members and donated them to striking workers in other parts of the country, even if they did not have direct ties to them. In November 1875, a dozen or so societies from the Central Valley and elsewhere collected 1,700 pesos, a sizeable sum, in support of strikers at the San Ildefonso factory in Mexico City.[129] Resistance societies enabled workers to forge imaginary ties with each other and to become aware of their commonalities. The experience of organizing and administering large strike funds provided workers with skills they used later to establish cooperatives.

125. "La Huelga justa," *La Firmeza,* 5 August 1874, 1.
126. Tomás Sarabia, "Querétaro," *El Hijo del Trabajo,* 15 March 1874, 3.
127. "La Huelga justa," 1.
128. "Derecho de los obreros," *El Socialista,* 11 April 1875, 2; and "La Huelga es una necesidad para el obrero," *El Socialista,* 22 August 1875, 2.
129. "Huelga," *El Socialista,* 7 November 1875, 1; also "Huelga," *El Socialista,* 10 October 1875, 1, and 17 October 1875, 1.

Producer and Consumer Cooperatives

The cooperative movement began in Mexico City in 1875 in response to a series of strikes that had taken place that year. In retaliation, owners organized a series of lockouts. Workers countered by calling on laborers and artisans to abandon their jobs, pool their money, and establish cooperatives. In order to accomplish this, they would also have to resign from resistance societies and mutual-aid groups and become committed solely to the cooperative:

> stop organizing [mutual-aid groups] and start organizing . . . cooperatives. This is the only way to improve our situation and transform ourselves from workers into co-owners of workshops, factories, textile mills, and railroads.[130]

Cooperatives were seen not only as an alternative to the factory and workshop system of the day but, more ambitiously, as an alternative model for organizing economic life.

Artisans were responsible for organizing the first cooperatives in the early 1870s, in Mexico City and other urban centers. Composed of tailors, the Sociedad de Sastrerías (1874) had fifty-five members, and in a short period of time succeeded in raising 4,000 pesos by selling shares of stock to other artisans and workers.[131] With this money, they rented a building and purchased a dozen sewing machines. Although financially successful, the Sociedad dissolved in 1876 when officers stole all the money in the treasury. The Sociedad de Sombreros (1874), composed of hatmakers, was more successful. It was established in order to provide striking colleagues with employment and a living wage. Members put out a new line of hats, "la huelga," which became all the rage among the elite. Thomas Unett, an Englishman sympathetic to Fabianism, visited the Sociedad Artística Industrial (1873), the country's largest and most successful cooperative, and recorded this description:

> Some years ago, the artisans of the city founded a society in which the members who were temporarily out of employment could obtain ad interim work at small wages; the excellent results eventually brought the institution under the notice of the government, which granted the society a large disused convent and adjoining buildings for their workshops, with the proviso that the society should take in a number of boys

130. Ricardo B. Velatti, "Discurso," *El Socialista*, 21 September 1873, 1. For other examples, see: Fernando Cuevas, "Boletín," *El Socialista*, 16 April 1882, 1; and Jesús A. Laguna, "Demos otro paso," *El Socialista*, 31 May 1882, 2.

131. "Sociedad de Sastres," *El Hijo del Trabajo*, 6 July 1872, 2; "Sociedad de Sastres," *Siglo XIX*, 16 October 1873, 3.

from the orphanages, industrial schools and kindred institutions of the city, and thoroughly instruct them in some trade. The place is now an immense workshop, including iron and brass foundries, carriage and cart mending, building and masonry, various branches of joinery and upholstery work, and silk and cotton hand weaving. Workmen are paid wages a trifle lower than the market price, and they had the advantage of instruction in their trade.[132]

Cooperatives retrained artisans and in the process also imbued them with democratic habits.

In late 1874 workers began organizing their own cooperative. The Compañía de Obreros (1874) sold 10,000 pesos worth of stock to its members. In addition to providing members with a job and salary, the Compañía used a portion of its funds to purchase plots of land on the outskirts of the city, turning them into truck gardens in order to feed members.[133] Textile workers in Tlaxcala organized the Compañía Linera (1874). Members bought 10,000 pesos in stock and used this money to rent a building, purchase machinery, and get production off the ground. Similar cooperatives also appeared in the cities of San Luis Potosí, Aguascalientes, Guadalajara, Morelia, and Puebla between 1871 and 1875.

Mexicans also organized housing cooperatives in several cities and towns across the country. In the country's capital, the Sociedad Progresista (1874) went from a founding membership of 200 to 4,000 members in two years. Members, mostly factory workers or artisans, pooled their money to buy a large tract of land from the municipality, and then took turns clearing trees, laying roads, dredging sewers, and cooking adobe bricks to build 500 homes. In addition to housing, "Colonia Buenavista," as this neighborhood came to be called, housed a central market in which produce from the collective gardens could be bought and sold, and cooperative workshops that offered employment opportunities for artisans. In 1878, a series of floods destroyed most of the homes, and because most residents did not have the funds to rebuild, they sold their land to wealthy real estate speculators.[134] Veracruz's Sociedad Protectora (1874), with about 600 members, established a similar community just outside the city's wall in what was called the "Negro quarter," where the descendants

132. Brockelhurst, *Mexico Today*, 36; also see: "La Sociedad Artística Industrial," *El Socialista*, 8 June 1873, 2; "La Sociedad Artística Industrial," *El Socialista*, 27 June 1873; and "Ahora sí Progresa la Sociedad Artística Industrial," *El Hijo del Trabajo*, 24 June 1876, 1.
133. "Bases aprobadas por la Compañía Cooperativa de Obreros," *El Socialista*, 5 April 1874, 3.
134. J. Muñuzuri, "Sociedad de Obreros de la colonia de Buenavista," *El Hijo del Trabajo*, 6 August 1876, 1; "Guerra a la Miseria," *El Hijo del Trabajo*, 20 August 1876, 1; "Colonia de Buenavista," *El Hijo del Trabajo*, 18 August 1878, 1.

of black slaves now lived.[135] The Compañía Colonizadora (1874), composed of workers and farmers, built 2,000 homes in the foothills that divided the states of Nayarit and Durango. Their slogan, "independence, liberty, and associations," summarizes the aims of the group.[136] Another housing cooperative was established in the small town of Tlalpizalco in the state of Mexico. The 120 families that made up the Colonia Cerícola (1887) owned all the land in common and were responsible for maintaining it; this included irrigation ditches and livestock corrals. Each member was also required once a month to stand watch at night and to join in hunting down insects and vermin that plagued the community.[137]

Joint-Stock Rural Corporations

Instead of dissolving their villages and privatizing their land as required by the government, indigenous peoples transformed their communities into joint-stock corporations (condueñazgos). According to Antonio Escobar Ohmstede, these corporations were far more important than "rural rebellions" in enabling small farmers to retain control of their land, forests, and water supplies.[138] This was the first time in the history of Mexico that large numbers of indigenous farmers organized joint-stock corporations. These corporations were the most significant innovation in social organization to have occurred in the countryside since Spanish officials organized the system of encomiendas and landowners the system of private haciendas some three hundred years previously.

The majority of these corporations appeared in the late 1870s in two regions: the Huasteca along the border between San Luis Potosí and Hidalgo, and Papantla in northern Veracruz.[139] Most of them were multiethnic, and when they were not it is because the area itself was not. Fifteen

135. "Las Sociedades de Socorros Mutuos de Veracruz," El Socialista, 17 May 1874, 1–2; "Impresiones de viaje de México a Veracruz," El Socialista, 19 July 1874, 1. Also see: Elizabeth Jean Norvell, "Elites, Artisans and Workers in the Making of the Port-City of Veracruz: 1873–1899" (Unpublished typescript, Columbia University, 1998).

136. "Compañía Colonizadora de Nayarit," El Socialista, 15 March 1874, 3.

137. Rosendo Rojas Coria, Tratado de cooperativismo Mexicano (Mexico City: Fondo de Cultura Económica, 1952), 240.

138. Antonio Escobar Ohmstede and Frans J. Schryer, "Las sociedades agrarias en el norte de Hidalgo: 1856–1900," Mexican Studies 8, no. 1 (winter 1992): 1–21; Emilio Kouri, "The End of Communal Landholding in Papantla, Mexico: 1870–1890" (Unpublished typescript, Dartmouth College, 1997); and Michael T. Ducey, "Liberal Theory and Peasant Practice: Land and Power in Northern Veracruz," in Liberals, The Church and Indian Peasants: Corporate Land and the Challenge of Reform in Nineteenth-Century Spanish America, ed. Robert Jackson (Albuquerque: University of New Mexico Press, 1977), 65–83.

139. Ohnstede and Scheyer, "Las sociedades agrarias," 10–21; Korri, "End of Communal Landholding." The agricultural societies that appeared in Chiapas, Chihuahua, Mexico, Sonora, Sinaloa, Oaxaca, and Michoacan have not been studied.

of the twenty-seven corporations in the Huasteca were fully integrated; they included Nahuatl-speaking peoples and mixed-bloods. For example, in the Sociedad de Centicapán (1878), 70 of the shareholders were of indigenous descent and the remaining 51 members described themselves as mixed-bloods. The size and ethnic composition of the Sociedad was common for this region. Nearby, in the sugar-growing town of Huejutla, an area where land and labor were much in demand, rural peoples competed for both by organizing the Sociedad de San Felipe (1875), with 250 members, and the Sociedad de San Antonio (1875), with 170. Both of these groups were multi-ethnic, with about half the shareholders describing themselves as mixed-bloods. The other twelve corporations in the Huasteca were ethnically segregated; according to indigenous peoples, mixed-bloods were trying to gain control of all the land in the area and to drive them away. The approximately twenty-five corporations that existed in the vanilla-growing area of Papantla were organized by Totonaco Indians.[140] All of them were also multi-ethnic. Women were also well-represented, accounting for a third of the shareholders in these societies.[141]

The transformation of an indigenous community into a joint-stock corporation was a long and drawn-out process, often taking three years or more from the moment the land was surveyed to when the stockholders were given their plots. The process was usually initiated by members of the village community themselves. After meeting several times, they would draft and vote on a charter that outlined the aims of the group. In 1875, the villagers of San Felipe Ixcatlan (Hidalgo), a Nahuatl-speaking community of sixty families, agreed to transform the village into a corporation, the Sociedad de Centicapán, and approved the following charter:

> all members have equal rights. . . . Each has the right to occupy the land they are on; those who need larger plots [due to the size of their family] can get more land from the administrator, although no one can exceed the limit of 2 fanegas; [nonresidents of the village] can rent land [from the corporation] but in order to do so they must live in the community of Ixcatlan . . . members cannot sell or transfer their plot to anyone outside the association . . . and all the profits from the rental of lands will be divided in equal parts among the members of the Sociedad [de Centicapán].[142]

140. Ohmstede and Schryer, "Las sociedades agrarias," 10–11; Kouri, "End of Communal Landholding," gives membership figures for seventy-five joint-stock associations.
141. Frans J. Schryer, *The Rancheros of Pisaflores: The History of a Peasant Bourgeoisie in Twentieth-Century Mexico* (Toronto: University of Toronto Press, 1980), 94; and Michael T. Ducey, "Tierras comunales y rebeliones en el norte de Veracruz antes del Porfiriato: 1821–1880," in *Anuario VI* (Jalapa, 1989), 209–29.
142. Quoted in Ohmstede and Schryer, "Las sociedades agrarias," 18.

Shareholders owned a percentage of the stock, but this did not give them exclusive rights to any one plot; it only granted them membership in the corporation. Any member who wished to rent a plot or work it for commercial purposes had to petition for approval from the board of director of the Sociedad. Shareholders could trade and sell stock amongst themselves in order to gain access to land, forests, and riverbeds owned by the corporation. However, they could not trade or sell shares to anyone who was not already a stockholder and a member of the corporation.

Agricultural societies were governed democratically. Shareholders elected the corporation's board of directors (Junta de Indígenas), who served for a year. The board was responsible for surveying the land, subdividing it into plots, and allocating it to members; protecting the rights of each member and those of the corporation; securing land deeds from the government; purchasing additional lands from bankrupt estates and municipal townships; and representing the corporation in legal disputes with nonmembers.

Members in rural corporations often used civic terms and phrases in everyday life. In the hamlet of Jilitla (Mexico), the Sociedad Agrícola la Benefactora (1874) explained its origins in this way: "the associative spirit . . . is the leverage we need to improve our country and overcome our inertia."[143] Improving the community was for them a way of developing the nation. The Junta de Agricultores (1872) also used civic rhetoric to describe their efforts:

> The old system, which was based on isolation and insecurity, never worked and is now in ruins. The modern system, based on the spirit of association, is what inspires all our actions.[144]

Farmers were now using civic terminology to make sense of each other's public practices.

These corporations paved the way for the creation of the first nationwide organization of farmers. In July 1878, farmers from scores of towns and hamlets in the states of Mexico, Guanajuato, Querétaro, and Morelos organized the Comite Central Comunero (1878). At their first congress, the Comite issued a proclamation, "Ley del Pueblo," summarizing its twenty-six demands. The first one stated:

> Any Mexican family whose assets are worth less than 3,000 pesos, will receive from the national government a plot of land . . . a pair of mules and a plough for each son in the family. . . .[145]

143. "Sociedad Agrícola La Benefactora," *El Cultivador: Periódico de Agricultura,* 1 November 1874, 272–73.
144. "Junta de Agricultores," *Siglo XIX,* 31 August 1872, 2.
145. "Ley del Pueblo," *El Socialista,* 4 August 1878, 1.

Article 4 of the proclamation demanded that the Mexican government "purchase, distribute, and expropriate land whenever it was in the best interests of the nation." Articles 11, 12, and 13 called on the state to create an "Agricultural and Industrial Bank to indemnify estate owners . . . and provide rural producers with [affordable] loans."[146] After the delegates returned to their communities, they discussed the Ley with residents and voted in favor of it.[147] By 1877, the Comite had roughly ninety local chapters and 17,000 members across the country; it would go on to play an active role in political life [more on this in chapter 12].

Commercial Banks, Paper Money, and Financial Markets

Between 1875 and 1883, Mexicans established eight banks.[148] Half were owned by family clans from Chihuahua; the other half, including the Banco Nacional, the most important bank in the country, were owned by Mexican and foreign investors in the nation's capital.

Chihuahua's banks deserve special attention. The 1870s mining and cotton boom, propelled by the U.S. civil war, brought enormous wealth to Chihuahua's leading clans—Manceyra, Ansulso, and Terraza.[149] Of the three, the Terraza family invested a large portion of their money in banks. By the 1880s, they owned a majority of shares in the four local banks that they had created, and they were providing low-interest loans to the other three clans. The generous system of credit provided by Terraza's banks also benefited small and medium-sized businessmen. Their banks contributed to the spread of civic practice in the economic terrain in this part of the country.

This "Mexicanization" of the banking sector was felt as far away as Mexico City, where it was still controlled by foreign capitalists. In 1884, the Banco Nacional was established with Mexican and foreign capital. The former owned a majority of shares and often voted as a bloc in the annual meeting of stockholders, enabling them to remain in control of the

146. "Ley del Pueblo," 1; Gastón García Cantú, *El pensamiento de la reacción mexicana* (Mexico City: Universidad Nacional Autónoma de México, 1965), 226–29, 723–26.

147. Leticia Reina, *Las luchas populares en México en el siglo XIX* (Mexico City: Secretaría de Educación Pública, 1983), 13–171. Prior to 1876, there were on average five rebellions per year; between 1877 and 1881, the number jumped to sixteen, with the majority of them breaking out in those states where agricultural societies were strongest.

148. Leonor Ludlow, "Redes y agentes de crédito en el México central durante el segundo imperio," *Siglo XIX* 14 (July–December 1993): 157–65. The first two banks—Banco de Londres and Banco de México—appeared in the early 1860s during the French occupation. They were foreign-owned, although Mexicans bought stock in them.

149. Leonor Ludlow, "La primera etapa de formación bancaria, 1864–1897," in *Los negocios y las ganancias de la colonia al México moderno,* ed. Leonor Ludlow and Jorge Silva Riquer (Mexico City: Instituto de Investigaciones Dr. José María Luis Mora, 1993), 330–62.

Banco and, indirectly, to influence the state's monetary policy. Mexico's leading shareholders came from old wealthy families in the nation's capital and from upwardly mobile families from across the provinces who had made their wealth from speculating in urban real estate and from investing in railroads and other public works projects financed by the state. Their mutual commitment to nationalism made it possible for them to transcend these other socioeconomic differences and work together in order to retain control of the Banco. Despite considerable opposition from foreign shareholders, the Banco provided low-interest and long-term loans to Mexican entrepreneurs, enabling them to compete effectively against European and North American investors. The Banco was also instrumental in getting the government to approve legislation prohibiting foreign-owned banks from providing credit to the state.[150]

By the late 1880s, the Banco had fifty-four branches around the country and had launched a nationwide campaign to wean citizens from silver specie to paper money. The spread of money altered business practices, in some places instilling civility in buyers and sellers. All the other banks in the country followed suit. While there are no records showing the number of bank notes issued, it must have been enormous, according to the economic historian Enrique Sobal, who expressed puzzlement over the public's acceptance of them: "how strange it is to see paper currency circulating throughout and penetrating more deeply in the country but without the state playing an active role."[151] Mexicans were becoming accustomed to using paper currency, although it remained unregulated by the state, and the ratio between money and silver was arbitrarily set by each bank.

Because banks were solely responsible for determining the silver worth of each note, businessmen were reluctant to accept notes from banks outside their own region. According to John Foster, U.S. consul:

> The rate of exchange between the Capital and nearby cities was often as high as from three to five percent, and for the cities in distant parts of the Republic even ten percent.[152]

The price of silver and the value of paper money varied from one place to another, which created a barrier to the formation of nationwide markets in Mexico. The circulation of bank notes was determined by the loca-

---

150. Ludlow, "La primera etapa," 330–62. Also see José Antonio Batiz Vázquez, "Aspectos financieros y monetarios: 1821–1880," in *México en el siglo XIX*, ed. Ciro Cardoso (Mexico City: Editorial Nueva Imagen, 1980), 178–79.

151. Enrique Martínez Sobal, *Estudios elementales de legislación bancaria* (Mexico City Tipografía de la Oficina Impresora de Estampillas, 1911), 24–25.

152. John W. Foster, *Diplomatic Memoirs*, vol. 1 (New York: Houghton Mifflin, 1909), 73.

tion of each bank, with most of them concentrated in the cities of Veracruz (Veracruz), Monterrey (Monterrey), Chihuahua (Chihuahua), Merida (Yucatán), and Mexico (Mexico).[153] Paper money contributed to the spread of business confidence in each region, but entrepreneurs from other areas had faith only in their own currency and did not accept "foreign" currency.

In any case, the country's elite remained skeptical about the use of paper money and still preferred to transact business in silver. In 1880, Thomas Unett Brocklehurt, a British lawyer, when asked by one of his clients in Mexico about local banking practices, responded with this anecdote:

> As proof that Mr. Winston is right in regard to treasures being locked up [at home rather than in banks], I may mention the case of the worthy don who died lately leaving the mother-in-law of Señor Riva Palacios, Minister of Public Works, over five million dollars. Out of this sum, two million were found in specie in old trunks and boxes in the bedchamber of the deceased.[154]

Perhaps the elite had good reasons for preferring silver. Banks backed only 20 percent of all the bills they issued with silver; the remaining 80 percent were in fact worthless. As long as buyers and sellers continued to use them, however, there was no reason for anyone to doubt their worth.[155]

But in 1884 the bubble burst. The state had borrowed large sums of money to in order to pay for public works projects, and it could not repay its debt, provoking a devaluation of the currency and a run on banks.[156] Wealthy investors in Mexico City, Puebla, and other cities reacted swiftly, and in a few hours withdrew more than 2 million pesos from the banks, leaving them without any silver reserves. The bank's other customers, mainly small businessmen, took longer to react and were consequently stuck with millions of worthless pesos. They demanded that the Finance Minister intervene in the matter.[157] Later in the year, the minister proposed a "Commercial Code," the country's first, designed to regulate the

153. Mario Cerutti, "Comerciantes y generalización del crédito laico en México: 1860–1910," in *Anuario del IEHS*, vol. 7 (Tandil, 1992), 211–22.

154. Brockelhurst, *Mexico Today*, 246.

155. Ludlow, "La primera etapa," 353–56. For a different estimate, see Francisco Pimentel, *La economía política aplicada a la propiedad territorial en México* (Mexico City, 1866), 212.

156. Francisco Barrera Lavalle, *Estudios sobre el origen, desenvolvimiento y legislación de las instituciones de crédito en México* (Mexico City: Tipografía D. García and Co., 1909), 16–47.

157. Carlos Marichal, "El manejo de la deuda pública y la crisis financiera de 1884–1885," in *Los negocios y las ganancias,*ed. L. Ludlow and Jorge Silva Riquer (Mexico City: Instituto de Investigaciones Dr. José María Luis Mora, 1993), 424–34.

ratio of money in circulation to silver reserves and other banking practices. "Public opinion" wanted reforms, but the people opposed the proposals put forward by the minister, describing them as "antidemocratic"
because they gave the Banco an outright "monopoly" on the printing of
money. Newspapers led this campaign and, together with small businessmen, succeeded in defeating the Code.[158] The Minister was forced to re-
draft the Code. Business confidence was restored, as illustrated by the
dramatic growth in the use of money in economic life, from 2.2 million to
13 million pesos' worth between 1882 and 1888.[159]

In the early 1880s, the Banco provided President Porfirio Díaz's first
government large amounts of cash, enabling the Mexican state to repay
its debt to foreign and domestic creditors. John Foster sent the following
report to the U.S. ambassador:

> When Diaz assumed control of affairs, the financial situation of the
> country could hardly have been more desperate. No interest on its pub-
> lic debt had been paid for many years. Its bonds had no value at home
> or abroad, and were not quoted in the money-market of a single city of
> the world. But the financial improvement which Diaz inaugurated soon
> began to create confidence among foreign capitalists, and the rapidly
> growing revenues finally enabled Senor Limantour, the able Secretary
> of Finance, to reestablish the Government credit. The foreign indebted-
> ness of every character whose legitimacy could be shown, was funded,
> first, into gold bonds at six percent, afterwards at five percent, and later
> at four percent, until the credit of Mexico became equal to that of some
> of the first powers of Europe, and much above that of any other Latin-
> American Republic.[160]

Business confidence was restored. The economic situation in Mexico was
stable enough that investors pushed to create money markets. Although
these markets were new to Mexico, their development followed a path
similar to that taken in other countries a century earlier. According to Carlos Marichal, in Mexico the

> operation of money markets for public securities had a spillover effect,
> leading investors to move from government bonds to railway to private
> stocks. . . . Only after individuals realized that holding a piece of paper
> [treasury note] was as secure an investment as a house, farm, mine or
> factory, were they willing to accept stocks and bonds.[161]

158. "Bases de la ley de bancos," El Hijo del Trabajo, 31 December 1882, 1; Lavalle,
Estudios sobre el origen, 43.
159. Ludlow, "La primera etapa," 355.
160. Foster, Diplomatic Memoirs, 1.114.
161. Carlos Marichal, "Obstacles to the Development of Capital Markets in Nineteenth-
Century Mexico," in How Latin America Fell Behind, ed. Stephen Haber (Stanford, Calif.:
Stanford University Press, 1997), 120.

Mexican bank owners and stockholders provided the central state with the fiscal base it needed to emancipate itself from foreign merchants and restore business confidence in the country.[162]

Savings and Loans

Citizens of modest means organized savings and loans. A member of the Banco Popular de Obreros (1884), the largest savings and loan in the country, employed civic terminology to describe its purpose:

> Mexico's moral state has not developed in proportion to its economy, causing an imbalance between the two. The [system of] credit we have devised seeks to correct this problem.[163]

Citizens active in the savings and loans movement considered them to be a part of a broader effort to propagate civic habits in daily life.

Savings and loans were operated as cooperatives. The depositors themselves owned and managed them, and accrued all the interest earned from the money in their account. (In order to prevent hostile takeover by moneylenders and foreign capitalists, savings and loans prohibited such investors from buying stocks and opening accounts with them.) This system of governance, according to members, was designed to instill in working people notions of frugality, thereby enabling them to practice "freedom and autonomy" in economic life. This phrase was often used by depositors to describe the benefits of savings and loans; it was even the slogan to one of the oldest savings and loans, the Caja de Ahorro (1869) in Guanajuato.[164] In order to encourage workers to deposit their weekly salary, savings and loans extended their hours on payday. Most savings and loans initially served relatively small groups of depositors who worked in the same place and had close ties to each other.[165] But by the 1880s, a large number of working families without ties to each other were depositing their money in the same savings and loan, indicating that they were now capable of forging impersonal ties with institutions. The success of the Banco Nacional de Obreros (1883) and the Banco Popular Mexicano (1884) stimulated other working families to entrust their hard-earned money to savings and loans.[166]

---

162. Marichal, "Obstacles," 124, warns: "For the period 1860 to 1880, the paucity of . . . studies makes it unwise to make any categorical affirmations on the evolution of money markets."

163. "Banco Popular de Obreros," *El Socialista*, 8 February 1884, 1.

164. "Caja de Ahorro en Guanajuato," *Siglo XIX*, 28 February 1869, 2.

165. "Sociedad Mutual el Porvenir," *El Hijo del Trabajo*, 19 November 1882, 1. Also see "Banco de Empleados," *El Hijo del Trabajo*, 1 July 1883, 1.

166. Poliuto, "Banco de Obreros," *El Hijo del Trabajo*, 22 July 1883, 1. Also see Francisco de la Fuente, "Banco Popular," *El Socialista*, 8 February 1884, 2. These banks began with 30,000 pesos, and sold their shares at 10 pesos each, and only to workers.

Kinship Relations and Family Firms

Family clans had been important during the late colonial period, but in the nineteenth century they came to occupy a central place in economic life. In the words of the economic historian John Kicza,

> family-based enterprises achieved their greatest scope during the nineteenth century, encouraged as they were by the weakness and instability of the central government, inheritance laws, lack of effective financial and commercial institutions, and the dearth of systematic commercial legal codes.[167]

Latin American entrepreneurs used kinship networks and family firms to transact business, like their counterparts in Europe.[168] But in Mexico, families and clans diversified their portfolios, investing heavily in both "traditional" (agriculture, mining) and "modern" sectors (banking, industry) of the economy, in contrast to Europe, where families concentrated their wealth in one or the other. Kinship ties in Mexico contributed to defusing sociopolitical struggles among the elite; this is one of the key factors accounting for "oligarchic" rule in the region even today, whereas in Europe investment patterns and family relations were crucial in generating rivalry and decentralizing economic power among the elite. Mexicans created a "social economy," to use David Walker's phrase, while Europeans created what we call a "political economy."[169]

Mexico's modern sector was volatile but extremely profitable; in contrast, the traditional sector was relatively stable but not very lucrative. Clans invested in both sectors and moved their capital back and forth depending on the conditions in each. In the far north, in the city of Monterrey (Nuevo León), the center of economic growth for the entire area, the three most important clans—Vidaurri, Garza, and Sada—all had major investments in banking, industry, commerce, mining, agriculture, and ranching.[170] The same was true with the dozen or so other clans elsewhere in the country.[171]

167. John Kicza, "The Role of the Family in Economic Development in Nineteenth-Century Latin America," *Journal of Family History* (fall 1985): 236; Leticia Gamboa Ojeda, "Formas de asociaciones empresarial en la industria textil," in *Los negocios y las ganancias* ed. Leonor Ludlow and Jorge Silva Riquer (Mexico City: Instituto de Investigaciones Dr. José María Luis Mora, 1993), 179–96.

168. David S. Landes, "La estructura de la empresa en el siglo XIX: Los casos de Gran Bretaña y Alemania," in *Estudios sobre el nacimiento y desarollo del capitalismo*, ed. Victor Díaz López (Madrid, 1972), 131–32.

169. David W. Walker, *Kinship, Business and Politics: The Martinez del Rio Family in Mexico* (Austin: University of Texas Press, 1986), 24–26.

170. Alex M. Saragoza, *The Monterrey Elite and the Mexican State: 1880–1940* (Austin: University of Texas Press, 1988), 8–22.

171. Cerutti, "Comerciantes," 211–25.

Family clans were led by strong-willed patriarchs and organized in a hierarchical and centralized manner. Patriarchs were responsible for appointing family members to head a firm or manage a branch in the provinces. They were also directly responsible for training their sons in all aspects of business life. If the father found his sons lacking in entrepreneurial talent, he then searched for a successor among his nephews on the male side of the kinship ladder. Succession struggles in family clans were fierce and prolonged, and sometimes they caused irreparable damage. Most clans lasted less than fifty years before falling prey to succession struggles.[172]

Patriarchs also made all the major financial and administrative decisions, although they did so in a collegial manner, in consultation with the head of each family firm. The heads of these firms provided the patriarch with "local knowledge" about economic conditions in the various sectors. The patriarch was dependent on them for information, assembling the various bits and pieces together in order to design an investment strategy for the entire clan.[173] Family firms rarely borrowed from commercial banks, preferring instead to turn inward for cash and credit:

> family members were likely to lend money to their kin on flexible terms, without interest or at a low rate and with little or no collateral demanded, since ultimately all the possessions of the family [broadly defined] served to protect the security of the loan and . . . stood to benefit [from it].[174]

The head of each family firm was responsible for apprenticing his own sons and nephews and for promoting their careers by bringing them to the attention of the patriarch.

Strong-willed matriarchs were responsible for maintaining the clan's social and moral cohesiveness. They accomplished this in several ways. They socialized children into the norms of the group by training them from an early age to subordinate their own personal ambitions to the good of the clan. Matriarchs also arranged marriages and tried to get bachelors to marry their cross-cousins in order to keep the family wealth circulating within the clan. Matriarchs hosted birthday parties and dinners and planned the seating arrangement at the table in order to provide estranged

172. Larissa Adler Lomnitz and Marisol Pérez-Lizaur, *A Mexican Elite Family, 1820–1980: Kinship, Class and Culture* (Princeton, N.J.: Princeton University Press, 1987); Saragoza, *Monterrey Elite*; Charles H. Harris, *A Mexican Family Empire: The Latifundio of the Sanchez Navarro, 1765–1867* (Austin: University of Texas Press, 1975); Mark Wasserman, *Capitalists, Caciques and Revolution: The Native Elite and Foreign Enterprise in Chihuahua, 1854–1911* (Chapel Hill: University of North Carolina Press, 1984).

173. Cerutti, "Comerciantes," 211–28, and his "Empresarios y sociedades empresariales en el norte de México, 1870–1920," *Revista de Historia Industrial* 6 (1994): 95–103.

174. Kicza, "The Role of the Family," 237.

relatives an opportunity to resolve differences. Those who failed to do so were ostracized from clan-related activities until they displayed a willingness to reconcile themselves with other family members. Matriarchs also served as "foreign ministers" and were responsible for establishing fictive kinship relations with members of other clans.

Business clans relied on kinship ties, real and fictive, to build monopolies over key sectors of the economy, to break into new markets, and to transact business outside their home region, and they were responsible for the formation of national markets in Mexico.

CHAPTER 12

Andeanizing Democracy:
Peruvian Civil and Economic Society

Beginning in the mid-nineteenth century, Peruvians for the first time in their history organized a large number of civic and economic associations. The 1854 popular movement had enabled them to break with old habits. Associative life in Peru nevertheless remained embryonic, and it was not nearly as stable and dynamic as it had been in Mexico in the first half of the century. Civil and economic society in Peru, furthermore, was extremely racist. The vast majority of voluntary groups in the country excluded indigenous peoples, blacks, and Chinese, marginalized mixed-bloods, and remained relatively hierarchical in terms of the practice of democracy in daily life. In 1879, the Chilean army invaded Peru and occupied it for five years, causing public life to unravel.

Socio-institutional Structures

Between 1856 and 1885, Peruvians organized 403 new civic and economic groups. This activity proceeded more or less continuously until the Peruvian-Chilean War in 1879 (fig. 12.1).[1] From 1856 to 1860, Peruvians organized 56 new associations—three times as many as they had created in the previous twenty-five years.[2] During his journey to Lambayeque, Próspero Pereira Gambóa, a regular contributor to Lima's leading jour-

---

1. The data for the maps and tables in this chapter are from Carlos A. Forment, "Data-bank on Associative Life in Nineteenth-Century Peru" (Unpublished working document, Princeton University, 1997).
2. Shane Hunt, *Growth and Guano in Nineteenth-Century Peru* (Wilson School, Discussion Paper #34, Princeton University, 1973), on the relationship between income from guano and state-building. Guano revenues were highest in the late 1840s and in the 1860s. But the spread of associative life did not occur until the late 1870s, suggesting a weak correlation between the three.

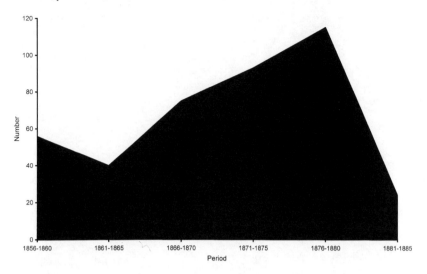

Figure 12.1   New Civic and Economic Associations, 1856–1885

nal, the *Revista de Lima,* published a summary of his observations. He noted:

> The people have embraced this [civic] spirit. Citizens have organized associations to study their rights and obligations and are using them to instill an egalitarian spirit in some of our public institutions [townships]. They have benefited from doing so, since these institutions have assisted them in their effort to organize primary schools and mutual-aid societies.[3]

This flurry of associative life was stimulated, as I suggested above, by the 1855 popular movement. From 1860 to 1865, the number of new associations being founded declined slightly, from 56 to 40. The movement's legacy was spent.

Between 1866 and 1879, the number of associations created in civil and economic society rose continuously from one five-year period to the next. Peruvians organized 75 groups from 1866 to 1870; 93 from 1871 to 1875; and 115 from 1876 to 1879, just prior to the war with Chile. The associations that surfaced after 1866 no longer relied on the 1855 movement for civic stimulation. Public life had become capable of sustaining itself and generating its own civic momentum.

Civil wars and popular rebellions continued to wrack Peru throughout the period under study, and although they hindered the development of

3. Próspero Pereira Gambóa, "Apuntes de un viajero," *Revista de Lima,* 13 June 1860, 641–45.

civic practices, military violence and sociopolitical instability no longer posed a mortal threat to the very existence of public life, as had been the case throughout the first half of the century. Despite adverse conditions, citizens remained active in public life. In 1867, Lima's regional commander was ordered to march his army to Arequipa, in the south, and wrest control of it from local commanders. After several days of battle, the local commanders yielded, and the citizenry resumed their normal lives. Several years later, in 1871, the editor of *El Eco del Misti,* the city's leading daily, summarized the main changes that had taken place in the recent past:

> It is now impossible not to feel the associative spirit and the enormous benefit it has had on us. This spirit is found in all our scientific bodies, our artistic societies, working people's mutual-aid associations, banks . . . and our insurance companies. . . .[4]

In 1872, Lima's residents took to the streets to protest the government's banning of congress, eventually toppling it and driving the army into their barracks. In October 1876, the Velada Literaria, a literary salon composed of free-spirited women, held their monthly meeting as always, although they were nervous after hearing rumors of an impending coup (which did not occur). One of the members described the gathering:

> We were frightened and convinced that our worst predictions would in fact come true . . . and on the same night [of our meeting], although this did not stop us from meeting.[5]

The ladies had reason to feel safe. The proliferation of associations in Peru enabled civilians and soldiers to distinguish clearly between public life and the military domain.[6] The development of civic life in the second half of the century reconfigured the moral landscape as much as it did the institutional.

But there were definite limits to what public life could endure. The invasion and occupation of Peru by the Chilean army wreaked havoc on public life between 1879 and 1884 (see fig. 12.1). The number of new associations plummeted to 24, a 75 percent drop from the previous five-year period. During the occupation, Peruvians organized 6 groups per year, 82 percent less than their average rate prior to the war. Public life in Peru remained moribund for several decades after the war.

4. "Espíritu de asociación," *El Eco del Misti* [Arequipa], 24 January 1871, 2.
5. "Velada Literaria," *La Opinión Nacional,* 3 August 1876, 2.
6. Víctor Villanueva, *Ejército Peruano: Del caudillaje anárquico al militarismo reformista* (Lima: Editorial Juan Mejía Baca, 1973), 62–97. The spread of civic life may have played a role in the creation of Peru's first military academy in 1870. The officers at the academy took courses in democracy and in the history of civil wars in Peru and their nefarious influence on public life.

Table 12.1   Membership in Civic and Economic
Associations, 1856–1885

Number of Members	Percentage of Associations
1–20	12
21–60	38
61–100	18
101 or more	30

Table 12.2   Duration of Civic and Economic
Associations, 1856–1885

Years	Percentage of Associations
1–3	21
4–6	15
7–9	20
10–12	13
13–15	5
16 or more	26

Another way of gauging the institutional contours of public life is by studying the average size and longevity of associations in Peru at this time. Only 30 percent of all groups had more than 100 members; 18 percent had between 61 and 100; 39 percent had between 21 and 60; and the remaining 13 percent had 20 or fewer (table 12.1). Most groups were small or medium-sized, enabling members to reshape each other's habits. The average duration of these civic and economic associations also varied considerably (table 12.2). Thirty-nine percent of the groups for which I found data lasted from 4 to 10 years; 24 percent lasted 17 years or more; 18 percent lasted between 10 and 16 years. The remaining 7 percent lasted less than 3 years. Associative life in Peru was relatively stable.

Associative life was evident throughout the country, but it was distributed unevenly (map 12.1). Eighty-three percent of the associations I found were concentrated either in Lima, the nation's capital, or in the nearby port of Callao, on the central coast. The other 17 percent were distributed sparsely across the provinces, with most of them concentrated in three places: Piura in the north, and Arequipa and Cuzco in the south. These three concentrations may reflect the fact that I did additional research in these three areas; had I studied other areas as closely, I might have uncovered more groups there as well.

Associative life was concentrated in the Lima-Callao corridor, one of

Map 12.1   Geography of Civic and Economic Life, 1856–1885

the areas where the 1855 movement had been strongest. The movement
also had broad support in the states of Junín, La Libertad, Ancash, and
Ica, although associative life in these states remained relatively undeveloped. After the revolution, large numbers of civic-minded families from
these areas migrated to Lima in search of new political and economic opportunities and spurred by the desire to live in a more cosmopolitan and

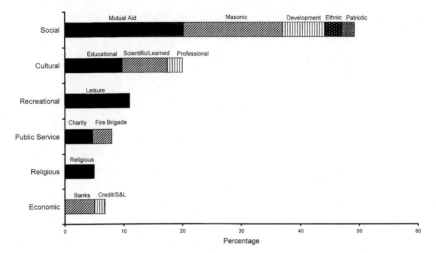

Figure 12.2   Civic and Economic Terrains, Fields, and Subfields, 1856–1885

civic milieu. Their presence enriched public life in Lima but impoverished it throughout the provinces.[7]

Civil society accounted for 86 percent of the associations in the country, with economic society claiming the other 14 percent. Figure 12.2 shows the various types of associations in both terrains, along with the relative percentages of groups for each field and subfield. Within civil society, the social field was the largest, accounting for 45 percent of groups; the cultural field comprised 19 percent, followed by the recreational (10 percent), public service (8 percent), and religious (4 percent) fields. The ratio of civic to economic groups was 6 to 1. Peruvians were much more inclined to practice democracy in civil society than in economic society.

Associative Practices in Civil Society

As figure 12.2 illustrates, associative activity in civil society may be broken down into five fields—Social, Cultural, Recreational, Public Service, Religious—each of which may also be broken down into various subfields. In this section we examine in greater detail the associative activities in these fields and subfields.

7. Manuel Atanasio Fuentes, *Estadística general de Lima* (Lima, 1858). Also see Dirección de Estadística, *Resumen del censo general de habitantes del Perú hecho en 1876* (Lima, 1878).

The Social Field

The social field was populated by mutual-aid and friendly societies, masonic lodges, patriotic groups, and ethnic-racial associations. By far the most democratic of these were the mutual-aid societies.

Mutual-Aid and Friendly Societies

Mutual-aid societies did not operate according to the ranking system used by citizens in public life. The Sociedad Amiga de las Artes (1869), for example, admitted any "person, male or female . . . regardless of national origin, race, class, or social standing."[8] Monthly dues for mutual-aid societies were within reach of most working families.[9] Some societies denied equal status to women, which in many cases prompted women to organize their own groups, such as the Sociedad Fraternal de San José (1873) and the Sociedad de Auxilios Póstumos (1873).[10] Internal practices in women's groups were as "particularistic" as they were in male-dominated societies, but in the former case these practices contributed, paradoxically, to making public life slightly more "universal" and egalitarian whereas in the latter they had the opposite effect, because of the misogynist nature of public life.

Mutual-aid societies encouraged members to respect the "private beliefs" of others in the group.[11] This was in direct violation of the Church's teachings, which prohibited Catholics from having contact with Protestants at all times, even in death: Lima's cemeteries remained segregated. Religion in Peru was still considered to be a public rather than a private matter. Citizens who violated these precepts were considered sinful; they were subject to excommunication and risked eternal damnation.[12] Despite these potential consequences, the members of the Sociedad Amiga (1869), among others, practiced religious tolerance, admitting immigrants into the group (immigrants were the only non-Catholics in Peru at the time). Mutual-aid societies provided members a place to fuse civic and religious notions, although the Church did not want them to do so. Mem-

---

8. Sociedad Amiga de las Artes, *Reglamento de la Sociedad Amiga de las Artes* (Lima, 1908), 4, 27; "Crónica," *El Comercio*, 8 February 1878, 2; "Sociedad Piadosa Nacional," *El Comercio*, 26 September 1858, 2.

9. "Sociedad Humanitaria," *El Artesano*, 15 April 1873, 2. The Sociedad Humanitaria charged members 1 sol per month. The Sociedad Fraternal del Rímac charged four times as much—see *Reglamento de la Sociedad Fraternal del Rímac* (Lima, 1863).

10. Jorge Basadre, *Historia de la República del Perú*, vol. 5 (Lima: Editorial Universitaria, 1968–1970), 2046.

11. *Reglamento de la Sociedad Amiga*, 3–4.

12. Fernando Armas Asín, *Liberales, Protestantes y Masones: Modernidad y tolerancia religiosa. Peru XIX* (Lima: Pontífica Universidad Católica del Perú, 1998), 51–104.

bers in these groups were not becoming "secular" in the strict sense of the term; they remained committed to Catholicism but were now critical of the Church. Peruvians became convinced that religious faith and civic tolerance were compatible.

Mutual-aid societies provided members a place to practice civic democracy in daily life. Annual elections for officers were usually competitive and were monitored by members themselves or by a committee selected by members. Ballots were tabulated at a monthly meeting, and in cases of fraud a new election was held.[13] In one case, the rank-and-file members of the Sociedad Humanitaria (1866) accused the entire leadership of fraud. According to a disgruntled member, the leaders' actions almost put an end to the group:

> we almost perished, but the majority . . . [of members] did their duty and demanded fair elections. The association was saved in this way; since then, we have been reforming our statutes [making it impossible for this to ever happen again].[14]

Members also monitored the treasurer; he was required to present monthly reports at meetings and had to allow any member to audit his books.[15] Citizens in mutual-aid societies became committed to fair elections and demanded that officials be responsive and accountable to those they represented.

Mutual-aid societies regulated the "speech acts" of their members. At monthly meetings of the Sociedad Tipográfica, the officers forbade members to "speak more than twice on the same subject," in order to discourage the elite from monopolizing the discussion and to provide the least experienced an opportunity to partake in them.[16] Some groups imposed a "gag rule" on members and prohibited them from discussing politics. Gabriel Corante, president of the Sociedad Fraternal, in his inaugural speech summarized his views:

> In order to avoid any further discord and disunity, it is best to avoid discussions about politics; in any case, our statutes forbid it. These discussions violate the wishes of our founders and the reason that brought us together. . . . Even more perilous than this, however, has been the

---

13. Juan Crisóstomo Mendoza, Francisco de Paula Secada, and P. J. Saavedra, *Reglamento de la Sociedad Fraternidad y Unión Militar* (Lima, 1874), 3–4; *Reglamento de la Sociedad Fraternal del Rímac*, 6.

14. "Sociedad Humanitaria," *El Comercio*, 23 July 1859, 2.

15. Mendoza, Secada, and Saavedra, *Reglamento*, 3; *Reglamento de la Sociedad Fraternal del Rímac*, 6.

16. Miguel Marisca, José María Monterola, and José Ramón Sánchez, *Reglamento de la Sociedad Tipográfica* (Lima, 1865), 12.

way our members have organized factions within our association. This has damaged our principles, made us neglect our duties, and led us to become entangled in personal matters.[17]

His electoral victory was proof that the rank and file supported his platform. The Sociedad Tipográfica was among the most successful in instilling in its members a sense of civility:

> Politics has never contaminated its internal affairs, which is why its members, all of whom are working men of modest means, have never been derailed. In their meeting hall, they only discuss issues directly related to their craft, the virtue and importance of work, and never the names of any [politicians].[18]

In 1875, the Sociedad Fraternidad held a general meeting to debate the issue of whether the group should become involved in the upcoming presidential elections. Four hundred members attended, and after a spirited discussion, defeated the proposal.[19] Members of the Sociedad Amiga voted in favor of a similar proposal but took appropriate measures to protect civic life within the group: they cancelled all meetings for the thirty days before election day and forbade members to discuss politics within a fifty-meter radius of their meeting place.[20] Mutual-aid societies instilled in their members an etiquette of self-restraint or "self-activating automatism," to use Norbert Elias's cumbersome phrase.[21]

Masonic Lodges

Peru's 2,000 masons were more or less evenly distributed among the twenty lodges across the country, making it, along with the Sociedad Católica, one of the two civic associations with a nationwide organization. In the early 1860s, a debate over religious tolerance factionalized the group and caused its demise, although it was restored in 1865.[22]

The social composition and governance structure of lodges were antidemocratic. Lodges attracted only elite groups, mainly "priests, military officers, merchants, state employees and property owners."[23] Like other members of the elite, masons had few, if any, social ties with those out-

---

17. Gabriel Corante, "Discurso pronunciado por el presidente de la Sociedad Fraternal de Artesanos," *La Patria,* 2 January 1873, 2.

18. "Editorial," *El Comercio,* 11 December 1876, 2.

19. "Sociedad Fraternidad y Unión Militar," *El Comercio,* 7 May 1875, 2.

20. Sociedad Amigas de las Artes, *Reglamento de la Sociedad Amiga de las Artes* (Lima, 1908), 27.

21. Norbert Elias, *The Civilizing Process,* trans. Edmund Jephcott (Oxford: Basil Blackwell, 1978), 257.

22. Carlos López Albújar, *Masones y Masonería en el Perú* (Lima, 1961).

23. "Iniciaciones," *El Heraldo Masónico,* 23 June 1862, 2.

side their own social circle, including artisans, whom they considered to be the embodiment of their own ideals of "virtue," "work," and "service." Dark-skinned artisans and fair-skinned masons did not mingle in public life nor in most civic and economic associations.[24] In any case, membership dues in most lodges were beyond the means of any artisan.[25]

Governance in most lodges was rooted in authoritarian ways of life. Outgoing officers, in consultation with their elders and other notables, were responsible for selecting their successors. They were responsible for making all decisions pertaining to the group, and they did so in private, behind closed doors.[26] Like the leaders, the rank and file practiced deference and respect for the elders in the group; younger members looked to their elders for advice and looked forward to the day when they would take their place. Gerontocratic practices gave lodges the organizational cohesion they needed to remain afloat despite the instability that continued to plague public life.

The status differences the Peruvian elite used to rank each other in public life also divided masons, with members often ranking each other by family lineage and wealth. Masonic rituals enabled the old and new elite to blur some of their differences. Peruvian lodges were "patented" by the Supreme Council in London in the early 1860s—that is, they were recognized as bona-fide members of the Scottish Rite. From that point on, lodges would have to adhere to protocol. Lodges "baptized" their members, and assigned them a new "name" and "age" (based on years in the group—1 for inductees), stripping them of their public identity. This and other rituals blurred status differences among the elite and eroded gerontocratic practices in each lodge.[27] At meetings, brothers were discouraged from "displaying wealth, titles and distinctions in an ostentatious manner" and encouraged "to establish contact . . . with brothers of inferior rank."[28] Lodges became active in charity work. The lodges in Lima spent almost 25 percent of their annual budgets providing the poor with food, housing, clothing, and medicine.[29] Their work with the needy made them aware of their own commonalities.

These rituals altered social relations in the lodges, although this did not become evident until 1862, during the debate on religious tolerance.[30]

24. Ibid., 2; "Untitled," *El Heraldo Masónico,* 4 June 1862, 2.
25. "Iniciaciones," 2; "Untitled," 2.
26. Albújar, *Masones y Masonería,* 329–30.
27. "Origen de la Masonería," *El Heraldo Masónico,* 22 February 1862, 1.
28. *Estatutos generales promulgados por el Supremo Consejo de SS. GG. II. GG. para le Rito Escocés Antiguo y Aceptado de la Orden Masónica en la República del Perú* (Lima, 1862), 3.
29. José Antonio G. y García, *Mensaje que dirige al Tall-Vir-y Uni* (Lima, 1861), 8.
30. "Revista de la semana," *El Heraldo Masónico,* 15 February 1862, 3–4.

The association split. The rank and file (new elite) favored tolerance, while the officers (old elite) opposed it and used their power in the group to defeat their rivals. Each lodge became factionalized. A member of the Estrella Polar (1862), a Lima-based lodge, described daily life in his lodge: the situation is one of "anarchy and disorder. Our discussions turn into disputes, and our elections into combat, and our rules into personal whim."[31] Lodges remained this way for three years, until 1865. By then, the old elite had abandoned the groups, so the new elite was able to reorganize them. The association remained elitist, but its system of governance, according to Carlos López Albújar, the leading scholar on the subject, "was democratized; power was decentralized and redistributed, giving members a greater voice."[32] Lodges also established a system of "trial by jury" in order to provide a means for members to settle disputes.[33] These reforms, in the words of a brother, "put an end to the hatred and . . . have diminished the rancor that existed within our group."[34]

Masonic lodges in Peru were not, clearly, as democratic in their daily practices or social composition as those in western Europe.[35] Nevertheless, Peruvian lodges provided elite groups an opportunity to overcome their status differences, to become sociopolitically unified, and to transform themselves into a "national elite" worthy of the name. This was the first elite to have been able to demilitarize public life and usher in civilian rule, which was quite an accomplishment. Recall that during the late colonial period the elite had been too divided to be able to secure Peru's independence from Spain, and that during the early republic their divisions had allowed the army to rule despotically over public life. Other associations assisted in making the Peruvian elite cohesive, but none of them contributed as much as the masons.

Patriotic Associations

The Sociedad de los Fundadores de la Independencia del Perú (1876), the Sociedad Defensores de la Independencia Americana (1862), and the Unión Americana (1862), among others, were responsible for organizing patriotic celebrations. Soldiers, veterans, and civilians were active in these groups, which gave individuals on both sides of the conflict a chance to

31. Julio M. del Portillo, *Mensaje que presenta a la R. L. Estrella Polar* (Lima, 1860), 4; Albújar, *Masones y Masonería*, 330; and Alfonso Harth Bedoya, *Ricardo Palma: El egregio tradicionalista e ilustre Masón* (Lima: Editorial San Marcos, 1992), 33.

32. Albújar, *Masones y Masonería*, 329–30.

33. *Estatutos generales promulgados por el Supremo Consejo*, 7–8.

34. "Iniciaciones," 2.

35. Margaret C. Jacobs, *Living the Enlightenment* (New York: Oxford University Press, 1991).

get to know each other during peacetime, rather than on the battlefield during civil wars, as they had always met before.[36]

The members of these groups practiced self-rule. A member of the Sociedad Defensores explained the importance of elections in keeping the group alive:

> Elections are of the utmost importance to us, since through them we select our officers, those who will be responsible for leading us. . . . The life and death of our association depends on us, and that is why we must all attend the meeting called for Wednesday. . . .[37]

The elite predominated in this association, but they were also among the most apathetic:

> our elected officers should be persons . . . of influence, those who have respect in the country. . . . But they seldom participate in the group. They refuse to attend meetings . . . which is why on other occasions we have selected citizens whose background is different from theirs.[38]

The non-elite played a leading role in patriotic groups.

The relationship between patriotic groups and the state changed over time. During periods of war, these groups subordinated themselves to the state: "we will fuse our power to the state in order to repel all foreign aggressors."[39] Once the crisis had passed, they would again reassert their autonomy. In 1864, they collected signatures among the residents of Lima and Callao demanding that the government immediately release four of their members who had been arrested for publishing a series of articles criticizing the Minister of Justice.[40] In May 1864, the Sociedad de Defensores organized a series of rallies in support of their jailed members. The largest rally brought out 4,000 citizens; the average turnout for the others was 2,000. During the rally, government troops surrounded the park, causing a great deal of concern among those present. The next day, the organizers of the event published an article in Lima's leading daily in which they wrote:

> What is the meaning of the army's sudden mobilization alongside a group of peaceful citizens? What does this indicate about the gov-

36. Villanueva, *Ejército Peruano.*
37. "Sociedad de Defensores de la Independencia Americana," *El Comercio,* 22 January 1866, 2.
38. Ibid., 2.
39. "Reglamento de la Sociedad Defensores de la Independencia Americana," *El Comercio,* 20 April 1862, 2.
40. "Sociedad Defensores de la Independencia," *La República,* 4 June 1864, 1–2.

ernment's attitude toward its own . . . people? Their distrust of us is regrettable.[41]

Patriotic associations moved sometimes in concert and other times at odds with the government.

Ethnic and Racial Associations

Associations based on race or ethnicity were committed to protecting the human and civic rights of the two most oppressed and vulnerable groups in Peruvian society: indigenous peoples and Chinese immigrants. Italian and Spanish immigrants also organized voluntary groups in order to assist their compatriots.

The Sociedad Amiga de los Indios (1866) was organized by Lima's elite in response to an indigenous-led uprising in Puno, in the Andean highlands. The aim of the organization was to make the public aware of the plight of native peoples. Members described their effort in civic terms: "the associative spirit has its advantages; this is why those of us in the Sociedad . . . came together, and why we now have chapters across the provinces and at the sub-provincial level."[42] Local chapters in Cuzco, Puno, and other states with large concentrations of indigenous peoples collected information on cases of abuse and sent it to the main office in Lima. The Lima group, with its offices in the back room of *El Comercio,* the country's leading daily, used these reports to publish articles and pamphlets, to debate in public forums, and to lobby congressmen.[43] The Lima group sent copies of their writings to all the local chapters. In Azángaro (Puno), where the rebellion had broken out, public opinion against indigenous peoples was strong, due to the enormous influence that landlords, regional commanders, and the two state senators had in the area. The local chapter wrote of their efforts to change this: "the uprising is now the focus of public opinion, and is being discussed and evaluated by all."[44]

The national and local chapters of the Sociedad became involved in other activities. Members translated many of their writings from Spanish into Quechua and read them in village communities and towns, in order to persuade indigenous peoples that they had popular support and were not alone in their struggle.[45] Local chapters hosted informal meetings

---

41. "La manifestación de ayer," *La República,* 25 May 1864, 1; "Reunión patriótica," *La República,* 20 April 1864, 3.

42. "Indios en el Senado," *El Comercio,* 16 September 1868, 2–3; reprinted in Emilio Vázquez, *La rebelión de Juan Bustamante* (Lima: Editorial J. Mejía Baca, 1976), 358–59.

43. Vázquez, *La Rebelión,* pp. 159–163, 174–75; Juan Bustamante, *Los Indios del Perú* (Lima, 1867).

44. Emilio Vázquez, *La rebelión,* 224.

45. Bustamante, *Los Indios,* 138–40.

with landowners in Cuzco and Puno in which they discussed the rebellion
and the need to recognize native peoples as citizens and to incorporate
them into public life:

> landlords are the only ones who are in direct contact with indigenous
> peoples; they are ideally positioned to bring about change and improve
> their situation. . . . In appealing to you, we do so in terms of patriotism
> and self-interest.[46]

The members reminded landlords that without indigenous laborers, they
would not be able to plant and harvest their fields nor graze their livestock.[47] The Sociedad initiated the first public debate in Peru on the "Indian question." It was also the first civic association to appeal directly to
public opinion to advance the native cause.

The Junta de Imigración Asiática (1870) and the Sociedad Colonial de
Beneficencia de China (1882) were committed to defending the civic and
human rights of Asian immigrants and to providing social and economic
assistance to those immigrants who chose to resettle permanently in the
country and to those who decided to return to their homeland.[48]

The Junta and the Sociedad offered immigrants low-interest loans, enabling them to buy back their freedom from landlords, who had paid for
their trip to Peru. These loans enabled Chinese immigrants to break free
from personal servitude rather than continue in bondage for another five
to ten years. These associations also found the newly emancipated employment as cooks, maids, shopkeepers, tailors, handymen, and launder-
ers and dry cleaners in Lima's thriving Chinatown and in Peruvian-owned
establishments. The Junta and the Sociedad also had a small staff of lawyers who volunteered their services. They were especially important in
the hinterlands, across La Libertad and Lima, where the word of the sugar
and cotton planters had become the law of the land. These lawyers pressured local magistrates to be impartial and fair in their decisions. The
Junta contributed to democratizing daily life in the countryside, where
authoritarianism remained entrenched.

The best way of evaluating the Junta's effort is through the comments
of their enemies, the sugar and cotton planters from the state of La Libertad and Lima, on their work:

46. Vázquez, *La rebelión*, 196–97.
47. Vázquez, *La rebelión*, 218–19, is a transcript of the Sociedad's meeting of February 11, 1868.
48. Humberto Rodríguez Pastor, *Hijos del Celeste Imperio en el Perú: 1850–1900*
(Lima: Instituto de Apoyo Agrario, 1988); and his *La rebelión de los Rostros Pintados*
(Huancayo: Instituto de Estudios Andinos, 1979).

There is a cancer spreading in the countryside. It is infecting agriculture, and jeopardizing our future. The Junta, composed of criminal elements, with support of a few . . . local intendants . . . [are responsible for this]. The latter have stopped prosecuting . . . Asians. They are no longer impartial nor capable of enforcing our laws and protecting justice. . . . Coastal landlords are being undermined. . . .[49]

The planters tried to discredit the Junta by claiming that they were fomenting racial hatred and planning a "caste war"—the same argument landlords had made against the Sociedad de Amigos de los Indios.

Organized by Italian immigrants and longtime residents, the Sociedad Italiana de Beneficencia y Asistencia (1862) was committed to providing its members with medical, health, and burial insurance, as well as employment and educational opportunities, including small loans to start a business or pay off a debt, information about jobs, and scholarships to enable their children to attend school. The main office of the Sociedad was in Lima, but it also had local branches in several provinces, and provided all of its 1,000 members with similar opportunities, a point worth underscoring since those who lived in the provinces were from relatively modest backgrounds whereas those who had stayed on in Lima and nearby were from elite families. Dues were modest and within the reach of even the poorest members; those unable to pay were subsidized by the group. Members who had already established themselves in Peruvian society remained committed to the group. They reimbursed the association, financially and socially, for loans they had borrowed, participated in its activities, and took immigrants into their homes for prolonged periods.[50] This type of "intergenerational" solidarity, binding one generation to another without any expectation for short-term gain, is, as Alan Wolfe argues, one of the most difficult to establish, and is a characteristic of the most developed civic groups.[51] The Sociedad was egalitarian and civic.

But it was not democratic in its governance. The rank and file seldom attended meetings, never ran for office, rarely voted in elections, and did not participate in public discussions pertaining to the group.[52] The wealthy elite were the only ones who participated in governance. They were oligarchic and patriarchal in how they went about making their

49. "Sublevación de los Asiáticos," *El Comercio,* 25 July 1870, 4.
50. Janet E. Worrall, "Italian Immigration to Peru: 1860–1914" (Ph.D. dissertation, Indiana University, 1972), 92, 145.
51. Alan Wolfe, *Whose Keeper: Social Science and Moral Obligations* (Berkeley: University of California Press, 1989), 79–89, 159–67.
52. Sociedad Italiana de Beneficencia y Asistencia, *Centenario de la Sociedad Italiana de Beneficencia y Asistencia* (Lima, 1962).

decisions.[53] But the fact that they dedicated their leisure time and income to the Sociedad rather than to economic gain, gambling, recreational pursuits, or their family suggests that they were more civic than their own practices suggest. Their involvement in community service, of course, was a way of gaining status in the community. Nevertheless, it is better for citizens to pursue "self-interest properly understood" than to have them pursue "egoistic" or "individualistic" goals, as Tocqueville argued. Like so many other civic groups in Peru, the Sociedad was the product of an odd mixture of civic and non-civic practices.

The Sociedad Española de Beneficencia (1862) provided similar benefits to its members. The Sociedad invested 40 percent of its annual income on immigrants who, after becoming settled in Peru, practiced the same type of intergenerational reciprocity mentioned above.[54] But unlike the Italians, the rank-and-file members of the Sociedad Española were committed to self rule and took an active interest in the governance of their group.[55] In 1862, the board of directors of the Sociedad were denounced by the rank and file and removed from office:

> our treasury is now in good shape but our society nearly went under due to the way . . . some individuals tried imposing their views on the rest of us, as if their views and opinions were infallible. This is the reason why some of us became apathetic [this year]. . . . We must learn to be tolerant and respectful of each other's views and to honor the agreements we have made with our members.[56]

The rank and file, in accord with new officials, voted to revise the constitution of the Sociedad in order to prevent future leaders from violating the compact they made with all the members of the group:

> without rules, our officers will continue thinking that the opinion of each member is nothing but a hindrance or obstacle to the development of the association, and they will continue interpreting official decisions simply as acts of favoritism. . . .[57]

After the reforms were implemented, membership in the group increased by 50 percent.

---

53. Worrall, "Italian Immigration," 153.
54. Sociedad de Beneficencia Española, *Memoria que la Junta Administrativa de la Sociedad de Beneficencia presenta a la Junta General* (Lima, 1862), 4; Sociedad Española de Beneficencia, *Reglamento de la Sociedad de Beneficencia Española* (Lima, 1862), 1.
55. Sociedad de Beneficencia Española, *Reglamento*, 16.
56. Sociedad de Beneficencia Española, *Memoria*, 2.
57. Sociedad de Beneficencia Española, *Memoria*, 2.

Community Development Groups

Throughout the provinces, citizens organized community development groups to promote socioeconomic development in the region, with the members taking turns working, or collecting funds and hiring local residents to clear land, build roads, erect dams, repair churches, and construct schools.

These groups surfaced in remote areas as well as in small towns. In Chachapoyas, near the Amazon jungle, local residents organized the Sociedad Patriótica (1858), which had a total of 80 members, and the Obreros del Porvenir de Amazonas (1883), which had 40 members.[58] The members of the Sociedad employed civic terminology to describe themselves: "we are fortunate that the associative spirit continues spreading its influence here."[59] Similar groups also appeared in less remote areas. In the town of Huánuco (Junín), farmers organized the Sociedad del Porvenir (1861).[60] Vineyard owners in the southernmost states of Moquegua and Tacna also organized similar groups, although these were short-lived. Civic life had surfaced here but would take several more decades to take root in this part of Peru.[61]

The Cultural Field

The cultural domain was populated by scores of educational, professional, scientific, and learned societies and literary salons. Its members, mainly schoolteachers, lawyers, scientists, engineers, architects, medical doctors, accountants, and the like, all came from the elite sectors of society, and were both producers and consumers of each other's writings.

Educational Associations

In 1876, the president and Congress approved a law creating the country's first educational system. Municipal townships were given the responsibility of financing, administering, and staffing all the primary schools in the country.[62] But the majority of townships were bankrupt, in disarray, and unable to provide schooling to children in their own community. The

58. Mariano Martín Albornoz, *Breves apuntes sobre las regiones Amazónicas* (Lima, 1885).
59. "Sociedad de patriotas de Amazonas," *El Comercio*, 1 October 1860, 2.
60. "Votos de gratitud," *Revista de Lima* 3 (1861): 32.
61. Luis Estévez, *Apuntes para la historia económica del Perú* (Lima, 1882), 19.
62. Basadre, *Historia*, 6.74 and 7.114–15; Eve Marie Fell, "La Constitución de la Sociedad Peruana: Estado y educación en el siglo XIX," in *America latina dallo stato coloniale allo stato nazionale,* vol. 2, ed. Antonio Annino and Marcello Carmagnani (Milan: F. Angeli, 1987), 809–21.

government's attempt to reform and decentralize the educational system turned out to be a complete failure. The number of primary schools across the provinces declined by 50 percent; the drop in Cuzco and Puno, the states with the largest concentration of indigenous peoples, was even greater. In contrast to Mexicans, citizens in Peru did not organize a significant number of educational groups across the provinces.[63] Manuel Vicente Villarán, the leading scholar on the subject, summarized his findings, based on a careful study of primary sources:

> municipalities never took an active interest in schooling. . . . Having grown accustomed to state tutelage . . . many of them had become inactive and, once the state withdrew aid, they shriveled and withered away. According to the dominant view [of citizens], the state was in charge of local affairs. Residents refused to assume responsibility for changing the educational situation in their community.[64]

Civic practices and democratic forms of life remained embryonic and were still too fragile to survive on their own.

According to Villarán, primary schooling in Lima and Callao (also in Junín, La Libertad, and a few other states) was considerably better, in large part because civic practices and associative life were much more developed in these places. Local townships in these areas had received a significant amount of money from the state, but in fact these municipalities were already energized by a high level of citizen participation. Funding from the state added financial stimulation to these townships, but it was local associations that were responsible for bringing them back to life in the first place. It was they who pressured the township to invest in schools, and it was they who monitored the spending of all state monies. Several associations even provided matching funds to schools that were not receiving adequate subvention from the township.[65]

Educational associations provided basic schooling to children of the working poor.[66] The Sociedad Hijos del Pueblo (1864) delivered on their

---

63. Manuel Vicente Villarán, "La instrucción primaria en el Perú: 1850–1873" and "La instrucción primaria en el Perú: 1873–1901," in *Páginas Escogidas* (Lima, 1962), 351–60 and 361–72. From 1874 to 1879, the number of schools in Cuzco declined from 209 to 52; in Loreto, from 88 to 51. In the states of Apurimac, Puno, La Libertad, Moquegua, Lambayeque, and Junín, the number of schools dropped to zero.

64. Villarán, "La instrucción primaria 1873–1901," 374.

65. Francisco de Paula González Vigil, "Importancia y utilidad de la educación popular," *El Constitucional*, 1–14 June 1858, 112–18; "Educación," *El Artesano*, 3 June 1873, 1–2.

66. Sociedad Amantes del Saber, *Reglamento de la Sociedad Amantes del Saber* (Lima, 1871), 3–5; "La imprenta," *El Obrero*, 5 June 1873, 2; Tomás Paredes, "Bibliotecas para los trabajadores," *El Obrero*, 10 April 1875, 2; "Sociedad Amantes del Saber," *El Artesano*, 15 April 1873, 1; "Una escuela nocturna," *El Artesano*, 1 August 1873, 1; Manuel A. Fuentes, *Estadística general de Lima* (París, 1866), 187; "Sociedad Amantes del Saber," *El Comercio*, 5 August 1874, 2.

commitment to "provide education to . . . artisans and to any other person regardless of social class or national origin." [67] Despite initial opposition from working families, they succeeded in schooling girls. [68] In addition to teaching children basic reading, writing, and arithmetic, these groups also drilled them in civic democracy. They used "catechisms," such as the one written by Francisco de Paula Gonzalez Vigil on commission from the township of Callao and reissued many times over, to inculcate democratic notions. [69] Educational groups campaigned to abolish corporal punishment at school and in the home. In the words of a member of the Sociedad de Amantes,

> we are against the regime of punishment that is still widely used in many of our schools, which is why our teaching methods are based on liberty, demanding only intellectual rivalry and hard work from our students, and nothing else. [70]

Corporal punishment and democratic liberty were antithetical concepts; students were to be stimulated and rewarded with prizes. But this method presented problems of its own. Lavishing attention on a student "at an early age, instilled in them a sense of superiority over others, and envy in all those around them." [71] The future of civic democracy in Peru depended on its children, which is why educational associations took such an active interest in instilling in them the proper habits. But there were simply not enough of these groups throughout the country to be able to carry out the task of resocialization.

Professional Associations

Medical doctors, engineers, and musicians organized associations of their own, although few of them played a major role in propagating civic practices.

The Sociedad Médica (1854), with 220 dues-paying members in the 1860s, was composed mainly of doctors, dentists, pharmacists, and phlebotomists. This was the only professional association that drew members from across the country, although the majority of them lived and worked in Lima. [72] Sixty-five percent of them were in the capital; the remaining

---

67. Mariano Bolognesi, *Constitución Reglamentaria de la Sociedad los Hijos del Pueblo* (Lima, 1864), 3–4; "Los Hijos del Pueblo," *Hijos del Pueblo*, 20 March 1864, 2.

68. "Prospecto," *Los Hijos del Pueblo*, 27 February 1864, 2.

69. Francisco de Paula González Vigil, *Catecismo patriótico para el uso de las escuelas municipales de la ciudad de Callao* (Callao, 1859).

70. "Sociedad Amantes del Saber," *El Comercio*, 5 August 1874, 2.

71. "Bases para la educación democrática," *La Revista de Lima* 3 (1861): 110–15.

72. José María Córdova y Urrutia, *Estadística histórica, geográfica, industrial y comercial de los pueblos que componen la provincias del departamento de Lima* (Lima, 1839), 45;

35 percent were scattered across the provinces, most of them concentrated in the cities of Arequipa and Cuzco.[73] The Sociedad tried to bridge the gulf between the two groups. In addition to sending them books, equipment, medicine, and journals with information on the latest advances in science, doctors in Lima gave their provincial colleagues technical advice and invited them to the capital to improve their medical and scientific skills. The Sociedad was also a mutual-aid society; it provided all its members the same insurance coverage and benefits. Although the majority of members in Lima and the provinces would never have any direct personal contact with each other, the two groups forged civic ties with each other. I call them civic because the notion of "professionalism" was not yet developed in the country. The Sociedad tried to democratize scientific knowledge and professional opportunities among medical doctors.

The members of the Sociedad practiced equality within the group, but they were exclusionary toward all other "health professionals," such as black phlebotomists, dark-skinned barbers, Chinese herbalists, and the many midwives who still were responsible for delivering babies and caring for pregnant women. Medical doctors in the Sociedad were seeking to improve their status in society, and in order to achieve this they needed to purge from their ranks health professionals who, because of skin color or gender, were considered an obstacle. But their campaign to drive such classes out of the Sociedad failed.[74]

Barbers and phlebotomists were purged. The Sociedad instituted certification requirements; the only way of fulfilling this requirement was by completing a course in the relevant field. These had to be taught by a licensed doctor from the Sociedad. Dark-skinned peoples and blacks were discouraged from enrolling in these courses, and those who did often failed them. Whether they failed because they lacked knowledge of basic science, such as chemistry and biology, or because their teachers, all members of the Sociedad, were trying to prevent them from joining the group is difficult to know and, in any case, may be one and the same reason. As I noted above, the Sociedad took appropriate measures to improve the skills of fellow members in the provinces but were not willing to do the same for those from the capital.

The Sociedad dealt with midwives and herbalists differently. Midwives were encouraged to enroll in courses taught by licensed doctors from the Sociedad and to become certified. Those who did, however, were not al-

Eduardo Carrasco, *Calendario y guía de forasteros de la República del Perú* (Lima, 1850), 95; Alfredo G. Leubel, *Anuario Nacional* (Lima, 1860), 262–65.

73. Alfredo G. Leubel, *El Perú en 1860* (Lima, 1861), 263.

74. Sociedad Médica, *Reglamento orgánico de la Sociedad Médica* (Lima, 1856).

lowed to join the Sociedad. Apparently, the doctors used these courses to learn from the midwives birthing techniques and other special skills and methods of healing women. After they had gained this knowledge, the doctors expelled the midwives from the Sociedad. In the case of herbalists, the Sociedad was unable to bar them from practicing homeopathic medicine. The dispute began soon after the Botanical Garden was opened in Lima in 1865 and doctors began taking an interest in "pharmacology" and the study of plants. The Sociedad and herbalists criticized each other in public, the former using the pages of the *Gaceta Médica,* their tabloid, and the latter relying on their clients to publish letters and articles on their behalf in *El Comercio.* The latter portrayed the former as "monopolists," as enemies of personal freedom and public liberty, as a remnant of the colonial past.[75] The dispute went on for years, and in 1869, during the yellow fever plague that brought death to so many families in Lima and Callao, the herbalists earned their respect. Whether they actually prevented additional casualties or cured anyone is, from a medical standpoint, difficult to know, but after the plague, public opinion swung to their side. The struggle between the Sociedad and herbalists for public status and control of medical knowledge continued for another two decades. The Sociedad was egalitarian in its treatment of its fair-skinned members, but not in its treatment of those they regarded as "polluted." This differential treatment in the association also deprived the Sociedad's minority members of a place in civil society and reinforced the racial, ethnic, and gender boundaries that divided citizens from one another.

Governance in the Sociedad was antidemocratic. In 1858, during presidential elections, the officers of the association met behind closed doors and without authorization from the rank and file appropriated most of the money in the treasury and turned it over to a political club. When the members found out what their officers had done, the majority resigned from the Sociedad.[76] For the next three and a half years, the Sociedad remained moribund: "no one attended meetings, no one took an interest in any of its projects; and the *Gaceta Médica* lost readers and was seldom published."[77] The leadership of the Sociedad remained authoritarian, but the rank and file, as indicated by the way they responded, demanded accountability. Whether this also made them into democrats is difficult to know.

75. Basadre, *Historia,* 6.262 on Botanical Garden; Leonardo Villar, "Informe respecto de los curanderos chinos," *Gaceta Médica* 4 (1878): 95–96 for the doctors' position; Pastor, *Hijos del Celeste Imperio,* 221–25 on herbalists.

76. "Sociedad Médica de Lima," *El Comercio,* 12 May 1858.

77. Manuel Atanasio Fuentes, *Estadística general de Lima* (Lima, 1866), 185.

The Colegio de Abogados (1821), a lawyers' association, dated all the way back to the colonial period, although it had not had much of a presence in public during the early republic because of the recurrent bouts of civil war that had destroyed public life and the extreme factionalism this had generated within the group. The Colegio only revived after the mid-1860s.[78] In 1867, at one of its peak moments, the Colegio had 260 dues-paying members, nearly all in the capital.[79] Lawyers from the provinces were usually denied admission because they were said to lack proper training. The members of the Colegio were competent, but they were also extremely corrupt: in the words of one of its own members, colleagues were "skillful . . . but they are neither fair or impartial in their verdicts; they are motivated by other reasons [than those of justice]."[80] In any case, the Colegio was, according to a contemporary, a "lifeless corpse on its way to extinction; its members do not attend meetings . . . it has no income and the treatises it publishes are worthless."[81] In the 1870s a new generation of lawyers entered the Colegio.[82] Members were no longer required to swear an oath of allegiance to the Catholic Church, nor did they have to present their certificate of baptism proving that they had been born to married parents. They organized public forums and invited members to debate controversial issues such as the need to reform the banking and judicial systems. Although these and other reforms they implemented contributed to the spread of civic practices in the Colegio, the association continued to occupy a minor place in civil society.

The Asociación de Ingenieros y Arquitectos (1872) brought together the country's engineers and architects. The Asociación came into existence at the same time that the state initiated what was to become its most ambitious public works project. The government of Peru invested a large portion of the money it had made from the guano trade in repairing roads and building a highway system between Lima and the various state capitals, and between them and the small towns in the region; in laying railroad tracks and erecting bridges to connect the people of the highlands with those who lived in the lowlands and coast; and in constructing harbors, docking facilities, and warehouses up and down the Pacific coast. The government invested heavily in all of these programs, convinced that

78. Geraldo Arosemena Garland, *Apuntes sobre el Colegio de Abogados* (Lima: n.p., 1947). The Colegio was formed in 1821.

79. *Matrículas del Ilustre Colegio de Abogados* (Lima, 1867).

80. Fuentes, *Estadística general de Lima,* 177.

81. Fuentes, *Estadística general de Lima,* 177.

82. Carlos Camprubi Alcázar, *Historia de los bancos en el Perú: 1860–1879* (Lima: Editorial Lumen, 1957), 190; Mariano Amezaga, *Refutación de una doctrina* (Lima, 1871); also see: Hugo Garavatio Amézaga, *El Santo Hereje: Mariano Amézaga y el radicalismo anti-clerical en el Perú del siglo XIX* (Lima: Ediciones El Virrey, 1986).

this would bring about socioeconomic development and national integration. The Asociación developed close ties to the Minister of Public Works. Many of the contracts went to the engineers and architects in the Asociación, which lured others to join the group in hopes of benefiting from its ties to the state. Corruption in the Asociación and the Ministry became rampant. Members of the group bribed public employees responsible for evaluating proposals and giving out contracts. An official of the Asociación, in a report written to the Minister and published in the Asociación's yearbook, summarized the situation: most of the contracts had been distributed based on "influence and favoritism . . . rather than intelligence and hard work. . . . [Our members have become accustomed to] living off public money."[83] In the scramble to make money, members presented proposals that were, from a technical point of view, ill-conceived:

> their proposals are flawed. . . . When their firm sells, for example, a railroad or irrigation project to the state, their plans are not based on a careful, serious and complete study.[84]

Public monies were squandered, and the government once again lost its credibility among the citizenry. Public opinion, in the form of newspaper articles, denounced the Asociación and the Ministry for having betrayed the shared ideal of modernizing Peru.

Civic-minded members of the Asociación joined together with their counterparts in the Ministry, and together they mounted a vigorous campaign to end corruption. The minister, with support from reformers in the group, transformed the Asociación into a separate wing of his agency.[85] As employees of the state, the minister now had the right to test them on their technical skills and practical knowledge. The thirty who failed to pass the exam were forced to resign from the Ministry; the other fifty were granted licenses to work as engineers and architects. The following year, most of them were sent to work on public projects outside of Lima, where they were needed, in

> localities along the coast and in the countryside where there is an absence of qualified persons, to places where private firms did not go because they had no interest in them, or to places where they charged too much money for their services.[86]

Some of the members resigned; those who remained in the Ministry and went to work for short periods of time in remote communities were not

83. *Anales del Cuerpo de Ingenieros*, vol. 1 (Lima, 1874), 6–7.
84. Junta Central del Cuerpo de Ingenieros y Arquitectos del Estado, *Memoria sobre las obras públicas del Perú* (Lima, 1874), 8.
85. *Anales del Cuerpo de Ingenieros*, 1.vii.
86. *Anales del Cuerpo de Ingenieros*, 1.52–53.

convinced that they were wanted there. Wherever they went, they were seen as agents of the central state and thus as a threat to the local autonomy of township officials: "local projects should be left in the hands of the municipality."[87] The minister yielded, and in the mid-1870s the "majority of them" were reassigned to Lima. This had disastrous consequences.[88] Construction projects in most communities ground to a halt. The return of engineers and architects to the capital did not generate local autonomy. If anything, it eroded it further by depriving local residents of the most basic public services, destroying what little faith they had in the townships.

The Sociedad Filarmónica (1863) was made up of musicians, both fair-skinned and dark-skinned. It had an average of 200 members, all from Lima, where the group was based. Most of them worked in other jobs but made additional income teaching music to the children of the elite, performing concerts, and providing entertainment at family or private gatherings; the light-skinned members were usually the only ones hired to play at such events. The members of the Sociedad took turns playing free concerts in public parks once a month; they considered this to be part of their civic duty, which is also why they described music as a public good rather than a private commodity for the few. This is the same reasons they sought financial support from the state, although their survival did not depend on it, judging from the steady increase in the Sociedad's membership. A member employed civic terminology to explain the group's request: they would continue to ask the "government for resources so that we can continue growing and developing, which is the right of any association that is working for the general good."[89] Most of the funds which they requested, and were never granted, were intended to send the group's most talented musicians to study for a brief period of time in a European conservatory. Like so many other groups, the Sociedad also functioned as a mutual-aid society, providing its members and their families with burial and unemployment insurance. All indications are that the Sociedad functioned in a relatively civic and democratic manner, which might explain why members were so active in the group and so committed to each other.[90]

Scientific and Learned Societies

Most scientific and learned associations were established between 1866 and 1875. The Academia Nacional del Perú (1867), a state-sponsored group, had sixty members, all influential men from the world of art and

87. *Anales del Cuerpo de Ingenieros,* 2.8.
88. Junta Central, *Memoria sobre las obras públicas,* 7.
89. *Reglamento de la Sociedad Filarmónica* (Lima, 1866), 5.
90. *Reglamento de la Sociedad Filarmónica,* 4–5.

literature. The aim of the Academia was to create what came to be called "national culture"—that is, an official version of the self-image of Lima's fair-skinned elite.[91] The Academia had considerable support from the state, but little influence in cultural life. Even the elite in the capital and throughout the provinces considered them a remnant of the colonial past. Their meetings, according to a contemporary, were an anachronism:

> Everything that is said at these meetings is garbed in elegance, and based on an etiquette that used to be typical of our old tertulias. . . . We need other types of gatherings, where there is greater liberty and where each person is free to express themselves, where women can help shape our country's literary traditions and play a more direct role.[92]

The Academia's notion of national culture excluded indigenous peoples and just about every other social group in the country, from women to men committed to civic democracy. The Academia's version of national culture was challenged from several quarters, and is itself evidence that their effort to produce a national culture, although misguided, was not unfounded.

The aim of the Cuzco-based Sociedad Arqueológica (1869), La Redentora (1869), and several other learned societies was to provide an Inca-centered vision of Peruvian culture. According to them, Cuzco was the heartland of Peru; Lima was the product of colonial violence and had been grafted onto the nation by the Spanish. Peru was now a sovereign republic, as in the days of the Incas; the time had come to move the capital from the coast to the highlands. Doing so would also enable Peruvians to understand their indigenous roots and to turn their backs on Eurocentric and foreign conceptions of nationhood. The Sociedad's members traveled throughout the Andes collecting and cataloguing Incan artifacts in support of their interpretation, and they published the results of their work in pamphlets and newspaper articles that were read by the local elite in Lima and elsewhere.[93] The Sociedad and the Academia put forward rival visions of what it meant to be Peruvian and competed for the hearts and minds of the country's elite.

The Sociedad's campaign to revalorize Andean tradition initiated a cultural movement in Lima and elsewhere. The "Yaraví," a melancholic tune played by the indigenous peoples of the Andes, became all the rage in elite gatherings. A contemporary noted:

91. Basadre, *Historia*, 6.313–14.
92. "Las tertulias literarias," *El Nacional*, 27 July 1876, 2.
93. Alberto Flores Galindo, *Buscando un Inca* (Habana: Casa de las Américas, 1986); Luis Enrique Tord, *El Indios en los ensayistas Peruanos: 1848–1948* (Lima: Editoriales Unidas, 1978).

Yaravís . . . are played in our tertulias, and have brought about a veritable revolution in musical tastes; yaravís will no longer be disdained [by our creoles].[94]

Incan dress, made of rough wool and decorated with Incan motifs, became fashionable and was worn at the fanciest balls in Lima, including the annual dance hosted by the members of the city's most oligarchic social club, the Club Unión (1868).[95] Writers and poets were smitten as well, and began portraying indigenous people in sympathetic terms and in protagonist roles in their works. The Academia had good reason to be uneasy.[96]

The Sociedad and Redentora made the Peruvian elite aware of the Incan roots of Peruvian culture. That so many of them embraced this Andean vision of public life had something to do with the fact that many of them, although enamored of things European, had since the spread of associations in public life become committed to nationalism, to turning Peru into a democratic and modern country. Turning inward toward the Incan past was their own way of "reimagining" Peru. Their conception of Andean culture was not the one proposed by the Sociedad and Redentora. These associations had an authoritarian reading of Incan life. They focused on the nobility and ignored the commoner; they marveled at the grandeur of the centralized state without displaying much interest in Incan society; and they praised the corporate and hierarchical nature of public life while overlooking some of the egalitarian elements.[97] This official account of Andean culture was no less canonical than the creole-centered identity put forward by the Academia.

The civic-minded elite rejected both alternatives. They gathered in the Bohemia Literaria (1865), the Club Literario (1872), the Veladas Literarias (1876), and similar groups. In the course of reading and commenting on each other's stories and poems, the participants shifted their attention from partisan politics to "belles lettres," enabling them to become increasingly moderate and tolerant in their views. A visitor to the Velada Literaria noted:

Those who had been separated by politics attend the meetings, put aside matters of ideology, and offer each other a handshake in an atmosphere of neutrality. . . .[98]

---

94. "Tertulias nacionales," *El Nacional,* 28 August 1876, 2.

95. Paulino Fuentes Castro, "Extremos del aura popular," *Revista Mundial,* 28 July 1921, n.p.

96. José Tamayo Herrera, *Historia del indigenismo Cuzqueño* (Lima: Instituto Nacional de Cultura, 1980), 130–60; Tord, *El Indio,* 27–42; Efrain Kristal, *The Andes Viewed from the City* (New York: Peter Lang, 1987), 27–65.

97. Herrera, *Historia del indigenismo Cuzqueño,* 149.

98. "Veladas Literarias," *El Comercio,* 7 September 1876, 2.

The elite relearned how to be civilians in these groups, instilling in each other civic etiquette and putting aside old hatreds. They accomplished this by renewing their "passion for literature . . . after a prolonged period of revolts and revolutions."[99]

Social equality and intellectual heterodoxy flourished in these gatherings. "Persons of different ages and social positions joined our group," wrote a member of one of Lima's most free-spirited salons, the Bohemia Literaria.[100] Juana Manuela Gorriti, the George Sand of Peru, ran a salon, Velada Literaria, that provided feminists a place to discuss issues related to gender discrimination in public life.[101] Men were also invited to the Velada. Men and women took turns "reading newspapers, playing music and engaging each other in instructive conversation."[102] Social relations between the sexes, in the words of a contemporary, were egalitarian: "we gathered at [Mrs. Gorriti's) house, and dealt with her in the same way we dealt with each other."[103] The Velada and other salons, as the members often noted, placed a premium on self-expression and self-cultivation rather than family lineage and "recreation," as in the family parlors of old.

The Club Literario (1872), more formal than the Velada, was the testing ground for those salonnières who had worked their way up through the ranks.[104] A visitor to the Club noted:

> Only finished works are presented in the Club Literario, that is, paintings which have already been retouched; this is the grand gallery of masters. But Mrs. Gorriti's [Velada] salon is more like a workshop, with beautiful [finished] pieces standing alongside rough sketches, simple drawings, and preliminary drafts. . . .[105]

Lima's public intellectuals flocked to the Club and developed a civic and democratic interpretation of Peruvian culture, thereby challenging the Academia's officialist and the Sociedad's neo-Incan versions of nationhood. A visitor was struck by the high-mindedness and earnestness of the Club:

99. Ricardo Palma, *La Bohemia de mi tiempo* (Lima: Ediciones Hora del Hombre, 1948), 7.

100. Palma, *La Bohemia,* 19.

101. Mercedes Cabello de Carbonera, "Necesidad de una industria para la mujer," *La Alborada,* 13 March 1875, 173–74; Francesca Denegri, *El abanico y la cigarrera* (Lima, 1996), 130–31.

102. "Tertulia literaria," *El Nacional,* 20 February 1876, 2. Also see Gertrude Yeager, "Women and Intellectual Life of Nineteenth-Century Lima," *Interamerican Review of Bibliography* 40, no. 3 (1990): 361–93.

103. Palma, *La Bohemia de mi tiempo,* 17.

104. *Estatutos del Club Literario* (Lima, 1872), 3.

105. "Las tertulias literarias," *El Nacional,* 27 July 1876, 2.

their conferences . . . are [of] a serious character, [lacking in our inclination for] informality, flexibility and ease. When we attend the Club,
we do so to hear and admire [the remarks made by the invited guest].[106]

The Club's concern for cultural authority contrasted sharply with the Velada's experimental approach, although the two nourished each other and
were part of the same effort to democratize public culture. That women
predominated in the Velada and men in the Club is significant, and is itself a reflection of the gendered nature of cultural production in Peru.[107]

The Recreational Field

Leisure-oriented clubs provided the elite a place to congregate outside
the home in a convivial and leisurely setting. The Club de Armas (1874),
for marksmen, and the Club de Ajedrez (1876), for chess players, to take
two examples, required that members take an oath swearing that in the
club house "they would not discuss political and religious issues in our
club."[108] Among men of wealth, power, and influence, target practice,
playing chess, and shooting pool were the acceptable ways of signaling,
without losing face, a readiness to "let bygones be bygones."

The club house offered the elite an ideal setting for this type of signaling. In contrast to family parlors, club houses were owned collectively by
the members, who purchased the building with money from the treasury
and supported it with monthly dues. Collective ownership of the home
meant that no one member could claim patriarchal authority over the
guests, as had been the case in salons in private homes. The house was
a neutral terrain. Its layout inside also reinforced this and fostered sociability. The common room, which took up the first floor, was a large space
furnished with sofas, chairs, and tables that were arranged in clusters
around the perimeter, with the central area left vacant for members to
greet each other. This design gave members privacy but in a context of
visibility. The game room and library were on opposite sides of the room.
Most of the signaling went on in the game room, where members

> passed the time playing billiards, chess, and the like; this is what occu-
> pies everyone's attention. It is rare to hear anyone discuss anything use-
> ful here. . . . The library is there but only for decoration; no one ever
> visits it.[109]

106. "Tertulia Literaria," *El Nacional,* 20 February 1876, 2.
107. "Tertulia Literaria," 2. The Velada was "freer and more expansive [than the male-
dominated Club]. Our discussions unfold in a context of mutual trust, inspiring all of us to
partake in the conversations, which is our way of cultivating [national] literature."
108. "El Club de Armas," *El Comercio,* 20 January 1875, 2; *Estatutos del Club de Ajedrez* (Lima, 1876), 4.
109. Capelo, *Sociología de Lima,* 3.268–71.

Leisure-oriented clubs depoliticized social relations among the Peruvian elite and also between them and their foreign counterparts. The Club Unión brought together civic leaders and army officers who had been on opposite sides in the civil wars, shooting at each other over the barricades.[110] The Club Nacional (1855) provided foreign merchants and Peruvian businessmen a place to meet.[111] In Piura, the capital of the state of the same name, in the far north, foreign and local businessmen gathered in the Club Piurano (1862), although the two groups not as accustomed to dealing with each other as were their counterparts in Lima, the center of import-export trade.[112] Prior to the 1850s, disputes between foreign and local businessmen often escalated into international incidents, to be settled by government officials either though diplomatic channels or by military means. From the 1870s onward, Peruvian and foreign merchants resolved most of their disputes in clubs amongst themselves. The smoother relations between them became, ironically, the more denationalized Peruvian economic society became, and the more exploitative relations between domestic producers and consumers became. Civicness in one subfield generated authoritarianism in another.

In comparison to family salons, leisure-oriented clubs were inclusive. Joaquín Capelo, the country's most astute observer of social life, remarked:

> in contrast to family salons, where guests had an intense and personal affection for each other, club members have relatively loose and relaxed social attachments [perhaps because] more individuals can participate in them.[113]

Women, however, were not admitted. Clubs prohibited them from entering the recreational field, and although women continued to host salons, attendance declined and they became increasingly feminized, with the majority of men abandoning them for clubs. The spread of clubs reinforced the gender differences between men and women and made the boundaries of public and private life all the more rigid.

The Public Service Field

Peruvians organized a number of welfare associations and fire brigades. These groups were dedicated to improving the quality of public life

110. Carlos Lemale, *Almanaque del Comercio* (Lima, 1876); Pedro Pablo Martínez, *El Club de la Unión a través de la historia* (Lima, 1965); *Historia del Club de la Unión en sus bodas de diamante* (Lima, 1843).

111. Club Nacional, *Estatutos* (Lima, 1913); Felipe Osma, *Reseña histórica del Club Nacional* (Lima, 1965).

112. Club Piurano, *Reglamento del Club Piurano* (Piura, 1862).

113. Capelo, *Sociología de Lima*, 3.268–71.

for the benefit of all citizens, regardless of socioeconomic status in the community.[114]

Welfare Associations

Municipal townships, in collaboration with local associations, were responsible for providing welfare relief to the poor, needy, and sick in the community. Neither of them did. In March 1869, González de La Rosa, one of Peru's most dedicated prefects, spent more than a month visiting and inspecting nearly every municipal township in southern Peru, in the states of Puno, Arequipa, Cuzco, and Ayacucho. At the end of his tour, he reported that almost all of them were without an administrative structure and financial base sufficient to enable officials to offer welfare relief to local residents. Although de la Rosa was a strong supporter of municipal life, he recommended that the central state assume full responsibility for providing public assistance.[115]

Municipal life throughout the provinces was moribund. But this in itself was, according to Manuel Carillo y Ariza, the prefect of Ancash, a result of the lack of civic spirit among local residents. The lack of civic-mindedness was manifested not only in their inability to breathe life into local townships, but in their failure to organize charitable and welfare groups of all types. According to him, local communities were still "lacking an associative spirit."[116] Other local officials within and outside the state made similar remarks about public life in their own townships.[117]

The Catholic Church continued to play a dominant role in this subfield. The Church provided "alms" to the country's poor and sick with "charity," but they no longer had the income to do so. The state had taken away most of the monies from confraternities, leaving them unable to provide for their members. Peruvians were left without public relief. Neither the state or the Church could provide citizens or the faithful, as

114. Elinor Ostrom, *Governing the Commons: The Evolution of Institutions for Collective Action* (New York: Cambridge University Press, 1990).

115. Manuel González La Rosa, *Informe que el inspector especial de todos los establecimientos de instrucción y beneficencia* (Lima, 1869), 4–53.

116. Manuel Carillo y Ariza, "Memoria del prefecto de Ancash," *El Peruano*, 28 November 1874, 1.

117. José Mercedes Izaguirre, "Memoria que presenta el sub-prefecto que subscribe, al señor prefecto del departamento del estado en que se encuentra la provincia del Cercado de Huaraz," *El Peruano*, 4 May 1874, 1; Tomás Montero, "Memoria del subprefecto de Luya," *El Peruano*, 3 July 1874, 1; Mariano Lorenzo Cornejo, "Memoria del prefecto del Departamento de Piura," *El Peruano*, 25 July 1874, 1; Prudencio del Castillo, "Memoria de la provincia de Urubamba," *El Peruano*, 13 November 1874, 1; Mariano Ybar, "Memoria del subprefecto de la provincia de Pauza," *El Peruano*, 24 November 1874, 1; Bernardo Pacheco, "Datos estadísticos de la provincia de Antabamba," *El Peruano*, 26 November 1874, 1; Mariano Torre, "Memoria del sub-prefecto de la Provincia de Chota," *El Peruano*, 22 November 1874, 1.

the case might be, with welfare rights based on notions of citizenship, or charity based on Christian notions of "mercy." Throughout the provinces, the poor became increasingly hostile toward municipal life and, more generally, toward civic democracy, inducing many to reaffirm their religious loyalty to the Church.[118]

Fire Brigades

During the Spanish-Peruvian War (1866), residents of Lima and Callao organized fire brigades to put out blazes caused by exploding cannonballs hurled from Spanish ships off the coast.

Immigrants, particularly Italians and Frenchmen, were especially active in these brigades. Anti-foreign sentiments were running high, and organizing brigades may have been a way of defusing them. After the war, immigrants continued to organize brigades, although by now the anti-foreign sentiment had subsided. The brigades they organized were, according to contemporary observers, much more numerous, better equipped, and more active in public life than those organized by Peruvians.[119] The imbalance became itself a new source of tension between Peruvian nationals and foreign residents, and a major source of embarrassment for Lima and Callao's municipal township. The townships tried remedying the situation by offering artisans living in neighborhoods without a brigade a subsidy to help defray the costs of organizing one:

> the authorities should protect and encourage [brigades]. It costs little to outfit an artisan unit; later on the unit can assume responsibility for financing itself.[120]

These townships wanted Peruvians to play a more active role in public life and to show that they were as civic-minded as foreign immigrants. The township agreed to pay for the cost of uniforms and firefighting equipment, the most expensive items, but artisans were unable to come up with matching funds.

The fire brigades were public-spirited in their relationship to the community at large. In addition to putting out fires, brigades provided other public services. In 1868, during the great yellow fever epidemic, they offered ambulance service and medical relief to the infirm; in 1874, they

---

118. Basadre, *Historia*, 4.1643–44, 1821.

119. "Bomberos," *El Comercio*, 9 July 1866, 4; Nestor A. Díaz, *Contribución a la historia general del cuerpo de bomberos voluntarios del Perú* (Lima, 1936), 18–80. An economist account of foreign involvement in fire brigades during the war might attribute it to self-interest: they were protecting their businesses. This explanation is incomplete for two reasons: Peruvian shops were located in the same areas, and after the war, when the threat had subsided, immigrants continued to organize fire brigades.

120. "La Sociedad de Artesanos," *El Comercio*, 5 April 1867, 3.

maintained law and order in the city during an attempted coup by the army against President Manuel Pardo; and in 1879, when the Chilean army invaded the country and the national army and local police stationed in Lima were battling them, the brigades rushed to Chinatown to protect local residents from what would become the worst outbreak of xenophobia yet seen in the nation's capital. Firefighters regarded themselves mainly as public servants, and this is why they often refused to serve as night watchmen for the boutique shops owned by foreign businessmen, even though the merchants had donated large sums of money to the brigades.[121]

Fire brigades were committed to self-rule, but they practiced civic democracy in an exclusionary manner. Governance in the Salvadora (1876), one of the most important brigades, was based, in the words of a member, on "those rules we ourselves approve; we will not recognize any officials other than those we have elected ourselves." [122] But election of officers in the Salvadora and all the other brigades was largely a function of wealth. Only the wealthiest members paid monthly dues, which were exorbitant and beyond the means of the rank and file. The former were given "active" voting rights in the brigade, whereas the latter had "passive" rights. Although they did not participate in elections, this did not mean that they had no voice in the group. In 1876, forty members resigned from the Salvadora in protest. The officials yielded to their demands and reincorporated them into the brigade.[123] Fire brigades practiced self-rule, although not all of them did so by relying on electoral means.

Fire brigades, like freemasons and unlike mutual-aid societies, drew their members from a limited social pool, which is why most of them were homogeneous. Members recruited friends, those in their own social circle, although admission into the brigade was somewhat meritocractic, with the firemen themselves voting for or against each candidate. Most brigades refused to admit military officers and soldiers, for fear that they would take over and make the brigade a part of the army.[124] The Compañía Nacional de Bomberos (1872), with a total of 127 members, admitted only one soldier.[125]

121. Compañía Salvadora Lima, *Reglamento Orgánico de la Compañía Salvadora Lima* (Lima, 1875), 61–62.
122. Compañía Salvadora Lima, *Reglamento*, 6.
123. "El comandante de la Compañía Salvadora," *El Comercio*, 11 August 1876, 2.
124. Daniel N. del Prado and Federico Lembcke, *Reglamento para la Compañía* (Lima, 1873), 6.
125. Compañía Nacional de Bomberos, *Reglamento para la Compañía Nacional de Bomberos* (Lima, 1872), 32–39.

The Religious Field

Although most Peruvians were devout Catholics and the Church continued to play a central role in public life, the relative number of voluntary associations they organized in this field remained quite small in relation to their numbers and influence. The reason is quite simple: despite the various attempts by government officials to secularize the state and introduce religious tolerance in society, the Catholic Church remained entrenched in daily life.

The Sociedad Católica (1868) and the Círculo Católico (1877) were organized by laypersons active in parish life in response to debates in congress on the separation of church and state.[126] Although committed to Catholic doctrine, members in both groups employed civic terminology to defend the role of religion in public life. Federico Panizo, a member of the Sociedad, outlined the group's views:

> The habit of obedience and whatever traces of public morality which remain among our citizens are the result of the harmony that exists between religious and civil society. . . . The state, regardless of the form and organization it takes, will always depend on religious principles in order to maintain and perfect itself. . . .[127]

The members of the Sociedad and the Círculo defended the role of religion in public life in sociopolitical rather than doctrinal terms. This was the first time a religious association linked to the Church had done this. Even authoritarian groups were now using a republican vernacular to defend their antidemocratic beliefs.

Governance in both groups was corporatist and hierarchical. In the words of Pilar García Jordán, the Sociedad was authoritarian

> from top to bottom. The Permanent Council was responsible for making all decisions; the Provincial Councils [received] orders and passed them on to . . . all the members, who were organized into divisions composed of legions, centurions, and decurions, like the Roman army. . . .[128]

Members did not vote. Officials in the Permanent Council, composed of laymen and priests, appointed new members to the council, and appointees served on it for life. They, in turn, were responsible for selecting mem-

126. Sociedad Católica Peruana, *Anales de la Sociedad* (Lima, 1868); Círculo Católico, *Estatutos del Círculo* (Lima, 1877).
127. F. Panizo, "Discurso pronunciado en la Universidad de San Marcos," in Sociedad Católica, *Anales* (Lima, 1869), 57.
128. Pilar García Jordán, *Iglesia y poder en el Perú contemporaneo, 1821–1919* (Cuzco: Centro de Estudios Regionales Andinos "Bartolomé de las Casas," 1992), 50.

bers to serve in the dozen or so Provisional Councils that existed across the country.[129] Although the Sociedad and the Círculo were authoritarian, they sometimes organized street marches, a strategy invented by democratic groups and based on their own notion of "sovereignty of the people." This fusion of authoritarian and democratic practices is another example of the hybrid nature of public life in Peru.

Admission into the Sociedad and the Circulo was relatively open but not very egalitarian. Candidates committed to the goals of the group were placed on probation for several months before they were inducted as full members. Monthly dues were affordable, between 10 cents and 1 sol, depending on the income of each person. What disqualified most candidates was the literacy requirement; few citizens could read or write. Cultural rather than economic factors shaped the social and ethnic composition of these groups, although, as I noted earlier, the two overlapped considerably.[130] The majority of members in the Sociedad were, according to one of them, "rich and philanthropic."[131]

After the war with Chile, citizens began once again to organize civic associations. However, according to Joaquín Capelo, Peru's first "scientific sociologist," these were devoid of civic life:

> Lima's citizens organize associations on a daily basis, although most of them lack purpose; their main reason for existing, it seems, is to allow members to draw up statutes and rules, after which they become as apathetic as always. Few of them express any regret when the group finally dissolves. The active spirit remains absent in them; statutes cannot sustain them, and that is why they wither and disappear so quickly. These associations are like lifeless cadavers.[132]

Public life in Peru remained relatively flat and barren for the next several decades.

Associative Practices in Economic Society

Daily life in economic society was, as in civil society, an odd fusion of civic and authoritarian practices. Hybrid forms of life were relatively stable and structured in the domestic sector, the subject of discussion below, and not just a transitional phase between tradition and modernity.

The Domestic Sector: Investing Dirty Money and Business Practices

Throughout the first half of the nineteenth century and for much of the second, the central state, having defaulted on all its foreign debts, was

129. Sociedad Católica, *Anales*, 9.
130. Sociedad Católica, *Anales*, 9.
131. Círculo Católico, *Estatutos*, 3.
132. Capelo, *Sociología de Lima*, 3.52.

forced to borrow money from moneylenders. The majority of them had either inherited their wealth and were part of the old, declining colonial elite, or had made most of their wealth by financing warring military chieftains during periods of civil strife and were part of the new-money elite. Heraclio Bonilla described Lima's moneylenders:

> they had a seigneurial mentality. Instead of investing their money in the productive sectors of the economy, they used it to profit from the government's fiscal debt. As speculators, they wanted to continue making money [in postcolonial Peru] in the same easy and comfortable way [that they were accustomed to].[133]

In return for cash and credit, state officials gave moneylenders the country's guano deposits off the coast as well as a large portion of the income from the sale of this nitrogen-rich fertilizer in the world market.

In 1866, the Spanish fleet attacked the port of Callao, forcing the Peruvian state to secure additional income to cover the costs of war. Peruvian moneylenders took advantage of the crisis and charged the government exorbitantly high interest rates, to be paid from revenues from the sale of guano. After the war, President Balta's government terminated the guano contract with Peru's greedy moneylenders and turned it over to the French-owned firm of Dreyfus and Brothers, which offered more favorable conditions.

Peruvian moneylenders were prone to "rent-seeking" behavior and were extremely corrupt in their business practices, as Bonilla argues, but they were also entrepreneurial, contrary to what he states. After losing the guano contract, moneylenders diversified their portfolios by investing heavily in different sectors of the domestic economy. From the mid-1860s to the late 1870s, they transferred much of the "dirty" guano money they had made from the state-controlled public sector to the private sector, bringing with them many of the corrupt practices they were prone to engage in, with predictable results:

> the guano wealth made from illicit deals . . . is now in the hands of our businessmen, foreign financiers, and railroad builders. . . . This money belongs to our national treasury, but it has been used to corrupt all our government officials, from the highest to the lowest ranks. This germ has also contaminated all of society. . . . The measure of how much we have prostituted ourselves can be seen in our courts, where bond holders actually sold the treasury bills they had stolen, making a double profit on them.[134]

133. Heraclio Bonilla, *Guano y Burguesía en el Peru* (Lima: Instituto de Estudios Peruanos, 1974), 70; J. A. Maiguashca, "A Reinterpretation of the Guano Age: 1840–1880" (Ph.D. dissertation, Oxford University, 1967), remains the best work on the subject.
134. Segundo Pruvonena, *Los hombres de bien* (Lima, 1872), 5.

Corruption and entrepreneurialism were fused. Nevertheless, the exact balance between them varied markedly from one branch of the domestic economy to the next (banking, manufacturing, commercial, agricultural, and so on). Moneylenders predominated in most branches, but not all.[135]

Joint-Stock Companies and Family Firms

Moneylenders invested their guano money in the domestic sector, and by the mid-1870s they had established more than a dozen joint-stock companies in the most dynamic sectors of the economy, in railroads, water works and harbor construction, roads, and the like. This was the first time Peruvian entrepreneurs had created so many joint-stock companies at one time. Nearly all of them were in fact joint ventures, with private investors owning more than half of the shares, and the rest owned by the government.[136] The editors of one of Lima's leading newspapers, *La Opinión Nacional,* a daily that was critical of most government policies, praised entrepreneurs for breaking out of their isolation, pooling their capital, and creating these companies:

> Peru owes almost all its progress to this spirit of association, which is now manifesting itself among us in the form of join-stock companies. . . . For an individual, pooling resources is the only way of overcoming isolation and impotence. . . . Credit has also contributed to making this possible. Without these companies, our private interests will continue floundering and will soon fade. . . .[137]

Joint-stock corporations altered the nature of business practices in Peru, forcing shareholders to make decisions in a collaborative and open manner and to settle their differences in a way that would not impede the functioning of their firm. Those who failed to do so went bankrupt. The influence of these companies on economic society must not be exaggerated; however, this should not lead us to dismiss them as insignificant. Although they were only a dozen in number, most of them were concentrated in the same sector of the economy and were among the largest and most financially powerful firms in the country. Moreover, these firms were man-

135. Bonilla claims that Pardo's Civilian Party was organized to defend the "class interest" of moneylenders. Many of them enrolled in this party, but so did artisans, retailers, professionals, and provincial elites who had no ties to the guano contract. Bonilla's argument, in any case, is internally inconsistent. He claims that Peru lacked a national bourgeoisie, but at the same time he says this non-bourgeoisie organized the party. A nonexistent class cannot organize a party.

136. "Sociedades Anónimas," *La Opinión Nacional,* 14 January 1874, 2. Scholars have not yet studied the development of joint-stock companies in Peru, which is why my remarks on them here are brief and sketchy.

137. "Sociedades Anónimas," *La Opinión Nacional,* 2.

aged and functioned unlike any of the businesses that had existed in the late colonial past, suggesting that shareholders had broken with some of their old habits and acquired associative ideas.

Peruvian entrepreneurs, even those in joint stock corporations, continued to transact a large portion of their business and to make a large percentage of their income through family-owned firms, which in Peru continued to occupy a central and dominant place in the domestic sector of the economy. The Commercial and Civil Code of 1855, in the words of Jorge Basadre, had

> individualized private property and forced wealthy families to distribute their wealth among inheritors, thereby undermining the economic foundations of the old aristocracy . . . and spreading equality [in economic society] more so than any other single piece of legislation.[138]

Wealth became divided among progenitors, who used it to create small firms, making economic society, as Basadre points out, slightly more egalitarian than before. But the Codes also encouraged family members to pool their resources and create business clans, much like those described in the section of chapter 11 on Mexican economic society. In contrast to joint-stock corporations, family firms were organized in a hierarchical and authoritarian manner, with the patriarch of each clan, in consultation with his junior partners—that is, his cousins and nephews—deciding on all business matters, informally at weddings, baptisms, and during Christmas dinner. The owners—or, to be more precise, the chief administrator of each family firm—would meet and provide each other with information on business deals and credit to enable them to maneuver and keep the family enterprise afloat in Peru's volatile economy.

The family clan provided income for all its members, productive and unproductive alike, including widowed wives, unemployed uncles, and bon vivant nephews and children. Socio-moral relations among clan members were relatively egalitarian, except at the top; relations between them and the patriarch and the owners of each family firm were based on patronage. These clans were very insular, making it difficult for anyone to enter or exit them. Although the men in the family controlled business life, the women were responsible for maintaining social cohesion in the clan and socializing the next new generation into its norms. Joaquín Capelo, a leading reformer of the period, criticized business clans in Peru, considering them one of the greatest obstacles to the spread of commercialization and the development of a national market:

138. Jorge Basadre, *Elecciones y Centralismo en el Perú* (Lima: Universidad del Pacífico, 1980), 15; and his *Historia*, 2.937–46.

The father in these families is a tribal chief, and he is expected to provide for all its members. . . . This is why even the most hard-working families are unable to save money and improve their situation; this is why there is so much poverty in Lima and why politicians are so corrupt. [In Lima], the ratio of productive persons to idlers is about 1 to 10, and this has influenced family life. Composed of rich and poor persons, these families have destroyed society's ranking system (based on wealth, prestige, and power) and disorganized public affairs. Instead of disappearing from public life, downwardly mobile persons find refuge in their family, who then find them a steady income from a charitable foundation, school, or public agency. . . . The reason the people of the United States of America have become a great nation is that they constitute their families differently, allowing only parents and children to be a part of them but excluding everyone else. . . .[139]

In encouraging members to minimize socioeconomic differences and to value relationships based on mutual reciprocity, these family clans may, despite their authoritarian nature, have eroded status ranking among the elite, thereby enabling them to become unified and cohesive.

Commercial Banks and Paper Currency

Peru's first commercial bank, Providencia, was founded in 1862 in Lima; it was followed by sixteen more in the next fifteen years. Ten of these banks were established in the provinces between 1870 and 1873. Lima became the financial center of Peru, but the spread of banks throughout the country provided credit and loans to large sugar and cotton planters and small farmers throughout the countryside.[140] Banks were privately owned joint-stock corporations. The main difference between them and the corporations discussed above was that the former, because they were authorized to issue paper money and lower and raise interest rates at will, had a major and direct impact on all of economic society rather than just a portion of it. Peruvian investors relied mainly on these indicators to gauge "business climate" in the country. In the absence of any other reliable statistical data, a run on banks or an increase in lending rates had profound consequences for Peruvian investors and consumers alike. Despite their importance, the Peruvian state had no "central bank" of its own, nor did it even try to regulate the printing of money. The banking sector in Peru was completely private.

According to Carlos Camprubi Alcázar, the leading scholar on the

---

139. Capelo, *Sociología de Lima*, 3.259–61.
140. For a list of banks that includes the year in which they were founded, see: Alcázar, *Historia de los bancos*, 37–113.

subject, the banking sector was regulated through public opinion, and although this approach in the end failed, it would be wrong to assume that this was merely a ploy by guano speculators to propagate corrupt practices in the financial sector. Although they were, as Bonilla has argued, devoid of a business ethic, the realities of banking in Peru forced these entrepreneurs to modify some of their old habits. In order to maintain a loyal clientele, the board of directors of each bank published long and detailed reports every so often, with information on their assets and holdings. These reports were widely distributed and commented on by shareholders in the press. After reviewing these articles, Camprubi Alcázar concluded:

> judging from the many newspapers articles written during this period, it was the public rather than the state that assumed responsibility for monitoring bank activities. . . . Public vigilance, not government control, was [the only form of regulation that existed at this time].[141]

Competition among banks was keen, and public opinion was crucial in swaying clients to do business with one rather than another.

Within each bank, shareholders played a key role in curbing the power of the board of directors and compelling guano speculators to alter their habits. Shareholders attended general meetings, lobbied members of the board, and were also known to defy bank policies if they had been established in an arbitrary manner and against the will of the majority. In 1877, for example, the stockholders of the Banco Nacional, during a general meeting, "made public their mistrust of the directors."[142] News of the incident was published in *El Comercio* and other leading dailies. The directors yielded to public opinion; to have resisted would have caused the shareholders to take their money elsewhere and would have discouraged new customers from signing on. Banks were not, clearly, democratic institutions, but they were not nearly as authoritarian as some scholars claim.

By the 1870s, banks were printing much more paper money than they should have, based on the amount of silver specie in their vaults. The practices had become customary:

> [Banks] always imagine that they have 2, 3, 4, and as much as 10 million soles [in reserve], and that is why they continue issuing large amounts of paper money. . . . But everyone knows that these bills are in fact worthless; they are not backed by real capital. . . .[143]

141. Alcázar, *Historia de los bancos,* 176.
142. "Gran Reunión de Accionistas," *El Comercio,* 5 May 1877, 2; Banco de Crédito Hipotecario, *Estatutos reformados del Banco de Crédito Hipotecario* (Lima, 1876), 17–20.
143. "La Libertad," *El Correo del Perú,* 25 January 1873, 1.

Merchants, businessmen, and agricultural producers all relied on this "fictive money" to transact business. All of them knew that only 20 percent of the money was backed by silver and that the remaining 80 percent was in fact worthless; the banks published this information in their reports. As long as the money kept circulating, and buyer and seller were willing to "suspend disbelief," fictive money was as good as real.[144] Fictive money, like fictive kinship, was "real" as long as everyone honored the rules of the game—in the case of money, as long as everyone kept passing on and receiving bills.

But the bubble burst in 1871, after the price of guano plummeted in the world market, making it difficult for the Peruvian government to repay its loans to the country's major banks. Clients ran to the banks to redeem their notes. But bank tellers only had enough silver to redeem one out of every four bills.[145] The banking community reacted to the crisis by organizing the "Board of Bankers." The Board, which was composed of bank directors and their staffs, fixed the ratio of bank notes to silver reserves. They also met periodically

> to decide whether or not to approve, on a case-by-case basis, the value of the notes [issued by each bank]. . . . The decisions made by this body are binding. . . . And the agreement reached must be posted by member banks, with copies sent also to any company planning on doing business with them.[146]

The board functioned as a regulatory agency. But the Peruvian state decided to also intervene directly and establish a legal framework to prevent a similar debacle from occurring again.[147] By 1874, the board and the state had restored business confidence. In his annual report to congress, the Finance Minister described the crisis as

> not just an economic crisis, but a very serious social and political one . . . with grave consequences for our most vulnerable classes. . . .[148]

144. On the relationship between money and social trust, see: Georg Simmel, *The Philosophy of Money* (London: Routledge and Kegan Paul, 1978), 178–79.

145. Juan Ignacio Elguera, "Memoria," in *Anales de la Hacienda Pública de Perú,* vol. 10, ed. P. Emilio Dancuart (Lima: Imprenta G. Stolte, 1908), 113–49; Alcázar, *Historia de los Bancos,* 88–100.

146. "Sociedades Anónimas," *El Correo del Perú,* 31 December 1873, 1–2.

147. Alcázar, *Historia de los bancos,* 176; Pablo Macera, *Trabajos de Historia,* vol. IV (Lima: Instituto Nacional de Cultura, 1977), 134–56; Bonilla, *Guano y burguesía,* 143–46, 172, 187; Alfonso Quiroz, *Domestic and Foreign Finance in Modern Peru: 1850–1950* (Pittsburgh, Pa.: University of Pittsburgh Press, 1992), chaps. 1–2. They also demanded that the state guarantee that it would not organize a central bank.

148. Elguera, "Memoria," 128; Alcázar, *Historia de los bancos,* 204–5.

The ratio of silver specie to paper money rose steadily, from 1:4 prior to the crisis to 1:2. According to the minister, "public trust in our currency had been restored." [149] Artisans concurred with his assessment and organized mass demonstrations in support of the policies that had been implemented.[150]

Savings and Loans and Cooperatives

Working families of modest means were the backbone of commercial life in urban areas throughout Peru. For many of them, savings and loans became the single most important type of economic association in their daily lives. They also organized cooperatives. Meanwhile, in the countryside, indigenous villagers and estate owners established a small number of agricultural cooperatives, with the former relying on them to protect their communal lands from the latter, and the latter turning to them in order to enlarge their land holdings.

The country's first savings and loan opened in Lima in 1869, and the second in Callao in 1878. Although we have no evidence of them in any of the provinces, it is likely that a few were also organized in Junín and other economically active towns.[151] Municipal townships played an important role in the creation of these savings and loans, providing them with start-up capital and administrative and legal assistance. Initially, the public refused to turn over their savings to these institutions, convinced that they would be losing all their money to rogues. Savings and loans were such a novelty that their proponents often had to explain their mission and purpose to the general public:

> our aim is to stimulate in the population a spirit of frugality. We must provide for ourselves, we must cease relying on state officials and assuming that we cannot accomplish anything without them. We must learn how to rely on ourselves, on the power of association, the engine that makes all else possible; our slogan has always been: "in unity there is power." [152]

The founding members of these savings and loans were always careful to link them to civil society, including municipal townships, rather than to the state, which the citizenry still held in mistrust. Lima's savings and loan was an instant success; by the end of its first year, it was handling 711 ac-

149. Alcázar, *Historia de los bancos,* 204–5.
150. "Gran Meeting Popular," *El Comercio,* 24 August 1877, 4; "Meeting Popular," *El Comercio,* 27 August 1877, 2.
151. Cajas de Ahorro, *Estatutos de la Caja de Ahorros establecida por la beneficencia pública de Lima* (Lima, 1888), 3–6.
152. Sociedad General del Perú, *Prospecto de la Providencia* (Lima, 1862), 8–9.

counts, with total deposits of 86,770 soles, for an average account value of 122 soles. The majority of customers came from the middle strata of economic life.[153] Savings and loans did not accept accounts worth more than a few hundred pesos, a policy designed to prevent bankers and the wealthy elite from gaining control of them; in the words of a founding member, "our aim is to improve the economic situation of working people, and this is why we only accept small sums."[154] Several banks offered to buy out Lima's savings and loan, guaranteeing customers a higher return on their money, but depositors rejected their proposal. Municipally backed savings and loans did much to improve the citizenry's life opportunities in the economic domain.

The Sociedad de Crédito (1871), with about 56 members, and the Asociación Económica de Empleados (1874), with 200 or so public employees, shared in the belief that "association and credit have become the main sources of change in our century."[155] The Sociedad provided affordable housing to its members; the Asociación was a consumer cooperative that offered affiliates basic food staples at wholesale prices. The Sociedad was invited by the Ministry of Public Works to become a semipublic institution under the patronage of the government, but its members rejected the generous offer. According to them, the Peruvian state "centralizes everything" in its path, and the only way for citizens to prevent this was for the poor and the wealthy to pool their resources:

> in order to prosper and satisfy our most basic necessities, the middle class, proletariat and wealthy must associate with each other. . . .[156]

According to the Sociedad, the wealthy, by virtue of their experience in economic society, were responsible for "guiding" the middle and lower classes. The Sociedad's version of associative life was rooted in a type of social "corporatism," based on reciprocity and hierarchy.

By 1873, there were ten commercial banks providing loans to small farmers and wealthy estate owners, charging interest rates 40 percent lower than those charged by moneylenders.[157] Farmers and planters in the

---

153. Carlos Camprubi Alcázar, *Un siglo al servicio del ahorro: 1868–1968* (Lima: Editorial Lumen, 1968), 52–55.

154. Alcázar, *Historia de los bancos,* 11; Basadre, *Historia,* 4.1808; Alfonso Quiroz, "Financial Development in Peru under Agrarian Export Influences," *The Americas* 47, no. 4 (April 1991): 447–76.

155. Ricardo Monti, *Proyecto de una Sociedad de Crédito para el desarollo de la propiedad pública y privada en el Perú* (Lima, 1871), 5, 10; "Asociación económica de empleados," *El Trabajo,* 26 September 1874, 2.

156. Monti, *Proyecto de una Sociedad de Crédito,* 24.

157. Alfonso Quiroz, "Financial Institutions in Peruvian Export Economy and Society" (Ph.D. dissertation, Columbia University, 1986); Macera, *Trabajos de historia,* 4.134–56. For an opposing view, see Bonilla, *Guano y burguesía,* 55–59.

coastal state of La Libertad, in the north, borrowed about 30 million pesos in a five-year period. With this money, they were able to purchase farm tools and equipment, hire more workers, and either buy or lease additional plots of land to increase their production. Banks were generous in their lending policies; rural producers were required to present land titles proving their ownership of the property, which was held by banks as collateral on their investment. The availability of credit and the formalization of property rights stimulated production, led to the commercialization of agricultural life, and prompted fierce competition for land, labor, and water rights between large and small property owners throughout the region.[158] A leading economist and influential reformer, J. Martinet, described the situation:

> the distribution of land along the coast is a serious problem, mainly because of the lack of water supply and the need for irrigation. . . . This has produced continuous quarrels and bloody confrontations among rural producers along the coast. Property owners have been expanding their holdings, gaining control of the valley, and driving out those [farmers] who had previously resided here.[159]

Indigenous villagers and estate owners organized cooperatives in order to defend and challenge each other's land and water rights.

In the northern state of Piura, indigenous villagers from the Lower Valley district, an area that included the town of Piura and the nearby farming communities of Sechura, Castilla, Tambogrande, and Catacaos, organized the Sociedad de Agricultura (1867) to protect their land and water rights from cotton planters who lived in the Upper Valley. In August 1867, the Sociedad summoned members from the area to a public meeting in the main plaza of Catacaos. More than two thousand "people of both sexes attended," noted a contemporary, and "after the national anthem was sung," Juan de la Rosa Castro, a leader of the Sociedad, addressed the crowd:

> under the Law, we have the right to assemble and that is why we are gathered here. . . . [Our] aim is to bring together anyone who owns a parcel of communal property, and who until now has been irrigating it by themselves, without any financial aid from the national government nor anyone else. . . . In order to defend our lands and waters, we need to have legal documents and it is imperative that we create a common fund. . . .[160]

158. Macera, *Trabajos de historia*, 4.91; Alcázar, *Historia de los Bancos*, 63–85.

159. J. B. Martinet, *La agricultura en el Perú* (Lima, 1877, 1977). Also see his articles in the *Revista de Agricultura* (1875–1876).

160. "Acta Popular" (28 July 1866), in Jacobo Cruz Villegas, *Cataccaos: Origen y Evolución Histórica de Cataccaos* (Piura: Centro de Investigación y Promoción del Campesinado, 1982), 269–70.

The Sociedad was opposed to having cotton planters build a dam along the Piura River. Diverting water to irrigate the cotton fields would leave the indigenous farmers without any—a serious problem in this semi-arid area.

The Sociedad organized local villagers into work brigades and had them take turns dredging a series of dikes and irrigation canals from the Piura River to their small cotton farms. The Sociedad also parceled out plots of land and had municipal authorities provide members with land titles for their farms. The Sociedad negotiated on behalf of all its members and prevented cotton planters from bribing individual villagers to sell their property and drive a wedge through the middle of the community.[161] The Sociedad enforced solidarity among its members in several ways. In exchange for access to water, members were required to work three days a month clearing and dredging irrigation canals; "if necessary, women and children could have their husbands, fathers, brothers or hired hands work in their place, and still have the same rights as anyone else." [162] Each work team had fifty members, all from the same neighborhood; on the day they worked, local taverns had to remain closed to prevent members from getting drunk or distracted. Each brigade elected its own leader, who was responsible for making certain that the members completed their tasks. The Sociedad invited tenant farmers to join them, offering them land and water in return for membership in the group, and incidentally depriving landowners of workers.[163] In the words of Nils Jacobsen, the people of Catacaos had

> created a complex set of institutions and identities: governed by a republican municipality, and representing their interests as property owners through a voluntary association, they defined themselves as native peoples . . . with their own "Indian" myths, festivities, and customs. The leading families of Catacaos aspired to be citizens of the republic, "progressive" farmer-agriculturalists and members of an Indian community at one and the same time.[164]

The Sociedad survived well into the 1890s, enabling local villagers to keep control of their land and water rights, despite the intense pressure from cotton planters, in an area that was responsible for more than 50 percent of Peru's total production.

Sugar and cotton planters in the Central Valley of Lima created the

161. Quoted in Villegas, *Cataccaos,* 258.
162. "Reglamento de la Sociedad de Agricultura," in Villegas, *Cataccaos,* 271–72.
163. Villegas, *Cataccaos,* 271–73.
164. Nils Jacobsen, "Liberalism and Indian Communities in Peru: 1821 to 1920," in *Liberals, the Church and Indian Peasants,* ed. Robert H. Jackson (Albuquerque: University of New Mexico Press, 1997), 152.

Sociedad Agrícola (1865) so that its "members would be able to borrow money without paying high interest rates."[165] A decade later, a second group of estate owners from the Valley organized the Sociedad de Agricultura (1875), in order to "to provide agriculturalists with a place to discuss common concerns and forge social ties."[166] As part of its program, the Sociedad published *El Agricultor,* a publication written by and for rural producers, the first ever in Peru. In the words of the editors,

> the spirit of association has spread amongst us . . . and has made it possible for us to form an accurate and precise idea of our common interest. . . . The aim of this publication is to replace our habit of isolation with associative habits, so that rural producers will learn how to form on their own other types of groups. . . .[167]

El Agricultor published articles of scientific and technical interest to farmers and planters. It also published letters to the editors and meeting announcements, enabling members to assemble and discuss shared concerns. But because of the fierce competition for land, labor, and water rights in the region, the Sociedad became the point group in a broader campaign by large estate owners and planters to drive small producers and indigenous villagers out of the countryside.

The invasion and occupation of Peru by the Chilean army caused enormous losses in the domestic sector of the economy and also damaged the moral fabric that had sustained it.[168] In 1896, José Clavero, a businessmen from Lima with a penchant for collecting data, estimated the losses inflicted on Peruvian economic life by the war with Chile. Prior to the war, there were eighteen millionaires in Peru; after the war there were none. Before the war, there were 11,587 wealthy individuals; after the war there were 1,725. Before the war, the country's middle class numbered 22,148, if you count only the male head of each family; after the war there were 2,000. Peru's working class, those who made a living wage, went from 1.2 million to 345,000. Peruvians tried to recover from the economic debacle in the same way they had after the wars of independence: by fusing kinship and business ties to extract and transfer public monies from the state to their family-owned firms and private joint-stock corporations. This initiated yet another round of corruption.

165. "Sociedad Agrícola," *El Comercio,* 1 May 1865, 2; "Sociedad Agrícola," *El Comercio,* 1 June 1875, 2.

166. Sociedad de Agricultura del Perú, *Estatutos de la Sociedad de Agricultura del Perú* (Lima, 1875), 1.

167. "Editorial," *El Agricultor: Organo de la Sociedad de Agricultura del Perú,* 13 September 1875, 3.

168. José Clavero, *El tesoro del Perú* (Lima, 1896), 51, cited in Bonilla, *Guano y burguesía,* 255–56.

CHAPTER 13

Democratizing Antipolitics:
Mexican Political Society

Mexicans organized many more voting clubs and participated more in presidential elections, municipal townships, and other forms of government-centered politics in the second half of the nineteenth century than they had in the first. The majority of citizens, however, were still more inclined to practice democracy in civil rather than in political society. Although the Ayutla Constitution (1857) had granted universal suffrage to all men, most Mexicans continued to live with disregard for the state, resulting in a radical disjuncture between everyday practices and institutional life. A member of Mexico City's Asociación Democrática Constitucionalista (1871), one of the largest clubs in the country, described the situation:

> The Ayutla Revolution and Constitution signal a new era. Unlike the other revolutions that have occurred in our country since independence, the Ayutla Constitution enabled us to break with our colonial habits and institutions. We have taken our first step on the road to democracy . . . however, many of our citizens and officials have not yet assimilated our Constitution and its principles.[1]

The expansion of male suffrage, contested elections, and associative life was accompanied by the democratization of antipolitics.

Socio-institutional Structures

Between 1856 and 1881, Mexicans organized 309 new voting clubs.[2] Nearly all of them appeared after the 1870s. Before then, associative life

---

1. "Asociación Democrática Constitucionalista," *El Mensajero,* 11 January 1871, 1–2.
2. Unless indicated otherwise, the data for the tables and maps in this chapter are from Carlos A. Forment, "Databank on Associative Life in Nineteenth-Century Mexico" (Unpublished working document, Princeton University, 1997).

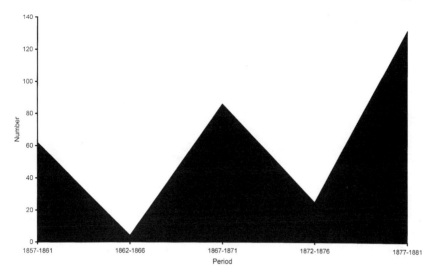

Figure 13.1 New Political Clubs, 1857–1881

was stunted by the Reform War (1858–1860), the bloodiest civil war the country had yet seen, and the Franco-Mexican War (1862–1867), when foreign troops invaded and occupied the country. In 1861 and 1868, immediately after each war, Mexicans held presidential elections, in the process organizing 65 and 12 voting clubs, respectively—not enough to restructure the nation's political practices (fig. 13.1).

Associative life spread across the political landscape from the 1870s onward but in a discontinuous and erratic manner. During the 1871–1872 elections, citizens organized 111 new clubs:

> no one can deny the progress the Mexican people have made when it comes to democracy. With each new election, the circle of citizens participating in them expands. This is an indication that we are now committed to resolving our political differences through electoral rather than military means. . . . Rival parties now accept the results of our elections, thereby preserving the stability needed to advance the cause of [democracy]. . . .[3]

Although elections were extremely corrupt, most voting clubs remained convinced that elections were the most appropriate way of transferring power from one government to the next. Club members described themselves as the loyal opposition and were committed to reforming and

3. "Las próximas elecciones," *Siglo XIX*, 14 June 1871, 1.

Table 13.1   Membership in Political Clubs,
1857–1881

Number of Members	Percentage of Associations
1–15	0
16–30	14
31–45	0
46–60	22
61 or more	64

democratizing elections. During the 1876 elections, voters organized only a dozen or so clubs. Citizens boycotted the elections in protest against the government's control of the electoral process:

> We predicted abstention, and the people went even further than we had expected in expressing their contempt for elections. . . . Everyone is of the opinion that we did not have an election.[4]

During the 1880 election, citizens created 132 clubs, the most to date. These clubs, for the first time in the country's history, were an appendage of the state—government officials used them to monopolize elections and establish Mexico's first modern dictatorship. In the 1870s, associative democracy had become widespread in political society, but it was never fully institutionalized, as it was across civil society.[5]

The duration and size of voting clubs supports this inference. Prior to the 1880s, voting clubs appeared every four years or so, during presidential elections, and operated for about four months. While the clubs themselves functioned only intermittently, social ties among club members were relatively stable; between elections, many of them continued to be active in the same civic or economic associations. The size of voting clubs provides additional insight into the structure of associative life. Sixty-four percent of all clubs had 61 or more members; of those, nearly all had 170 or more affiliates—almost twice as many as the clubs that had existed prior to mid-century (table 13.1).[6] Twenty-two percent of all clubs had between 46 and 60 members; the remaining 14 percent had from 16 to 30 activists. Although most clubs had grown in size, they remained relatively

4. "La farsa electoral," *Monitor Republicano*, 27 June 1876, 1.
5. Robert Dahl, *Democracy and Its Critics* (New Haven, Conn.: Yale University Press, 1980), 315, defines political institutionalization as the uninterrupted growth of associations, contestation, and participation for twenty or more years.
6. I obtained reliable data on 5 percent of the clubs.

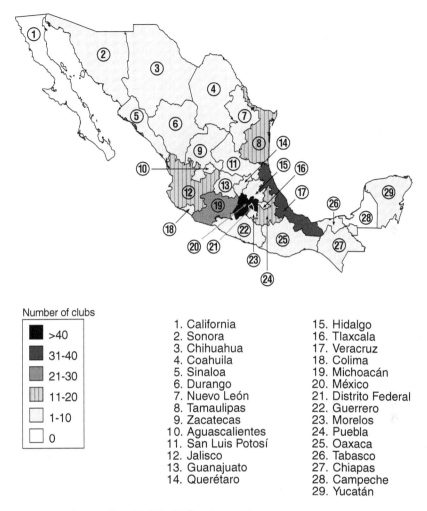

Number of clubs

■	>40
▨	31-40
▨	21-30
▦	11-20
☐	1-10
☐	0

1. California
2. Sonora
3. Chihuahua
4. Coahuila
5. Sinaloa
6. Durango
7. Nuevo León
8. Tamaulipas
9. Zacatecas
10. Aguascalientes
11. San Luis Potosí
12. Jalisco
13. Guanajuato
14. Querétaro

15. Hidalgo
16. Tlaxcala
17. Veracruz
18. Colima
19. Michoacán
20. México
21. Distrito Federal
22. Guerrero
23. Morelos
24. Puebla
25. Oaxaca
26. Tabasco
27. Chiapas
28. Campeche
29. Yucatán

Map 13.1   Geography of Political Life, 1857–1881

small until the late 1880s when President Díaz's dictatorship monopolized the electoral field and organized the country's first nationwide political party.

The regional distribution of voting clubs provides additional evidence that associative life had not yet become institutionalized. Voters in the state of Mexico (including Mexico City) organized the most clubs (35 percent) in the country, followed by voters in the state of Veracruz (12 percent), Michoacán (7 percent), Jalisco (6 percent), and Puebla (5 percent). Associative life in the other states remained undeveloped, although together they accounted for 31 percent of the clubs (map 13.1).

Most clubs surfaced in large cities and attracted only a small number of voters:

> Political clubs now play an important part in elections, but the majority of them have appeared only in our nation's capital and state capitals, and they appeal only to a small circle of citizens.[7]

By the mid-1870s, voting clubs had spread to small towns and attracted a large percentage of commoners, but in general Mexican citizens persisted in their disregard for the state and for government-centered politics.

Associative Practices in Political Society

During the War of Reform and the Franco-Mexican conflict, democratic life became rooted in rural communities under the control of Benito Juárez's rebel militias. During the postwar period, under Presidents Benito Juárez (1867–1872) and Sebastian Lerdo de Tejada (1872–1876), democratic practices migrated to urban areas and surfaced mainly in electoral clubs. During Porfirio Díaz's first government (1877–1880), associative practices migrated back to rural areas, with small farmers playing a key role in democratizing municipal life, the new epicenter of political life. Democratic life declined under the government of Manuel Gonzalez (1880–1884) and during President Díaz's second and third administrations (1884–1888, 1889–1993).

Militias, Citizenship, and Nationhood

In rebel-held enclaves, local militias promoted democratic habits at a time when the rest of political society was militarized and authoritarian groups controlled the central state. My discussion examines the emergence of these militias, their internal structure, and their influence on daily life across several of these enclaves in Puebla's northern highlands and central plateau and in northern Veracruz.[8]

Public-spirited citizens who had been active in civic groups and economic networks before the war played a prominent role in organizing and leading militia units.[9] Schoolteachers who had been active in educational

---

7. "Las Elecciones," *Siglo XIX*, 5 June 1869, 1.

8. Guy P. C. Thomson with David G. LaFrance, *Patriotism, Politics, and Popular Liberalism in Nineteenth-Century Mexico: Juan Francisco Lucas and the Puebla Sierra* (Wilmington, Del.: Scholarly Resources, 1999), 109: "There were two periods of intense fighting... between September and December 1863, and... [between] January and July 1865...."

9. For a partial list of militia leaders in Puebla and Veracruz, see: Thomson with LaFrance, *Patriotism*, 19–22, 320; and Michael T. Ducey, "From Village Riot to Regional Rebellion: Social Protest in the Huasteca, Mexico, 1760–1870," vol. 2 (Ph.D. dissertation, University of Chicago, 1992), 351–53.

and community development groups were responsible for organizing militia units in Zacualtipán (Veracruz) and Tetela.[10] Xochiapulco's militia unit was organized by Nahuatl-speaking peoples who before the war had established a Masonic lodge in their village.[11] Prior to the war, one of Puebla's senior commanders, Miguel Alariste, son of a poor tailor and an accomplished country lawyer, had been a member of the Academia de Literatura.[12] All of them had used the organizational skills, personal contacts, and civic practices they had acquired in these associations to organize militia units in their own communities and throughout the region.

Economic associations and networks were also a breeding ground for future militia leaders. Indigenous farmers who served on the boards of directors of several joint-stock corporations in Papantla, Huautla, and Yahualica (Veracruz) were responsible for organizing and leading their militias.[13] Prior to the war, family clans such as the Rivera and Luna of northern Puebla controlled the production and sale of brown sugar, cane liquor, and syrup, and provided credit to farmers, muleteers, and store owners with whom they did business.[14] The goods and credit that circulated among them made them interdependent; the success of each depended on everyone else in the network honoring financial and business obligations in a timely manner. Members reaffirmed their civic ties by serving as godfathers and godmothers to each other's children, providing coparents an additional credit line they might use during moments of economic duress. Business associates also practiced ritualized gift-giving. During each transaction, buyers and sellers invested large amounts of money and time exchanging jars of cane syrup, inviting the other for drinks, and pledging loyalty to each other, further cementing social ties among them.[15] The Rivera and Luna networks extended across the entire state of Puebla and included dark-skinned and fair-skinned persons. The militias that grew out of them were socially cohesive and financially solvent, and they coordinated military strategy and the collection and distribution of food, arms, medical supplies, and information.

Whether a militia unit was egalitarian and democratic depended on whether public life in the community had been civic before the war. In communities with a tradition of civic-mindedness, roughly 40 percent of all adult males (between the ages of seventeen and fifty-five) volunteered

10. Thomson with LaFrance, *Patriotism*, 20; Florencia Mallon, *Peasant and Nation: The Making of Postcolonial Mexico and Peru* (Berkeley: University of California Press, 1995), 391; Ducey, "From Village Riot to Regional Rebellion," 2.352–53.

11. Thomson with LaFrance, *Patriotism*, 20, 57–58.

12. Thomson with LaFrance, *Patriotism*, 61–64.

13. Ducey, "From Village Riot to Regional Rebellion," 2.374–79.

14. Thomson with LaFrance, *Patriotism*, 36–37.

15. Thomson with LaFrance, *Patriotism*, 37, 93.

for service and remained active in the unit for twenty years; the rate was slightly higher in small farming communities where residents were in conflict over land with large estate owners (see below).[16] Almost all the militias were socio-ethnically mixed, but this did not always make them egalitarian. In elections for officers, members of Tetela, Zacatlán, and several other units often voted for indigenous peoples; units from Zacapoaxtla and Cuetzalan were always led by fair-skinned commanders.[17] Elections were held every two years. In addition to personal courage and military skills, candidates were evaluated in terms of their commitment to "freedom, dignity, and equality"; the most popular candidates were those who opposed corporal punishment and personal services (harvesting the crops of officers while on reserve or active duty). The rank and file negotiated with commanders for greater democracy in the unit prior to elections and before and after a major battle. In general, militia units across Puebla's northern highlands and central plateau and throughout the northern half of Veracruz were far more democratic than those outside these areas.[18]

Militia units also democratized socioeconomic life in rebel-held areas. They privatized and nationalized between 100 and 150 million pesos worth of Church property, municipal lands, and estates owned by collaborators.[19] This massive transfer of land broadened Juárez's base of support among elite and non-elite groups in urban and rural areas. In the state of Mexico, the wealthy elite benefited the most from these transfers, but in Puebla, Veracruz, Hidalgo, Jalisco, and Michoacán, artisans, sharecroppers, peons, and shopkeepers—many of whom were militiamen—and their widowed wives acquired the lion's share of the land.[20] Many of them

16. Ducey, "From Village Riot to Regional Rebellion," 2.343, 349; and Thomson with LaFrance, *Patriotism*, 27, 67, 96.

17. Thomson with LaFrance, *Patriotism*, 27, 90; Ducey, "From Village Riot to Regional Rebellion," 2.342–43, 349.

18. Mallon, *Peasant and Nation*, 32–53; Thomson with LaFrance, *Patriotism*, 13–30; Ducey, "From Village Riot to Regional Rebellion," 2.340–60.

19. For estimates, see: Jan Bazant, *Alienation of Church Wealth in Mexico: Social and Economic Aspects of the Liberal Revolution, 1856–1875*, ed. and trans. Michael P. Costeloe (Cambridge: Cambridge University Press, 1971); and Robert J. Knowlton, *Church Property and the Mexican Reform: 1856–1910* (DeKalb: Northern Illinois University Press, 1976).

20. For the best studies on the relative benefit the elite and the non-elite derived from the land reform, see: Michael Ducey, "Liberal Theory and Peasant Practice: Land and Power in Northern Veracruz, Mexico, 1826–1900," in *Liberals, the Church and Indian Peasants*, ed. Robert Jackson (Albuquerque: University of New Mexico Press, 1971), 65–85; Jennie Purnell, "With All Due Respect: Popular Resistance to the Privatization of Communal Lands in Nineteenth-Century Michoacan," *Latin American Research Review* 34, no. 1 (1999): 85–113; Donald J. Fraser, "La política de desamortización en las comunidades indígenas, 1856–1872," *Historia Mexicana* 21, no. 4 (April–June 1972): 615–52; Charles Berry, "The Fiction and Fact of the Reform: The Case of the Central District of Oaxaca, 1856–1867," *The Americas* 26, no. 3 (January 1970): 277–90; Jan Bazant, "La división de las grandes

came to identify property rights with democratic citizenship. In March 1864, José Maldonado, commander of Zacapoaxtla's miltia, met with Nahuatl-speaking villagers from Xochitlan, Nauzontla, and Cuetzalan and explained to them that the purpose of the reform was to

> convert national property into private holdings so that a multitude of families might be enriched . . . distribute communal lands equally among all the villagers so that they might be able to fulfill their needs . . . [and punish] officials who have taken the best communal lands to the detriment of the villagers.[21]

Indigenous peoples fused democratic notions of property with their own ancestral ideas to create a hybrid third way: communal democracy. Although the majority of residents in rebel-held areas could neither read nor write, and fewer still had an understanding of the legal and political foundations of the 1857 Constitution, they became loyal to it. Militiamen played a key role in translating the Constitution into local terms, enabling rural peoples to develop a sense of nationhood.

Militiamen also undermined the public authority of the Church in rebel-held areas, although it was local residents who determined how and to what extent this would be done. In rebel-controlled areas, priests were forbidden to wear religious tunics in public; to demand personal services from parishioners; to lead religious processions and ring church bells without prior authorization; and to bury the faithful in church grounds. Local officials also assumed responsibility for recording the number of births, deaths, and marriages in the community and denied priests access to the civil registry. The first thing militiamen did after capturing the town of Zacapoaxtla, a bulwark of conservatism in Puebla's highlands, was to imprison the parish priest.[22] In other communities, the conflict between citizen-soldiers and churchmen was less dramatic but no less important. In the radical town of Tetela, residents volunteered their labor (*faena*) to build a sanctuary for their patron saint, which they had removed from the parish Church. Every fortnight, they paraded the saint through the middle of the town, collected "eggs, maize kernels, and other little things" for it from residents, and sold them in the market, using the money they had

---

propiedades rurales mexicanas en el siglo XIX," in *Después de los latifundios,* ed. Heriberto Moreno García (Mexico City: Colegio de Michoacán, 1982), 37–41; Antonio Padilla, "La reforma y los bienes de la iglesia en Chiapas," *Secuencia* 12 (September–December 1988): 29–38; Frank Schenck, "La desamortización de las Tierras Comunales en el estado de México: 1856–1911," *Historia Mexicana* 45, no. 1 (1995): 3–37; Héctor Díaz Polanco and Laurent Guye Montandon, "La reforma y la desamortización de los bienes de la iglesia," *Revista de Historia de América* 97 (January–June 1984): 175–217.

21. Mallon, *Peasant and Nation,* 101 and 60.
22. Thomson with LaFrance, *Patriotism,* 61.

earned to maintain the sanctuary and to pay for masses in Church in honor of the saint.[23] Radical democrats remained devout Catholics, although they were now also critical of the Church and its priests.

The relationship between militiamen and churchmen in communities with a tradition of civic-mindedness was different. In San Francisco Ixtacamaxtitlan, the priest, José María Cabrera, was director of the most democratic school in the entire state of Puebla.[24] Cuauximaloyan's residents donated more money and labor to the Church than to the school, to the dismay of radical militiamen:

> They are more interested in building a Church . . . than in building a temple to science. . . . Each person has donated a peso (8 reales) for the Church, but only a real for the school. . . .[25]

Chignahuapan's residents also admired their parish priest, a man known for his civic commitment.[26] Daily practices, not abstract ideology, shaped the relationship between local residents and parish priests.

Residents in rebel-controlled communities used a Civic Catholic vernacular in daily life. After capturing the religious stronghold of Tlatlauquitepec, a citizen-soldier exclaimed: "this mystical settlement reminds me more of a monastery than a civil society."[27] In the 1880s in Xochiapulco, Rafaela Bandala, a schoolteacher attending the funeral of Miguel Mendez, a militia leader, paid homage to his deceased father, Juan, and their comrade, Bonilla, who had been active in the same unit. The oration ended like this: "In our state, the Liberal party, for whom Juan Francisco is the Father, Juan Méndez the Son, and the late Juan Bonilla the Holy Ghost, has freed Mexico from friars and other poisonous snakes."[28] The audience was familiar with the civic-religious terms and imagery the teacher used in his oration. That he had characterized militia leaders as the Holy Trinity and churchmen as snakes, the devil incarnate, is additional evidence that the Civic Catholic rhetoric was used in daily life even in small, relatively remote farming communities across the highlands of Puebla, one of the most religious states in the country, and used in a way that subverted the traditional moral codes espoused by the Church.

After defeating and expelling the French from Mexico, Juárez's rebel

23. Thomson with LaFrance, *Patriotism*, 17; and Mallon, *Peasant and Nation*, 292–93.
24. Thomson with LaFrance, *Patriotism*, pp. 19–21.
25. "Informe del Juez Municipal de Xociapulco, Juan Francisco Dinorín (14 December 1870)," quoted in Mallon, *Peasant and Nation*, 291.
26. Mallon, *Peasant and Nation*, 95, 127–28.
27. Ramón Sánchez Flores, *Zacapoaxtla: Relación histórica* (Zacapoaxtla: Editorial de Puebla, 1984), 174.
28. Guy Thomson with David G. LaFrance, *Patriotism*, 21.

army established a "transitional government."[29] This government was responsible for purging collaborators from the public bureaucracy and the national army. It also slashed the army's budget by 45 percent; reduced the number of men in uniform by 180,000; replaced disloyal state governors with patriotic ones; and stripped citizens who had supported the French of many of their civic, political, and economic rights, including the right to run for public office, vote in national elections, and reclaim property that had been nationalized by the rebel government during the war.

In communities across the country, local militias and patriotic associations also ostracized collaborators from public life. Their names were published in tabloids and posted on public buildings on all the major thoroughfares. Civic and economic associations used these lists to expel old members and deny candidates admission into the group.[30] Authoritarian-minded citizens were forced to withdraw into private life:

> The war that was formerly waged everywhere with steel and powder is now a battle of words in private homes; instead of provinces and capitals, it is the control of the rising generation for which Liberals and Ultramontanes now contend.[31]

Authoritarianism migrated from political society to family clans, where it became entrenched, with matriarchs now serving as its main carriers:

> It is widely known that women are largely responsible for the resurgence of [authoritarianism]. In the conservative party, the men are passive and cowardly; the women, in contrast, are active, brave, and in control of everything.[32]

Democratic writers "feminized" authoritarianism by depicting its men as having lost the ability to act rationally, as indicated by their antipatriotism during the war and their passivity during the postwar period. They were, practically speaking, no different from women and indigenous peoples, and were therefore unfit to participate in politics. By reworking the colonial dichotomy of reason and passion, democrats were able to strip

29. Daniel Cosío Villegas, *Historia moderna de México: La república restaurada, vida política*, vol. 1 (Mexico City: Editorial Hermes, 1955–1974), 81–82, 189–95; Laurens Ballard Perry, *Juárez and Díaz: Machine Politics in Mexico* (Dekalb: Northern Illinois University Press, 1978), 7–8, 39–41. In reaction to these reforms, regional chieftains organized forty or so barrack revolts.

30. "El Traidor Almonte borrado del registro," *Siglo XIX*, 2 May 1862, 3; "Junta Patriótica," *Siglo XIX*, 14 March 1863, 3; "Academia Nacional," *Siglo XIX*, 16 July 1867, 2. Also see: Walter V. Scholes, *Mexican Politics during the Juárez Regime: 1855–1872* (Columbia, Mo.: University of Missouri Press, 1957), 130–31.

31. John Lewis Geiger, *A Peep at Mexico* (London, 1874), 307.

32. "Editorial," *Siglo XIX*, 7 September 1872, 1.

authoritarians of their status as citizens. For the first time in the country's history democrats had achieved socio-moral consensus and political dominance in public life; it was the first time any group had done so by relying mainly on citizens rather than the support of the Church, the army, and the aristocracy.

Voting Clubs and Electoral Contestation

The transitional government also oversaw the first presidential elections of the postwar period. Juárez and his supporters were convinced that the only way to modernize the state and democratize public life was by turning Mexico into a "centralist-presidentialist" regime. During the 1867 elections, the government put the matter directly before voters in a referendum.[33] Juárez won the presidency but lost the plebiscite.[34] For the next decade or so, voting clubs and state officials used elections to challenge each other's vision of democratic life.[35]

Nearly all the political clubs organized during the second half of the century were against centralization.[36] Members of the Amigos de la Union (1867) in Guadalajara and the Círculo Progresista (1868) in Zacatecas expressed commitment to federalism by swearing loyalty to the "1857 constitution" and by declaring support for "local militias," "associative life," and "public opinion." [37] Joining a club was fraught with moral risks. In San Juan Bautista (Tabasco), the Club Libera (1870) required candidates to swear allegiance in public to the Laws of the Reform that had deprived the Church of its property and stripped priests of their authority. Churchmen retaliated by prohibiting club members from receiving the Holy Sacraments and threatening them with eternal damnation. The fact that Mexico's God-fearing voters subjected themselves to this "baptism by fire" is an indication of their commitment to Civic Catholicism.[38]

Daily life in voting clubs was based on a mixture of civicness and clientelism. Durango's Borrego Club (1867) and Club Electoral (1867) distrib-

33. Manuel Dublan and José M. Lozano, *Legislación Mexicana,* vol. 10 (Mexico City, 1876–1904), 40–44. The plebiscite weakened the legislative branch by dividing congress into an upper and a lower chamber. It also strengthened the executive branch by increasing its veto power; by allowing it to decree new laws when congress was not in session; and by protecting cabinet ministers from appearing before congress.

34. Villegas, *Historia moderna de México,* 1.168–90; and José Fuentes Mares, "La Convocatoria de 1867," *Historia Mexicana* 14, no. 3 (January–March 1965): 423–44.

35. Villegas, *Historia moderna de México,* 2.345–50.

36. "Club," *La Voz de México,* 17 February 1877, 1. The first centralist club, "Díaz y Chacón," did not appear until 1877, during Díaz's first government, in Morelia, homeland of authoritarianism. Few followed, until after 1881.

37. "Círculo Progresista," *Siglo XIX,* 28 September 1868, 3; and "Zacatecas," *Siglo XIX,* 7 October 1868, 3.

38. "Club Liberal de Tabasco," *Siglo XIX,* 17 February 1870, 2–3.

uted large amounts of liquor to plebeians in exchange for their ballots.[39] Patronage ties continued to pervade most clubs, but they were not as hierarchical as they had been:

> No one believes any more in personalism, only in platforms and programs. . . . Conspiratorial circles are a thing of the past; in our parties, a notable who acts despotically and violates public opinion . . . will lose support even among his followers. . . . Instead of relying on false prophets and ambitious impostors, party leaders now find it necessary to court public opinion. . . . This change has come about because of direct elections, popular suffrage, and the press. . . .[40]

In exchange for their loyalty, those on the bottom were demanding more from the elite. In 1875, the rank and file of Jalisco's ten largest voting clubs rallied together around their officials, defending them from the governor, who threatened them with military conscription.[41] Political clubs had their own judicial system to determine whether or not a member had violated the norms and statutes of the group. Elite and commoner took turns serving as jurors and deciding each other's innocence or guilt, thereby blurring the socio-ethnic differences that divided them.

Club members learned to deliberate about public concerns. In Mexico City, members attending the weekly meetings of the Sociedad Democrática Universal (1872) discussed issues such as "democratic morality, suffrage, municipal townships, schooling, employment, and the death sentence."[42] In July 1870, all the clubs in the state of Zacatecas held a "convention" in Fresnillo, the capital, at the Coliseum, the city's largest theater, with a seating capacity of several hundred persons. During one of the sessions,

> a humble artisan . . . stood up and went to the podium. He then spoke with admirable clarity, and accused the [Juarista] Governor of sending armed thugs to occupy the city's voting booths. . . .[43]

Indigenous peoples also acquired deliberative skills. During the 1876 elections, voters from forty-eight farming communities in and around Matehuala (San Luis Potosí) drafted, circulated, and signed a petition denouncing local officials for depriving them of the ballot. They also collected

---

39. "Francisco Gómez Palacios to B. Juárez (22 October 1867)," in *Benito Juárez: Documentos, discursos y correspondencia,* ed. Jorge L, Tamayo (Mexico City: Editorial Libros de México, 1964–1972), 12.703–5.
40. "Círculos políticos," *Siglo XIX,* 19 January 1868, 1.
41. "Jalisco," *El Sufragio Libre,* 5 November 1875, 2.
42. Sociedad Democrática Universal, *Estatutos de la Sociedad . . . organizada en la capital de la República Mexicana* (Mexico City, 1872), 5–6, 92–93; and Amigos de la Unión, "Bases de los trabajos," *Siglo XIX,* 25 September 1867, 2. Also see: "Algo sobre elecciones," *Siglo XIX,* 21 April 1869, 1; "Electores," *Siglo XIX,* 30 January 1861, 3.
43. "Convención Zacatecana," *El Siglo XIX,* 23 July 1870, 2.

money and paid for a small delegation to travel all the way to Mexico City to present the petition to their congressmen. The "secretary of the assembly refused to read the letter," but several deputies pressured him;

> it was written in a plain and simple style, without any trace of hyperbole [characteristic of the writings by scribblers and other public intellectual], but it was forceful and made an enormous impression on everyone who heard it. . . .[44]

Indigenous farmers were far more outspoken about their political rights than they had ever been in the past.

Voting clubs introduced several innovations in the way citizens practiced electoral politics. From the late 1860s on, clubs organized district- and statewide conventions. The 1868 Convention held in Saltillo was attended by ninety or so delegates from a dozen clubs across the state of Coahuila. The Cuernavaca Convention of 1877 attracted about 220 delegates from fifty clubs scattered throughout the state of Morelos.[45] The 1869 Convention in Veracruz was composed "exclusively of artisans, farmers and merchants," mainly mixed-bloods. Conventions enabled club members to forge vertical ties with others in the same electoral district and horizontal ties with those in the state capital. These district- and statewide conventions prepared the way for the development of national parties in the mid-1880s.

Conventions also provided club members an opportunity to learn how to negotiate their political differences in a strategic manner. Despite "constant bickering and factionalism," delegates to the Saltillo convention overcame their differences and agreed on a single slate of candidates.[46] In order to reconcile their differences, club delegates at the 1870 Tabasco convention organized a formal "grievance committee." Composed of two members from each club, the committee met behind closed doors and drafted a "statement" outlining their commonalities, then presented it to the delegates at large for discussion.[47] Conventions also democratized governance inside each club. Delegates were encouraged to consult with their own rank and file on whether or not to support a candidate or an issue.[48]

Voting clubs introduced a second major innovation. During electoral campaigns, clubs held public rallies and marches in all the major cities of

44. "Hasta los indios," *Monitor Republicano*, 23 September 1876, 3.
45. "Convención Progresista de Coahuila," *Siglo XIX*, 3 May 1868, 1; "Convención electoral," *Monitor Republicano*, 12 January 1877, 3.
46. "Club Liberal de Tabasco," 2–3;
47. "Clubs," *El Sufragio Libre*, 5 November 1875, 2.
48. "La Convención Progresista," *Siglo XIX*, 13 September 1867, 3. Also see: "Convenciones Progresistas," *Siglo XIX*, 7 March 1868; "Convención electoral de Cuernavaca," *Siglo XIX*, 10 January 1877, 3; "Otra convención Progresista," *Siglo XIX*, 6 June 1868, 1.

the country. Mexico City's Club Central (1871) sponsored a rally in the central plaza that drew more than 4,000 residents.[49] Earlier in the year, the club had also led a march from the Principal Theater to the other end of the city and back again; about 1,500 citizens participated:

> The marchers carried brilliantly colored banners with slogans such as "1857 Constitution" and "Citizen Porfirio Díaz for President" emblazoned across them. They paraded in an orderly manner down all the major streets of the city yelling out the name of their candidate. . . . The participants were enthusiastic, but the march itself was at all times peaceful and orderly. This is the first time local residents in the nation's capital have expressed support for a candidate in this way. . . . There was no looting, robbing, nor disorder of any kind; even the merchants did not feel threatened by the march and kept their stores opened. . . . They were certain that so many honest and decent citizens would never subvert the public order.[50]

In contrast to the York-led marches in 1830, these marches were peaceful. However, unlike the "monster demonstrations" organized by the English Chartists in the 1830s in support of popular suffrage, these marches were relatively small, limited to urban areas, and they attracted mainly "honest and decent people."[51]

Voting clubs contributed to demilitarizing political life. During the 1871 election, the most corrupt and violent yet held in Mexico, clubs discouraged members from joining the "Noria rebellion," a minor revolt led by Porfirio Díaz from his estate in Oaxaca.[52] Even his most loyal supporters in his home state refused to take up arms. Weeks before the uprising, the Club de Artesanos (1871) and the Club de Estudiantes (1871) held a public rally in Oaxaca's central plaza. It was attended by commoners and elite; some were there for the free liquor, others to hear what Pirote, the town barber and president of Artesanos, had to say regarding the rebellion. He had fought valiantly against the French; local residents considered him a patriot. Pirote mounted the podium and, after reminding his audience of his war record and political credentials, stated

> that this time he would not take up arms. . . . His remarks were in response to those made by Rosalino Cruz, another member of the Club, who had spoken earlier and had told voters the opposite.[53]

49. "Clubs," *El Mensajero*, 6 June 1871, 2–3.
50. "5 de febrero de 1871," *La Oposición*, 9 February 1871, 2.
51. Charles Tilly, *Popular Contention in Great Britain, 1758–1834* (Cambridge: Cambridge University Press, 1995), 14–15, 41.
52. Daniel Cosío Villegas, *Porfirio Díaz en la Revolución de Noria* (Mexico City: Editorial Hermes, 1953), 19, 59–61, 94, 168.
53. Perry, *Juárez and Díaz*, 255.

Far away from Díaz's home state, in the indigenous village of Huamantla (Tlaxcala), members of the local Porfirista club met in the theater to discuss the same issue, whether to participate in the rebellion or remain loyal to the constitution. The club's president, in a letter to Porfirio Díaz, wrote: "they were prepared to revolt . . . but I persuaded them not to." [54] Voting clubs remained committed to elections and to the 1857 Constitution, which during the war had been a symbol of nationhood and patriotism. [55]

Voting clubs connected political life at the local-community and elite-congressional levels as never before. In the 1871 election, the opposition ran two candidates (Porfirio Díaz and Sebastian Lerdo de Tejada) against President Benito Juárez, who was seeking reelection. Although these elections were the most corrupt to date, they were also the most closely contested. Juárez failed to get a plurality of votes from the country's 208 district-level electoral colleges, many of which were controlled by voting clubs. [56] Prior to the elections, Porfirista and Lerdista deputies in Congress closed ranks and approved a law granting legislators the right to select the country's next president if none of the candidates gained a majority of votes. [57] The "Liga," as the congressional coalition came to be called, had been the work of local voting clubs. [58] But as election day approached, factionalism broke out in various districts across the state of Puebla, where the Liga had been strongest, sending shock waves throughout other parts of the country and through congress, and the Liga unraveled. [59] The Liga represented the first time in the country's history that opposition clubs had created a coalition amongst themselves and forged horizontal ties across the country between local voters and politicians in congress.

Despite the spread of voting clubs, there is no denying that the vast majority of Mexicans remained inactive and uninvolved in electoral life. Their reasons for practicing antipolitics varied considerably, and it would be worthwhile to consider them individually in some detail.

54. "Pedro Junco to P. Díaz (13 July 1871)," in *Archivo del General Porfirio Díaz: Memorias y documentos,* ed. Alberto María Carreño (Mexico City: Universidad Nacional Autónoma de México, 1947–1951), 9.203–4.

55. "Editorial," *Siglo XIX,* 9 July 1869, 3: "A democracy can exist despite electoral abuses, falsification of ballots, debased officials and a plundered national treasury. The great problem for us is to remedy these problems legally and peacefully without any military violence."

56. Villegas, *Historia moderna de México,* 1.588–90.

57. Thomson with LaFrance, *Patriotism,* 184–85.

58. Basilio Pérez Gallardo, *Cuadro comparativo de las elecciones de presidente de la república* (Mexico City, 1872), 5–6. The Liga was strongest in Puebla, Oaxaca, Chiapas, San Luis Potosí, Zacatecas, Guanajuato, and Jalisco.

59. Villegas, *Historia moderna de México,* 1.614–17. Congress voted for Juárez over Díaz (103–57).

A large group of citizens remained attached to their colonial habits; they were as uninvolved in public life as their parents and grandparents had been during Spanish rule. A second group had broken with their past, now practicing democracy in civil and economic society, but they continued to ignore the state and electoral politics. In Civic Catholic terms, these citizens were active in civic and economic associations and relied on horizontal forms of solidarity to restrain their passions, while avoiding all forms of state-centered politics based on domination. A third, much smaller group had practiced a Jacobin brand of democracy during the war in rebel-controlled enclaves and now found it difficult to make the transition from "citizen-soldier" to "civilian-voter." After the war, President Juárez's government spent large sums of federal funds in agricultural credit to encourage militiamen to disarm.[60] Most units accepted and used the money to purchase additional land, seeds, farm tools, and the like. However, radical units across Puebla's highlands refused the offer. A government official who spent months negotiating unsuccessfully with them summarized their reasons for resisting: they claim they have

> always used their weapons in defense of republican institutions . . . [and that by disarming them], the chief of the nation . . . is humiliating and depriving [militiamen] . . . the laurels that they had earned . . . during the siege of Querétaro, Puebla, and Mexico. As members of citizen-militias, they consider it their duty to protect their honor . . . defend the general interest of the district and the private interests of each person and family. . . .[61]

The places where radical democracy had been strongest during the war became epicenters of antipolitics during the postwar period. These three groups prepared the way for the resurgence of authoritarianism across the electoral field.

In October 1870 the National Congress issued a general amnesty allowing collaborators to run for office, vote in national elections, and work in the local, state, and federal bureaucracy. White-collar professionals were in short supply, and without them government officials would be unable to rebuild the state and centralize power. The president's secretary received a "brutally frank" letter from a supporter in Veracruz summarizing the amnesty's impact in his home state:

---

60. Thomson with LaFrance, *Patriotism*, 130–31; Francisco Bulnes, *El verdadero Díaz* (Mexico City: E. Gomez de la Puente, 1920), estimates the number of "active" militiamen during the war at 40,000; after demobilization, there were 20,000 on "reserve."

61. "Col. Pilar Rivera to Lauro Luna (22 July 1868)," quoted in Thomson with La France, *Patriotism*, 138; Mallon, *Peasant and Nation*, 85, 113–14.

The amnesty has opened the door to many who had been allied with the Empire and who are now seeking a post in congress. . . . Many of them are men of talent, experience, and skill. . . . Instead of letting them go and running the risk of having them assist the opposition . . . we should use them for our own cause.[62]

Authoritarian politicians reentered political life through informal networks but never organized themselves into a voting club, as this would have provoked enormous resistance and perhaps another civil war.

Collaborators were hired to work as schoolteachers, mail clerks, public bureaucrats, and, most importantly, political chiefs. In addition to implementing federal and state laws, collecting taxes, and promoting economic development, political chiefs were responsible for overseeing municipal and presidential elections and presiding over the township. In administrative terms, political chiefs were at the bottom of the totem pole, but this is exactly why they were important: without them, the central state would not have been able to penetrate so deeply into political life. Political chiefs were also pivotal in enabling the state to shift from a military to an electoral system of control.[63] During the 1871 presidential elections, the most closely contested to date, Manuel María Zamacona addressed his nervous colleagues from the floor of congress and reassured them that it was unnecessary to send troops against various electoral districts:

two or four years ago, maybe we would have needed them, but a few men with sharp sticks is all that is needed to domesticate those villages and ensure that they vote accordingly.[64]

Physical violence was still used to intimidate voters, but even in these cases it was deployed by political chiefs in a characteristically democratic manner, by mobilizing "armed mobs" rather than relying on local notables.[65]

Elections became the centerpiece of this new political system.[66] Politi-

---

62. "Gonzalo A. Esteva to P. Santicilia (26 September 1870)," in *Benito Juárez: Documentos*, 14.780–81; Ducey, "From Village Riot to Regional Rebellion," 2.353–56, 400–401.

63. Lázaro Pavia, *Ligeros apuntes biográficos de los jefes políticos de los partidos* (Mexico City, 1891). Juárez created the chiefs in 1861 but because of the war they did not become fully operative until after 1870.

64. "Manuel María Zamacona (16 March 1871)," quoted in Perry, *Juárez and Díaz*, 19.

65. "Crónica electoral," *Monitor Republicano*, 13 June 1873, 3; "Manifestación que hace la mayoría del colegio electoral del estado de Tabasco," *Monitor Republicano*, 10 March 1873, 1; "La libertad de las próximas elecciones," *Siglo XIX*, 8 June 1871, 1; "Editorial," *Monitor Republicano*, 29 December 1876, 1.

66. Elections were indirect and two-tiered. Citizens voted for primary electors, who in turn voted for township officials. Every two years, the electors gathered in the district capital and selected from among their own ranks secondary electors to serve in the states' elec-

cal chiefs used a variety of methods, from the relatively crude to the sophisticated, to ensure that the government's candidate (for governor, electoral college, and municipal township) won a majority of votes in the district. Voting clubs used similar methods to challenge them. In 1875, the political chief responsible for Mexico City (Mexico) and Jalisco (Guadalajara) erased the names of eligible voters from the voting roll and added the names of ineligible citizens.[67] Jalisco's clubs resisted by compiling their own rolls, establishing their own electoral station, and posting handbills throughout the city inviting citizens to vote.[68] In Mixcoac (Mexico), Chalchicomula, Llanos, Zacapoaxtla, Matamoros, Tehuacán (Puebla), and countless other villages and towns, political chiefs distributed premarked ballots among indigenous peoples.[69] Mixcoac's clubs walked away with the ballots and filed a complaint with congress, which was forced to disqualify the results.[70] Political chiefs in towns such as Ayala (Morelos), Cerritos (San Luis Potosí), Tehuacán (Puebla), and elsewhere would often move the voting booth to nearby towns where voting clubs were weak.[71] Electoral clubs used this same tactic of "doubling" to prevent government supporters from casting their vote.[72]

Between 1861 and 1876, the government increased the number of electoral districts (one district per 40,000 voters) from 188 to 231, although the number of eligible voters in most of these districts had not grown accordingly. Politics rather than demographics seems to have determined which states got additional districts. The states with the most active clubs, including Jalisco, San Luis Potosí, Zacatecas, Oaxaca, Guanajuato, Puebla, and Veracruz, gained few districts; Mexico, Querétaro, and Michoacán, where voters supported the government, gained many more districts than their populations would warrant.[73] In addition to gerryman-

---

toral colleges. These electors picked all the congressional deputies to the state and national legislature. The Tuxtepec Revolution (1876) changed the system of voting (see below).

67. "Elecciones," *Monitor Republicano,* 3 and 7 July 1875, 1; "Farsa electoral," *Monitor Republicano,* 5 July 1875, 1; "Libertad electoral," *Sufragio Libre,* 4 August 1875, 1.

68. "Carta," *Monitor Republicano,* 9 July 1875, 3.

69. "Elecciones," *Monitor Republicano,* 7 July 1875, 1; "Crónica electoral," *Monitor Republicano,* 13 June 1873, 3.

70. "Mixcoac," *El Pájaro Verde,* 28 June 1876, 3.

71. "Crónica electoral" and "Elecciones en Xochimilco," *Bandera de Juárez,* 28 June 1873, 1; "Elecciones en Morelos," *Monitor Republicano,* 14 July 1873, 1; "Elecciones," *Siglo XIX,* 8 July 1869, 1.

72. "Elecciones duplas," *Sufragio Libre,* 6 August 1875, 1; "Las elecciones de ayuntamiento," *Siglo XIX,* 21 December 1870, 1.

73. Marcello Carmagnani and Alicia Hernández Chávez, "La ciudadanía orgánica mexicana: 1850–1910," in *Ciudadanía política y formación de las naciones,* ed. Hilda Sábato (Mexico City: Fondo de Cultura Económica, 1999), 371–401, explain the increase in the number of electoral districts in terms of democratization.

dering, chiefs in Veracruz and elsewhere denied club members the right to vote in electoral colleges at the district level:

> As is well known, the liberty-loving voters in the port of Veracruz have always elected trustworthy persons to serve in their electoral college. If in this city, renowned for its public spirit, government officials have usurped the elections, imagine what it must be like in other districts where the practice of liberty is far less developed.[74]

But this strategy was risky and often backfired. Club members began to boycott all pro-government colleges, depriving them of the quorum congress required to certify their ballots. The "absentist" movement reached its apogee during the 1876 elections when congress disqualified 136 of the country's 231 districts.[75] Under conditions of democracy, political chiefs were more likely to tamper with electoral laws, voting rolls, ballots, and other symbols of sovereignty than to launch physical attacks against voters.

The bureaucratization of politics by political chiefs brought about a decline in the political influence of voting clubs. Although they never won an election, clubs were relatively strong in a significant number of districts throughout the country prior to 1876. Table 13.2 gives the percentage of voting districts (by state) in which antigovernment candidates obtained 30 percent or more of the votes from the local electoral college during the elections of 1867, 1871, and 1876.[76] The decline of voting clubs from 1876 onwards was directly related to the political chief's capacity to monopolize the electoral field:

> no one believes any more in mass suffrage. Instead of elections, what we have in reality is a system of appointments that is only slightly more complicated than the one used to hire office clerks and secretaries.[77]

Elections were corrupt throughout the second half of the century, but after 1876 they were no longer participatory and contested, as they had been in the recent past.

Voting clubs toward the end of the nineteenth century shifted their attention from national to local government:

> Few citizens take any interest in political life, unless they are seeking employment in the state. Federal elections go unnoticed in most villages

---

74. Emilio Velasco, "Exposición presentado por el C. . . . acreditando que no habido elecciones para presidente de la república," *Siglo XIX*, 19 September 1876, 1–2.

75. "Elecciones," *Monitor Republicano*, 13 July 1875, 4; "Hernández to P. Díaz (8 August 1871)" and "Club Porfirio Díaz to P. Díaz (12 July 1871)," in *Porfirio Díaz: Memorias*, 9.236 and 197–99; Gallardo, *Cuadro comparativo*, 5.

76. See Gallardo's *Cuadro comparativo de las elecciones de la república* for 1872, 1876, and 1877.

77. "Elecciones," *Monitor Republicano*, 9 July 1875, 1. Also see: "Editorial," *Siglo*

Table 13.2 Voting Clubs and Electoral Contestation

States	Percentage of Voting Districts with Strong Opposition		
	1867	1871	1876
Aguascalientes	25	50	0
Baja California	100	0	0
Chiapas	0	0	0
Distrito Federal	0	10	0
Guanajuato	27	77	22
Hidalgo	4	100	0
Jalisco	0	29	0
México	25	56	6
Michoacán	26	46	13
Morelos	25	100	25
Nuevo León	25	75	0
Oaxaca	68	100	0
Puebla	45	60	0
Queretaro	0	50	0
S. Luis Potosí	33	83	0
Sinaloa	0	100	0
Sonora	0	100	0
Tamaulipas	66	33	0
Tlaxcala	66	33	0
Veracruz	18	36	0
Zacatecas	4	40	20
Average	27	56	4

and towns. Municipal elections, in contrast, continue to attract local residents. The nation is identified with townships and with its administrative matters, rather than with congress and its laws.[78]

Political clubs now encouraged voters to place their sovereign will in local townships rather than in the central state. Municipal life became the new terrain in which voting clubs and political chiefs would challenge one another's federalist and centralist visions of democratic life.[79]

Local practices more than any other factor shaped the political geography of municipal life—even more than demographics or proximity to the central state in Mexico City, for which some contemporaries claimed primacy.[80] Municipal liberty flourished in Sonora, Durango, Nuevo León,

XIX, 3 July 1876, 1; "El pueblo no vota," *Monitor Republicano,* 24 June 1876, 1; "La abstención," *Siglo XIX,* 10 June 1876, 2.

78. "El ayuntamiento," *La Comuna Mexicana,* 20 August 1874, 2.

79. "Abusos electorales en la capital del estado de Hidalgo," *Monitor Republicano,* 31 July 1873, 3; Thomson with LaFrance, *Patriotism,* 206, 218, 221, 234, 261; and Perry, *Juárez and Díaz,* 205–6.

80. "Independencia de los municipios," *Siglo XIX,* 20 December 1871, 1; "Elecciones municipales," *La Comuna Mexicana,* 25 November 1874, 1.

and several other northern states; in Veracruz on the Gulf Coast; and in Hidalgo and Tlaxcala, near the nation's capital.[81] In these states, in urban and

> rural communities . . . the head of the family . . . is honored to serve [as township official]; the rest of the citizenry keeps an eye out on them and considers it their duty to ensure that they are fulfilling their obligations. . . . Although township officials come from modest backgrounds, from occupations such as doctors, priests, judges, tailors, barbers, and carpenters, they are respected and everyone in the community seeks their advice on matters ranging from domestic squabbles to public affairs. . . . If an official turns out to be incompetent or corrupt, the residents themselves suffer the consequences of their mistake. . . . As the saying goes: sinning brings with it its own worst penance. . . . This is why they take an interest in public life. . . .[82]

In contrast, township life remained moribund in Zacatecas, San Luis Potosí, Yucatán, Oaxaca, and Guerrero:

> Anyone who has visited these dreary townships comes away with an overwhelming feeling of sadness at the mere sight of so much passivity and backwardness. Democracy has not penetrated them, nor has liberty washed away the imprint left behind by the old regime.[83]

Municipal townships across the states of Aguascalientes, Puebla, and Mexico were in the process of renewing themselves.[84] Since the early 1870s, political chiefs and township officials had been struggling for control of municipal life.[85]

In January 1876, Porfirio Díaz and militia units loyal to him in the northern and southern parts of the country rebelled in defense of municipal townships and fair elections.[86] The "Tuxtepec revolt" was insignificant in military terms, but in political terms it prepared the way for the ruralization of democratic life.[87]

81. Alicia Hernández Chávez, *La tradición republicana del buen gobierno* (Mexico City, 1993), 68–85.

82. "El poder municipal," *Siglo XIX,* 29 March 1873, 1.

83. "Editorial," *Siglo XIX,* 17 June 1874, 1.

84. Chávez, *Tradición republicana,* 68–85.

85. "Editorial," *Siglo XIX,* 22 August 1876, 1: "We are in the midst of a phenomenon of the first order: the government has lost its prestige and earned the wrath of all social classes, especially those in the provinces where President Lerdo's appointed governors had ruled their state tyrannically. . . ."

86. "Plan de Tuxtepec," *Monitor Republicano,* 22 November 1876, 1.

87. Villegas, *Historia moderna de México,* 1.798–800; Laurens Perry, "The Dynamics of the Insurrection of Tuxtepec: Mexico in 1876" (Ph.D. dissertation, University of Michigan, 1971). Rather than a civil war, the uprising was a "vote of no confidence" against the government. The country's leading newspapers supported it. The uprising claimed few lives and destroyed little property, making it easy for Mexicans to return to civilian life.

Municipalizing and Indianizing Democracy

Following Tuxtepec, government officials and their middle-class urban supporters retained control of national politics, while rural people became active in local government like never before. In his memoirs, John Foster, chief of the U.S. delegation during the regimes of Presidents Díaz and Manuel Gonzalez, noted:

> During my seven years' residence in Mexico, I often visited the polling places on election days, but I never saw a citizen deposit a ballot, and rarely did I find any persons at the polls besides the election officers. An American merchant, who had resided many years in the city of Oaxaca and possessed the esteem of the people, in answer to my inquiry about the elections, said that one of the polling places was always held near his store, and that he generally passed most of the election day chatting in company with the officers of the "mesa" [election board]. He stated that it was a very rare occurrence that any citizen came to the polls to vote. . . . These comments . . . do not apply to all elections; often in local and municipal contests there is an animated campaign and a free exercise of the ballot.[88]

The municipalization of democratic life refigured the way Mexicans imagined and practiced popular sovereignty.

In the state of Mexico, where municipal life had been undeveloped, indigenous peoples and mixed-bloods in small farming communities became active in township life. Local residents living in small communities across the northern half of the state (Jilotepec, Acambaro, Timilpan, Acuclo, Temascalcingo, San Felipe, Jiquilpico, Ixtlahuaca, San Bartolo, San Miguel, Malinalco) created fourteen new townships.[89] They also participated in township elections. In the 1871 election, before Tuxtepec, less than 10 percent of Malinalco's residents had participated. By 1880, 38 percent of the residents of Aculco (six head-towns and sixteen neighborhoods), participated in municipal elections. Fifty-one percent of the voters worked as salaried peons (*jornaleros*) in landed estates; 9 percent described themselves as potters (*alfareros*); 8 percent were small farmers (*agricultores*); the remaining voters came from equally humble back-

---

88. John Foster, *Diplomatic Memoirs*, vol. 1 (Boston, 1909), 54–55.

89. María del C. Salinas Sandoval, "Transformación o permanencia del gobierno municipal: Estado de México" (Ph.D. dissertation, El Colegio de México, 1993), 80–81. Townships were created in three ways: fusion, secession, and annexation. In some cases, several hamlets would fuse and become a single community, giving it the 4,000 residents required by law to establish a township. In other cases, a community would break away from an existing township and create its own, or a community would incorporate itself to an existing township.

grounds—charcoal-makers, mule-pack drivers, haulers, and domestics.[90] The proliferation of townships provided rural peoples in Mexico and other states an opportunity to shed their old habits and become active in public life.

Across the highlands of Puebla, another state where municipal life had languished, indigenous peoples in small towns such as Cuetzalan, Zautla, and Zacatlán became active in local government:

> a certain brand of egalitarian liberalism, emphasizing self-government and constitutional guarantees against arbitrary government, held a strong appeal among the Nahua population, especially within barrios (hamlets) subject to cabeceras (head-towns) controlled by non-Indians. The . . . popular elections for municipal councils offered barrios an opportunity to increase their autonomy from cabeceras. . . . Popular elections even introduced a possibility for the barrios, where most people lived, to propel one of their own into the municipal presidency, as had occurred in Zautla in 1878 and 1884 with the election of José Máximo and Manuel Francisco Bonifacio. All this rocked the traditional hierarchy of ethnic power in the Sierra.[91]

Municipal life in these communities shifted the balance of power away from mixed-bloods toward indigenous peoples, and away from head-towns toward surrounding hamlets.

In Chihuahua, Sonora, Hidalgo, Tlaxcala, and other states with a long tradition of municipal liberty, townships redefined the office of political chief. Chiefs were downgraded and no longer allowed to serve as township president, collect municipal taxes, undertake public works projects, and oversee elections (see below).[92] Instead of having the state governor appoint all the chiefs, local residents voted for them. These elections were organized by townships and based on direct rather than indirect voting, making it difficult for political chiefs to intervene in them.[93] Townships were also granted the right to petition congress, which gave them another way of checking chiefs and removing them from office. As agents of the central state, political chiefs remained loyal to the president and the governor, but in order to implement federal policies in the region they served, chiefs had to collaborate with township officials; those who did not found it difficult to fulfill their duties and ran the risk of losing their jobs.[94]

Indigenous peoples from Tlaxcala, Hidalgo, Michoacán, Guanajuato,

90. Sandoval, "Transformación o permanencia," 114–30.
91. Thomson with LaFrance, *Patriotism,* 258–59.
92. Thomson with LaFrance, *Patriotism,* 202, 209, 250.
93. Sandoval, "Transformación o permanencia," 111–27; and Chávez, *Tradición republicana,* 68–85.
94. Thomson with LaFrance, *Patriotism,* 202, 209, 234, 250.

and other states with a strong tradition of municipal liberty organized the country's first nationwide political association: the Gran Comité Comunero (1877). The Comité began with about 17,120 members and had local branches in eighty-six communities; the majority (65 percent) of the branches were in the state of Guanajuato.[95] The following year, indigenous peoples from Mexico and adjacent states organized a second, smaller association: the Sociedad de los Pueblos Unidos (1878).[96] Both groups had grown out of the interpersonal ties forged by members in townships, civic and economic associations, and militia units.

The Comité and the Sociedad worked to secure land titles for members. Membership dues were used to pay lawyers and to send local residents (with power of attorney) to the state capital and all the way to Mexico City to do research in the National Archive, where land titles and maps were kept.[97] After a lengthy stay in the capital, Leonardo Pérez returned to his hometown of San Pedro, in the district of Jilotepec (México). He was greeted by hundreds of residents at the edge of the forest and escorted for several kilometers to the main plaza with "music and whistles as if he were a saint."[98] When Cayetano Rodríguez returned to Santiago with copies of land titles, the political chief complained: "residents treat him as if he were an official; they have lost all respect for me."[99] In addition to protecting the property rights of rural peoples, local branches of the Sociedad and the Comite, as one of their petitions reads, demanded that

> the government suppress any ruling or decision that has been based on the notion that we are minors, since they violate our interests and rights.[100]

The political struggle for land was part of a broader cultural struggle over the moral meaning of citizenship. In their petitions for land and water rights, members of the Comité and the Sociedad, including those who lived near the San Nicolás and Santa Catarina estates in the state of Mexico, used the term "civil society."[101] Civic Catholic terminology circulated even in small farming communities deep in the countryside.

The Comité and the Sociedad also assisted farmers without land titles

95. *Defensa del derecho territorial patrio elevado por el pueblo mexicano al Congreso General de la Nación* (Mexico City, 1877).

96. "Boletín," *Monitor Republicano,* 20 November 1878, 2.

97. "Aparece la luz," *El Hijo del Trabajo,* 30 September 1877, 1.

98. "San Pedro Denxi al Ayuntamiento de Aculco (2 August 1877)," quoted in Sandoval, "Transformación o permanencia," 295.

99. "Presidente Municipal de Chapa de Mota al Presidente Municipal de Aculco (18 May 1877)," quoted in Sandoval, "Transformación o permanencia," 287.

100. "Exposición de varios pueblos al presidente de la república (24 September 1877)," quoted in Sandoval, "Transformación o permanencia," 331–46.

101. "Justas aspiraciones," *El Hijo del Trabajo,* 11 November 1877, 1–2.

who had owned their plots "from time immemorial" and were losing them to landowners who had paid political chiefs to obtain fraudulent deeds on them. In these cases, the Comité and the Sociedad organized local residents into armed units and took over, surveyed, and divided landed estates and their riverbeds, woodlands, and pastures. Before the coming of the Comité and the Sociedad, there had been on average three land takeovers per year between 1872 to 1876; for the years from 1877 to 1881, when the two groups were functioning, the rate increased to sixteen per year; and after they dissolved, the number fell back to six per year. The majority of these takeovers took place in the states in which the Comité and the Sociedad were strongest.[102] Political chiefs, estate owners, petty tradesmen, parish priests, and a great many farmers reacted to them by closing ranks and convincing state governors, congressional deputies, and the president that the Comité and the Sociedad were in the process of organizing a "caste war" throughout the countryside. Rural guards were sent to "pacify" the countryside, and congress declared itself unqualified to evaluate any more petitions from rural communities or to draw up any legislation related to land reform.[103]

By 1878, the Comité and the Sociedad had withdrawn their support from President Díaz's government, but rather than retreating to civil and economic society, the usual pattern for Mexicans, they remained active in political life. Díaz's government, like all earlier regimes, considered indigenous peoples irrational and, therefore, "unrepresentable" as citizens. The Comité and the Sociedad challenged the state by organizing an alternative legislature, the "Indigenous Congress," and drafting a radically different constitution, the "Mexican Confederation of United Peoples," thus providing indigenous peoples a new institution in which to deposit their own sense of sovereignty. This new charter provided a blueprint for turning Mexico into a confederation.[104] In this new government, townships would be made into a "fourth power," and would be granted institutional autonomy from and parity with the other three branches of government (executive, legislative, and judicial). The Constitution also required members to renounce military violence and to rely only on legal means to bring about the political and administrative changes they wanted.

The Indigenous Congress met annually between 1877 and 1880 in

102. Leticia Reina, *Las luchas populares en México en el siglo XIX* (Mexico City: Secretaría de Educación Pública, 1983), 13–32, 165–68.

103. Moisés González Navarro, *Historia moderna de México: El Porfiriato, vida social* (Mexico City: Editorial Hermes, 1957), 207–8; and Paul Vanderwood, *Disorder and Progress: Bandits, Police, and Mexican Development* (Lincoln: University of Nebraska Press).

104. "Los pueblos unidos de la Confederación Mexicana," *Monitor Republicano*, 14 June 1879, 1.

Mexico City. Hundreds of delegates from countless farming communities across the country attended each meeting.[105] According to the organizers, the congress was far more democratic than any of the existing state institutions:

> our national institutions claim to be committed to sovereignty of the people, and to the principle of majority rule. According to our most recent census, our population is composed mainly of mixed-bloods and indigenes, with the latter numbering nine million and, therefore, in the majority. This is why national sovereignty resides with our country's indigenous peoples.[106]

These congresses provided, for the first time ever, a nationwide institution in which rural townships and those they represented could deposit their individual and collective will, withdrawn long ago from the existing legislature and other branches of the central government. In symbolic terms, the Indigenous Congresses were making a bid to represent the will of the nation. The conservative and moderate press described the 1879 Congress in this way:

> last week a great many Indians came to Mexico as representatives of their communities, all of which are involved in struggles over land. They have come to establish an Agrarian League, a type of (Paris) Commune, one that will have horrific consequences on our republic: a caste war.[107]

Prior to each congress, the central government instructed political chiefs to arrest delegates living in their region. In the district of Jilotepec (Mexico), local chiefs arrested the delegation from Villa Carbón and nearby communities.[108] Democratic life flourished at the roots of political society while authoritarianism became entrenched at the top and down through the middle of the pyramid.

The Resurgence of Authoritarian Politics

The spread of rural unrest and the inability of the landed elite to regain control of the countryside made the governments of Manuel González and Porfirio Díaz doubly determined to turn Mexico into a centralist regime. State officials and politicians had broad support among the elite and non-elite, who were just as frightened by rumors of an impending caste war, and with good reason: several racial-ethnic conflicts had erupted in parts

105. "La cuestión indígena," *El Hijo del Trabajo*, 1 June 1879, 1; "Los pueblos unidos," 1.
106. "Carta de Tiburcio Montiel," *El Monitor Republicano*, 26 June 1879, 2.
107. "Congreso de indígenas," *La Voz de México*, 14 March 1879, 1.
108. "Indígenas del estado de México," *Monitor Republicano*, 18 October 1879, 1.

of the country, which led public intellectuals across the entire political continuum to assume that this was the beginning of a civil war similar to the one that had pitted north against south and torn apart the United States, a country far more stable and powerful than Mexico.

Despite enormous pressure from radical democrats, Díaz's Tuxtepec government did not purge any public officials from the federal, state, and municipal bureaucracy, although most of them had been loyal to the deposed government and had also collaborated with the French during the occupation:

> The ministers, customs officers, treasury officers, pay-masters, and all the political chiefs and local administrators in all the districts and states across the country . . . are the same ones who had served in Lerdo's government. . . .[109]

They had only basic reading, writing, and arithmetic skill, but because white-collar professionals remained in short supply, politicians depended on them to maintain control of the electoral field and to modernize the state.

Public employees organized themselves into a political party, the Junta Central Porfirista. This was the first time in Mexico's history that public bureaucrats had a party of their own; it also marked the first time a nationwide party had taken root. The Junta surfaced and recruited most of its leaders from local voting clubs in Díaz's home state of Oaxaca and sent them to staff government offices throughout the country:

> Oaxacans have been assigned to serve in congress . . . as state governors, as justices of the peace, as political chiefs, as treasury officials, as tax administrators and inspectors, as secretaries general in all branches of the federal government, [and so on]. They are for the state what the Jesuits are for the Pope: keepers of the faith and guardians of the dogma: "Abolish politics, and replace it with Administration."[110]

By the late 1880s, "scientific politics" had triumphed.[111] The Junta accomplished this by establishing local chapters at all levels of the federal, state, and municipal governments throughout the country. Composed primarily of public bureaucrats, politicians, and government officials, the Junta recruited heavily among the new middle class in major cities and

109. "Jesús Cuentas to P. Díaz (26 January 1877)," in *Porfirio Díaz: Memorias,* 17.63–65.

110. Francisco Bulnes, *El verdadero Díaz y la revolución* (Mexico City: E. Gomez de la Puente, 1920), 181–82.

111. Leopoldo Zea, *El positivismo en México* (Mexico City: Universidad Nacional Autónoma de México, 1968); and William D. Raat, *El positivismo durante el Porfiriato: 1870–1910* (Mexico City: Secretaría de Educación Pública, 1975).

smaller towns across the country. The majority of the recruits had lived with with disregard for the state, but the Junta incorporated them into political life. The Junta also channeled them into state-centered forms of life and instilled certain authoritarian habits, thereby limiting the pool of potential recruits for antigovernment clubs.

Unlike previous clubs, the Junta was an appendage of the state and was committed to defending government policies. In the 1880 presidential elections, Manuel González, the Junta's candidate, won with 78 percent of the votes. During the 1884 elections, Porfirio Díaz ran unopposed; during the 1892 elections, he won 99 percent of the votes.[112] In addition to putting an end to electoral contestation, the Junta pressured the government to reform the electoral system by increasing the number of electors and by raising literacy and income requirements for voters. Between 1880 and 1892, the number of district-level college electors rose from 15,026 to 17,301 (one elector per 500 voters). In other words, the government had extended the franchise to 1.14 million new voters. However, because suffrage laws were now stricter, voting was restricted to the elite and middle-class sectors of society—the same members who formed the backbone of the Junta.[113] This "desktatorship," as it was called, incorporated the privileged few into the political system and in this respect increased their participation while at the same time putting an end to electoral contestation.

Public employees, the most active members in the Junta, pressured Díaz's government to increase the size of the federal, state, and municipal bureaucracy. Government administrators accounted for 20 percent of the state's annual budget in 1868; by 1910 they took 40 percent of all federal monies, an increase that benefited mostly white-collar professionals. In 1868, 12 percent of professionals were on the state's payroll; in 1876, the proportion had risen to 16 percent. By 1910, roughly 60 percent of Mexico's middle class was employed by the state.[114] In a private gathering at the home of Jorge Hammeken Mejía, President Díaz described these civil servants:

> they wake up and arrive late to the office; spend their day searching for patrons [who might promote them]; they often take paid sick-leaves to attend bullfights with friends . . . they are keenly interested in obtaining

112. Villegas, *Historia moderna de México,* 2.8–10, 39–47, 313–14, 362–65, 442, 570, 595–96, 602–3; Carmagnani and Chávez, "La ciudadanía orgánica," 371–401.

113. Villegas, *Historia moderna de México,* 2.8–10, 39–47, 313–14, 362–65, 442, 570, 595–96, 602–3.

114. Bulnes, *El verdadero Díaz,* 42. A mathematician by training, Bulnes was also a committed public intellectual. His figures are probably inflated; nevertheless, they are useful for understanding the subordination of the middle class by the state. Jose Maria Vigil, who had radically different views, and other contemporaries made very similar observations. See: Villegas, *Historia moderna de México,* 1.410–11, 423, 672.

public awards and special honors from prestigious institutions [to improve their social standing]; they marry young, have lots of children, and spend more than they make . . . thereby driving themselves further into debt. The head of these large families are the government's most loyal supporters; they are motivated by fear [of unemployment] and their own inertia rather than by oppression. . . . The bureaucratic slave, white or dark-skinned, is abominable. Haunted by the same ghost of unemployment, he lives in constant fear that his chief does not consider him loyal and in favor of [the president's] reelection. A bit of malicious gossip is enough to sink him and his family forever.[115]

These white-collar professionals enabled politicians to bureaucratize the state and to shift the balance of power within it from the military to the civilian wing.[116]

The Junta's members also staffed municipal townships throughout the country. The township of Tetela (population 13,000), in the highlands of Puebla, provided employment to 340 of its residents (3 percent). In addition to receiving a salary, township officials acquired public lands at below market price; obtained land titles to plots owned by farmers without legal documentation; and secured state contracts to build or repair public roads and bridges in the area. The Junta's local members enabled political chiefs to regain their power and turned townships into centers of antidemocratic life:

township elections, like all others, are left each year to the same individuals; their names are so firmly planted in our memory that anyone can recite them at any time. . . . Political chiefs, public employees, and elected officials . . . always pick the same elector for the same college each year. They occupy these posts in perpetuity . . . [and have] the right to pass them on to their descendants after their death.[117]

The same pattern was also evident in other nearby towns, including Tlatlauqi and Texiutlán.

The Junta's sociopolitical tentacles extended to the National Congress and the office of state governor. Roughly 62 percent of the congressmen were from Oaxaca. They had taken up residence in other states and now represented those states in congress. The Junta's local chapter selected one of their own to serve as state governor, and had the difficult task of getting the state's oligarchy, many of whom were members of the party, to agree on the candidate, who

---

115. Bulnes, *El verdadero Díaz,* 39, 48.

116. Porfirio Díaz, *Informe que en el último día de su periodo constitucional a sus compatriotas* (Mexico City, 1896). Also see Bulnes, *El verdadero Díaz,* 33, 165–68, 292–330.

117. *El Progreso de Zacatlán,* 1 February 1884, quoted in Thomson with LaFrance, *Patriotism,* 243–44.

relied on personal friends among the state's great landlords, industrialists, and merchants to secure letters of recommendation [as required by the president].[118]

The Junta also had the delicate task of mediating between the state's elite and the central government. As of 1910, two-thirds of all state governors (26) had been in office for fifteen or more years, an indication of the Junta's success in accomplishing both tasks.[119] Prior to elections for state governor,

> the [candidate] and local notables travel together to Mexico City to confer privately with the president. . . . But sometimes it is impossible for them to meet; in these cases the president sends them a telegram with his instructions. . . .[120]

The thousands of kilometers of railroad tracks and telegraph lines that now crisscrossed the country served at once to extend and to centralize the Junta's sociopolitical networks. The Junta's "indirect" networks were far more flexible and efficient than the "direct" networks used by voting clubs prior to the 1870s.[121] Even technology seemed to be on the side of dictatorship.

As long as Mexicans continued to live "with their backs toward the state," they would not be able to keep state officials from propagating authoritarian practices across political society:

> The Mexican people have demonstrated repeatedly that they have the power and the will to prevent dictatorship from becoming rooted in our country, but we have not been able to extirpate it once and for all. Each time it appears, the public has exploded against it.[122]

The practice of antipolitics weakened democratic life; however, it also enabled citizens to continue imagining and practicing sovereignty of the people even under adverse conditions.

118. Bulnes, *El verdadero Díaz*, 44.
119. Bulnes, *El verdadero Díaz*, 357.
120. "Gobernadores," *El Lunes*, 18 July 1881, 1.
121. "J. I. Álvarez to B. Juárez (6 July Up to that point, clubs had relied on personal couriers to communicate with each other, but letters were often lost or intercepted.
122. "Organización del Partido Liberal," *El Combate*, 24 June 1880, 2.

CHAPTER 14

Fragile Democracy and Tattered Nationhood: Peruvian Political Society

The 1854 popular rebellion in Peru contributed to the decentralization of administrative life, enabling Peruvians to establish municipal townships and voting clubs throughout the country. Citizens used both to challenge the army's continued control of political life at the local, state, and national levels:

> Citizens want a civilian for president. Since Independence, we have been ruled by military men, but we are now ready to resolve our problems and settle our differences differently than in the past. . . . From now on, any civilian government will have to secure support from the people and . . . public opinion rather than from the army.[1]

The proliferation of townships and clubs also encouraged Peruvians to break with their old habits and to become active in public life. The invasion and occupation of the country by Chilean troops (1879–1883) put an end to these developments. During the war, patriotic Peruvians organized guerrilla groups in several regions; these regions offered rebels a place to practice self-rule and collective sovereignty at a time when the rest of the country was under foreign rule. For Peruvians, the formation of municipal townships, electoral clubs, and guerrilla groups represented a major political innovation; however, all of them proved to be short-lived and without broad support. The overwhelming majority of Peruvians remained as antipolitical, antidemocratic, and antinationalist as they had been in the first half of the century.

---

1. Unos Republicanos, "Candidatura civil," *El Comercio,* 19 June 1861, 2.

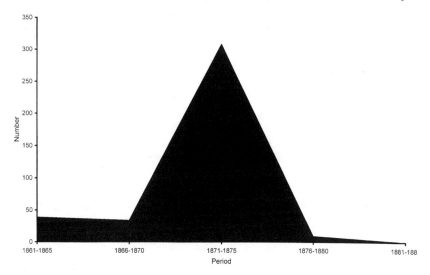

Figure 14.1   New Political Clubs, 1861–1885

Socio-institutional Structures

Peruvians created 390 new voting clubs between 1861 and 1885, almost all of them in preparation for the 1872 presidential election (fig. 14.1).[2] A meager 35 clubs appeared in 1862 and another 40 during the 1868 election—not nearly enough to restructure institutional life and daily practices across political society. However, in the months before the 1872 election, Peruvians created roughly 320 new clubs, signaling the start of a new political era. The Chilean-Peruvian War, however, put an end to the electoral cycle and halted the spread of associative life. It would be three decades before Peruvian political life regained its civic momentum.

There are several reasons why Peruvians organized so few voting clubs between 1856 and 1870. Some were rooted in the country's past, the rest were rooted in the state of affairs at the time. Although the 1854 rebellion contributed to the spread of associative life in civic and economic society, it was less successful in altering public practices in political society, where the legacy of colonialism remained entrenched. In the words of Francisco Laso, one of the country's most influential publicists,

> citizens do not yet understand that they should participate in the political life of our republic. The habits they have inherited from the

2. Unless otherwise indicated, the data for the figure, tables, and map in this chapter are from Carlos A. Forment, "Databank on Associative Life in Nineteenth Century Peru" (Unpublished working document, Princeton University, 1997).

colonial past remain with them, and make them assume that the government should continue to take care of everything as the government of Spain did. These indolent and egoistic persons have no right whatsoever to criticize our public life. If they want to change things they must realize that they have power and are responsible for steering the state. . . .[3]

Laso's remarks were directed primarily toward the elite, but they applied just as well to the non-elite.

Peru was no longer a military dictatorship, but the army continued to have enormous influence over most government institutions at the local, state, and federal levels, which discouraged even the most civic-minded citizens from participating in political life.[4] Township officers were responsible for organizing elections and used a variety of fraudulent methods—stuffing ballot boxes; destroying marked ballots; bribing plebeian and indigenous voters with liquor, food, and money in exchange for their ballots—in order to maintain control of the electoral field.[5] Electoral corruption was especially widespread in rural areas:

> The majority of Indians in the countryside . . . are hostile toward officials; however, they will oppose their clever tricks only in the most extreme cases. The rest of the time they capitulate and vote for the candidate they are told to vote for. Instead of giving Indians ballots, election officials will often keep and mark them themselves. . . .[6]

The same things occurred in most cities and small towns throughout the provinces.

The voting clubs that appeared during the 1860s were neither numerically significant nor sufficiently developed organizationally to be able to challenge the government's monopoly of the electoral field. In fact, they were so weak that club members had to resort to physical violence in order to wrest control of the voting booth from state officials:

3. Francisco Laso, "Croquis sobre las elecciones," *La Revista de Lima* 3 (1863): 104–5.

4. "Consejos," *La República*, 10 January 1864, 2–3: "nearly all our prefects and subprefects are in the military. In fact, the practice is so common that until now I had assumed that the Constitution required it." Also see: Jorge Basadre, "Los hombres de traje negro," in *Letras*, vol. 1 (Lima, 1929), 29–59.

5. For numerical estimates and descriptive accounts of ballot-box stuffing during the 1862, 1868, and 1876 elections see: "Cuadro sinóptico de las elecciones de 1862," *El Comercio*, 26 June 1862, 2; "Elecciones," *El Comercio*, 1 October 1868, 2; and M. A. Fuentes, *Estadística electoral y parlamentaria del Perú: 1870–1876* (Lima, 1878), 1–30.

6. Ernst Middendorf, *Perú: Observaciones y estudios del país y sus habitantes durante una permanencia de 25 años*, vol. 1 (Lima: Universidad Nacional Mayor de San Marcos, 1973), 251. Also see: "La política sin máscara," *El Comercio*, 6 December 1871, 2; "Editorial," *El Comercio*, 29 August 1877, 2.

Brute violence has taken over the electoral field. Instead of relying on the will of the people to decide public affairs, we have been forced to rely on violence, since this is the only way of winning an election.[7]

The following description of voting day in several parishes from Lima is worth quoting:

> the plebeians spent last night drinking, and at dawn they armed themselves and gathered in the main plaza of the parish. Once they were assembled, they moved in and assaulted the electoral table, taking the urn and all the marked ballots inside it. . . . There was always intense competition among rivals to control these tables. Whoever triumphed was sure to win the election. . . . The most effective way of gaining control of them was by fighting, shooting and expelling your opponent from the plaza. . . . Those who were allowed to vote enjoyed the benefits of an orderly election, albeit a simulacra of a real one.[8]

Electoral violence in the provinces was even worse—it resembled the type of "ritualized combat" practiced by indigenous peoples that was discussed in an earlier chapter. The majority of Peruvians, elite and nonelite, in urban and rural areas, rarely participated in elections, since the "benefits" of voting were not worth the "risks."[9] Prior to 1872, voting clubs never succeeded in winning a single municipal or presidential election. Members of these clubs used physical violence against state officials to challenge their control of political life, but in the long run this tactic may have discouraged their own sympathizers from participating in elections, thus ironically strengthening the government's monopoly over the electoral field.

The 1872 presidential election signaled the beginning of mass politics in Peru and encouraged a great many citizens to become politically active. This was the first time an antigovernment candidate (Manuel Pardo) had won—a victory made possible by the hundreds of political clubs that had been organized across the country. This flurry of associative life stemmed more from a change in the socio-moral judgment of citizens than from

7. "Sociedad Orden e Independencia," *El Comercio,* 7 July 1859, 2. Also see J. M. Quimper, "Memoria que el Secretario de Estado . . . presenta al Congreso," *El Peruano,* 23 February 1867, 1.

8. Manuel Vicente Villarán, "Costumbres Electorales," in his *Páginas escogidas* (Lima: n.p., 1962), 198. For descriptions of electoral violence in other parts of the country see all the articles titled "Elecciones" in *La República* published on the following dates: 15 November 1863, 4–5; 22 November 1863, 3; and 6 December 1863, 3. Also see "En Tarapacá," *La República,* 3 January 1863, 6; and N. N. and N. N., *Elecciones populares en Trujillo* (Lima, 1860).

9. Frank O'Gorman, "Campaign Rituals and Ceremonies: The Social Meaning of Elections in England, 1780–1860," *Past and Present* 135 (May 1992): 79–115, on the relationship between violence and voting.

any dramatic transformation in electoral laws.[10] A member of Lima's professional class summarized his own change:

> Before now, I had never belonged to any political club and had been only concerned with my own career, but I have decided to participate [in this election].[11]

The majority of Peruvians now saw themselves as rational adults capable of self-rule, and they were prepared to demilitarize the state and to invest their sense of sovereignty in government institutions:

> the army is no longer the main symbol of public life; it has become a second-class career like any other. From now on, the country's true sons are represented by artisans, merchants, agriculturalists, and anyone who dedicates himself to scientific and literary pursuits.[12]

In order to accomplish this, citizens for the first time in their history organized hundreds of voting clubs and used them to participate in elections.[13] Manuel Pardo, the Civilian Party's presidential candidate, summarized the change in his countrymen:

> Until today, the military government had centralized public life and had succeeded in liquidating any trace of personal initiative. Each man felt like an isolated and helpless atom, and each believed it was impossible to challenge [the state]. . . . However, the day we began to join together we became aware that we were in fact the source of all power.[14]

The proliferation of voting clubs and the incorporation of so many voters made it difficult for the military to retain control of the electoral field and encouraged large numbers of Peruvians to break with their old habits.

The size and distribution of voting clubs in the country varied considerably. Table 14.1 provides an estimate of the number of dues-paying members in a large sample of voting clubs.[15] Thirty-five percent of all clubs had more than a hundred affiliates; 34 percent had between 61 and 100 members; 30 percent had between 21 and 60; the remaining 1 percent

---

10. Jorge Basadre, *Elecciones y centralismo en el Perú* (Lima: Universidad del Pacífica, 1980), 1–30; Gabriella Chiaramonti, "Reformas electorales y centralización del espacio político nacional en el Perú: 1860–1919" (Unpublished typescript, University of Padua, 1993); Vincent Peloso, "Liberals, Electoral Reform, and the Popular Vote in Mid-Nineteenth-Century Peru," in *Liberals, Politics and Power,* ed. Vincent Peloso and Barbara A. Tenenbaum (Athens: University of Georgia, 1996), 186–211.

11. "Elecciones: Dos partidos," *El Comercio,* 4 October 1866, 2.

12. Guillermo Seoane, *La revolución de julio* (Lima, 1872), 6.

13. "La prensa," *El Correo del Perú,* 11 January 1874, 1.

14. Manuel Pardo, "Discurso," *El Comercio,* 6 August 1872, 2.

15. This sample includes 14 percent of all the voting clubs in my databank that appeared in 1872.

Table 14.1   Membership in Political Clubs,
1856–1885

Number of Members	Percentage of Associations
1–20	1
21–60	30
61–100	34
101 or more	35

had less than 20. The clubs were large enough to constitute an effective challenge to local government officials.

Associative life spread unevenly and took root unevenly (map 14.1). Fifty-four percent of all political clubs surfaced in Lima and Callao on the central coast, indicating that associative life remained very concentrated. The remaining 46 percent were scattered thinly across the provinces. Of this second group, 38 percent were in the northern provinces of Ancash, La Libertad, and Lambayeque; 25 percent were in Ayacucho and Cuzco in the south; and 14 percent were clustered in Junín and Huancavelica in the center of the country. The remaining clubs (23 percent) were scattered across the other eleven states.

Associative Practices in Political Society

Citizens practiced government-centered politics mainly in municipal townships and voting clubs, relying on those institutions to demilitarize political life. During the war with Chile, Peruvians adopted a Jacobin notion of politics and construed themselves as "the nation-at-arms," which led them to practice democracy primarily in guerrilla groups. In this section, I examine all three types of practices and forms of political life.

Regional Councils, Municipal Liberty, and Administrative Decentralization

After the 1854 popular rebellion, citizens throughout the provinces demanded that the central government decentralize administrative life by creating regional councils and municipal townships. Councils were supposed to provide the elite of each state a place to discuss common concerns pertaining to the socioeconomic and institutional development of each region and to pressure the federal government to provide them with the financial resources and technical assistance they needed to modernize public life in the provinces. Civic-minded democrats all over the country regarded these councils as the ideal vehicle for transforming Peru into a

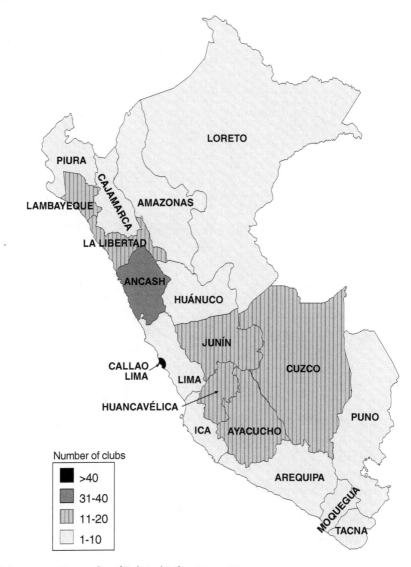

Map 14.1   Geography of Political Life, 1861–1885

federalist republic. When these councils were first formed in 1856, Francisco de Paula Gonzales, a supporter of them, described them as

> the best hope we have for republican democracy. . . . While absolutist governments centralize power, the goal of democratic regimes is to create multiple centers of authority and to make each one responsible for

protecting local interests. . . . This is why during the 1854 revolution, the people demanded the creation of regional councils. . . .[16]

The councils provided Peruvians with their first experience in federalism, but they were abolished a year or so after they were created. The authoritarian elite in each state had gained control of them and used them to forge alliances with military chieftains in their region in order to prevent voting clubs from democratizing political life. The great constitutional lawyer and scholar José Santiesteban, author of the most widely used textbook in the country's law schools, described these regional councils as "a congress for oligarchs."[17] Local notables (*gamonales*) used these councils to implant a decentralized and despotic system of rule—one that Tocqueville never imagined, since he assumed that local autonomy and political liberty always went together. Federalism in Peru was fraught with political danger for civic-minded democrats.

The 1854 popular movement also succeeded in getting congress to establish municipal townships. In 1856, the central government approved the "Municipal Law," authorizing any town with a thousand or more residents to establish a township; citizens residing in communities smaller than this were incorporated and represented by the township nearest to them.[18] The law resembled closely one that was implemented about the same time in post-Napoleonic France and that had contributed greatly to the decentralization of administrative life in that country. The Peruvian government almost overnight established more than 600 townships across the country. The number of new townships and the size of each varied by region and was, as I noted above, determined mainly by demographic factors (table 14.2).The southern states—that is, Cuzco, Puno, Ayacucho, and Arequipa—accounted for one-third of all municipal governments. The states in the central region of the country accounted for an additional 31 percent, followed by the northern states (26 percent) and Lima-Callao (10 percent). Most municipal governments had between five and seven delegates, although Lima, the largest township in the country, had almost ten times as many officials.

Townships provided citizens a place to break with their anti-civic habits and to acquire democratic inclinations. Initially, the vast majority

16. Francisco de P. Gonzales Vigil, "Juntas Departamentales," *El Comercio*, 23 February 1859, 1. Also see: Manuel T. Ureta, Pío B. Mesa, and Rafael Hostas, *Ley orgánica de 2 de enero que detalla la organización y modo de las Juntas Departamentales* (Lima, 1857).

17. José Silva Santiesteban, *Curso de derecho constitucional* (Lima, 1874), 355. Also see: Manuel A. Fuentes, *Guía del viajero de Lima* (Lima, 1861), 56–64; "Consejos," *La República*, 10 January 1864, 2–3; and Jorge Basadre, *Historia de la República del Perú*, vol. 5 (Lima: Editorial Universitaria, 1961), 2052–57.

18. *Ley orgánica de municipalidades* (Lima, 1856).

Table 14.2 Regional Distribution of
Municipal Townships, 1856–1860

Regions	Number of Townships	Average and Total Number of Township Officials
North	161 (26%)	5 (805)
Central	196 (31%)	6 (1176)
Lima and Callao	62 (10%)	7 (434)
South	210 (33%)	5 (1050)
Total	629 (100%)	5 (3465)

of citizens, even in Lima where the nation's elite resided, remained unin-terested in municipal life. Their apathy was so great that the editors of *El Comercio* rebuked them in print:

> The apathy and coldness of our citizens is astonishing. They have re-fused to occupy their posts in the municipality even after they were summoned repeatedly. Yesterday, we even heard them complaining about the lack of municipal services. . . . Although they always make ostentatious displays of patriotism, when the institution really needs them they do little for it. For the last time, I implore you to go and fulfill your duties—if, that is, you still can overcome your egoism . . . and have any appreciation for public opinion. . . .[19]

Municipal life in the provinces remained moribund in the early years of the townships' existence. Tomás Dávila summarized the situation: "much has been said in favor [of townships], but in many places they remain nonexistent and have not provided citizens with any services."[20]

Citizens became active in municipal life shortly thereafter. During his month-long tour of the state of Piura in the far north, Próspero Pereira Gamba, a public intellectual from Lima, wrote:

> As evidence that decentralization is occurring in our country, I am de-lighted to report that there is a functioning township in 21 of the 24 dis-tricts [in the state of Piura]. . . . They are having a beneficial effect on public life; however, in order for them to survive, they must be given greater autonomy and control over local affairs. Until this happens, res-idents will continue to rely on the central state to fulfill all their needs.[21]

19. "Municipalidad," *El Comercio*, 25 April 1857, 3.
20. Tomás Dávila, "Instrucción Primaria," *Revista de Lima*, 13 June 1860, 590–91.
21. Próspero Pereira Gamba, "Memoria geográfica sobre el Departamento de Piura," *Revista de Lima* 6 (1862): 241–46.

Municipal life had even taken root in the southern Andean highlands in Puno, the poorest state in the country. Clements R. Markham, the naturalist, who spent a year or so in the region collecting flora and fauna, noted:

> I saw signs of municipal activity. . . . At Lampa, they were attempting to reestablish a manufactory of glazed tiles in that town; in Azangaro, they were collecting subscriptions for a bridge across the river, one of the members of the body had contributed half the required sum; and in Sandia they were drawing up a report on the state of the roads, with an estimate of the sum required for thorough repair and bridging. . . . The municipal townships of Sandia and Quiaca, especially the latter one, took measures to prevent me from procuring a supply of chinchona plants or seeds, influenced by motives which exposed their ignorance of political economy, while it displayed their activity and patriotic zeal.[22]

Townships were fast becoming part of the public landscape and providing residents an opportunity to transform themselves into civic-minded citizens.

Despite the relative success of the townships, there is no denying that municipal life was from the very outset fraught with difficulties. Some of them were financial, others were racial, civic, and political; all were closely related. To finance the creation of townships, the central state authorized local officials to nationalize and transfer all the money and property owned by religious confraternities to the municipal government. By the late 1860s most of the initial resistance had subsided and the law had been implemented in most places, providing townships the startup capital they needed to pay for schooling, welfare relief, public works, and other municipal services.[23] From here onward, townships were expected to become financially self-sufficient by collecting municipal taxes from local residents, from property owners, from business and professional licenses, from the rental of public lands, and from bullfights and other sources.

Most Peruvians, especially those in the Andes where indigenous peoples predominated, were simply too poor to pay their taxes, which is why so many townships were bankrupt and unable to provide citizens with even the most basic services. In mid-1869, Manuel González de la Rosa, a government official of uncommon dedication, spent a month or so vis-

---

22. Clements R. Markham, *Travels in Peru and India* (London, 1862), 223–24.
23. Mark Thurner, "From Two Nations to One Divided: The Contradictions of Nation-Building in Andean Peru; the Case of Huaylas" (Ph.D. dissertation, University of Wisconsin, 1993), 107–8, for a case study of Huaylas.

iting townships in the states of Puno, Cuzco, Ayacucho, and Arequipa. In his report, he urged the central state to provide them with funding.[24] The president and members of the National Congress had already approved a bill allocating to townships a portion of the income the state had earned from the recent sale of guano.

Most of these funds, however, were used to subsidize wealthy townships that served fair-skinned creoles rather than the poorest townships, which served indigenous peoples. Members of Cuzco's municipal government complained bitterly and repeatedly about this but without any success:

> If we are all equal under the law, then all our countrymen deserve to . . . share in the same sufferings and delights. . . . Since our guano islands began yielding fabulous amounts of money, Congress, which has the responsibility for financing public works and other projects related to the needs of our countrymen . . . has deprived [Cuzco and the other provinces in the Andes their] due share . . . while allocating enormous sums to the townships of Arequipa, Tacna, Lima, and Callao. . . .[25]

Even the bishop of Puno, José Ambrosio Huerta, who had oposed the creation of townships because it involved the confiscation of funds from confraternities and so undermined the Church, now invoked religious arguments in defense of municipal life in the Andes:

> Would Peruvians be better off if they had been transformed into a nation of merchants like England, which has so many paupers? Today, almost all the Protestant countries suffer from this malaise.[26]

The main problem, however, was not related to regionalism or religion, as Cuzco's township officials and the bishop of Puno asserted; rather, it was related to racism. The majority of fair-skinned Peruvians lived in Lima, Callao, Arequipa, and Tacna, whereas the majority of indigenous peoples lived in Cuzco, Puno, and Ayacucho, in the states that made up the so-called "Indian stain." The central government used townships to establish a dual system of administration: one system provided local autonomy to fair-skinned creoles, and the other was designed to prevent indigenous peoples from participating in public life.

Municipal life was threatened in other ways. Corruption and fraud were clearly a problem; however, they were not nearly as corrosive of

---

24. Manuel González La Rosa, *Informe que el inspector especial de todos los establecimientos de instrucción y beneficencia* (Lima, 1869), 4–53.

25. Pío B. Mesa, "Intereses del Cuzco," *La República*, 13 March 1864, 2–3.

26. Juan Ambrosio Huerta, *Instrucción pastoral que el obispo de Puno da a sus amados diocesanos* (Puno, 1867), 5.

local government as was the citizenry's complete lack of confidence in all public institutions. The majority of townships, as noted above, were simply too poor to provide corrupt officials with sufficient income; in any case, now that the central state was partially subsidizing townships, their financial records were monitored regularly.[27] The main problem with most townships, based on the sources I studied, was that most citizens did not trust public officials. This is not surprising given the historical lack of civic commitment in the country. After being falsely accused of misappropriation of funds, Huanuco's municipal officials responded:

> In our community everyone is more or less poor, and there is little difference between those who provide relief and those who seek it. . . . And as you already know, we often have to beg in order to cover our most basic expenses. . . .[28]

In Huanuco, one of the most destitute communities in the country, this was in fact the case. Similar accusations were frequently made against the members of Lima's municipal government. Although its treasury was relatively well supplied and its officials were wealthy and politically ambitious, the primary and secondary sources I consulted do not offer any evidence of corruption. Yet local residents were always accusing municipal officials of venality and graft:

> our township is wealthy, but this is not reason enough to accuse us of corruption. . . . This crass error . . . is getting propagated by public opinion. The ease with which the public is always attacking and undermining our public institutions is serving to destroy them.[29]

State officials and public intellectuals throughout the country remarked frequently on the citizenry's complete distrust of local government, which made it difficult to enlist support for government institutions.[30] The lack of confidence in public institutions became so widespread that the editors of *El Comercio* launched a campaign on their behalf:

27. *Documentos relativos a la suspensión de la beneficencia de Ica* (Lima, 1876), 5–6, 25–27, for an example of financial corruption.
28. "Interior," *El Comercio*, 16 February 1877, 1; "Sociedad Benéfica de Huánuco," *El Comercio*, 22 January 1864, 2.
29. José Casimiro Ulloa, *Comentarios sobre la memoria presentada a la Sociedad de Beneficencia por el Vice Director* (Lima, 1856), 10.
30. Manuel Carillo y Ariza, "Memoria . . . de Ancash," *El Peruano*, 28 November 1874, 1; José Mercedes Izaguirre, "Memoria . . . del Cercado de Huaraz," *El Peruano*, 4 May 1874, 1; Tomás Montero, "Memoria . . . de Luya," *El Peruano*, 3 July 1874, 1; Mariano Lorenzo Cornejo, "Memoria . . . de Piura," *El Peruano*, 25 July 1874, 1; Prudencio del Castillo, "Memoria . . . de Urubamba," *El Peruano*, 13 November 1874, 1; Mariano Ybar, "Memoria . . . de Pauza," *El Peruano*, 24 November 1874, 1; Bernardo Pacheco, "Datos . . . de Antabamba," *El Peruano*, 26 November 1874, 1; Mariano Torre, "Memoria . . . de Chota," *El Peruano*, 22 November 1874, 1.

we will never hesitate to criticize [any township official] whenever they have betrayed the public interest; however, we shall never accuse them of any wrongdoings unless we have evidence to support our claims.[31]

Public cynicism became a self-fulfilling prophecy that fed on itself and devoured everything in its path, including municipal life.

During presidential elections, government officials politicized municipal governments, contributing to the erosion of what little trust the public had in them. Township officials played a key role in elections: they were responsible for compiling voting lists, setting up electoral tables and voting booths in each district, and collecting and forwarding all the marked ballots to Lima, where they were tabulated and verified by members of congress. Instead of using the limited funds they received from the central state to provide health care, schooling, and other basic services to residents, township officials used this money to purchase liquor and food and to bribe voters to support government candidates:

> the funds belonging to our municipal townships have been spent in organizing political conspiracies. . . . In order to put an end to this, we demand that the public have full access and be allowed to inspect their financial records. . . . According to rumors, in some townships, officials have erased the original entry, rewritten the information and in some cases even removed several pages from the ledger. . . . We have not taken full advantage of our townships, which were created by the 1854 revolution. . . . The Council of Ministers should intervene at once to reform them. . . .[32]

It is likely that even the poorest residents in the Andean highlands would have paid at least a portion of their municipal taxes if they had been convinced that the money would be invested in improving public life rather than in subsidizing the electoral campaigns of government candidates.

Township officials also used their administrative power to punish residents who voted for the antigovernment candidate, thereby discouraging others from doing the same. In Junín, Huancayo, and Huaraz, municipal officials organized mass levies and conscripted members who were active in political clubs into the army:

> Jauja is responsible for providing the army with 60 recruits, but recently the authorities conscripted . . . 300; they were sent because of their political affiliations. Public opinion is the only force capable of

---

31. "Municipalidad," *El Comercio,* 16 May 1868, 2; also see: "Protesta del Pueblo de Lima," *El Comercio,* 1 August 1861, 2; "Municipalidades," *El Comercio,* 11 January 1862, 2; "Municipalidades," *El Comercio,* 4 February 1862, 2.
32. "No hay municipalidad," *El Comercio,* 17 July 1857, 2.

correcting this situation and erecting a barrier between citizens and misgovernment. . . .[33]

Citizens in the most politicized townships were the least likely to break with their old habits and become active in public life.

Municipal life was fraught with problems; however, by the mid-1870s, in large part because of the campaign launched by *El Comercio* and other national and regional newspapers and by the Civilian Party, which now ruled the country, the most blatant and worst abuses had been curbed. According to Jorge Basadre, the leading historian of Peru, municipal townships contributed substantially to decentralizing political life and would have transformed Peru into a federalist country if not for the war with Chile.[34]

Electoral Clubs and the Demilitarization of Government

After nearly three decades of military dictatorships and continuous civil war, most Peruvians agreed that the best means for transferring power from one government to its successor was through elections and that civilians ought to govern the country. Even state officials and professional politicians who were seeking to modernize the state realized that the only way of accomplishing this was by slashing the military budget, reducing the size of the army and driving it back into the barracks.[35] In the second half of the century, whatever unity and cohesiveness existed among members of electoral clubs derived from their commitment to demilitarizing political life rather than from organizational structure, ideological outlook, and social composition, all of which remained vague and amorphous.

Electoral clubs became the vehicle Peruvians used to transform social into political power.[36] In the words of Manuel Pardo, the future president of the country, clubs

> are our political schools. They teach the nation how to organize its social power and its public opinion and how to use them in order to win [state power]. . . . [Clubs] initiate citizens into the mysteries of self-government . . . transforming their wills into engines of change.[37]

33. "Recluta," *La República*, 20 March 1864, 149–50; "Reclutamiento," *La República*, 6 March 1864, 140; "Huancayo," *La República*, 13 March 1864, 144.

34. Basadre, *Historia*, 5.2052–56.

35. "La prensa," *El Correo del Perú*, 11 January 1874, 1.

36. "Club Liberal," *El Comercio*, 11 November 1859, 2; "Elecciones," *El Comercio*, 9 August 1858, 2; "Sociedad de Orden e Independencia," *El Comercio*, 8 June 1858, 2; "Sociedad Constitucional," *El Comercio*, 13 February 1868, 2; "Club Liberal," *El Comercio*, 1 October 1866, 2.

37. Manuel Pardo, "Discurso al asumir la Presidencia del Colegio Electoral en Lima," *El Comercio*, 16 November 1871, 2.

Voting clubs would modernize political life in the same way that the steam engine had modernized economic life. The Civilian Party had hundreds of local branches throughout the country, each relatively independent from the rest. The clubs that made up this loose, umbrella-type, nationwide organization had little contact with each other, and even less political cohesiveness. In the words of Pardo, its presidential candidate,

> the Civilian Party includes men of diverse and sometime even contradictory opinions. Despite their differences, they all agree on a single, basic point: the need to elect a civilian to the executive office, and to use constitutional means to transform society. . . . This is why in our Party, men of very sophisticated ideas sit next to those who have retrograde and even reactionary ones.[38]

In 1871, the Civilian Party organized a public meeting in Lima. More than six hundred rank-and-file members attended. Carmen McEvoy studied their occupational backgrounds and found that they included artisans (35 percent), small shopkeepers (25 percent), military officers (11 percent), white-collar professionals (12 percent), public employees (7 percent), farmers (5 percent), students (4 percent), and other groups (3 percent), including fishermen, scribblers, and water-carriers.[39] The leadership of the Party included government officials, landlords, and wealthy merchants.

Social relations among members in the Civilian Party, as in all the other voting clubs that appeared in the second half of the century, were based on clientelism. Lewis Taylor's description of political life in the provincial town of Hualgayoc is relevant to understanding Peruvian electoral practices:

> Although divisions along class lines did occur, the population most commonly decided its allegiances on the basis of personal acquaintance or social expediency. . . . [Peruvian] society was . . . vertically segmented on "political" issues, so that any given moment every small town, village or rural parish tended to be divided into two or even three rival bands, with each political group a poly- class amalgam, in which landlords, merchants, small holding peasants, quasi-urban artisans and rural laborers participated. At the [level of the state], factional leaders were normally the most important landowners or wealthier mine owners and merchants, with leadership in the [districts] usually assumed by medium-scale farmer-merchants or [country] lawyers. The [bottom]

---

38. "Los partidos," El Comercio, 17 September 1872, 2.
39. Carmen McEvoy, Un proyecto nacional en el siglo XIX (Lima: Pontífica Universidad Católica del Perú, 1994), 284–85.

tier in a faction's informally organized hierarchical structure was most commonly composed of . . . richer peasants or the more prosperous artisan-farmers, who nurtured their own and their superiors' political and economic ambitions at the hamlet level.[40]

The political elite of Peru needed the "masses" in order to demilitarize the state and to improve their socioeconomic opportunities in daily life. Each side had to make concessions to the other, and when they did not, the patronage ties between them unraveled, creating an opening for democratizing relationships to emerge.

Artisans played a key role in most voting clubs. In Lima in preparation for the 1866 elections, more than "600 known and honorable artisans" from different voting clubs, including the Club Liberal (1866), the Sociedad de Orden (1866), and the Club Democrático (1866), held a meeting in the atrium of the Convent of San Francisco to discuss common concerns and to agree on a candidate.[41] Since the late 1850s, Lima's artisans had been trying to organize their own political clubs, convinced that this was the most effective way of advancing their own political demands: an end to military conscription and to state protection of national industry; schooling for their children; and legal recognition of all civic and economic associations.[42] Despite repeated efforts, they never succeeded in gaining political autonomy from the elite:

> Open your eyes and do not be deceived by [their voting clubs]. Instead of joining their clubs and attending their banquets and barbecues, flee from them; they are trying to corrupt you. Let us organize our own associations . . . where we will be able to read our own newspapers and to find out about the political program of each candidate.[43]

Because 25 percent of Lima's working people were unemployed, and 75 percent of all workshops in the city had gone bankrupt in the preceding decade, artisans could not press their demands within any of the voting clubs.[44]

Nevertheless, without them the Civilian Party could not demilitarize political life. The Party, which now controlled Lima's municipal township

40. Lewis Taylor, *Bandits and Politics in Peru: Landlord and Peasant Violence in Hulgayoc* (Cambridge: Center for Latin American Studies, Cambridge University, 1996), 13.

41. "Artesanos," *El Comercio,* 12 October 1866, 2.

42. Lorenzo Pérez, "Sociedad de Artes y Oficio," *El Comercio,* 21 December 1858, 2; "Artesanos," *El Comercio,* 22 December 1858; "Los artesanos de Lima al público," *El Comercio,* 26 December 1858, 2.

43. "La cuestión eleccionaria y la Clase Obrera," *El Obrero,* 5 June 1873, 2.

44. Paul Gootenberg, *Imagining Development: Economic Ideas in Peru's "Fictitious Prosperity" of Guano, 1840–1880* (Berkeley: University of California Press, 1993), 128–30, 153.

and several government agencies, agreed to finance a number of public works programs. In addition to providing state jobs to 40,000 artisans, the government hired many of them as soldiers, militiamen and civil servants. The editors of *El Artesano*, which was published by and for artisans, remarked:

> artisans have quit their workshops and are living off public money. They have corrupted our customs and eroded public morality. . . . Passion has replaced patriotism, and tainted the reputation of all working people. . . . There is an overabundance of public employees and all of them are getting paid with public monies.[45]

The Civilian Party was correct in its assessment of the situation. In 1872, the Minister of War, Tomás Gutiérrez, in a last desperate attempt to prevent the Civilian Party from winning, mobilized the national army, dissolved congress, and cancelled elections. More than 7,000 soldiers refused to follow orders and joined Lima's working poor in erecting barricades across the city. After five days of fighting, the troops that had remained loyal to the government surrendered, and the Minister of War and his brother were captured and shot.[46] According to a contemporary,

> Next morning, they were hoisted and hung from the Cathedral tower . . . where they remained for several hours, for viewing by the entire population of Lima—the best behaved crowd I have ever seen before such a spectacle. . . .[47]

This was the first time Peru's history that a political party had succeeded in leading a relatively bloodless rebellion against the army; the country was thereby spared another bout of civil war.

Cuzco's artisans succeeded, after trying for more than a decade, in wresting control of the local branch of the Civilian Party from textile mill owners. In 1877, the artisans sent a cabinet-maker, Francisco González, to represent them in congress. This was the first time an artisan from the provinces was elected to serve in the national legislature. Cuzco's artisans called their victory a triumph of "popular sovereignty."[48] The editors of *El Comercio* congratulated them for successfully challenging the party's leadership in Cuzco:

45. "Artesanos," *El Artesano*, 15 March 1873, 1.
46. Margarita Giesecke, *Masas urbanas y rebelión en la historia: Golpe de estado en Lima, 1872* (Lima: Centro de Divulgación de Historia Popular, 1977), 13–15, 118–23.
47. Thomas J. Hutchinson, *Two Years in Peru*, vol. 2 (London, 1873), 15–16.
48. "La clase obrera," *El Rodadero* (Cuzco), 11 August 1877, 2. Also see Thomas Kruggeler, "Unreliable Drunkards or Honorable Citizens: Artisans in Search of Their Place in Cuzco Society" (Ph.D. dissertation, University of Illinois, 1987), 227–41.

Those who call themselves republicans and democrats are continuously undermining the interests of working people, and that is why we organized ourselves. . . . Despite fierce opposition, Cuzco's artisans won peacefully, legally, and civilly, thereby proving to everyone that no one can kill public opinion. . . .[49]

Cuzco's skilled workers were politically far more independent than their counterparts in Lima.

Indigenous groups became increasingly active in voting clubs throughout the provinces, although the majority of them were used by fair-skinned notables against their rivals. In the 1870s, the Civilian Party sent organizers to Vilque and other regional fairs across the southern Andes to recruit indigenous voters.[50] In the town of Guzmango in the northern state of Cajamarca, the Sociedad de Fuerza Mutua (1877), the local branch of the Civilian Party, relied on indigenous voters to defeat their rival. In the words of an official:

The Indians . . . are threatening to attack . . . my predecessor, the sub-prefect, Don Francisco Plascencia. . . . They are one hundred strong, and although poorly armed, they have been greatly encouraged by the results of the recent Congressional elections in which Don José Mercedes Alva won a seat. His local backers have published news of his victory and are celebrating their triumph by shouting "Death to Plascencia's band."[51]

Lima's Club Liberal (1868) supported Vargas Machuca, a candidate for the post of vice president. According to members of the club, Machuca "was a defender of indigenous peoples, a group which is oppressed by our own government officials."[52] Whether some of the members of this club were themselves of indigenous descent remains unclear.

Electoral clubs organized mass demonstrations, thereby introducing Peruvians to a new type of political practice. During the presidential campaign of 1871, the Civilian Party held a march and rally in the Acho Plaza that was attended by 14,000 citizens. In a private letter to a friend, one of the organizers remarked:

You have no idea what an impression this march has produced all across the city. . . . As you know, our party is divided into sections, each of them composed of between 5 and 10 decurions; in Lima alone there

49. "Las elecciones de Cuzco y la clase obrera," *El Comercio*, 13 November 1877, 3; "La diputación por el Cuzco," *El Comercio*, 15 February 1877, 2.
50. McEvoy, *Un proyecto nacional*, 115.
51. Lewis Taylor, "Society and Politics in Late Nineteenth-Century Peru: Contumaza, 1876–1900" (Working Paper, Institute of Latin American Studies, University of Liverpool, 1990), 27.
52. "Club Central Liberal," *El Comercio*, 20 February 1868, 2.

are 200 sections. On the day of the march, the leaders of each section met in the homes of their respective chiefs, and from here they went to their parishes, where they were met by their followers. At exactly 1:30 P.M., they began marching toward . . . Acho, with each leader at the head of his group, from the various parishes of Lima. This parade of people . . . was so long that those bringing up the rear where still in the Plaza Merced when the first marchers entered Acho. . . . The organizers of the event had instructed everyone to maintain absolute silence throughout the march, and they did.[53]

The marchers were the very embodiment of sovereignty of the people. The fact that they had behaved in an orderly manner was additional evidence that plebeians were rational adults. Similar marches were organized in Callao, Cuzco, Puno, Arequipa, Pasco, Trujillo, Huaraz, Piura, Tarma, and Huancayo.[54]

Warfare and Citizenship

The war with Chile forced Peruvians to shift the form and style of their practice of politics from municipal townships and voting clubs based on representative forms of electoral democracy to guerrilla groups based on the Jacobin notion of the "nation-in-arms." Political life had been militarized in the first half of the century too, but now it was citizens, not soldiers, who were the main carriers of democracy and nationhood and who would practice sovereignty of the people in this manner. The war, in the words of Nelson Manrique, was

> the only event since independence which was national in scope, and felt equally by residents of Tumber [in the far north], Tarapacá [in the far south], Iquitos [in the Amazon jungle] and Puno [in the Andean highlands]. Although each of them experienced the war differently, its overall effect on Peruvians was as traumatic as the Spanish conquest.[55]

Going into the war, the Peruvians and Chileans were more or less evenly matched, but after only a few weeks of fighting it became abundantly clear that Chile would win.[56] One of the most important reasons for their

53. Quoted in McEvoy, *Un proyecto nacional,* 82.

54. For descriptions of marches in the capital and across the provinces, see: "Los meetings," *El Correo del Perú,* 24 September 1864, 2; "El meeting," *El Correo del Perú,* 20 August 1876, 1; "Callao," *El Comercio,* 21 March 1878, 2; "Reunión popular," *El Comercio,* 11 April 1877, 2; "Callao," *El Comercio,* 6 February 1877, 2; "Chincha," *El Comercio,* 30 October 1876, 3; "Huancavelica," *El Comercio,* 9 September 1876, 3; "Meeting," *El Comercio,* 19 August 1876, 2.

55. Nelson Manrique, *Yawar Mayu: Sociedades terratenientes serranas, 1879–1910* (Lima: Instituto Francés de Estudios Andinos, 1988), 25.

56. Ronald Bruce St. John, *The Foreign Policy of Peru* (Boulder, Colo.: L. Rienner Press, 1992), 109.

victory is related to the relative lack of associative skills and civic dispo-sition among the Peruvian elite and non-elite in urban and rural areas across the country.

The national elite in Lima remained factionalized before, during, and after the Chilean invasion. In October 1879, weeks before the invasion, Spencer St. John, of the British consulate in Lima, wrote a private memo-randum to the Foreign Secretary in London, describing the situation:

> At present there does not seem to be any government. . . . Peruvians have been seized with paralysis. The people are indifferent toward their future, as are the ruling groups, all of whom are more concerned with their own personal ambitions than anything else.[57]

Lima's elite even refused to donate money or provide loans to the munic-ipal township, which was responsible for financing the military defense of the city. The million pesos the township was able to collect came mainly from the non-elite.[58] The elite remained divided after the Chileans occu-pied Lima, according to Ricardo Palma, who was one of their own. In a private letter to a friend, he complained of the "political intrigue" and "rot" that continued to "fester" among the local elite, and he closed with a telling phrase: "patriotism is nothing but a myth among us."[59]

While large number of Lima's elite remained unpatriotic, an equally sig-nificant number paid dearly for their nationalism, including the Dávalos-Lisson family, one of the city's wealthiest and most privileged clans. All five brothers in this family took their places in the front lines alongside in-digenous peoples and plebeians, and they fought valiantly against Chilean troops in the battles of Miraflores, Chorrillos, and San Juan in the out-skirts of the capital. After the Chileans overpowered them and occupied Lima, the brothers retreated and hid in their parents' home. The Davalos-Lisson family celebrated their return. Pedro, the oldest brother, described it like this:

> My mother presided at the head of the table; she, my father and sisters queried me about the battle. . . . Later on, two of my brothers, Enrique and Florecio, arrived unexpectedly. They told us the sad news that our other brother, Carlos, had died in the battle of San Juan. . . . Despite our grief, we felt fortunate. All the families we knew also lost a loved one in the war.[60]

57. Quoted in Heraclio Bonilla, *Guano y burguesía en el Perú* (Quito, 1994), 222–23.
58. Bonilla, *Guano y burguesía*, 225.
59. Ricardo Palma "Letter (11 October 1881)," in his *Cartas Inéditas* (Lima: C. Milla Batres, 1964), 65–66.
60. Pedro Dávalos y Lisson, *Por qué hice Fortuna?* vol. 1 (Lima: Editorial Gil, 1947), 7–9.

If the experience of the Dávalos-Lisson family was as common as its members suggest, then most elite families in Lima lost one of their own in defense of the homeland. I am not claiming that the elite were unified and patriotic.[61] Recall that during the war, the elite organized three different rebel governments, each with its own legislature and army, each proclaiming itself to be the sole representative of the Peruvian nation.[62] Some of Lima's most privileged families were mainly concerned with preserving their own private interests and did little to protect their homeland; however, even the most patriotic families seemed to lack the political experience and associative skills required to create a rebel government under conditions of war.

Peru's regional elite was also factionalized, though for different reasons. After capturing Lima in January 1881, the Chilean army sent half of its troops north to occupy the rich sugar plantations in the state of Cajamarca, and the other half east to conquer Junín, Peru's most economically dynamic state. In preparation for the invasion, local notables in and around Hualgayoc (Cajamarca) met to plan the town's defense. But age-old animosities resurfaced and divided the group into two factions. Members on each side armed themselves, recruiting workers from their estates, and opened fire against those in the other faction.[63] In Junín's Mántaro Valley and Cerro de Pasco, the majority of estate owners (nineteen and sixteen, respectively) were accused by local peasants and indigenous peoples of collaborating with the Chileans.[64] Whether it was true or not is difficult to know. Rebel patriots confiscated, divided, and distributed their land and livestock among themselves, causing widespread panic among local notables throughout the country. Many of the elites supported Miguel Iglesias, one of Cajamarca's wealthiest landowners; in order to regain control of rural life, they agreed to cede the nitrate-rich state of Tarapacá to Chile in exchange for an end to the war.[65] The negotiations between Iglesias and Chilean General Patricio Lynch aggravated deep divisions among the regional and national elite and led members of each group to organize rival governments. Those who opposed the trans-

61. Margarita Guerra Martinière, *La ocupación de Lima* (Lima: Pontífica Universidad Católica del Perú, 1993), 305–14.

62. Martinière, *La ocupación de Lima*, 75–77, 204–10: Francisco García Calderón established his Miraflores government in 1881; Nicolás de Pierola established his Ayacucho government in 1880; and Miguel Iglesias established his Cajamarca Assembly in 1882.

63. Taylor, *Bandits and Politics*, 16.

64. Nelson Manrique, *Las guerrillas de indígenas en la guerra con Chile* (Lima: Centro de Investigación y Capacitación, 1981), 179, 198–99, 399–400; and Bonilla, *Guano y burguesía*, 229.

65. José Dammert Bellido, *Cajamarca durante la guerra del Pacífico* (Cajamarca: Imprenta MACS, 1983), 109–14.

fer, the so-called "Reds," were led by Andrés Cáceres; those who favored it, the "Blues," were led by Iglesias. In October 1883, the Blues, with military and logistical assistance from the Chileans, fought and defeated the Reds at the Battle of Huamachuco.

Soon after, Iglesias appointed himself president. On their way out of the country, Chilean troops stopped in each town and replaced Red with Blue officials, enabling President Iglesias to take administrative and political control of the country.[66] An English diplomat noted: "General Iglesias is relying on Chilean bayonets to establish his authority in the country."[67] Once they had consolidated their power, the Iglesistas held a plebiscite ratifying the transfer of Tarapacá to Chile. Local notables in Cerro de Pasco (Junín), Huánuco (Ayacucho), Chincha Alta (Ica), Cuzco and Vilcabamba (Cuzco), Cajamarca (Cajamarca), and several other towns led popular rebellions against the Blue coalition, regarding it as nothing more than a puppet government.[68]

Patriotism was also in short supply among the country's non-elite. At the beginning of the war, more than 20,000 Quechua- and Ayamara-speaking Indians from the Andean highlands were forcibly conscripted, taken from their villages and marched all the way to Lima on the coast. They were responsible for defending the nation's capital from the invading Chileans. Few of them had any idea of who they were fighting or why. Adriana de González Prada, wife of one of Peru's leading writers, spent several days visiting and talking with the newly arrived recruits. Her sympathetic description of them is worth quoting:

> Lima had been transformed into a military camp, with Indian recruits from the Andes everywhere in sight; they looked exhausted from their long journey. . . . The people of Lima took pity and would often approach them, asking them why they had traveled to the capital. Most of them did not know. They had come, they said, to "kill Chileans," which they went on to describe as a "large animal with boots."[69]

During the battles of Miraflores, Chorrillo, and San Juan, the majority of indigenous soldiers threw down their arms, removed their uniforms, and deserted. Lieutenant Carey Brenton, a British officer and advisor to the Peruvian army, explained why:

66. Manrique, *Guerrillas indígenas,* 132–60, 237–40, 244–45, 262.
67. Quoted in Bonilla, *Guano y burguesía,* 255. Also see: Manrique, *Guerrillas indígenas,* 236–51.
68. Manrique, *Guerrillas indígenas,* 222–27, 248, 262, 298–99; and Bonilla, *Guano y burguesía,* 226–27, 254.
69. Adriana González de Prada, *Mi Manuel* (Lima: Editorial Cultura Antártida, 1947), 83.

nearly all the officers are from [aristocratic] . . . families of Spanish lineage and have little in common with their men, which is why there is so little esprit-de-corps among them. . . . Many of the [soldiers] have no idea why they are fighting. They assume that this war is no different than any of the other civil wars that have been fought in the country, except that this one is being led by generals "Chilli" and "Piérola." Many of them have stated that they will not risk being shot for the sake of any Whites.[70]

After the Chileans secured Lima, General Lynch invited French Admiral Du Petit Thouars, an observer, on a tour of their military hospital. They went from one ward to another asking Chilean and Peruvian soldiers the same question:

And why did you fight? The Peruvians replied: I fought for don Nicolas [Pierola], or I fought for don Miguel [Iglesias]. Then he approached two Chileans and asked them the same question. They responded: for my country, my general. Lynch turned to the French admiral and said: This is the reason why we won. We fought for our homeland, they fought for Mr. X and Mr. Y.[71]

The majority of Quechua- and Aymara-speaking peoples who defended Lima were far away from their homes in the Andes and had no ties to Lima or its residents.

Across the provinces, in the state of Junín, indigenous peoples practiced a type of peasant nationalism in a triangular area that measured forty by forty by sixty miles, with the town of Jauja at its apex, and Chongos and Comas on opposite sides of the base. Prior to the war, the Mantaro Valley was exceptional in that residents had a rich and complex tradition of civic democracy, as indicated by the dynamism of municipal life and voting clubs.[72] During the war, the Valley's residents organized half a dozen guerrilla groups (and cavalry units called *montoneras*). Their social composition and governance structure varied greatly. Those around Comas attracted indigenous peoples and were relatively egalitarian; those around Jauja were multiracial and socioeconomically diverse but hierarchical and clientelistic, with fair-skinned creoles in charge of them and the rank and file composed mainly of mixed-bloods and indigenous peoples. With the intensification of the war, the different guerrilla groups in the Valley were forced to band together and assist each other in defending their respective communities. This encouraged rebel fighters and their

70. Quoted in Bonilla, *Guano y burguesía,* 237.
71. Quoted in ibid., 213–14.
72. Florencia Mallon, *Peasant and Nation: The Making of Postcolonial Mexico and Peru* (Berkeley: University of California Press, 1995), 180–81.

families in each area to view themselves as Peruvians, and not only in ethnic or communal terms. Indigenous and non-indigenous rebels in this area elevated national sovereignty above racial, ethnic, and class differences, assaulting landowners not because of their skin color but because they were antipatriotic.[73] This enclave of Jacobin democracy is significant in showing that peasant nationalism in Peru and elsewhere is possible under certain special conditions; however, it did not transform political life in any lasting way.[74]

Expressions of patriotic nationalism were also rare among Chinese-Peruvians in Lima. Racial and ethnic hatred was especially intense among plebeians, and the war provided them an opportunity to express these sentiments with a ferocity uncommon during peacetime. In the summer of 1881, several days before the Chilean army occupied Lima, the Chinese community celebrated the defeat of the Peruvian army. Daniel Riquelme, a Chilean general, described what happened:

> when [the Chinese] learned that we had won in Miraflores, they hoisted flags of their homeland above their stores, assuming that Peruvians would not notice . . . and celebrated our victory behind closed doors. Once the festivities got underway, hordes of plebeians descended on the Chinese neighborhood . . . ripped down their flags and forced their way inside their stores. During the rampage, they looted and burned and killed more than 200 Chinese.[75]

In fact, the rampage resulted in the deaths of three hundred residents and 5 million pesos in property damage.[76] If the city's fire brigades had not intervened and cordoned off the area, the massacre would have been far worse. Similar massacres took place throughout the provinces (see discussion in chapter 15).

The war had a catastrophic effect on political life; it would be another three decades before Peruvians climbed out of the carnage and regained their civic and associative momentum. In the words of Joaquín Capelo, the country's first social scientist,

> Most of our public institutions remain petrified. They lack vitality because they lack spirit and organization. What little dynamism they

73. Manrique, *Guerrillas indígenas*, 179, 198–99, 207, 380–83, 399–400; Bonilla, *Guano y burguesía*, 229; Mallon, *Peasant and Nation*, 176–220; Antonia Moreno de Cáceres, *Recuerdo de la campaña de la Breña* (Lima: C. Milla Batres, 1974), 46–47, 78–79.

74. Taylor, *Bandits and Politics*; Manuel Burga and Alberto Flores Galindo, *Apogeo y crisis de la república aristocrática* (Lima: Ediciones Rikchay Perú, 1979), 8; Emilio López Albújar, *Los caballeros del delito* (Lima: Compañía de Impresiones y Publicidad, 1936), 75–76, 92–93, 120–24, 268–75.

75. Daniel Riquelme, *La expedición de Lima* (Santiago: Editorial del Pacífico, 1967), 148–49.

76. Martinière, *La ocupación de Lima*, 59–71.

possess was bequeathed to them by the previous generation; none of these institutions are capable of generating their own. . . . Worker bees built our hives but now they have died and only the drones remain. Instead of replenishing [our public energies] all they do is sap them. Even our most virtuous institutions function on self-interest and exploitation . . . and are devoid of any vitality. The meanness we experience in society is because we no longer have any public spirit. If we are to succeed in reviving public life, we must replace our old institutions with new ones. . . . The only way to accomplish this is to engage in collective action. This can take one of two forms: individual- or state-centered. The French invented the first approach in 1789, and the Japanese introduced the second in our own time. Which of the two Peru should adopt is the most important question before us.[77]

The state-centered approach to political life had become dominant and widespread by the turn of the century, and it remains prevalent in contemporary Peru, regardless of the presence or absence of President Alberto Fujimori.

77. Joaquín Capelo, *Sociología de Lima*, vol. 3 (Lima, 1899), 238–40.

CHAPTER 15

Critical Deliberation:
The Mexican Public Sphere

By the second half of the nineteenth century, Civic Catholicism had become the vernacular of public life in Mexico. Citizens in urban and rural areas now used this vocabulary to make sense of one another's differences in daily life and to interpret their nation's history. Newspapers published by and for artisans and workers, women and indigenous peoples, white-collar professionals and other social groups contributed substantially to the spread of Civic Catholicism. Voluntary associations also played a major role in the development of new deliberative sites, providing citizens from all walks of life with alternative places to congregate and discuss common concerns. The consolidation of Civic Catholicism in Mexico was accompanied by sociopolitical pluralization, cultural diversification, and the decentralization of public opinion. In the late 1880s, however, Porfirio Díaz's dictatorship put an end to this.

Socio-institutional Structures

Between 1857 and 1886, Mexicans produced a total of 1,104 newspapers and tabloids, with the bulk of them appearing in the postwar period after 1867 (fig. 15.1).[1]

---

1. My estimates are based on the following sources: Enrique Dávila Diez and Silvia María Soledad Zubillaga, *La prensa en México* (Mexico City, n.d.); Archivo General de la Nación, *Catálogo de la Hemeroteca* (Mexico City: n.p., n.d.); Biblioteca Nacional, *Catálogo de la Hemeroteca: Fondo reservado* (Mexico City: n.p., n.d.); Florence Toussaint Alcaraz and Rosalba Cruz Soto, *Índice hemereográfico: 1876–1910* (Mexico City: Universidad Nacional Autónoma de México, 1985); Fernando Castañón Gamboa, *La Imprenta y El periodismo en Chiapas* (Tuxtla: Universidad Autónoma de Chiapas, 1983); Margarita Luna García, *La prensa del estado de México en el Siglo XIX* (Mexico City: Secretaría de Educación Pública, 1986); José Lama, *La imprenta y el periodismo en el estado de Veracruz* (Veracruz: Universidad Autónoma de Veracruz, 1987); Francisco Madrid Santos and

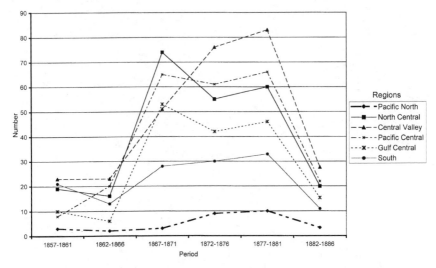

Figure 15.1   Newspaper Production and Public Opinion, 1857–1886

The Reform War (1855–1858) and the Franco-Mexican War (1862–1867) led to the militarization of public life and discouraged citizens from publishing new publications between 1857 and 1866. During each five-year period, they produced 80 or so tabloids and newspapers; nearly all of them were created by patriotic groups with the purpose of instilling nationalist sentiments in the populace (fig. 15.1).

During the postwar period, according to Daniel Cosío Villegas and other leading scholars, the public sphere gained institutional autonomy, as indicated by the almost unlimited freedom enjoyed by the press.[2] After the war, the number of new publications in the country rose dramatically, to 274 in 1867–1871, and for the next ten years it remained more or less at this same level: 280 in 1872–1876, and 297 in 1877–1881. This indicates that the demand for publications was being met. Newspaper produc-

Carlos Sánchez Silva, *Un siglo de prensa en Oaxaca: 1835–1943* (Oaxaca: Universidad Autónoma "Benito Juarez" de Oaxaca, 1987); and Florence Toussaint Alcaraz, *Escenario de la prensa en el porfiriato* (Mexico City, 1989).

2. See the following works by Daniel Cosío Villegas: *Historia moderna de México: República restaurada, vida política* (Mexico City: Editorial Hermes, 1959), 53, 69–70, 351, 492, 500; *Historia moderna de México: El Porfiriato, vida política interior,* vol. 1 (Mexico City: Editorial Hermes, 1970), 723–30; and *Historia moderna de México: El Porfiriato, vida política interior,* vol. 2 (Mexico City: Editorial Hermes, 1972), 235–39, 525. Also see: Laurens Ballard Perry, *Juarez and Diaz: Machine Politics in Mexico* (DeKalb: Northern Illinois University Press, 1978), 184–86; and Stanley Ross, *Fuentes de la historia contemporánea de México: Periódicos y revistas,* vol. 1 (Mexico City: El Colegio de México, 1965), xxi.

tion dropped to 99 in 1882–1886 as a result of the modernization of the printing industry and the competition it generated among publishers.

In regional terms, the Central Valley accounted for 26 percent of the newspapers and tabloids in the country; the North Central produced 21 percent; the Pacific Central region added another 19 percent; the Gulf Central and the South each contributed 16 percent; and the Pacific North added 2 percent.[3] Residents of different parts of Mexico now had information about each other, and they were able to follow debates on national as well as local matters. The decentralization of newspaper production contributed to the pluralization of the public sphere and is further evidence of its institutionalization.

Illiteracy and linguistic differences continued to prevent most Mexicans from partaking in public discussions. According to the most reliable estimates, in the mid-1890s 14 percent of Mexican citizens over the age of six were literate, with the overall percentage for men slightly higher than for women (17 and 11 percent, respectively).[4] Literacy in Mexico City (40 percent), Puebla (40 percent), Veracruz (34 percent), and other urban areas was roughly three times the national average, while in rural areas it was about 7 percent, although this could vary greatly from one community to the next even within the same state.[5] By the mid-1870s, according to the editors of *Siglo XIX,* twenty thousand indigenous people had learned to read and write while serving in the army and militia; most of them had returned to their communities and become active in public affairs.[6] In general terms, literacy was most advanced in the northern and central states (with literacy rates of 25 and 17 percent, respectively), and least developed in the southern states (10 percent) where the vast majority of indigenous peoples lived.[7]

Linguistic differences also prevented many Mexicans from participating in the public sphere. Roughly 20 percent of citizens spoke only Nahuatl, Otomi, Maya, Mixtec, or Zapotec; almost all of them lived in the

3. The six regions are: Central Valley (D.F., Mexico, Tlaxcala); Pacific Central (Jalisco, Guerrero, Michoacán, Morelos, Colima); Gulf Central (Guanajuato, Queretaro, Hidalgo, Veracruz, Puebla); South (Yucatán, Campeche, Chiapas, Tabasco, Oaxaca); North Central (Chihuahua, Coahuila, Durango, Nuevo León, Tamaulipas, San Luis Potosí, Aguascalientes, Zacatecas); Pacific North (Sonora, Sinaloa, California, Nayarit).

4. Moisés González Navarro, *Historia moderna de México: El Porfiriato, vida social* (Mexico City: Editorial Hermes, 1957), 532–55.

5. Navarro, *Historia moderna de México,* 532–55; Mary Kay Vaughan, "Economic Growth and Literacy in Late Nineteenth-Century Mexico: The Case of Puebla," in *Education and Economic Development since the Industrial Revolution,* ed. Gabriel Tortella (Valencia: Generalitat Valenciana, 1990), 89–101; Albert S. Evans, *Our Sister Republic: A Gala Trip through Tropical Mexico, 1868–1870* (Hartford, 1870), 482–83.

6. "La escuela y el cuartel," *Siglo XIX,* 22 August 1874, 1.

7. "La escuela," 1.

southern states of Yucatán, Oaxaca, Campeche, and Chiapas. The remaining 80 percent of Mexicans were fluent in Spanish; half of them also spoke another, native tongue.[8] Spanish predominated in the public sphere across the central and northern states; however, a great many indigenous peoples in both areas resisted using it, considering it the language of exploitation and domination:

> Indigenous peoples use Spanish when dealing with outsiders. . . . But because these exchanges occur in a context of subordination, with a superior giving orders to an indigene, they are invariably mean-spirited and hateful. . . .[9]

Women played a pivotal role in preventing the spread of Spanish into the private domain and teaching their children their mother tongue:

> The Indian, in his necessary intercourse with the Mexican, naturally acquires a knowledge of . . . Spanish; but they jealously avoid speaking [it] unless compelled. . . . I have gone through whole villages and not found a single woman or child who could speak Spanish. I have also observed on large haciendas, where hundreds of Indians are employed and where they daily hear Spanish spoken, many of the women who come weekly to the pay office to take up their husband's miserable salaries, although understanding Spanish, nothing will induce them to speak it. . . . So great is the chasm which separates Mexicans from Indians, that the title, "people of reason," is given to the former. Nothing is more common than the expression: "Is he an Indian?" No, he is "de razón."[10]

Indigenous peoples still considered Spanish the language of domination and their native tongue as the language of friendship and solidarity. Codeswitching between the two was shaped by moral rather than purely linguistic or even "self-interested" factors, contrary to what David Laitin maintains.[11]

President Porfirio Díaz's government, like all previous regimes, subsidized a great many newspapers, even those critical of its policies.[12] But

8. Navarro, *Historia moderna de México,* 530-32.

9. Ignacio Ramírez, "Discurso sobre la discusión de la Constitución (7 July 1856)," in his *Obras de Ignacio Ramírez,* vol. 1 (Mexico City: Centro de Investigación Científica Jorge L. Tamayo, 1960), 207-8.

10. Gilbert Haven, *Our Next Door Neighbor* (New York, 1875), 463-64. Also see "Guerra de Castas," *Siglo XIX,* 1 August 1848, 3.

11. David D. Laitin, *Identity in Formation: The Russian-Speaking Populations in the Near Abroad* (Ithaca, N.Y.: Cornell University Press, 1998), 248-51.

12. Alcaraz, *Escenario de la prensa,* 21-34; María del Carmen Ruiz Castañeda, Luis Reed Torres, and Enrique Cordero y Torres, *El periodismo en México* (Mexico City: Edimex, 1974), 217-18. In the late 1880s, Diaz's government was spending roughly 40,000

Diaz's administration began in the mid-1880s to finance only those newspapers, such as *El Imparcial* and *El Mundo,* that used the funds they were given to purchase rotary presses, telegraphs, linotype machines, and other modern technology.[13] The modernization of the printing industry in Mexico resulted in lower production costs; the price of a single issue dropped from six cents to one. Newspapers became an item of mass consumption, driving into bankruptcy the less efficient dailies, such as *El Siglo* and *Monitor,* the oldest papers in the country. Newspapers became profitable, with the bulk of their income drawn from the sale of advertisements. By the turn of the century, the advertisement section of dailies had grown from 30 to 50 percent, roughly the same proportion that Michael Schudson found in U.S. newspapers.[14] The penetration of the market into the public sphere drew intense monitoring and censorship by President Diaz's government.[15] By the mid-1880s, the public sphere had lost its institutional autonomy. The modernization and commercialization of the press saw an attendant decline in freedom of expression.

Communicative Networks

Public intellectuals contributed greatly to the spread of critical deliberation and instilled in citizens a sense of tolerance, thereby making public debates far more "reasonable."

Reading and Writing Practices

The "Prensa Asociada" (1872), composed of newspaper writers from Mexico City and the provinces, had 165 dues-paying members of all political persuasions, from radical democrats to orthodox Catholics:

> Despite religious and political differences, our weekly meetings are fraternal. For a brief moment, writers are able to put aside their differences and listen attentively to each other. Here one finds the editors of *La Voz* [a Catholic weekly], *El Socialista* [a working-class weekly], and *El*

pesos monthly in subsidies to thirty newspapers in Mexico City; state governors subsidized an additional twenty-seven papers from their own coffers.

13. Phyllis Lynn Smith, "Contentious Voices amid the Order: The Porfirian Press in Mexico City, 1876–1911" (Ph.D. dissertation, University of Arizona, 1996), 30–84. Rotary presses had the capacity to print three times as many issues per hour as the old mechanical presses; additionally, the Megantheler Linotype machine could cast six times faster than an experienced compositor was able to do by hand. The government also contributed to the modernization of the press by granting certain newspapers free use of its own telegraph lines, which they used to send articles on late-breaking news from around the country, and to gain access to the wire services, which carried international news.

14. Smith, "Contentious Voices," 183–84, compares the Mexican and U.S. cases.

15. Castañeda, Torres, and Torres, *El periodismo en México,* 216–19.

Correo de las Doce [a pro-government publication] discussing common concerns together.[16]

Even indigenous writers sometimes participated in these meetings.[17] By regulating themselves, the members of the Prensa succeeded in preserving free speech and avoided the intrusion of government censorship. Newspaper men who had been slandered or wrongly criticized in the press were judged by a jury of their peers and given an opportunity to defend their "personal honor." In the 1890s, the phrase "the personal honor of the editorial staff has been offended" began to appear regularly in all the leading newspapers.[18] The writer or reader responsible for insulting the staff member was now informed of the situation and was expected to make a public apology.

If such an apology was not forthcoming, then the two parties resolved matters the way honorable men settled their differences—in a duel. As Pablo Piccato notes:

> Through dueling, journalists of diverse status and persuasion had to acknowledge each other. In 1897, Francisco Montes de Oca, director of the liberal penny papers *Gil Blas* and *El Popular,* accused a rival newspaper, *El Imparcial,* of receiving subsidies from the government. . . . Montes de Oca faced *El Imparcial*'s director, Rafael Reyes Spindola, on the field of honor. . . . Rather than teaching journalists, as in the Italian case, the guidelines for using their "new-found freedom," the duel in Mexico simply gave journalists such as Montes de Oca greater prominence, by introducing them into the group of public men concerned about their honor.[19]

The number of duels fought in Mexico went from two in 1870–1879 to ten in 1880–1889, and to twenty in 1890–1899, with many of them directly or indirectly related to public opinion.[20] Personal honor and social equality became inextricably intertwined among public intellectuals, and this prepared the way for the professionalization of newspapers. By the late 1890s, the editor of *El Combate* was lamenting the consequences of all this:

16. "Editorial," *El Monitor del Pueblo,* 12 April 1885, 2.
17. "Prensa asociada," *Monitor Republicano,* 22 October 1890), 3, and 24 October 1890, 3.
18. "Editorial," *El Noticioso,* 12 December 1894, 2.
19. Pablo Piccato, "Politics and the Technology of Honor: Dueling in Turn-of-the-Century Mexico," *Journal of Social History* 33, no. 2 (winter 1999): 341.
20. Piccato, "Politics and the Technology of Honor," 341.

Instead of newspaper writers, men of letters, and poets, all that is left are "reporters." The learned, invincible, and sharp-tongued polemicist has been replaced by the ignorant and illiterate reporter.[21]

The Prensa succeeded in instilling in newspaper writers simutaneously a democratic and an aristocratic ethos, preparing the way for the professionalization of the public sphere.

The Sociedad Católica, a militant defender of the Church, had its own official publication, *La Voz.* Many of the articles it published were then reprinted by Catholic tabloids throughout the country, such as the *Artesano Católico,* which was produced in Merida and circulated across the Yucatán peninsula.[22] Ignacio Altamirano, a radical democrat who often polemicized with the editors of *La Voz,* noted:

> It is a pleasure to polemicize with the Sociedad Católica, and all its writers; they know how to express themselves vigorously and elegantly.[23]

La Voz and *El Pájaro Verde,* the second most important Catholic weekly, often criticized the policies of the Sociedad. In the late 1870's, these newspapers initiated a two-year-long debate on whether the group should remain a civic association or break with the Catholic Church and turn itself into an independent political party:

> The conservative party must abandon its extremist demands and become tolerant. . . . It can accomplish this only by disassociating itself from the Catholic Church. There are Catholics who are not conservatives, and conservatives who are not Catholic. The political fortunes of the conservative party should be based on its needs rather than on those of the Church.[24]

The rank-and-file members of the Sociedad, like many other citizens, had become relatively heterodox in their public opinions.

Voting clubs also contributed to improving the quality of public debate by providing members an opportunity to acquire the skills they needed to deliberate publicly:

> Workers and artisans in our cities have acquired considerable education not only in matters of production, but also in . . . public affairs. Today we see them taking part in electoral campaigns, participating in voting clubs, and discussing the merits of each candidate. Discussions in club

21. "Agonía de la prensa y de las letras," *El Combate,* 8 August 1898, 2.

22. *Memoria de la Sociedad Católica* (Mexico City, 1875), 22–23; "La Sociedad Católica," *Siglo XIX,* 6 March 1875, 2.

23. Ignacio Altamirano, "Sociedad Católica," *Siglo XIX,* 13 November 1869, 3.

24. José María Lozano, "Carta," *El Pájaro Verde,* 20 April 1877, 3.

meetings have enabled them to encounter new ideas, refine their language, and polish their manners. This has allowed them to overcome their sense of inferiority . . . and to become confident and poised. . . .[25]

Most voting clubs published their own tabloids, which they used to mobilize supporters and to monitor local elections, publishing articles exposing fraud on the part of state officials, especially in remote communities where it was most common and where there were few other safeguards available.[26] Clubs sent copies of these articles to leading dailies in Mexico City, which reprinted them, forcing the National Congress to investigate the charges and to disqualify the ballots received from those districts in which electoral laws had been violated.[27] Often, in districts where the government candidates had broad support, local voting clubs would lodge false accusations of corruption in order to invalidate their victory. Leading dailies published articles denouncing such activities, thereby eroding the credibility of offending clubs and prompting others to mend their ways.[28]

Cultural and professional groups encouraged members to develop an authentic "creole" style in everything from music and architecture to mining and medicine. Contrary to what most scholars claim, nationalism contributed to the spread of tolerance. The new editor of *El Propagador Industrial,* published by the Sociedad Minera (1876), which included wealthy and middle-class mine owners across the country, issued the following directives to all future contributors:

> We will not engage in polemical exchanges with anyone, and will only publish scientific and technical works in our magazine. . . . When members of the editorial board or the Sociedad Minera find it necessary to polemicize, they can do so by expressing their views in a different publication. All the articles appearing in our journal must carry the author's name, unless they represent the views of the entire association.[29]

25. "Las clases obreras," *La Firmeza,* 30 January 1875, 1. Also see "Asociación de Artesanos," *Siglo XIX,* 14 January 1868, 3.
26. Amigos de la Unión, "Bases de los trabajos," *Siglo XIX,* 25 September 1867, 2–3. Also see: "Diego Flores to B. Juárez (9 October 1867)," in *Benito Juárez: Documentos, discursos y correspondencia,* ed. Jorge L. Tamayo, vol. 12 (Mexico City: Editorial Libros de México, 1964–1972), 617–18; "Los libres pensadores de Chiapas," *Siglo XIX,* 27 November 1874, 2; and Romeo Rojas Rojas, "Periódicos electoreros del porfiriato," *Revista Mexicana de Ciencias Políticas y Sociales* 28, no. 109 (July-September 1982): 31–38.
27. "Crónica electoral," *Monitor Republicano,* 13 June 1873, 3; "Chiapas," *Siglo XIX,* 24 April 1869, 2–3. Also see: Walter V. Scholes, "El Mensajero and the Election of 1871 in Mexico," *The Americas* 5 (1948): 61–67.
28. "Crónica electoral," *Monitor Republicano,* 9 August 1871, 1–2; "Editorial," *Siglo XIX,* 20 January 1872, 1.
29. "Introducción," *El Propagador,* 16 April 1875, 1.

Nationalism enabled them to enforce the sociocultural boundary between public and private life.

Most social groups published their own newspapers. Workers and artisans, to begin with, published forty or so weeklies, including *El Socialista,* the leading paper, which had roughly 10,000 subscribers and circulated in ninety cities and towns across the country.[30] The editors of *El Pueblo,* another leading working-class tabloid, noted:

> Newspapers are, without a doubt, the best way to influence public opinion; they are also the most effective pedagogical tools we have to educate ourselves. Because they circulate freely from one person to another and are written in a simple language, nobody refuses to read them.[31]

Newspapers had become part of working-class life, although the majority of skilled and unskilled laborers could neither read nor write (see the next section).

Indigenous peoples had their own publications, including *El Indio* and *El Filopolita,* published in Jalisco, and *La Justicia* of Puebla, which described itself as "defending Indians, artisans, workers, farmers and poor people."[32] *La Comuna* and other working-class tabloids also published countless articles on indigenous groups. An article on the subject of citizenship, written in Nahuatl, began by exhorting readers to "memorize these pages and teach them to your children."[33] As these examples and my discussion below of reading circles indicate, a growing number of newspapers were now circulating among indigenous peoples.

Women, Protestants, and Masons also had their own publications. Elite women in Mexico City, Leon (Guanajuato), Merida (Yucatán), Jalapa (Veracruz), Monterrey (Nuevo León), and other large cities produced twenty new publications between the mid-1870s and the mid-1880s.[34] *El Socialista* and other working-class weeklies frequently included articles on the plight of women in cigarette factories and abused

30. Juan Felipe Leal and Jose Woldenberg, *Del estado liberal a los inicios de la dictadura porfirista* (Mexico City: Siglo Veintiuno, 1980), 179–95; "Subscripción," *El Socialista,* 2 April 1876, 1; Gastón García Cantú, *El socialismo en México* (Mexico City, 1969), 120–23.

31. "Editorial," *El Pueblo,* 14 March 1874, 1.

32. "Publicación," *Siglo XIX,* 8 April 1885, 3; Ignacio Altamirano, "Crónicas de la semana," *Siglo XIX,* 4 September 1869, 4; "La raza indígena," *Siglo XIX,* 28 October 1872, 1.

33. "A los indios," *La Comuna Mexicana,* 10 July 1874, 3; and "A los indígenas," *La Comuna Mexicana,* 20 December 1874, 3.

34. María de la Luz Pacero, *Condiciones de la mujer en México durante el siglo XIX,* Mexico City: Instituto Nacional de Antropología e Historia, 1992, 223–37.

wives, thereby making public their special problems and concerns. Protestants and Masons had several publications (eight and three, respectively), which they used to denounce intolerant Catholics and to defend free speech in Mexico.[35] *El Siglo, Monitor Republicano,* and other nationwide dailies often reprinted articles from and debated with all these specialized publications, which helped to amplify their influence on public opinion.[36]

Counter-Publics and the Proliferation of Deliberative Sites

The proliferation of deliberative sites enabled workers, artisans, and indigenous peoples to enter the public sphere and broaden its agenda. Artisans' and workers' groups established "reading circles" in cities and towns throughout the country. Members took turns reading aloud to each other from *El Socialista, El Demócrata,* and other newspapers. In the 1890s, the editor of *El Demócrata* visited one of these circles in Mexico City, and left this description:

> Groups of thirty, fifty, and more workers from the city would assemble in a place beyond the reach of their bosses . . . and wait until the reader arrived. After he finished with *El Demócrata,* the audience . . . would ask him to read the paper several more times. They memorized its content, and repeated it to their friends and neighbors.[37]

Reading circles also surfaced inside textile factories and artisan workshops, prompting Catholic workers to organize their own circles under the auspices of the Asociación Católica Industrial (1873) in order to "maintain morality on the shop-floor . . . and prevent bad reading materials from reaching [the hands of co-workers]."[38]

Factory owners in Mexico City, Veracruz, Puebla, and other major centers of industrial production became alarmed by the spread of these circles. Any worker who participated in one during the work day was fined 50 cents the first time, and fired from their job for a second of-

---

35. Jean-Pierre Bastian, *Los disidentes: Sociedades protestantes y revolución en México, 1872–1911* (Mexico City: Fondo de Cultura Económica, 1989), 344–45.

36. Also see: Cantú, *El socialismo en México;* Juan Leal and Jose Woldenberg, *La clase obrera en la historia de México* (Mexico City: Siglo Veintiuno, 1980); Antonio Escobar Ohmstede and Teresa Rojas Morales, *La presencia del indígena en la prensa capitalina del siglo XIX,* vols. 1–4 (Mexico City: Instituto Nacional Indigenista, 1992); Pacero, *Condiciones de la mujer en México;* Bastian, *Los disidentes;* and José María Mateos, *Historia de la masonería en México desde 1806 hasta 1884* (Mexico City: Editorial Herbasa, 1884).

37. Samuel Kaplan, *Combatimos la tiranía: Conversaciones con Enrique Flores Magón,* trans. Jesús Amaya Topete (Mexico City: Instituto Nacional de Estudios Históricos de la Revolución Mexicana, 1958), 36–37.

38. Sociedad Católica, *Bases para la formación de la Comisión de Artesanos y Obreros* (Mexico City, 1873), 3.

fense.[39] Striking workers, in their negotiations with factory owners, often included in their list of demands the right to have a reading circle.

Voluntary associations also established scores of reading cabinets across the country in cities such as Mexico City, Puebla, and Guadalajara, and small towns like Juchitán (Oaxaca), Villa de Marín (Nuevo León), and Zumpango (Mexico). These libraries provided elite and commoner alike a place to read newspapers, novels, and technical-scientific manuals.[40] The "May 5th" library in Mexico City was the most important of these cabinets. It was well-stocked with all three types of publications, and was open daily from 8:00 A.M. to 10:00 P.M., including Sundays and holidays. In 1873, it was visited by 6,350 readers, the majority of whom were from "the poorest sectors of society."[41] Guadalajara's library served 16,432 readers in 1886; more than a third of them consulted newspapers, another third read novels, and the rest selected technical-scientific manuals.[42] The public library in Morelos was one of the smallest, used in 1887 by only 630 readers, the majority of whom requested novels—an indication that the majority of its patrons were from the elite sectors of society.[43]

These libraries altered reading practices by allowing users to read whatever they wanted without having to seek the approval of the local parish priest or having the text interpreted for them. According to a contemporary, libraries were based on the

> free method of learning [that was opposed by the Church]. Although the most serious vices and errors are rarely discussed openly, we now have the opportunity to do so [in our libraries], and when we shine light on them we are no longer confused by them.[44]

Library reading enabled commoners to develop their critical faculties in ways the Church had discouraged, but which Lancasterian groups had propagated among their students. The majority of library users had been taught to read and write by Lancasterians according to the new "Hollendorf" method, which emphasized reasoning over rote memorization of facts, enabling them to overcome the fear they still felt when reading texts that had not been approved by the Church.[45]

---

39. "Primer Ataque al Socialista," *El Socialista,* 4 August 1872, 2.
40. "Compañía Lancasteriana," *Siglo XIX,* 23 March 1870, 3.
41. Compañía Lancasteriana, *Memoria que presenta la Compañía . . .* (Mexico City, 1871), 6, 13, 21; Compañía Lancasteriana, *Memoria que presenta la Compañía . . .* (Mexico City, 1872), 7, 11; Compañía Lancasteriana, *Memoria que presenta la Compañía* (Mexico City, 1874), 6–8.
42. Navarro, *Historia moderna de México,* 688.
43. Navarro, *Historia moderna de México,* 688.
44. C. José María Iglesias, *Discurso pronunciado por el C . . .* (Mexico City, 1872), 7.
45. "La lectura y la moral," *La Firmeza,* 9 December 1874, 1; and "Unos cuadernos,"

The Sociedad de Historia Natural (1869), the Academia de Literatura (1875), the Sociedad Arqueológica (1893), and other elite groups launched an ambitious campaign to revalorize the country's pre-Hispanic roots as part of their broader campaign to create a "national culture." According to them, Mayan and Aztec civilizations were as "advanced" as those of classical Greece and Rome but had declined after the Spanish conquest and were now in the process of regaining their rightful place as a world civilization.[46] "Indigenism" was used by the elite to propagate cultural nationalism, but it also enabled rural peoples to gain recognition in public. Members in these learned and scientific societies began to study Nahuatl, Otomí, Maya, and other indigenous tongues and published roughly fifty dictionaries and grammar manuals on them—quite a switch from just a few decades earlier when they had expressed concern at the way "Mexicanisms" had deformed Castilian Spanish.[47]

The indigenous intellectual Ventura de las Casas, from the small town of Coyotepec, contributed to this effort by publishing his own dictionary of Nahuatl. He and others like him persuaded schoolteachers in the countryside and the director of Normal School in Mexico City, where they had been trained, to use indigenous languages in the classroom and to make them part of the curriculum.[48] Ignacio Ramírez, himself of indigenous stock, was the most ardent champion of multilingualism:

> The best means of elevating Indians to the rank of citizens and providing them an opportunity to influence public affairs is by separating them according to their languages. . . . They must be allowed to continue using their tongues, and we must learn to use them as well.[49]

Ramírez's articles appeared regularly in all the leading dailies and often generated lively discussion.[50] What had begun as a scholarly debate among the cultural elite became a pressing matter for rural teachers and was discussed in regional and national conferences. Delegates to the First

La Firmeza, 6 February 1875, 1, on artisans refusing to read a pamphlet that had been condemned by the bishop.

46. Sociedad Mexicana de Historia Natural, *Estatutos de la Sociedad* (Mexico City, 1869), 2–3; "Informe," in *La Naturaleza*, vol. 1 (Mexico City, 1869–1870), 391–412; "Editorial," *Monitor Republicano*, 29 March 1890, 3.

47. "Arte de lengua Maya," *Siglo XIX*, 28 May 1889, 3. Also see Manuel Germán Parra y Wigberto Moreno, *Bibliografía indigenista de México y Centroamérica: 1850–1950* (Mexico City: Instituto Nacional Indigenista, 1950), 63–107; and Shirley Brice Heath, *Telling Tongues: Language Policy in Mexico, Colony to Nation* (New York: Teacher's College Press 1978), 68–77.

48. "Nota," *Siglo XIX*, 22 November 1893, 3, and 19 July 1894, 3.

49. Ignacio Ramírez, *Obras de Ignacio Ramírez*, vol. 2 (Mexico City, 1889), 207–8.

50. "Editorial," *Monitor Republicano*, 22 November 1879, 1, and 26 November 1879, 1.

Congress of Instruction (1889) recommended the adoption of multilingualism and pressured the Ministry of Education into changing its language policy.[51]

In the countryside, the Comité Comunero (1877) and the Sociedad de los Pueblos Unidos (1878) were responsible for incorporating indigenous peoples into the public sphere. The money these groups collected from membership dues went to hire country lawyers and to pay for villagers to do research in Mexico City's National Archives, where land titles were kept:

> Indians have descended on the National Archive in search of their deeds; estate owners have done the same.[52]

Local chapters of the Comité and the Sociedad also drafted and circulated petitions denouncing estate owners and government officials for violating their property rights. Copies of these petitions were then hand-delivered to the president's secretary, members of the National Congress, and the reporting staff of *El Siglo* and other leading newspapers in Mexico City. After publishing a dozen or so petitions from a group of rural communities that was defending its land in a relatively remote part of the state of San Luis Potosí, the editors of *El Hijo* announced:

> This is to inform the representatives of these communities that we will not be publishing any more articles on their case; they should retrieve the documents they sent us recently or tell us what to do with them.[53]

Educational and Protestant groups also encouraged indigenous peoples to become literate.[54]

In the late 1870s, a number of national newspapers published in Mexico City, including the *Monitor,* an independent weekly, and *La Libertad,* a government-controlled daily, began regularly publishing articles denouncing local tabloids in different parts of the country for instilling "Indians with the absurd idea that they are the natural owners of the land."[55] These articles were discussed in reading circles that had been organized by the Comité, the Sociedad, and other political and civic associations. The following description of one such circle was provided in the early 1900s by the lawyer of Ricardo and Enrique Flores Magón, the editors of *La Regeneración:*

51. "Circular," *Monitor Republicano,* 7 January 1890, 3, and 23 January 1890, 3; "Escuela," *Siglo XIX,* 31 August 1892, 3. Also see Heath, *Telling Tongues,* 70–79.

52. "Restitución," *Bandera Negra,* 5 February 1878, 1.

53. "Lo social y los indígenas," *El Hijo del Trabajo,* 30 June 1878, 4.

54. "Editorial," *El Monitor Republicano,* 25 July 1883, 1.

55. "Los agitadores de los indios," *La Libertad,* 20 November 1878, 2; and "La guerra social," *La Libertad,* 1 March 1879, 2.

one day, while traveling deep in the countryside in the state of Chihuahua . . . I came upon a group of about 100 Indians. They were silent as statues, except the one that was standing in the middle. He was reading a newspaper . . . *Regeneración*. The words came out slowly and his reading skills were not one hundred percent. I witnessed similar scenes time and again during my travels across the state of Sinaloa and in Tepic.[56]

Although the Comité and the Sociedad had long since vanished from public life, their influence on reading and writing practices among indigenous groups in the countryside lingered on.

Verbal and Visual Practices

Indigenous associations in rural areas enabled small farmers to transform their oral traditions into written texts. Archeological museums and public monuments and statues commemorating indigenous heroes were also established across the country, enabling rural peoples to see themselves reflected positively across the public landscape. Newspapers carrying satirical drawings also enabled nonliterate plebeians in urban areas to participate in public debates about common concerns.

The Comité Comunero and the Sociedad de los Pueblos Unidos assisted small farmers who had never registered their land and who lacked any legally valid document proving that they were the rightful owners of their plot. With local branches across the country, these associations held public meetings and had residents give an oral history of land tenure in each region from "time immemorial."[57] They used the information to produce maps and land titles, enabling indigenous peoples to transform "local knowledge" into "legal-rational" texts and thus to protect their lands from predatory estate owners.[58]

The spread of nationalism among the cultural elite also led them to establish archeological museums in the nation's capital, in all the state capitals, and in several small towns across the country, such as Sinaloa (Sinaloa) and Tampico (Veracruz).[59] Antonio García Cuba, a member of

56. Kaplan, *Combatimos la tiranía*, 158.

57. Alicia Hernández Chávez, *Anenecuilco: Memoria y vida de un pueblo* (Mexico City: Fondo de Cultura Económica, 1993), 23–25, 33–48; and María Salinas Sandoval, "Transformación o permanencia" (Ph.D. dissertation, El Colegio de México, 1993), 273–87.

58. William Roseberry, "El Estricto Apego a la Ley: Liberal Law and Communal Rights in Porfirian Patzcuaro" (Unpublished typescript, New School for Social Research, 1998).

59. Antonio García Cubas, *Cuadro geográfico y estadístico, descriptivo e histórico* (Mexico City, 1884), 105; Manuel Rivera Camba, *México Pintoresco*, vol. 1 (Mexico City, 1880–1883), 180–81; "Arquelogía," *El Correo de los Estados*, 12 April 1877, 1; "Antigüedades," *La República*, 6 June 1880, 3.

the Sociedad de Historia, offered this description of Mexico City's Museo Nacional, the country's largest:

> The bottom floor of the Great Gallery includes the . . . newly acquired statue of Chac Mool, king of the Itzaez (Mayan). The figure appears in a reclining position, with a plate directly above his groin, and is similar to all the other ones that have been found recently in other parts of the country. . . . Nearby are serpent heads made of plumes and scales, which I myself found while excavating underneath the atrium of the Cathedral. . . . The Palenque Cross [from Chiapas] came from the ruins of the same name. . . . On display in the two main rooms on the upper floor is an impressive collection of objects: figurines from the Yucatán, feather headdresses, and a variety of pottery and other artifacts from Mitla [Veracruz]. Next to them are several deities, including . . . Izcozauhqui, the Tlaloc, the Toltec goddess of water, and, possibly, Huitzilopochtli, as well as a funeral urn. . . . There are also several hieroglyphics, including the most important one of all, "Pilgrimage of the Aztec Tribe" . . . along with several depicting cities, battles, and warriors. . . . In the second, smaller room, there are shelves filled with offensive and defensive weapons, banners, clubs, musical instruments, amulets, stamps, pipes, and masks. . . .[60]

According to contemporary accounts, non-elite families often visited the museum; given that by the 1880s almost half of the city's population was made up of rural migrants, the majority of visitors were the descendants of the same indigenous peoples on display.[61] Even plebeians who made a living from selling counterfeit artifacts to museums and amateur archeologists gained an appreciation for indigenous peoples, though perhaps in ways the elite had not intended.[62]

In Mexico City and elsewhere, indigenous heroes were immortalized in public monuments. Local residents from the neighborhood of Viga, one of the poorest in the nation's capital and home to a great many indigenous peoples and mixed-bloods, collected money and got the township to erect a monument in the main plaza. John Geiger visited the Viga in the late 1870s and left this description:

> This part of . . . Mexico . . . has changed the least since the days of Moctezuma. . . . [The] visitor finds himself bewildered by the utter change, and transported into the midst of sights and sounds which have nothing in common with the half-European life of the capital. In the

60. Cubas, *Cuadro geográfico*, 296–97.
61. Robert A. Wilson, *Mexico: Its Peasants and Its Priests* (New York, 1856), 271.
62. "Nota de Puebla," *El Universal*, 25 January 1890, 3; and "Gacetilla," *El Monitor Republicano*, 26 January 1890, 3.

paseo stands a recently erected monument to Guatemozin, the last of the Aztec sovereigns. It is a colossal bust, supported by a square pedestal, which on the side facing the city bears an inscription, in Spanish, and on the opposite one the translation of it in old Mexican.[63]

In the center of the city, along the elegant and tree-lined Reforma boulevard, the city's elite also erected a statue in honor of the great Aztec warrior, Cuauhtemoc. The statue included a series of bas-reliefs depicting the capture, imprisonment, and torture of Cuauhtemoc by Hernán Cortés and his men. According to contemporary accounts, the statue was to commemorate the many indigenous peoples who had died defending Mexico against the French.[64] In 1890, Juan Maxtlis and other indigenous peoples in the nation's capital organized a patriotic group that hosted day-long celebrations on civic holidays. They paraded "allegorical floats," performed pre-Hispanic dances, and delivered rousing speeches in front of Cuauhtemoc's statute. These celebrations attracted large numbers of workers and artisans of different ethnic backgrounds, giving indigenous peoples additional visibility in the public sphere.[65]

El Hijo de Ahuijote, La Tarántula, and *La Orquesta,* among others, published only satirical drawings denouncing public corruption and caricatures of government and Church officials.[66] Although most of the *Hijo*'s audience were illiterate, it carried articles satirizing journalists and newspapers that received government subsidies.[67] These papers were very popular among the non-elite and were read in cafes and taverns:

> The table in front is occupied by a rustic with his children and wife wrapped in a shawl [used by the lower classes]; all of them are drinking lemon-flavored iced shavings. . . . Next to them is a table of retired military officers with broad moustaches; all of them are reading the *Revista Universal* and drinking strong coffee with cognac. . . . At another table is a group of lads; they have invited dancers and circus performers to drink ajenjo, torino, or grosella with seltzer water. . . . Across from them are groups of artisans; they have just returned from a meeting at

---

63. John Lewis Geiger, *A Peep at Mexico* (London, 1874), 274; Cambas, *México pintoresco,* 3.184; "Del 28 de febrero al 6 de marzo de 1869," *El Monitor Republicano,* 7 March 1869, 1–3; and "Por el Paseo de Vigas," *Siglo XIX,* 17 March 1875, 3.

64. Cubas, *Cuadro geográfico,* 311–15; and Cambas, *México pintoresco,* 1.234–35, 261.

65. "Fiesta," *Siglo XIX,* 19 August 1887, 3; "Fiesta," *Monitor Republicano,* 23 May 1890, 3, and 24 August 1890, 3; "Fiesta," *Monitor Republicano,* 22 August 1891, 3; "Fiesta," *Monitor Republicano,* 22 August 1893, 3.

66. Esther Acevedo, *El surgimiento de la caricatura como lenguaje crítico de la ideología* (Mexico City: Círculo de Arte, 1979), 5–15; Villegas, *Historia moderna de México: El Porfiriato, vida política interior,* 2.239.

67. "Cántico de los Periodistas," *El Hijo de Ahuijote,* 27 September 1885, 1; and "Escritores del gobierno," *El Hijo de Ahuijote,* 18 March 1884, 1.

the Junta and Lancasterian Association. They are insulting the waiter, reading the latest issue of *La Tarantula* and *The Orquestra,* discussing the upcoming elections, and they use the term "Indian" when referring to [President] Juarez. The artisans are drinking café au lait and eating cold cuts, while their female companions . . . look on, take drags from their cigars and blow smoke around them. . . .[68]

The importance of these satirical papers can be gauged by the fact that in the mid-1880s, when President Díaz's government began censoring the press, the *Hijo's* editor, Daniel Cabrera, was jailed more often than any other writer.[69]

Civic Catholic Narrative

In the closing decades of the century, public writers continued to use Civic Catholicism to make sense of each other in civil, economic, and political society, but now they were far more ambitious in their uses of its narrative resources. In urban areas, newspaper writers used Civic Catholic terminology and phrases to develop a new theory of Mexican history based on the changing nature of associative life and to develop a set of standards by which citizens culd evaluate each other's actions in public. In the countryside, indigenous intellectuals also began to use Civic Catholic terms, although not in the same way.

Interpreting History and Classifying Citizens

Public writers used Civic Catholicism to propose a radically new interpretation of Mexican history. A relatively obscure writer by the name of Fernando Garrido published an essay in the *Siglo* titled "The Family, the State and the Associative Principle," in which he expressed and summarized the views held by a prominent group of thinkers. His article was among the first and, without a doubt, the most explicit attempts to reinterpret Mexican history from an associative perspective:

> It is a mistake to continue believing that the state is a mirror image of family life, and that the state is to the nation as a father is to his children. This idea came to us from Islam and Christianity [via Spain]. . . . Society is composed not only of the family and the state, but of countless associations that exist between the two and have been created by individuals in order to satisfy the needs they have outside these two other domains. . . . In fact, the form the state now takes depends to a

68. "Del 31 de enero al 6 de febrero de 1869," *El Monitor Republicano,* 7 February 1869, 1–2. Also see: "Mendigos," *La razón de México,* 3 November 1864, 3.
69. Alcócer, *Reseña histórica,* 28; and Kaplan, *Combatimos la tiranía,* 35, 59–60, 74.

large extent on the shape of associative life itself. . . . History has shown that changes in the character of each state—theocratic, warrior, aristocratic, oligarchic, industrial, and commercial—are directly related to changes in associative life.[70]

Garrido's interpretation is steeped in positivist notions of progress and sociological notions of public life that were prevalent across the modern West. He uses them to shed new light on Mexico's particular experience.

Public writers also used Civic Catholic notions in order to provide citizens a new set of socio-moral categories by which to evaluate each other's actions. One of the most succinct discussions of them appeared in an unsigned article titled "Classifications," published in the working-class weekly *El Socialista*. The author sorted citizens into three categories:

> active, egoist, and apathetic. The first type, although in the minority, are responsible for all the improvements that have been made in our voluntary groups. These persons are responsible for maintaining unity and instilling in all members a sense of duty and obligation. . . . Next are the egoists. Although they pay their monthly dues, they are deeply utilitarian in their actions and never participate in the affairs of the group. . . . The last type, the apathetic . . . portray themselves in public as civic and enlightened, but in real life they tend to isolate themselves from others in the group and shirk their duties. During general meetings, they rarely participate in any discussion and retreat into themselves in order to avoid conflict.[71]

The number of Mexicans who were active in associative life had increased to the point that citizens had to develop new, more refined categories to evaluate and classify each other. Public life in Mexico was now populated with citizens rather than colonial subjects, and civic participation had replaced religious piety as the main virtue. Public writers now used Civic Catholic notions in order to make sense of broad, historical changes as well as discrete, individual behavior, linking the two to produce a single, coherent account of Mexican democratic life.

In the countryside, indigenous writers still used the old colonial dichotomy of passion and reason; however, some of them began also to use Civic Catholic terminology in their own distinctive way. From the late 1870s to the mid-1880s, the Comité and the Sociedad encouraged indigenous communities to challenge government officials who wanted to

---

70. Fernando Garrido, "La familia y el estado y el principio de asociación," *Siglo XIX*, 27 March 1878, 1–2.
71. "Clasifiquemos," *El Socialista*, 16 May 1886, 2.

downgrade their municipal townships and turn them into third-tier institutions. Doing so would have deprived them of many public services, including primary schooling, and easy access to justices of the peace:

> to claim that indigenous peoples are still perpetual minors incapable of attending to their affairs, the way that we had been portrayed in colonial legislation, violates our Constitution . . . which protects the rights of all citizens to assemble freely, to move about, and to pursue their interests without having to seek advice from or render accounts to any so-called tutors, including government officials, court judges, and legislators.[72]

The "people of reason" continued to construe indigenous peoples as "prerational." Although the linguistic field inhabited by these two groups had changed little, indigenous peoples who lived deep in the countryside were for the first time using Civic Catholic terminology in public life.

Smaller farmers who lived near the San Nicolás and Santa Catarina estates (Mexico) drafted and sent a petition to the state legislature demanding a municipal township. The petition was signed by 200 (of a total of 350) families from the region. The petitioners argued that they wanted to live as "free citizens" and "protect our families" in "civil society" rather than continue to live as "peons."[73] For these indigenous farmers, family life, citizenship, and municipal liberty were the building blocks of civil society.

72. "Carta de Tiburcio Montiel," *El Monitor Republicano*, 30 October 1879, 2.
73. "Justas apreciaciones," *El Hijo del Trabajo*, 11 November 1877, 1–2.

CHAPTER 16

Opinion-Making: The Peruvian Public Sphere

In the second half of the nineteenth century, Peruvians began using Civic Catholic keywords, in public discussions and in daily life, to make sense of their differences in civil, economic, and political society. Citizens discussed public affairs in practical terms and not just by invoking abstract, rarefied principles. Artisans, women, indigenous peoples, plebeians, white-collar professionals, and other groups had their own publications, which contributed to the pluralization of public debate and to the erosion of government and Church control of cultural life. The socio-ethnic diversification of the public sphere also contributed to its deradicalization and helped to make citizens more tolerant and moderate in their views. Despite these and other changes, however, the overwhelming majority of Peruvians continued to practice civic democracy more readily in civil society than in the public sphere—or, for that matter, in any of the other terrains.

Socio-institutional Structures

Peruvians published 211 new newspapers and tabloids between 1856 and 1875, with the bulk of them (69 percent) appearing during the first decade (fig. 16.1).[1] The number of newspapers in the country declined from 72 in 1856–1860, to 59 in 1861–1865, and to 33 in 1866–1870, before increasing again to 47 in 1871–1875. *El Comercio*, Peru's largest selling daily, had roughly three thousand subscribers—three times as many as in the 1840s. Most of the other newspapers published in Lima had less than

---

1. All the data presented in this paragraph are based on my tabulations of Mariano Felipe Paz Soldán's *Biblioteca Peruana* (Lima, 1879).

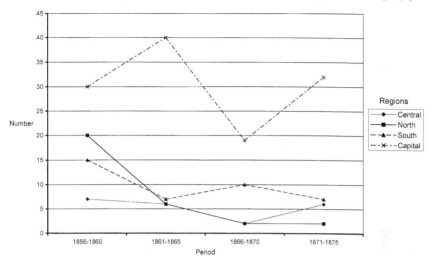

Figure 16.1   Newspaper Production and Public Opinion, 1856–1875

half that number.[2] The pool of readers remained relatively small, and the price of newspapers was beyond the reach of most citizens, especially during the 1860s when economic depression buffeted the country. From 1876 to 1880, the number of publications dropped to ten or so, the lowest to date, as a result of the invasion and occupation of Peru by the Chilean army. It would take another decade or so for public opinion to recover:

> Public opinion remains undeveloped in Lima. Although it continues to play an important role in society, it is not contributing to our progress. . . . If we succeed in reviving it and introducing it in our schools, salons, and electoral clubs, our current efforts to disseminate truth, justice, and good will yield positive results, enabling us to change the face of Peruvian society.[3]

Newspaper production remained depressed until the turn of the century. Newspaper production and public opinion continued to be centralized and concentrated in Lima. The nation's capital accounted for 58 percent of all publications. Most of them continued to circulate in the area and were read mainly by local residents. The southern states accounted for 19 percent, most of them produced in and read by the residents of Arequipa.

2. Héctor López Martínez, *Los 150 años de El Comercio, 1839–1989* (Lima: Edicion "El Comercio," 1989), 67, 197.
3. Joaquín Capelo, *Sociología de Lima*, vol. 3 (Lima, 1895), 73–74.

The northern states produced 14 percent, and the central states accounted for the remaining 9 percent.

Communicative Networks

Because of the limited number of readers in the country, public writers remained dependent on the government for subsidies and were unable to carve out for themselves a stable and autonomous place in Peruvian society. Although their situation remained precarious, those who were active in civic, economic, and political associations succeeded in preserving their independence.

Reading and Writing Practices

Newspaper writers and public intellectuals remained dependent on state officials, without a place in public life even in Lima, where they were most influential because of the city's relatively large media market. Nationwide the market for newspapers, books, and magazines was so limited that even the most prolific and popular writers could not make a living from their work:

> writers lack a well-defined role in our society, and literary pursuits are not yet a stable profession, making it impossible for anyone engaged in them to survive on the proceeds from their own work. And I do not mean by this to profit from it, I only mean to survive. . . .[4]

Public intellectuals relied on state officials for subsidies. During the late 1850s, the Minister of State, Miguel Carpo, offered the members of the Bohemia Literaria, the most important writer's group of this period, lucrative jobs in the public sector:

> the Bohemians secured any [government job] they wanted, although we were never unreasonable in our requests to the Minister. [Some of our members were] given officer's rank in the army, which provided them with a salary of thirty-two pesos per month.[5]

The salaries these writers earned were modest, so they were forced to secure employment in several different government agencies at the same time, drawing an income from each without working for any of them. State officials also used indirect, market-based subsidies to support public intellectuals: "when congress or one of the government agencies wants to express their backing for the work of a particular author, they will

4. Alfredo G. Leubel, *El Perú en 1860 o sea anuario nacional* (Lima, 1861), 273.
5. Ricardo Palma, *La Bohemia de mi tiempo* (Lima: Ediciones Hora del Hombre, 1971), 20.

purchase a quantity of copies of it."[6] The subsidy was sometimes given to the entire staff of a publication. The writing staff of *La Revista de Lima* (1859–1863), the country's leading journal, benefited from this arrangement:

> it was indispensable for us to solicit the government's support [for our journal]. . . . We were not demanding . . . a great deal. . . . Eighty or one hundred subscriptions from the Minister, about the same amount he offered many other publications. . . .[7]

Despite their close ties to government officials, some public writers were able to maintain their autonomy, as indicated by their criticisms of their own patrons and their policies. The most independent writers were active in associative life and relied on the socio-moral support of members of their associations to buffer themselves from the pressure sometimes placed on them by state officials. Members sometimes met with them privately and tried to convince them to let up.

From the 1860s on, public deliberation in Lima became far more moderate and critical than it had ever been. Manuel A. Fuentes, one of the country's most perceptive intellectuals, published an article in the late 1860s describing this change:

> Between 1821 and 1856, Lima had a total of 128 newspapers; most of them did not meet even minimal [journalistic] standards. . . . The few that did were of inferior quality . . . vitriolic comments filled their pages. . . . The decline in the quality of our newspapers began in 1833 when sectarian writers used them to attack their rivals. . . . This practice became generalized. . . . In October 1862, the editors of *El Comercio* changed the situation when they began . . . protecting the privacy of individuals. . . . In doing so, they have encouraged society to practice self-restraint. . . .[8]

The change in style was reflected in the physical layout of *El Comercio* and other newspaper. Up to that time, government propaganda, personal slander, news articles, and editorials appeared together on the same page, suggesting that the sociocultural boundary between public and private life remained indistinct. By the early 1860s, *El Comercio* and other leading dailies had

> three sections: (1) general interests; (2) public spectacles; and (3) personal matters. Before [then], all three sections had appeared together in a confusing manner, but after 1859 they were separated from each

6. Leubel, *Perú en 1860,* 274.
7. Ricardo Palma, "Última Página," *La Revista de Lima* 7 (1863): 405–6.
8. Manuel Atanasio Fuentes, "Andar," *El Murciélago* 3 (1866): 194–95.

other and placed in different parts of the newspaper. . . . This brought us closer to our goal of enlightenment and morality. Anyone who now reads the section dedicated to personal matters can attest to this.[9]

Newspapers altered deliberative practices in Peru.

Voluntary groups undermined the cultural and moral influence of the state and the Church on public debate. The Sociedad Amigos del Indio, a human-rights group discussed in an earlier chapter, sent members on fact-finding missions and published reports, pamphlets, and newspaper articles in order to prove that governors, priests, and landlords were violating the rights of indigenous groups:

> in contrast to those government officials that [Congress sends] to investigate the situation of indigenous groups, who return without any reliable information, the Sociedad is collecting accurate information and passing it on to legislators so that they might use it to draft legislation. . . .[10]

Civic groups also challenged religious orthodoxy. In 1871, Mariano Amezaga, a member of the Colegio de Abogados, delivered a speech to the group demanding that they evaluate all candidates using only professional and academic standards, and not religious standards. His speech was published in all the leading dailies and also circulated as a pamphlet, causing considerable alarm among the Church's hierarchy and its supporters in the Colegio.[11] The editors of *El Artesano* wrote countless articles against religious intolerance:

> the beliefs of atheists, Jews, and other idolatrous peoples do not concern us. We respect them the same way they respect us. Although we are convinced that they are wrong in holding these beliefs, we must not attack them. . . . We have only one duty: to associate with each other. . . .[12]

Civic groups transformed the "universalistic" assertions of state and church officials into "particularistic" claims, thereby contributing to the moral and cultural differentiation of the public sphere.

Associations also contributed to sociopolitical pluralization by providing artisans, women, indigenous peoples, and poor families an opportu-

9. Leubel, *Perú en 1860*, 287.
10. "Indios en el Senado," *El Comercio*, 16 September 1868, 2–3, in Emilio Vázquez, *La rebelión de Juan Bustamante* (Lima: Editorial J. Mejía Baca, 1976), 358–59.
11. Pedro Gual, *El abogado del Señor Barrenechea y el Doctor Tovaro o sea el racionalismo liberal y el catolicismo* (Lima, 1871); Mariano Amezaga, *Refutación de una doctrina* (Lima, 1871), 2, 9. Also see: *Anales del Cuerpo de Ingenieros*, vol. 1 (Lima, 1879), ix.
12. "La asociación es un deber," *El Artesano*, 15 June 1873, 1.

nity to express their demands publicly. Some of the largest voluntary groups in the country were now publishing their own tabloids:

> there is not a single political, religious, scientific, or industrial association that today does not have its own publication, filled with statistical data, inventions, and whatever else may be of moral, material, or scientific interest to its members. . . .[13]

Artisans in Lima, Cuzco, Arequipa, and other cities published their own newspapers. The editor of one of them noted:

> from now on we will put aside our working tools, if only for a brief moment, to [publish our newspaper]; labor might provide us with material sustenance, but the goal of our publication is to provide moral nourishment, which we have lacked until now. . . . The aim of our newspaper is to represent the artisan's viewpoint in all public debates, especially those related to our own interests. We will defend our views in public against those seeking to dominate us. . . . Eloquence is a gift, but it is not required to shape public opinion. In any case, the [nation's political leaders] have always used it to manipulate us rather than to make things better.[14]

In distinguishing between mere "eloquence" and public opinion, artisan writers were trying to establish their own credibility while undermining that of the elite.

Elite women in the city of Lima published several tabloids, and also became staff writers for several leading newspapers. Written by and for women, *La Alborada,* among other tabloids, championed the cause of female emancipation. Its writers demanded equality in "civil and political life" and called for an end to "tyranny" in domestic life.[15] They also encouraged women to "participate in associations . . . as this is the only way of revolutionizing society."[16] Members of the feminist salon Velada Literaria met and pressured the editor of *El Correo del Perú,* one of the nation's most influential dailies, to hire a woman writer.[17] Her articles on the "woman question" were the only ones that reached a mass audience composed of men and women.

The Sociedad Amiga de los Indios, discussed in an earlier chapter, refuted the interpretation of the landed elite and the army that the indigenous-led uprising that had broken out in 1867 in half a dozen

13. "Indios en el Senado," *El Comercio,* 16 September 1868, 2–3.
14. "Editorial," *El Artesano,* 15 March 1873, 1.
15. Abel de la E. Delgado, "Educación social de la mujer," *La Alborada,* 1 April 1875, 29.
16. Teresa González de Fanning, "Trabajo para la mujer," La Alborada, 2 May 1875, 12.
17. Francesca Denegri, *El abanico y la cigarrera* (Lima: Instituto de Estudios Peruanos, 1996), 130–31.

communities in the state of Puno in the southern Andean highlands was a "caste war" aimed at exterminating all the fair-skinned creoles in the region. In addition to gathering information on the uprising and local living conditions of indigenous peoples in the area, the Sociedad published countless articles in numerous newspapers throughout the entire country in their defense: "the uprising is now the focus of public opinion; everyone is debating and evaluating it." [18] The Sociedad translated into Quechua many of the reports it presented in congress and had its own members distribute them to indigenous communities across the Andes. The groups also pressured the central government into publishing about a thousand copies of Jose de Anchorena's Spanish-Quechua dictionary.[19] This enabled villagers with reading and writing skills to improve their command of Spanish and to teach others in their communities.

In 1885, another indigenous-led rebellion broke out in the small town of Huaylas (Ancash), about forty-five miles north of Lima. Once again, the landowners and state officials in the region and officers in the national army depicted the uprising as a "caste war" against fair-skinned creoles. The majority of public writers in Lima came out in support of the indigenous rebels:

> If it is true that the Indian-led rebellion is a caste war against the White sector, which forms less than a sixth of the country's total population, then we are in the midst of a national crisis of formidable dimensions. . . . We have been studying the matter and publishing the facts available to us, and these lead us to think otherwise. . . . This is not a caste war, only an armed protest, and a justifiable one at that, against the abuses perpetrated against indigenous peoples by some government officials.[20]

Soon after, *El Comercio* published the following letter to the editor. It summarizes quite well the change that had taken place in the public sphere in relation to indigenous peoples:

> It is heartening to discover that in Peru someone is actually interested in the Indians of this country, and not just in what occurs in Russia, Turkey, or the Sudan. The author's appreciation for Peruvian Indians is all the more noteworthy, because it stands in direct contrast to the way our big capitalists boast about the need to kill . . . and replace them with Chinese coolies. Without these Indians, do these gentlemen really think that Peru can govern or defend itself?[21]

18. Vázquez, *La rebelión de Juan Bustamante*, 138–40, 224.
19. José de Anchorena, *Gramática y diccionario Español-Quechua* (Lima, 1873).
20. Quoted in William W. Stein, *El levantamiento de Atusparia*, trans. Jessica McLauchlan (Lima: Mosca Azul Editores, 1988), 105–6, 148–49.
21. Un Mestizo, "Letter to the Editor," *El Comercio*, 30 May 1885, 3. The author shifts

Indigenous peoples now occupied a place in public debate, although this does not seem to have significantly improved their life situations. Educational associations organized a literacy campaign in Lima and elsewhere to encourage poor families to send their children to school. Teachers frequently ridiculed illiterate families, generating resentment and fear among husbands.[22] Most of them worked and could not attend school, and they feared they would lose their authority once their children and wives became literate. Members in educational groups visited their homes and reassured them that this would not occur:

> Education for men and women is always useful. In the case of boys, once they learn to read and write, they can spend their leisurely moments studying technical manuals and morally uplifting literature. . . . In the case of women, schooling is an even more pressing need . . . she is the one person responsible for educating our children. It is simply wrong to assume that education will awaken envious and ambitious sentiments, and nothing else. After all, the education we are proposing is moral as well as intellectual. . . .[23]

As part of this campaign, civic groups organized neighborhood libraries and encouraged children and adults to visit them:

> It is not enough for a small, educated elite to lead the dark, gray masses into enlightenment; the age of tutelage has ended and science and learning are no longer aristocratic privileges. . . . Books have destroyed all forms of slavery . . . and, with the invention of the printing press, they can be purchased at affordable prices. . . . Books must be given the opportunity to penetrate our consciousness, and should not remain the exclusive patrimony of the elite. . . . Of all our democratic institutions, public libraries best fulfill the needs of our inferior classes, who need instruction more than other groups. . . . The associative spirit has aided us in creating public libraries and our own desire to become educated has increased their numbers. . . .[24]

Primary schools required students to read Francisco de Paula Gonzales Vigil's political catechism, *Importance of Civic Associations*. It was reissued as a pamphlet for students ten times between 1858 and 1880 and was reprinted countless times by newspapers throughout the country at

---

back and forth in the letter, referring to the Indians sometimes as "them" and other times as "us." Although the writer was probably not an indigenous person, he might have been a "mixed-blood," as his pseudonym indicates and his syntax seems to suggest.

22. Francisco García Calderón, "La instrucción pública en el Perú," *La Revista de Lima* (June 1860): 306–7; L. F. Zegeras, "Bases para la educación democrática," *La Revista de Lima* (January 1861): 114–15, 127.

23. García Calderón, "La instrucción pública."

24. "Bibliotecas populares," *El Nacional,* 21 February 1879, 2.

the request of schools who could not afford to buy copies of it. Newspapers and pamphlets played an important role in influencing public opinion, but the overwhelming majority of Peruvians remained illiterate and unable to speak Spanish.

Visual Signaling and Nationhood

Religious celebrations, patriotic festivities, public monuments, and museums provided Peruvians a place in public life to reflect on the meaning of nationhood and democracy.

Religious festivities declined in importance, and no longer served as sociocultural glue. In Lima,

> for several years now, the number of religious processions has declined, and so has their grandeur. Even the celebrations held during Holy Week are now just a shadow of what they once were. . . .[25]

Between the mid-1860s and early 1870's, Lima's elite launched a citywide campaign to abolish carnivals and recruited their counterparts across the provinces to do the same. Manuel Fuentes was responsible for organizing and leading the campaign. He explained why he and his supporters wanted them abolished: carnivals undermine "social hierarchy . . . and promote social equality."[26] After considerable debate in the press, congress decided against banning them. It did, however, approve legislation designed to make them less unruly. Fuentes complained, and claimed that they had been defeated by "public opinion," which had succeeded in portraying all of them as "enemies of the people." According to Fuentes, many of Lima's elite had backed down when they were accused by newspapers of displaying antidemocratic sentiments.[27]

In the countryside, the decline of religious celebrations had an even greater impact on public life. In the small town of Huaylas (Ancash), deep in the Santa Valley, about a day's ride north from Lima, local residents, as always, had spent the better part of the year saving money and preparing for the celebration in honor of the Holy Virgin, which usually lasted an entire month. The contemporary festivity became "racially" and "ethnically" divided, and lost whatever integrative function it once had:

25. Manuel A. Fuentes, *Lima: Apuntes históricos, descriptivos, estadísticos y de costumbres* (Lima, 1867), 111.

26. Manuel A. Fuentes, *Guía histórico-descriptiva, administrativa, judicial y de domicilio de Lima* (Lima, 1861), 266.

27. Manuel A. Fuentes, "El carnaval y sus glorias," *Aletazos del Murciélago* (Paris, 1866), 292. Also see: "Los carnavales," *El Comercio*, 21 January 1876, 2; "Correspondencia," *El Comercio*, 28 February 1877, 2.

The entire population [at the outset of the celebration] divided itself into two camps, with Indians and mixed-bloods on opposite sides; even the main plaza was divided in half, with those on one side mingling with those of their own race and separated from those on the other side, who were of a different race. The fiesta was celebrated in four stages, each one lasting for eight days, which means that the celebration went on for more than a month. On the principal days of the fiesta, there are processions, but these, too, are performed separately. On Assumption Day, the Virgin was carried in a procession by Indians and surrounded by dancers in lavish costumes, with their faces covered in masks resembling fierce animals. Eight days later, the Virgin was once again taken out in a procession, but this time mixed-bloods carried her; they fire rockets and light fireworks. If the parish priest is not a stickler [for religious orthodoxy], he is allowed to join in; otherwise he is ignored and the icon is taken from the chapel without his consent.[28]

As in Lima, churchmen had lost much of their public authority.

The carnival celebrations in several sugar plantations in the late 1870s in the Valley of Cañete, just outside Lima, turned into one of the most horrifying massacres in the history of postcolonial Peru. Blacks and mixed-bloods butchered more than 1,500 Chinese workers in a single afternoon. A contemporary described the massacre in this way:

The blacks and cholos of this place have for thirty years hated [Chinese] immigrants. . . . The immediate pretext that provoked this latest round of killings had to do with a disagreement between a Chinese man and a black woman, after she threw water at him during carnival. The celebration turned violent and bloody. . . . The Asians did not know why they were being clubbed, hacked with machetes and knives, and stoned to death. . . . Their corpses were thrown down in the middle of the plantation's main patio. . . . Women and children gathered round them and began mutilating them in a bacchanalian atmosphere of ludic revelry. . . . Many of the black women who were now stuffing the severed limbs and body parts of their victims into their mouths had once had sexual relations with them. . . .[29]

The inter-class violence that had permeated Peruvian society after decades of civil war had been turned into intra-class violence and internalized among plebeian groups. Racial and ethnic xenophobia among them was far stronger than any sense of nationhood.

---

28. E. W. Middendorf, *Perú: Observaciones y estudios del país ys sus habitantes durante una permanencia de 25 años*, trans. Ernesto More, vol. 3 (Lima: Universidad Nacional Mayor de San Marcos, 1973), 46.

29. Juan de Arona, *La inmigración en el Perú* (Lima, 1891), 99–102.

Manuel A. Fuentes explained why he had not included a discussion of patriotic celebrations in his otherwise exhaustive account of public life in Lima: "Civic fiestas are far from deserving any . . . attention."[30] The only time a large number of residents in Lima participated enthusiastically in a civic celebration was in 1876, to commemorate Peru's naval victory over Spain in 1872.[31] It was attended by a great many

> blackies . . . indians and whites, sons of the Enlightenment which now dwells amongst us. . . . Equality is no longer a lie. Education, the bright sun of the democratic system, is now shining upon us.[32]

The celebration was financed and organized by the municipal township rather than the central government:

> In the past, civic celebrations were in the hands of government officials, today they are in the hands of municipal townships, and this is praiseworthy and deserving of recognition. . . .[33]

The fact that the township chose to celebrate May 2 rather than the war of independence is itself significant. Civilians played a prominent role in the former, whereas military chieftains predominated in the latter.[34] An eyewitness provided a detailed description of the celebration that is worth quoting at length:

> The figure of Liberty was dragged across the plaza [by stevedores] on a van normally used to haul [bulk]. . . . She was draped in a coconut-white gown . . . the person representing her greeting those on the parade route, telling them that it did not matter that the statue of Liberty was being towed in the stevedores' van, and that the only thing that mattered was our motherland and nothing else. Following the figure of Liberty, was the fire brigade company known as Lima and . . . several civic leaders; all of them rode in a fire engine. . . . However, the most important float was the one led by Dr. Bambarén. . . . It was dragged by two large, panting horses representing a steam engine. . . . They were led by a blackie. . . . The occupants of this float, Melchior and Gaspar [the magi who, along with Baltazar, brought gold, frankincense, and myrrh to the boy Jesus], symbolized the liberty of both races (white and black) and of both worlds (New and Old). . . .

30. Manuel Atanasio Fuentes, *Estadística general de Lima* (Paris, 1866), 454–55.

31. Próspero Pereira Gamba, "Apuntes de un viajero," *La Revista de Lima*, 13 June 1860, 642, claims that Lambayeque's patriotic celebrations were celebrated with "great pomp."

32. Fuentes, *Estadística General de Lima*, 454–55.

33. "El solféo cívico," *El Correo del Perú*, 2 August 1873, 249.

34. Manuel Pardo, *Memoria que presenta el alcalde municipal . . . de los actos realizados por la municipalidad de 1862* (Lima, 1863); Francisco Laso, "Croquis sobre las elecciones," *Revista de Lima* 7 (1863): 106; Fuentes, *Guía histórico-descriptiva*, 255.

[After an intermission] the celebration started again in the afternoon. . . . The marchers were arranged in the following order: four honor guards, then a band, Lima's fire brigade . . . the stevedores . . . a number of artisan-led associations carrying the portrait of Sucre and Pardo [the Peruvian President], a second military band . . . students from the Technical School, students from the school of Guadalupe, students from San Marcos . . . another band . . . a float with the portrait of Bolivar and La Mar . . . then the members of the Sociedad de Amantes, the Club Literario, a group carrying the flag of each Latin American country, another band . . . military officers and soldiers followed by veterans from the wars of independence . . . a float with portraits of San Martín and Páez, without any Peruvian heroes. . . .[35]

Interpreting each frame provides a clue to the way Peruvians imagined themselves.

The stevedores' flatbed, an old, rickety cart, was unworthy of the task of hauling "Liberty" across the plaza, but this did not rob the display of its dignity. The person garbed as Liberty on the cart provided bystanders with an authoritative, "canonical" reading of this incongruity. The second float, carrying the magi, was based on a religious motif (Epiphany). Blacks and whites were placed next to each other, to represent the encounter between the Old and New Worlds and the notion of social equality and racial liberty. The presence of blacks in this float camouflaged the "indigenous" question, which remained a more intractable problem for Peruvians.

In the afternoon, the celebration shifted from an allegorical to a literal mode, one in which citizens were invited to represent themselves.[36] Students, teachers, and associations occupied a prominent place in the parade, whereas the army, which as the observer notes has not produced a single hero since independence, was relegated to the rear of the line. Civilians rather than soldiers were now considered to be the source of patriotism.[37]

Indigenous peoples were rarely represented in public monuments and archeological museums, and when they were it was in the most degrading and contemptuous fashion, making it difficult for them to envision themselves as part of public life. In 1868, Ignacio Manco Ayllón, an artisan of indigenous descent, launched a campaign in Lima to build a public statue in honor of Huaina Cápac, an Incan nobleman whose bodily remains had

35. "Día 29: Monumento al 2 de Mayo" and "Crónica," *La Opinión Nacional*, 31 July 1876, 2–3.
36. Hannah Fenichel Pitkin, *The Concept of Representation* (Berkeley: University of California Press, 1967), 60–111.
37. "La procesión cívica y el monumento del 2 de Mayo," *La Patria*, 1 August 1874, 1–2.

been recently disinterred during a public works project. In order to generate support and collect funds for this project, Ayllón organized public lectures, circulated petitions, published articles in *El Comercio* and other newspapers, and even appeared before the members of congress. They had spent a sizeable sum of money to erect a statue in honor of Christopher Columbus, he argued, and now they should do the same for Huaina Cápac:

> In Europe and America . . . the venerable remains of Kings, Emperors, and great men . . . are customarily stored in distinguished places, such as a mausoleum, a statue, or a pyramid, in this way immortalizing their names from generation to generation. . . . Huayna Cápac is no less deserving [of a monument] than Cristobal Colón or Bolivar.[38]

Congress rejected his request. Incan mummies belonged in museums, the repository of dead history, but not in public life, the place of living memory.

Completed in 1872, the Palace of National Expositions was located on Lima's southern edge. It was an impressive building for an impressive collection of archeological objects, flora, and fauna from throughout the country. Modeled after a renaissance-style Italian palazzo, the Palace stood in the middle of a vast field and was enclosed on all sides by a concrete wall fifteen meters high. Visitors gained access to the Palace through three porticos.[39] A large number of exotic and regional plants, trees, and bushes were on display along the four sides of the courtyard, each one marked clearly with its scientific and common names and an indication as to where in Peru it came from. This was the first public exhibit of Peruvian flora. It seems likely that visitors identified with flora from their home state and associated the regional diversity in plant life with political federalism, but I did not find any documentary evidence in support of this.

Off to one side of the courtyard stood the main pavilion, a long two-story building that housed the main exhibits. On display on the first floor near the entrance were an assortment of machines, tools, and technological gadgets invented or produced by Peruvians. The exhibit was to honor the "genius" of Peruvians and to show that the nation was on its way to becoming modern and industrial. Most of the second floor was taken up with a display of Incan mummies and artifacts and stylized, "creole"

38. Ignacio Manco Ayllón, "Private Letter (4 November 1868)," Biblioteca Nacional, D2632; quoted in Natalia Majluf, *Escultura y espacio público: Lima, 1850–1879* (Lima: Instituto de Estudios Peruanos, 1994), 33.

39. Middendorf, *Perú*, 1.441–44.

paintings of Quechua- and Aymara-speaking peoples from the Andes. This exhibit reaffirmed the Peruvian elite's description of itself as modern and forward-looking. More than four thousand visitors made their way to the Palace during the first week; from then on it remained deserted. Newspaper writers attributed the sudden and steep decline in visitors to the lack of "civic spirit" among Lima's residents.[40] The elite and their families were the only ones who identified with the Palace's visual representation of the nation.

Democratic Narrative

Public intellectuals described the development of associative life in Peru as a "second independence," as momentous as the first, which had led to sovereignty from Spain:

> We must conquer and overcome our own egoism by organizing associations. . . . Let us come together as our forefathers did before us to reclaim their independence and liberty from Spain. . . .[41]

Civic leaders called on all voluntary groups to contribute to the self-organization of society and the development of public life:

> Sovereignty resides in the association itself, and it does not recognize any laws other than those its own members have given themselves. . . . Our association is autonomous and independent of all political and ecclesiastical authorities. In our discussions, we will honor only those agreements the members have arrived at freely. . . .[42]

Associative life was now considered the most effective way of democratizing Peru. Public writers were sometimes grandiloquent in their remarks about associative life and civic democracy, but they were also practical and realistic regarding how they might achieve this and the many obstacles that still remained.

Associative Life in Civil and Economic Society

Civic groups campaigned against the racial, ethnic, religious, and nationalist xenophobia that was growing and spreading across the country. *El Hijo del Pueblo*, the leading artisan newspaper, outlined their views:

---

40. "Apertura de la Exposición," *La Patria*, 12 July 1872; "Palacio de la Exposición," *El Comercio*, 13 March 1876, 3.
41. "Nuestras aspiraciones," *El Obrero*, 27 March 1875, 2.
42. Sociedad Liberal Piadosa, *Reglamento de la Sociedad Liberal Piadosa y de auxilios mutuos de la villa de Chorillos* (Lima, 1874); also see: Sociedad Amiga de las Artes, *Reglamento de la Sociedad Amiga de las Artes* (Lima, 1908), 4.

> The spirit of association is beginning to spread among us. . . . For some time now, different types of associations have been appearing; all of them have very praiseworthy goals. . . . However, many of them remain exclusionary, anti-egalitarian, and egoistic in their statutes and founding principles. . . . One of the requirements for membership in these associations is that the person must be of such and such nationality, have such and such trait, or occupy such and such a place [in public life]. . . . While it is true that homogeneity is conducive to associative life, this should be understood only in terms of the . . . goals of the group, not in terms of the candidate's ranking or nationality. For example, mutual-aid societies that have been organized by Peruvians should admit into their ranks non-Peruvians. . . . The Sociedad understands that the true basis of sociability is universality and homogeneity, and that is why it will not exclude anyone. . . . We have only one requirement: that the person contribute to the country's moral progress. . . .[43]

The stability and success of associative life, they claimed, depended on the ideals and goals of the citizenry rather than on their socio-ethnic traits.

Juan Copello and Luis Petriconi's *Studies on the Economic Independence of Peru* was arguably the single most influential work published during this period on the subject of economic development. It summarized the main problems facing the members of Peru's financial and business establishment. In chapter 16, the authors summarize their findings and provide practical policy recommendations. They underscore two issues: the need to increase "labor productivity" and the need to develop the "spirit of association." According to the authors,

> Initially, our businessmen did not have any experience [with joint stock ventures], and this is why they exploited each other. But this is changing. Whether the associative spirit continues to grow in our country will depend on our business leaders, on their ability to make these firms profitable, and on the willingness of . . . [stockholders] to assume responsibility for them.[44]

Copello and Petriconi's views were representative of the country's wealthiest and most entrepreneurial businessmen and financiers.

Fernando García Calderón, a distinguished lawyer and active member of the Civilian Party, also stressed the importance of joint-stock companies for the development of economic life in Peru; however, he was interested in them as a vehicle for decentralizing wealth and democratizing property and authority relations:

43. "La Sociedad de los Hijos del País," *El Hijo del Pueblo: Periódico Popular, Literario, y Político,* 12 March 1864, 1.

44. Juan Copello and Luis Petriconi, *Estudios sobre la independencia económica del Perú* (Lima, 1876), 36–38.

There is in reality a common goal among those who form part of the same association. . . . For there to be a genuine associative spirit, employers and employees must have the opportunity of participating in each other's duties and tasks. When someone works for a salary . . . they are usually uninterested in the task assigned to them. However, the opposite is the case when an employee is made to share in the profits and losses of his association; this arrangement encourages each individual to be interested in the welfare of all. . . . [Our] most successful commercial houses and factories have prospered and are stable because their members have adopted this associative model. . . . Only by implementing this organizational model across the industrial, agricultural, and commercial sectors . . . will we be able to bring about material progress in our country.[45]

This associative model of economic life was never implemented in Peru.

Public intellectuals also discussed the issue of credit. Nearly all of them were convinced that the existing system was authoritarian and had to be reformed at once. José Martín de Cárdenas, an influential businessmen from Lima, described the situation:

Credit is in the economic realm what steam has become in the mechanical one: the prime mover of all action. [But in order for our system of credit to have a similar effect], it needs to be democratized. Although Peru is a republic, our system of credit remains aristocratic. . . . A few merchant houses remain in control of credit in our country, demanding usurious rates and imposing them on the rest of society. . . .[46]

The democratization of credit was inextricably linked to the spread of social trust in the economic realm:

in countries where credit has become a powerful economic tool, debtors are assumed to be honorable, solvent, and competent in their business dealings. . . . In these countries, credit has the effect of converting the moral qualities of lenders into circulating capital. . . . True credit lives off social trust; usury, on the other hand, thrives precisely where there is a lack of trust. . . .[47]

Economic progress and moral development were seen as mutually dependent. In the 1870s, economists and businessmen published numerous newspaper articles and gave expert testimony in congress in support of credit system reform.

---

45. Francisco García Calderón, *Diccionario de la legislación Peruana*, vol. 1 (Lima, 1860), 228–29.
46. Quoted in Pablo Macera, "Las plantaciones azucareras andinas," in *Trabajos de Historia*, vol. 4 (Lima: Instituto Nacional de Cultura, 1977), 136.
47. Joaquín Copelo, *Sociología de Lima*, vol. 3 (Lima, 1899), 129–31.

Democratizing Political Life

Public intellectuals and newspaper writers focused on the role of associations in presidential elections, in the development of municipal townships, and in decentralizing administrative and political power. During his presidential campaign, Manuel Pardo explained the role of electoral clubs in these terms:

> The impact of associations on political life is just as great as in industrial life. The work of one man alone cannot produce enough power to overcome even the most minor obstacle in his path; however, the work of a thousand of them, when harnessed and organized, will yield great results, like the Trans-Andean railway [that was recently completed]. To take another example: the life savings of a family hidden away in their chest of drawers represents a great loss to society at large, but when it is combined with the savings of other families, then, in five years or so, it will [accrue enough interest to] finance a railroad line all the way from the Atlantic to the Pacific coast. This is our main task today: to associate groups and unify their power, which until recently had been inert and passive.[48]

Electoral clubs generated social power and transformed it into political power. Participation was the only way for citizens to democratize the state and reclaim it for the nation.

Many of Pardo's supporters, including the editor of *El Comercio,* also wrote countless newspaper articles and pamphlets in support of municipal townships and federalism. In providing municipal services to local residents, townships were also infusing them with civic-mindedness:

> democratic regimes entrust townships with the sacred duty of providing citizens with health, sustenance, good habits, and education. . . . Those which fulfill this mandate become sentinels of freedom and wipe away our [tendency toward] egoism and individualism.[49]

Municipal liberty transformed egoistic individuals into citizens. The editor of *El Comercio* went further, connecting the development of townships to federalism and both to nationhood:

> The ties of friendship between a person from Puno and one from Bolivia are stronger than those the former has with his own compatriots

---

48. Manuel Pardo, "Sociedad Independencia Electoral," *El Comercio,* 30 May 1871, 2.
49. Antonio Gutiérrez de la Fuente, *Exposición que hace la Honorable Municipalidad de Lima al Supremo Gobierno* (Lima, 1863), 7.

in the central and southern parts of the country. . . . This is why we are in favor of decentralizing the government, turning Peru into a federation of provinces . . . and creating as many autonomous centers of power as possible, each one responsible for local affairs. Federation does not lead to chaos and disorder as some claim; in fact, it is the only practical way of ensuring that our republican government works. The central government is incapable of attending to the local needs of our communities . . . and the proof of this is that many of those whom it selects as prefects, sub-prefects, and governors behave like sultans in their regions, contributing absolutely nothing to improving the moral and material conditions of life, looking out only for their own self-interests. . . . This monocentric system harms all our provinces. . . .[50]

Municipal liberty and nationhood went together.

In the scale of social power, municipal power is by far the oldest and most important, since it is the one responsible for the local needs of residents. Before we can attend to our general needs and contribute to the national good, we must fulfill our municipal needs. Townships are born to satisfy the needs and customary practices of local residents, and their continued existence is assured by their capacity to reconcile communal interests with those of the nation. . . .[51]

According to this interpretation, national integration would only come about to the extent that citizens were able to practice popular sovereignty at the local level, in townships.

Civic groups were concerned with the way the central state and some of its local representative were overpoliticizing municipal townships, robbing them of their ability to attend to their administrative duties. Residents from countless communities throughout the country denounced government officials for undermining municipal liberty. The editors of *El Comercio* agreed and supported them:

Municipal townships have nothing to do with politics. Local interests are what should move them, and nothing else. . . . But as things now stand, it is our politicians who select most of our councilors, employing partisan criteria to select them. . . . This is why these bodies are rarely capable of representing the general and common needs of local residents. . . .[52]

50. "La Federación," *El Comercio*, 20 February 1874, 2; also see: "La Federación," *El Comercio*, 23 February 1874, 2.

51. "Disolución de la Municipalidad de Ayacucho," *El Comercio*, 14 January 1858, 2.

52. "Editorial," *El Comercio*, 3 January 1877, 2.

Citizens who supported federalism also wanted administrative life to remain immune to political strife. After more than six decades of political apathy, Peruvians had become active and committed to electoral life; however, the more they participated in it the more they wanted to de-radicalize it and to preserve and protect administrative life from radical extremists.

 CONCLUDING REMARKS

Rethinking Tocqueville:
A Latin American Perspective

Tocqueville never journeyed to Latin America, but judging from the many passages contained in his published books, notebooks, and private correspondence, he was keenly interested in the fate of civic democracy in this part of the world as well as in the United States and elsewhere. His assessment of the region could not be bleaker, and the gloomier it was, ironically, the more satisfaction he derived from knowing that his general argument about the predominance of habits over laws (institutions) in shaping democratic life had been vindicated yet again:

> There are people whose early education has been . . . vicious and whose character [is] . . . a strange mixture of passions, ignorance, and mistaken notions on all subjects. . . . People are astonished to see the new nations of South America convulsed by one revolution after another. . . . The Mexicans . . . took the federal Constitution of their Anglo-American neighbors as a model and copied it almost completely. . . . They borrowed the letter of the law, [but] . . . could not at the same time transfer the spirit that gave it life. In fact, at present, Mexico is constantly shifting from anarchy to military despotism and back. . . .[1]

While North Americans were advancing steadily toward democracy, Latin Americans were marching inexorably toward dictatorship.

This chapter is written "after the fact." The historical chapters have provided a Tocquevillian account of Latin American public life; the purpose of this one is to provide a Latin American account of Tocqueville. My aim is to use the case of Latin America to underscore key aspects of his argument that have escaped notice or comment in the work of his most

---

1. Alexis de Tocqueville, *Democracy in America*, trans. George Lawrence, ed. J. P. Mayer (Garden City, N.Y.: Doubleday, 1969), 165 and 226. Hereafter abbreviated as *DA*.

perceptive critics.[2] Along the way I also take issue with the work of some contemporary Tocquevillians. My discussion is in six parts. In the first, I account for the disjunction between daily habits and institutional structures in Latin America; in the second, I discuss the asymmetrical nature of public life and why citizens flocked to civil society more than any other terrain; in the third, I discuss the development of democratic selfhood from a performative perspective; in the fourth, I explain the fragmentation of democratic life in terms of the racial, ethnic, and gendered divisions that prevailed among citizens; in the fifth, I examine the Catholic narrative and its relationship to the development of a civic democracy idiom in order to understand the hybrid nature of Latin American cultural life; and in the sixth, I discuss the role of popular movements, civic and economic associations, and voting clubs in enabling citizens to democratize public life.

Daily Habits and Institutional Structures: Disjunction

Tocqueville attributed the success of democracy in New England to the fit between daily practices (habits) and institutional structures (laws).[3] As he saw it, Latin Americans were in a double bind: their practices were anticivic and their institutions were unstable.

Habitual Practices

Tocqueville grants centrality to habits, but remains vague as to what they are.[4] Nor have his followers, including Edward C. Banfield and Robert Putnam, done much to clarify matters.[5] I have enlisted the arguments of several authors to help us along in the discussion. Michael Oakeshott's account of habitual practices is one of the clearest, and therefore it is an appropriate place to begin the discussion:

2. Seymour Drescher, *Dilemmas of Democracy: Tocqueville and Modernization* (Pittsburgh, Pa.: University of Pittsburgh Press, 1968); Roger Boesche, *The Strange Liberalism of Alexis de Tocqueville* (Ithaca, N.Y.: Cornell University Press, 1987); Jean Claude Lamberti, *Tocqueville and the Two Democracies,* trans. Arthur Goldhammer (Cambridge: Harvard University Press, 1989); Pierre Manent, *Tocqueville and the Nature of Democracy,* trans. John Waggoner (Lanham, Md.: Rowman and Littlefield, 1996). Sheldon S. Wolin, *Tocqueville between Two Worlds: The Making of a Political and Theoretical Life* (Princeton, N.J.: Princeton University Press, 2001) reached me after I had written this chapter.
3. Tocqueville, *DA,* 287, 307–8.
4. Tocqueville, *DA,* 287, 308.
5. Edward C. Banfield, *The Moral Basis of a Backward Society* (Glencoe, Ill.: The Free Press, 1950); and Robert Putnam, *Making Democracy Work: Civic Traditions in Modern Italy* (Princeton, N.J.: Princeton University Press, 1993). Jane Schneider, *Italy's Southern Question: Orientalism in One Country* (Oxford: Berg, 1998), 1–27, situates their work in the Italian context as part of an ongoing debate that began in the 1860s with "Reunification."

We acquire habits of conduct, not by constructing a way of living upon rules or precepts that are learned by heart and subsequently practiced, but by living with people who habitually behave in a certain manner: we acquire habits of conduct in the same way as we acquire our native language. . . . What we learn here is what may be learned without the formulation of rules.[6]

Tocquevillians scholars concur with Oakeshott's account, although they remain divided over the substantive content of these habitual practices. This is not surprising. Like any other "contested concept," the notion of habit has several meanings, all of which are more or less credible as long as they are situated in the appropriate "language game" and are used in accordance with local practices.[7] These games, as Oakeshott suggests, are themselves expressions of alternative forms of life. When scholars study habitual practices, they are doing more than analyzing them "objectively"; they are also manifesting, through their writings, their own manners, morals, and ways of life.

Scholars who study habits conceive them in one of two ways: as mechanical behavior or as improvised action. Tocqueville and Oakeshott exemplify the first approach. Their emphasis on the impulsive-compulsive nature of habitual practices has a family resemblance to how Max Weber, Talcott Parsons, and "neo-modernization" scholars discussed the behavior of peasants and other "traditional" peoples.[8] Even Pierre Bourdieu's work on Algerian peasants, according to William Sewell Jr., "retains precisely the agent-proof quality that the concept . . . is supposed to overcome."[9] All five thinkers remain fixated in their understanding of habits.

6. Michael Oakeshott, *Rationalism in Politics* (New York: Basic Books, 1962), 62. For the French perspective (mentalities) see: Roger Chartier, *Cultural History*, trans. Lydia G. Cochrane (Ithaca, N.Y.: Cornell University Press, 1988), 19–52.

7. W. B. Gallie, "Essentially Contested Concepts," in *The Importance of Language,* ed. Max Black (Englewood Cliffs, N.J.: Prentice-Hall, 1962), 121–46.

8. Charles Camic, "The Matter of Habit," *American Journal of Sociology* 5 (March 1986): 1039–87, traces the way sociologists, from Weber on, impoverished our understanding of habit. N. Brett, "Human Habits," *Canadian Journal of Philosophy* 11, no. 3 (1981): 369, surveys the discussion in philosophy, and concludes: "The category of habitual activity is . . . comprised of a continuum of cases ranging from those which involve blind and stereotyped responses to nearly identical situations, to those in which attentiveness and variation are an essential part." Why they retained a capacious understanding of habits when sociologists and political scientists did not is related to the forms of life in each field.

9. William Sewell Jr., "A Theory of Structure: Duality, Agency and Transformation," *American Journal of Sociology* 98, no. 1 (July 1992): 15: "In Bourdieu's habitus, schemas (mental structures) and resources (material structures) so powerfully reproduce one another that even the most cunning or improvisational actions undertaken by agents necessarily reproduce the structures. . . . Although Bourdieu avoids either a traditional French structuralist ideal determinism or a traditional Marxist material determinism, he does so only by erecting a combined determinism that makes significant social transformation seem impossible."

This suggests that "modern" scholars are as likely as "traditional" peasants to think and behave in a mechanistic fashion. Contrary to what scholars claim, "repetition" and "creativity" are constitutive of habits, and both are distributed more or less evenly among social groups. The precise balance between the two changes over time and from one situation to the next, in large part as a result of the experience we have already acquired in transforming our old habits into new ones.

Like a jazz musician who improvises a new melody from an old tune, Latin Americans used their own judgment to reconcile their own vision of the future with their memory of the past in terms of the constraints and opportunities they faced in the present.[10] My study of public life in the region has emphasized the ways citizens created new practices and ways of life in order to challenge the dominant interpretations in the field, which emphasize the opposite. During the postcolonial period, Latin Americans maneuvered across public life in novel ways. They organized a great many (a) civil, economic, and political associations; (b) municipal townships; (C) multi-ethnic, multi-class and multi-regional rebellions aimed at toppling the central government; and (d) semi-competitive elections. Citizens also (e) deliberated publicly and challenged each other's understanding of nationhood and democracy; and (f) created a variety of new socio-moral practices rooted in notions of self-rule and collective sovereignty. Latin Americans sometimes behaved in a traditional manner, but they were just as likely to act in a modern way, more often than not fusing the two in complex ways that rendered the dichotomy altogether meaningless. Whether citizens broke with their habits or not was, as my historical evidence shows, wholly contingent on the type of socio-moral relations that existed in the mass movements or voluntary associations they were a part of (see below).

Institutional Structures

According to Tocqueville, public life in Latin America also lacked stable institutions. No one has done more to develop this argument than Samuel Huntington:

> the crucial distinction between a politically developed society and an underdeveloped one is the number, size, and effectiveness of its organizations. If social and economic change undermine or destroy traditional

10. John Dewey, "Creative Democracy: The Task Before Us," in *The Philosopher of the Common Man: Essays in Honor of John Dewey to Celebrate His Eightieth Birthday*, ed. Sidney Ratner (New York: G. P. Putnam's Sons, 1940), 220–28. Robert Westbrook, *John Dewey and American Democracy* (Ithaca, N.Y.: Cornell University Press, 1991), remains the best guide.

bases of association, the achievement of a high level of political development will depend upon the capacity of the people to develop new forms of association. . . . The primary problem [in Third World countries] is not liberty but the creation of a legitimate public order. Men may, of course, have order without liberty, but they cannot have liberty without order. Authority has to exist before it can be limited, and it is authority which is in scarce supply in those modernizing countries where government is at the mercy of alienated intellectuals, rambunctious colonels, and rioting students.[11]

But the foreign support given to postcolonial states by First World democracies has usually been used to implant authoritarianism. From Max Weber onward, scholars had always assumed that "parliamentary democracy" and "bureaucratic domination" were in tension if not in outright conflict with each other. Huntington was the first to conflate them.[12]

Weber's argument is worth repeating, since Tocquevillians have not given it the attention it deserves. According to Weber, state and party officials will use whatever material and symbolic resources they have to refashion citizens in their own image and likeness. In the course of formulating, implementing, and evaluating policies, institutional managers extend the same type of "patron-client" ties that exist in their organization to the citizenry at large, predisposing them to behave in a servile manner toward their superiors and in an autocratic manner toward those below them. The point of bureaucratic domination, however, is not just to control but to "deskill" citizens, destroying their capacity for judgment, rendering them unfit to participate in public life, and making it necessary for "experts" to intervene to prevent democracy from turning into "mob rule."[13]

Contrary to what Tocqueville would have expected, democratic life in Latin America arose from the fissures between daily practices and institutional structures. Recall that during the first half of the nineteenth century, and through much of the second, democratic-minded citizens

---

11. Samuel Huntington, *Political Order in Changing Societies* (New Haven, Conn.: Yale University Press, 1968), 31 and 7–8.

12. Max Weber, *Economy and Society: An Outline of Interpretive Sociology*, vol. 2, trans. and ed. Guenther Roth and Claus Wittich (Berkeley: University of California Press, 1978), 956–1003, 1393–1431, 1442–62.

13. For examples of deskilling among urban workers and rural farmers, see: Harry Braverman, *Labor and Monopoly Capitalism: The Degradation of Work in the Twentieth Century* (New York: Monthly Review Press, 1975), 59–69, 85–123, 139–54; and James Scott, *Seeing Like a State: How Certain Schemes to Improve the Human Condition Have Failed* (New Haven, Conn.: Yale University Press, 1998), 6–7, 49, 54–58, 88–89, 125–29, 310. Also see John Dewey, *The Public and Its Problems* (New York: Henry Holt, 1927), on the role of technocrats and universities in deskilling citizens.

migrated to civil society, claiming it as their "internal domain" (to borrow Partha Chatterjee's phrase) and yielding political society to authoritarian groups because they considered it part of the "external domain." [14] Because civil society had not yet developed any nationwide structures, it was difficult for democratic groups to nourish and sustain their practices over time. The institutional structures of political society, including the government, church, and army, provided authoritarian groups with a way of propagating their practices in daily life. Although these institutions were certainly fragile, they provided authoritarians with the additional support they needed to gain control of public life. Latin Americans invested their sense of sovereignty horizontally in each other rather than vertically in government institutions, which created a radical disjunction between the two.

The Latin American case has direct relevance for how we understand Tocqueville's work and, more generally, how we study postcolonial life. Contemporary Tocquevillians assume there is a one-to-one correspondence between daily practices in civil society and institutional structures in political society. Their understanding of this relationship, in fact, is similar to the "base-superstructure" model of orthodox Marxism. Tocqueville himself is partly responsible for this, but he was also far more circumspect in his formulation than his followers recognize:

> There can . . . be . . . equality in civil society, though . . . none in the world of politics. . . . There can even be a sort of equality in the world of politics but without any political freedom. . . . One can easily invent several other hypotheses in which a great deal of equality is easily combined with institutions more or less free, or even not free at all. . . . Freedom is found at different times and in different forms; it is not exclusively dependent on one social state, and one also finds it elsewhere than in democracies.[15]

Public life in Latin America was bifurcated during the first half of the nineteenth century and for much of the second half. Democratic practices throughout the region surfaced through the cracks and crevices between daily habits and institutional structures.

---

14. I am indebted to Partha Chatterjee, *The Nation and Its Fragments: Colonial and Postcolonial Histories* (Princeton, N.J.: Princeton University Press, 1993), but we differ in our conceptions of the "internal" and "external" domain and, more generally, on the nature of colonial and postcolonial life.

15. Tocqueville, *DA*, 503–4.

Civil Society and Public Life: Asymmetrical

Prior to the 1870s, Latin Americans practiced democracy primarily in civil and economic society, although they did so most readily and intensely in civil society. There were sociocultural reasons for this. Citizens were "suspended in webs of significance." [16] Latin Americans used Catholicism, the language of public life, to give shape to what Albert Hirschman calls "passions" and "interests," in the same way that Puritanism and Republicanism enabled western Europeans and North Americans to make sense of theirs. [17]

Latin Americans described themselves as driven by a "dominant passion"—that is, by a ceaseless drive to control all those around them. This passion was dominant, and hence constitutive of all human beings (like "sin" and "free will") and far stronger than any of the secondary or "artificial" desires, for economic wealth, political power, social honor, and knowledge. Catholics had their own distinctive way of turning "private vice" into "public virtue." In contrast to New Englanders, who relied on *doux commerce* (economic society), and French Republicans, who relied on state governance (political society), Latin Americans relied on sociability (civil society). [18]

Democratic-minded Latin Americans gravitated to civil society, the one public terrain where they felt they could practice civic solidarity and assist each other in restraining their dominant passion. Individuals could not by themselves domesticate their own passion to seek glory and dominate others, but by forging bonds of solidarity with those around them they could impose external restraints on themselves and so also protect the community. In the language of Catholicism, humans were by nature social animals who needed to live in community rather than, as Puritans claimed, alone and isolated. The only way for people to overcome their dominant passion (sin) was by entering civil society and practicing mutual reciprocity with those around them.

In Latin America, democratic-minded citizens flocked to civil society, making it the "symbolic center" of public life, in Edward Shils's sense, relegating the other public terrains (economic society, political society, and the public sphere) to "peripheral" status. [19]

16. Clifford Geertz, *The Interpretation of Cultures* (New York: Basic Books, 1973), 5.
17. Albert O. Hirschman, *The Passions and the Interests: Political Arguments for Capitalism before Its Triumph* (Princeton, N.J.: Princeton University Press, 1977).
18. Tocqueville, *DA,* 51, 285, 551–60, 621, 633; and his *The Old Regime and the French Revolution* (Gloucester, Mass.: Peter Smith, 1978).
19. Edward Shils, *Center and Periphery: Essays in Macrosociology* (Chicago: University

Creating Citizens: Performing Trust

According to Tocqueville, the single greatest challenge confronting modern democracy was to find a way of turning egoistic individuals into civic-minded citizens:

> it is not an easy task to bring together fellow citizens who have lived for centuries aloof from, or even hostile to, each other and to teach them to collaborate and cooperate in their own affairs.[20]

New Englanders accomplished this by relying on their own rational "self-interest."[21]

Before one can have an "interest," one must have an "identity"; without a sense of self, it is impossible for one to know, much less strategize about, one's preferences. Individuals develop an identity in a social context through a process of "mutual recognition." In the words of Alessandro Pizzorno:

> In order to have an interest, a person must first assume that his criteria for evaluating his preferences, to use the language of economics, will be identical at the moment when he is calculating their costs and reaping their benefits. This is plausible only if these two moments coincide temporally, or if the person has a formula that allows him to convert the worth of his preference at time one in terms of his preferences at time two. In other words, the person has to assume that his identity will be constant over time. Hume showed why this assumption is untenable. Selfhood can only be secured through a process of identification with other individuals in the context of a particular group, a general public or another type of collectivity.[22]

Membership in a group offers individuals the social and narrative resources they need to give coherence to their otherwise discontinuous selves.

Latin Americans refashioned themselves into democratic citizens in voluntary associations. Members staged "performative acts" in these

---

of Chicago Press, 1975), 3–16, 34–47. I find his distinction between center and periphery illuminating but do not subscribe to the "active-passive" dichotomy that underlies it.

20. Tocqueville, *The Old Regime*, 107.
21. Tocqueville, *DA*, 641. For a rationalist account, see: Putnam, *Making Democracy Work*, 174, 171–73. Also see Margaret Levi, "Social and Unsocial Capital: A Review Essay of Robert Putnam's *Making Democracy Work*," *Politics and Society* 24, no. 1 (March 1996): 45–56.
22. Alessandro Pizzorno, "Sul Intertemporale delle Utilita," *Stato e Mercato* 16 (April 1986): 3–25.

groups, using whatever sociocultural resources they had on hand to choreograph them.[23] Senior and junior democrats took turns "representing" democracy, sometimes playing the role of actor and sometimes that of spectator, teaching each other alternative ways of practicing social equality, political liberty, and mutual recognition. Routinization turned these performances into mimetic acts—that is, into "twice behaved behavior"—and encouraged citizens to translate their own particular concerns (aesthetic) into intersubjective ones (communicative), to recall Hannah Arendt's argument.[24] For example, during the anticolonial struggles, Latin American citizens "objectified" their understanding of democracy by organizing popular movements, whereas during the postcolonial period they represented democracy by creating civic, economic, and political associations.[25] Failure to follow local conventions would have deprived them of the support they needed to "move cultural material from one order of signification to another."[26] Whether a citizen succeeded in developing a new "repertoire of action" was contingent on the type of socio-moral practices that existed in the association or movement of which they were a part.[27]

But the question still remains: how did citizens initially break with their predatory past? In Latin America, senior democrats (commoner and elite) imbued with moral authority mentored novices, guiding them from one stage to the next and along the way providing them with the "tacit knowledge" and "practical skills" they needed to become civic- minded

23. Richard Schechner, *Performance Theory* (New York: Routledge, 1988), 280, 155, 120, 194. Schechner discusses its four aspects: temporality, staging, purpose, and audience. Jonas Barish, *The Anti-Theatrical Prejudice* (Berkeley: University of California Press, 1981), for a history of scholarly and theological hostility toward theater and, more generally, the performative perspective.

24. Marcia Calkowski, "A Day at the Tibetan Opera: Actualized Performance and Spectacular Discourse," *American Ethnologist* 18, no. 4 (1991): 644; Hannah Arendt, *Between Past and Future: Eight Exercises in Political Thought* (New York: Penguin Books, 1977), 153–55; and her *Human Condition* (Chicago: University of Chicago Press, 1958), 176–200. In contrast to her account, I have emphasized the role of "mutual recognition" rather than "individual virtuosity."

25. Donald Brenneis, "Aesthetics, Performance and Enactment of Tradition in a Fijian Indian Community," in *Gender, Genre and Power in South Asian Expressive Traditions*, ed. Arjun Appadurai (Philadelphia: University of Pennsylvania Press, 1991), 362–78.

26. Robert Cantwell, *Ethnomimesis: Folklife and the Representation of Culture* (Chapel Hill: University of North Carolina Press, 1993), 5.

27. Charles Tilly, *Popular Contention in Great Britain* (Cambridge: Harvard University Press, 1995), 41–42, defines a repertoire as a "limited set of routines that are learned, shared, and acted out. . . . People learn to break windows . . . stage public marches, petition, hold formal meetings, and organize special-interest associations." Although I am indebted to his account, it remains overly behaviorist. I am also skeptical that repertoires develop linearly from "competitive" to "reactive" to "proactive."

citizens.[28] Those who completed this apprenticeship emerged from it transformed, having undergone a type of *Bildung*.[29] This account enables us to make better sense of Tocqueville's own argument, which, as I noted above, is implausible.

New Englanders developed democratic habits in stages. In the first, senior members drilled novices in the most rudimentary form of "self-interest":[30]

> they follow the doctrine of self-interest, of which they have only a crude idea, and [as a way] to better guard their interest, [although they continue to] neglect the main one of them, that is, to remain their own masters.[31]

Short-term gain enabled novices to break with their egoism and practice what Isaiah Berlin calls "negative liberty."[32] This brand of self-interest is rudimentary, and although

> by itself cannot make a man virtuous. . . it disciplines and shapes a lot of orderly, temperate, moderate, careful and self-controlled citizens. If it does not lead the will directly to virtue, it establishes habits which unconsciously turn it that way.[33]

The second stage was slightly more demanding. Entry into associative life resembled a *rite de passage*.[34] Senior democrats played a key role, guiding novices through it:

> men who have as yet little skill in the technique of association and do not understand the . . . rules thereof . . . are afraid the first time they combine in this way, that they may pay dearly for their experience. . . . But they cannot belong to such associations for long without discovering how to maintain order among large numbers and what procedures enable men to advance in methodical agreement toward a common aim.[35]

28. Michael Polanyi, *The Tacit Dimension* (Garden City, N.Y.: Doubleday, 1966), 4, 87. Also see Thomas Kuhn, *The Structure of Scientific Revolutions* (Chicago: University of Chicago Press, 1962).

29. Hans Georg Gadamer, *Truth and Method*, trans. Garrett Braden and John Cummings (New York: Seabury Press, 1975), xvi, 10–17, 318–20.

30. Tocqueville, *DA*, 526.

31. Tocqueville, *DA*, 540.

32. Isaiah Berlin, *Four Essays on Liberty* (London: Oxford University Press, 1969), 129–30.

33. Tocqueville, *DA*, 526–27.

34. Victor Turner, *The Forest of Symbols* (Ithaca, N.Y.: Cornell University Press, 1967), 96.

35. Tocqueville, *DA*, 521–22.

Members who had already broken with their previous habits but had not yet acquired democratic ones relied heavily on their mentors to transit through this "liminal" corridor. Those who reached the other side were now able to practice civicness consistently. In the third and final stage, senior democrats invited graduates to participate alongside them in public life, enabling them to learn to reconcile group interests (based on class, status and party) with national interests:

> Every citizen . . . may be said to transfer the concern inspired in him by his little republic into his love of the common motherland. In defending the Union, he is defending the increasing prosperity of his district. . . .[36]

Among advanced democrats, selfhood and nationhood sustained each other.

Public prestige in aristocratic regimes had been the patrimony of the "few," but in democratic regimes personal dignity had become the birthright of the "many."

Caste Democracy and Nationhood: Fragmented

According to Tocqueville, citizens who practiced self-rule and collective sovereignty in an exceptional manner were granted special recognition in public life:

> when the public governs, all men feel the value of public goodwill and . . . try to win it [for themselves] by gaining the esteem and affection of those among whom they must live.[37]

Latin Americans practiced democracy in daily life and ranked each other accordingly, except in the case of indigenous peoples, blacks, mixed-bloods, and women. Although many of the popular movements and voluntary associations discussed in the historical chapters were pluralistic, there is no denying that public life remained segregated along racial, ethnic, and gender lines. Even senior democrats considered members of these groups to be "morally polluted" and therefore unworthy of public recognition.[38]

The Latin American case sheds new light on Tocqueville's remarks on New England and, more importantly, on the nature of modern democracy:

> a natural prejudice leads a man to scorn anybody who has been his inferior, long after he has become his equal; the real inequality . . . is

---

36. Tocqueville, *DA*, 162.
37. Tocqueville, *DA*, 568, 510–11, 540.
38. Mary Douglas, *Purity and Danger* (New York: Praeger, 1966).

always followed by an imagined inequality rooted in mores. . . . Race prejudice seems stronger in those states that have abolished slavery than in those where it still exists, and nowhere is it more intolerant than in those states where slavery was never known. . . . In the north, the white man no longer clearly sees the barrier that separates him from the degraded races, and he keeps the Negro at a distance all the more carefully because he fears lest one day they be confounded together.[39]

Informal habits were responsible for this "natural prejudice." Servitude had ended, but the memory of it lingered on, depriving indigenous peoples, blacks, women, and other marginalized groups of the public recognition they deserved.

These persons were committed to democratic life, but they were penalized for remaining loyal to their own communities. The experience of indigenous groups in the United States is directly relevant to understanding the Latin American case. Anglo-Americans have

dispersed their families, obscured their traditions and broken the chain of memories; [they] also changed their customs and increased their desire beyond reason making them more disorderly and less civilized than they had been before.[40]

Citizenship was granted only to individuals who had severed all prior ties to their community and transformed themselves into an "unencumbered self," to recall Michael Sandel's argument.[41] Those who refused to do so were banished to the margins of public life, where they served as a symbolic reminder to the next generation of citizens of the risks of remaining attached to their communities. Democratic life in Latin America and North America became an example of what Lewis Coser calls "greedy institutions."[42]

Caste democracy in the New World was based on a type of exclusionary nationalism:

A nation stands apart from the rest of mankind, as well as the general wants common to all humanity, when it has some particular interests and needs. Certain opinions peculiar to this community about what should be praised or blamed are immediately established, and these are what the citizens call honor. A caste comes to be established within the

39. Tocqueville, *DA,* 343.
40. Tocqueville, *DA,* 318–24.
41. Michael J. Sandel, "The Procedural Republic and the Unencumbered Self," *Political Theory* 12, no. 1 (February 1984): 91–96.
42. Lewis A. Coser, *Greedy Institutions: Patterns of Undivided Commitment* (New York: Free Press, 1974), 4. These institutions require "exclusive and undivided loyalty from members, [and] erect strong boundaries between insider and outsider so as to hold the insider in close-bonds to the community to which he owes total [allegiance]."

same nation, and it in turn keeps itself apart from all other classes and contracts particular needs, which again give rise to special opinions. Among this caste, honor is composed of a strange mixture of the peculiar notions of the nation and the even more peculiar notions of the caste. . . . This is the extreme point of the argument, from which we must now return.[43]

Tocqueville became increasingly interested in caste democracy, and this led him to study the nature of postcolonial regimes.[44] In Latin America, the citizenry's habits pertaining to marginalized groups remained the least changed (most mechanistic), which accounts for the radically fissured and fragmented nature of public life in the region.

Religion and Citizenship: Cultural Hybridity

In Tocqueville's account, religion served to restrain passions and instill citizens with patriotic sentiments.[45] In order for religion to have a positive influence on democratic life, the Church had to remain separated from the state. In Latin America, the Church was allied with both the old regime and the new authoritarian one, and although democratic-minded citizens became hostile to their institutions, they continued to rely on Catholicism to challenge authoritarianism in the region.

Catholicism was the language of public life, and like any other grand narrative, including Puritanism and Islam, it was "polyvocal."[46] Latin Americans pronounced its keywords—"free will," "passion," "divine will," and so on—with slightly different accents, generating alternative "language games": call them Neo-Colonial Catholicism and Civic Catholicism.[47] These two vocabularies influenced the way citizens maneuvered across the public landscape. Neo-Colonials continued to describe their compatriots like unruly children, beholden to their passions and therefore morally and sociopolitically unfit to partake in public life. Neo-

43. Tocqueville, *DA*, 626.
44. Carlos A. Forment, "Tocqueville, Peripheral Peoples and Post-Colonial Regimes in the Modern World" (Public lecture, Institute for Advanced Study, 1997).
45. Tocqueville, *DA*, 36–39, 287–94. "It is . . . of immense importance to . . . have fixed ideas about God, their souls, and their duties toward their Creator and their fellows, for doubt about these first principles would leave all their actions to chance and condemn them, more or less, to anarchy and impotence. . . ."
46. Paul Ricoeur, "Structure, Word, Event," in *The Conflict of Interpretation* (Evanston, Ill.: Northwestern University Press, 1974), 84–93.
47. On the affinity between Puritanism and democracy, and between Catholicism and authoritarianism, see: Michael Walzer, *The Revolution of the Saints* (Cambridge: Harvard University Press, 1965), 301–3; David Little, *Religion, Order and Law* (Oxford: Oxford University Press, 1970), 132, 222–23, 309–13; and Talcott Parsons, *The Evolution of Societies* (Englewood Cliffs, N.J.: Prentice-Hall, 1977), 199–204.

Colonials were committed to using "law and order" to inculcate "self-discipline."[48] Neo-Colonials still construed their fellow citizens as colonial officials had portrayed them prior to independence. However, because the sociopolitical context (democratic republics) had changed so radically, their narrative resources were now embedded in a different situation, leading them to pronounce its phrases and terminology and to maneuver across public life in different ways. Neo-Colonials retained their mental habits but were forced, because of changes in public life, to alter their cultural and sociopolitical practices.

Democratic-minded citizens construed citizens as rational adults. According to them, Latin Americans had broken with their old habits and were now capable of restraining their passions and practicing self-rule. The mass movements they had organized during the wars for independence had brought together tens of thousands of citizens, which according to them constituted proof that they were capable of channeling even their most violent passions toward a single goal: national sovereignty. Their ability to organize thousands of voluntary associations after independence was additional evidence that they were capable of ruling themselves without an enlightened despot lording over them. The mass movements and voluntary groups that had surfaced in the region were "real," but they were also part of a much broader symbolic struggle taking place across the continent between democrats and authoritarians for the hearts and minds of citizens. Although democrats had broken with their old habits, they continued to live with disregard for the state, as their predecessors had done during the late colonial period under Spanish rule. Although their actions seemed to be rooted in traditional habits, they were in fact a novel response to a new sociopolitical configuration that had emerged in the postcolonial period. Democratic groups across the region practiced the "politics of antipolitics" and lived with their backs toward the state in order to prevent government officials from colonizing civil and economic society and destroying the associations they had created. Authoritarians and democrats remained attached to some of their old habits, modified others, and broke free from some, enabling them to invent new ways of "in-habiting" public life.

Civic Catholicism enabled citizens to "signal" and recognize each other as members of the same imagined community: the democratic nation.[49] This vocabulary was shaped, to be sure, by power struggles against

48. Brian Loveman, *The Constitution of Tyranny: Regimes of Exception in Latin America* (Pittsburgh, Pa.: University of Pittsburgh Press, 1993), discusses the legal foundations of authoritarian rule.
49. Michael Spence, *Market Signaling: Informational Transfers in Hiring and Related Screening Processes* (Cambridge: Harvard University Press, 1974).

authoritarian groups. But it would be an oversimplification to claim, as James Scott does, that the narrative resources of Civic and Authoritarian Catholicism were nothing more than the result of "ideological" (verbal) or "hegemonic" (nonverbal) struggles.[50] Jean and John Comaroff explain why:

> Since it is possible, indeed inevitable, for some symbols and meanings not to be hegemonic—and impossible that . . . hegemony can claim all the signs in the world for its own—culture cannot be subsumed within hegemony. . . . Meaning may never be innocent, but it is also not merely reducible to the postures of power.[51]

Narrative resources are what economists call a "public good"—that is, a good owned by a collective entity but not controlled by any one member or subgroup.[52]

Sovereignty of the People: Creating Social Power

According to Tocqueville, Latin Americans lacked civic habits and stable institutions during the late colonial and postcolonial period. Prior to independence, associative life was stunted; however, during the postcolonial period, Mexicans, Peruvians, Argentines, and Cubans broke with their old habits and organized thousands of civic, economic, and political associations.

Breaking Old Habits: Mass Movements

The various anticolonial movements that surfaced across Mexico, Cuba, and Argentina provided citizens a place to break with their old habits and acquire civic ones, in contrast to the movements that broke out in Peru. In other words, the connection between popular movements and civic life is contingent on the type of practices that existed in them. In the Mexican, Cuban, and Argentine cases, after the anticolonial movements had dissolved, ex-rebels and sympathizers returned to their families, neighborhoods, and workplaces and disseminated the civic habits they had acquired among those with whom they now shared daily life, extending the radius of civic-mindedness far beyond its original scope. This connection between movements and civic-mindedness was, as I noted in the historical chapters, strongest during the independence struggles but weakened

50. James Scott, *Domination and the Arts of Resistance* (New Haven, Conn.: Yale University Press, 1990), 1–16, 20.

51. Jean and John Comaroff, *Of Revelation and Revolution* (Chicago: University of Chicago Press, 1991), 21–24.

52. Elinor Ostrom, *Governing the Commons: Evolution of Institutions for Collective Action* (New York: Cambridge University Press, 1990).

during the postcolonial period. The proliferation and diversification of civic and economic groups made it possible for them to develop their own internal sources of civicness.[53]

Acquiring New Habits: Voluntary Associations

From the 1840s on, the number of voluntary associations rose steadily and spread gradually across Latin America, at a time when most governments were antidemocratic. The growth and spread of associative life was accompanied by its diversification. With each passing decade, citizens created new types of civic and economic associations: mutual-aid and friendly societies; community development groups; moral improvement and religious groups; human rights organizations; literary, educational, and professional societies; Masonic lodges; fire brigades; patriotic groups; ethnic and racial associations; joint-stock companies; recreational clubs; and so on. By the 1860s, Latin Americans had organized thousands of civic and economic associations and used them to shuttle back and forth between public and private life. But these groups were more than "organizational facts"—they were "socio-moral facts."

Citizens congregated in these democratic temples to practice social equality, mutual recognition, critical deliberation, and self-rule, carving out a place for themselves in public life in which they might break with their old habits and acquire democratic ones. Latin Americans turned these civic groups into what James Scott calls sites of "everyday resistance,"[54] providing the nation a place to deposit its "sovereign will," having already deemed all government institutions unworthy of the honor on account of their commitment to authoritarianism. Associative life enabled Latin Americans to block state officials from extending a "great arch" over the nation, to reverse Philip Corrigan and Derek Sayer's argument.[55] Democratic life had become rooted throughout public life except in political society, which remained under the control of authoritarian groups.

Consolidating Democratic Habits: Electoral Clubs

Dankwart Rustow, borrowing from Tocqueville, argues that elections serve to "habituate" citizens to believing that "democracy . . . is the only

53. Michael T. Hannan and Glenn R. Carroll, *Dynamics of Organizational Populations* (New York: Oxford University Press, 1992) on the interplay of institutional fields and organizations.

54. Scott, *Domination*, 123, 183–228.

55. Philip Corrigan and Derek Sayer, *The Great Arch: English State Formation as Cultural Revolution* (Oxford: Oxford University Press, 1985).

56. Dankwart Rustow, "Transition to Democracy: Toward a Dynamic Model," *Comparative Politics* 2, no. 3 (April 1970): 337–63.

game in town."[56] But this argument is unpersuasive; elections occur too infrequently and when they do are too brief to be able to alter daily habits. Tocqueville himself was far more skeptical of elections than were his followers:

> Under this system [of elections], the citizens quit their state of dependence just long enough to choose their masters and then fall back into it. . . . It really is difficult to imagine how people who have entirely given up managing their own affairs could make a wise choice of those who are to do that for them. One should never expect a liberal, energetic, and wise government to originate in the votes of a people of servants. . . .[57]

Instead of focusing on the voting act itself, as most scholars of democracy tend to do, we would be better served to explore the everyday practices and ways of life in which elections are embedded.

Beginning in the late 1860s, a significant number of Mexicans, Peruvians, Argentines, and Cubans organized voting clubs, participated in national elections, and became active in other forms of government-centered politics in an ongoing manner. Latin Americans participated in political life despite the fact that their governments were too poor to provide them with any short-term, material benefits. Members of the same civic and economic group sometimes became active in the same electoral club and voted for the same candidate as a way of reaffirming their ties of solidarity with each other.[58] For these citizens, politics was rooted in and was an extension of social life. But this does not explain the action of those citizens who belonged to different groups but voted for the same candidate, nor the action of citizens who belonged to the same group but supported different candidates. Voting in these cases was related to matters of practical judgment and collective identity.[59] In practicing politics, citizens were transforming their own individual sense of insecurity into collective uncertainty, thereby socializing the risk they felt and making it bearable. Although this was the first time that a large number of Latin Americans became active in political society, the overwhelming majority of them, as I argued in the historical chapters, continued to boycott elections.

At once the greatest strength and the greatest weakness of democratic life in nineteenth-century Latin America stemmed from a single source: antipolitics, the tendency for citizens to live with their backs toward the

57. Tocqueville, *DA,* 693–94.
58. Murray Edelman, *The Symbolic Uses of Politics* (Chicago: University of Chicago Press, 1964).
59. Alessandro Pizzorno, "Sulla razionalita della scelta democratica," *Stato e Mercato* 7 (April 1983): 3–46.

state. On the one hand, antipolitics enabled Latin Americans to create and preserve democratic life, but on the other hand, it prevented them from extirpating authoritarianism in political society. Despite the many limitations and flaws that characterized democratic life in the region, there is no denying that by the late nineteenth century a great many citizens were committed to practicing social equality, mutual reciprocity, and political liberty in daily life.

In my judgment, the most enduring contribution Latin Americans have made to the theory and practice of modern democracy is their faith in civic democracy. They have remained committed to it while living in conditions of poverty, bureaucratic authoritarianism, inefficient state institutions, corrupt politicians, and unresponsive government officials. Without in any way minimizing the difficulties and accomplishments of citizens in North America and western Europe, their loyalty to modern democracy has not been subjected to such extreme and recurrent trials as has that of their counterparts in Latin America. If one's commitment to democracy can only be proven under conditions of duress, then it is safe to say that Latin Americans remain unrivaled in their faith in democracy. And as the old saying goes: "Creer es poder."

Index